The Biology and Utilization of Shrubs

The Biology and Utilization of Shrubs

Edited by

Cyrus M. McKell

NPI
University Research Park
Salt Lake City, Utah

Academic Press, Inc.
Harcourt Brace Jovanovich, Publishers
San Diego   New York   Berkeley   Boston
London   Sydney   Tokyo   Toronto

ACADEMIC PRESS, INC.
San Diego, California 92101

United Kingdom Edition published by
ACADEMIC PRESS LIMITED
24-28 Oval Road, London NW1 7DX

Library of Congress Cataloging-in-Publication Data

The Biology and utilization of shrubs.

Includes index.
1. Shrubs.   2. Shrublands.   3. Shrubs—Utilization.
I. McKell, C. M.
QK475.B55   1988   582.1'7   88-3477
ISBN 0-12-484810-9   (alk. paper)

PRINTED IN THE UNITED STATES OF AMERICA
88 89 90 91   9 8 7 6 5 4 3 2 1

Contents

Part II. Environmental Influences and Plant Responses

Part III. Genetic Variability in Shrubs

Part IV. Physiological Adaptation of Shrubs

Part V. Multiple Uses of Shrubs

Part VI. Shrub Establishment and Management

Part VII. Social and Economic Aspects of Shrubs

Contributors

G. MICHAEL ALDER   NPI, Salt Lake City, Utah 84108

ROBERTO M. BÓO   Departamento de Agronomía and Centro de Recursos Naturales Renovables de la Zona Semiárida, Universidad Nacional de Sur, 8000 Bahía Blanca, Argentina

JERRY D. BUDY   Range, Wildlife, and Forestry, University of Nevada, Reno, Nevada 89512

FRANCIS PAINE CONANT   Human Ecology and Remote Sensing Laboratory, Department of Anthropology, Hunter College, City University of New York, New York, New York 10021

K. M. M. DAKSHINI   Department of Botany, University of Delhi, Delhi 110007, India

OMAR DRAZ   Agricultural Research Center, Crops Research Institute, Forage Section, Cairo University, Giza, Egypt. (Deceased). Inquiries may be sent to C. M. McKell, editor.

CLAIRE GABRIEL DUNNE   Absaroka Seed Company, Manderson, Wyoming 82432

RAYMOND A. EVANS   Agricultural Research Service, U.S. Department of Agriculture, Reno, Nevada 89512

OSVALDO A. FERNÁNDEZ   Departamento de Agronomía and Centro de Recursos Naturales Renovables de la Zona Semiárida, Universidad Nacional de Sur, 8000 Bahía Blanca, Argentina

EDMUNDO GARCIA-MOYA   Rama Botanica, Colegio de Post Graduados, Escuela Nacional de Agricultura, Chapingo, Mexico

JOSEPH R. GOODIN   College of Arts and Science, Texas Technological University, Lubbock, Texas 79409

A. A. GUBB   East London Museum, East London, Republic of South Africa

DENNIS J. HANSEN   NPI, Salt Lake City, Utah 84108

LIU HUAXUN   Institute of Geography, Chinese Academy of Sciences, Beijing, China

HENRI N. LE HOUÉROU   Centre d'Ecologie Fonctionelle et Evolutive, CEPE Louis Emberger, F-34033 Montpellier, Cedex, France

E. DURANT MCARTHUR   Shrub Sciences Laboratory, Intermountain Research Station, USDA Forest Service, 735 North 500 East, Provo, Utah 84601

CYRUS M. MCKELL   NPI, Salt Lake City, Utah 84108

C. V. MALCOLM   Resource Management Division, Department of Agriculture, South Perth 6151, Western Australia

E. J. MOLL   Botany Department, University of Cape Town, Rondesbosch 7700, Republic of South Africa

ZEV NAVEH   The Lowdermilk Faculty of Agricultural Engineering, Technion–Israel Institute of Technology, Haifa, 32000 Israel

RONALD J. NEWTON   Department of Forest Science and the Texas Agricultural Experiment Station, Texas A&M University System, College Station, Texas 77843

G. ORSHAN   Department of Botany, The Hebrew University of Jerusalem, Jerusalem, Israel

W. KENT OSTLER   NPI, Salt Lake City, Utah 84108

HORST PAETZOLD   2500 Rostock 1, Tremsenplatz 1, German Democratic Republic

LUIS F. SÁNCHEZ   Departamento de Agronomía and Centro de Recursos Naturales Renovables de la Zona Semiárida, Universidad Nacional de Sur, 8000 Bahía Blanca, Argentina

ZHAO SONGQIAO   Institute of Geography, Chinese Academy of Sciences, Beijing, China

V. R. SQUIRES   Faculty of Natural Resources, Roseworthy Agricultural College, Roseworthy, South Australia

HOWARD C. STUTZ   Department of Botany and Range Science, Brigham Young University, Provo, Utah 84602

PHILIP J. URNESS   Range Science Department, Utah State University, Logan, Utah 84322

GORDON A. VAN EPPS   Departments of Range and Plant Science, Utah State University, Logan, Utah 84322

BRUCE L. WELCH   Shrub Sciences Laboratory, Intermountain Research Station, USDA Forest Service, 735 North 500 East, Provo, Utah 84601

NEIL E. WEST   Department of Range Science and the Ecology Center, Utah State University, Logan, Utah 84322

JAMES A. YOUNG   Agricultural Research Service, U. S. Department of Agriculture, Reno, Nevada 89512

Preface

The Biology and Utilization of Shrubs is the culmination of several years of study and writing on behalf of the many authors who have contributed chapters. Each of the authors has been a "champion of the cause" to bring to the scientific and resource management community information from around the world that will foster wise utilization and long-term management of shrubs. The phenomenal increase in knowledge about shrubs is countered by preconceived notions that shrubs are of little value. The major goal of this book is therefore to bring together the wide range of information about shrubs from many disciplines and world locations. Even so, there is so much to share that not all published papers could be included.

The intended audience is more extensive than research scientists, and includes geographers, land managers, resource policy makers, economists, social scientists, and students in these disciplines. It is the hope of the authors that the book will not only be a source of information but also a stimulus to further scholarship and enlightened management.

In preparing the book, our outlook has been positive. We believe that shrubs have many unique features and that important uses and products can be obtained from shrubs under positive management practices.

This book is written from a worldwide perspective. Even though some chapters draw upon regional examples to illustrate certain principles, we hope they can be applied to solve problems internationally.

In Section I, shrublands of the world are described in nine chapters. Scientists who are familiar with the distribution, climate, soils, and traditional uses of shrubs for each continental region prepared these chapters.

In Section II, environmental influences and plant responses are described in four chapters. Given the diversity in stature, unique structural features, secondary metabolites, and vigorous plant growth, shrubs are able to persist and even flourish in many harsh environments of the world.

In Section III, genetic variability is considered from an evolutionary point of view; subsequent chapters deal with the utilization of diverse germ plasm for breeding of new plant types.

In Section IV, physiological adaptations of shrubs are examined as major factors for their persistence in stress environments. Adaptation to temperature extremes and drought, plus photosynthetic and respiratory efficiency, are attributes that enable shrubs to survive where other life forms perish. In a later chapter, the discussion on shrub productivity in saline environments completes the overview of physiological stress tolerance.

In Section V, evidence is given to substantiate the claim that the many virtues of shrubs provide a basis for sustaining shrub use for livestock fodder, wildlife habitat, reclamation and erosion control, fuel, and naturalized landscaping.

In Section VI, practical instructions are outlined for seed harvesting, seed plantations, propagation in a nursery, field establishment in a saline environment, and management of shrub-dominated lands for multiple-use purposes.

In Section VII, one chapter describes cultural adaptation to shrub use in a livestock-dominated primitive culture, and the following chapter provides a detailed economic analysis of establishing shrub plantations to improve livestock production.

The challenge for the future is to learn more about how shrubs adapt and prosper in the diverse habitats they occupy. We are constantly improving ways to manage shrubs more efficiently for the benefits they can provide to humans as well as to the natural ecosystem. Utilization of new research techniques will quicken an already fast pace of research, yielding replies to questions we despaired of answering in past generations. As unique genotypes are identified, we can now clone them *in vitro* rather than wait for the slow results of conventional plant breeding. When we find superior traits in shrubs that are desired in other plant forms, we can look forward to transferring the genes for these characters through new techniques in genetic engineering. New soil inoculants will enable resource managers to obtain high rates of success in plant establishment and plant growth through the biological action of improved strains of mycorrhizae, bacteria, and actinomycetes tailored especially for shrubs. Indeed, the future looks bright!

I am grateful for the contributions of the chapter authors as well as those who assisted them in preparing their work. I also express gratitude to former colleagues at Utah State University and to my fellow officers and staff at NPI (formerly Native Plants, Incorporated) for their encouragement and discussions. Finally, I express my sincere appreciation to my wife and partner, who assisted in reading, typing, and correspondence during preparation of the book. The pathway to publication has been long—long enough for me to have an artificial lens implant in one eye and succeed in a bout with cancer. I hope our effort will be of significant value to our readers.

I

Shrublands of the World's Continents

The chapters in this section give expert viewpoints on the major shrublands found on each of the vegetated continents. Authors have attempted to give an overview of the dominant shrubland types as well as the associated features of soil and climate that influence the geographic distribution of major shrub species.

Each chapter was prepared by a scientist who has worked many years with the various shrub species of his region and is familiar with the ways that shrubs are used by humans. Surprising to some may be the fact that shrubs provide a substantial portion of the fodder consumed by domestic livestock, especially during seasons when grass forage is limited in volume or low in protein content. Shrubs are also used for fuel, construction of huts and enclosures, fiber, and as sources of crude medicinal extracts. Because of their aggressive growth habits, shrubs are often maligned and overlooked as a valuable resource rather than given due credit for their importance in sustaining human life.

1

North American Shrublands

Cyrus M. McKell
Edmundo Garcia-Moya

I. Introduction

A. Geologic Influences

The patterns of occurrence for North American shrublands are based on many historical factors extending through geologic time. The area's geography and climate have undergone drastic changes as a result of significant geologic alterations. These changes since the pleistocene period have been especially influential on present-day vegetation, during which time human impacts have also been added. However, the last 125 years have seen more rapid change than in any other short period of history because of the degrading effects of exploitive grazing use. Intensive utilization of shrublands and grasslands by domestic livestock has shifted the balance from a shrub- and grass-dominated vegetation to shrub dominance in many sites and encouraged desertification processes. However, advances in natural resources research have provided answers to vexing problems of plant response to utilization and improved management practices that help to avoid repeating the mistakes of previous generations.

The present Cascade, Sierra, and Sierra Madre Oriental ranges are a part of the geologic mountain-building upheaval that created a rain-shadow effect in the path of the prevailing westerly wind currents, causing a gradual but significant change to a drier climate east of the mountains. Axelrod (1940) speculated that during the Tertiary period the climate changed from temperate to warm-temperate to tropical and finally, at the end of the Tertiary, to a dry and relatively cool climate similar to the present. At higher elevations in the Rocky Mountain chain, glaciation occurred. The plant fossil record documents the progression of vegetation types during the climatic changes. Many mesic species failed to survive but those related to the present chaparral and desert shrubland types were common in the Tertiary flora and the more xeric species gradually became climax and now dominate vast desert areas that were formerly woodland in more mesic geologic periods.

B. Factors in Present-Day Shrub Distribution

Marine influences from the great inland ocean are evident on landform and chemical composition of the soils of western North America. Mountain faces show sedimentary stratification and marine deposits. Weathered rocks and soils yield salts from marine formations that eventually accumulate in closed basins to form salinized soils or increase the salinity content of streamflow (McKell *et al.*, 1984). Thus, many halophytic or salt-tolerant shrubs have evolved in the salt-enriched environment of western North America.

Moisture-laden winds blowing east from the Pacific Ocean drop some of their water as land is encountered and further amounts are lost on the slopes and mountain tops of the western mountain ranges, leaving relatively little precipitation for the millions of hectares of desert lands east of the mountains. This pattern of precipitation is further modified by the buildup of a high-pressure air mass in the summer months that redirects westerly traveling storms to the north. Another important precipitation pattern of western North America is the northward flow of moist semitropical air masses from the South Pacific and Gulf of Mexico during spring and summer months. Storms in this pattern are erratic and not always a dependable source of moisture. Of the three main climatic factors, moisture, temperature, and wind, moisture is the most variable and definitive for the occurrence of shrublands. According to Good (1947), plant distribution is controlled by climate, particularly the extremes. With their greater adaptation to drought through deep root systems, timing of growth and reproduction, and morphological features for conserving moisture and regulating temperature, shrubs are a suitable life-form to dominate the arid and semiarid lands of western North America. They are found on the xeric slopes of mountains and down into the broad valleys. Shrubs dominate saline valleys and dry deserts, where only the most adapted bunchgrasses and annuals can compete with them.

II. Types of Shrublands

A. *Classification of Shrublands*

Several systems have been developed for classifying vegetation types using life-form as the main criterion. Other factors of importance are geographical units and ecological relationships. Shreve (1917) and Shantz and Zon (1924) described natural vegetation types in their map of U.S. vegetation. Küchler (1964) delineates 106 major plant communities based on present occurrence but also considers the potential vegetation that could exist in areas where degradation and ecological change have produced a deviation from what might be considered the climax or natural potential. Rzedowski (1978) divided Mexico into 10 major plant communities, of which the xerophilous desert scrub occupies 80×10^6 ha. The Küchler system was used as the basis for the report of the Forest-Range Task Force (1972). Utilizing criteria from several systems of vegetation classification as well as those appropriate to animals and other ecosystem components, a group of public agency and university experts in Arizona organized a description of the biotic communities of the American Southwest that includes both the United States and Mexico. The resulting publication (Brown, 1982a) contains information on Mexican shrublands that previously has not been available. Particularly useful are the numerous references and photographs. A recent description and delineation of vegetation types of North America was compiled by Bailey and Cushwa (1981), which shows the extension of shrubland types into Mexico and Canada (Fig. 1). This classification utilizes a combination of vegetation, climate, and landform to provide a uniform tool for management and resources planning. Bailey's classification system consists of five main "domains": Polar, Humid, Temperate, Dry, and Humid Tropical. Eleven ecological provinces are dominated by shrubs, all of which are in the western part of the continent (Table I). Other plant communities such as forests and grasslands have a component of shrubs in them but the major emphasis of the biological relationships and management practices are on the other plant types and not the shrubs.

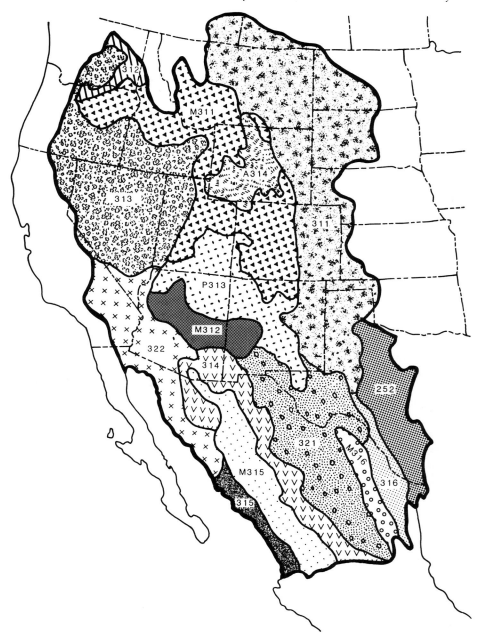

Figure 1.   Vegetation types of North America. (After Bailey and Cushwa, 1981).

Table I. Shrubland vegetation types of North America

Map code	Province and section	Area (km^2)
252	Prairie Brushland Province	217,360
2521	Mesquite–buffalo grass	83,720
2522	Juniper–oak–mesquite	62,660
2523	Mesquite–acacia	70,980
M262	California Chaparral Province	86,800
313	Intermountain Sagebrush Province	528,840
3131	Sagebrush–wheatgrass	233,480
3232	Lahontan saltbush–greasewood	86,580
3133	Great Basin–sagebrush	121,940
3134	Bonneville saltbush–greasewood	57,720
3135	Ponderosa shrub forest	29,120
314	Mexican Highland Shrub Steppe Province	45,325
315	Sinaloa Coast Province	60,000
316	Rio Grande Shrub Steppe Province	90,000
P313	Colorado Plateau Province	246,200
3131	Juniper–pinyon woodland + sagebrush–saltbush mosaic	102,960
3132	Gramma–galleta steppa + juniper– pinyon woodland mosaic	143,260
A314	Wyoming Basin Province	109,980
3141	Wheatgrass–needlegrass–sagebrush	34,060
3142	Sagebrush–wheatgrass	75,920
321	Chihuahuan Desert Province	166,660
3211	Gramma–tobosa	47,200
3212	Tarbush–creosote bush	119,340
322	American Desert Province	201,500
3221	Creosote bush	95,420
3222	Creosote bush–bur sage	106,080
M321	Baja California Province	62,720

Source: Bailey and Cushwa (1981).
Note: Canada is not included in the totals given. For geographic locations see Fig. 1.
Area values are from Bailey (1978) and Rzedowski (1978).

B. Shrubland Types, Descriptions, Species, and Uses

Because of the continental coverage of Bailey's "Ecoregions of North America" this system will be followed, in general, in describing shrublands of the continent (Bailey and Cushwa, 1981). Valuable information about North American shrublands was compiled by Brown (1982a) and his co-authors, who reviewed extensively the abundant literature describing vegetation features, uses, and history of management in the plant communities of southwestern North America. The occurrence of animals in western habitat types was summarized by McKell and his colleagues

(Institute for Land Rehabilitation, 1978). The following descriptions do not include such remote shrubland types as arctic–boreal scrub trees and bog shrubs or the mixed forest types, tropical rain forest, or subtropical deciduous forests, where shrubs constitute a major portion of the understory species, depending on the degree of disturbance.

1. Prairie Brushland Province

a. Mesquite–Buffalo Grass. Located in west-central Texas south of the Red River, the 51,500-km^2 mesquite–buffalo grass type is one of three variants of the Prairie Brushland province that extend prairie grassland species into the southwestern limit of their range of adaptability. Shrub species such as *Prosopis glandulosa* and *Quercus havardii* occur where grassland dominance by such midgrass species as *Buchloe dactloides, Bouteloua curtipendula,* and *Schizachyrium scoparium* gives way to allow the development of scrub thickets in some of the drier ecological sites. Küchler (1964) used the term "shinnery" for this type. Grazing is a major use and was estimated by the Forest-Range Task Force (1972) to be possible at a level of 0.57 AUM/ha (animal unit months of grazing per hectare on a sustained yield basis).

b. Juniper–Oak–Mesquite. In a 62,660-km^2 area south of the mesquite–buffalo grass area in south-central Texas, the density of shrubby species increases and *Juniperus ashei* and *Quercus virginiana* become important components of the vegetation. Many of the species found in the previous type also occur but the grasses are in lesser abundance. Küchler (1964) describes this area as Texas savanna. Mesquite is a dominant species and causes numerous problems in land management because of its aggressive nature and resprouting habit. Rootplowing is one of the most effective methods of controlling mature plants (Drawe, 1977) but new plants established from seeds readily perpetuate mesquite. Grazing potential is about 0.85 AUM/ha (Forest-Range Task Force, 1972).

c. Mesquite–Acacia. The mesquite–acacia type extends for 70,980 km^2 from the Prairie Brushland to the Gulf of Mexico through the southern rolling hills and coastal plains of Texas. *Acacia rigida* and *A. farnesiana* add diversity to the clumps of dense shrub cover of *Prosopis glandulosa, Juniper* species, and *Quercus virginiana,* while at the same time there is a further diminution of grass dominance characteristic of the southern prairie, but prickly pear cactus, *Opuntia* spp., can be a problem in grazing management. The major climatic pattern of this area is a long, hot, and humid summer with precipitation during the growing season. Whereas considerable research has been devoted to methods for control of mesquite (Schifres, 1980), a benefit of *Prosopis* is its production of high-protein seed pods for livestock use (Felker, 1979). Control of mesquite by mechanical means is a recommended practice for raising the average animal carrying capacity from the existing status, which is normally about 0.85 AUM/ha.

2. California Chaparral Province

Occupying the foothills of the Sierra Nevada, the coastal and southern mountains of California, and extending south into Baja California, Mexico, the California chaparral occupies 86,800 km² in the United States (Bailey, 1978). Chaparrel species are well adapted to a moist mild winter and a dry summer Mediterranean climate (Mooney, 1977). This type prospers over a wide range of precipitation extremes, from a low of 305 mm at San Juan de Dios in Baja California, Mexico, to 702 mm at San Gabriel Dam in the mountains north of Glendora, California. Chaparral shrub species are tolerant to long periods of summer drought, are non deciduous, and have sclerophyllous leaves. Pase (1982) describes several series of chaparral communities based on the most abundant genera: *Adenostema, Ceanothus, Arctostaphylos,* and *Quercus.* Some of the most abundant species include *Adenostema fasculatum, Artemisia californica, Ceanothus leucodermis, Salvia melifera, Arctostaphylos glauca, Quercus dumosa,* and *Castanopsis sempervirens.*

Extremely dense vegetative cover in many chaparral stands prevents access by larger animals, especially domestic livestock. Shrub density also poses a safety hazard when ignited by natural or man-made fire. Passage of fire to adjacent and distant flammable structures under the influence of high-velocity, dry desert winds, as well as serious damage from soil erosion from steep, denuded slopes after a fire, justifies a high priority for resource management of the chaparral type. Fire-resistant root crowns that can regenerate rapidly after fire are the result of evolutionary development. Considerable reseach has been done on ways to use fire as a management tool, with the objective of converting from shrub to grass for grazing and improved watershed use Bentley, 1967: Love *et al.,* 1960). Policy questions regarding aesthetics may be raised as well as the desirability of maintaining a natural ecosystem. Productivity of chaparral in areas of favorable rainfall for grazing averages 0.17 AUM/ha, which can be increased to 0.52 AUM/ha under intensive management (Forest-Range Task Force, 1972).

3. Intermountain Sagebrush Province

a. Great Basin Sagebrush–Wheatgrass. Of five shrubland types in the Intermountain Sagebrush Province, the 233,480-m² sagebrush–wheatgrass type is the largest. This type occupies most of southern Idaho, southeastern and central Oregon, central Washington, and northern Nevada in the rain shadow of the Sierra Nevada and Cascade mountains. Summer precipitation occurs as infrequent thundershowers, while winters are cold and precipitation is in the form of snow. Average annual moisture ranges from 150 to 400 mm. Species diversity is low; the main shrub is sagebrush, *Artemisia tridentata* ssp. *tridentata*, and the main grasses are *Agropyron spicatum, Festuca idahoensis, Stipa comata, Sitanion hystrix,* and *Poa sandbergii.* In shallow, rocky, or sandy soil other shrubs such as *Chrysothamnus nauseosus, Purshia tridentata, Ceratoides lanata,* various *Atriplex* species, or smaller *Artemisia* species may partially substitute for the dominant *A. tridentata.* Under intense grazing the codominance between sagebrush and the grasses has given way to a shrub-dominated system. Livestock carrying capacity of this northern portion of the Great Basin is 0.31 AUM/ha (Forest-Range Task Force, 1972), but by applying various range improvement practices such as burning, disking, chaining, and applying herbicides (Valentine, 1979), the production of forage can be more than doubled.

b. Lahontan Saltbush–Greasewood.   Located directly east of the Sierra Nevada in western Nevada, the 86,580-km^2 Lahontan saltbush–greasewood shrub type occupies desert valley bottoms in the general area formerly occupied by the Pleistocene lake Lahontan (Bailey, 1978). The soils of the area are saline and deep in the desert valley bottoms but shallow on the alluvial slopes of the desert mountains. Precipitation is limited primarily to the winter months and the yearly total is less than 200 mm. The dominant low-growing chenopod shrubs *Atriplex confertifolia, A, nuttalii,* and *Ceratoides lanata,* as well as the taller *Sarcobatus vermiculatus,* are very tolerant to saline soils and drought. Some of the associated grasses include *Elymus cinereus, Sporobolus airoides,* and *Distichlis stricta* (Roundy and Young, 1985). Much of the area occupied by this shrub type is in closed-drainage basins. In the bottom of these basins, salt content may be so high as to preclude the growth of any plants except the most salt-tolerant halophytes such as *Allenrolfia, Salicornia,* and *Suaeda.* The productivity of the area is limited by aridity and only wildlife habitat and grazing are the main uses. *Halogeton glomeratus,* a poisonous herbaceous annual weed from Central Asia, invaded the Nevada desert about 1934 and has caused many livestock deaths (Williams, 1973). Carrying capacity is less than 0.08 AUM/ha. Range improvement methods are limited to grazing management to effect better distribution and avoiding overuse.

c. Great Basin Sagebrush.   Situated in the eastern half of Nevada, the 121,940-km^2 Great Basin sagebrush type is a mosaic of low shrubs in the broad valley bottoms, taller shrubs on the slopes of the desert mountains, and a shrub understory to juniper trees on the mountainsides. This type is in the center of the Basin and Range geographic province described by Fenniman (1929). Annual precipitation ranges from 125 mm in the valleys to 250 mm in the higher elevations of the desert mountains. *Artemisia tridentata* is the principal shrub on the deep and near-neutral soils, while low-growing chenopod shrubs occupy the saline valleys. The principal uses of this shrub type are wildlife habitat and livestock grazing, primarily in the winter, when the high-protein stem tips and leaves of the chenopod shrubs are consumed. Carrying capacity is low at 0.36 AUM/ha with little opportunity to increase productivity by use of mechanical equipment and seeding (Bleak *et al.*, 1965).

d. Bonneville Saltbush–Greasewood.   Occupying 57,720 km^2 in the western half of Utah in the old Lake Bonneville lake bed, the Bonneville saltbush–greasewood type is analogous to the saltbush–greasewood type in western Nevada. Many of the same species are present and many of the same saline soil conditions prevail. Precipitation is slightly higher, ranging from 150 to 300 mm, because of the influence of the Wasatch Mountains in slowing down the flow of the storm fronts as they move across the Great Basin. The land is used for livestock grazing, wildlife habit, and recreation. The latter is important because of the proximity of small cities on the eastern margin of the shrub type at the foot of the mountains. Urban influences have had a significant impact on the composition of the vegetation through grazing and clearing of land for dryland farming or irrigated farming where mountain streamflow was sufficient. Livestock carrying capacity is approximately 0.30 AUM/ha. Extensive range improvement projects have been carried out on sites of suitable soil, usually where the presence of *Artemisia tridentata* indicated a potential for improved productivity (Cook, 1958).

e. Ponderosa Shrub Forest.   Shrubs are an important component of the 29,120-km^2 ponderosa shrub forest located along the eastern foothills of the Cascades and Sierra Nevada in northern California and central Oregon. Annual precipitation ranges from 250 to 450 mm. Farther up the slopes of the forest, the shrub understory gives way to a dense *Pinus* and *Pseudotsuga* forest. The open *Pinus ponderosa* forest has a dense to scattered understory of *Purshia tridentata*, *Artemisia tridentata*, and *Chrysothamnus nauseosus*. Extensive logging has removed the choice old-growth timber, leaving a dense understory of *Pinus contorta* to occupy many productive sites. The type provides excellent big game habitat as well as livestock grazing. Carrying capacity averages 0.18 AUM/ha.

4. Mexican Highland Shrub Steppe Province

The 45,325 km^2 of Mexican highland shrub steppe are located in the high plains of southeastern Arizona and southwestern New Mexico, extending to Queretaro, Mexico, along the eastern slopes of the Sierra Madre

Oriental. A local term for the type is "encinal," which is derived from the Spanish designation meaning place of live oaks. The type is highly variable and occurs along the slopes and mesas of the Sierra Madre Oriental. Brown (1982b) describes several variations that include *Quercus emoryii, Q. viminea,* and *Q. hypoleucoides* in association with *Juniperus* and cactus species that give way to pine forests at the higher elevations. The more prevalent grass species are *Muhlenbergia emersleyi, Elyonurus barbiculmis,* and *Eragrostis intermedia.* Carrying capacity varies considerably and may be as low as 0.9 AUM/ha.

5. Sinaloa Coast Province

This province takes its name from the state of Mexico where it is mostly found. Floristically it is also reported in southeastern Sonora, Tamaulipas (Rzedowski, 1978; Brown, 1982b), and Guanajuato (Rzedowski, 1978). It covers an area of ~60,000 km^2 in southwestern North America. The precipitation ranges from 300 to 500 mm, most of it during the summer (Brown, 1982b).

The florist lists available for this province (Gentry, 1942; Shreve, 1951; Rzedowski, 1978; Brown, 1982a) clearly demonstrate the dominance of tree species such as: *Prosopis velutina, Acacia cymbispina, Lysoloma divaricata, Cercidum sonorae, C. torreyanum, Bursera odorata, B. laxiflora, Fouquieria macdougalii, Pachycereus pecten-aboriginum, Ipomoea arborescens, Cassia attomaria, C. emarginata, Zizyphus sonorensis, Pithecellobium sonorae, Caesalpinia platyloba, Lonchocarpus megalanthus, Jatropha cordata,* and *Piscidia mollis.* In Sinaloa, *Acacia cymbispina* is the dominant and most widely distributed and forms park-type vegetation or dense forests (Shreve, 1937).

Miranda and Hernández (1963) consider this province as thorny scrubland where *Acacia cymbispina* is the dominant species. Brown (1982b) in his revision of the Sinaloan Thornscrub, refers to an abundance of shrubs and increased participation of short microphyllous trees as two criteria for the definition of this vegetation type. COTECOCA (1976) refers to five vegetation types dominated by shrubs.

Herbaceous vegetation is found in interspaces and it is composed of annuals. COTECOCA reports a carrying capacity of 1.3–2.9 AUM/ha with an average of 2.12 AUM/ha.

6. Rio Grande Shrub Steppe Province

This province, also called Tamaulipan Brushlands, occupies approximately 90,000 km^2. The topography varies from level to rolling, elevations range from 0 to 300 m, and precipitation averages 630 mm. The most important elements of the vegetation are: *Prosopis glandulosa* var. *glandulosa, Opuntia engelmannii, Celtis pallida, Karwinskia humboldtiana, Condalia hookeri, Leucophyllum texanum, Acacia farnesiana, A. rigidula, A. berlandieri,* and *Cordia boissieri.* The presence of grasses will depend on the range sites (Gould, 1962).

This province is the most productive of all three referred to by Bailey and Cushwa (1981) for Mexico, 1.75 AUM/ha (COTECOCA, 1978). Overgrazing has led to invasion of mesquite and cacti, thus lowering the carrying capacity and making brush control and range seeding with exotics necessary to recover its potential up to 0.3 AUM/ha.

7. Colorado Plateau Province

a. Juniper–Pinyon Woodland and Sagebrush–Saltbush Mosaic. Occupying a major portion of western Colorado and north-central New Mexico, this variable mosaic of 102,096 km² covers a large part of the Colorado Plateau, where precipitation averages 500 mm. Pinyon–juniper also occupies many of the desert mountains of the Great Basin (Tueller *et al.,* 1979). *Juniperus osteosperma* and *J. scopulorum* along with *Pinus edulis* and *P. monophylla* form a pygmy forest canopy interdigitating with open shrub-dominated valleys of *Artemisia, Atriplex, Cercocarpus, Eriogonim, Chrysothamnus,* and herbaceous species. Old stands of pinyon–juniper and associated sagebrush are not as biologically productive as younger stands, where species diversity is high (Gifford and Busby, 1975). Land use opportunities are limited and soil erosion may be a problem in old stands. Because of the potential for increasing the productivity of this ecosystem, hundreds of thousands of hectares have been treated to control old tree and shrub growth and subsequently seeded to forage grasses and shrub species (Plummer *et al.,* 1968). The average animal carrying capacity of 0.13 AUM/ha can be increased to 1.9 AUM/ha (Aro, 1971).

b. Gramma–Galleta Steppe and Juniper–Pinyon Woodland Mosaic. The southern portion of the Colorado Plateau and low mountains of northern Arizona and New Mexico are occupied by 143,260 km² of a warm-season grass steppe and open pygmy forest. Generally more open than the pygmy forest to the north, this mixed steppe–forest has an important shrub component but is partially dominated by the warm-season grasses *Hilaria mutica, Bouteloua curtipendula,* and *Oryzopsis hymenoides. Atriplex canescens, Ceratoides lanata, Quercus* spp., and *Berberis fremontii* are some of the shrubs that add diversity to this mixed tree–shrub–grass type. Livestock carrying capacity varies significantly because of site variability, soil depth, and local climatic factors. Compared with the juniper woodland type farther north, effectiveness of the average annual precipitation of less than 400 mm is reduced because a greater portion of the annual precipitation occurs in the summer months when evapotranspiration is highest. Animal carrying capacity is 0.15 AUM/ha.

8. Wyoming Basin Province

a. Wheatgrass–Needlegrass–Sagebrush. Situated in the north-central portion of Wyoming, at elevations ranging from 1800 to 2400 m, this 34,060-km^2 shrub–grass type is an important variant of the *Artemisia tridentata*–bunchgrass plant community. Because of its location in a precipitation zone of 250 to 400 mm, which is more favorable than other sagebrush areas, the carrying capacity is greater than 0.35 AUM/ha. Along with the dominant shrub, *Artemisia tridentata* ssp. *tridentata*, *Atriplex confertifolia*, and *A. gardnerii* are associated with the grasses *Agropyron smithii*, *A. spicatum*, and *Stipa columbiana*. Dominant use of this area is for grazing, although it is prime habitat for antelope (*Antilocapra americana*) according to Long (1965).

b. Sagebrush–Wheatgrass. The southwestern quarter of Wyoming is occupied by 75,920 km^2 of *Artemisia tridentata* ssp, *wyomingensis* and *Agropyron* species. Locally called the Red Desert, the terrain is characterized by bold sandstone buttes and mesas with extensive valleys in between. Annual precipitation of less than 300 mm limits productivity for grazing to less than 0.30 AUM/ha. Genetic diversity of sagebrush in its many locations has been recognized taxonomically (Ward, 1953). Studies of the three main big sagebrush subspecies by Barker and McKell (1983) indicate that basin big sagebrush, *Artemisia tridentata* ssp. *tridentata*, occupies valley bottoms and deep soils, while subspecies *wyomingensis* is the most xeric and occupies warmer and drier sites on somewhat more saline soils such as those of the Wyoming plains. Subspecies *vaseyana* is the most mesic of the three and occupies cooler and wetter sites in mountain valleys.

9. Chihuahuan Desert Province

a. Gramma–Tobosa. Comprising 47,200 km^2 in south-central New Mexico (Bailey, 1978) and extending southward into Mexico west of Ciudad Juarez, the gramma–tobosa grassland area is hot in the summer and often cold in the winter. Average precipitation at Las Cruces, New Mexico, is 140 mm, of which 46 mm occurs in the summer months. Topography is that of high plains with internal drainage leading to saline playas (Brown, 1982a). Although in appearance it is a grassland type, the shrubs *Larrea tridentata*, *Flourensia cernua*, and *Yucca elata* are abundant. In areas of sandy hummocks, low forms of *Prosopis glandulosa* var. *glandulosa* and *Ephedra trifurcata* add to the diversity. Grazing use is only conducted on an extensive basis with a carrying capacity of 0.47 AUM/ha for areas in good condition.

b. Tarbush–Creosote Bush. Extending south from the gramma–tobosa type, 75,920 km^2 of the *Flourensia cernua–Larrea tridentata* type are located in southwest Texas and along the lower plains of the Rio Grande. In Mexico this type continues southward through eastern Chihuahua, western Coahuila, and the far eastern margin of Durango. The climate is arid and hot, characterized by that of Camargo, Coahuila with an annual precipitation 318 mm, with 71% occurring in the five summer months (Brown, 1982a). *Larrea* is the most prevalent shrub but *Flourensia cernua, Acacia neovernicosa, Fouquieria splendens, Parthenium incanum,* and *Agave lecheguilla* add variety to extensive ridges, slopes, and plains. Highly calcareous and saline barren playas and shallow marshes in the center of large basins were once pluvial lakes. Carrying capacity for livestock grazing is less than in the gramma–tobosa type.

10. American Desert Province

a. Creosote Bush. The Mojave desert of southern Nevada and southeastern California sustains 95,420 km^2 of *Larrea tridentata* and its xeric associated species of *Yucca brevifolia, Cloeogyne ramosissima, Acacia gregii,* and perennial bunchgrasses *Hilaria jamesii* and *Oryzopsis hymenoides.* On the margin of the desert, other shrub communities such as *Atriplex polycarpa, Artemisia tridentata,* and *Juniperus californica* form associations with the dominant *Larrea.* The desert is rich in ephemeral annual species that germinate and produce a carpet of color in the occasional year of adequate late winter and early spring precipitation (Turner, 1982). Average precipitation is less than 150 mm. Topographically the desert is a series of extensive basins with low mountains separating them. Many of the basins are closed and in wet years ephemeral playas develop. Soils are sandy and saline and the limited nitrogen fertility is concentrated in "islands of fertility" under the canopy of shrubs (Garcia-Moya and McKell, 1970). Grazing use is very limited, and the average carrying capacity is as low as 0.7 AUM/ha.

b. Creosote Bush–Bur Sage. Continuing south of the creosote bush type with average rainfall of 130 mm, the *Larrea–Flourensia* type occupies 105,000 km^2 in extreme southwestern Arizona, southeastern California, and extending into Mexico along the Sonora coastal plain as far south as Los Mochis. According to the report by Turner and Brown (1982), many species of the Sonoran desert shrub type are derived from subtropical elements that evolved to fill the void left by the demise of more mesic types following the Holocene shift to a desert climate. Dominant shrubs are *Larrea tridentata* and *Ambrosia dumosa,* as well as *Cercidium microphyllum, Foquieria splendens, Jatropha cuneata,* and the columnar cactus,

Carnegiea gigantea, which are more abundant along the minor rills. Carrying capacity is 0.012 AUM/ha.

11. The Baja California Province

The Baja California Province includes four of the seven desert communities reported by Shreve and Wiggins (1964): microphyllous, sarcocaulescent, sarcophyllous, and arbocrassicaulescent. Turner and Brown (1982) regard only the first three as desert scrub. This idea is very much in line with what has been worked out by COTECOCA (1974, 1975) in the delimitation of range sites for the entire peninsula. It covers 62,720 km^2 and has precipitation values from 30 to 450 mm falling in summer, winter, or both seasons. The province has unique vegetational features imparted by the presence of *Idria (Fouquieria) columnaris, Pachycormus discolor, Fouquieria peninsularis, Pachycereus pringlei, Yucca valida, Agave shawii, Viscainoa geniculata,* and *Glaucotea armata* (Shreve and Wiggins, 1964). It is the province with the lowest carrying capacity, with values from 2.9 to 4.5 ha/AUM with an average of 3.9 AUM. (COTECOCA, 1974, 1975).

III. Development and Management of Shrublands

A. *Historical Aspects*

Human occupation of the arid and semiarid shrublands of North America has had a varied history. Indigenous peoples learned to live with the constraints of aridity and low plant productivity. Each of the American Indian tribes adapted ways by which the meager plant resources could be used for human food and domestic animal feed. Most of the meat protein was derived from wildlife killed by hunting parties. Nuts, berries, and seeds collected from wild plants were stored for use in periods of winter and stress. Compared with present-day land use practices, the native Indians lived in harmony with nature. Conquerors and settlers from Europe took control of the land either by means of land grants from a foreign power, such as the Spanish Land Grants of Mexico, or by the extension of sovereign power over large tracts of "public land." To encourage settlement of the western desert the U.S. Congress passed the Enlarged Homestead Act of 1911 and the Stock Raising Homestead Act of 1916 that permitted entry of 320- and 640-acre homesteads, respectively (R. G. Brown, 1948). Coming as they did from climates and vegetation dissimilar to that of the shrublands, settlers had a slow and sometimes painful learning process. Misinformation of the basic productivity of the land and competition for use of a relatively free and common resource led to crowding of livestock on land at rates in excess of carrying capacity. The result was deterioration of land productivity through overgrazing of forage grasses, a decrease in high palatability shrubs, and accelerated erosion.

In the late 1800s and early 1900s sheep numbers in the United States reached peak levels and created intense competition for grazing land. Jackman and Long (1982) described how in 1930 Lake County, Oregon, had about 175,000 sheep as compared with the permitted number of 40,000 in 1980. During the days of unregulated grazing, additional sheep were trailed in for "itinerant" winter grazing on the shrubs.

Against this background of intense use, abuse, and lack of understanding, research attention began to be directed to solving problems of biology and management. In 1934 the U.S. Congress authorized the formation of the U.S. Grazing Service. One year later it became the Bureau of Land Management (BLM), which was charged with the responsibility of setting grazing use standards and regulating uses. Although it operated on a policy of managing for multiple uses, the BLM had to await passage of the Federal Land Policy and Management Act of 1976 to clarify its role in managing arid and semiarid public lands for sustained multiple uses. For the past 150 years there has been a gradual evolution of utilization, research, and management of shrublands in the United States. A somewhat similar transition has taken place in Mexico, although land degradation may have reached lower levels than in the United States and the development of research and management began later.

B. General Productivity and Management Problems

The generally low productivity of shrublands in contrast with other vegetation types creates special problems for management. In areas of limited precipitation, particularly so with regard to the often long periods of drought, lack of sustained productivity is a serious problem for management. Even though shrubs are well suited to endure as well as produce more biomass than other plant groups such as annual and perennial grasses during periods of environmental stress, the level of production may not be sufficient to sustain a consistently high level of uses. Thus, the rule developed by professional resource managers is to set the level of use close to the minimum level of cyclic production to avoid damage to the resource in times of stress.

C. Special Uses

Perhaps no single vegetation type has been so neglected, abused, and even cursed as the shrublands. Yet modern livestock producers and wildlife managers are acutely aware of shrub values. As reviewed in "Wildland Shrubs: Their Biology and Utilization" (McKell *et al.*, 1972), there are many uses of shrublands for the benefit of man, among them animal feed, erosion control, industrial products, ornamentals, medicinal sources, and maintaining ecosystem functions.

1. Browse and Forage Use

In the foregoing descriptions of North American shrublands, the carrying capacity of each has been mentioned in terms of the numbers of animal unit months of grazing that could be obtained per hectare on a sustained yield basis. These figures can also be used to compare one type with another. The data for carrying capacity were compiled on the basis of the total amount of forage available for animal consumption, sometimes ignoring the values contributed by shrubs during periods not traditionally considered as prime grazing time when grasses and forbs are the mainstay for the grazing animal. Cook (1972) cited data to show that except for digestible energy, shrubs have higher values for protein, phosphorus, lignin, and carotene than grasses or forbs and are most important for fall and winter grazing, when grasses and forbs are not available in quantity and, as a result, the forage value of shrubs increases. Desert shrublands are used in a transhumant grazing pattern (McKell and Norton, 1981), whereby livestock are herded in the mountains during the late spring and summer, in the foothills in the fall, and in the desert shrublands in the winter. Where topographic variety does not include mountainous areas, animals must be herded year-round on desert shrub–grasslands at a lower stocking rate. In most areas, wildlife species must compete with livestock for forage and browse. One of the most important challenges of wildlife and range managers is to manage animal numbers to be commensurate with the productivity of the vegetation. Differences in species preferences of the various animals provide opportunities for management to balance the general level of use placed on shrubland species. When the most unpalatable plants receive little or no grazing use, they increase in density, creating very difficult management problems for sustaining useful productivity.

2. Erosion Control

Although shrubs are not a first choice of soil conservation specialists for controlling soil erosion, shrubs have valuable features such as a deep root system and a spreading habit that are present during all seasons and provide benefits sometimes not common to traditional conservation species. The tendency in the past has been to choose grasses because of their ease of establishment and availability of seeds, but now that seeds and methods for establishment of shrubs are available, greater use will be made of this valuable resource. Species of all shrub types and areas of ecological adaptation are being used for reclamation of areas drastically disturbed in the development of surface coal mines, pipelines, petroleum resources, and industrial facilities.

3. Industrial Products

Some shrubs contain economically attractive levels of secondary metabolic products that have industrial uses. Several North American shrubs receiving research and development attention may be important in the future. The most notable example is jojoba (*Simmondsia chinensis*), a native of the southern California chaparral and Colorado–Sonoran desert, which produces seeds containing a valuable long-chain fatty acid. Over 16,000 ha have been planted in the United States, plus substantial areas in suitable climates in Mexico, Israel, Australia, South Africa, and Latin American countries. Problems and opportunities of a fledgling jojoba industry have been discussed annually at international jojoba conferences.

Potential products from other shrubs such as *Parthenium argentatum* and *Prosopis* spp. have been described in many reports summarized in publications by the National Academy of Sciences (1975), in symposium proceedings edited by Ritchie (1979) and by Goodin and Northington (1979), and in a report prepared by Theisen *et al.* (1978), to mention a few.

4. Ornamentals

Increasing demands for low-maintenance, low-water-consumption landscaping plant materials prompt a careful examination of shrubs with aesthetic appeal. Stark (1966) brought native shrubs to the attention of highway landscape planners who subsequently included them in their specifications. The report of the Natural Vegetation Committee of the Arizona Chapter of the Soil Conservation Society of America (1973) described the many opportunities to utilize shrubs in landscape plans for the arid Southwest.

5. Medicinal Sources

Few commercial uses of shrubs have been documented but indigenous peoples make use of shrubs in many ways. The pharmaceutical industry appears to be very interested in jojoba oil as a base for various preparations as soon as a dependable supply is assured. Steroidal sapogenins have been extracted from *Yucca* species and could be available as a main product in relation to an expanded program of *Agave* and *Yucca* for their fibers (Dominguez, 1968). The big problem in development appears to be lack of adequate information.

6. Maintaining Ecosystem Functions

The importance of shrubs in maintaining ecosystem functions should not be overlooked. Processes such as nutrient cycling are vital as Garcia-Moya and McKell (1970) pointed out in describing the immediate area under the canopy of desert shrubs as "islands of fertility," whereas the interspace area is almost devoid of soil nitrogen. Subsequent work reviewed by West and Skujins (1978) elaborated many of the details of nutrient turnover in desert shrubland systems. Each shrub creates a microsystem in which it influences temperature, cycles nutrients, reduces wind speed, adds organic matter as well as chemical breakdown products, and thus adds stability to the plant–soil–animal complex.

D. Perspectives for the Future

Although shrublands of North America appear to be influenced adversely by unwise and exploitative management, greater knowledge of the ecological potential of individual species and improved management practices give reason for optimism. Indiscriminate and broad-scale chemical control of all shrub species is no longer a main objective of range improvement programs. Inclusion of valuable fodder shrub seeds in seed mixtures is becoming a common practice now that quality seeds are available. Shrublands considered to be areas of critical wildlife habitat have been identified and are often under management appropriate for the dominant wildlife use. Commercial development for industrial products, biomass, fibers, or other materials brings a heightened awareness for the need to better understand the biology of shrubs and to better manage them for optimum and sustained production. Inasmuch as the major use of shrublands is still for grazing, there is need for better understanding of the ways in which sustained use can be obtained while maintaining productivity of all ecosystem components.

IV. Summary

North American shrublands represent one of the most extensive plant resources of the continent, yet they are one of the least understood and possibly the poorest managed. Productivity ranges from a low of less than 0.012 AUM/ha for the southern desert shrub to 0.85 AUM/ha for mesquite–buffalo grass. Eleven shrubland types occupy the southwestern portion of the United States and all of northern Mexico. Historical development of each country has involved extensive use and abuse of shrubland resources. Livestock and wildlife use of shrubs constitute the major uses, and possibilities for development of shrubs for industrial products, landscape ornamentals, biomass, and medicinal products remain largely in the future as knowledge of shrublands increases.

References

Aro, R. S. (1971). Evaluation of pinyon–juniper conversion to grassland. *J. Range Manage.* **24**, 188–189.

Axelrod, O. F. (1940). Historical development of the woodland climax in western North America. *Am. J. Bot.* **27**, 21.

Bailey, R. G. (1978). "Descriptions of the Ecoregions of the United States." USDA For. Serv. Intermountain Region, Ogden, Utah.

Bailey, R., and Cushwa, C. T. (1981). "Ecoregions of North America." USDA Forest Service and USDI Fish and Wildlife Service, U. S. Geological Survey National Mapping Division, Reston, Virginia.

Barker, J. R., and McKell, C. M. (1983). Habitat differences between basin and Wyoming big sagebrush in contiguous populations. *J. Range Manage.* **36**, 450–454.

Bentley, J. R. (1967). Conversion of chaparral areas to grassland. *U. S., Dept. Agric., Agric. Handb.* **328**.

Bleak, A. T., Frischknecht, N. C., Plummer, A. P., and Eckert, R. E., Jr. (1965). Problems in artificial and natural revegetation of the arid shadscale vegetation zone of Utah and Nevada. *J. Range Manage.* **18**, 59–65.

Brown, D. E., ed. (1982a). "Biotic Communities of the American Southwest: United States and Mexico," Desert Plants, Vol. 4, Nos. 1–4. University of Arizona, Tucson.

Brown, D. E. (1982b). Sinaloan Thornscrub. *Desert Plants* **4** (1–4), 101–105.

Brown, R. G. (1948). "Historical Geography of the United States." Harcourt Brace, New York.

COTECOCA (1974). "Coeficientes de Agostadero de la República Mexicana. Estado de Baja California." Comisión Técnico Consultiva para la Determinación Regional de los Coeficientes de Agostadero, Secretaria de Agricultura y Ganadería, México, D. F.

COTECOCA (1975). "Coeficientes de Agostadero de la República Mexicana. Estado de Baja California Sur." Comisión Técnico Consultiva para la Determinación Regional de los Coeficientes de Agostadero, Secretaria de Agriculture y Ganadería, México, D. F.

COTECOCA (1976). "Coeficientes de Agostadero de la República Mexicana. Estado de Sinaloa." Comisión Técnica Consultiva para la Determinación Regional de los Coeficientes de Agostadero, Secretaría de Agricultura y Ganadería, Mexico, D. F.

COTECOCA (1978). "Tamaulipas." Comision Tecnico Consultiva para la Determinación Regional de los Coeficientes de Agostadero, Secretaría de Agricultura y Recursos Hidraúlicos, Subsecretaría de Ganadería, México, D. F.

Cook, C. W. (1958). Sagebrush eradication and brushland seeding. *Bull. — Utah Agric. Exp. Stn.* **404**.

Cook, C. W. (1972). Comparative nutrient values of forbs, grasses and shrubs. *In* "Wildland Shrubs: Their Biology and Utilization" (C. M. McKell, J. P. Blaisdell, and J. R. Goodin, eds.), USDA For. Serv. Gen. Tech. Rep. INT-1, pp. 303–310. Utah State University, Logan.

Dominguez, X. R. (1968). Industria racional de las plantas nativas de zonas aridas. *In* "International Symposium on Increasing Food Production in Arid Lands" (T. W. Box, and P. Rojas-Mendosa, eds.), pp. 225–236. Texas Tech Univ. Press, Lubbock.

Drawe, D. L. (1977). A study of five methods of mechanical brush control in south Texas. *Rangeman's J.* **4** (2), 37–39.

Felker, P. (1979). Mesquite: An all-purpose leguminous arid land tree. *AAAS Sel. Symp.* **38**, 89–135.

Fenniman, N. M. (1929). Physiographic divisions of the United States. *Anna. Assoc. Am. Geogr.* **18**, 261–353.

Forest-Range Task Force (1972). The nation's range resources—A forest range environmental study. *For. Resour. Rep. (U. S., For. Serv.)* **19.**

Garcia-Moya, E., and McKell, C. M. (1970). Contribution of shrubs to the nitrogen economy of a desert wash plant community. *Ecology* **51**, 81–88.

Gentry, H. S. (1942). Rio Mayo plants: A study of the flora and vegetation of the valley of the Rio Mayo-Sonora. *Carnegie Inst. Washington Publ.* **527.**

Gifford, G. F., and Busby, F. E., eds. (1975). "The Pinyon–Juniper Ecosystem: A Symposium." Utah State University, Logan.

Good, R. (1947). "The Geography of Flowering Plants." Longmans, Green, London.

Goodin, J. R., and Northington, D. K., eds. (1979). "Arid Land Plant Resources." International Center for Arid and Semiarid Land Studies, Tesas Tech Univ. Press, Lubbock.

Gould, F. W. (1962). "Texas Plants—A Checklist and Ecological Summary." Texas Agricultural Experiment Station, Texas A & M University, College Station.

Institute for Land Rehabilitation (1978). Rehabilitation of western wildlife habitat: A review. *U. S., Fish Wildl. Serv., off. Biol. Serv. [Tech. Rep.] FWS/OBS* **FWS/OBS/78–86.**

Jackman, E. R., and Long, R. A. (1982). "The Oregon Desert." Caxton Printers, Caldwell, Idaho.

Küchler, A. W. (1964). Potential natural vegetation of the coterminus United States. *Am. Geogr. Soc., Spec. Publ.* **36.**

Long, C. H. (1965). The mammals of Wyoming. *Univ. Kans. Publ. Mus. Nat. Hist.* **14**, 493–758.

Love, R. M., Berry, L. J., Street, J. E., and Osterli, V. P. (1960). Planned range improvement programs are beneficial. *Calif. Agric.* **14** (6), 2–4.

McKell, C. M., and Norton, B. E. (1981). Management of arid resources for domestic livestock forage. *In* "Arid Land Ecosystems: Structure, Functioning and Management" (D. W. Goodall, and R. A. Perry, eds.), Vol. 2, IBP 17. Cambridge Univ. Press, London and New York.

McKell, C. M., Blaisdell, J. P., and Goodin, J. R., eds. (1972). "Wildland Shrubs: Their Biology and Utilization." USDA For. Serv. Gen Tech. Rep. INT-1. Utah State University, Logan.

McKell, C. M., Goodin, J. R., and Jeffries R. L. (1984). Saline land of the United States of America and Canada. *In* "Proceedings of Seminar on Forage and Fuel from Salt Affected Wasteland." Western Australia Dept. Agric., West Perth.

Miranda, F., and Hernández, E. (1963). Tos tipos de vegetatcion de Mexico y su clasificacion. *Bol. Soc. Bot. Mex.* **28**, 29–179.

Mooney, H. A. (1977). Southern coastal scrub. *In* "Terrestrial Vegetation of California" (M. G. Barbour and J. Major, eds.), pp. 471–489. Wiley, New York.

National Academy of Sciences (1975). "Underexploited Tropical Plants with Promising Economic Value." Panel of Advisory Committee on Technology Innovation, Board of Science and Technology for International Development, Washington, D. C.

Natural Vegetation Committee, Arizona Chapter, Soil Conservation Society of America (1973). "Landscaping with Native Arizona Plants." Univ. of Arizona Press, Tucson.

Pase, C. P. (1982). California (coastal) chaparral. *Desert Plants* **4** (1–4), 91–94.

Plummer, A. P., Christensen, D. R. and Monsen, S. B. (1968). Restoring big game range in Utah. *Utah Div. Fish Game, Publ.* **68–3.**

Ritchie, G. A., ed. (1979). "New Agricultural Crops," AAAS Sel. Symp., No: 38. Westview Press, Boulder, Colorado:

Roundy, B. A., and Young, J. A. (1985). Salt deserts of the Great Basin. *Proc. Sel. Pap., 38th Annu. Meet. Soc. Range Manage.,* pp. 39–49.

Rzedowski, J. (1978). "Vegetacion de Mexico." Limusa, Mexico, D. F.

Schifres, C. J. (1980). "Brush Management: Principles and Practises for Texas and the Southwest." Texas A & M Univ. Press, College Station.

Shantz, H. L., and Zon, R. (1924). The natural vegetation of the United States. *In* "Atlas of American Agriculture," Sect. 7. USDA, Washington, D. C.

Shreve, F. (1917). A map of the vegetation of the United States. *Geogr. Rev.* **3,** 119–125.

Shreve, F. (1937). The vegetation of Sinaloa. *Bull. Torrey Bot. Club* **64,** 605–613.

Shreve, F. (1951). Vegetation and flora of the Sonoran Desert. Vol. 1. Vegetation. *Carnegie Inst. Washington Publ.* **591.**

Shreve, F., and Wiggins, L. (1964). "Vegetation and Flora of the Sonoran Desert," Vol. 1. Stanford Univ. Press, Stanford, California.

Stark, N. (1966). "Review of Highway Planting Information Appropriate to Nevada," Coll. Agric. Bull. b–7. Desert Res. Inst., University of Nevada, Reno.

Theisen, A. A., Knox, E. G., and Mann, F. L. (1978). "Feasibility of Introducing Food Crops Better Adapted to Environmental Stress," Vols. I and II. National Science Foundation, Washington, D. C.

Tueller, P. T., Beeson, D., Tausch, R. J., West, N., and Rea, K. H. (1979). Pinyon–juniper woodlands of the Great Basin: Distribution, flora, vegetal cover. *USDA For. Serv. Res. Pap. INT* **INT–229.**

Turner, R. (1982). Mojave desert scrub. *Desert Plants* **4** (1–4), 152–168.

Turner, R. M., and Brown, D. E. (1982). Sonoran desertscrub. *Desert Plants* **4** (14), 181–220.

Valentine, J. F. (1979). "Range Development and Improvements," 2nd ed. Brigham Univ. Press, Provo, Utah.

Ward, G. H. (1953). *Artemisia,* section *Seriphidium* in North America—A cytotaxonomic study. *Contrib. Dudley Herb.* **4,** 155–205.

West, N., and Skujins, J. (1978). "Nitrogen in Desert Ecosystems." Hutchinson & Ross, Stroudsburg, Pennsylvania.

Williams, M. C. (1973). Halogeton—Sheep killers in the West. *Weeds Today* **4,** 10–22.

2

South American Shrublands

Osvaldo A. Fernández
Roberto M. Bóo
Luis F. Sánchez

I. Introduction

South America extends from latitude 12° N to 56° S, with a length of 7500 km. It is 5000 km at its widest part and the highest mountains reach 7000 m. Therefore, an extraordinary variability may be expected in the sequence of vertical and horizontal biogeographical zones, which range from the equatorial tropical rain forests to the Puna de Atacama desert to the cold austral subantarctic regions.

This chapter is dedicated to Anibal N. Balmaceda, a former researcher of the Universidad Nacional del Sur and the Province of Río Negro, who, despite his youth, was an academician in the classic sense, and an independent and original experimenter. He was a person of immense warmth and was respected and cherished by friends and colleagues.

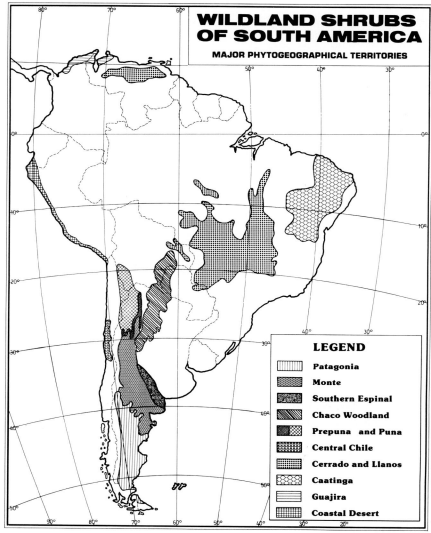

Figure 1. Major phytogeographical territories of the wildland shrubs of South America. This map has been compiled from the following sources of information: Cabrera (1976), Cabrera and Willink (1980), Cochrane and Sánchez (1981), Gómez Molina and Little (1981), Morello (1968), OEA (1971), and Quintanilla (1981).

In extensive areas of this continent the environmental conditions allow for the development of a more or less continuous vegetation cover, but many areas are frequently too dry to permit regular soil cultivation. Features characterizing these areas are usually associated to semiarid ecosystems in terms of structure and function. The vegetation is commonly a combination of herbaceous and woody species in which shrubs frequently constitute the dominant plant strata.

The major phytogeographical territories in which shrubs are present at least in part as the dominant plant forms are shown in Fig. 1. Within these large areas there are naturally large variations in the environmental factors and vegetation, making each of them unique in several ways. Some of these territories, such as the Monte, have a shrub climax as the dominant community, whereas others, such as Chaco Woodland, though essentially a tree community, have very strong shrub elements.

A brief description of each territory, including its climate, relief, types of soils, and vegetation, is given. The climate seasonal courses are shown in the ecological climate diagrams of Fig. 2. Because of limited space only one climate seasonal diagram is represented for each phytogeographical region.

Soils are classified under two main systems, the one developed by the Soil Survey Staff (1975) of the United States Department of Agriculture and that elaborated by FAO–UNESCO (1971) for the Soil Map of the World. They are referred to in the text as "Soil Taxonomy" and "FAO Legend," respectively.

In each discussion the greatest emphasis is given to palatable shrubs. However, a brief consideration is given to shrubs that can be useful for pharmaceutical properties, industrial purposes, and as protectors of microenvironments for other valuable species. We will also refer to present management practices and human impact on shrubs and shrubland types.

Land use mainly based on the utilization of natural vegetation is a common feature of the wildland shrubs in South America. The geographical territories described here may seem limitless since they occupy a significant part of South America, however, their wildland ecosystems are fragile and easily injured by abusive use. Should the vegetation cover be damaged, a downward succession begins toward desertification.

Land use is retrograde, in the sense that little modern technology is applied and management practices are simple. Grazing and browsing pressure by livestock is more remarkable in some places than in others, but in general wildlands have not been devastated as in the arid and semiarid lands of other parts of the world. We can foresee improvements that might increase the productivity of these territories.

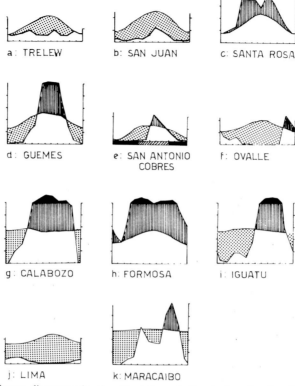

Figure 2. Climate diagrams showing 11 stations in South America for the major shrub phytogeographical territories: (a) Patagonia, (b) Monte, (c) Southern Espinal, (d) Chaco Woodland, (e) Prepuna and Puna, (f) Central Chile, (g) Llanos, (h) Cerrado, (i) Caatinga, (j) Coastal Desert, and (k) Guajira. (From Walter *et al.*, 1975.)

II. Patagonia

The Patagonia is one of the few cold arid and semiarid regions of the world. It extends throughout southern Argentina, from the Atlantic Ocean to the Andean piedmont in the west. Huge masses of marine and continental sediments that accumulated over crystalline ancient rocks were eroded by winds and waters to create deep valleys and gulches. The resulting landscape consists of plateaus and hills of flattened surfaces and stepped slopes that constitute the typical "tabular" relief of the extra-Andean Patagonia. An outstanding feature characterizing the plateau surfaces is the presence of Patagonic or "tehuelches" boulders related to fluvioglacial origin. These boulders form a desert pavement; in these areas the winds are very strong and prevent any deposition of material.

The Patagonian central plateaus show a typical arid temperate climate with four well-defined seasons. Strong winds are frequent and rainfall ranges from 100 to 200 mm/yr. In the southernmost areas of this territory the climate can be considered as cold-temperate arid. In the northern plateaus, comprising the Colorado and the Limay–Negro rivers and the coastal oceanic border, rainfall increases slightly, though it remains below 300 mm/yr. For the Patagonia area as a whole, the annual average temperature ranges from 6° to 14°C. Absolute maximal temperatures vary from 30° to 40°C and the absolute minimal ones range from −15° to −20°C and lower, while the average annual potential evapotranspiration ranges from 550 to 750 mm/yr. All these values decrease from the northeast toward the southwest. The frost average annual frequency is 60 or more days. The snowfall average annual frequency is 5 to 20 days, mainly falling in the west and the south.

Monteith and Laya (1970) describe the presence of lithological discontinuities, boulders throughout the profile, sandy-textured topsoils, and clay accumulations in the subsoil related to paleoclimatic origin as the main characteristics of the Patagonic soils. Volcanic ash is a parent material in some cases, though it frequently appears as superficial or buried layers. The subsoil pH is neutral, though there exist moderate to strong alkalinity conditions in the topsoil. Small valley ("mallin") soils are subject to floods and are partly bog soils, grassland soils, Solonetz, and Solonchaks (Papadakis, 1963).

The Soil Map of the World (FAO–UNESCO, 1971) shows that the dominant soils of Patagonia are Luvic Yermosols associated with Calcic Yermosols and Orthic Solonchaks. In the province of Neuquén (northwest Patagonia), Eutric Regosols are dominant. In the southern Patagonia, Luvic Kastanozems associated with Eutric Regosols are reported. The valley bottoms of the great Patagonian rivers contain Eutric Fluvisols (FAO Legend). A soil map of Argentina compiled by Etchevehere (1971) shows the Patagonic zone soils as an association of Petrocalcic Calciothids and Psamments, with dominant Calciorthids. Also large Lithosols areas and other smaller isolated areas with Fluvents and Natrustolls are mentioned. The valley bottoms of the great rivers are associated with Fluvents (Soil Taxonomy). Soil humidity and temperature regimes for the whole Patagonia were determined as aridic and thermic, respectively, by Van Wambeke and Scoppa (1976).

A detailed study on the geology, soils, vegetation, and animal life on the Patagonia has been published by Soriano (1983). In terms of phytogeographical units, most of this territory is quoted by Cabrera (1976) as the

Patagonian Province. A study and mapping of the vegetation units of Central Patagonia have been carried out by Bertiller *et al.* (1987, 1981a, 1981b).

Studies on the ecotone vegetation of the north of this territory together with that of the Monte have been published by Soriano (1949, 1950) and Ruiz Leal (1972). The shrubs *Larrea divaricata, L. nitida,* and *Bougainvillea spinosa* are dominant in this transition area. The Patagonia vegetation is characterized by a low shrubby steppe intermingled with tussock grasses. In large areas, the shrubs are the physiognomically dominant plant species. The most frequent shrubs are: *Chuquiraga avellanedae, Colliguaya integerrima, Mulinum spinosum, Senecio filaginoides, Verbena tridens, Pseudoabutilon bicolor, Berberis heterophylla, B. cuneata, Baccharis darwinii, Anarthrophyllum rigidum, Nassauvia glomerulosa, Lycium chilense,* and others.

The Patagonian rangelands are mainly used for sheep production. The stocking rate varies between 400 and 2500 sheep per square league (2500 hectares). The shrubs contribute significantly to the actual diet of sheep; the species preferentially browsed are: *Lycium chilense, Verbena ligustrina, Ephedra ochreata, Adesmia campestris, Atriplex sagittifolium, Trevoa patagonica,* and *Nassauvia glomerulosa.* They are notably hedged and are frequently eaten almost to the ground.

Tinto (1977) cited *Lycium chilense* and *Ephedra ochreata* as valuable fodder species for the arid and semiarid environments. The digestible protein for these two species was reported as 2.26 and 6.85% respectively, on a dry matter basis (Abiusso, 1962). Continuous overgrazing has provoked either the decrease of the area occupied by useful shrubs or their replacement by others having low palatability and less nutritive value. Remarkably, some of the most frequent shrubs such as *Chuquiraga avellaneadae* and *Colliguaya integerrima* are not eaten by domestic animals or only used in very moderate amounts.

Mulinum spinosum, a common cushion shrub of the north and center of the Patagonia, has been mentioned (Soriano, 1956) as an indicator of soil moisture. Its color can vary from deep green to brownish yellow. This species blossoms in summer and its flowers are eaten by sheep, thereby conferring to the meat a disgusting taste. One of the biggest shrubs of the Patagonia is *Schinus polygamus.* Adult plants can reach 3 m in height. This species used to be an abundant representative of the flora of the southern Patagonia. However, because of its excellent qualities as firewood it was indiscriminately overexploited and has disappeared from many places.

Abusive use of land by overgrazing for over 100 years has caused soil erosion and range degradation to such an extent that in extended areas the most desired species are almost extinguished, scarce, or continue growing only in places where livestock can hardly reach them. After more than three generations of careless land use, ranchers are inclined to think the present degraded rangeland conditions are a natural situation and not the result of many years of mismanagement. Fortunately, in many places it is still possible to reverse the continuous degradation process if simple conservation range improvement practices are followed.

III. Monte

The territory called Monte extends from north to south in central and western Argentina (Fig. 1). It is a vast, almost continuous and uniform area of shrublands comprising about 50 million hectares. Its boundaries with other large phytogeographical formations are marked by the development of wide ecotones.

Three main physiographical regions can be differentiated. The northern one presents a typical landscape of "bolsones" (intermontane depressions related to tectonic origin), valleys, and slopes belonging to the pampean hills. Rivers are intermittent and salty flats over large areas are common. The central portion is an undulating to depressed loessic plain related to fluvial, lacustrine, and Quaternary eolic origin. The third region forms the southernmost portion of the Monte and occurs on a plateau landscape in northeastern Patagonia. The climate of the Monte is dry and warm in the north, gradually becoming cooler toward the south.

Aridity in the northern portion of the Monte is related to its physiographical position between two mountain chains: the Andes to the west and the pampean hills to the east, which intercept the wet winds from the Pacific and the Atlantic, respectively. The large inner bolsón experiences very high solar radiation and evapotranspiration. Rains occur mainly during the summer and range from 80 mm up to slightly more than 200 mm/yr. The annual number of days with a clear sky is high, from 100 to 120 and sometimes more. Annual average temperatures range between 15° and 19°C and the frost average annual frequency is less than 60 but more than 5 days. Potential evapotranspiration decreases from 1000 mm in the west to 700 mm in the east. Soils are classified as Haplic Yermosols, Regosols, and Haplic Kastanozems (FAO Legend). Etchevehere (1971) reports them as Psamments, Calciorthids, Paleorthids, and Salorthids (Soil Taxonomy).

The climate of the intermediate region is warm and is influenced by warm, dry winds coming from the west. An accentuated continentality exists with very warm summers, when absolute maximum temperatures may reach 40° to 45°C. The absolute minima can decrease to −15° or

−20°C. The average annual temperature is 14° to 16°C. Rainfall ranges from 250 to 500 mm/yr. The annual number of days with a clear sky is 60 or more. The average annual potential evapotranspiration is 800 to 850 mm/yr. Soils have been formed from more or less recent accumulations of sands and finer materials and are classified as Calcic Xerosols and Haplic Yermosols (FAO Legend). The Soil Map of Argentina compiled by Etchevehere (1971) reports an extensive Quartzipsamments area in the north. Psamments and Salorthids occur toward the west, whereas toward the south an association of Petrocalcic Calciustolls, Aridic Haplustolls, and Calcixerolls exists.

Finally, the Patagonic southern portion of the Monte formation has a cold and arid climate. Its average annual temperatures range between 12° and 14°C. Rainfall is scanty, with 200 to 300 mm/yr or less concentrated in winter and spring. The average annual potential evapotranspiration decreases to 700 mm. The reported soils are Luvic Yermosols associated with Lithosols (FAO Legend). They are also classified as Calciorthids, Paleorthids, and Psamments.

A classic study on the Monte vegetation is that by Morello (1958). Other works on vegetation of the central-western portion of this territory have been published by Roig (1970), Ruiz-Leal (1972), and Böcher *et al.* (1972), and by Balmaceda (1979) of the southern portion. The Monte vegetation can be classified as a steppe scrub dominated by microphyllous xerophytic shrubs ranging from 1 to 3 m high. Height tends to decrease westward. Representatives of the Zygophyllaceae family are clearly dominant and *Larrea* is the most abundant genus. Associated with this community are several *Prosopis* spp. The Cactaceae family is also well represented, especially by the *Opuntia* and *Cereus* genera, whose abundance increases northward. Aphylly is a characteristic frequently found in the vegetation of this territory, in which photosynthesis is carried out mainly in the green stems and branches. Examples of aphyllous shrubs are *Bulnesia retama, Cassia aphylla, Monttea aphylla,* and *Neosparton aphyllum.*

The plant community most characteristic of the Monte is the "jarillal." It is a vegetal association dominated by *Larrea divaricata, L. cuneifolia,* and *L. nitida.* These evergreen shrubs preserve their leaves even through the most severe droughts. Other evergreen shrubs often found are *Atamisquea emarginata* and *Zuccagnia punctata.* Important deciduous species are *Plectrocarpa rougesii, Prosopis alpataco, Prosopidastrum globosum, Lycium chilense,* and *Geoffroea decorticans.*

The chemical composition and nutritive value of several shrubs found in this territory have been reported by Wainstein and González (1971) and Wainstein *et al.* (1979) (Table I). Species are grouped in several categories according to their potential as fodder for livestock. However, regardless of

Table I. Nutritional value of several shrubs of the Monte

Botanical name	Proteins		Fiber	Free nitrogen extract	Ash	Ca	P	Fodder value	Browsing preference
	Total	Digestible							
Prosopidastrum globosum	12.01	9.94	38.23	33.79	5.84	0.59	0.14	Very good	High
Ephedra ochreata	12.10	9.63	44.90	29.04	6.63	1.30	0.09	Good	Very high
Psila retamoides	8.84	7.13	34.20	40.41	4.93	0.71	0.21	Regular	—
Brachychlados lycioides	7.17	5.60	24.66	46.83	6.21	0.96	0.09	Inferior	High
Verbena aspera	14.37	12.90	23.90	37.54	11.25	1.62	0.24	Excellent	Medium
Bougainvillea spinosa	11.20	9.41	27.37	35.83	15.56	3.59	0.10	Very good	Medium
Lycium ovalilobum	10.65	8.35	37.69	10.45	27.91	7.32	0.07	Good	—
Lycium chilense	13.12	11.08	32.29	33.84	10.36	2.04	0.11	Very good	Very high
Lycium tenuispinosum	11.80	9.28	30.44	25.94	20.24	4.41	0.13	Very good	Medium
Tricomaria usillo	11.02	9.41	22.44	48.16	5.67	1.11	0.12	Good	—

Source: Adapted from Wainstein *et al.* (1979).
Note: Air dry moisture free %.

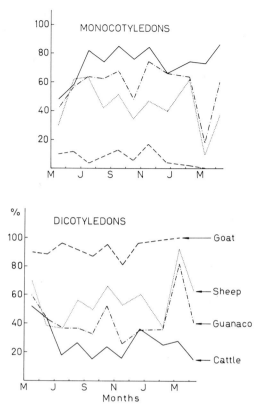

Figure 3. Yearly percentage consumption by goat, sheep, guanaco, and cattle of monocotyledons and dicotyledons of the Monte. (From Balmaceda and de Digiuni, 1981.)

nutritive value or abundance of a species, it is of no use unless animals eat it. Selective feeding by livestock does not necessarily correlate with the nutritive value of the plant tissue. For example, although *Brachyclados lycioides* is considered to be of poor nutritive value, it is eagerly sought by animals and heavily browsed. The chemical composition of several shrubby species of the Monte including the three above-mentioned *Larrea* species has been studied by Abiusso (1962). Various shrubs of the Monte have been cited by Tinto (1977) as a possible fodder resource for livestock.

Although shrubs in this territory produce most of the available plant biomass, little is known about selective feeding by livestock and wildlife. Some wildland shrubs have acquired a reputation as fodder plants as they appear to be consistently browsed by livestock. Poor management of the shrubby community may result in the replacement of these species for less valuable ones. This situation may seriously affect the stocking rate capacity.

Pioneering research on selective feeding on a steppe scrub in Monte rangeland has been reported by Balmaceda and de Digiuni (1981, 1982). The monthly free food intake of cattle, sheep, goat, and guanaco (*Lama guanicoe*) was ascertained using microhistological feces analysis. Figures 3 and 4 show the feeding preferences of animals including details for four of the most frequently browsed shrubs in the study area. Other species included in this study and not shown in Fig. 4 were *Hyalis argentea*, *Prosopis alpataco*, and *Larrea divaricata*. The total yearly percentage consumption of dicotyledons averaged 26.6 for cattle, 43.6 for guanaco, 56.4 for sheep, and 92.3 for goats.

Figure 4. Yearly percentage consumption by goat, sheep, guanaco, and cattle of four commonly browsed shrubs of the Monte. (From Balmaceda and de Digiuni, 1982.)

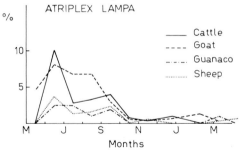

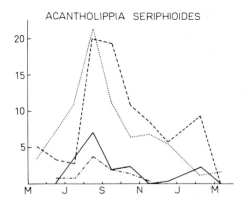

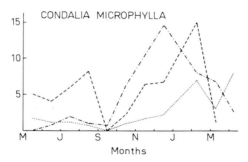

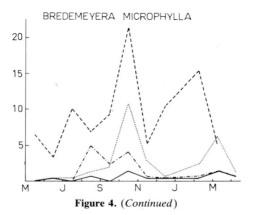

Figure 4. (*Continued*)

Studies on the aboveground primary productivity and caloric content in the Monte community of the mendozinian plains have been carried out by Braun *et al.* (1979) and Braun and Candia (1980). The primary productivity fluctuates around 1600 kg per hectare per year, with 90% due to woody species. The cattle stocking rate for this area has been estimated at about 25 to 30 hectares per animal unit (Guevara *et al.*, 1977).

Particular attention has been given to *Larrea* species because of their abundance and capacity to establish in the driest and warmest zones of the semiarid regions of South and North America, where they can become dominant over vast areas. An International Biological Program contribution was devoted to the biology, chemistry, and distribution of *Larrea* spp. Timmermann (1977) summarizes several interesting possible and practical uses of this plant. Varied chemical treatments (Duisberg, 1952; Abiusso, 1971; Tinto, 1977) can transform *Larrea* tissues into a nutritious feed for livestock after eliminating the high resin content that renders it unpalatable to animals.

The human impact in the Monte has been great. Areas containing trees have been frequently exploited almost to their extinction. The primary biomass productivity of the Monte can be increased by applying conservation land management practices, preventing rangeland erosion, and replacing less valuable shrubs with those with useful characteristics.

IV. Southern Espinal

In terms of phytogeographical units this territory coincides approximately with the southern part of the Espinal Province known as Cabrera's (1976) Calden District, or Parodi's (1964) Bosque Pampeano. The Southern Espinal is a level to gently undulating plain covered with recent sandy and loessic sandy sediments of eolian origin. There are endorheic basins and few permanent streams. The climate is temperate semiarid, and the aridity increases westward and southward. Summers are dry while spring and fall are rainy. Average rainfall is 400–600 mm/yr and average annual temperature is 15°–16°C. The absolute maximum is 42°C, whereas the absolute minimum is −10°C. The frost average annual frequency is 30 to 60 days.

Soils are more or less sandy and parent materials are rich in $CaCO_3$. They usually have a petrocalcic horizon ("tosca") with a hard, abrupt upper limit at a depth from 0.5 to 2 m. Originally they were called Prairie soils intergrading toward Brown soils. Papadakis (1963) named them Non-Chernozem Steppe soils lacking an argillic horizon and having a calcareous hardpan. In the depressions, some salty Humic Gley, Solonchaks, and Solonetz usually present a calcareous hardpan. These are also called Haplic Xerosolls, petrocalcic phases (FAO Legend).

This territory is physiognomically characterized by the presence of *Prosopis caldenia* (Caldén), which is the typical and almost exclusive representative tree. Caldén is a xerophytic deciduous tree that may exceed 10 m in height. Advancing southward in this territory, the presence of trees decreases and shrubs become the predominant woody representatives. The shrub layer is very rich and the most frequent species are: *Condalia microphylla, Lycium chilense, L. gilliesianum, Prosopis alpataco, Atamisquea emarginata, Prosopidastrum globosum, Ephedra ochreata, E. triandra, Baccharis ulicina, Geoffroea decorticans,* and *Larrea divaricata.* Under good range management, the herbaceous ground cover is abundant and very rich in perennial grasses of good forage value. The presence of halophilous steppes is frequent in poorly drained areas, where shrubs such as *Cyclolepis genistoides,* and *Atriplex* spp. appear.

One of the main causes of changes in the floristic composition has been the disturbance caused by man. During the first decades of this century, damage was due to overgrazing by cattle and the clearing of trees and shrubs for soil cultivation.

Because of climatic, soil, and vegetation conditions, this territory has a potential for more intense development of livestock activity than the Monte territory, with which it borders on the west. In general, the use of rangelands is very severe and only occasionally are appropriate range management techniques used.

Natural grasslands are normally overstocked with cattle, particularly during the dry summer season. At that time, the shrubby species represent a valuable fodder resource. Covas (1971) carried out an inventory of the woody species from which cattle and sheep feed: *Lycium chilense* and *Ephedra triandra* are possibly the two most palatable shrubs in this territory. Other shrubs frequently browsed are: *Ephedra ochreata, Atriplex lampa, A. ondulata, Croton parvifolius, Bredemeyera microphylla, Junellia aspera,* and *J. ligustrina.* Legume trees and shrubs are important fruit suppliers. The caldén are valuable for the production of pods. However, *Prosopis alpataco* and *P. flexuosa* pods are more palatable. *Geoffroea decorticans* drupes are also eaten by livestock.

Natural or accidental wildfires occur at irregular intervals in this territory and may be considered as an unpredictable environmental factor. As a rule, when associated with high summer temperatures and droughts, wildfires may cover thousands of hectares. Braun and Lamberto (1974) observed that fire caused a reduction of the shrubby cover but this effect was considered beneficial for the understory herbaceous vegetation. In the same area Willard (1973) reported that 58% of all woody plants were killed by headfire, while 36.5% died by backfire. Mortality ranged from 82% for *Schinus fasciculatus* to 38% for *Geoffroea decorticans* in the headfire area. Since wildfires are a common phenomenon throughout this territory, they play an important role in controlling shrub density and expansion. However, information on the beneficial effects of fire on shrubby vegetation is inadequate (Bóo, 1980).

Cattle raising is the most important economic activity in this territory. It has been threatened by the slow and relentless advance of *G. decorticans* on the native understory grassland vegetation. This species is a very aggressive shrub or small tree that propagates by seed and vegetatively from its roots, forming islets that can join among themselves in an advanced state of invasion. Primary productivity below the canopy of this species is always very low. In the last 50 years this woody species, originally confined to reduced areas, has become a weed that is advancing on a vast region of the temperate semiarid zone of Argentina (Fig. 5). The reasons for the *G. decorticans* invasion are all attributed to human activity. According to Anderson (1977), the most significant are (a) fire elimination, (b) extensive culture with alfalfa and cereal crops in marginal lands and subsequent abandonment, and (c) overgrazing.

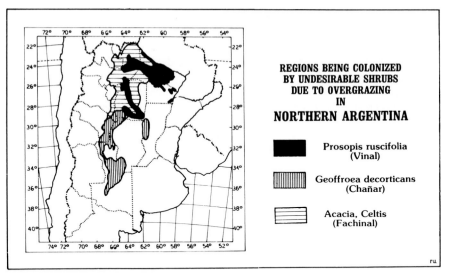

Figure 5.   Woody plants that are increasing in subhumid and semiarid regions of Argentina. (From Morello, 1975.)

V. Chaco Woodland

The Gran Chaco is a huge outwash plain built up of sediments derived mainly from the eastern Andes flank and filled with loessic, fluvial, and lacustrine quaternary materials. It comprises the north of Argentina, the west of Paraguay, and the southeast of Bolivia, broadly coinciding with the Biogeographic Chaqueña Province described by Cabrera and Willink (1980).

In Fig. 1, only the west portion of the Gran Chaco has been indicated. This region is referred to as Chaco Woodland. It represents the driest part of this huge sedimentary basin, whereas the wetter east portion is covered by forests, savannas, marshes, and tropical wet forests. The Chaco Woodland limits correspond on the Argentine side to those established by Morello (1968) for the Chaco Leñoso and they broadly overlap with those of the Parque Chaqueño Occidental described by Ragonese and Castiglione (1970) or the Distrito Chaqueño Occidental by Cabrera (1970).

The Chaco Woodland is characterized by its hot, wet summers and mild, dry winters. Rain ranges between 500 and 800 mm/yr, reaching lower values in the western boundaries (320 mm/yr). The wet season extends from October to April and the dry season from May to September.

Maximum absolute temperatures reach very high values (48.9°C in Rivada-
via, Salta, Argentina), while the minimum absolute temperatures go to
−8°C in the meridional portion. The average annual frequency of frost is
0–5 days and 5–30 days in the north and south of the Chaco Argentinian
portion, respectively.

The predominant soils of the Chaco Woodland are coarse textured, of a
high base status, lack an argillic horizon, but have an epipedon darkened
by organic matter. There are also alluvial soils on the floodplains of the
rivers. Over large depressions, soils having high sodium content occur. The
Soil Map of the World (FAO–UNESCO, 1971) classifies the predominant
soils as Haplic and Calcic Xerosols and Haplic and Calcic Kastanozems.
Over the alluvial sediments, Eutric Fluvisols associated to Gleyic Solonchaks and Mollic Solonetz are developed, while in the depressions
Solonetz and Solonchaks appear (FAO Legend). In the Soil Map of
Argentina, compiled by Etchevehere (1971), the soils of the northern
Chaco Woodland were classified as Ustolls and Ustalfs, whereas in the
south an association of Calciorthids, Salorthids, and Orthents exists. Never-
theless, in a computerized study of climatological taxa of the argentine soils
(Van Wambeke and Scoppa, 1976), the soil moisture regime was determined
as aridic. The soil temperature regime is hyperthermic for the Argentine
Chaco Woodland, except for the southern end, which has a thermic regime.

The vegetation of this territory is characterized by the presence of trees
that can exceed 20 m in height and 1.20 m in diameter. However, since
shrubs are very significant secondary components, they will be discussed in
relation to this important region of South America. In these vast regions,
trees have been intensely exploited and now shrubs are the predominant
species.

The vegetation type of this territory is the xerophytic deciduous woodland, with an abundance of shrubs, and also *Cactaceae* and *Bromeliaceae*.
Among the woody vegetation, there grows a prairie rich in grasses of very
good forage value. Red (*Schinopsis lorentzii*) and white (*Aspidosperma
quebracho blanco*) quebracho woods constitute the climax association of
this territory. The most frequent shrub species are: *Bulnesia foliosa,
B. bonariensis, Bougainvillea praecox, B. indesta, Castela coccinea, Ruprech-
tia apetala, R. triflora, Schinus piliferus, S. sinuatus, Vallesia glabra, Acacia
caven, A. praecox, Mimosa detinens, Larrea divaricata,* and many others.

Morello and Saravia Toledo (1959a) studied the vegetation of this territory and the changes suffered from human influence. The natural ecosystems of this territory are very altered because of indiscriminate forest
exploitation and overgrazing of the understory grassland vegetation. Cattle
raising constitutes the main use of the wildlands of this territory. In many
locations both the primitive wood characterizing the climax situation and
the herbaceous cover have disappeared. When grass shortage is extreme,

cattle increase browsing on young trees, tree seedlings, and shrubs. In regions strongly degraded by livestock action, cattle are replaced by goats, which are capable of browsing on any type of available new growth. This sequence in rangeland use terminates in the extinction of desirable species and their replacement by a thorny chaparral that is useless for forage. Frequently, these degraded zones are invaded by *Larrea divaricata*.

One of the few reports on the use of shrubs as fodder has been prepared by Morello and Saravia Toledo (1959b). They found that cattle feed on grasses and low shrubs during summer and fall, for example; *Justicia echegarayi, Beloperone squarrosa*, and several *Ruellia* species. During the winter season, when grass forage is scarce, livestock browse on young plants of several tree species, particularly, red quebracho, as well as such shrubby species as *Maytenus spinosa, Atamisquea emarginata, Grabowskia duplicata, Capparis retusa, C. tweediana*, and *Achatocarpus nigricans*. From July onward, a significant part of the cattle diet is the fruit of trees and shrubs, such as *Geoffroea decorticans* and *Prosopis torquata*. Ragonese (1967) indicated that cattle eat fruits of various Leguminosae such as *Prosopis algarrobilla, Acacia aroma*, and *Prosopis vinalillo*.

An excellent example of good rangeland use by cattle was reported by Anderson (1980). By regulating cattle stocking rate and proper timing of use, in less than 10 years an improvement in range condition and constant increase in meat productivity took place. In the same study, a positive correlation was reported between the existence of woody species and the presence of a valuable understory herbaceous vegetation, such as *Thrichloris crinita* or *Setaria leucopila*. The elimination of woody species modifies the edaphic and climatic parameters of the microenvironment in such a way that desirable grasses growing in close association with woody species tend to disappear. García Moya and McKell (1970) observed a similar situation in California, where the soil nitrogen content decreased significantly as a function of the radial distance from the center of the canopy of shrubs.

A common result in the vegetation changes produced by anthropogenic actions is the invasion of wildland areas by thorny shrubs. Figure 5 shows the regions where these woody colonizers are expanding. Vinal (*Prosopis ruscifolia*) is a good example of a species that expanded in a few years to occupy areas that formerly were useful rangelands. The vinal colonizing mechanism has been studied by Morello (1970) and Morello *et al.* (1971), who believe that before the introduction of cattle, the natural ecosystems were subject to two periodical pulses, fire and floods, which hindered the advance of this shrub. With the coming of cattle, biomass production sufficient to support combustion and spread of fire disappeared. Elimination of periodical fires and the changes in floods allowed the explosive invasion of this species, which has become one of the most important woody weeds in South America. The area covered by vinal on this continent is estimated at approximately 200,000 km², of which 80,000 km² are in Argentina (Morello *et al.*, 1971). Other genera that form dense shrubby communities locally known as "fachinal" (Fig. 5) are *Acacia, Celtis,* and other *Prosopis* spp. in addition to the above-mentioned vinal.

Many species belonging to more than 150 genera of Argentina, mainly woody species and among them several shrubs of this territory, are cited as ornamentals for parks, gardens, and streets by Parodi (1934).

VI. Puna and Prepuna

The extensive region known as the Puna or Altiplano is represented by the vast high plateaus of the central Andes extending over several thousand kilometers from latitude 8° to 27° S through Perú, Bolivia, and northernmost Argentina and Chile. The Puna or Andean Altiplano is a large high-level intermontane basin, at present covered with the sediments of extinct or shrunken lakes. Aridity increases southward with rainfall of 800–1000 mm/yr in the humid northern Puna and culminating in northern Argentina and Chile and southern Bolivia in the arid Puna, also known as the Puna de Atacama. An interesting overview on the geoecology of the Andes mountains has been recently prepared by Gómez-Molina and Little (1981).

Only the arid Puna (see Fig. 1) is considered in this discussion. This territory covers plateaus, high plains, and slopes of the Andes at elevations between 3200 and 4400 m. The peripheral belt of mountains gives it a basin character, although interior mountain ranges create subbasins with average elevations of 3500 m above sea level. For this reason, a distinct feature of the arid Puna is internal drainage. Dunes and long, narrow salt flats are frequent. Extensive colluvial–alluvial accumulations with low and level areas of salty soils are also common.

The arid climate of Puna de Atacama is characterized by precipitation lower than 200 mm/yr, high insolation, wide daily temperature range, and reduced seasonal amplitudes. Precipitation is concentrated in a single wet summer season of variable length, diminishing from north to south and from east to west. Snowfall average annual frequency is less than 5 days. The mean annual temperatures are generally below 10°C and frosts are common, especially during the dry season. Night temperatures are below 0°C during the whole year. The mean annual potential evapotranspiration varies from 500 to 600 mm/yr. Winds are very strong.

The eastern Puna border, known as the Prepuna, is a narrow belt of mountain ranges of the eastern Andes, with peculiar valleys and gulches. It stretches from the Puna high plateau in the west to the lower sub-Andean hills in the east, which are covered by the Tucumano–Oranense jungle. This region has a rough topography, with elevations reaching from 1500 to 3000 m above sea level. Its climate is temperate with moderate thermic amplitudes, both daily and seasonal. Rainfall is mainly in summer between October and March and ranges from 500 to 1500 mm/yr, depending on height and direction of the hills. Summer showers are violent and unpredictable and produce mudflows that endanger everything in their way.

The desert soils of the Puna, except for those of a sandy texture, have unusually darkish topsoils, with Luvic Yermosols and Haplic Yermosols dominant (FAO Legend). The former have argillic sub-superficial horizons, whereas the latter may present sodic phases over extensive flat areas. Associated with these, Orthic Solonchaks and Vitric Andosols have developed over minor areas and are generally derived from andesithic ash and basaltic sands. Their allophane content is low except in some deep buried layers. For the Argentine Puna, Etchevehere (1971) reports Haplargids and Paleorthids (Soil Taxonomy). In the Prepuna, Lithosols are dominant.

The flora and ecology of the Argentine Puna have been studied by Cabrera (1957). Most plants of the desert Puna are adapted to drought, salt, and frost. The vegetation is further influenced by the intense solar radiation, low oxygen pressure, and wide daily variations of temperature. The Puna vegetation is represented by a steppe rich in shrubby species, floristically related to the Patagonian flora. The predominant forms are nanophanerophytes from 30 to 100 cm high, which grow far apart leaving large soil spaces between them. The most abundant shrubs are *Fabiana densa, Adesmia horriduscula, A. spinosissima, Junellia seriphioides, Baccharis incarum,* and *B. boliviensis.* Vegetation cover does not usually exceed 15%, although in isolated wet areas it can be greater (Gomez Molina and Little, 1981). In salty plains *Atriplex microphylla* is dominant, reaching 30–40 cm in height.

The high plateaus of the Puna are actively exploited by assorted livestock, including goats, sheep, llamas, donkeys, and cattle. This is the main activity since land cultivation is rare or null.

The Prepuna vegetation is a thorny shrubby steppe. The dominant species are *Gochnatia glutinosa, Aphyllocladus spartioides* of the Compositae family, and also an aphyllous Leguminoseae, *Cassia crassiramea.* Other shrubs frequently found are *Cercidium andicola, Churquiraga erinacea, Adesmia inflexa, Lycium cliatum,* and several others. Cactaceae are very abundant, and the *Trichocereus pasacana* silhouettes are striking. *Prosopis ferox,* a thorny shrub that may bear the form of either a shrub or a small tree, appears in gulches.

The phytogeographical distribution, physiognomy, morphology, and phenology of 115 species of the Prepuna, Puna, and the high mountain belt were described by Ruthsatz (1974). Information is also given about the fodder qualities of the shrub vegetation and other uses such as firewood and pharmaceutical properties. Twenty-five percent of all shrubs included in the study have a high or medium value as fodder plants. Some of the more palatable species for livestock are *Ephedra breana, E. rupestris, Krameria iluca, Buddleja hieronymi,* and *Acantholippia hastulata.* Frequently these species grow malformed because of the intensive browsing. As a result of the unsatisfactory management of this natural resource, degradation, such as loss of valuable species and soil erosion, is evident everywhere.

Plants with therapeutical value are: *Ephedra americana, E. breana, Azorella compacta, Salvia gilliesii, Pellaea nivea, Chenopodium graveolens, Artemisia copa,* and *Haplopappus rigidus* (Cabrera, 1957; Ruthsatz, 1974).

VII. Central Chile

The area included in Central Chile corresponds to the "matorral" formation, which is depicted in the chart on the main vegetation formations of Chile published by Quintanilla (1981). A more detailed map for a reduced area appears in the "Chile–California Mediterranean Scrub Atlas" edited by Thrower and Bradbury (1977). In both works, the physiognomic dominance of shrubs and the most predominant changes of vegetation due to altitude are shown throughout the east–west transects.

The climate of this scrub region is Mediterranean with warm dry summers and mild, wet winters. Climates similar to that in Central Chile occur only in California, southern and southwestern Australia, the Cape Town region in South Africa, and the territories surrounding the Mediterranean Sea. January is the warmest month in Santiago (Chile), with an average temperature of 20.5°C; June is the coldest month, with an average temperature of 7.5°C. Frosts are infrequent and winter temperatures are pleasantly mild. Rainfall increases from the north (25–200 mm/yr) to the south (342 mm/yr, in Santiago) and from the coast inland. The principal rainy season occurs between May and September at a low-irradiation time of the year when evaporation losses are much smaller. For this reason, the natural vegetation reflects better the subhumid than the arid climatic types and plants are more adapted to low temperatures than to drought (Eidt, 1968).

Physiographically, the southern portion of Central Chile is formed by a central valley and plains, which are associated with Vertisols, Mollic

Gleysols, and Fluvisols. To the east, on the Andes foothills, Humic Andosols developed on thick layers of volcanic ash. To the west, on the low hills of the coastal ranges, are Chromic Luvisols and Eutric and Dystric Cambisols. Kaolin, gibbsite, and halloysite are common in the horizons. In the northern portion of Central Chile, the topography becomes more abrupt, and Lithosols associated with Haplic Yermosols are dominant. An extensive plain with a Haplic Yermosol, sodic phase, is confined among Lithosols with a steeply dissected to mountainous topography in the northern end of Central Chile (FAO–UNESCO, 1971).

In the Mediterranean climatic region of Chile, shrubs are frequently the dominant species. Mooney *et al.* (1977) prepared a list of over 50 woody plants with their absolute and relative average cover from three sites: the Mediterranean interior, the Mediterranean coastal, and the coastal desert. Studies on the biomass, phenology, growth, water utilization, photosynthesis, and mineral nutrition for several shrub communities of this region have been recently published in a book edited by Miller (1981). The phenological pattern for 97 species, many of which were shrubs, from three vegetational belts in the high Cordillera de los Andes in Central Chile was reported by Arroyo *et al.* (1981).

In the past, the wildland areas of this region had a high proportion of desirable species. Continuous overgrazing by livestock has caused rangeland degradation and changes in the botanical composition of the regional flora. The most useful and palatable shrubby species have been replaced by others with less desirable characteristics. Gastó and Contreras (1972) proposed replacing these species by others with higher productivity and nutritive quality; they suggested over 20 woody species as promising.

Special attention has been given to *Atriplex repanda,* a native shrub of the central zone of Chile, between 28° and 32° S. A comprehensive review of the research carried out on this species has been published by Olivares and Gastó (1981). Previously, *A. repanda* was widely distributed, but because of overutilization by livestock, its natural population was drastically reduced and now only isolated individuals are found in secluded areas. Owing to its high productivity, palatability, tolerance to browsing and diseases, and high nutritive value, *A. repanda* appears to be one of the most promising species as a fodder resource in the semiarid and arid zones of Chile and, possibly, of other regions in the world. Human-planted pure stands of this shrub demonstrate the feasibility of its utilization for sheep grazing. The individual productivity of 18-month-old *A. repanda* plants increased as stand density increased from 697 to 1307 individuals per hectare. At 42 months plants showed an identical trend. The productivity per unit area continued to increase to maximum plant density of 18,518 individuals per hectare. The phenology and growth analysis for *A. repanda* in three-year-old plants was presented by Fraile (1973). *In vitro* dry matter digestibility of the leaves of this shrub ranged from 60.9% in July to 65.7% in January; digestible energy was constant through the year with a value of 2.12 kcal/g, except for January, in which it was greater (Silva *et al.*, 1976).

Researchers using fistulated sheep grazing a rangeland area planted with *A. repanda* (Silva *et al.*, 1976; Concha *et al.*, 1977a,b) demonstrated the importance of this species as a supplement during critical nutritional periods for sheep. The liveweight increase obtained was attributed to the presence of this shrub. The relationships between production and the most important Chilean soil variables during establishment were studied by Gargano (1978). *Atriplex repanda* shows promising reseeding characteristics. Although a high proportion of its fresh mature seeds are dormant, seed and soil treatments may improve germination significantly (Cristi and Gastó, 1971; Olivares and Johnston, 1978).

Quillay (*Quillaja saponaria*) is a valuable species of the Central Chile region and extends up to latitude 38° S. It is a tree or a shrub and grows in the Mediterranean interior up to elevations of 2000 m (Vita, 1974; Prado *et al.*, 1980). Its cortex is used as a source of saponins for industrial purposes, and exports amounted to 1000 tons in 1979 with an approximate value of a million dollars (Prado *et al.*, 1980). It is not surprising that such a valuable species has been seriously overexploited.

VIII. Cerrado and Llanos

The Cerrado and Llanos are two large, well-drained savannas of the central lowlands of tropical South America where shrubs are significant vegetation (Fig. 1). The Cerrado occupies about 180 million hectares of the central Brazilian plateau, comprising almost all the state of Goias, a great part of Mato Grosso, and the west of Minas Gerais. Small areas of this region extend into Paraguay and Bolivia. The Llanos in the north includes the central and eastern parts of the region known as the Venezuelan Llanos. The poorly drained western Llanos extending into Colombia (Apure Plains) and the well-drained high plains south of the Meta River are not included since they are mainly treeless savannas. Of the four ecological regions in which Sarmiento and Monasterio (1969) divided the Venezuelan Llanos, that included in Fig. 1 broadly corresponds to the authors' dry savanna region.

A. Cerrado

The climate of the Cerrado is tropical and frost-free and has heavy rains in the warm prehumid season (summer) and an extremely dry, cool season (winter). It is a region with more than 1000 mm/yr and a 4- to 6-month-long dry season, generally from May to September. The average annual temperatures vary from 20° to 25°C. Soil moisture regime is ustic; soil temperature regimes are isothermic (high savannas) and isohyperthermic (low savannas).

The Cerrado vegetation occurs in a landscape of ancient erosion surfaces of various ages modeled on the Brazilian shield at a general altitude of 750 m. The mantles of soil material subsequently developed are extremely weathered and deep. The soils related to these ancient erosion surfaces, probably the oldest in the world (30 million years), are classified as Acric Ferralsols, Rhodic Ferralsols, Orthic Acrisols, and Ferric Luvisols (FAO Legend) or as Acrustox, Haplustox, Haplustults, and Rhodustults. There are also important areas of sandy soils with sparse vegetation and with few trees and shrubs.

The Cerrado presents many serious limitations related to acid soil infertility. Soil pH ranges from 3.8 to 5.5 with high exchangeable aluminum saturation and common aluminum toxicity. Phosphorous fixation is high, while base status and cation-exchange capacity are low. Mineral deficiencies are widespread and micronutrient deficiencies are common. Fortunately, the physical properties of the well-drained soils are relatively good. However, low soil moisture-holding capacity is a common physical problem in these soils and causes drought damage to crops and pastures when the typical erratic periods with little rainfall occur, locally referred to as "veranicos," during the wet season in central Brazil.

Considerable controversy exists regarding the origin of the Cerrado vegetation. Its existence is an enigma that is only partially explained by edaphic, climatic, geomorphic, biotic, and anthropic theories or a combination of them. It was presumed that an edaphic gradient of fertility existed among the savannas and adjacent forests as well as within the savannas themselves (from "campo limpo" through "campo sujo" and "campo cerrado" to "cerradão"). Those soils supporting a high biomass would have a higher fertility status (Goodland, 1970a; Lopes and Cox, 1977). At present, data show that in their natural state there is often little difference between the chemical composition of soil under forests or savannas (Cochrane *et al.,* 1980) or soil under savannas with a different proportion of woody biomass (Cochrane and Sánchez, 1981). The savanna region can be defined as an area with a strong 4- to 6-month dry season. Nevertheless, in some regions of the central lowlands of tropical South America, semievergreen seasonal forests exist with a 4-month dry season, in contrast to other locations with a 6-month drought where drier types of vegetation such as the deciduous forests or the "caatinga" type are found. It is evident that simple duration of the dry season does not offer an adequate explanation of the differences.

In spite of their dispersed geographical distribution, the well-drained savannas occupy a well-defined habitat limited by the climatic potential for growth. They can be distinguished from other physiognomical vegetation classes on the basis of total wet season potential evapotranspiration. Within these savannas, there is no significant difference in the mean total wet season potential evapotranspiration between groups with 6, 7, or 8 months of wet season (Cochrane and Sánchez, 1981). Figure 6 summarizes the dependence of vegetation classes with respect to the total wet season potential evapotranspiration (TWPE) and wet season mean monthly temperature (WSMT). The latter parameter effectively separates lowland (isohyperthermic) from higher (isothermic) savanna. The savanna vegetation appears in Fig. 6 as an elongated band in the center of the diagram and is characterized by a narrow range of TWPE of 901 to 1060 mm. Thus, the climate of the well-drained savanna, according to the studies carried out in CIAT (Centro Internacional de Agricultura Tropical) by Cochrane and co-workers, appears to be remarkably constant when described as an area with 6 to 8 months of wet season and a total wet season potential evapotranspiration of 901 to 1060 mm.

In Brazil, there is increasing interest in the potential of the Cerrado. Various official organizations are devoting great efforts to develop this region, largely to accommodate the demographic expansion of recent years. The vegetation of the Cerrado region has some peculiar characteristics and has been classified as savanna. This word confers different meanings in different regions of the world. Here it is used in a very broad sense (Eiten, 1972). Even though it is not well known yet, the Cerrado is one of the most important regions of Brazil from the viewpoint of its vegetation. Several authors have conducted partial studies (Rawitscher, 1948; Rizzini, 1963; Goodland, 1970b; Eiten, 1972).

A peculiar characteristic of the Cerrado vegetation is its xeromorphism, mainly regarding its woody components. Generally, these are either species with evergreen leaves or species that lose their leaves during very short periods individually and alternatively in the dry season. Trees and shrubs have a thick bark and their trunk is generally tortuous. It is very difficult to differentiate trees from shrubs (Goodland, 1971) since the same species appear as a tree in one place and as a shrub in another.

The Triângulo Mineiro is the best known area within the Cerrado. Goodland (1970b) mentions 600 species with 336 genera belonging to 83 families. The family best represented in this region is the Leguminosae with 107 species. Other families with a great number of species are Gramineae, Compositae, Rubiaceae, Bignoniaceae, Vochysiaceae, and Apocynaceae. Other families that are very characteristic or have endemic species in the Cerrado are Caryocaraceae, Cochlospermaceae, Ebenaceae,

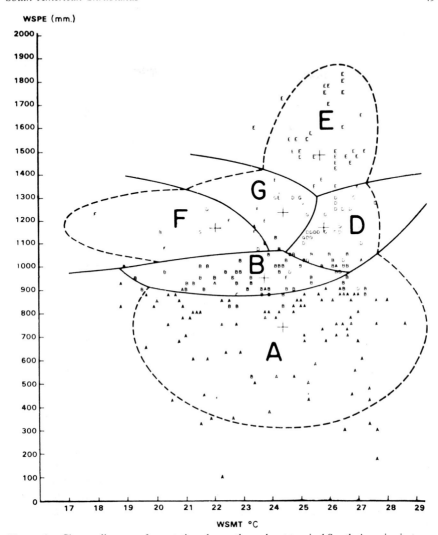

Figure 6. Cluster diagram of vegetation classes throughout tropical South America in terms of total wet season potential evapotranspiration (WSPE) and wet season mean monthly temperature (WSMT). (A) Deciduous forest, (B) well-drained savanna, (D) semievergreen seasonal forest, (E) tropical rain forest, (F) subtropical semievergreen forest, (G) subtropical evergreen forest. Solid lines show equiprobability of assignments. Dashed lines are 95% confidence ellipsoids for the vegetation classes. (From Cochrane and Jones, 1981.)

Guttiferae, Malvaceae, Protaceae, and Opiliaceae. Shrubs are very abundant in the floristic composition of the Cerrado. Some of the most common genera cited by Eiten (1972) are *Anacardium, Andira, Annona, Bauhinia, Crotalaria, Croton, Eriosema, Jacaranda, Lantana, Mimosa, Serjania,* and *Vernonia.*

There are significant variations in the density and height of the vegetation, yielding several physiognomical forms. Most authors recognize the following four main forms:

1. Cerradão: Dense Cerrados with an average tree height of 15 m or more. Many species that have the trunk ramified from the base in the cerrado present a well-formed trunk in the cerradão. The tree crown cover is 30–40%.
2. Cerrado: This word confers two meanings. In a broad sense it defines the whole region, including all structural forms of vegetation. In a restricted sense it refers to areas with a tree crown cover of 30–40% but with woody species that do not exceed 7 m high.
3. Campo cerrado: The woody crown cover is open and less than 30–40% and is composed of scattered low trees and shrubs whose height does not exceed 5 m.
4. Campo sujo: It is almost open grassland, with very few and very scattered low trees and shrubs. When there are no woody species it is called campo limpo.

Goodland (1971) studied the types of vegetation of the Cerrado based on seven physiognomical characteristics. The characteristic that best explained the variation was the basal area of trees per hectare, which is related to the biomass.

One of the first activities in the Cerrado region was cattle raising under natural grazing conditions. According to dos Santos *et al.* (1980), 36% of the Brazilian cattle population is concentrated in the central-west region and in Minas Gerais State, where 135 million hectares constitutes approximately 74% of the Brazilian Cerrado. Natural vegetation occupies 84% of this area and is of great importance for cattle feeding. The use of the Cerrado as a natural grazing area is far from efficient. According to de Freitas (1980), productivity is very low, approximately 20 kg of meat per hectare per year. According to Kornelius *et al.* (1979), the carrying capacity of the native Cerrado vegetation varies from 0.2 to 0.6 animal units per hectare per year. Overgrazing and the excessive use of fire are degrading factors. To improve production, fertilization with phosphorous is suggested as a means of increasing the native legumes. It is also advisable to subdivide the land into management units and develop watering stations.

Since the ground-layer vegetation is seasonal, the contribution of the woody species to cattle diet during the dry season is very important. This fact was verified in a study of diets with fistulated steers carried out in Minas Gerais by Macêdo *et al.* (1978). During the months of fodder scarcity a vine, *Serjania gracilis,* and a tree, *Piptadenia communis,* were significant in the diet.

The Leguminosae family is very numerous in the Cerrado and many shrubs belonging to this family are eaten by cattle. Some genera cited by Ferreira (1980b) are *Aeschynomene, Centrosema, Crotalaria, Desmodium, Eriosema, Stylosanthes,* and *Zornia.* Ferreira (1980a) also mentions 51 native species in the Cerrado that are common and produce edible fruits. This list includes several shrub species, such as *Campomanesia adamantinum, C. coerulea, Eugenia dysenterica, Psidium bergiana,* and *Anacardium humile.*

The increasing interest in the Brazilian Cerrado has encouraged research work carried out during recent years. Ferri (1980) reviewed the main research in the V. Symposio Sobre o Cerrado. Interestingly, most of the contributions deal with crop production, for which elimination of the natural vegetation is a necessity. In view of the increasing perturbations of the natural ecosystems due to agricultural expansion, Ferreira (1981) proposed the establishment of natural reserves to preserve the existing plant germ plasm, which is in danger of extinction.

B. Llanos

The well-drained Venezuelan Llanos consists of the so-called Llanos Mesas, which are low and flat-topped tablelands or terraces of Tertiary soft shales covered with more recent alluvial, fluvial, and eolian depositions. The climate is similar to that of the Cerrado. The dry season extends from November through April. Average annual rainfall varies between 1000 and 1400 mm. The soil mean annual temperature is higher than 22.5°C and has been classified as isohyperthermic. This can be expected since the Llanos are lowland tropical savannas between 75 and 150 m above sea level.

Soils are classified as Orthic Acrisols associated with Ferric Acrisols and Ferralic Arenosols. In fact, the Llanos soils do not appear to be as infertile as those of the Brazilian Cerrado. In recent studies carried out by the Centro Internacional de Agricultura Tropical (Cochrane *et al.,* 1980), soils were classified as Haplustalfs, Haplustox, and Hapludults.

Sarmiento and Monasterio (1971) conducted a broad study covering 300,000 ha in the Calabozo Plains to analyze the relationship among vegetation, geomorphology, and soils. The type of vegetation of this region was defined as "bunchgrass savanna" by Myers (1933). Within this relative homogeneity of the herbaceous layer, different physiognomical types can be recognized from the variation in density and height of the woody layer components. Similar to what was described for the Cerrado, these variations range from open grassland to woodland. The most common woody species are *Curatella americana, Byrsonima crassifolia,* and *Bowdichia virgilioides.* Other woody species that can be found are *Copaifera officinalis* and *Vochysia venezuelana.*

Because of edaphic limitations, the main use of this region has been almost exclusively as rangelands in extensive systems of management. The human impact has been in general slight, except for overgrazing and, in certain areas, the excessive use of fire.

IX. Caatinga

The Caatinga is a distinctive type of vegetation that occurs in the northeastern Brazilian Uplands (states of Ceará, northern Bahía, southeastern Piauí, and western Rio Grande do Norte, Paraiba, and Pernambuco). Generally, average annual rainfall varies from 400 to 750 mm; however, approximately 25% of the region has less than 40 mm (Eidt, 1968). Some of the variation in rainfall seems to be reflected in the height of the Caatinga vegetation, which may vary from 1 to 10 m. Rainfall distribution is variable and the dry season may extend for five months from May to September (Cabrera and Willink, 1980), four months from June to September (Eidt, 1968), or seven months from June to December (FAO–UNESCO, 1971). Moreover, recent long-term climatological data compiled by Hancock *et al.* (1979) suggest that the dry season is frequently longer, up to eleven months beginning in June or August. The erratic character of rainfall, with some years lacking rain and others with heavy showers, produces alternative droughts or floods that are responsible for severe agricultural damage, and promote rural population migration to a great extent.

The topography is gently undulating, but the relief is broken by inselbergs, isolated mountains, and escarpments. The Soil Map of the World (FAO–UNESCO, 1971) shows the distribution of the different soils of the region. The so-called "Caatinga Latosols" (Orthic Ferralsols) are dominant and occur on the "chapadas" over ancient sedimentary rocks, having a medium to high base status, in both the surface and subsoil. Toward the east and north, Chromic and Ferric Luvisols predominate, which were developed over ancient Precambrian metamorphic rocks exposed after the sedimentary cover was eroded. They appear associated with moderately deep alkaline soils, mostly solodized Solonetz. Ferric Luvisols and Xanthic Ferralsols are widespread in the region.

The term Caatinga means open forest (Cabrera and Willink, 1980) and is used to define several physiognomical forms of xerophytic vegetation. Environmental differences are responsible for these variations in the vegetation nature and composition (Cole, 1960). In the drier areas, an open savanna form with a shortgrass layer and low shrubs and cacti is called "seridó." However, the most typical vegetation of the natural caatinga is a closed scrub (Eiten and Goodland, 1979). In the drier areas, the level surfaces support a characteristic low scrub type called "sertão" composed of *Mimosa* legumes, the giant cactus *Pilocereus gounelle, Opuntia* spp., and several small cacti and bromelias. The moister Caatinga portion in the east is called the "agreste" and is characterized by the dominance of *Caesalpinia pyramidalis* (caatingueira), associated with the giant cacti *Cereus jamacaru* (mandacaru) and *C. squamosus* (fareiro). On the mountain slopes, where rainfall is higher and soil conditions are better, the typical Caatinga vegetation is replaced by a semideciduous forest with trees.

Large areas of the caatinga are used for extensive grazing by cattle and, to some extent, by goats and sheep. In the dense Caatinga areas the grass layer is poor and hence browsing is the main feeding source for livestock.

X. Guajira

Guajira is a complex region of thorny woodland and cactus scrubland that includes the Guajira peninsula itself and the coastal formations of northern Colombia and Maracaibo Lake, the Gulf of Venezuela, and the northern part of Falcon State in Venezuela. The climate is that of a tropical desert. The Colombian portion of this region is dry and tropical semiarid along the coasts of the Gulf of Venezuela and northern Maracaibo Lake. The Paraguaná península and the adjacent Colombian coasts are also dry with a somewhat lower temperature (FAO–UNESCO, 1971). There is a double rainy period interspersed with a double dry season. The average annual temperatures are generally over 27°C. The most common soils of the Guajira region reported by the Soil Map of the World are Calcic Xerosols, Calcic Yermosols, and Eutric Regosols (FAO Legend). These last soils occur mainly on the Guajira peninsula itself.

Vegetation comprises forbs, shrubs, small trees, and cacti. The species frequently found are *Calotropis procera, Prosopis juliflora, Capparis odoratissima,* and *Cercidium praecox.* Cactaceae are very abundant, the most common species being *Lemaireocereus griseus, Melocactus* spp., and *Pereskia colombiana* (Instituto Geográfico "Agustín Codazzi," 1977).

Adverse climatic characteristics have compelled the inhabitants of this territory to develop a simple survival life-style based on goat grazing.

Sometimes overgrazing destroys the forb and shrub vegetation and turns wildlands into deserts that are difficult to recover (Instituto Geográfico "Agustín Codazzi," 1977).

XI. Coastal Desert

The Pacific Coastal Desert is a narrow belt 75 to 150 km wide that stretches from northern Peru (4° S) to the south of Coquimbo in Chile (31° S). It is a subtropical desert with almost no rainfall but considerable fog. Summer days are warm and nights are cool, with no frost during the whole year. Temperature decreases gradually from the north of Peru (Piura, 24.5°C) to the south (Coquimbo, 16.4°C). Precipitation also diminishes from north to south, falling to zero in the extreme north of Chile. The outstanding feature of the climate of this region is the regular coastal fog in the desert zones of Chile and Peru.

Most of the Chilean coastal portion lacks vegetation. In the Peruvian coastal desert, there is a typical vegetation called "loma" on a hilly coastal range located immediately behind the marine terraces. Along this coastal shelf zone, precipitation is almost nonexistent and occurs only every few years. The coastal hills constitute a cloudy zone with rain intervals of 5 to 10 years. A few kilometers inland of these hills the fog disappears, giving way to extended desert plains where rains falls only at intervals of many years (Bowman, 1916, quoted by Cabrera, 1955). Soils have been reported as Lithosols and Regosols, with smaller areas occupied by Yermosols, Fluvisols, and Solonchaks (FAO Legend).

The mists, known as "garúas" in Peru, occur frequently on the hills at heights between 150 and 1500 m above sea level and sustain the periodical loma vegetation already mentioned, which consists of euphemerophyte and geophyte species. Plants with perennial external organs are rare. In central Peru, on favorable sites located between 500 and 700 m above sea level, the persistent fogs support real xerophyte forests formed by shrubs of up to 6–7 m in height (*Carica candens, Caesalpinia tinctoria, Acacia macracantha,* and *Eugenia* spp.).

An important species growing in the coastal area is *Prosopis tamarugo.* It is mentioned here because of its fodder value in the arid zones, even though it is not a shrub but a tree. This legume tree can be found in northern Chile between latitude 19°30' to 22°15' S, this zone being characterized by the lack of rain. The plant gives its name to a region of over a million hectares called La Pampa of the Tamarugal (Elgueta and Calderón, 1971). Extraordinary drought resistance is a characteristic of this species and its water balance has been subject to many investigations. Sudzuki

(1969, 1977) reported that the plant is capable of absorbing water from the air through its leaves and transporting it downward to the roots.

The plant community of *P. tamarugo* is characterized by its high litter productivity, which consists of approximately equal quantities of leaves and fruits on a weight basis. This litter, averaging 1.5 kg/m² of crown projection, has very good nutritive value and high palatability for sheep, goat, and cattle (Elgueta and Calderón, 1971). Because of the dryness of the area, the leaves and fruits remain preserved on the soil surface and form a thick mulch layer that can be used as fodder by animals throughout the year.

References

Abiusso, N. G. (1962). Composición química y valor alimenticio de algunas plantas indígenas y cultivadas en la República Argentina. *Rev. Invest. Agríc.* **16,** 93–247.

Abiusso, N. G. (1971). Digestibilidad de las "jarillas" (*Larrea* spp.) y su posible aprovechamiento en la alimentación del ganado. *Rev. Fac. Agron., Univ. Nac. La Plata* **47,** 37–44.

Anderson, D. L. (1977). Las causas de la invasión del chañar en el área medanosa de pastizales e isletas de chañar. *In* "Limitación en la Producción Ganadera de San Luis debido a las Leñosas Invasoras." Agencia Extensión Rural San Luís, Instituto Nacional de Tecnología Agropecuaria, Argentina.

Anderson, D. L. (1980). "Manejo Racional de un Campo en la Región Arida de los Llanos de la Rioja (República Argentina)." Instituto Nacional Tecnología Agropecuaria, Buenos Aires.

Arroyo, M. T. K., Armesto, J. J., and Villagran, C. (1981). Plant phenological patterns in the high Andean cordillera of central Chile. *J. Ecol.* **69,** 205–223.

Balmaceda, N. A. (1979). Vegetación. *In* "Estudio de clima, geomorfología, suelos vegetación y erosión," Ser. Estud. Doc. No. 6, pp. 74–93. Ministerio de Agricultura, Ganadería y Minería, Provincia Río Negro, Argentina.

Balmaceda, N. A., and de Digiuni, J. N. P. (1981). Comparación de la dieta del guanaco en la zona de monte bajo dos condiciones diferentes. *In* "Anales de la IV Convención Internacional sobre Camelidos Sudamericanos" Punta Arenas, Chile. Noviembre 1981.

Balmaceda, N. A., and de Digiuni, J. N. P. (1982). "Estimación de la dieta de vacunos, ovinos, caprinos y guanacos en la zona de monte por el método microhistológico," Internal Report. Ministerio de Agricultura, Ganadería y Minería, Provincia Río Negro, Argentina.

Bertiller, M. B., Beeskow, A. M., and Irisarri M. del P. (1977). Caracteres fisonómicos y florísticos de las unidades de vegetación del Chubut. *IDIA, Supl.* **35,** 247–296.

Bertiller, M. B., Beeskow, A. M., and Irisarri, M. del P. (1981a). Caracteres fisonómicos y florísticos de la vegetación del Chubut. 1. Sierra de San Bernardo, llanura y valle aluvial del río Senguer, Pampa de María Santísima, Valle Hermoso y Pampa del Castillo. Contribución No. 40, Centro Nac. Patagónico, Pto. Madryn, Argentina. 26 pp.

Bertiller, M. B., Beeskow, A. M., and Irisarri, M. del P. (1981b). Caracteres fisonómicos y florísticos de la vegetación del Chubut. 2. La Península Valdés y el Istmo Ameghino. Contribución No. 41, Centro Nac. Patagónico, Pto. Madryn, Argentina. 20 pp.

Böcher, T. W., Hjerting, J. P., and Rahn, K. (1972). Botanical studies in the Atuel valley area, Mendoza Province, Argentina. Part III. *Dan. Bot. Ark.* **22,** 195–358.

Bóo, R. M. (1980). El fuego en los pastizales. *Ecología* **4,** 13–17.

Bowman, I. (1916). "The Andes of Southern Peru," Vol. 8. Am. Geogr. Soc., Washington, D. C.

Braun, R. H., and Candia, R. J. (1980). Poder calorífero y contenidos de nitrógeno y carbono de componentes del algarrobal de Ñacuñan, Mendoza. *Deserta* **6,** 91–99.

Braun, R. H., and Lamberto, S. A. (1974). Modificaciones producidas por incendios en la integración de los componentes leñosos de un monte natural. *Rev. Invest. Agropecu., Ser. 2* **11,** 11–27.

Braun, R. H., Candia, R. J., Lieva, R., Páez, M. N., Stasi, C. R., and Wuilloud, C. F. (1979). Productividad primaria aérea neta del algarrobal de Ñacuñan (Mendoza). *Deserta* **5,** 7–43.

Cabrera, A. L. (1955). Latin America. *Arid Zone Res.* **6,** 77–113.

Cabrera, A. L. (1957). La vegetación de la Puna Argentina. *Rev. Invest. Agríc.* **11,** 317–412.

Cabrera, A. L. (1970). La vegetación del Paraguay en el cuadro fitogeográfico de América del Sur. *Bol. Soc. Argent. Bot.* **11,** Supl., 121–131.

Cabrera, A. L. (1976). Regiones fitogeográficas argentinas. *In* "Enciclopedia Argentina de Agricultura y Jardinería," pp. 1–85. Editorial ACME S.A.C.I., Buenos Aires.

Cabrera, A. L., and Willink, A. (1980). "Biogeografia de América Latina," 2nd ed. Ser. Biol., Monogr. 13. Organización de Estados Americanos, Washington, D. C.

Cochrane, T. T., and Jones, P. G. (1981). Savannas, forests and wet season potential evapotranspiration in tropical South America. *Trop. Agric. (Trinidad)* **58,** 185–190.

Cochrane, T. T., and Sánchez, L. F. (1981). Clima, paisajes y suelos de las sabanas tropicales de Suramérica. *Interciencia* **6,** 239–244.

Cochrane, T. T., Jones, P. G., and Sánchez, L. F. (1980). "The Land Resource Inventory of Tropical America for the Evaluation and Transfer of Germplasm Based Agrotechnology," Annu. Rev. 1980. Land Resources Unit, Centro Internacional Agricultura Tropical, Cali.

Cole, M. M. (1960). Cerrado, caatinga and pantanal: The distribution and origin of the savanna vegetation of Brazil. *Geogr. J.* **126,** 168–179.

Concha, R. R., Silva, M., Bonilla, S., and Cabrera, R. (1977a). Uso del *Atriplex repanda* como refuerzo de una pradera natural mediterránea semiárida pastoreada con ovinos en periodos secos. I. Consumo y ganancia de peso vivo. *Av. Prod. Anim.* **1,** 11–22.

Concha, R. R., Silva, M., Cabrera, R., and Bonilla, S. (1977b). Uso del *Atriplex repanda* como refuerzo de una pradera natural mediterránea semiárida pastoreada con ovinos en periodos secos. II. Digestibilidad y energía del forraje. *Av. Prod. Anim.* **2,** 85–98.

Covas, G. (1971). Arboles y arbustos forrajeros nativos de la Provincia de La Pampa. *In* "IV Reunión Nacional para el Estudio de las Regiones Aridas y Semiáridas," Resúm. Comun. Univ. Nac. La Pampa Santa Rosa, La Pampa.

Cristi, A., and Gastó, J. (1971). Alteraciones ambientales y del fruto en la germinación de *Atriplex repanda* Phil. Univ. Chile, Fac. Agron. Est. Exper. Agron. *Bol. Tec.* **34,** 25–40.

de Freitas, L. M. M. (1980). Alternativas de uso do cerrado. *In* "Cerrado: Uso e Manejo" (D. Marchetti and A. D. Machado, eds.), pp. 279–316. Editorial Editerra, Brasilia.

dos Santos, C. A., Estermann, S., Estermann, P., and Estermann, A. (1980). Approveitamento da pastagem nativa no cerrado. *In* "Cerrado: Uso e Manejo" (D. Marchetti and A. D. Machado, eds.), pp. 419–435. Editorial Editerra, Brasilia.

Duisberg, P. C. (1952). Development of a feed from the creosote bush and the determination of its nutritive value. *J. Anim. Sci.* **11,** 174–180.

Eidt, R. C. (1968). The climatology of South America. *In* "Biogeography and Ecology in South America," (E. J. Fittkau, J. Illies, H. Klinge, G. H. Schwabe, and H. Sioli, eds.), pp. 54–81. Dr. W. Junk Pub., The Hague.

Eiten, G. (1972). The cerrado vegetation of Brazil. *Bot. Rev.* **38,** 201–341.

Eiten, G., and Goodland, R. (1979). Ecology and management of semi-arid ecosystems in Brazil. *In* "Management of Semi-arid Ecosystems" (B. H. Walker, ed.), pp. 277–300. Elsevier, Amsterdam.

Elgueta, H., and Calderón, S. (1971). Estudio del tamarugo como productor de alimento del ganado lanar en la Pampa del Tamarugal. Instituto Forestal, Santiago, Chile. *Inf. Tec.* **38.**

Etchevehere, P. H. (1971). "Mapa de Suelos. República Argentina." Instituto Nacional de Tecnología Agropecuaria, Buenos Aires.

FAO-UNESCO (1971). "Mapa Mundial de Suelos," Vol. IV. America del Sur. UNESCO, París.

Ferreira, M. B. (1980a). Frutos comestíveis nativos do Cerrado em Minas Gerais. *Inf. Agropecu.* **61,** 9–18.

Ferreira, M. B. (1980b). Cerrado: Fonte de forrageiras. *Inf. Agropecu.* **61,** 25–27.

Ferreira, M. B. (1981). Formações vegetais naturais em Minas gerais e sua importância. *Inf. Agropecu.* **80,** 45–49.

Ferri, M. G. (1980). Breve histórico das mais importantes linhas de pesquisa no cerrado. *In* "Cerrado: Uso e Manejo" (D. Marchetti and A. D. Machado, eds.), pp. 25–35. Editorial Editerra, Brasilia.

García-Moya, E., and McKell, C. M. (1970). Contribution of shrubs to the nitrogen economy of a desert-wash plant community. *Ecology* **51,** 81–88.

Gargano, A. O. (1978). "Influencia de algunas variables de suelos del norte chico en el crecimiento inicial de *Atriplex repanda* Phil." Tesis Magister Ciencias Agropecuarias, Universidad de Chile, Santiago.

Gastó, J., and Contreras, D. (1972). Bioma pratense de la región mediterránea de pluviometría limitada Univ. Chile, Fac. Agron. Est. Exper. Agron. *Bol. Téc.* **35,** 3–29.

Gómez Molina, E., and Little, A. V. (1981). Geoecology of the Andes: The natural science basis for research planning. *Mt. Res. Dev.* **1,** 115–144.

Goodland, R. J. A., ed. (1970a). "The Savanna Controversy," Publ. 15. McGill University, Savanna Research Project, Montreal.

Goodland, R. J. A. (1970b). Plants of the cerrado vegetation of Brazil. *Phytologia* **20,** 57–78.

Goodland, R. J. A. (1971). A physiognomic analysis of the "cerrado" vegetation of central Brazil. *J. Ecol* **29,** 411–419.

Guevara, J. C., Candia, R. J., and Braun, R. H. (1977). Inventario de los recursos pastoriles de Mendoza. *IDIA, Supl.* **35,** 330–336.

Hancock, J. H., Hill, R. W., and Hargreaves, G. H. (1979). "Potential Evapotranspiration and Precipitation Deficits for Tropical America." Centro Internacional Agricultura Tropical, Cali.

Instituto Geográfico "Agustín Codazzi" (1977). "Zonas de Vida o Formaciones Vegetales de Colombia," Vol. 13, No. 11. Bogota.

Kornelius, E., Saueressig, M. G., and Goedert, W. J. (1979). Pastures establishment and management in the cerrado of Brazil. *In* "Pasture Production in Acid Soils of the Tropics" (P. A. Sanchez and L. E. Tergas, eds.), pp. 147–166. Centro Internacional Agricultura Tropical, Cali.

Lopes, A. S., and Cox, F. R. (1977). Cerrado vegetation in Brazil. An edaphic gradient. *Agron. J.* **69,** 828–831.

Macêdo, G. A. R., Ferreira, M. B., and Escuder, C. J. (1978). "Dieta de novilhos em pastagem nativa de cerrado." Empresa de Pesquisa Agropecuária de Minas Gerais, Belo Horizonte.

Miller, P. C., ed. (1981). "Resource Use by Chaparral and Matorral." Springer-Verlag, New York.

Monteith, N. M., and Laya, H. A. (1970). Estado actual y programa general de la cartografía y clasificación de suelos en la Patagonia. *Rev. Agron. Noroeste Argent.* **7,** 385–388.

Mooney, H. A., Kummerow, J., Johnson, A. W., Parsons, D. J., Keeley, S., Hoffmann, A., Hays, R. I., Giliberto, J., and Chu, C. (1977). *US/IBP Synth. Ser.* **5,** 85–143.

Morello, J. (1958). La provincia fitogeográfica del monte. *Opera Lilloana* **2**, 3–155.

Morello, J. (1968). Las grandes unidades de vegetación y ambiente del Chaco Argentino. Primera parte. Objetivos y metodología. *Ser. Fitogeogr.* **8**, 1–125.

Morello, J. (1970). Modelo de relaciones entre pastizales y leñosas colonizadoras en el Chaco Argentino, *Inf. Invest. Agríc* **276**, 31–52.

Morello, J. (1975). El punto de vista ecológico y la expansión pecuaria. *Cienc. Investi.* **31**, 168–178.

Morello, J. H., and Saravia Toledo, C. (1959a). El Bosque chaqueño. I. Paisaje primitivo, paisaje natural y paisaje cultural en el oriente de Salta. *Rev. Agron. Noroeste Argent.* **3**, 5–81.

Morello, J. H., and Savaria Toledo, C. (1959b). El Bosque chaqueño. II. La ganadería y el bosque en el oriente de Salta. *Rev. Agron. Noroeste Argent.* **3**, 209–258.

Morello, J. H., Crudelli, N. E., and Saraceno, M. (1971). Los vinalares de Formosa. *Ser. Fitogeogr.* **11**, 1–159.

Myers, J. G. (1933). Notes on the vegetation of the Venezuelan llanos. *J. Ecol.* **21**, 335–349.

OEA (1971). "Cuenca del Plata. Estudios para su Planificación y Desarrollo." OEA, Washington D. C.

Olivares, E., and Gastó, J. (1981). "*Atriplex repanda.* Organización y Manejo de Ecosistemas con Arbustos Forrajeros." Cienc. Agríc. No. 7. Universidad de Chile, Facultad de Ciencias Agrarias, Veterinarias y Forestales, Santiago.

Olivares, A., and Johnston, M. (1978). Alternativas de mejoramiento en la emergencia de *Atriplex repanda* Phil. *ΦYTON* **36**, 129–137.

Papadakis, J. (1963). Soils of Argentine. *Soil Sci.* **95**, 356–366.

Parodi, L. R. (1934). Las plantas indígenas no alimenticias. *Rev. Argent. Agron.* **1**, 165–212.

Parodi, L. R. (1964). Las regiones fitogeográficas argentinas. *In* "Enciclopedia Argentina de Agricultura y Ganadería," Vol. 2, Chapter 1, pp. 1–14. Editorial ACME S.A.C.I., Buenos Aires.

Prado, J. A., Barros, S., Rojas, P., and Barros, D. (1980). "Análisis del desarrollo del Quillay (*Quillaja saponaria* Mol.) en la zona árida y semiárida chilena." Instituto Forestal, Santiago, Chile.

Quintanilla, V. G. (1981). "Carta de las Formaciones Vegetales de Chile," Contri. Cient. Tecnol. No. 47. Area Geociencias I, Universidad Técnica del Estado, Santiago, Chile.

Ragonese, A. E. (1967). "Vegetación y Ganadería de la República Argentina," Colecc. Cient. No. 5. Instituto Nacional de Tecnología Agropecuaria, Buenos Aires.

Ragonese, A. E., and Castiglioni, J. C. (1970). La vegetación del parque chaqueño. *Bol. Soc. Argent. Bot.* **11**, Supl., 133–160.

Rawitscher, F. (1948). The water economy of the vegetation of the "campos cerrados" in southern Brazil. *J. Ecol.* **36**, 237–268.

Rizzini, C. T. (1963). A flora do cerrado. *In* "Simpósio sôbre o cerrado" (M. G. Ferri, ed.), pp. 125–177. Editôra Universidade de São Paulo, São Paulo.

Roig, F. A. (1970). Flora y vegetación de la reserva forestal de Ñacuñan. *Deserta* **1**, 25–232.

Ruiz Leal, A. (1972). Flora popular mendocina. *Deserta* **3**, 9–296.

Ruthsatz, B. (1974). Los arbustos de las estepas andinas del noroeste argentino y su uso actual. *Bol. Soc. Argent. Bot.* **16**, 27–45.

Sarmiento, G., and Monasterio, M. (1969). Studies on the savanna vegetation of the Venezuelan llanos. I. The use of association analysis. *J. Ecol.* **57**, 579–598.

Sarmiento, G., and Monasterio, M. (1971). "Ecología de las sabanas de América Tropical." Cuad. Geogr. No. 4. Universidad de los Andes, Mérida.

Silva, G. M., Dimarco, A., O., and Cerda, D. (1976). Consumo y preferencia ovina estacional en un bioma biestratificado con *Atriplex repanda*. *Av. Prod. Anim.* **1**, 129–140.

Soil Survey Staff (1975). "Soil Taxonomy. A Basic System of Soil Classification for Making and Interpreting Soil Surveys," Handbook No. 436. Soil Conservation Service, USDA, Washington, D.C.

Soriano, A. (1949). El límite entre las provincias botánicas Patagónica y Central en el territorio del Chubut. *Lilloa* **20**, 193–202.

Soriano, A. (1950). La vegetación del Chubut. *Rev. Argent. Agron.* **17**, 30–66.

Soriano, A. (1956). Aspectos ecológicos y pasturiles de la vegetación patagónica relacionados con su estado y capacidad de recuperación. *Rev. Invest. Agric.* **10**, 349–372.

Soriano, A. (1983). Deserts and Semi-Deserts of Patagonia. *In* "Ecosystems of the World, Vol. 5, Temperate Deserts and Semi-Deserts." (N. E. West, ed.), pp. 423–460. Elsevier. Amsterdam.

Sudzuki, F. (1969). Absorción foliar de humedad atmosférica en Tamarugo, *Prosopis tamarugo*. Univ. Chile, Fac. Agron. Est. Exper. Agron., *Bol. Téc.* **30**, 1–23.

Sudzuki, F. (1977). Captación y economía del agua en plantas que viven en ambientes de desierto. *IDIA, Supl.* **34**, 212–217.

Thrower, N. J. W., and Bradbury, D. E., eds. (1977). "Chile–California Mediterranean Scrub Atlas," US/IBP Synth. Ser. 2. Dowden, Hutchison & Ross, Stroudsbourg, Pennsylvania.

Timmermann, B. N. (1977). Practical uses of *Larrea*. *US/IBP Synth. Ser.* **6**, 252–256.

Tinto, J. C. (1977). Recursos forrajeros leñosos para zonas áridas y semiáridas. *IDIA, Supl.* **34**, 182–196.

Van Wambeke, A., and Scoppa, C. O. (1976). Las taxas climáticas de los suelos argentinos. *Rev. Invest. Agropecu., Ser. 3,* **13**, 7–19.

Vita, A. (1974). Algunos antecedentes para la silvicultura del Quillay (*Quillaja saponaria* Mol.). Univ. Chile, Fac. Cs. Forest., *Bol. Téc.* **28**, 1–18.

Wainstein, P., and González, S (1971). Valor nutritivo de plantas forrajeras del este de la Provincia de Mendoza (Reserva Ecológica Ñacuñan). II. *Deserta* **2**, 77–85.

Wainstein, P., González, S., and Rey, E. (1979). "Valor nutritivo de plantas forrajeras de la Provincia de Mendoza. III," Cuad. Téc. No. 1, pp. 97–108. Instituto Argentino de Investigaciones de las Zonas Aridas, Mendoza.

Walter, H., Harnickell, E., and Mueller-Dombois, D. (1975). "Climate Diagrams Maps of the Individual Continents and the Ecologic Climatic Regions of the Earth." Springer-Verlag, Berlin and New York.

Willard, E. E. (1973). Effect of wildfires on woody species in the monte region of Argentina. *J. Range Manage.* **26**, 97–100.

Zuñiga Fraile, M. (1973). Determinación de curvas de crecimiento en *Atriplex repanda* Phil. en función de la densidad poblacional. Thesis, Facultad de Agronomia, Univ. Católica de Chile, Santiago, Chile.

3

Australia: Distribution, Characteristics, and Utilization of Shrublands

V. R. Squires

I. Introduction

The ancient land mass of the Australian continent encompasses 7.7×10^6 km^2 and spans 30 degrees of latitude with the Tropic of Capricorn lying roughly across the middle. This vast area makes Australia the fifth largest country in the world. The environment of Australia is an unusual one. It has unique flora (Burbidge, 1960; Barlow, 1981), but many aspects, including geology and geomorphology (Mabbutt, 1969), climate (Gentilli, 1978), and fauna (McKnight, 1975), are peculiar.

Much of the uniqueness is a function of the long period of isolation of Australia from any other landmass. It is believed that Australia separated from Gondwanaland over 90 million years ago (Raven and Axelrod, 1972; Barlow, 1981). Over the successive millenia Australia has drifted north into warmer and drier latitudes (Fig. 1).

Biologically, the continent is a world of its own, yet a region in which all the world is interested. But "Australia is not a biological asylum where ancient forms of life persist. . . Rather than being ancient, much of the present flora and fauna are recent developments in response to climatic change" (Gill, 1975, p. 255).

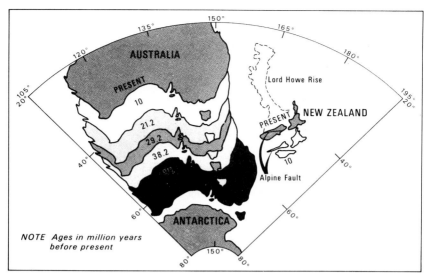

Figure 1. Australia's drift north according to plate tectonics theory. [Adapted from Ludbrook (1980). Reproduced with permission of the South Australian Department of Mines and Energy, Adelaide.]

Figure 2. During the early Cretaceous Australia was inundated by a marine incursion—the so-called epicontinental sea. [Adapted from Ludbrook (1980). Reproduced with permission of the South Australian Department of Mines and Energy, Adelaide.]

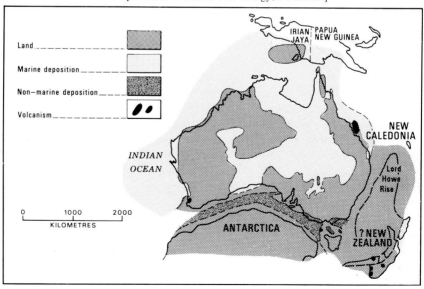

The Australian continent as we know it today came into existence in the Upper Cretaceous, some 60–70 million years ago. Australia achieved its continental unity with the withdrawal of the Lower Cretaceous epicontinental sea (Fig. 2), which had previously turned the region into a group of islands, changed its climate, and isolated its biota. Gill (1975) postulated that as the invading seas withdrew, the great river systems such as the Murray/Darling (Fig. 3) were created. However, the greater humidity of the Tertiary fed much larger river systems than now. The copious acidic water deeply leached the country rock. Australia's flora and fauna evolved to cope with the impoverished deeply leached soils. With the change from the humid Tertiary climate to the modern relatively dry one, the flora and

Figure 3. The Murray/Darling river system is Australia's largest. It drains an area of over 1 million km², about one-seventh the size of Australia. [Adapted from Hills (1974). Reproduced with permission of Angus and Robertson Publishers, Sydney.]

fauna also had to cope with drought (Barlow, 1981; Friedel and Squires, 1982).

The presence of Tertiary laterite is consistent with the steady northward drift of Australia as shown in Fig. 1, but at variance with the notion that the climate can be *both* wetter and drier as lower latitudes are reached. The "explanation is probably that world climate altered, and that a wider tropic belt existed in the mid-Tertiary. There is much evidence round the world that this was actually so" (Gill , 1975, p. 226). See also Kemp (1981).

Although the present-day climates of Australia vary from temperate in the south to monsoonal in the north, there is not as much variation as one would expect from a continent of its size. Latitudinal effects are modified by the concentric zonation of rainfall (Fig. 4), the predominantly gentle terrain, and the major geological trend from ancient to younger land

Figure 4. Average annual rainfall. Note the concentric zonation, which tends to be rather independent of latitude. (Adapted from the map by the Bureau of Meteorology and reproduced with permission.)

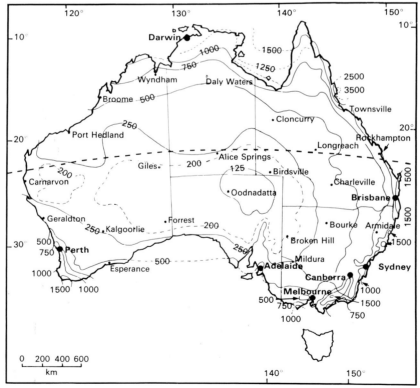

surfaces from west to east. Even so, according to the Köppen classification of climate, there are 23 major climatic zones. It is worth noting that a large expanse of the central western coast has the arid climate typical of continental western coasts in mid latitudes.

Apart from recent mountain-building activity on the east coast, Australia has been free of major tectonic activity. As a consequence, relief is subdued and stable conditions have allowed widespread peneplanation (Mabbutt, 1969). Because of the ancient nature of surface layers, the levels of soil fertility are low by world standards (Hubble, 1970). Phosphorus and nitrogen are particularly low. Beadle (1966) postulated that many of the morphological and physiological adaptations of Australian plants are due to low phosphorus and not aridity per se. The most obvious adaptations relate to xerophily and scelerophylly.

The present-day flora is characterized by widespread desertic and sclerophyll types of vegetation. Current knowledge concerning the origin, distribution, and elements of the Australian flora has been thoroughly reviewed by Barlow (1981). The plate tectonics interpretation is that as Australia was rafted northward into a zone of warmer and drier climate plant genera such as *Acacia, Eucalyptus, Casuarina, Melaleuca, Hakea,* and *Eremophila* adapted to a progressively drier, more continental climate. And, as drought continued to spread over the interior, new opportunities arose for temperate Austral families that evolved a wholly new flora composed of desert and desert-border alliances restricted to the drier parts of Australia (Axelrod and Raven, 1972).

The absence of native ungulate fauna has had a profound effect on the evolution of herbaceous and woody plants. Few species of shrubs or trees are equipped with spines, even among the *Acacia*. This absence is thought to reflect the very different conditions under which Australian trees and shrubs evolved. There is little evidence of a major browsing pressure on any plant prior to the introduction of domestic ungulates about two centuries ago. The niche traditionally occupied in other continents by ungulates has to a certain extent been filled by macropod marsupials (McKnight, 1975). Of these, the red kangaroo (*Megaleia rufa*) and the grey kangaroo (*Macropus robustus*) have come closest to filling the niche for a grazing/browsing animal (Dawson, 1977).

II. Australian Shrublands

Shrublands in Australia occupy a significant proportion of the Australian continent, especially in the arid zone (Fig. 5). In addition, the heathlands occupy the humid margins (Carnahan, 1976). Shrublands in Australia are

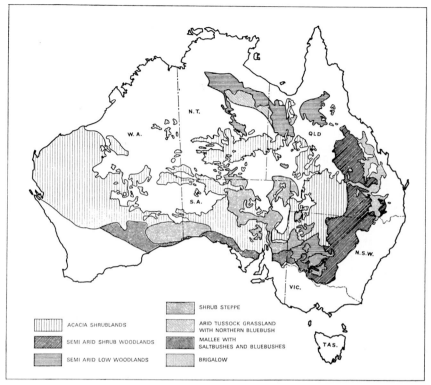

Figure 5. Distribution of useful wildland shrubs in Australia. [After Moore (1972). Reproduced with permission of Angus and Robertson Publishers, Sydney.]

characterized by a high proportion of species edible to livestock, and the peculiar absence of true succulents such as cactus or *Euphorbia* species. Peculiar too is the dominance of the genus *Acacia* in arid zone shrublands. In this regard, Australian shrublands are more akin to those in Africa (Walter, 1971; Werger, 1978) than those of North America despite the similarity in rainfall patterns (Yeaton and Cody, 1979). Another aspect worthy of comment is the high proportion of woody plants in Australia's arid zone (Perry, 1970). The principal families of edible shrubs are Caespalpinaceae, Mimosaceae, Sapindaceae, Capparidaceae, Sterculiaceae, and Chenopodiaceae. Moore (1972) reviewed the literature and mapped the distribution of individual species of useful shrubs in relation to soils and other site factors (Fig. 5). For the purposes of this chapter, the climate of Australia's inland regions is classified in one of three zones, winter rainfall, summer rainfall, or nonseasonal (Fig. 6). Three genera,

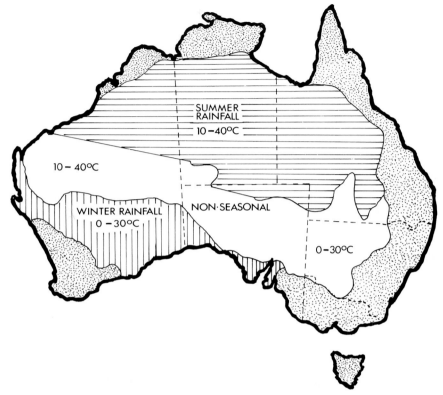

Figure 6. Map of Australia showing grazing lands with summer, winter, and nonseasonal rainfall, and mean minimum and maximum temperatures for the coldest and warmest months.

Acacia, Atriplex, and *Maireana* (*Kochia*), dominate the plant communities of the Australian inland. The two chenopod shrubs, *Atriplex* and *Maireana,* are distributed in a broad band across the southern (winter rainfall) regions of Australia, while *Acacia* is dominant in the summer rainfall regions.

The major vegetation formations in terms of life-form, height, and projected foliage cover of the tallest stratum of inland Australia are semiarid low woodlands represented by low *Acacia* shrublands, *Casuarina–Heterodendrum–Callitris* low woodlands, chenopodiaceous low shrubland or shrub steppe, and arid hummock grassland. Between the arid zone and the humid margin of the continent are the *Eucalyptus* shrub woodlands and tussock grasslands (Specht, 1979). These formations are defined and described by Leigh and Noble (1969), Moore *et al.* (1970), and Moore and

Perry (1970). The humid fringe supports a variety of heath formations (Specht, 1979).

Australian shrubs are predominantly evergreen. Their leaves are, in general, hard and tough (sclerophylls), and many are small or reduced; "ordinary" leaves (orthophylls) are prominent in only a few vegetation types. Commonly true leaves are replaced by scales (*Casuarina* and *Allocasuarina*), or phyllodes (some *Acacia* spp.).

A. Distribution and Characteristics

Maps showing the distribution of Australian plant formations have been prepared by several authors, the most recent by Carnahan (1976). A useful summary at the subformation level is also available (Leigh and Noble, 1969).

1. Chenopodiaceous Low Shrubland

The chenopod shrublands occur mainly in the winter rainfall zone (150–500 mm per annum) of southern Australia, where they occupy

Figure 7. Chenopod shrublands comprising principally *Atriplex* and *Maireana* spp. are widespread in southern (winter rainfall) regions of Australia. (After Squires, 1971.)

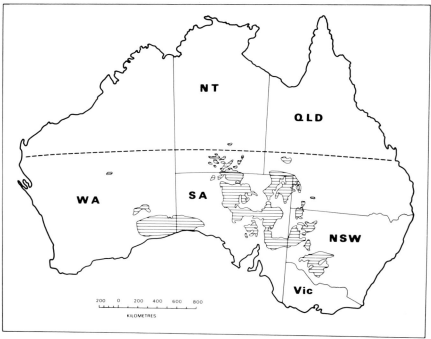

308,000 km² or 5% of the land area of Australia (Oxley, 1979) (Fig. 7). The main species are *Atriplex vesicaria* (bladder saltbush), *A. nummularia* (oldman saltbush), *A. rhagodioides* (Oodnadatta saltbush), *Maireana sedifolia* (pearl bluebush), *M. pyramidata* (black bluebush), *M. aphylla* (cotton bush), *M. astrotricha* (southern bluebush), *Rhagodia spinescens* (thorny bluebush), and *R. nutans* (climbing saltbush). At the northern limit of the chenopod shrublands, which has a stronger summer rainfall component, *Chenopodium auricomum* (northern bluebush) is the most important chenopod species but it is restricted in occurrence to ephemeral swamps and areas of aggregated drainage (Oxley, 1979).

Generally, the shrubland consists of gray, blue-gray to dull green, well-spaced shrubby plants. They may be described as xeromorphic halophytes growing up to 1.5 m tall, although *A. nummularia* may reach a height of 3 m (Figs. 8 and 9). Where the shrubs are dense, there is little or no grass or forb growth.

Williams (1979) listed the regional descriptions of chenopod communities and commented on soil type as a factor affecting distribution. *Maireana* communities tend to be restricted to the deeper and lighter soils, while *Atriplex* grows on soils that range from heavy clay to stony desert soils. The relative distributions of *Atriplex* and *Maireana* are apparently correlated

Figure 8. *Atriplex vesicaria* is the most widespread chenopod shrub. The shrubs grow to a height of about 1 m.

Figure 9.   *Atriplex nummularia* is the tallest chenopod shrub and may reach a height of 3 m.

with the depth to which the soil is normally wetted by rain. *Maireana* is deep rooted and grows in soils which can be wetted to 65 cm, whereas *Atriplex* may grow where the soil is wetted to 30 cm (Perry, 1972).

A feature of some *Atriplex* communities is that they show some form of spatial patterning. Patterning in *A. vesicaria* is characterized by well-defined "bands" of vegetation separated by bare or sparsely vegetated interbands that follow terrestrial contours (Valentine and Nagorka, 1979).

The resistance of these chenopod shrubs to high water stress is recognized as one of the major attributes of the shrubs (Hasick, 1979). Hence their ability to withstand drought periods is an important stabilizing influence in the pastoral industry of inland Australia (see Section B,2).

Chenopod shrublands occur in pure stands, as with *A. vesicaria* on the Riverine Plain in western New South Wales (Fig. 7), or as an understory to various woodland communities. Boundaries between chenopodiaceous low shrub and the arid low and medium woodlands dominated by *Acacia*, *Casuarina*, and *Eucalyptus* spp. are imprecise because a slightly modified low shrubland becomes an understory (Fig. 10).

2. *Acacia* Woodlands and Shrublands

Acacia-dominated communities occupy 26% of Australia, about 2 million km^2, and are represented by subformations that range from low woodland

Figure 10. Chenopod shrubs are often found as an understory in arid low and medium woodlands dominated by *Eucalyptus*.

of 5–10 m height through tall shrubland to dense scrub of 2–8 m height. The density of the tall shrub layer varies from only one individual per hectare to over 8000 per hectare. The main *Acacia* species are *A. aneura* (mulga), *A. pendula, A. sowdenii, A. cambagei, A. georginae, A. bracystachya,* and *A. kempeana.*

The most extensive and important *Acacia* communities are those dominated by *A. aneura* (Fig. 11). These communities occupy 1,500,000 km^2

Figure 11. *Acacia aneura* (mulga) is widely distributed throughout the arid zone of Australia.

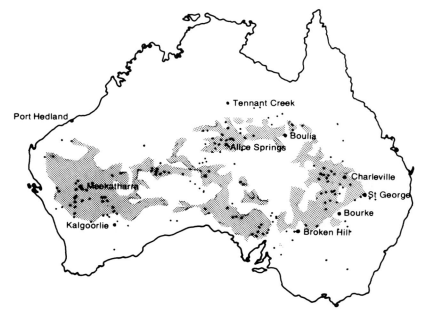

Figure 12.   Distribution of *Acacia aneura* shrublands in Australia. [After Nix and Austin (1972). Reproduced with permission of the Tropical Grasslands Society.]

(Fig. 12). The remaining area of *Acacia* woodlands is classified variously as *A. cambagei–A. harpophylla* and *A. georginae* and associated *Acacia* communities in northern Australia.

Nix and Austin (1972) examined *A. aneura* distribution on a continental scale in relation to the water regime. At the regional level, strong interactions with soil type and climate are readily demonstrated. *Acacia aneura* tends to grow on medium to coarse-textured neutral to acid soils and varies from a fairly dense woodland with a grass/forb understory to a sparse woodland with an understory of chenopodiaceous shrubs. At tree densities of <1/ha the woodland is, for all practical purposes, either a chenopod shrubland or a grassland. Where the trees are dense there is little or no grass or forb growth even in good seasons. This had led to an approach, especially in Queensland, where *A. aneura* density is drastically reduced by thinning (Beale, 1973). However, the attainment of maximum forage yield from the ground layer was at tree densities that provided little browse.

A feature of *A. aneura* communities in parts of inland Australia is the patterning that occurs in response to microtopographic differences, which lead to soil moisture redistribution (Wilcox, 1972). *Acacia aneura* communities on gentle slopes in central and Western Australia exhibit a grove pattern in which contour-aligned groves of dense shrubs alternate with almost bare intergroves (Graetz, 1973; Boyland, 1973). In addition to the community structure that maximizes water redistribution through groving, there is also the well-documented phenomenon of stemflow, which is common in *A. aneura*. Rainfall is intercepted by the shrubs and it is channeled to the base of the plant (Fig. 13). Significant quantities of water channeled down *A. aneura* stems to the surrounding soil (about 18%). By capturing precipitation on the plant surfaces *A. aneura* modifies its hydrological cycle within its immediate vicinity and increases its chances of survival in an arid environment (Pressland, 1976, 1978).

Acacia aneura is a polymorphic species (Pedley, 1978) and is variable in both phyllode width and gross morphology (Lamont and Fox, 1981). Phyllodes vary in width from 1 mm to 1 cm with lengths up to 12 cm. Everist (1969) recognizes four distinct types of *A. aneura* in Queensland. Graetz (1973) lists the characteristics of some of the forms that vary in height, width of phyllodes, and the extent to which multiple stems are characteristic.

Figure 13. Water budget of *Acacia aneura*. Stemflow is a significant factor. P is precipitation, T is throughfall, S is stemflow, and E is evaporation. [After Sabbath and Quinnell (1981). Reproduced with permission of Longman Cheshire Publishers, Melbourne.]

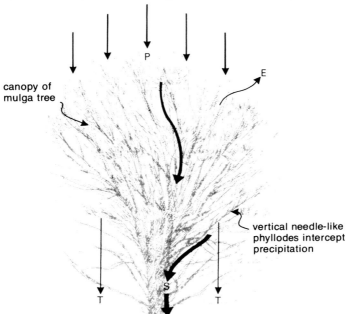

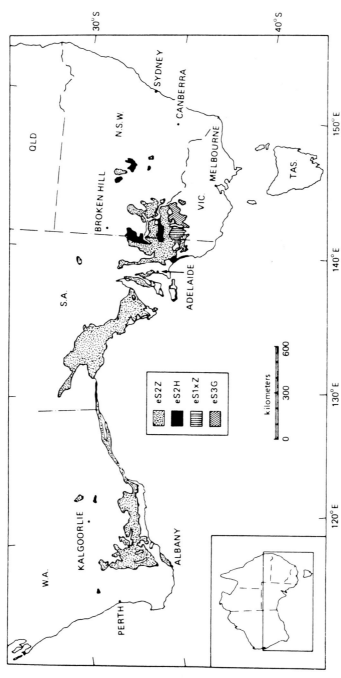

Figure 14. Eucalyptus tall shrubland is widely distributed in southern Australia. Collectively these are known as mallee. eS2Z, tall shrubland with low shrubs; eS2H, tall shrubland with hummock grasses; eS1xZ, tall open shrubland with low shrubs; eS3G, tall shrubland with tussock grasses and graminoids. [After Noble *et al.* (1980). Reproduced with permission of the Australian Rangelands Society, Perth.]

3. *Eucalyptus* Tall Shrubland

Eucalyptus tall shrublands with associated low shrubs have a widespread distribution in southern Australia, mainly under annual rainfall in the range 200–450 mm and especially on solonized brown soils and solodized solonetz soils and some deep sands (Fig. 14). There are also some examples on rocky soils in mountainous areas. The dominant *Eucalyptus* are many and varied, with some of the more widespread examples being *E. oleosa, E. socialis, E. dumosa, E. gracilis,* and *E. incrassata* (Carnahan, 1976). Under high rainfall the lower stratum is usually dense and the low shrubs are characteristically sclerophyllous and often ericoid. There is a very wide range of species, including species of *Acacia* and members of the families Proteaceae and Myrtaceae (especially species of more open areas), consisting of fewer species. There may be a sparse ground cover, including tussock grasses. The low shrub layer tends to be dominated by species of Chenopodiaceae.

A characteristic of these *Eucalyptus*-dominated communities is that their dominants are dwarf multistemmed eucalypts, known colloquially as "mallee" (Barrow and Pearson, 1970). A significant feature of all mallees is the presence of a large underground storage organ, the ligno-tuber. This imparts considerable fire tolerance (Burbidge, 1950).

4. *Eucalyptus populnea* Communities

Although structurally *Eucalyptus populnea* communities are classified as woodlands, they are nonetheless relevant to this review because many of the 31 plant associations that have been recognized (Beeston *et al.,* 1980) have a significant shrub understory. *Eucalyptus populnea* associations cover 160,000 km² in eastern Australia as shown in Fig. 15 (Beeston *et al.* 1980). They occur under a wide range of environmental conditions from the coast to more than 1000 km inland and between latitudes 20° to 34° S. Rainfall generally is between 300 and 750 mm per year. The climatic gradient from coast to the inland is related to both decreasing rainfall and increasing evaporative demand.

The principal *E. populnea* communities in Queensland, where shrubs are significant, are characterized by an upper layer of *E. populnea* with an average density of 170 trees per hectare, and a shrub layer of *Eremophila mitchelli.* The most common other shrubs are *Acacia excelsa, Atalaya hemiglauca, Carissa ovata, Canthium oleifolium, Capparis lasiantha, Geijera parviflora,* and *Heterodendrum oleifolium.* Further south, in New South Wales, the shrub layer is more variable, with *Eremophila sturtii* and *E. longifolia* being the most common species.

Hodgkinson (1980) reviewed information on the biology of 25 shrubs that occur as an understory in *E. populnea* lands. The distributions of 17 of

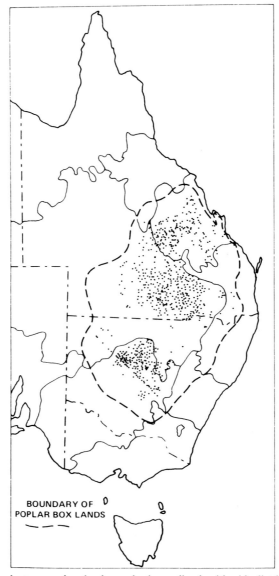

Figure 15.   *Eucalyptus populnea* lands are shrub woodlands with wide distribution in eastern Australia. [After Webb *et al.* (1980). Reproduced with permission of the Australian Range-lands Society, Perth.]

these shrubs that are considered to be "woody weeds" are shown in Fig. 16. The shift from grass to shrub dominance in the understory as a result of year-long grazing by sheep and cattle is considered to be the major biological problem facing ranchers in the *E. populnea* lands (Anonymous, 1969; Moore, 1969).

Undeniably, shrubs have increased in many parts of the *E. populnea* lands since the beginning of settlement, and the process is still going on. Harrington *et al.* (1979) reviewed the effects of settlement and livestock on the shift in botanical composition within the *E. populnea* lands. They conclude that the direct effects of grazing and trampling cause changes in soil fertility and that suppression of fire facilitates the replacement of herbage by woody plants.

5. Heaths

Heaths are communities of shrubs, often less than 2 m high with ericoid, microphyllous, or sclerophyllous leaves, and few or no herbaceous species. They occur from the tropics to the southernmost part of Australia and include alpine variants (Specht, 1979). Common genera of lowland heaths are *Banksia, Leptospermum, Calytrix,* and *Hakea,* while in the tropics the dominants are principally dwarf Protaceae, Epacridaceae, Leguminoseae, and Myrtaceae (Bryan, 1970). In the alpine regions there is a large selection of mainly Epacridaceae and Myrtaceae (Costin, 1970).

Soil and climate relationships of heathlands are more complex than for any other shrub formation so far described (Specht, 1979). Generally, the soils are those which at least for part of the year are liable to be water-logged and in addition they are commonly very high in silica and deficient in both major and minor elements. Heaths are the only shrub communities so far discussed that occur in Tasmania (Fig. 17).

B. Utilization

Despite the fact that most woody plant species in Australia are palatable to livestock, they tend to be viewed largely as a source of reserve forage, especially during the recurrent droughts that are a feature of Australia. Nonetheless, both *Acacia* and chenopod shrublands have contributed signficantly to the grazing industry (Graetz, 1973; Squires, 1981). Other functions, such as reduction of wind erosion in susceptible landscapes (Marshall, 1979), have contributed to maintenance of stable and productive rangeland (Friedel and Squires, 1982).

1. Chenopod Shrublands

Much has been written about the chenopod shrublands and they are comprehensively reviewed in Graetz and Howes (1979). The arrival of

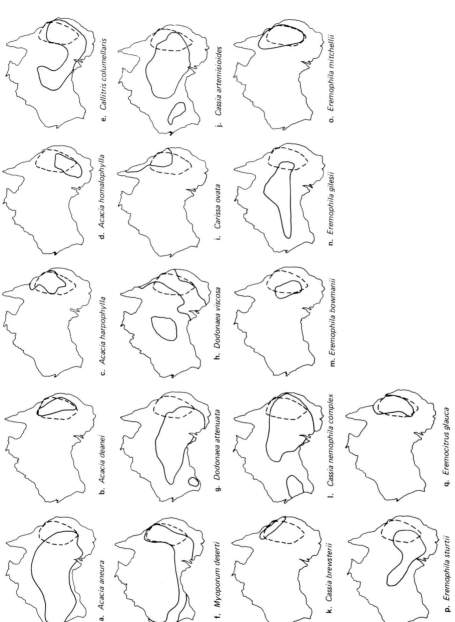

Figure 16. Map showing the distribution of 17 shrub species that have reached the status of "woody weeds" in *Eucalyptus populnea* lands. The *E. populnea* lands are delineated on these maps by a dashed line and the distributions of individual shrubs by solid lines. [After Hodgkinson (1980). Reproduced with permission of the Australian Rangelands Society, Perth.]

a. *Acacia aneura*

b. *Acacia deanei*

c. *Acacia harpophylla*

d. *Acacia homalophylla*

e. *Callitris columellaris*

f. *Myoporum deserti*

g. *Dodonaea attenuata*

h. *Dodonaea viscosa*

i. *Carissa ovata*

j. *Cassia artemisioides*

k. *Cassia brewsterii*

l. *Cassia nemophila complex*

m. *Eremophila bowmanii*

n. *Eremophila gilesii*

o. *Eremophila mitchellii*

p. *Eremophila sturtii*

q. *Eremocitrus glauca*

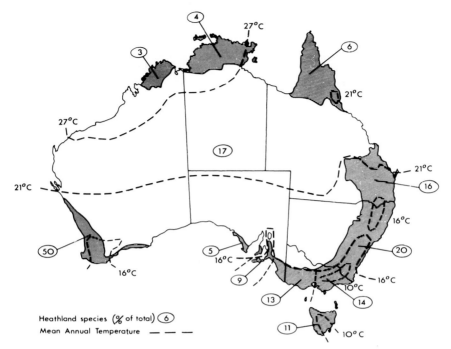

Figure 17. Distribution of heath communities (over 3700 species) in Australia. [After Specht (1979). Reproduced with permission of Elsevier, Amsterdam.]

Europeans with their introduced hard-footed herbivores and the European rabbit produced significant changes in the shrubland communities.

Grazing of rangelands in Australia occurs on an extensive basis. Livestock are free-ranging within large fenced paddocks containing one or more watering points. Paddock size varies but is commonly from 500 to >5000 ha (Squires and Hindley, 1970). The pattern of utilization of the forage species is determined largely by the behavior patterns of the stock alone (Squires, 1981). Over the years the uneven distribution of animals produces, through grazing and trampling, a recognizable pattern within the vegetation that is centered on the watering point. Osborn *et al.* (1932) were the first to report on the grazing pattern in chenopod shrubland in South Australia. Lange (1969) coined the term "piosphere" for the zone of stock influence around a watering point. The piosphere develops as the result of the interaction of the maintenance and social behavior of domestic livestock and feral and native herbivores with the vegetated laandscape in which the watering point is established (Graetz and Ludwig, 1978). In a uniform *A. vesicaria* community in southwest New South Wales a gradient of stocking pressure developed that was greatest near the watering point

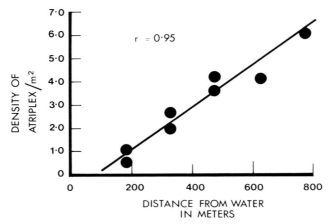

Figure 18. The density of the chenopod shrub *Atriplex vesicaria* increased linearly with distance from the watering point in a study in southwest New South Wales (After Squires, 1971.)

and decreased as a function of distance from it (Fig. 18). Graetz and Ludwig (1978) hypothesized that, in general, the relationship between distance from water and response of many vegetation and soil resources is likely to be sigmoid. Data from an *A. vesicaria* community, grazed by sheep for more than 50 years, demonstrate the general validity of this hypothesis (Fig. 19).

Apart from broad generalizations about herbivore influence on vegetation there is also the aspect of differential grazing pressure on individual plants of the same species. Graetz (1978) describes the greater browsing pressure on female than on male bushes of *A. vesicaria*. The contribution of chenopod shrubs to sheep production in Australia's arid zone has been reviewed by Wilson (1974). He concluded that the intake of shrubby species varied widely with season, the total forage available, and type of animal involved. Wilson and Graetz (1980) indicate that there is no apparent relationship between a high shrub component and high animal productivity.

Shrubs contribute only a small proportion to the diet of livestock grazing multilayered rangeland in average seasons. However, in poor seasons shrubs contribute significantly to intake, especially when the annual field layer fails (Squires and Siebert, 1983). During drought, livestock depend on sources of forage other than the field layer species for survival and the chenopod shrubs provide a valuable fodder resource (Wilcox, 1979). In addition to being a potential forage source, shrubs have other attributes. These include influences on landscape stability and nutrient cycling, and as guides to range condition assessment.

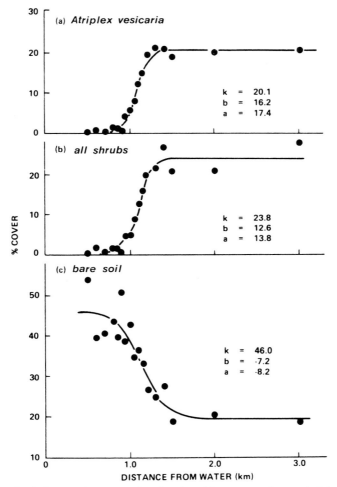

Figure 19. Logistic equation curve fits the sigmoid responses in an *Atriplex vesicaria* community in southwest New South Wales that has a history of grazing by sheep for more than 50 years. [After Graetz and Ludwig, (1978). Reproduced by permission of the Australian Rangelands Society, Perth.]

Marshall (1972) emphasized the need to maintain a cover of perennial shrubs in arid rangelands to prevent wind erosion. He derived formulae for determining the potential stability of a site from the size and spacing of the roughness elements (shrubs) upon it. Erosion of the surface layers or rangeland soils can remove the majority of readily available plant nutrients (Charley and Cowling, 1968) and create conditions that favor development of denuded areas. The soil mounds that commonly develop at the base of

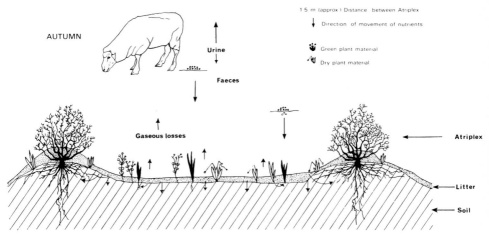

Figure 20. Mounds of organic matter accumulate around the base of *Atriplex vesicaria* grazed by sheep. [After Rixon (1970). Reproduced with permission of CSIRO, Melbourne.]

shrubs (Fig. 20) have higher total nitrogen and organic carbon and support more forage-producing species (Rixon, 1970) than the interspaces.

Because there is a near absence of spines or other protective devices and ready access by browsing animals to the unprotected primordia, it is not too surprising that many chenopod species are destroyed by overgrazing. There is considerable variation both between and among species, and some have a low acceptability to domestic livestock that offsets inability to withstand severe defoliation (Graetz and Wilson, 1979). Leigh and Mulham (1971) established that complete defoliation of *A. vesicaria* killed the plants of this species because they lack the ability to produce viable lateral or epicormic buds. Field observations suggest that *M. sedifolia* regenerates readily after heavy browsing, and epicormic buds can be produced from stem stumps. A similar situation seems to exist with *A. nummularia,* whereas *M. asrotricha,* a species that is almost identical to *M. sedifolia* in morphology and grazing acceptability, succumbs to grazing or to grazing and drought combined (Perry, 1972).

2. *Acacia*-Dominated Communities

Acacia in Australia, even within the same species, can occur as either trees or shrubs. Many are edible to livestock but there is considerable disagreement about forage value, palatability, and even toxicity of individual tree and shrub species, even within an individual species (Harrington, 1979).

The edible parts of *Acacia aneura* and other *Acacia* spp. (the phyllodes and seed pods) are frequently too high for sheep to reach and in drought times these shrubs and low trees may be pushed over or the branches lopped to provide a source of forage (Everist, 1969). The practice of drought feeding with *A. aneura* is particularly well developed in Queensland. In other than drought seasons it is not the shrub layer but rather the field layer species that provide the forage for livestock. Stocking rates vary from one sheep to 2 ha to one sheep to 12 ha. Cattle are grazed at about one to 40 ha (Moore, 1972). The associations that contain browse species have been mapped (Fig. 5) by Moore (1972).

The value and limitations of *A. aneura* as feed are discussed by Graetz (1973). McLeod (1973) determined the chemical composition and digestibility of the leaves of some tree and shrub species that are commonly used for drought feed. Results show that *A. aneura* phyllodes have value as a survival ration only. The data reveal that there is considerable variation between seasons. Leigh *et al.* (1978) concluded from a study of seasonal variation in the quality of leaves of four species of browse, including *A. homalophylla,* that the nutritive value was very low. The digestibility of *A. aneura* and *A. kempeana* from a site in central Australia was about 30%, despite the high proximate analysis (Siebert *et al.,* 1968). The major criticism of chemical analyses are that they fail to measure carbohydrate constituents and ignore cell wall lignification. *In vitro* digestibility provides a more relevant measure of potential forage value (Wilson, 1969).

Because woody plants appear to have their greatest potential value as a drought reserve it is a matter of concern that some trees and shrubs are failing to regenerate over whole regions (Lange and Purdie, 1976). Reasons for this include the impact of rabbits, grazing pressure by sheep and/ or cattle, changed fire regimes, and the interaction of drought with some or all these factors (Friedel and Squires, 1982).

Stability of *Acacia* shrublands is dependent on recruitment of new plants to the population (Fox, 1980). With such long-lived perennials it is not essential that recruitment occur every year or even every decade. Recruitment once every 25–50 years would probably be adequate to ensure that desirable shrub species persist.

3. *Eucalyptus* Communities

Eucalyptus woodlands and shrublands are quite diverse. They sustain many millions of livestock, especially in Queensland and New South Wales. However, as with the *Acacia* communities discussed earlier, livestock are dependent on the ground layer grasses and forbs and any edible browse in the shrub layer.

Little published information is available on the utilization of various mallee communities and this reflects their lesser significance for animal production (Noble *et al.,* 1980).

Merino sheep are the principal livestock grazed in the *Eucalyptus* woodlands and shrublands but these communities also support a substantial population of feral goats. Cattle are less common but in some districts they can be significant. Harrington (1978) and Squires (1982) have examined the diet of sheep, cattle, and goats that were grazing in common on an *E. populnea* community. Both the botanical and chemical compositions of the diet were assessed. Up to 96 species (including browse) were present on occasion but only 18 were detected in the extrusa from esophageal fistulas. The diets of the three animal species contained various quantities of browse. Goats ate the most, more than 50% on average, and sheep the least. Table I shows the maximum contribution made by selected browse species on any occasion during the 12-month study. From the information available it is clear that the field layer is ephemeral and the yield of forage dry matter is low (Squires, 1980; Johns, 1981). Livestock are forced to eat browse on occasion.

It is clear from Table I that some browse species contribute significantly to the diet of livestock at certain times of the year and that there is great disparity among animal species in which browse they prefer. Significant too is the fact that in the *Heterodendrum–Casuarina* woodlands studied by Wilson *et al.* (1975), sheep and goats showed a similar hierarchy of

Table I. Maximum contribution by selected browse species to the diets of sheep, cattle, and goats grazing a *Eucalyptus populnea* community[a]

Species	Maximum percentage in the diet		
	Sheep	Cattle	Goat
Scelerolaena diacantha[b]			
Scelerolaena convexula	29.6	51.4	0.7
Chenopodium anidiophyllum	16.6	34.2	1.8
Acacia aneura	12.1	6.0	49.4
Dodonaea viscosa	18.4	17.4	83.1
Acacia excelsa	0.0	0.0	8.2
Acacia homalophylla	11.1	11.9	13.3
Apophyllum anomalum	16.1	58.6	39.7
Cassia nemophila	6.3	3.1	16.6
Eremophila bowmanii	0.5	2.3	21.9
Eremophila mitchelli	0.0	4.9	0.6
Exocarpus aphyllus	0.0	0.0	42.5
Geijera parviflora	1.6	0.4	2.3

[a] From Squires (1980).
[b] *Scelerolaena* syn. *Bassia*

Figure 21. Woodlands dominated by *Heterodendrum* and *Casuarina* have a shrub under-story. Some of the understory shrubs are useful browse plants but many are unpalatable and have the status of woody weeds.

preference for the browse species. The site studied by Wilson *et al.* is farther south than the *E. populnea* community but has a similar suite of shrubs in the understory (Fig. 21).

4. Heathlands

Because of the great disparity between coastal and alpine heaths it is difficult to generalize. Generally, heathlands are not used extensively by livestock (Specht, 1981). Many areas of heathland are either unused for any form of agriculture or have been cleared of native vegetation and replanted to improved pastures or to crops. Their value as wildlife habitat is considerable and has been ably reviewed by Dwyer *et al.* (1979) and Kikkawa *et al.* (1979). Fire is a regular feature of heathlands and wildlife need special adaptations to allow them to cope (Main, 1981). Toxic substances in plant tissues make herbivory hazardous and the few browsing and grazing vertebrates on heathlands tend to utilize the seasonal or postfire growth of young foliage (Kikkawa *et al.*, 1979).

C. Unexploited Useful Wildland Shrubs

Apart from the value of shrubs to wildlife and livestock as browse and shelter there is a wide range of human uses, from food to fiber, that is at present not widely recognized. This lack of recognition is not because the information is not documented. Several books (e.g., Cribb and Cribb, 1981) have been written on the value of Australian wildland plants as well as numerous research papers and articles.

The value of plants is usually judged on the basis of their utility to people. There are many fewer species used commercially now than a century ago. Australian aboriginals were, and to a considerable extent still are comprehensive users of plants. About 170 species were used for a multiplicity of purposes (Latz and Griffin, 1978). Friedel and Squires (1982) reviewed the known uses of shrubs and other plants by aboriginals in central Australia. Uses include food, shelter, fiber, gum, drugs, weapons, tools, and fuel.

1. Ornamental and Amenity Planting

In Australia the potential of indigenous species for amenity plantings has been slow to be realized. Hall (1972) brings together a considerable amount of information on plants for shade, shelter, ornament, low-maintenance landscaping, and soil stability. Some genera, notably *Acacia, Banksia, Leptospermum, Callistemon, Cassia,* and *Melaleuca,* have long been valued as ornamentals. Many species have been commercialized. In the arid inland the value of tree plantings to ameliorate the harsh environment is particularly appreciated. Mining towns such as Broken Hill in western New South Wales, Mt. Isa in western Queensland, and Kambalba in Western Australia have benefited by extensive plantings of shrubs and trees, including salt- and drought-tolerant species of *Eucalyptus* and *Atriplex.*

Recently, attention has been focused on other indigenous shrubs, notably the various species of *Eremophila,* which have great potential as ornamentals. Many other species are now being screened for their landscaping potential.

2. Honey and Beeswax

An important use of shrubs in Australia is for honey and beeswax production. Australia is one of the four leading honey-producing countries of the world. Leigh (1972) listed the species from which high yields of nectar and pollen are obtained. Honey and beeswax are produced mainly from various species belonging to the genus *Eucalyptus* but many *Acacia, Melaleuca,* and *Hakea* are important pollen-producing species. Apiarists frequently take advantage of known environmental differences by traveling with their hives. For example, apiarists commence extracting operations in South Australia in early summer, where, because of high temperatures in early spring, flowering commences first. As flowering diminishes they move with their hives eastward, where flowering is later.

3. Hydrocarbon Potential

Latex-rich plants have a high hydrocarbon content that makes them potentially valuable as a source of liquid fuels. The plants of highest interest are species of *Euphorbia* and *Asclepias,* although some *Sarcostemma* species are also under study. As with guayule (*Parthenium argentatum*) and jojoba (*Simmondensis chinensis*) of North America, the Australian wildland species have a potential for commercial exploitation on a large scale. Preliminary trials at Roseworthy Agricultural College in South Australia have shown that some of the indigenous shrubs could be used for production of fuel, fiber, hydrocarbons, oils, and waxes. Recovery of hydrocarbons from the indigenous shrub *Asclepias rotundifolia* has been quite promising. In addition to the latex extracts, the cellulosic residues have been tested for bioconversion to either alcohol or fatty acids or for synthesis of alternative liquid fuels (van der Sommen and Jamieson, 1984).

4. Other Uses

Essential oils highly valued in medicine, pharmacy, and industrial applications are also well represented in Australia's indigenous shrubs (Cribb and Cribb, 1981). Essential oils are more or less homogeneous substances, but are usually a mixture of a wide range of alcohols, aldehydes, ketones, phenols, esters, and terpenes. *Eucalyptus* yields a valuable oil and is perhaps best known but other species have potential as well (Cribb and Cribb, 1981). Until the commencement of the present century eucalypt essential oil was used in Australia mainly for medicinal purposes, especially for the treatment of colds and as a mild disinfectant that could be used as a mouthwash. Subsequent use extended to solvents for substances such as tar, grease, and paint. Other uses include perfumery, industrial uses such as mineral recovery (through flotation), and as inexpensive, nontoxic disinfectants.

III. Conclusions

Australian shrublands are diverse and widespread. They have evolved in isolation from the mainstream of the world's flora, and as such have developed an interesting set of adaptations to low soil nutrient status, aridity, and fire. The absence of ungulates or other browsing animals during all but the most recent times has made them more vulnerable to the on-slaught of sheep, cattle, goats, donkeys, horses, camels, and the rabbits that accompanied Europeans in successive waves of colonization beginning less than two centuries ago.

In the Australian arid zone there is a higher proportion of shrub-dominated communities than is common in comparable world regions. The dominance of Australian arid zone shrublands by two genera, *Acacia* and *Atriplex,* is noteworthy. Both genera are edible to the introduced ungulate livestock that wrought, in the space of less than 200 years, great changes to the Australian rangelands.

Because of the value of most of the shrublands for livestock production, emphasis in the past has been on their forage value. More recently, attention has been directed to the role of shrubs in stabilizing the plant communities. Nutrient cycling and protection from wind and water erosion are but two important ecosystem functions.

Changing demands for alternative fuels and other chemicals have led to renewed interest in screening a wide range of indigenous plants. Interest is also growing in the potential of indigenous shrubs for ornamental and amenity plantings. In short, it can be said that shrubs play a significant role in the stability, productivity, and aesthetics of Australian rangelands and that this role is becoming increasingly recognized.

References

Anonymous (1969). "Report of the Inter-Departmental Committee on Shrub and Timber Regrowth in the Cobar–Byrock District and Other Areas of the Western Division of New South Wales." Government Printer, Sydney.

Axelrod, D. I., and Raven, P. H. (1972). Evolutionary biogeography viewed from the plate tectonic theory. *In* "Challenging Biological Problems: Directions Towards Their Solution" (J. A. Behnke, ed.), pp. 218–236. Oxford Univ. Press, London and New York.

Barlow, B. A. (1981). The Australian flora: Its origin and evolution. *In* "Flora of Australia," Vol. 1, Introduction, pp. 25–75. Bureau of Flora and Fauna, Australian Government Publishing Service, Canberra.

Barrow, P. M., and Pearson, F. B. (1970). The mallee and mallee heaths. *In* "Australian Grasslands" (R. M. Moore, ed.), pp. 219–227. Aust. Natl. Univ. Press, Canberra.

Beadle, N. C. W. (1966). Soil phosphate and its role in molding segments of the Australian flora and vegetation, with special reference to exeromorphy and sclerophylly. *Ecology* **47**, 992–1007.

Beale, I. F. (1973). Tree density effects on yields of herbage and tree components in south-western Queensland. *Trop. Grassl.* **7**, 135–142.

Beeston, G. R., Walker, P. J., Purdie, R., and Pickard, J. (1980). Plant communities of the poplar box (*Eucalyptus populnea*) lands of eastern Australia. *Aust. Rangel. J.* **2**, 53–58.

Boyland, D. E. (1973). Vegetation of mulga lands with special reference to south-western Queensland. *Trop. Grassl.* **7**, 35–42.

Bryan, W. W. (1970). Tropical and subtropical forests and heaths. *In* "Australian Grasslands" (R. M. Moore, ed.), pp. 101–111. Aust. Natl. Univ. Press, Canberra.

Burbidge, N. T. (1950). The significance of the mallee habit in *Eucalyptus. Proc. R. Soc. Queensl.* **62,** 73–78.

Burbidge, N. T. (1960). The phytogeography of the Australian region. *Aust. J. Bot.* **8,** 75–212.

Carnahan, J. A. (1976). Natural vegetation. *In* "Atlas of Australian Resources," 2nd ser. Department of National Resources, Canberra.

Charley, J. L., and Cowling, S. W. (1968). Changes in soil nutrient status resulting from overgrazing and their consequences in plant communities in semi arid areas. *Proc. Ecol. Soc. Aust.* **3,** 23–38.

Costin, A. B. (1970). Sub-alpine and alpine communities. *In* "Australian Grasslands" (R. M. Moore, ed.), pp. 191–198. Aust. Natl. Univ. Press, Canberra.

Cribb, A. B., and Cribb, J. W. (1981). "Useful Wild Plants in Australia." Collins, Sydney.

Dawson, T. J. (1977). Kangaroos. *Sci. Am.* **237**(2), 78–89.

Dwyer, P. D., Kikkawa, J., and Ingram, G. J. (1979). Habitat relations of vertebrates in subtropical heathlands of coastal southeastern Queensland. *In* "Heathlands and Related Shrublands: Descriptive Studies" (R. L. Specht, ed.), pp. 281–299. Elsevier, Amsterdam.

Everist, S. L. (1969). "Use of Fodder Trees and Shrubs." Advis. Leafl. No. 1024. Division of Plant Industry, Department of Primary Industries, Brisbane, Queensland.

Fox, J. E. D. (1980). Stability in the mulga zone. *Trop. Ecol. Dev.,* pp. 79–90.

Friedel, M. H., and Squires, V. R. (1982). Plants as a resource. *In* "Man in the Centre" (G. Grook, ed.). CSIRO, Melbourne.

Gentilli, J. (1978). "Australian Climatic Patterns." Nelsons, Melbourne.

Gill, E. D. (1975). Evolution of Australia's unique flora and fauna in relation to the plate tectonics theory. *Proc. R. Soc. Victoria* **87,** 215–234.

Graetz, R. D. (1973). Biological characteristics of Australian *Acacia* and chenopodiaceous shrublands relevant to their pastoral use. *In* "Arid Shrublands: Proceedings of the Third Workshop of The United States/Australia Rangelands Panel" (D. N. Hyder, ed.), pp. 33–39. Society for Range Management, Denver, Colorado.

Graetz, R. D. (1978). The influence of grazing by sheep on the structure of a saltbush (*Atriplex vesicaria* Hew ex Benth.) population. *Aust. Rangel. J.* **1,** 117–125.

Graetz, R. D., and Howes, K. M. W., eds. (1979). "Studies of the Australian Arid Zone. IV. Chenopod Shrublands." CSIRO, Melbourne.

Graetz, R. D., and Ludwig, J. A. (1978). A method for the analysis of piosphere data applicable to range assessment. *Aust. Rangel. J.* **1,** 126–136.

Graetz, R.D., and Wilson, A. D. (1979). An assessment of herbivore diets in the chenopod shrublands. *In* "Studies of the Australian Arid Zone. IV. Chenopod Shrublands" (R. D. Graetz and K. M. W. Howes, eds.), pp. 144–159. CSIRO, Melbourne.

Hall, N., (ed. (1972). "The Use of Trees and Shrubs in the Dry Country of Australia." Forestry and Timber Bureau, Australian Government Printer, Canberra.

Harrington, G. N. (1978). The implications of goat, sheep and cattle diets to the management of an Australian semi-arid woodland. *Proc. Int. Rangel. Congr. 1st,* pp. 447–450.

Harrington, G. N. (1979). The effects of feral goats and sheep on the shrub populations in a semi-arid woodland. *Aust. Rangel. J.* **1,** 334–345.

Harrington, G. N., Oxley, R. E., and Tongway, D. J. (1979). The effects of European settlement and domestic livestock on the biological system in poplar box (*Eucalyptus populnea*) lands. *Aust. Rangel. J.* **1,** 271–279.

Hasick, D. J. (1979). Heat and water vapour fluxes in an arid zone community. *In* "Studies of the Australian Arid Zone. IV. Chenopod Shrublands" (R. D. Graetz and K. M. W. Howes, eds.), pp. 54–60. CSIRO, Melbourne.

Hills, E. S. (1974). The physiographic setting. In "The Murray Waters, Man, Nature and River System" (H. J. Frith and G. Sawer, eds.), pp. 1–12. Angus & Robertson, Sydney.

Hodgkinson, K. J. (1980). The shrubs of the poplar box (*Eucalyptus populnea*) lands. *Aust. Rangel. J.* **1**, 280–295.

Hubble, G. D. (1970). Soils. In "Australian Grasslands" (R. M. Moore, ed.), pp. 44–58. Aust. Natl. Univ. Press, Canberra.

Johns, G. G. (1981). Hydrological processes and herbage production in a shrub invaded poplar box (*Eucalyptus populnea*) woodland. *Aust. Rangeland J.* **3**, 45–55.

Kemp, E. M. (1981). Tertiary paleogeography and the evolution of Australian climate. In "Ecological Biogeography of Australia" Vol. 1. (A. Keast, ed.). pp. 33–46. Junk, The Hague.

Kikkawa, J., Ingram, G. J., and Dwyer, P. D. (1979). The vertebrate fauna of Australian heathlands—An evolutionary perspective. In "Heathlands and Related Shrublands: Descriptive Studies" (R. L. Specht, ed.), pp. 221–279. Elsevier, Amsterdam.

Lamont, B. B., and Fox, J. E. D. (1981). Spatial pattern of six sympatric leaf variants and two size classes of *Acacia aneura* in a semi-arid region of Western Australia. *Oikos* **38**, 73–79.

Lange R. L. (1969). The piosphere, sheep track and dung patterns. *J. Range Manage.* **22**, 396–400.

Lange, R. T., and Purdie, R. (1976). Western myall (*Acacia sowdenii*) its survival prospects and management needs. *Aust. Rangel. J.* **1**, 64–69.

Latz, P. L., and Griffin, G. G. (1978). Changes in aboriginal land management in relation to fire and to food plants in central Australia. In "The Nutrition of Aborigines in Relation to the Ecosystem of Central Australia" (B. S. Hetzel and H. J. Frith, eds.), pp. 77–85. CSIRO, Melbourne.

Leigh, J. H. (1972). Honey and beeswax production in semi-arid and arid Australia. In "The Use of Trees and Shrubs in the Dry Country of Australia" (N. Hall, ed.), pp. 264–283. Forestry and Timber Bureau, Australian Government Printer, Canberra.

Leigh, J. H., and Mulham, W. E. (1971). The effect of defoliation on the persistence of *Atriplex vesicaria*. *Aust. J. Agric. Res.* **22**, 239–244.

Leigh J. H., and Noble, J. C. (1969). Vegetation resources. In "Arid Lands of Australia" (R. O. Slatyer and R. A. Perry, eds.), pp. 73–92. Aust. Natl. Univ. Press, Canberra.

Leigh, J. H., Wilson, A. D., and Mulham, W. E. (1978). Seasonal variations in the leaf fall and quality of the leaves of four Australian fodder trees. *Aust. Rangel. J.* **1**, 137–141.

Ludbrook, N. H. (1980). "A Guide to the Geology and Mineral Resources of South Australia." Department of Mines and Energy, Adelaide.

Mabbutt, J. A. (1969). Land forms of arid Australia. In "Arid Lands of Australia" (R. O. Slatyer and R. A. Perry, eds.), pp. 11–32. Aust. Natl. Univ. Press, Canberra.

McKnight, T. (1975). Friendly vermin—A survey of feral livestock in Australia. *Univ. Calif., Berkeley, Publ. Geogr.* **21**.

McLeod, M. N. (1973). The digestibility and the nitrogen, phosphorus and ash contents of the leaves of some Australian trees and shrubs. *Aust. J. Exp. Agric. Anim. Husb.* **13**, 245–250.

Main, A. R. (1981). Fire tolerance of heathland animals. In 'Heathlands and Related Shrublands: Analytical Studies" (R. L. Specht, ed.), pp. 85–90. Elsevier, Amsterdam.

Marshall, J. K. (1972). Principles of soil erosion and its prevention. In "The Use of Trees and Shrubs in the Dry Country of Australia" (N. Hall, ed.), pp. 90–107. Forestry and Timber Bureau, Australian Government Printer, Canberra.

Marshall, J. K. (1979). Plant weight to density relationships in chenopod shrublands. In "Studies of the Australian Arid Zone. IV. Chenopod Shrublands" (R. D. Graetz and K. M. W. Howes, eds.), pp. 75–82. CSIRO, Melbourne.

Moore, C. W. E. (1969). Application of ecology to the management of pastoral leases in northwestern New South Wales. *Proc. Ecol. Soc. Aust.* **4**, 39–53.

Moore, R. M. (1972). Trees and shrubs in Australian sheep grazing lands. *In* "Plants for Sheep in Australia" (J. H. Leigh and J. C. Noble, eds.), pp. 55–64. Angus & Robertson, Sydney.

Moore, R. M., and Perry, R. A. (1970). Vegetation. *In* "Australian Grasslands" (R. M. Moore, ed.), pp. 59–73. Aust. Natl. Univ. Press, Canberra.

Moore, R. M., Condon, R. W., and Leigh, J. H. (1970). Semi-arid woodlands. *In* "Australian Grasslands" (R. M. Moore ed.), pp. 228–245. Aust. Natl. Univ. Press, Canberra.

Nix, H. A., and Austin, M. P. (1972). Mulga: A bioclimatic analysis. *Trop. Grassl.* **7,** 9–21.

Noble, J. C., Smith, A. W., and Leslie, H. W. (1980). Fire in the mallee shrublands of western New South Wales. *Aust. Rangel. J.* **2,** 104–114.

Osborn, T. G. B., Wood, T. G., and Paltridge, T. B. (1932). On the growth and reaction to grazing of the perennial saltbush, *Atriplex vesicarium*. An ecological study of the biotic factor. *Proc. Linn. Soc. N. S. W.* **57,** 377–402.

Oxley, R. E. (1979). The perennial chenopod pasture lands of Australia. *In* "Studies of the Australian Arid Zone. IV. Chenopod Shrublands" (R. D. Graetz and K. M. W. Howes, eds.), pp. 1–4. CSIRO, Melbourne.

Pedley, L. (1978). A revision of *Acacia* Mill in Queensland. *Austrobaileyea* **1,** 75–234.

Perry, R. A. (1970). Arid shrublands and grasslands. *In* "Australian Grasslands" (R. M. Moore, ed.), pp. 246–259. Aust. Natl. Univ. Press, Canberra.

Perry, R. A. (1972). Native pastures used by sheep in South Australia and the Northern Territory. *In* "Plants for Sheep in Australia" (J. H. Leigh and J. C. Noble, eds.), pp. 25–37. Angus & Robertson, Sydney.

Pressland, A. J. (1976). Soil moisture re-distribution as affected by throughfall and stemflow in an arid zone shrub community. *Aust. J. Bot.* **23,** 965–976.

Pressland, A. J. (1978). Soil moisture distribution and evapotranspiration of a mulga (*Acacia aneura* F. Muel.) scrubland in south-western Queensland. *In* "Studies of the Australian Arid Zone. III. Water in Rangelands" (K. M. W. Howes, ed.), pp. 129–138. CSIRO, Melbourne.

Raven, P. H., and Axelrod, D. I. (1972). Plate tectonics and Australasian paleobiogeography. *Science* **176,** 1379–1386.

Rixon, A. J. (1970). Cycling of nutrients in a grazed *Atriplex vesicaria* community. *In* "Studies of the Australian Arid Zone. I. The Biology of *Atriplex*," pp. 87–95. CSIRO, Melbourne.

Sabbath, M. D., and Quinnell, S. (1981). "Ecosystems, Energy and Materials. The Australian Context." Longman, Cheshire, Melbourne.

Siebert, B. D., Newman, D. M. R., and Nelson, D. J. (1968). The chemical composition of some arid zone pasture species. *Trop. Grassl.* **2,** 31–40.

Specht, R. L., ed. (1979). "Heathlands and Related Shrublands: Descriptive Studies." Elsevier, Amsterdam.

Specht, R. L. (1981). Conservation: Australian heathlands. *In* "Heathlands and Related Shrublands: Analytical Studies" (R. L. Specht, ed.), pp. 235–240. Elsevier, Amsterdam.

Squires, V. R. (1971). A study of a bladder saltbush (*Atriplex vesicaria*) community grazed by sheep. Master's Thesis, University of New England, Armidale, Australia (unpublished).

Squires, V. R. (1980). Chemical and botanical composition of the diets of oesophageally fistulated sheep, cattle and goats in a semi-arid *Eucalyptus populnea* woodland community. *Aust. Rangel. J.* **2,** 94–103.

Squires, V. R. (1981). "Livestock Management in the Arid Zone." Inkata Press, Melbourne.

Squires V. R. (1982). Dietary overlap between sheep, cattle and goats when grazing in common. *J. Range Manage.* **35**, 116–119.

Squires, V. R., and Hindley, N. L. (1970). Paddock size and location of watering points as factors in the drought survival of sheep on the central Riverine Plain. *Wool Technol. Sheep Breed.* **17**(11), 49–54.

Squires, V. R., and Siebert, B. D. (1983). Botanical and chemical components of the diet and liveweight change in cattle on semi-desert rangeland in central Australia. *Aust. Rangel. J.* **5**, 28–34.

Valentine, I., and Nagorka, B. N. (1979). Contour patterning in *Atriplex vesicaria* communities. *In* "Studies of the Australian Arid Zone. IV. Chenopod Shrublands" (R. D. Graetz and K. M. W. Howes, eds.), pp. 61–74. CSIRO, Melbourne.

van der Sommen, F. J., and Jamieson, R. R. A. (1984). "The Potential of Euphorbiaceae to Provide Petroleum Substitutes in South Australia." South Australian Energy Research Advisory Committee, Adelaide.

Walter, H. (1971). "Ecology of Tropical and Sub-tropical Vegetation." Oliver & Boyd, London.

Webb, A. A., Walker, P. J., Gunn, R. H., and Mortlock, A. T. (1980). Soils of poplar box (*Eucalyptus populnea*) communities of eastern Australia. *Aust. Rangel. J.* **2**, 17–30.

Werger, M. J. A. (1978). Vegetation structure in the southern Kalahari. *J. Ecol.* **66**, 933–941.

Wilcox, D. G. (1972). The use of native pastures by sheep in Western Australia. *In* "Plants for Sheep in Australia" (J. H. Leigh and J. C. Noble, eds.), pp. 45–54. Angus & Robertson, Sydney.

Wilcox, D. G. (1979). The contribution of the shrub component in arid pastures to production from sheep. *In* "Studies of the Australian Arid Zone. IV. Chenopod Shrublands" (R. D. Graetz and K. M. W. Howes, eds.), pp. 170–177. CSIRO, Melbourne.

Williams, O. B. (1979). Ecosystems of Australia. *In* "Arid Land Ecosystems: Structure, Functioning and Management" Vol. 1. (D. W. Goodall and R. A. Perry, eds.), pp. 145–212. Cambridge Univ. Press, London and New York.

Wilson, A. D. (1969). A review of browse in the nutrition of grazing animals. *J. Range Manage.* **22**, 23–28.

Wilson, A. D. (1974). Nutrition of sheep and cattle in Australian arid areas. *In* "Studies of the Australian Arid Zone. II. Animal Production" (A. D. Wilson, ed.), pp. 74–84. CSIRO, Melbourne.

Wilson, A. D., and Graetz, R. D. (1980). Cattle and sheep production on an *Atriplex vesicaria (saltbush)* community. *Aust. J. Agric. Res.* **31**, 369–378.

Wilson, A. D., Leigh, J. H., Hindley, N. L., and Mulham, W. E. (1975). Comparison of the diets of goats and sheep on a *Casuarina cristata–Heterodendrum oliefolium* community in western New South Wales. *Aust. J. Exp. Agric. Anim. Husb.* **15**, 45–53.

Yeaton, R. I., and Cody, M. L. (1979). The distribution of cacti along environmental gradients in the Sonoran and Mohave deserts. *J. Ecol.* **67**, 529–541.

4

Mediterranean Europe and East Mediterranean Shrublands

Zev Naveh

I. Introduction

According to the International Classification and Mapping of vegetation (UNESCO, 1973), Mediterranean shrublands belong to the formation class "scrub" (or thicket), called "evergreen broad-leaved sclerophyllous shrublands." They are characterized by the dominance of evergreen phanerophytes with broad, but mostly small, thick, stiff and leathery sclerophyllous leaves. Sometimes these shrublands have an overstory of small trees with one stem, but most of the taller sclerophylls have shrubby growth habit with ramifications from the base. These can eventually be trained into a one-stemmed tree by cutting, pruning, and prevention of regeneration of suckers. In their more open phases they have an understory of chamaephyte dwarf shrubs and herbaceous perennial hemicryptophytes and geophytes and annual therophytes.

Such sclerophyll shrublands can be considered as the *natural potential* vegetation of all those regions with typical Mediterranean climates. These are characterized by dry, warm to hot summers with high solar radiation and high rates of evaporation, alternating with humid, cool to cold winters with low solar radiation and low rates of evaporation. According to Ashmann (1973), the annual precipitation ranges from 250 (in coastal regions) to 350 mm (in warmer interior regions), at least 65% of this concentrated in the winter half. Köppen (1923) called this the Cs (mild humid winter and dry summer) "olive climate," because the sclerophyll evergreen olive tree around the Mediterranean Basin corresponds quite well with the climate type.

In addition to the Mediterranean, four other widely separated regions of the world, chiefly between 30° and 40° north and south latitudes on the west coasts of the continents, with similar bioclimates have comparable sclerophyll shrublands: the chaparral in California, the matorral in Chile, the mallee in Australia, and the renosterveld in South Africa. This Mediterranean sclerophyll zone makes up roughly 1% of the world's terrestrial vegetation and about half of this is concentrated around the Mediterranean Sea.

II. Distribution and General Description

This chapter will be confined to the Mediterranean shrublands of Europe and the Near East. Those of North Africa will be discussed in Chapter 5. The present shrubland area in the former region has been estimated by Le Houérou (1981) together with Mediterranean forests to be around 300,000 km². As indicated in Fig. 1, they are distributed along the coast of all countries bordering the Mediterranean Sea. But in the Iberian peninsula these shrublands also reach the Atlantic Coast and inland, covering the largest area of any country. In southern France they reach the southern slopes of the Cevenne Mountains and extend far into the Rhone valley. In Italy they spread inland along the Zerno and Tiber rivers. They are also very widespread in Greece and its islands as well as in Cyprus and Turkey. But with the exception of the Dalmation coast, they occupy only a very

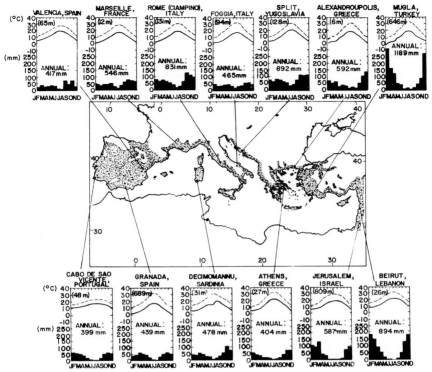

Figure 1. Distribution of Mediterranean shrublands and mean monthly precipitation (mm) and temperatures (°C) in European and Near East countries. (Modified from Quezel, 1981, and McCutchan, 1977.)

narrow belt along the Adriatic coast in Yugoslavia. In Syria, Lebanon, and Israel they cover chiefly the western slopes of the mountains along the coast, but in Jordan they occur far inland.

Different vernacular names have been given to these shrublands, such as *maquis* in France, *macchia* in Italy, *matorral* in Spain, *xerovini* in Greece, and *choresh* in Israel. Lower shrub vegetation is called *gariga* in Israel and other Mediterranean countries, but in France the term *garrigue* has been resticted to the low scrub formation, dominated by the *Quercus coccifera* on calcareous soils and rocks. The lower, and more xeromorphic heath-landlike shrublands, dominated by chamaephytes and subshrubs, are called *phrygana* in Greece, *batha* in Israel, *tomillares* in Spain, and sometimes *lande* in France. Their counterpart in California is the *coastal sage* (Naveh, 1967) and on oligotrophic soils in the Cape region of South Africa they are called *fynbos* (Kruger, 1979).

Tomaselli (1981) has suggested adopting the Spanish *matorral* term. According to height (H) and cover (R) he distinguished between high ($H > 2$ m), middle (0.60 m $< H <$ 2 m), and low ($H <$ 0.60 m) matorral and dense ($R > 75\%$), discontinuous (50% $> R > 75\%$), and scattered matorral (25% $< R <$ 50%). He described in detail their structure by diagrams and collected examples of each type from all Mediterranean countries.

The high matorral is usually called "maqui," namely, a dense, impenetrable tall shrubland of xerophilous, sclerophyll evergreen—but sometimes deciduous—low trees. A typical example is the *Quercus calliprinos*-dominated maquis of the Near East (Fig. 2). The distinction between these and the sclerophyll forest is not always clear and many phytosociologists and foresters regard these shrublands as degraded stages of the Mediterranean sclerophyll forest climax, which can be restored by protection (Tomaselli, 1981).

For the middle matorral the above-mentioned *Quercus coccifera* garrigue in southern France is most representative. Also the *Olea–Ceratonia* and *Ceratonia–Pistacion* formations are parklike middle matorral shrub-

Figure 2. Typical East Mediterranean mixed, middle matorral on very rocky terra rossa. The multilayered stratification is maintained by moderate browsing, wood cutting, and periodic burning. The taller, scattered shrubs are *Quercus calliprinos* and *Pistacia palaestina*, mixed with *P. lentiscus* and *Rhamnus palaestina*. The trees in the cultivated valley are *Ceratonia siliqua*.

lands and the same is true for the *Pinus halepensis* and *P. brutia* forests of scattered pine trees with a sclerophyll shrub understory. The browsed, semiopen scattered middle motorral shrublands are probably the most abundant shrubland type of the East Mediterranean. Low matorral are either heavily grazed and browsed sclerophyll shrublands or heatherlike dwarfshrublands, dominated by *Sarcopoterium spinosum* and/or aromatic *Cistus* and *Labiatae* species. These are very abundant in Greece and the East Mediterranean. An example of a typical shrubland community forming a closely interwoven mosaic of regeneration and degradation stages is shown in Fig. 3.

Mediterranean woodlands and their open, parklike savanna phases, dominated by oak trees, such as the deciduous *Quercus macrolepis* in Turkey and *Q. ithaburensis* in Israel, as well as the evergreen *Q. suber* in the West Mediterranean, all of which have a dense grass understory, cannot be considered matorral shrublands and will not be discussed here, in spite of their great economic importance and biological richness.

Important information on Mediterranean shrubland ecosystems, is contained in the volume "Origin and Structure of Mediterranean Ecosystems"

Figure 3. Typical East Mediterranean low matorral ("batha"), dominated by *Sarcopoterium spinosum* on pale rendzina, near an Arabic village. In the past, this highly flammable dwarf shrub has been cut as fuel for lime kilns but now the only usage is for goat grazing in spring and after burning. Note the neglected terrace walls of patch cultivated fields and the removal of soil on the opposite slope. Olive trees are still cultivated on the deepest soils in the valley.

(di Castri and Mooney, 1973) and in the more recent compilation devoted to Mediterranean shrubland ecosystems (di Castri *et al.*, 1981). A lucid overview of the Mediterranean sclerophyll vegetation and its ecophysiological peculiarities has been presented by Walter (1968). Comprehensive regional studies of this vegetation have been provided by Horvat *et al.* (1974) for south east Europe and by Zohary (1973) for the Near East. Very intensive phytosociological studies have been carried out in the West Mediterranean shrublands by ecologists from the SIGMA group at Montpellier under the late J. Braun-Blanquet. Much of this information has been summarized in the above-mentioned compilation by Tomaselli (1981), Quezel (1981), and Le Houérou (1981).

III. Physical Environment

A. *Physiographic Features and Soils*

The physiographic and gemorphological features of Mediterranean uplands, occupied mostly by these shrublands, have been summarized by Paskoff (1973) and Bradbury (1981). These uplands characterized by massive, young orogenic systems that evolved in the Mesozoic era, but attained their maximum relief of moderate to steep slopes in the Cenozoic. The lower, coastal areas exhibit a striking alternation of complex stream-eroded mountains and hills and alluvial, cultivated plains. Natural vegetation has remained only on nontillable uplands too steep and too rocky for cultivation. Their soils are highly complex and vary in depth, but most are shallow and heavily eroded, especially those that were terraced, cultivated, and later neglected (Naveh and Dan, 1973). Most important shrubland soils are rather fertile and well-structured *terra rossa* soils, derived from hard limestone and dolomite of Upper Cretaceous and Tertiary rocks, and *dark rendzinas,* derived from soft limestone with hard calcareous Nari crusts (Fig. 4). Much poorer are the highly calcareous *pale rendzinas,* derived from soft limestone, chalk, and Eocenic marls, which are abundant in the Near East and Turkey, as well as *noncalcareous brown soils,* derived from granitic rock, sandstone, and metamorphic rocks, which are associated with the more important shrubland soils in the West Mediterranean.

Among the different varieties of terra rossa soils, the *red-brown* variety is most typical for these shrublands. These soils are mostly shallow with many rock outcrops and after the destruction of the woody vegetation canopy, the upper, humus layer has been lost and only a skeleton lithosol remains (Dan *et al.*, 1972). The A horizon has in general a granular structure and

Figure 4. Brown rendzina soil on hard nari limestone rock in the Judean foothills (described in Table I).

the B horizon a blocky one. The texture is clayey, the limestone content low, and bases are slightly unsaturated; the reaction is slightly acid to mildly alkaline and the minor clay is chiefly montmorillonite with some kaolinite.

One of the most characteristic features of these Mediterranean uplands, covered mostly by shrubland, is their rugged topography and the formation of karst, especially in Cenomanian–Turon formations. Here, permeable dolomite and crystalline limestone are covered with a very shallow terra rossa or brown rendzina soil mantle in irregular pockets. Closer inspection reveals that vertical erosion of fine, well-structured silt and clay particles, rich in organic matter, as well as caps of soft chalk and marl lenses ensure favorable fertility and moisture conditions for the deeply penetrating shrub roots.

According to Oppenheimer (1956) roots can dissolve even hard rocks. The cumulative moisture withdrawal of a dense cover of high mattoral, dominated by *Q. calliprinos* and *Pistacia lentiscus,* ranged between 541 mm in a wet year with 760 mm rainfall to 408 mm in a dry year with 630 mm. During the same period, the control plot from which the woody vegetation had been cleared withhdrew ony 285 and 256 mm. We can, therefore, conclude that in contrast to most other sclerophylls, these Mediterranean shrubs are relying chiefly on moisture storage in the rock layer. Their adaptation to these heterogeneous microsites and rock niches and their ability to withdraw "rock moisture" are two of the most unique features with far-reaching ecological implications (Shachori *et al.,* 1968).

B. Bioclimate

The overall pattern of Mediterranean bioclimates is affected very much by the surrounding regions and especially from the moist air carried from the Atlantic, cold air from Central Europe and Turkey, and the hot air from the Sahara. These different and locally very diverse wind regimes are not expressed effectively in pluviothermic and ombothermic diagrams used by Mediterranean ecologists (Nahal, 1981) but have great influence on plant life. Thus, the cool "mistral" and "bore" blowing down from central Europe limit the extension of sclerophylls to the north and, on the other hand, the hot and dry desertic "sharav" (the counterpart of the North Africa "sirroco" in Israel), the "etesian" in Greece, and the "meltemi" in Turkey cause heavy summer drought stress.

Nahal (1981) has given many examples of Mediterranean bioclimate and has attempted to improve the pluviothermic quotient of Emberger for a general classification. Di Castri (1981), in his introduction to Mediterranean-type shrublands, reviewed all earlier attempts for such a classification and suggested a simplified subdivision of the UNESCO (1963) bioclimate classification of six major types from perhumid to perarid. He concluded that the distribution of sclerophyll shrubs seems to correspond to the semiarid and arid types. But as these terms are applied in a different way in classifications of arid climates (Meiggs, 1964), we shall use for these types

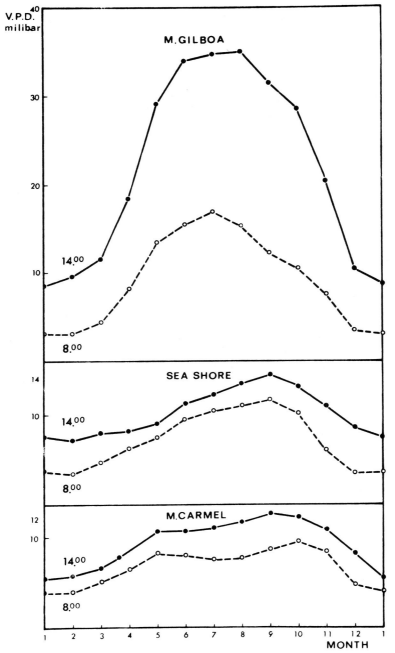

Figure 5. Vapor pressure deficit (V.P.D.) throughout the year in three Mediterranean shrubland habitats in Israel. (For climate characteristics, see Table I.)

Table I.   Climatic characteristics of three Mediterranean shrubland habitats in Israel

	Mt. Gilboa	Mt. Carmel	Coastal plain
Annual precipitation (mm)	450	650	600
Average monthly evaporation (mm)			
January	35	50	50
June	260	220	150
Average monthly temperature (°C)			
January at 0800	11	11	10
June at 0800	28	20	21
January at 1400	18	14	15
June at 1400	33	22	23
Average number of sharav days per year			
(less than 35% relative humidity)	60	39	18

the original UNESCO terminology of thermomediterranean and xerother-momediterranean shrubland bioclimates. In this, a xerothermic index (x) is used for hot weather drought and biological dry days, calculated from the sum of monthly indices of dry months, in which total precipitation is equal or lower than half of the temperature. For most of these shrublands this xerothermic index ranges from 200 to 100. According to Naveh (1973) this is the "true Mediterranean fire climate" in which severe fire hazard for dense sclerophyll stands, as well as for conifers and dry herbaceous vegetation, prevails for 4 to 8 months.

The great bioclimatic heterogeneity that characterizes these shrublands, even across distances of less than 50 km, is well demonstrated by a comparison of three representative shrubland sites in northern Israel, all dominated presently by *Pistacia lentiscus:* the subhumid sea shore near Cesarea and Carmel Mountain, both mapped as accentuated thermo-mediterranean, and the semiarid Mt. Gilboa, mapped as xerothermo-mediterranean (Fig. 5 and Table I).

IV. Evolution and Dynamics of Mediterranean Shrublands

A. *Evolution of the Sclerophyll Geoflora*

According to Axelrod (1973) the Mediterranean sclerophylls, like their North American counterparts of the Madro–Tertiary geoflora, had their origins in the southwestern parts of the continent by late Cretaceous (and earlier) time. These regions are presently deserts but were then well watered even though there was a dry season in winter.

As a response to the general continental uplift in transitional Oligo–Miocene time, greater extremes of temperatures began to develop and precipitation was reduced over the interior. It was about this time that taxa representing species similar to those of the present Mediterranean sclerophyll vegetation first appear in the floras of southern Europe, increasing in diversity during the Miocene and Pliocene. At the beginning of the Tertiary, the Mediterranean Sea originated as the result of the contraction of the Tethys (the shallow inland sea that occupied the central Asiatic area during the Mesozoic), and at the end of the Tertiary, the geographical situation was more or less similar to that at present. However, the climate was somewhat warmer and the Tertiary geoflora had a subtropical character with many tropical elements, including evergreen sclerophylls. The Mediterranean climate regime developed only later, in the Pleistocene, and as emphasized by Axelrod (1973) those sclerophylls that survived have been *preadapted* to summer drought and did not evolve as a result of it like most of the herbaceous plants.

B. Dynamics of Shrubland Degradation and Regeneration

Following the functional–factorial approach by Jenny (1961), the evolution of Mediterranean shrublands as part of the cultural landscape has been described as a series of multivariate functions of independent and driving ecosystem state factors on their dependent soil and biotic variables (Naveh, 1982). In the evolution of the natural Mediterranean landscape, drought and fire as climatic factors and grazing as a biotic factor are recognized as important selective forces in these biofunctions. However, the increasingly dominant role of humans in controlling state factors by hunting, gathering, and burning in the Upper Pleistocene and by agropastoral land uses during historical times turned these functions into *anthropogenic biofunctions*. In these, the introduction of human-made cultural artifacts, such as terrace walls, as dependent variables created the cultural Mediterranean landscape and its seminative and semiagricultural shrublands.

As shown by Naveh and Dan (1973) and Le Houérou (1981), present accelerating landscape degradation biofunctions in heavily populated upland regions are leading to the creation of bare soil and *Asphodelus* (a fire- and grazing-resistant geophyte) rock deserts. This process does not occur, in general, in a sequence of well-defined "regressive successional stages." It is the direct and immediate result of the mechanical removal and *uprooting* of the woody plants, together with plowing out of the herbaceous canopy on patch-cultivated, steep, and unterraced slopes, or the destruction and neglect of existing terrace walls. Sclerophylls like *Pistacia lentiscus, Quercus calliprinos,* and *Q. coccifera,* together with highly resilient perennial grasses, such as *Poa bulbosa* and *Hordeum bulbosum,* provide efficient soil protection, even in a stunted and heavily browsed stage, as long as their underground parts and extensive root systems are intact.

As could be expected, the harsher and more fragile the environment and its habitat state factors, the more far-reaching and irreversible are these human-induced changes in the other state variables and the slower and more difficult is the recovery process. This is especially true for shallow soils covering hard rock, where soil recovery processes are extremely slow and may take many thousands of years, much longer than is required for the striking recovery and redominance of dense high matorral and forest "climax" communities of *Quercus ilex* or *Q. calliprinos* after release of human and animal pressures.

C. Effects of Prolonged Noninterference, Abandonment, Complete Protection, and Afforestation on Biological Diversity

As mentioned earlier, cessation of traditional agropastoral activities of cultivation, woodcutting, grazing, and periodic burning, resulting from the depopulation of rural uplands, distorts the dynamic equilibrium between the different herbaceous and woody vegetation strata. In its early stages this leads to a recovery in height and density of the herbaceous and woody plant cover, but very soon aggressive tall grasses and perennial thistles crowd out the smaller herbs, and a dense, species-poor and highly combustible weed thicket establishes itself in open woodlands and grasslands. In shrublands, the above-described, vigorous vegetative sclerophyll regeneration is followed, in general, by the gradual encroachment of the taller shrub canopy, resulting in the almost total suppression of the herbaceous understory and the loss of its biological and scenic values.

After extensive studies of shrublands in the Near East, Zohary (1973) concluded that such undisturbed *Quercus calliprinos* "climax communities" are extremely monotonous and species-poor. From the more humid, Adriatic *Quercus ilex* forests, Horvat *et al.* (1974) reported that these have lost their open appearance and their floral and faunistic richness after the cessation of intensive agropastoral uses. This was confirmed recently by Ilijanic and Hecimovic (1981) in a study of the plant succession on the island of Lokrum near Dubrovnik in Yugoslavia, protected since 1948 as a nature reserve. They concluded that without renewal of these human

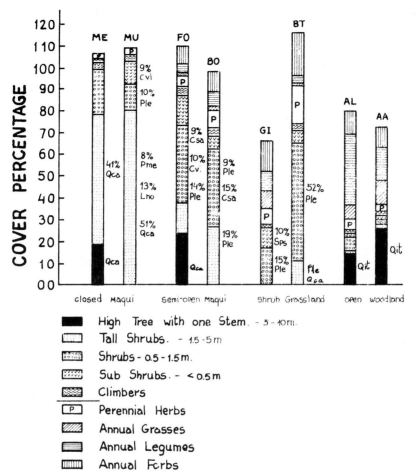

Figure 6. Plant cover by strata and growth forms in shrubland samples, northern Israel 1975–1976. Major species are abbreviated: *Quercus calliprinos, Q. ithaburense, Pistacia lentiscus, Sarcopoterium spinosum, Cistus salvifolia, C. villosa, Laurus nobilis, Phillirea media.* (After Naveh and Whittaker, 1979.)

activities, the richest and most attractive low and middle matorral "degradation" stages will be lost forever and this island will conserve only a species-poor *Q. ilex* forest.

Comparisons of protected and disturbed tall matorral and moderately and heavily grazed middle matorral in Israel are shown in Fig. 6. The dense and almost impenetrable tall shrub maqui canopies on the Mt. Meron Nature Reserve (ME) and the muhraqa on Mt. Carmel (MU) were dominated by *Quercus calliprinos* with relatively few subordinate shrubs. The most monotonous muhraqa community, protected for 40 years, had the lowest values for total and stratified woody species richness per 1000 m^2 (21). Here also the lowest diversity values of evenness and highest dominance concentrations were calculated and the faunal abundance and species richness were lowest.

D. *Optimization of Overall Adaptive Resistance*

During the long duration of the agropastoral biofunctions, humans changed not only the initial habitat factors of slope and exposure but also the biotic flux potential of plant and animal species. This encouraged the invasion of more xeric elements from adjacent drier regions (Zohary, 1973), and the selection and evolution of those biotypes that had the best chance to survive and prosper in spite of environmental rigor and constant defoliation pressures of fire, grazing, and cutting. We can assume, therefore, that in all sclerophylls, as well as in other woody species, a high degree of adaptive resistance has evolved, not only for specific stress factors, such as drought (Margaris, 1981; Rundel, 1977) or fire (Trabaud, 1981; Gill, 1977), but also for their *combined* impact.

In Mediterranean shrublands, adaptive responses to the catastrophic pyric destruction of all aboveground phytomass are aimed chiefly at survival through postfire regeneration, induced by positive feedback responses. Both hydroecological groups also differ in this respect: the drought-*enduring* sclerophylls rely solely on *vegetative resprouting* from their extensive root systems and are therefore *obligatory resprouters*. But the drought-*avoiding* shrubs and dwarf shrubs as well as perennial herbaceous plants have *double vegetative* and *reproductive* regeneration mechanisms, both from underground and protected buds and from seeds that avoided the fire or are even stimulated by it and its aftereffects (Figs. 7 and 8). Both groups are shown in Table II. In general, the vigorous resprouting of sclerophylls from suckers, from dormant buds of the root crown, or from lateral roots and shoots that were not destroyed by the fire is initiated almost immediately after the fire—as well as after cutting— even in the middle of the summer. These defoliation stresses, like the drought stress, are apparently overcome by positive feedback responses that mobilize stored carbohydrates and possibly also metabolized water in the roots. This enables immediate and simultaneously renewed photosynthetic activity and root growth, as observed by Swarzboim (1978) in

Figure 7. Fire and ash-stimulated development of seedlings of *Salvia triloba* (control from unburned plot on the right).

Pistacia lentiscus. On the other hand, in facultative resprouters the post-fire feedback responses like those after summer drought are postponed until the onset of the rainy season in late fall with the renewed supply of soil moisture. At that time the rate of growth, of both resprouting shoots and new seedlings, is very high.

Figure 8. Fire- and ash-stimulated development of seedlings of *Sarcopoterium spinosum* (control on the left).

Table II.   Regeneration behavior after fire of some common
Mediterranean woody plants in Israel

Plant	Resprouting	Spreading by seeds[a]
Trees		
Pinus halepensis Mill.	−	+
Quercus calliprinos Webb.	+	−
Quercus ithaburense (Decne.) Boiss.	+	−
Quercus boisseri Reut	+	−
Ceratonia siliqua L.	+	−
Styrax officinalis L.	+	−
Laurus nobilis L.	+	−
Arbutus andrachne L.	+	−
Rhamnus alaternus L.	+	−
Pistacia palaestina Boiss.	+	−
Phyllirea media L.	+	−
Cercis siliquastrum L.	+	−
Shrubs		
Pistacia lentiscus L.	+	−
Rhamnus palaestina Boiss.	+	−
Calycotome villosa (Dor) Lk.	+	+
Dwarfshrubs		
Sarcopoterium spinosa L.	+	+
Cistus salvifolius L.	+	+
Cistus villosus L.	+	+
Salvia triloba L. fil.	+	+
Teucrium creticum L.	+	+
Majorana syriaca L.	+	+
Satureja thymbra	+	+
Thymus capitata L.	+	+
Climbers		
Rubus tenuifolia D' Urv	+	−
Smilax aspera L.	+	−
Tamus communis L.	+	−
Asparagus aphyllus L.	+	−
Clematis cirrhosa L.	+	−
Lonicera etrusca Santi.	+	−
Prasium majus L.	+	−

[a] Only plants with pronounced postfire germination.

V. Multipurpose Afforestation, Brush Range Conversion, and Multiple Land Use Patterns

A. *Multipurpose Afforestation*

The improvement of dense or semiopen shrublands can be achieved mainly by burning or by manipulation and controlled utilization of the existing woody plant cover. However, large portions of Mediterranean shrublands have already reached such an advanced stage of deterioration of the existing woody cover that their rehabilitation can be achieved only by much more far-reaching and intensive methods. Up to now this was attempted mainly by afforestation with drought-resistant, fast-growing, and wood- and fiber-producing conifer trees, such as *Pinus halepensis* and *P. brutia*. Now, as a result of introduction trials carried out since 1970 in degraded low matorral sites on very shallow and rocky rendzina and terra rossa soils in northern Israel, alternative ways have been developed for multipurpose reclamation and afforestation (Naveh, 1975, 1982). As opposed to the one-layered, monotonous, and vulnerable conifer planta-tions, the aim is to create a new type of seminatural, multilayered, and stable park-forest with multiple ecological, economical, and social benefits. At the same time, they could be of greater economical and ornamental value by the replacement of inferior indigenous woody plants by more valuable introduced shrubs and trees.

Although it is still too early for any final conclusions, there are already available a number of highly promising plants that can be established and maintained like pine trees with minimum care and without any sup-plemental irrigation. In this, the planting of shrubs and trees is combined with the reconstitution of the stunted sclerophyll remnants by pruning and thinning. These plants belong to three main ecological groups.

1. *Fast-growing, soil-protecting, low cover subshrubs* that can replace and compete successfully with dwarf shrubs like *Sarcopoterium spinosum* and herbaceous weeds in the driest, rockiest, and/or highly calcareous microsites. Among these are *Rosmarinus officinalis,* a highly ornamental and valuable honey plant from the West Medi-terranean, *Myoporum multiflorum,* a prostrate, highly ornamental, and low-flammability plant from Australia, and *Atriplex glauca,* a valuable fodder shrub from Australia.

2. *Deep-rooted, evergreen or summer green, taller shrubs* for slightly better microsites. These faster-growing, more palatable and produc-tive shrubs have higher ornamental values but similar drought and limestone tolerance, regeneration capacities after fire and grazing, and soil amelioration capabilities than the indigenous sclerophylls. Most promising among these are *Cotoneaster franchetti* and *C. pannosa*

ornamental shrubs from China, which proved themselves as highly palatable and productive fodder shrubs; *Atriplex nummularia*, one of the most valuable, limestone-tolerant fodder shrubs from Australia, which also competes successfully with *Sarcopoterium spinosum* under heavy goat grazing on highly calcareous poor pale rendzina; *Medicago arborea,* a valuable West Mediterranean leguminous fodder shrub, and several promising *Acacia* species from Australia, which combine fodder value with ornamental values.

3. *Slower-growing but persistent tall shrubs and trees* for the most favorable microsites. These shrubs have high fodder and/or forest and ornamental value and can serve as shade trees in recreation forests. Here, local trees, like *Ceratonia siliqua, Pistacia atlantica, Cercis siliquastrum,* and several Australian *Acacia* trees, show great promise.

B. Brush Range Conversion and Improvement

Methods for conversion and improvement of pastoral shrubland areas and a rationale for utilization of Mediterranean shrublands as investigated in Israel have been described in detail by Naveh (1973, 1974), in Greece by Liacos (1981), and for the Mediterranean as a whole by Le Houérou (1981).

By applying the practices developed in California for chaparral conversion using a combination of prescribed burning and seeding of desirable perennial grasses, very encouraging early results have been achieved in Israel and in Greece (Liacos, 1981). A four to five times increase in pasture and livestock production has been obtained in the first 3 years. In Greece, pastures have provided 120 kg meat of yearling goats per hectare and the equivalent of 150 kg meat of beef cattle per hectare in Israel. However, as shown in Fig. 9, the success of reseeding high-yielding perennial grasses, and especially *Phalaris tuberosa*, which does not occur naturally in shallow and rocky shrubland soils, depends on the prevalence of well-developed sclerophylls before burning. Sites that received 3- to 4-year rotations of burning without reseeding shifted to low production and a mixed dwarf shrub and herbaceous plant cover (Papanastasis, 1980). A more intensive method of improvement is by replacing the undesirable woody plants with productive fodder shrubs, which might be the most promising means of pastoral improvement (Fig. 10).

C. Multiple Land Use Patterns

To ensure the greatest possible overall benefit from these different management and improvement options and to reconcile differences between these often clashing land use demands, flexible multipurpose

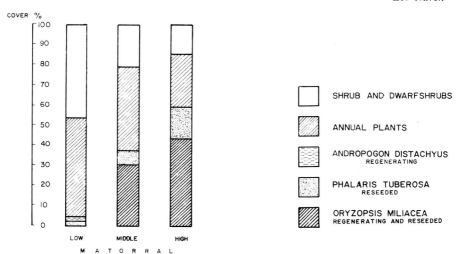

Figure 9. Success of reseeded and regenerating perennial grasses after burning in three different shrub habitats. (Mazuba–Western Galilee, 1954). The dominating woody plants in low matorral were *Sarcopoterium spinosum,* in middle matorral *Pistacia lentiscus* and *Phamnus palaestina,* and in high matorral *Quercus calliprinos.*

strategies should be applied according to site potentials and local and national requirements. This could be realized in practice by the creation of *closely interwoven networks of multiple land use patterns.* For this purpose, flow charts of management strategies and cybernetic models of the mutual impacts of these options and their production are needed. Protection, regulation functions, and environmental variables should be prepared (Naveh, 1978, 1979). From these models and a preliminary balance sheet of costs and benefits, multiple use benefits can be projected for environmental and watershed protection, fire hazard resistance, biotic diversity, recreation amenity, forest and livestock production, and water yields from seminatural multilayered park-forests. Because of their overwhelming impact, managerial interest in maximal forestry and livestock production should be weighed carefully against all other expected benefits.

VI. The Need for New Approaches and Attitudes in Shrubland Management

The introduction of sound, rational, and conservative management and improvement practices, described earlier, face severe socioeconomic constraints. The first and foremost one is the public and communal ownership

Figure 10. Promising fodder shrubs for multipurpose afforestation of degraded shrublands on shallow and rocky slopes: *Cotoneaster franchetti* and *Atriplex nummularia.* Both shrubs were planted in winter 1970 and have been heavily grazed in fall 1975, 1976, 1977, and 1978. Photo was taken 14 months after last browsing.

or tenure of the greatest parts of all Mediterranean shrublands (as well as woodlands and grasslands), which allows unrestricted grazing for everybody, according to the classic model described by Hardin (1968) as the "tragedy of freedom for the commons." The adverse effects of pasture deterioration on livestock are now partly eliminated by supplemental fodder. They detract, therefore, only a small fraction from the benefit gained by the individual, who exploits these shrublands and other open upland ranges as much as possible. Another constraint is the general neglect and indifference of politicians, decision makers, their advisors, and, chiefly, economists toward these untillable Mediterranean uplands. In general, all development and improvement schemes are directed to the more productive agricultural lands, where the ratio between investments in research and resources and the expected short-term benefits seem to be much more favorable. If there are any efforts and investments made in these uplands, they are directed toward forest production and commercial recreational uses, with little direct benefit for local and chiefly pastoral shrubland users.

VII. Discussion and Conclusions

From the description of Mediterranean shrublands and their evolution, it is obvious that their striking organic variety in space and time, coupled with their great resilience, should be regarded as their most outstanding and unique features. This multidimensional heterogeneity and resilience can be regarded as a result of the coevolution of Mediterranean humans and their cultural landscapes. In these, sclerophyll shrublands occupy that part that is closest to nature and its spontaneously evolving and self-organizing bioecosystems, although constantly modified by fire, humans, their goats, and the axe. The dynamics of such semi-natural ecosystems can best be described as a series of anthropogenic degradation and regeneration biofunctions. These do not fit into any classical or modern theories of deterministic, progressive successions toward a stable and mature climax after cessation of these human perturbations. On the contrary, the quantification of some of the biotic ecosystem variables of plant and animal species abundance and diversity showed clearly that disruption of the traditional agropastoral biofunction, not only by overuse, but also by complete protection, may lead to a less natural and lower stage of scenic attractiveness and economic utility. The decline in productivity, the rise in the ratio between dead and living biomass, the absence of young plants, and the loss of structural, floristic, and faunistic diversity of the closed and high matorral maqui-thicket cannot be regarded as attributes of a mature self-maintaining ecosystem. It is a sad fact that presently not only in the densely populated uplands of the developing Near East countries, with the exception of Israel, but also in developed European countries like Italy and France, hundreds of thousands of hectares of Mediterranean shrubland are left to the fate of negligence and despoilation.

To reconcile these needs for dynamic conservation and optimization both of soft and hard landscape values with the needs of the local populations and the national economy, comprehensive regional and national master plans are required. Decisions should be based on landscape ecological determinism in making land use priorities and multiple management strategies. In preparing master plans, highest priorities should be given to the *establishment of nature reserves and bioreserves,* as promoted in the UNESCO Man and Biosphere (MAB) program, and to the efficient protection and conservative management of sites with unique biological, geological, and cultural values. In these, special provision should also be made to enable long-term and integrated ecosystem studies and ecological manipulations to attain highest biological diversity.

The introduction of new multiple-use strategies for the management and rehabilitation of the open shrublands will require a formidable educational and research effort and great financial and moral support from local and national authorities in order to have any impact in the near future.

The most important conclusion is that there is hope for the future development of these neglected and desolate Mediterranean shrublands and their resources if we can succeed in changing the attitudes of those responsible for their fate and if we are able to educate a new generation of interdisciplinary land managers and developers to replace the single-minded foresters, graziers, recreationalists, and economists who predominate today.

References

Ashmann, H. A. (1973). Distribution and peculiarity of Mediterranean ecosystems. *In* "Mediterranean-Type Ecosystems, Origin and Structure" (F. di Castri and H. A. Mooney, eds.), pp. 11–19. Springer-Verlag, Berlin and New York.

Axelrod, D. I. (1973). History of the Mediterranean ecosystems in California. *In* "Mediterranean-Type Ecosystems, Origin and Structure" (F. di Castri and H. A. Mooney, eds.), pp. 225–277. Springer-Verlag, Berlin and New York.

Bradbury, D. A. (1981). The physical geography of the Mediterranean lands. *In* "Mediterranean-Type Shrublands: Ecosystems of the World" (F. di Castri, D. W. Goodall, and R. L. Specht, eds.), Vol. 11, pp. 53–62, Elsevier, Amsterdam.

Dan, J., Yaalon, D. H., and Koyumdjisky, H. (1972). Catenary soil relationships in Israel. 2. The Bet Guvrin Catena on chalk and Nari Limestone crust in the Shefela. *Isr. J. Earth Sci.* **21**, 99–114.

di Castri, F. (1981). Mediterranean-type shrublands of the world. *In* "Mediterranean-Type Shrublands: Ecosystems of the World" (F. di Castri, D. W. Goodall, and R. L. Specht, eds.), Vol. 11, pp. 1–52. Elsevier, Amsterdam.

di Castri, F., and Mooney, H. A., eds. (1973). "Mediterranean-Type Ecosystems, Origin and Structure, "Ecological Studies: Analysis and Synthesis, Vol. 7. Springer-Verlag, Berlin and New York.

di Castri, F., Goodall, D. W., and Specht, R. L., eds. (1981). "Mediterranean-Type Shrublands," Ecosystems of the World, Vol. 11: Elsevier, Amsterdam.

Gill, A. M. (1977). Plant traits adaptive to fires in Mediterranean ecosystems. *In* "Proceedings of the Symposium on the Environmental Consequences of Fire and Fuel Management in Mediterranean Ecosystems," U. S. For. Serv. Gen. Tech. Rep. WO–3, pp. 17–26. USDA, Washington, D. C.

Hardin, G. (1968). The tragedy of the commons. *Science* **162**, 1243–1248.

Horvat, I., Clavac, V., and Ellenberg, H. (1974). "Vegetation Suedost-Europa." Fischer, Stuttgart.

Ilijanic, L. J., and Hecimovic, S. (1981). Zur Sukzession der Mediterranean Vegetation auf der Insel Lokrum bei Dubrovnik. *Vegetation* **46**, 75–81.

Jenny, H. (1961). Derivation of state factor equation of soils and ecosystems. *Soil. Sci. Soc. Am. Proc.* **25**, 385–388.

Köppen, W. (1923). "Die Klimate der Erde." de Gruyter, Berlin.

Kruger, F. J. (1979). South African Heathlands. *In* "Heathlands and Related Shrublands: Descriptive Studies" (J. Specht, ed.), pp. 19–80. Elsevier, Amsterdam.

Le Houérou, H. N. (1981). Impacts of man and his animals on Mediterranean vegetation. *In* "Mediterranean-Type Shrublands: Ecosystems of the World" (F. di Castri, D. W. Goodall, and R. L. Specht, eds.), Vol. 11, pp. 479–522. Elsevier, Amsterdam. .

Liacos, L. (1981). Grazing management of evergreen brushlands in Greece. *In* "Proceedings of the Symposium on Dynamics and Management of Mediterranean-Type Ecosystems," U. S. For. Serv. Gen. Tech. Rep. WO–3, pp. 289–398. USDA, Washington, D. C.

McCutchan, M. H. (1977). Climatic features as a fire determinant. *In* "Proceedings of the Symposium on the Environmental Consequences of Fire and Fuel Management in Mediterranean Ecosystems," U.S. For. Serv. Gen. Tech. Rep. WO-3, pp. 1–5. USDA, Washington, D. C.

Margaris, N. S. (1981). Adaptive strategies in plants dominating Mediterranean-type ecosystems. *In* "Mediterranean-Type Shrublands: Ecosystems of the World" (F. di Castri, D. W. Goodall, and R. L. Specht, eds.), Vol. 11 pp. 309–316. Elsevier, Amsterdam.

Meigs, P. (1964). Classification and occurrence of Mediterranean type dry climates. *In* "Land use in Semi-arid Mediterranean Climates," pp. 17–21. UNESCO, Paris.

Nahal, I. (1981). The Mediterranean climate from a biological view. *In* "Mediterranean-Type Shrublands: Ecosystems of the World" (F. di Castri, D. W. Goodall, and R. L. Specht, eds.), Vol. 11, pp. 63–86. Elsevier, Amsterdam.

Naveh, Z. (1967). Mediterranean ecosystems and vegetation types in California and Israel. *Ecology* **48**, 445–459.

Naveh, Z. (1973). The ecology of fire in Israel. *Annu. Tall Timber Fire Ecol. Conf.*, pp. 131–170.

Naveh, Z. (1974). The ecological management of non-arable Mediterranean uplands. *J. Environ. Manage.* **2**, 351–371.

Naveh, Z. (1975). Degradation änd rehabilitation of Mediterranean landscapes. *Landscape Plann.* **2**, 133–146.

Naveh, Z. (1978). A model of multi-purpose ecosystem management for degraded Mediterranean uplands. *Environ. Manage.* **2**, 31–37.

Naveh, Z. (1979). A model of multiple-use management strategies of marginal and untillable Mediterranean upland ecosystems. *In* "Environmental Biomonitoring, Assessment, Prediction and Management" (J. Cairns, G. P. Patil, and W. E. Waters, eds.), pp. 219–239. International Cooperative Publishing House, Burtonsville, Maryland.

Naveh, Z. (1982). Mediterranean landscape evolution and degradation as multivariate biofunctions: Theoretical and practical implications. *Landscape Plann.* **9**, 125–146.

Naveh, Z., and Dan, J. (1973). Human degradation of Mediterranean landscapes in Israel. *In* "Mediterranean-Type Ecosystems, Origin and Structure" (F. di Castri and H. A. Mooney, eds.), pp. 373–390. Springer-Verlag, Berlin and New York.

Naveh, Z., and Whittaker, R. H. (1979). Structural and floristic diversity of shrublands and woodlands in northern Israel and other Mediterranean areas. *Vegetatio* **41,** 171–190.

Oppenheimer, H. R. (1956). Penetration active des racine debuisons méditerranéen dans le roches calcaires. *Bull. Res. Counc. Isr., Sec. D* (Bot), **5,** 219–222.

Papanastasis, V. P. (1980). Effects of season and frequency of burning on a phryganic rangeland in Greece. *J. Range Manage.* **33,** 251–255.

Paskoff, R. P. (1973). Geomorphological processes and characteristic landforms in the Mediterranean regions of the world. *In* "Mediterranean-Type Ecosystems, Origin and Structure" (F. di Castri and H. A. Mooney, eds.), pp. 53–60. Springer-Verlag, Berlin and New York.

Quezel, P. (1981). Floristic composition and phytosociological structure of scleropyllous matorral around the Mediterranean. *In* "Mediterranean-Type Shrublands: Ecosystems of the World" (F. di Castri, D. W. Goodall, and R. L. Specht, eds.), Vol. 11, pp. 107–121. Elsevier, Amsterdam.

Rundel, P. W. (1977). Water balance in Mediterranean sclerophyll ecosystems. *In* "Proceedings of the Symposium on the Environmental Consequences of Fire and Fuel Management in Mediterranean Ecosystems," U. S. For. Serv. Gen. Tech. Rep. WO–3, pp. 95–106. USDA, Washington, D. C.

Shachori, A. Y., Rosenzweig, D., Israeli, M., and Stanhill, G. (1968). Study of difference in effects of forests and other vegetative cover on water yield. Annual Report No. 3, USDA, A-10–FS-13.

Swarzboim, I. (1978). Autecology of *Pistacia lentiscus.* Ph. Sc. Thesis, Technion, Israel Institute of Technology, Haifa (in Hebrew, with English summary).

Tomaselli, R. (1981). Main physiognomic types and geographic distribution of shrub systems related to Mediterranean climates. *In* "Mediterranean-Type Shrublands: Ecosystems of the World" (F. di Castri, D. W. Goodall, and R. L. Specht, eds.), Vol. 11, pp. 95–104. Elsevier, Amsterdam.

Trabaud, L. (1981). Man and fire: Impacts on Mediterranean vegetation. *In* "Mediterranean-Type Shrublands: Ecosystems of the World" (F. di Castri, D. W. Goodall, and R. L. Specht, eds.), Vol. 11, pp. 523–538. Elsevier, Amsterdam.

UNESCO (1963). "Bioclimatological Map of the Mediterranean Zone." Arid Zone Research, UNESCO, Paris.

UNESCO (1973). "International Classification and Mapping of Vegetation." UNESCO, Paris.

Walter, H. (1968). "Die Vegetation der Erde in oke' physiologischer Betrachtung," Vol. 2. Fischer, Jena.

Zohary, M. (1973). "Geobotanical Foundations of the Middle East." Fischer, Stuttgart.

5

The Shrublands of Africa

Henri N. Le Houérou

I. Introduction

This chapter is concerned with Africa north of the Tropic of Capricorn; southern Africa is covered in Chapter 6. The present chapter thus deals with about 96% of the African continent, including the islands, that is 28.2 million km^2. This is almost four times the acreage of the conterminous United States.

This huge area is extremely varied and encompasses the following climates:[1] Mediterranean, tropical, equatorial, subtropical, subequatorial, montane, and afro-alpine (Le Houérou and Popov, 1981). Most soil classes of the world are represented (Food and Agriculture Organization, 1974, 1978). The African flora comprises some 36,000 species of which 30,000 are in the intertropical zone and about 9000 of them are shrubs and trees (Wickens, 1980). About 75% of the latter are browsed (Whyte, 1947) and over 4500 have been recorded as being useful to man (Wickens, 1980).

A symposium on the browse species aspects only was held in Addis Ababa in April 1980 and gathered some 50 scientists from 10 disciplines, 25 countries, and 5 continents; the 500 pages of procceedings were made available to the public in late 1982 (Le Houérou, 1980a).

II. The Major Native Shrub Communities

A. Overview

Shrublands occupy approximately $10,000^3$ km², that is, 35% in the area under study, the remainder being desert (36%), forest (22%), and cropland (7%) (Le Houérou, 1980e). Shrubland is actually synonymous with grassland plus open woodland, as most of the African savannas are more or less wooded and more or less sparsely dotted with shrubs; open woodlands also encompass an often dominant understory of shrubs. North of the Tropic of Cancer, so-called "forest" lands are essentially bushland or shrubland with more or less sparse trees, or no trees at all, while most of the steppes of the Mediterranean arid zone are dominated by dwarf shrubs.

B. North of the Tropic of Cancer

North African flora comprises some 600 species of shrubs and trees (Le Houérou, 1980b). The areas occupied by shrublands in northern Africa are shown in Table I. In addition to these native shrublands there are substantial areas of shrub plantations, particularly for forage production. These include *Cactus, Acacia,* and *Atriplex,* mainly, which altogether may amount to half a million hectares, 80% of which is spineless cacti (*Opuntia ficus-indica*). The main natural shrub ecosystems and their areas in North Africa are shown in Tables II and III.

[1] Mediterranean = Winter rains, summer drought.
   Tropical   = Summer rains, monomodal pattern, no frost.
   Equatorial   = Summer rains, bimodal pattern, no frost.
   Subtropical = Summer rains, monomodal pattern, occurrence of frost.
   Subequatorial = Summer rains, bimodal pattern, occurrence of frost.
   Montane   = Summer rains, various patterns, moderate temperature, elevation.
   Afro-alpine = Various rainfall patterns, yearlong night frost.

Table I. Area of North African shrublands (in 10^3 km^2)

Country	Total	Semiarid to humid shrublands $R^a > 400$ mm	Arid steppic shrublands $400 > R > 100$ mm	Desert dwarf shrublands $R < 100$ mm
Algeria	345.6	25.6	120.0	200.0
Egypt	125.0	—	25.0	100.0
Libya	240.7	0.7	80.0	160.0
Morocco	142.0	32.0	80.0	30.0
Tunisia	87.2	7.2	45.0	35.0
Total	940.5	65.5	350.0	525.0

[a] R = mean annual rainfall in mm.

1. Shrubland Ecosystems of the Semiarid to Humid Zones ($R^* > 400$ mm)

Apart from a few thousand hectares of dense timber forest, all the "woodlands" are shrublands (shrubs alone) or bushland (shrubs + sparse trees) devoted to grazing, fuel gathering, charcoal making, distillation (tars, essential oils), and cork production. Grazing represents 60 to 80% of the utilization of these lands in terms of economic output.

a. The Cedrus Atlantica Series. The *Cedrus atlantica* series includes a series of plant communities derived from the pristine *Cedrus atlantica* climax forest, which occurs on various substrata from granite to limestone. This series, or dynamic sequence, occurs in higher elevations above 1200–1500 m and up to 2000–2800 m with annual rainfall above 600 mm, 1 to 3 months of snow cover in winter, and 60 to 120 days of hard frost. Summer drought is relatively short, 2–4 months. Pristine forests of *Cedrus* produce high-grade timber and summer grazing. Degraded forest and shrubland produce firewood, charcoal, browse, and honey, in addition to some game hunting. There are some 10 common and more or less dominant browse species and many grass, grasslike, and legume species (Le Houérou, 1980b).

b. The Quercus faginea/Quercus suber Series. The *Quercus faginea/Quercus suber* series occurs with rainfall usually above 600 mm, on more or less acidic soils derived from crystalline, metamorphic rocks or sandstone. While pristine forest produces timber, cork, firewood, wildlife, and grazing, degraded woodland produces cork, firewood, browse, wildlife, and some honey. There are about 15 common and more or less dominant browse species in the woodlands, bushlands, and shrublands. Some species

*R = mean annual rainfall, mm.

Table II. Major shrubland ecosystems in the semiarid to humid ecoclimatic zones of North Africa (in 10^3 ha)

Country	Qercus faginea	Quercus suber	Quercus ilex and coccifera	Cedrus atlantica	Pinus halepensis	Tetraclinis articulata	Olea ceratonia and Pistacia lentiscus	Total
Algeria	70	650	700	30	850	160	100	2560
Egypt	—	—	—	—	—	—	—	—
Libya	—	—	10	—	10	—	50	70
Morocco	10	400	1350	120	70	750	500	3200
Tunisia	30	130	120	—	340	30	70	720
Total	110	1180	2180	150	1270	940	720	6550

Table III.   Major shrubland ecosystems in the arid ecoclimatic zone of North Africa

Type of ecosystem	Area (10³ ha)
Juniperus phoenicea garrigue (chaparral)	2,300
Argania sideroxylon parkland (Southwest Morocco)	700
Artemisia herba alba steppes (silty soils)	7,000
Artemisia campestris/Helianthemum lippii steppes (sandy soils)	4,000
Gymnocarpos decander/Atractylis serratuloides steppes (shallow soils)	12,000
Nanophanerophytic steppes (*Lygos, Ziziphus, Atriplex, Tamarix, Calligonum, Nitraria*)	2,000
Crassulescent halophytic steppes (*Salsola, Suaeda*, etc.)	4,000
Wormwood subdesertic steppes (*Hammada, Anabasis, Traganum*, etc.)	3,000
Total	35,000

such as the ash tree (*Fraxinus oxyphylla*) are pollarded. Some dynamic ecological stages in the succession closely related to repeated burning and dominated by *Cistaceae* produce little forage and virtually no firewood. Transformation of this vegetation to a highly productive grassland has been successfully achieved in several countries: Portugal, Spain, Tunisia, Morocco, Algeria, and France (Corsica). In these areas productivity has been multiplied by a factor of 5 to 18 depending on techniques used and local conditions (Le Houérou, 1978, 1981).

c. The Quercus ilex Series.   Holm oak shrublands occupy large areas in northern Africa (about 21,000 km^2) between the 400- to 800-mm isohyets of annual rainfall. The main utilization is for charcoal, firewood, browse, wildlife, and beekeeping. Browse production from over 30 species of "trubs" is of the order of one to two sheep equivalent/ha/yr. Potential honey production is estimated to be around 3 kg/ha/yr. Firewood and charcoal production account for 400–600 kg dry wood-equivalent/ha/yr (Le Houérou, 1981).

d. The Olive/Carob and Olive/Mastik Series.   The Olive/Carob and Olive/Mastik series occupy over 7200 km^2 in the lowlands between the isohyets of 300 and 1000 mm of annual precipitation, on deep soils or soft geological rocks for the latter and on hard rock, mainly limestone, for the former. Most of the primeval Olive/Mastik vegetation type has been converted into cropland, mainland cereals and annual crops for the past 2500 years, while large areas of the Olive/Carob type have been converted into orchards during the same period (Le Houérou, 1981). The main types of utilization are charcoal, firewood, browse, beekeeping, and wildlife cover. Approximately 30 major browse species are recorded (Le Houérou, 1980b).

e. The Aleppo Pine Series.   Aleppo pine (*Pinus halepensis*) woodland, bushland, and shrubland occupy 13,000 km^2 in the semiarid and subhumid (300–800 mm) ecoclimatic zones of North Africa. There are 30 to 35 major browse species. The main utilization is for firewood, charcoal, browse, distillation (junipers, rosemary), beekeeping, wildlife, and recreation.

f. The False Thuya Series.   False Thuya (*Tetraclinis articulata*) extends over 9000 km^2 in the mild-to-warm winter lowlands of the semiarid ecoclimatic zone, particularly in western Morocco. Firewood, charcoal, browse, wildlife cover, beekeeping, and recreation are the main uses; there are about 35 major browse species.

2. Shrublands and Dwarf Shrublands of the Arid Zone ($100 < R < 400$ mm)

a. The Red Juniper Substeppic Series.   The Red Juniper substeppic series occupies 15,000 km^2 on the hills and low mountains in the arid zone. It constitutes a transition between the shrublands and the chamaephytic steppes, an ecotone between arid and semiarid ecoclimatic zones. The main utilization is for browse involving 45 major species; of less importance is firewood, alfa grass collection (for paper mills), and beekeeping. Red juniper (*Juniperus phoenicea*) is distilled for tar for medicinal uses.

b. The White Sage Steppic Series.   A complex group of plant communities is dominated by white sage (*Artemisia herba alba* = *A. inculta*). This series includes most of the alfa grass steppes of North African highlands (Le Houérou, 1969). The various plant communities in the series cover 210,000 km^2 on silty soils of the steppic zone of North Africa (and beyond the borders of North Africa to southeast Spain and the Near East). The main utilization is grazing on 15 to 20 major forage species.

c. Field Sage Series.   A complex of plant communities has developed on sandy soils of the steppic zone that is dominated by *Artemisia campestris* subsp. *glutinosa* and its relative in northern Egypt, *Artemisia monosperma*. This series extends over 40,000 km^2. The main utilization is grazing on 25 to 30 forage species and occasional cereal cultivation in favorable years, with subsequent stubble and fallow pasturing.

3. The Desert Shrublands ($R < 100$ mm)

North African desert shrublands are located along the northern fringe of the Sahara along the stream network and in the depressions benefiting from runoff or having a permanent water table within reach of roots. Desert shrublands are essentially grazing lands. Winter and spring grazing involve small stock while camels may graze year-round. There are some 20 major browse species such as the "Dhamran" (*Traganum nudatum*), the "Had" (*Cornulaca monacantha*), or "Askaf" (*Nucularia perrini*). These three Chenopodiaceae are particularly relished by dromedaries.

4. Halophytic Steppes

Halophytic Steppes occur over more than 20,000 km^2 and are grazed mainly by camels in summer and fall; they are spread over the arid and desert zones in depressions having saline soils and waters. Most of the browse species are Chenopodiaceae such as *Atriplex halimus*, *Salsola* spp., *Suaeda* spp., *Arthrocnemum indicum*, and *Salicornia* spp.

5. Introduced Species

Many shrub species have been introduced in the region since the late 19th century, particularly browse species such as Australian "wattles" (phyllodineous acacias), saltbushes (*Atriplex* spp.) (Franclet and Le Houérou, 1971), mesquites (*Prosopis* spp.), and honey locust (*Gleiditshia triacanthos*). The cacti, mainly spiny and spineless types of *Opuntia ficus-indica*, were introduced after Columbus's second expedition and spread over the entire Mediterranean during the 16th to 18th centuries (Monjauze and Le Houérou, 1965). The spineless type is widely used as emergency fodder for dry spells, and as such is planted in "fodder orchards" over large acreages in the arid and semiarid zones below 1000 m of elevation. Other shrubs were introduced for sand dune stabilization programs such as *Acacia saligna (= A. cyanophylla)*. Over 100,000 seedlings of the latter were annually planted around Tripoli (Libya) as early as 1916 to 1920 (Leone, 1924). This species has now been planted over more than half a million hectares in Morocco, Algeria, Tunisia, Libya, and Egypt. It turned out to be a good browse plant (Dumancic and Le Houérou, 1981). Another important sand-binding species, particularly adapted to seashore dunes and sea spray, is *Acacia cyclops;* another promising drought-hardy species for mild winter arid zones is *Acacia salicina*. These species, however, can hardly be considered as browse, except for camels and goats over short periods.

6. Value of North African Shrubs and Shrublands to Humans

Grazing represents 60 to 80% of the economic output of North African shrublands. Of minor importance (but locally important) are cork production, fuel gathering, charcoal production, distillation (rosemary, junipers), and beekeeping (5000 tons of honey are produced annually from the whole region; *Eucalyptus* plantations and *Citrus* groves play an important role in the latter). Browse, on the other hand, contributes about 40% of the overall livestock diet in the region (Floret and Le Floch, 1980; Le Houérou, 1980b, 1981).

The livestock population of the region represents 100 million sheep equivalents with a value of $5 billion (1980 dollars). With an offtake rate of 30%, the economic output of shrublands in the livestock sector is thus around $1.5 billion U.S. per annum. The total net economic output of the 940,000 km² of North African shrublands is thus probably in the vicinity of $2.5 billion U.S. per year or $2.1 per/ha/yr. The shrublands in the semiarid to humid ecoclimatic zones alone probably yield some $10–15 billion U.S.

The potential output could be considerably increased, probably by a factor of 3 to 5, through improved management. For instance, estimated honey production could reach over 3 kg/ha/yr from shrubland alone; while at present the production from shrubland is negligible, most of the honey coming from *Eucalyptus* woodlots, *Citrus* groves, other orchards, and cropland. Browse and grazing production could likewise be increased considerably using adequate management tools that have been shown to be successful in field-scale demonstration trials. Other uses, although quite substantial, are difficult to quantify because of their lack of measurable product, such as amenities and recreation, protection against erosion, and wildlife use. The development outlook, however, remains bleak in spite of the potential because of socioeconomic and political reasons linked to land ownership and management structures inherited from pastoral and communal exploitation traditions combined with the lack of know-how on the part of the users of the shrublands.

C. Intertropical Africa

1. General, Climate

This huge area (22 million km²) comprises a number of ecoclimatic zones according to precipitation and temperature regimes (Le Houérou and Popov, 1981). Precipitation occurs during the long-days season, that is "summer," but there are two main regimes: monomodal and bimodal, corresponding to one or two rainy seasons. The former characterizes a group of climates called "tropical" and the latter another group called "equatorial." Both tropical and equatorial climates have dry (desert) and wet (rain forest) subtypes that tend to become "amodal"—either no rain or continuous rain. Tropical climates occur between latitudes 10° and 30° on both sides of the tropics (23°27′) and equatorial climates occur on both sides of the equator between 10° N and 10° S, hence the names.

On higher elevations frost may occur during shorter or longer periods depending on elevation and latitude. This, again, gives rise to subtropical

Table IV. Ecoclimatic zonation of shrublands in intertropical Africa (in 10^3 km^2)

Zone	Tropical	Subtropical	Equatorial	Subequatorial	Montane	Afro-alpine	Total
Hyperarid	3,170	50	423	—	—	—	3,643
Arid	1,572	118	460	—	—	—	2,150
Semiarid	1,085	268	541	6	4	—	1,904
Subhumid	1,676	600	416	20	10	5	2,727
Total							10,424

or subequatorial (frost occurring) climates, according to whether there is one or two rainy seasons. Higher elevations are characterized by montane and afro-alpine climates, which bear many climatic and floristic similarities to Mediterranean and temperate zones, respectively.

The shrubland ecosystems are distributed across the hyperarid, arid, semiarid, and subhumid zones under tropical, subtropical, equatorial, subequatorial, montane, and afro-alpine climates, over some 10 million km^2, that is, one-half of the intertropical zone. These ecoclimatic zones occupy the areas shown in Table IV (Le Houérou and Popov, 1981).

2. Tropical/Equatorial Desert Shrublands

Desert shrublands occur below the 100-mm isohyet of annual precipitation toward the southern fringe of the Sahara as well as toward the northern rim. Desert shrublands also occur in eastern Africa under equatorial eco-climates, particularly in Ethiopia, Djibuti, Somalia, and Kenya. Shrublands are then restricted to drainage systems: runnels, water courses, wadis, alluvial fans, and depressions, where run-in compensates rainfall deficiency.

a. West Africa. In West Africa and the Republic of Sudan, at the edge of the Sahara and the Sahel, the major species are: *Acacia tortilis raddiana, A. ehrenbergiana, Capparis decidua, Moerua crassifolia, Balanites aegyptiaca, Grewia tenax, Salvadora persica, Ziziphus lotus saharae, Leptadenia pyrotechnica, Ochradenus baccatus, Aerva persica, Tamarix aphylla, Cornulaca monacantha, Nucularia perrini, Traganum nudatum,* and *Moringa peregrina,* which are dotted over steppes of perennial grasses. (Boudet, 1975).

b. East Africa. In East Africa the dominant shrub species are: *Acacia tortilis tortilis, A. tortilis spirocarpa, A. reficiens misera, A. oliveri, A. horrida benadirensis, A. edgeworthii, A. nubica, Balanites aegyptiaca, Leptadenia pyrotechnica, Ochradenus baccatus, Duosperma eremophilum, Indigofera spinosa, Salvadora persica, Sericocomopsis hildebrandtii, Lagenantha nogalensis, Suaeda monoica,* and *Zygophyllum* spp., with the companion perennial grasses *Chrysopogon plumulosus, Panicum turgidum, Cenchrus ciliaris,* and *Andropogon kelleri.*

3. Arid Zone Shrublands

These shrublands occur between the isohyets of 100 and 400 mm approximately. They are primarily grassland savannas more or less densely dotted with shrubs and some trees as well. Shrub density is usually 100–1000 per hectare depending on moisture availability and dynamic status; canopy cover may vary from about 5% in open savannas on flat land or rolling country to more than 30% in depressions or around temporary ponds. This vegetal formation is called the "Mimosaceae savanna" (Chevalier, 1912, 1933; Aubreville, 1949), which is the characteristic vegetation of the Sahel from the Atlantic Ocean to the Red Sea. The physiognomically similar vegetation type in East Africa is called the "*Acacia/Commiphora* bushland" (ecoclimatic zone 5: Pratt *et al.,* 1966).

a. The Sahel (tropical ecoclimatic zone 6 of Le Houérou and Popov, 1981). Dominant species are: *Acacia tortilis raddiana, A. erhrenbergiana, A. senegal, A. nubica* (eastern Sahel), *A. mellifera* (eastern Sahel), *Maerua crassifolia, Salvadora persica, Ziziphus mauritiana, Balanites aegyptiaca, Commiphora africana, C. quadricincta, Cordia sinensis, Grewia tenax,* and *Bosci senegalensis;* the shrubs overlay a more or less continuous understory of annual grasses.

b. Eastern African (equatorial ecoclimatic zone 6 of Le Houérou and Popov, 1981). Major species in the *Acacia/Commiphora* bushlands are: *Acacia tortilis spirocarpa, A. tortilis tortilis, A. seyal fistula, A. bussei, A. mellifera, A. senegal, A. reficiens, A. edgeworthii, A. asak, A. nubica, Dichrostachys cinerea, Balanites glabra, B. orbicularis, Commiphora* spp., *Ziziphus mucronata, Z. abyssinica, Maerua crassifolia, Cadaba farinosa, C. gladulosa, C. rotundifolia, Boscia minimifolia, Dobera glabra,* and *Salvadora persica,* which overlay a more or less continuous layer of perennial and annual grasses.

4. Semiarid Zone Shrublands

Semiarid zone shrublands are distributed approximately between the 400- and 600-mm isohyets in both West and East Africa (tropical ecoclimatic zone 5 and equatorial ecoclimatic zone 5 of Le Houérou and Popov, 1981). In both cases the dominant vegetation type is a "Combretaceae savanna" of soft, broad-leaved trees and shrubs, as opposed to the spiny microphyllous "Mimosaceae savanna" and "*Acacia/Commiphora* bushland" of ecoclimatic zone 6 described earlier. It is actually a mixture of evergreen broad-leaved species with deciduous microphyll species such as *Acacia* and *Dichrostachys*. Typical dominant species in the southern Sahel are: Combretaceae—*Combretum glutinosum, C. nigricans, C. micranthum, C. ghazalense, C. aculeatum, C. geitonophyllum, Guiera senegalensis, Terminalia avicennoides, T. brownii, Anogeissus leiocarpus;* Tiliaceae—*Grewia bicolor, Grewia* spp.; Mimosaceae—*Acacia tortilis, A. senegal, A. mellifera, A. seyal seyal, A. sieberiana, A. ataxacantha, Faidherbia (Acacia) albida, A. laeta, A. nilotica, Parkia biglobosa, Entada africana, Dichrostachys cinerea;* Capparidaceae—*Boscia angustifolia, B. salicifolia, B. senegalensis, Cadaba farinosa, C. glandulosa, Capparis corymbosa, Crataeva adansonii, Maerua crassifolia, M. angolensis, M. angustifolia, M. oblongifolia;* Rubiaceae—*Mitragyna inermis, Feretia apodanthera, Gardenia* spp. In East Africa the major shrubs are: *Acacia bussei, A. etbaica, A. nilotica, A. seyal, A. drepanolobium, A. hockii, A. xanthophloea, Combretum molle, C. aculeatum, Terminalia brownii, T. sericea, T. orbicularis, T. prunoides, Grewia bicolor, G. mollis, G. villosa,* and *Tarchonanthus camphoratus*. The grass layer is primarily perennial.

5. Subhumid Zone Shrublands

Subhumid zone shrublands occur between the 600- and 1200-mm isohyets. They constitute more or less wooded bushland savannas usually with an understory of perennial grasses; they are subject to bushfires almost every year. This corresponds to the so-called "Sudanian" ecological zone located between the Sahel to the north and the "Guinean" ecological zone to the south; the Sudanian zone corresponds to the "Miombo" woodland south of the equator (ecoclimatic zones 3 (600–800 mm) and 4 (800–1200 mm) of Le Houérou and Popov 1981). Dominant and characteristic species of trees and shrubs are: *Khaya senegalensis, Butyrospermum paradoxa, Parkia biglobosa, P. clappertoniana, Borassus ethiopum, Bombax costatum, Burkea africana, Piliostigma thinningii, Pterocarpus erinaceus, Acacia seyal, Faidherbia (Acacia) albida, Terminalia macroptera,* and *Detarium microcarpum.* Perennial grasses provide a substantial cover (Nebout and Toutain, 1978). The equivalent zone of East Africa and southern Africa to ecological zones 3 and 4 (III of Pratt *et al.* (1966)) is the Miombo, which extends over some 4 million km^2 in Kenya, Tanzania, Mozambique, Malawi, Zimbabwe, southern Zaire, Zambia, and Angola (Lawton, 1980). The Miombo is a multistory formation of trees 10–15 m tall, shrubs 1–5 m high, and grasses and herbs 0.5–2.5 m high. Miombo vegetation is dominated by *Caesalpinieae* trees and some Fabaceae. Under the trees is an important story of shrubs, many of them from the Combretaceae and Capparidaceae families. Perennial grasses are numerous, particularly from the Andropogoniodeae subfamily.

6. Humid Zone Shrublands ($R > 1500$ mm)

Shrubs are often considered as invaders in the humid zone and are therefore given low value compared with industrial crops such as coffee, cocoa, sisal, cotton, banana, tea, henna, pineapple, hevea, etc., or food crops such as cassava, mango, guava, custard apples, plantain banana, etc. Many species, however, are actually used by local populations, especially for their fruits, which are consumed by humans, or their leaves and fruits which are consumed by livestock (Audru, 1980; Carew *et al.*, 1980; Wickens, 1980). Among the major species are: *Daniellia oliveri, Ficus thonningii, Lophira lanceolata, Cussonia barteri, Bridelia ferruginea, Cordyla pinnata, Lannea shimperi,* and *Parinari curatellifolia.* Invading undesired shrubs are: *Annona senegalensis, Arthrosamanea eriochari,* and *Harungana madagascariensis.*

7. Montane Shrublands (> 1500 m above sea level)

Montane shrublands occupy some 45,000 km^2; they occur in the equatorial zone in East Africa above an elevation of 1500–1800 m, up to 3000–3500 m. These shrublands constitute degraded stages of an evergreen montane forest of *Juniperus procera* and *Podocarpus gracilior.* Rainfall may vary from 600 to 1500 mm. Main species are microphyll or mesophyll sclerophyllous evergreens, while some are deciduous, macrophyll, and malacophyllous.

8. Alpine and Subalpine Shrublands

Alpine and subalpine shrublands occur above 2800–3500 m of elevation, depending on latitude; they cover some 5000 km^2. Dominant shrubs are: *Arundinaria alpina* (Montane bamboo), *Hypericum revolutum, H. lanceolatum, Erica arborea, Lobelia* spp., *Dendrosenecio* spp., and *Phillipia* spp. The grass layer contains many temperate-climate genera: *Trifolium* spp., *Medicago lupulina, Alchemilla* spp., *Potentialla* spp., *Festuca* spp., *Avena* spp., *Anthroxanthum* spp., *Lolium perenne,* and *Dactylis glomerata* (S. L.).

III. Traditional Uses of Intertropical Shrubs and Shrublands

A. *General Use*

Traditional uses of shrubs are innumerable; they may be grouped into 13 main headings.

- Food and drink for humans
- Browse for livestock and wildlife

- Beekeeping and honey production
- Source of energy: firewood and charcoal
- Building and fencing material
- Fiber for cloth, ropes, and handicrafts
- Tools for agriculture and cottage industry
- Handicraft, art, and religious objects
- Dye and tanning
- Drugs, medicinal and veterinary uses
- Shade and shelter for plants (cover crops), animals, and humans (palaver trees)
- Protection against erosion, maintenance of soil fertility and productivity
- Water storage (*Baobab*)

B. The Browse Component

The browse aspect was reviewed by Lamprey *et al.* (1980) for East Africa, by Walker (1980) for southern Africa, by Lawton (1980) for the Miombo woodlands, and by Le Houérou (1980b,c) for northern and western Africa. There are about 200 main browse species in intertropical Africa. Special mention should be made of legumes (Mimosaceae and Caesalpiniaceae mainly), Capparidaceae, Combretaceae, Tiliaceae, Rubiaceae, and Rhamnaceae, in decreasing order of importance in animal diets. Chemical composition and feed value were reviewed by Mabey and Rose-Innes (1964 a,b,c,1967), Dougall *et al.* (1964), and Le Houérou (1980 e,d) over some 850 samples. Reports show that values are comparable in East and West Africa. Average composition over 850 samples reported in the literature is crude protein, 13%; crude fiber, 24%; fat, 4%; nitrogen-free extract, 48%; ash, 11%; phosphorus, 0.18%; calcium, 1.75%. Capparidaceae show an average crude protein content of over 20%, while legumes average 16%; crude protein contents of 30% are routinely reported from the leaves of Capparidaceae, while 44% was observed (and confirmed) in a species of Acanthaceae, *Justicia salvioides* (Lawton, 1980). Overall productivity is estimated to be about 1 kg dry matter (DM) per hectare per year and per millimeter of rain fallen (i.e., consumable biomass produced). This figure is obviously liable to enormous variations depending on shrub density and the species concerned (range: 0.1 to 5.0 kg DM/ha/yr/mm). Production of 5000 kg DM/ha/yr has been reported in riverine conditions in East Africa (Pellew, 1980). Individual "trub" production averages 1 kg DM/yr, with a range of 0.08 to 50.0 kg, and most figures between 0.5 and 5.0 kg (Bille, 1977; Poupon, 1980; Hiernaux, 1980; Dayton, 1978; Pellew, 1980; Kennan, 1969; Rutherford, 1978). Browse may represent an important part of stock diet in the arid zone during the dry season (Dicko, 1980;

Pellew, 1980), and even in family small stock husbandry in the humid equatorial zone (Carew *et al.*, 1980; Mecha and Adegbola, 1980). Among the major species, *Faidherbia (Acacia) albida* should be mentioned because of its traditional use in agroforestry systems in West and East Africa semiarid and subhumid zones. *Faidherbia albida* has been the subject of many studies and publications (Giffard, 1964, 1972). Densities of 25 to 50 trees per hectare would increase millet yield by a factor of 2.5 as compared to otherwise treeless fields and in the absence of chemical fertilization, while supporting an additional stocking rate of 40–60 kg of liveweight per hectare year-round (Le Houérou, 1978). A similar agroforestry system exists with *Acacia tortilis* subsp. *spirocarpa* in the mid-rift valley of Ethiopia (Le Houérou and Corra, 1980). A somewhat different agroforestry system based on *Acacia sengal* that combines grazing, millet/sorghum cropping, and the production of gum arabic has been in use for decades in the Republic of Sudan (Kassas, 1970; Mubarak and Seif el Din, 1970).

C. The Screen Function

The screen function is obvious from field observation: animals seek shade in the midday hot hours when standard shelter temperatures reach 35–45°C. In the degraded rangelands of the arid zone, grass layer production is usually much higher (up to twice or more) under shade than in the open, and it remains green 4 to 6 weeks longer at the end of the rainy season. Measurements by Pratchett in the semiarid zone of Botswana ($R = 550$ mm, lat. 25° S, long. 25°50′ E, altitude 1000 m) over several years showed that under a canopy of *Peltophorum africana*, *Acacia tortilis*, and *Grewia flava*, solar radiation and windspeed were reduced by about 50% as compared to a nearby test area. As a consequence, potential evapotranspiration was reduced by 70%, while in the continuous grass layer of *Panicum maximum*, production increased by 26% when grazed and 12% when ungrazed. Bille (1977) reported that in the Sahel zone of Senegal, production of the grass layer is twice as great in the shade as compared to the open, that is, when shrub and grass productivity are added, the photosynthetic efficiency during the growing season was 1.4%, whereas it barely reached 0.3% in the surrounding open grassland (global radiation = 180 kcal/cm^2/yr (752 kj); incident radiation = 90 kcal/cm^2/yr (376.2 kj); 1 g DM = 4.2 kcal/cm^2/yr (17.6 kj); NPP = maximum standing crop + 25%). The efficiency of the ecosystem is thus 4.6 times greater in a multistory vegetation structure as compared to a monostratum grass layer. These facts, however, should not be overgeneralized, as there are instances where shrub cover may reduce production from the understory

(Harrington and Wilson, 1980). It is not clear under what precise circumstances grass production is increased or reduced under shade. The nature of the cover, whether shrub or tree, and the light interception of its foliage seem to play a determining role as well as the nature of the grass layer, the dynamic status of the range, and the nature and dynamic status of the soil surface. Generally speaking, depleted ranges would yield more under the protection of a tree/shrub layer. Otherwise, range in good condition would tend to be more productive in the absence of a "trub" layer.

D. Other Uses

Many other uses of African shrubs and trees, belonging to the domain of ethnobotany, were reviewed by Wickens (1980).

IV. Browse Plantations in the Tropics

The planting of *Faidherbia* (*Acacia*) *albida* and of *A. senegal* has been discussed by several authors (Giffard, 1964; Seif el Din, 1979; von Maydell, 1983) as well as the natural regeneration of native stands (Delwaulle, 1975, 1978; Catinot, 1967a,b). Many medium- and large-scale afforestations have been achieved successfully using these two species in areas with a mean annual rainfall higher than 400 mm. Other native species such as *Acacia tortilis* have also been used in spectacular afforestations on a small scale: at M'bidi (400 mm) in Senegal, for instance, or at Birkaner (180 mm) in Rajasthan. Among exotic species, striking successes have been achieved with *Prosopis juliflora* (Mauritania, Senegal, Sudan, Cape Verde Islands), but only in coastal or subcoastal areas with high atmospheric moisture or in sites having a more or less deep water table. *Parkinsonia aculeata* has achieved spectacular results with rainfalls as low as 200 mm in the Cape Verde Islands, but under conditions of high atmospheric moisture and deep water table Lepape, 1980). *Acacia aneura,* the Australian "mulga," seems to have achieved moderate results in the Sahelian zone of the Sudan. On the other hand, Hamel's introduction trials in Senegal have given rise to considerable hopes of using phyllodineous acacias from northwest Australia in the Sahel. Successful introduction of "wattles" at M'bidi (400 mm) and Bandia (600 mm) included *Acacia linaroides, A. tumida, A. salicina, A. coriacea, A. bivenosa, A. holosericea, A. sclerosperma,* and *A. pyrifolia* (Hamel, 1980). In the subhumid and humid Sudanian ecoclimatic zone of West Africa, many species can be planted and will normally thrive, including *Faidherbia albida, Leucaena leucocephala, Pithocellobium dulce, P. saman, Stylosanthes scabra, S. hamata,* and *S. viscosa.* Among native species some are promising (Piot, 1979; Piot *et al.*, 1980; Hiernaux *et al.,* 1979; Gosseye, 1980), particularly in the 400- to 800-mm belt: *Combretum aculeatum, Bauhinia refescens,* and *Ziziphus mauritiana.* Other species that have high feed value should be studied more thoroughly, particularly their ability for reproduction and their growth rate. These include *Maerua crassifolia, Boscia angustifolia, Pterocarpus lucens, Salvadora persica, Cadaba farinosa, C. glandulosa, Grewia bicolor,* and *Balanites aegyptiaca.*

Planting cost with nursery-grown seedlings averages $300–350 U.S. in 1980 for a density of 600 trees per hectare at M'bidi in Senegal, that is, approximately $0.50 U.S. per tree/shrub established. This cost includes soils preparation, nursery operations, transportation to planting site, and two plowings per year over 3 years to eliminate competition from grass cover. Of course this may vary from one country to another, especially regarding the cost of labor, which constitutes 70 to 80% of the overall operation expense. Such costs are obviously beyond the means of the small African farmer. Research should therefore be focused on less expensive establishment methods, such as direct sowing, a method which has sometimes proven successful in particular situations (Piot, 1980) but has more often failed in the dry tropics (Gosseye, 1980) (see Note added in proof). With some shrubs such as *Leucaena, Cajanus cajan,* or *Stylosanthes scabra,* direct sowing does not seem to constitute any serious problems in the subhumid and humid ecoclimatic zones; these species should enable fallows to be greatly improved in terms of fertility and productivity for the subsequent crop. Planting of *Leucaena leucocephala* in the humid tropics of Africa has been shown to be economically feasible (Beale, 1980) now that technical problems have been solved (Savory *et al.,* 1980; Taylor, 1980). Yields are 5 to 10 metric tons of fodder DM/ha/yr. Grazing systems combining *Leucaena* and *Panicum maximum* (Guinea grass) or *Brachiaria ruziziensis* have been advocated for small-scale estates in the humid tropics of the Ivory Coast (Audru, 1980). Other promising fodder shrubs for the semi-arid and subhumid intertropics of Africa are the stylos recently selected and bred in Australia, *Stylosanthes hamata, S. scabra, S. sericea,* and *S. viscosa,* while *S. guyanensis* is already being used in the more humid zones (above 1000–1200 mm of mean annual rainfall). Spineless cacti are a routine arid zone fodder crop in South Africa (De Kock, 1980).

V. Biology, Multiplication, and Utilization of Intertropical Shrubs

Some multiplication experiments carried out at Niono, Mali, under the ILCA program, have given the results shown in Table V. Multiplication

Table IV. Germination rates and striking rates of some Sahelian shrubs and trees

Species	Germination rate after treatment in boiling water	Striking rate in nursery			
		Apex cuttings	Lignified cuttings	Bottom cutting	Rootstock
Combretum					
aculeatum	78	0	0	0	34
Acacia seyal	78	0	3	0	35
Faidherbia					
albida	60	0	0	0	63
Sclerocarya					
birrea	53	0	0	0	—
Bauhinia					
rufescens	30	0	0	0	26
Pterocarpus					
lucens	0	0	0	0	21
Ziziphus					
mauritiana	32	0	0	0	20
Balanites					
aegyptiaca	—	0	0	3	32
Cadaba farinosa	—	0	0	0	—
Grewia bicolor	—	0	12	19	60
Boscia angustofolia	—	0	11	5	60

Source: Gosseye (1980)

trials using seedlings grown in polyethylene bags in nursery have produced variable site establishment results in the conditions of Niono (southern Sahel ecoclimatic zone, mean annual rainfall 500 mm). Various utilization trials are being continued as part of the same research program involving utilization methods and patterns and the effects of pruning and cutting back at various intensities and at various seasons. Preliminary results with *Feretia apodanthera, Combretum aculeatum,* and *Cadaba farinosa* clearly show that with faster utilization, production falls. Total utilization has a marked depressive effect on output as compared with partial utilization. Protein content is in direct ratio to utilization frequency. In addition, the trials show that pruning and cutting back are likely to lengthen the utilization period considerably around the second half of the dry season, particularly with *Pterocarpus lucens.* Cool dry season pruning (November–January) has a more favorable effect than hot dry season pruning (March–May). In every case pruning ensures a higher production than cutting back. The facts are less clear with *Acacia seyal,* although, again, cool dry season pruning seems more favorable to total production and sustained production throughout the second half of the dry season.

VI. Present Evolution of African Shrublands and Long-Term Consequences

All monitoring studies in the Sahel and East Africa show a considerable regression of the ligneous cover during the last 30 years, caused by the combination of two phenomena: prolonged droughts since 1969 and overutilization due to exponential growth of human and stock populations at a rate of about 2.5% per annum or more. The comparison of aerial photo coverages taken at about 20-year intervals provides absolute proof of the substantial decline of the shrub cover in Chad, Sudan, Niger, Mali, Upper Volta, Senegal, Ethiopia, Somalia, and Kenya. The decline has been 20 to 35% between 1954 and 1975 (Le Houérou and Wilson, 1978; Haywood, 1981; De Wispelaere, 1980; De Wispelaere and Toutain, 1980; Gaston, 1981; Barral *et al.*, 1983; Barry *et al.*, 1983; Lamprey, 1975, 1983; Lusigi, 1981; Boudet, 1972, 1977; Le Houérou, 1980a, e, 1981; Peyre de Fabregues and De Wispelaere, 1984; Gillet, 1980, 1985; Le Houérou and Gillet, 1985; Pratt and Gwynne, 1977). These results are confirmed by field surveys over the whole Sahel and large parts of East Africa. In the Sahel, for instance, the mean mortality of trees and shrubs during the 1969–1973 drought has been estimated at 40 to 50%. Over limited areas the die-off was total. Detailed research on the functioning of Sahelian ecosystems conducted at Fete Ole in northern Senegal (Bille, 1977, 1978; Poupon, 1980) over a peroid of 10 years, including the 1969–1973 drought, showed an average mortality of 20% under conditions of total protection. Naturally, under current conditions of utilization in the Sahel, the situation is much worse, with mortalities often reaching 50%. A demographic study of the plant populations shows that 30 years would be required to offset the effects of the 1969–1973 drought and to bring back production to its pre-1970 level (Bille, 1978). But the subsequent 1980–1985 drought was still worse (Tucker *et al.*, 1985; Le Houérou and Gillet, 1985). According to most ecologists familiar with the Sahelian situation, the Sahel might never recover from these two consecutive droughts (Peyre de Fabregues and De Wispelaere, 1984).

The lack, or the weakness, of regeneration after the drought can be explained by three main factors:

1. A great many trees were badly pruned or lopped to make foliage available to animals during the drought. Many trees did not survive, mainly because cutting was done over the whole canopy or using methods that harmed branches and stems, leaving canopies hanging from the stem like a half-closed umbrella thus contributing to the

"cooking" of the tree when the inevitable bushfires occur during subsequent years (Piot, 1980).

2. Seeds and seedlings were consumed by hungry animals.
3. Individual trees or shrubs located toward the arid border of the geographic area of distribution of their own species cannot withstand the drought stress and whole stands perished, thus preventing any regeneration.

Firewood gathering has a disastrous effect on browse production and the development of populations of browse species. Wilson (1980) showed that the small town of Niono (central Mali), with a population of 15,000 inhabitants (growing by 12% annually), consumes the equivalent of the annual production of 37,000 ha of *Pterocarpus lucens* in firewood (this species is the best ligneous forage in the Sahel, and is also sold as such on markets during the dry season). If the present demographic growth of the town remains unchanged over the next 15 years, the firewood consumption will reach the equivalent of the production from 400,000 ha by the year 2000, thus reducing the stock capacity of the zone by 60,000 heads of cattle. Assuming there will be three drought periods in the next 100 years (there were four since the beginning of the present century), it is feared that the ligneous cover of the Sahel will be reduced to an absolute minimum over the next 50 years.

If environmental degradation worsens, the Sahel will become unexploitable by livestock outside the rainy seasons, unless the animals are provided with concentrates and/or urea and with minerals to offset the shortage of browse. Given the meat prices at the producer's level and offtake rates in pastoral production systems currently prevailing, scarcely any investment is economically feasible (though slight differences exist between countries). In fact one cannot see any way in which animals could be supplemented economically for 8 to 9 months a year with the present meat and concentrate prices. The destruction of the ligneous cover would therefore lead to a deadend for the livestock industry in the Sahel and parts of East Africa. This could happen before the middle of the next century and perhaps locally before the end of the present one, if the population growth rate continues as it is. Generally speaking, the situation is not yet as bad in East Africa as it is in West Africa, but some local situations are just as bad and the overall situation is worsening very fast, particularly in Somalia, Southeast Ethiopia, and parts of northern Kenya. There is, for instance, a clear shift in herd composition toward larger proportions of browsers (goats and camels), which is a classic indicator of environmental deterioration.

VII. Conclusion: Toward Ecological Management of Shrubland Ecosystems

For nutritional and economic reasons browse should represent 20–25% of ruminant intake (30% in the dry season and 5% in the rainy season) in the arid and semiarid zones of Africa. How could this balance be ensured and how could sound management be established on the principle of sustained maximum output? At the conceptual and planning level, the philosophy and objectives ought to be clearly defined and the strategy and means to attain the objectives should be selected and described. This implies a dynamic livestock policy including stratification, a marketing policy, and thus a price policy in favor of quality products.

In the field, the problem is theoretically very simple—if not very easy. It is a question of adapting pasture stocking rates to the long-term productivity of the ecosystems, that is, an offtake of no more than 25–30% of the primary production. In practice this would mean that human and animal densities would be controlled and that simple techniques such as deferred grazing, periodic exclosures, and the adaptation of watering regimes to the density and seasonal occurrence of watering points would be applied. This kind of management naturally implies choices and daily decisions, that is, the notion of responsibility. Yet the present situation in dry Africa is characterized by a generalized lack of responsibility at the resources management level, in other words, a communal ownership of land and water prevails. Water and pasture are actually common public resources and it is in every user's short-run interest to draw a maximum and immediate profit from the common resource without bothering about what may happen in the long run. Such a situation results in the looting of the common resources for the individual's immediate benefit.

It is quite obvious that no traditional system of any kind can be implemented without the concept of responsible management, whether by individuals or groups. Meeting these responsibilities involves fundamental land reforms in terms of land tenure and of land and water usufruct. If drastic sociopolitical reforms are not implemented without delay to ensure the rational management of shrubland ecosystems, the arid and semiarid zones of Africa will have to face a very profound crisis that will threaten their present main resource.

The situation in the subhumid and humid ecoclimatic zones is certainly less gloomy, and development prospects are much better, at least on deep soils. But what will happen to the immense areas of shrublands and forests growing on shallow ferruginous or lateritic (ferralitic) hardpans? At present browse plays an important part in livestock production, especially during the second half of the dry seasons.

References

Aubreville, A. (1949). "Climats, forêt et désertification de l'Afrique tropicale." Soc. Ed. Geogr. Marit., Paris.

Audru, J. (1980). Ligneous and subligneous forage and fruit species in the Guinean Ecoclimatic Zone: prospects for utilization in animal production. *In* "Browse in Africa: The Current State of Knowledge" pp. 115–122. (H. N. Le Houérou, ed). International Livestock Center for Africa, Addis-Ababa, Ethiopia.

Barral, H., and 17 colleagues (1983). "Systèms de production d'élevage au Sénégal, dans la région du Ferlo." GERDAT/ORSTOM, Paris.

Barry, J. P., and 6 colleagues (1983). "Etudes des potentialités pastorales et de leur évolution en milieu sahélien du Mali." GERDAT/ORSTOM, Paris.

Beale, C. I. A. (1980). Economic aspects of developing *Leucaena* as a cash crop, a review of pre-investment studies in Malawi (1974–79). *In* "Browse in Africa: The Current State of Knowledge" (H. N. Le Houérou, ed.), International Livestock Center for Africa, Addis-Ababa, Ethiopia.

Bille, J. C. (1977). Etude de la production primaire nette d'un ecosystème sahélien. *Trav. Doc. ORSTOM* **65**.

Bille, J. C. (1978). Woody forage species in the Sahel, their biology and use. *Proc. Int. Rangel. Congr., 1st,* pp. 392–395. 14–18 Aug. 1978, Denver, Colorado.

Boudet, G. G. (1972). Désertification de l'Afrique tropicale seche. *Adansonia, Ser. 2* **12**(4), 505–524.

Boudet, G. G. (1975). The inventory and mapping of rangeland in West Africa. *In* "Proceedings of the International Symposium on Evaluation and Mapping of Tropical African Rangelands," pp. 57–77. International Livestock Center for Africa, Addis-Ababa, Ethiopia.

Boudet, G. G. (1977). Désertification ou remontée biologique au Sahel? *Cah. ORSTOM, Ser. Biol.* **12**(4), 293–300.

Carew, B. A. R., Misi, A. K., Mba, A. U., and Egbunike, G. N. (1980). The potential of browse plants in the nutrition of small ruminants in the humid forest and derived savanna zones of Nigeria. *In* "Browse in Africa: The Current State of Knowledge" (H. N. Le Houérou, ed.), pp. 307–312. International Livestock Center for Africa, Addis-Ababa, Ethiopia.

Catinot, R. (1967a). Sylviculture tropicale dans les zones seches de l'Afrique. *Bois For. Trop.* **111**, 19–32.

Catinot, R. (1967b). *Bois For. Trop.* **112**, 3–29.

Chevalier, A. (1912). Carte botanique, forestiere et pastorale de l'A. O. F. *La Geographie* **26**.

Chevalier, A. (1933). Le territoire géobotanique de l'Afrique tropicale nord-occidentale et ses subdivisions. *Bull. Soc. Bot. Fr.* **80**, 4–26.

Dayton, B. R. (1978). Standing crop of dominant *Combretum* species at three browsing levels in the Kruger National Park. *Koedoe* **21**, 67–76.

De Kock, G. C. (1980). Cultivation of drought tolerant fodder shrubs. *In* "Browse in Africa: The Current State of Knowledge" (H. N. Le Houérou, ed.), pp. 399–410. International Livestock Center for Africa, Addis-Ababa, Ethiopia.

Delwaulle, J. C. (1975). Le rôle du forestier dans l'amenagement du Sahel. *Bois For. Trop.* **160**, 3–22.

Delwaulle, J. C. (1978). "Plantations forestieres en Afrique tropicale seche," Bois For. Trop., Nos. 181–184. CTFT, Nogent sur Marne.

De Wispelaere, G. (1980). Les photographies aériennes temoins de la degradation du couvert ligneux dans un écosystème sahelien sénégalais. Influence de la proximité d'un forage. *Cah. ORSTOM, Ser. Sci. Hum.* **17**(3–4), 155–166.

De Wispelaere, G., and Toutain, B. (1981). Etude diachronique de quelques geosystèmes sahéliens en Haute Volta septentrionale. *Rev. PhotoInterpretation* **81**, 1/1–1/5.

Dicko, M. (1980). Measuring the secondary production of pasture: An applied example in the study of an extensive production system in Mali. *In* "Browse in Africa: The Current State of Knowledge" (H. N. Le Houérou, ed.), pp. 247–254. International Livestock Center for Africa, Addis-Ababa, Ethiopia.

Dougall, H. W., Drysdale, V. M., and Glover, P. E. (1964). The chemical composition of Kenya browse and pasture herbage. *East Afr. Wildl. J.* **2**, 86–121.

Dumancic, D., and Le Houérou H. N. (1981). *Acacia cyanophylla* Lindl. as a supplementary feed for small stock in Libya. *J. Arid Environ.* **4**, 161–176.

Floret, C., and Le Floch, E. (1980). Contribution of browse species to the pastoral value of southern Tunisia steppes. *In* "Browse in Africa: The Current State of Knowledge" (H. N. Le Houérou, ed.), pp. 131–134. International Livestock Center for Africa, Addis-Ababa, Ethiopia.

Food and Agriculture Organization (1974). "Soil Map of the World," Vol. 1. Legend, Food and Agriculture. United Nations, Viale de Terme di Caracalla, Rome.

Food and Agriculture Organization (1978). "Soil Map of the World," Vol. 3. Africa. Food and Agriculture, United Nations, Viale de Terme di Caracalla, Rome.

Franclet, A., and Le Houérou, H. N. (1971). "Les Atriplex en Tunisie et an Afrique du Nord." F. A. O., Rome (English translation by U. S. Forest Service available at FAO Doc. Cent. Microfich No. 17909 El, FAO, Rome).

Gaston, A. (1981). "La végétation du Tchad: Evolutions récentes sous influences climatiques et humaines." Thèse Doct. Sci., Univ. Paris XII, IEMVT, Maisons-Alfort.

Giffard, P. L. (1964). Les possibilities de reboisement en *Acacia albida*. *Bois For. Trop.* **95**, 21–33.

Giffard, P. L. (1972). Le rôle de l'Acacia albida dans la régénération des sols en zone tropicale aride. *Congr. For. Mondial, 7th.*

Gillet, H. (1980). Observations on the causes of devastation of ligneous plants in the Sahel and their resistance to destruction. *In* "Browse in Africa: The Current State of Knowledge," pp. 117–130. (H. N. Le Houérou, ed.). International Livestock Center for Africa, Addis-Ababa, Ethiopia.

Gillet, H. (1985). "La secherese au Sahel," Suppl. Encyclopoedia Universalis.

Gosseye, P. (1980). Introduction of browse plants in the Sudano–Sahelian zone. *In* "Browse in Africa." The current State of Knowledge (H. N. Le Houérou, ed.), pp. 393–398. International Livestock Center for Africa, Addis–Ababa, Ethiopia.

Hamel, O. (1980). Acclimatation of phyllodineous acacias from Australia in Senegal. *In* "Browse in Africa: The Current State of Knowledge." (H. N. Le Houérou, ed.), pp. 361–374. International Livestock Center for Africa, Addis–Ababa, Ethiopia.

Harrington, G. N., and Wilson, A.D. (1980). Methods of measuring secondary production from browse. *In* "Browse in Africa: The Current State of Knowledge" (H. N. Le Houérou, ed.), pp. 255–260. International Livestock Center for Africa, Addis–Ababa, Ethiopia.

Haywood, M. (1981). "Evolution de l'utilisation des terres et de la végétation dans la zone Soudano–Sahelienne du projet CIPEA au Mali" (mimeo), Doc. Trav. No. 3. CIPEA/ILCA, Addis–Ababa, Ethiopia.

Hiernaux, P. (1980). Inventory of the browse potential of bushes, trees and shrubs in an area of the Sahel in Mali: Methods and initial results. *In* "Browse in Africa: The current State of Knowledge" (H. N. Le Houérou, ed.), pp. 197–204. International Livestock Center for Africa, Addis–Ababa, Ethiopia.

Hiernaux, P., Cisse, M. I., and Diarrz, L. (1979). "Rapport annual d'activité de la section d'écologie" (mimeo), restricted. International Livestock Center for Africa, Bamako, Mali.

Kassas, M. (1970). Desertification versus potential for recovery in certain circum-saharan territories. *In* "Arid Lands in Perspective" (H. E. Dregne, ed.), pp. 123–139. Am. Assoc. Adv. Sci., Washington, D.C.

Kennan, T.C.D., (1969). The significance of bush grazing of land in Rhodesia. *Rhod. News* **3,** 331–336.

Lamprey, H. F. (1975). "Report on the Desert Encroachment Reconnaissance in the Northern Sudan" (mimeo). UNEP, Nairobi.

Lamprey, H. F. (1983). Pastoralism yesterday and today: The overgrazing problem. *In* "Tropical Savanna: Ecosystems of the World" (F. Bourliere, Ed.), Vol. 13, Chapter 1, pp. 643–666. Elsevier, Amsterdam.

Lamprey, H. F., Herlocker, D. J., and Field, C. R. (1980). Report on the state of Knowledge on browse in East Africa in 1980. *In* "Browse in Africa: The Current State of Knowledge" (H. N. Le Houérou, ed.), pp. 33–54. International Center for Livestock in Africa, Addis–Ababa, Ethiopia.

Lawton, R. M. (1980). Browse in the "Miombo." *In* "Browse in Africa: The Current of State Knowledge" (H. N. Le Houérou, ed.), pp. 33–54. International Center for Livestock in Africa, Addis–Ababa, Ethiopia.

Le Houérou, H. N. (1969). La végétation de la Tunisie steppique, avec référence aux végétations analogues d'Algérie, de Libye et du Maroc. *Ann. Inst. Natl. Rech. Agron. Tunis.* **42,** (5), 1–624.

Le Houérou, H. N. (1978). The role of shrubs and trees in the management of natural grazing lands (with particular reference to protein production). *World For. Congr. 8th,* position Pap. Item No. 10.

Le Houérou, H. N., ed. (1980a). "Browse in Africa: The Current State of Knowledge." International Livestock Center of Africa, Addis–Ababa, Ethiopia.

Le Houérou, H. N. (1980b). Browse in Northern Africa. *In* "Browse in Africa: The Current State of Knowledge" (H. N. Le Houérou, ed.), pp. 55–82. International Livestock Center for Africa, Addis Ababa, Ethiopia.

Le Houérou, H. N. (1980c). The role of browse in the Sahelian and Sudanian zones. *In* "Browse in Africa: The Current State of Knowledge" (H. N. Le Houérou, ed.), pp. 83–102. International Livestock Center for Africa, Addis Ababa, Ethiopia.

Le Houérou, H. N. (1980d). Chemical composition and nutritive value of browse in West Africa. *In* "Browse in Africa: The Current State of Knowledge" (H. N. Le Houérou, ed.), pp. 261–290. International Livestock Center for Africa, Addis–Ababa, Ethiopia.

Le Houérou, H. N. (1980e). The grasslands of Africa: Classification, production, evolution and development outlook. *Proc. Int. Grassl, Congr., 13th, 1977,* pp. 99–116.

Le Houérou, H. N. (1981). Impact of man and his animal on Mediterranean vegetation. *In* "Mediterranean-Type Shrublands: Ecosystems of the World" F. di Castri, D. W. Goodall, and R. L. Specht, eds.), Vol. 11, Elsevier, Amsterdam.

Le Houérou, H. N., and Corra M. (1980). Some browse plants of Ethiopia. *In* "Browse in Africa: The Current State of Knowledge" (H. N. Le Houérou, ed.), pp. 109–114. International Livestock Center for Africa, Addis–Ababa, Ethiopia.

Le Houérou, H. N., and Gillet, H. (1985). "Conservation versus Desertization in African Arid Lands," *In* "Conservation Biology. The Science of Scarcity and Diversity" (M. Soulé, ed.), pp. 444–461. 2nd Conf. Conserv. Biol. School of Nat. Res., Univ. of Michigan, Ann Arbor.

Le Houérou, H. N., and Popov, G. F. (1981). "An Ecoclimatic Classification of Intertropical Africa," Plant Prod. Pap. No. 31 FAO, Rome.

Le Houérou, H. N., and Wilson, R. T., eds. (1978). Study of the Traditional Livestock

Production Systems in Central Mali (Sahel and Niger Delta)" (mimeo), restricted. International Livestock Center for Africa, Addis–Ababa, Ethiopia.

Leone, G. (1924). Consolidamento ed imboschimento delle zone dunose dell Tripolitania. *Agric. Coloniale,* **18** (9), 299–308.

Lepape, M. C. (1980). Browse in the Cape Verde Islands. *In* "Browse in Africa: The Current State of Knowledge" (H. N. Le Houérou, ed.), pp. 123–126. International Livestock Center for Africa, Addis–Ababa, Ethiopia.

Lusigi, W. J. (1981). "Combating Desertification and Rehabilitating Degraded Production Systems in Northern Kenya." IPAL, UNESCO, Nairobi.

Mabey, G. L., and Rose-Innes, R. (1964a). Studies in Browse plants in Ghana. *Emp. J. Exp. Agric.* **32** (126), 114–130.

Mabey, G. L., and Rose-Innes, R. (1964b). Studies in Browse plants in Ghana. *Emp. J. Exp. Agric.* **32** (127), 180–190.

Mabey, G. L., and Rose-Innes, R. (1964c). Studies in Browse plants in Ghana. *Emp. J. Exp. Agric.* **32** (128), 274–278.

Mabey, G. L., and Rose-Innes, R (1967). Studies in Browse plants in Ghana. *N. Ser.* **2** 27–32, 112–117.

Mecha, I., and Adegbola, T. A (1980). Chemical Compostition of some southern Nigeria plants eaten by goats. *In* "Browse in Africa: The Current State of Knowledge" (H. N. Le Houérou, ed.), pp. 303–306. International Livestock Center for Africa, Addis–Ababa, Ethiopia.

Monjauze, A., and Le Houérou, H. N. (1965). Les rôles des *Opuntia* dans l'économie agricole nord-africaine. *Bull. Ec. Natl. Super. Agron. Tunis.* **8–9,** 85–164.

Mubarak, O., and Seif el Din, A. G. (1970). Ecological studies of the vegetation of the Sudan: *Acacia senegal* (L.) Willd. and its natural regeneration. *J. Appl. Ecol.* **7,** 507–518.

Nebout, J. P., and Toutain, B. (1978). "Etude sur les arbres fourragers dans la zone sahélienne (Oudalan Voltaique)." CTFT/IEMVT, Nogent sur Marne and Maisons–Alfort.

Pellew, R. A. (1980). The production and consumption of acacia browse and its potential for animal protein production. *In* "Browse in Africa: The Current State of Knowledge" (H. N. Le Houérou, ed.), pp. 223–232. International Livestock Center for Africa, Addis–Ababa, Ethiopia.

Peyre de Fabregues, B., and De Wispelaere, G. (1984). Sahel, la fin d'un monde pastoral? *Marches Trop.,* pp. 2488–2491.

Piot, J. (1979). Paturage servien au utilisation des ligneux pour les bovines. *Rev. Ect. Med. Vet. Phys. Trop.* **23;** 503–512.

Piot, J. (1980). Management and utilization methods for ligneous forage: Natural stands and plantations. *In* "Browse in Africa: The Current State of Knowledge" (H. N. Le Houérou, ed.), pp. 339–350. International Livestock Center for Africa, Addis–Ababa, Ethiopia.

Piot, J., Nebout, J. P., Nanot, R., and Toutain, B. (1980). "Utilisation des ligneux sahéliens par les herbivores domestiques." CTFT/IEMVT, Nogent sur Marne and Maisons-Alfort.

Poupon, H., (1980). Structure et dynamique de la strate ligneuse d'une steppe sahélienne au Nord du Senegal. *Trav. Doc. ORSTOM.*

Pratt, D. J., and Gwynne, M. D., eds. (1977). "Rangeland Management and Ecology in East Africa." Hodder Stroughton, London.

Pratt, D. J., Greenway, P. J., and Gwynne, M. D. (1966). A classification of East Africa rangelands, with an appendix on terminology. *J. Appl. Ecol.* **3,** 369–382.

Rutherford, M. C. (1978). Primary production ecology in Southern Africa. *In* Biogeography and Ecology of Southern Africa" (M. J. A. Werger, ed.), pp. 621–660. Junk, The Hague.

Savory, R., Breen, J. A., and Beale, C. I. A. (1980). *Leucaena* as a forage crop on small farms in Malawi. *In* "Browse in Africa: The Current State of Knowledge" (H. N. Le Houérou, ed.), pp. 411–414. International Livestock Center for Africa, Addis–Ababa, Ethiopia.

Seif el Din, A. G. (1979). "Rainfall Distribution and Vegetation in the Sahel," pp. 43–50. Report of IDRC, Ottawa.

Taylor, M. S. (1980). Initial performance of *Leucaena* at a subhumid, midaltitude location in Ethiopia. *In* "Browse in Africa: The Current State of Knowledge" (H. N. Le Houérou, ed.), pp. 415–418. International Livestock Center for Africa, Addis–Ababa, Ethiopia.

Toutain, B. (1980). The Role of browse plants, in animal production in the Sudanian zone of West Africa. *In* "Browse in Africa: The Current State of Knowledge" (H. N. Le Houérou, ed.), pp. 103–108, International Livestock Center for Africa, Addis–Ababa, Ethiopia.

Tucker, C. J., Vanpraet, C. L. Sharman, M. J. and Van Ittersum, G. (1985). Satellite remote sensing of total herbaceous biomass production in the senegalese Sahel: 1980–1984. *Remote Sens. Environ.* **17,** 233–249.

von Maydel, H. J. (1983). "Arbres et arbustes du Sahel," Publ. No. 147. GTX, German Technical Assistance Organization, Eschborn, West Germany.

Walker, B. H. (1980). A review of browse and its role in livestock production in southern Africa. *In* "Browse in Africa: The Current State of Knowledge" (H. N. Le Houérou, ed.), pp. 7–24. International Livestock Center for Africa, Addis–Ababa, Ethiopia.

Whyte, R. O. (1974). The use and misuse of shrubs and trees as fodder. Africa. Imperial Agricultural Bureau, Joint Publication No. 10.

Wickens, G. E. (1980). Alternative use of browse species. *In* "Browse in Africa: The Current State of Knowledge" (H. N. Le Houérou, ed.), pp. 155–184. International Livestock Center for Africa, Addis–Ababa, Ethiopia.

Wilson, R. T. (1980). Fuel wood in a central Milian town and its effects on browse availability. *In* "Browse in Africa: The Current State of Knowledge" (H. N. Le Houérou, ed.), pp. 473–476. International Livestock Center for Africa, Addis–Ababa, Ethiopia.

Note added in proof: Recent research in Senegal showed that direct field sowing of pregerminated *Acacia* seeds in moist soils (with 30–50 mm of infiltrated rains) is a most promising technique. It would considerably reduce establishment cost and thus make fodder shrub plantation affordable on small farms in Africa.

6

Southern African Shrublands

E. J. Moll
A. A. Gubb

I. Introduction

The most extensive continuous area of shrubland in southern Africa occurs in the phytochorological Karoo–Namib Region, which is further
subdivided into four domains: the Namib, Namaqualand, Western Cape,
and Karoo Domains. This region is characterized by a fairly rich and dry
flora (Werger, 1978). It consists largely of an open to closed low shrub
formation (Karoo bushes), with taller woody shrubs on the hill and
mountain slopes (Werger, 1978; Vorster and Roux, 1983) (Plates 1–8).
The name Karoo is derived from the Hottentot name Karu—meaning dry
or arid land (Compton, 1929; Vorster and Roux, 1983). Today the term
Karoo is synonymous with the vast and monotonous semiarid central and
western area of the Cape Province that is flat to undulating, generally
uniform in topography, and repetitive in structure of the vegetation
(Talbot, 1961). Taller shrublands (1.5 to 3.0 m tall) occur in the adjacent
Kalahari Transitional Zone of the northern Cape and Botswana, but are

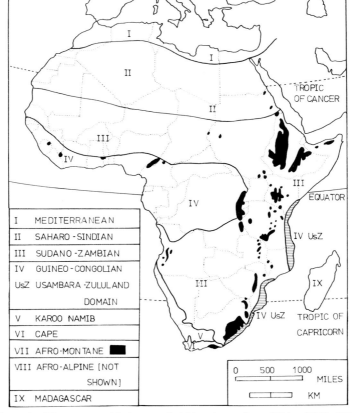

Figure 1. Phytogeographical map of Africa drawn from White (1965, 1971).

not included here. Some scattered shrublands are also present in the
Sahelian extension of the Oriental Domain of the Sudano–Zambezian
Region (see Figs. 1 and 2) (White, 1965, 1971). Since the authors are most
familiar with the southern African shrublands a discussion of these will
form the bulk of this chapter.

Shrublands in southern Africa support numbers of domestic animals. In
East Africa, pastoralism in the semiarid and arid zones is vital for the
survival of a large number of people (Pratt and Gwynne, 1977). In many
areas the carrying capacity is exceeded and desertification is proceeding at
an alarming rate (U.N. Conference on Desertification, 1977). In South
Africa the situation is a little different. There only a few, relatively wealthy
European farmers own most of the livestock (except in Namaqualand) and

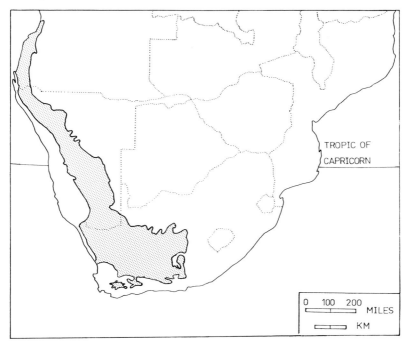

Figure 2. Map of southern Africa showing the distribution of shrublands. (From White, 1965, 1971; Vorster and Roux, 1983.)

government aid programs are fairly easily available in times of stress (Roberts, 1969), so the sophistication of land management has remained low in both regions. The position regarding desertification is similar (Anonymous, 1951, 1978; Acocks, 1953; Talbot, 1961; Jarman and Bosch, 1973; Downing, 1978).

Since the major environmental factors determining the distribution and spread of shrublands into adjacent more productive rangeland are generally acknowledged to be soil moisture availability and management practices, these factors will be emphasized here. Moisture availability is dependent not only on the amount and seasonal distribution of rainfall, and in some cases fog precipitation (particularly the west coast of southern Africa), but also on soil physical properties. The rainfall is erratic with respect to amount, duration, and time between rains. A clayey substrate and deep Kalahari sands (both with low rainfall) will have remarkably different vegetation cover (see Figs. 3 and 4). The clayey substrate will support only dwarf xerophytic shrubs, scattered perennial grasses, and some annuals, while the sand will support scattered trees in an open to

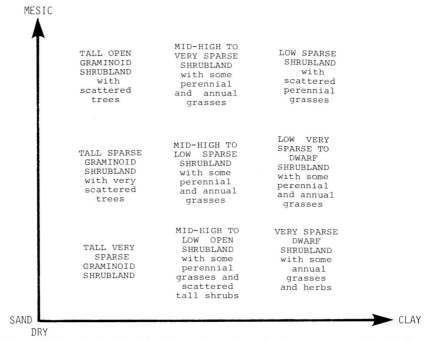

Figure 3. Hypothetical shrubland dynamics under optimal management regimes in South Africa. Structural terminology follows that of Campbell *et al.* (1981).

Figure 4. Hypothetical shrubland dynamics resulting from poor management practices in South Africa. Structural terminology follows that of Campbell *et al.* (1981).

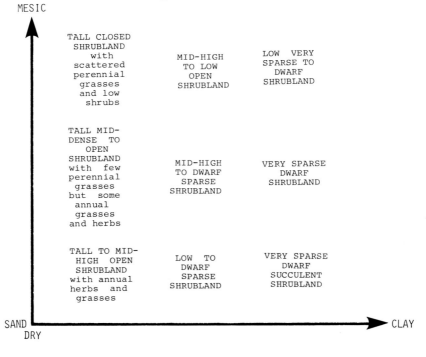

closed tall shrubland (1.5 to 3.0 m) with a good understory of perennial grasses (0.5 to 1.2 m). In the short term, the impact of poor management on the clayey soils is to reduce shrub cover drastically, eliminate perennial grass cover, and cause some changes in species composition. In the long term, there is invasion and proliferation of unpalatable dwarf shrubs, an increase in annual grasses, and a major change in species composition. On the sandy soils poor management tends to lead to thicket development of unpalatable species and a corresponding decrease in perennial grass cover (see Fig. 4).

II. Physiography and Geology

The geology of the Karoo is composed of sedimentary rocks, mainly shales, mudstones, and some fine sandstones, with some tillite of the Dwyka formation (Hamilton and Cooke, 1960). Intrusive Karoo dolerites occur frequently. This geology has had a major influence on the topography, which is generally relatively flat with scattered, low hills and inselbergs (Werger, 1973a). Most of the Karoo basin is drained by the Orange River, which rises in the highlands of Lesotho (at some 3500 m) and flows west to the Atlantic Ocean.

III. Climate

The rainfall pattern over South Africa is characterized by an increase in precipitation from west to east with the mean annual precipitation being close to zero on the west coast (e.g., Oranjemund and Swakopmund) and reaching 400 mm some 600 km inland (e.g., Carnarvon and Beaufort West). However, on the west coast rainfall is supplemented by coastal fog (121 fog days per year at Swakopmund), which can penetrate as far as 100 km inland on occasions. Fog data are, however, generally poor (Nagel, 1956, 1962) despite the fact that the importance of fog for the maintenance of certain communities is acknowledged (Walter, 1979). In the extreme southwest of the country the climate is of a Mediterranean type with rain falling in winter. Areas covered by shrubland generally have an annual water deficiency exceeding 400 mm (Figs. 5 and 6) and correspond to Köppen's types BWh and BWk (arid zone desert with a mean annual temperature of >18°C and <18°C, respectively), BSk (arid zone steppe with a mean annual temperature of <18°C), and to some extent to Csb and Csa (warm temperature having a dry summer season with the warmest month >22°C and <22°C, respectively). Summers are generally warm

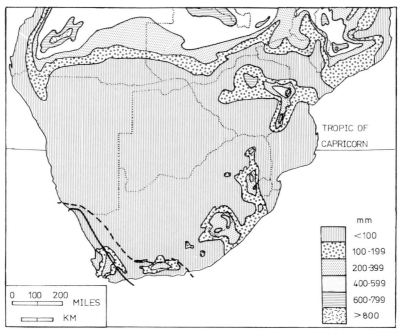

Figure 5. Annual water surplus. (Drawn from Schulze and McGee, 1978.) Rainfall in southern Africa occurs in summer except for the southwest corner which has rainfall all year (dotted line) or in winter (solid line).

Figure 6. Annual water deficiency. (Drawn from Schulze and McGee, 1978.)

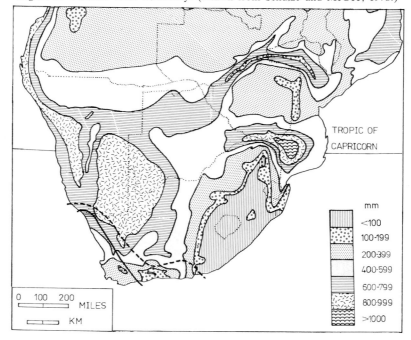

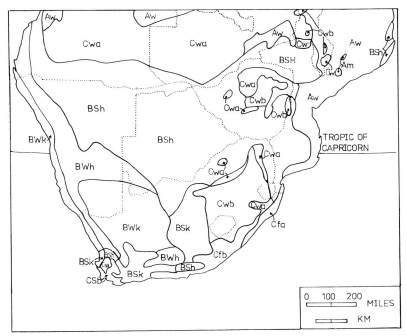

Figure 7. Climates according to Köppen. (Drawn from Schulze and McGee, 1978.)

(January mean daily maximum is 20–35°C) and winters are cool (July mean daily minimum is 0–7.5°C) with severe frost in depressions (Fig. 7).

In East Africa most shrublands experience a bimodal rainfall season with peaks in April and November. The mean annual rainfall seldom exceeds 700 mm, typically less than 600 mm, but because of the low elevation (mostly below 1200 m) and high temperature (annual mean of 25–30°C), potential evaporation (which may be up to 2000 mm) exceeds rainfall.

IV. Soils

The soils are mainly alkaline desert soils with some Kalahari and solonetzic soils in the north and east, respectively. Extensive "desert pavements" (vast areas covered by pebbles and rocks) and large pans are common in areas (Vorster and Roux, 1983), the soils of the latter often being brackish (Isaac and Gershill, 1935). In South Africa, shrublands generally occur on shallow lithosols, or in localized depressions on saline soils, or on very weakly developed soils (von M. Harmse, 1978) derived *in situ* from weathered shales, mudstones, and tillite. Some exceptions do occur where shrublands now grow on relatively deep, structured clays (e.g., red mont-morrillonitic clays) and sandy loams (usually solonetzic and planosolic soils), but in most cases this is due to degradation of rangeland and subsequent scrub encroachment.

Because most of the soils that support shrubland vegetation have a high clay content they are usually nutrient rich but with poor physical properties—notably having poor water infiltration and holding capacity, so climate and soil compound the droughty nature of the plant environment. With poor management practices, which have led to increased soil compaction and erosion, this existing droughty environment has been made even harsher.

In East Africa the soils are mostly sandy to sandy loams (Pratt and Gwynne, 1977), and although not particularly rich in nutrients, they have better physical properties that facilitate water infiltration and holding capacity. East African soils tend not to be as droughty as clays nor as prone to the same degree of compaction under poor management regimes. Thus the process of desertification could perhaps be more easily rectified with intensive management, simply because of the better physical properties of the soils.

V. Historical Perspective

Prior to the arrival of European settlers in 1652 the shrublands in South Africa supported only a sparse population of humans. These were the nomadic Hottentots, who had relatively small herds of cattle and flocks of fat-tailed sheep (Burchell, 1822–1824), and the San, who were hunter-gatherers. But since the shrubland environment was relatively hostile with little perennial surface water, the utilization of the region was minimal and the impact of humans was low, despite the fact that the region is known to have supported large numbers of indigenous mammals (Skead, 1980).

During the last 300 years those once-minimal utilization patterns have changed drastically with improved communications, advanced agricultural technology, and population growth. The unrestricted migration of the indigenous herbivores (Cattrick, 1957) has been replaced by fenced farms and domestic stock (Downing, 1978). With this change in the patterns of utilization from pulse to continuous disturbance, the vegetation, which once comprised a mixture of perennial grasses and shrubs, has been selectively overgrazed and abused to the extent that the grasses have all but disappeared (Fig. 8) and only the more unpalatable shrubs remain (Acocks, 1966; Werger, 1973a). Desertification of once well-vegetated areas and the alarming spread of the shrublands into adjacent grasslands

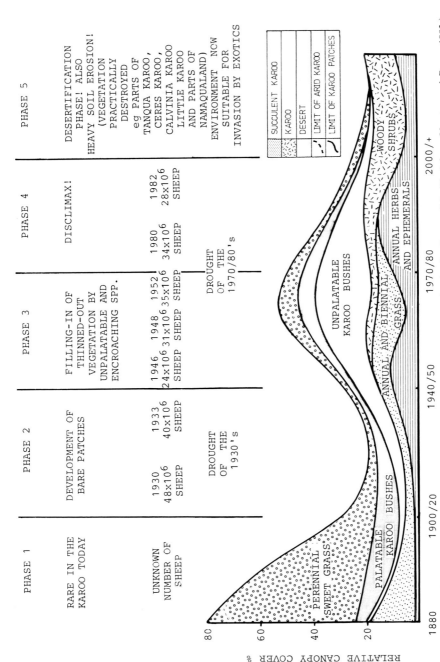

Figure 8. Five phases of change in cover of the main components of vegetation in the Karoo. (Modified from Vorster and Roux, 1983.)

have proceeded apace (de Klerk, 1947; Tidmarsh, 1948, quoted by Roux, 1979) despite the recognition of the causal factors and the scientific knowledge to reclaim and rehabilitate the land.

Improvement of shrublands is hampered by a general lack of response by farmers to the application of veld management systems. There is an unwillingness to change from traditional methods of management, even in the face of the obvious effects of veld deterioration (Roberts, 1969). Statistics show that a surprisingly low proportion of farmers apply any system of veld management, even though as early as 1934 the concept of veld management was developed in the karroid shrublands. Many farmers do not even employ simple, inefficient rotational grazing systems because the physical requirements (e.g., fencing, water points, etc.) do not exist. Yet, a small percentage of successful farmers have adapted management systems accepted by the Department of Agriculture or have undertaken systems that have not been given departmental support, such as nonselective grazing, controlled selective grazing, and short duration grazing. The latter systems are all based on a set of principles of veld reclamation and maintenance (Acocks, 1966; McNaughton, 1967, 1969; Roux, 1967; Roberts, 1969). Unfortunately, management systems are judged on production per animal rather than on veld improvement, increased carrying capacity, or greater production per hectare. State-aid schemes are now

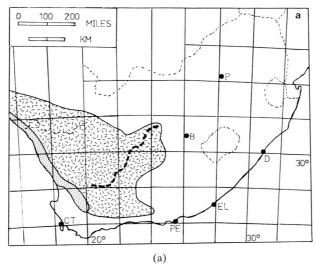

(a)

Figure 9. Vegetation trends in South Africa. (From Acocks, 1953.) (a) State of vegetation in A.D. 1400? (b) Vegetation in A.D. 1950. (c) Vegetation in A.D. 2050? (d) Vegetation under scientific management.

traditional and during times of stress (e.g., drought) are practically demanded as a right by the politically dominant rural electorate (Talbot, 1961).

The classic predictions of Acocks (1953) and his worst fears for the year 2050 (Fig. 9) have been realized more than 50 years ahead of his con-

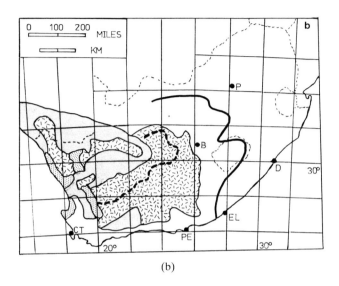

(b)

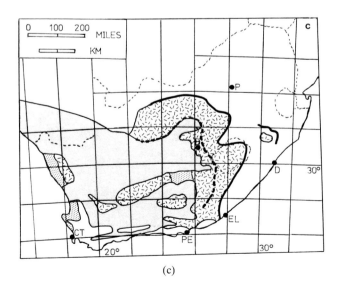

(c)

Figure 9. (*Continued*)

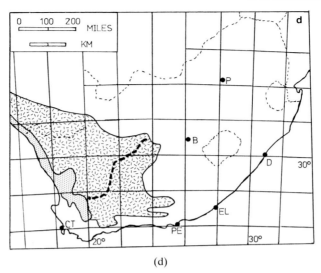

(d)

Figure 9. (*Continued*)

servative estimates, and all this has occurred during stable climatic conditions (Adamson, 1938; Tyson, 1978).

In East Africa the impact of European technology has had less direct effect on shrublands. Indirectly, better health care of humans and their livestock and the general concern for people in the "Third World" have led to overpopulation of the area by both people and their domestic stock. This increased pressure on the land has accelerated desertification with the acute problems being accentuated during a prolonged drought in the West African region during the 1970s. However, there is evidence to suggest that subsequent conservation measures have been reasonably successful, and that the situation today is not as bad as it was.

VI. Vegetation

Floristically the Karoo–Namib Region supports a rich and distinct flora that is generally acknowledged to have a northern origin (Levyns, 1950; Goldblatt, 1978), or it originated as a mixture of the southern and northern floras (Axelrod and Raven, 1978; Werger, 1978). In the south and southeast it is mixed with the vegetation in the adjacent Capensis and Sudano–Zambezian regions, respectively (Werger, 1978; Cowling, 1983). On this southern boundary a non-Karoo–Namib shrubland occurs that is the Renosterveld—composed essentially of the dominant species *Elytro-*

pappus rhinocerotis (Boucher and Moll, 1981). The Karoo–Namib flora itself is characterized by the presence of genera in such families as Asteraceae (*Pentzia, Eriocephalus, Pteronia, Felicia, Chrysocoma,* and *Osteospermum*), Poaceae (*Aristida, Stipa, Eragrostis, Enneapogon, Stipagrostis,* and *Themeda*), Mesembranthemaceae and Aizoaceae with ±50 endemic genera (Goldblatt, 1978) such as *Ruschia, Lampranthus, Galenia,* and *Sphalmanthus,* and Sterculiaceae (*Hermannia*).

Typically the vegetation is composed of evergreen, small, narrow-leaved sclerophyllous or succulent dwarf shrubs, with the presence of grass varying greatly, depending on climate and management regimes (past and present). The South Africa karroid shrublands (Plates 1–8) can be broadly divided into three main divisions (Venter and Theron, 1983): Central and Upper Karoo (Plate 1), Western Succulent Karoo (Plate 5), and False Karoo (formerly occupied by mainly tropical grasslands) (Plate 8). Most succulents occur on the western boundary, where most fog occurs (e.g., Succulent Karoo): along the Karoo–Namib ecotone in the Little Karoo (excluding Renosterveld, which occurs on more specialized sites) (Boucher and Moll, 1981), on the Karoo–Mountain Fynbos ecotone, and on the southeastern boundary (e.g.,

Plate 1. Central Upper Karoo (Acocks, 1953) near Victoria West. Note the exposed rock, a result of sheet erosion. The shrubs are mainly *Eriocephalus* and *Pentzia* spp.

Plate 2. False Upper Karoo (Acocks, 1953) near Calvinia, an area that has been severely overgrazed and where sheet erosion has exposed the underlying Ecca shale saprolite. Sparse vegetation is mainly *Galenia africana*.

Plate 3. False Upper Karoo (Acocks, 1953) on the agricultural experimental farm near Middelburg. The paddock on the left has been subject to nonselective grazing while that on the right to continuous grazing. Note that there are few shrubs in the grassland.

Plate 4. Succulent Karoo (Acocks, 1953) on the Beaufort shales near Laingsburg. Note the solonetzic soil in the depression.

Noorsveld) (Acocks, 1953). In the central and northern part the vegetation comprises mainly dwarf shrubs (e.g., Central Upper Karoo) with grasses being more conspicuous on the dolorite hills and ridges on the northern boundary (where the Kalahari Sands overlie the shales of the Karoo System) and on the eastern boundary (where the karroid shrublands have invaded the true grasslands of the Highveld) (Acocks, 1953).

The major difference between the East African shrublands and those in South Africa is that they are generally much taller (up to 3–4 m compared to <1 m) and have a more conspicuous grass component of essentially tropical C_4 genera such as *Cenchrus, Chloris,* and *Chrysopogon.* In fact they are much more similar to the Kalahari shrublands in the northern Cape, which occur on calcrete overlying dolomite bedrock, and have as the dominant tall shrub species (1.5 to 3.0 m tall) *Tarchonanthus camphoratus, Rhus ciliata, R. undulata,* and *R. tridactyla.* The East African shrublands can be divided into two major types: those dominated by *Commiphora* on more sandy, red soils, and those dominated by *Acacia* on dark, heavier soils. In the *Commiphora* type the more common shrub genera in the understory are *Lannea, Combretum, Cordia,* and *Grewia,* while in the *Acacia* type the shrub genera are *Acacia, Euphorbia,* and *Sansevieria*

Plate 5. Succulent Karoo (Acocks, 1953), which is dominated by mesembs, with few trees or large shrubs.

Plate 6. Karroid Broken Veld (Acocks, 1953) in which bushy succulents are dominant Grasses are scarce. The dominance of the mesembs is an artificial phenomenon resulting fron selective overgrazing and consequent soil erosion.

Plate 7. Western Mountain Karoo (Acocks, 1953) is situated in very stony shale, sandstone and granite country. The dominant and characteristic shrubs are *Pentzia* spp.

Plate 8. False Upper Karoo (Acocks, 1953) near Richmond. This vegetation type represents the disasterous conversion of 52,000 km^2 of productive grassland into dwarf karroid shrubland. The hills are still essentially grass covered. The pioneer of the False Upper Karoo is *Chrysocoma tenuifolia*.

(Pratt and Gwynne, 1977). Since these last two genera are succulent and may form dense thickets, the vegetation here could be compared to that of the Noorsveld and the Orange River Broken Veld in South Africa (Acocks, 1953). However, it is structurally and floristically more similar to those down-graded vegetation types that occur well north of the Karoo–Namib Region of southern Africa in the Indian Ocean Coastal Belt (Moll and White, 1978), and in the Sudano–Zambezian Region (Werger and Coetzee, 1978). In addition *Commiphora* is more characteristic of the Namib Desert area (Werger, 1973b, 1978). The conclusion regarding the East African shrublands is that they are essentially the arid fringe of the typical tropical to subtropical savanna types of Central Africa and not, therefore, as structurally and floristically distinct as the karroid shrublands in South Africa.

VII. Utilization

Only data from the Karoo are readily available, so the discussion will be restricted to these southern African shrublands.

Today most of the domestic stock are either sheep or goats. Roberts

(1969) recorded that with degradation following the settlement of the land, there has been a changing trend in the kinds of domestic stock. Initially the chief herbivores were cattle, horses, and sheep, but by the early 1900s most of the livestock were Merino sheep and wool was the major product. There was a dramatic increase from six animals in 1789 to approximately 50 million by 1930 (Talbot, 1961; Hugo, 1968). Owing to degradation, livestock carrying capacity has been reduced by almost one-half. The carrying capacity ranges from 1 to 2 ha/SSU[1] in the southeast to ≥6 ha/SSU in the northwest (Roux, 1979). Today, however, rangeland condition is so poor that most sheep are kept for mutton production and on the poorer rangeland, especially in the west, karakul are becoming more common, and in the southeast goats are the main domestic herbivores. Today cattle play a minor role and are primarily found along the eastern fringe in the higher rainfall zone (Roux *et al.*, 1981).

Today the most important shrubs, arranged more or less in order of palatability, are:

Most palatable shrubs
- *Nenax microphyllum*
- *Osteospermum sinuatum*
- *Phymaspermum parvifolium*
- *Plinthus karooicus*
- *Salsola glabrescens*
- *Felicia muricatus*

Moderately palatable shrubs
- *Atriplex semibaccata*
- *Hermannia multiflora*
- *Indigofera sessilifolia*
- *Pegolettia polygalaefolia*
- *Pentzia incana*
- *Salsola nigrescens*
- *S. tuberculata*
- *Sutera albiflora*
- *Selago speciosa*
- *Tetragonia arbuscula*
- *Walafrida geniculata*
- *Zygophyllum microphyllum*

Slightly palatable shrubs
- *Eriocephalus ericoides*
- *E. spinescens*
- *Euryops multifidus*
- *Helichrysum pentzoides*
- *H. dregeanum*
- *Galenia africana*
- *Lightfootia albens*
- *Nestlera conferta*
- *Pteronia glauca*
- *Suaeda fruticosa*
- *Sutera atropurpurea*
- *Zygophyllum flexuosum*

Unpalatable shrubs
- *Chrysocoma tenuifolia*
- *Gnidia polycephala*
- *Hertia pallens*
- *Nestlera prostrata*
- *Pentzia globosa*

Few data are available on primary production of various Karoo types but Rutherford (1978) gives data from the Arid Karoo at Carnarvon

[1] SSU = small stock unit. (This equates to one-fifth of a regular animal unit.)

(3700 kg/ha), False Upper Karoo at Middleburg (4800 to 5600 kg/ha), and Succulent Karoo at Worcester (7500 kg/ha). In general Karoo species are low in protein and important elements such as phosphorus, manganese, and potassium (Henrici, 1935; Louw, 1969). In the southeast many of the important and dominant species are low in sodium and phosphorus (Louw *et al.*, 1968a). Although the above elements may be adequate for sheep during the summer months, moderate to low deficiencies in nutrient content and digestibility may prevail throughout the karroid shrublands during the winter months (Vorster and Roux, 1983). (For a more detailed discussion of the food value of selected species see Buttner, 1961–1964, 1965; Louw *et al.*, 1968b; Steenkamp and Hayward, 1979.)

As far as the important growth periods of the component vegetation types are concerned (Bosch, 1983), the grass species grow in spring and summer (October to February) while the shrub species generally show a bimodal growth in spring (October to November) and autumn (March to May) (Fig. 10). Growth is largely dependent on moisture availability. Perennial grass species flower during late summer and autumn (February to May), the palatable shrub species flower during spring (October to November) and/or autumn (March to May), and the unpalatable and invader shrubs flower during winter (June to September) (Vorster and Roux, 1983) (Fig. 10). Most dwarf shrub seeds require an after-ripening period during which germination inhibitors are broken down (Henrici, 1935; van Rensburg, 1983). Many shrub species have extensive and deep root systems (Scott and van Breda, 1938) and this fact, as well as further adaptations such as differential germination, seed longevity, seed diversification, and complex germination mechanisms, makes them ideally suited to an environment experiencing unreliable water conditions (Werger, 1978). Some species are extremely plastic, becoming xerophytic (small leaves, very low transpiration rate) during dry years and more mesophytic (large leaves, high transpiration rate) during favorable years (Henrici, 1939). Furthermore, these species may be deciduous (dry years) or evergreen (wetter years). Many of the dwarf shrubs, for example, *Plinthus karooicus* and *Pentzia* spp., reproduce vegetatively by longitudinal splitting and secondary growth of the main stem into several "daughter stems" (Theron *et al.*, 1968). From data on the utilization of the vegetation by sheep it is apparent that grasses are most palatable in spring and summer, and that shrub browse is used in autumn and winter (Louw, 1968). Fire as a management tool is used by farmers in rugged mountainous habitats, resulting in the removal of unpalatable, invasive, woody species and the encouragement of young palatable growth. Generally the arid plains vegetation does not burn because of the meager and widely spread fuel reserves.

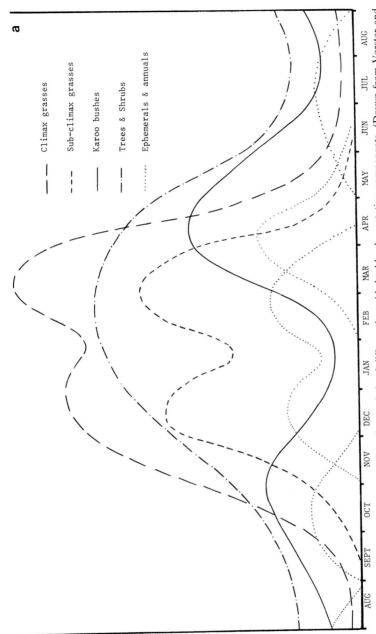

Figure 10. Average growth cycles and flowering periods of different karroid shrubland vegetation components. (Drawn from Vorster and Roux, 1983.) (a) Average growth cycles. (b) Average flowering activity.

RELATIVE GROWTH ACTIVITY

Climax grasses

Sub-climax grasses

Karoo bushes

Trees & Shrubs

Ephemerals & annuals

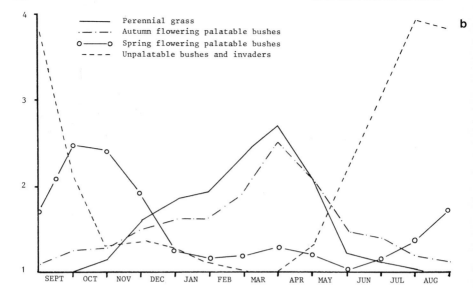

Figure 10. (*Continued*)

Little is published on the utilization of the karroid shrublands by indigenous mammals. The karroid shrublands once supported a vast spectrum of herbivores (Puzo, 1978) each with their own grazing habits and preferences, but all to a certain degree dependent on the presence of natural surface waters (Shaw, 1875; Acocks, 1955, 1976; Talbot, 1961; Downing, 1978). These great herds migrated naturally from the center and south to the north and west, following the rains and green pastures (Talbot, 1961). As the large herds moved freely, they grazed the veld[2] evenly (Acocks, 1976). Regulating mechanisms were drought, disease, and predation. Destruction of the game and their subsequent rapid decline in numbers occurred during the latter part of the 19th century as a result of the popular belief that they competed with domestic stock. The present-day ratio of domestic grazers to browsers is higher than that which occurred with the indigenous herbivores. This has resulted in the destruction and conversion of 52,000 km[2] of dense productive grassland into false eroded karroid shrubland (Acocks, 1953; Downing, 1978) and the continuing extension of the drier western shrubland types into the moister

---

[2] The term "veld" (pronounced "felt") means the countryside of natural vegetation.

Plate 9. The Springbok (*Antidorcas marsupialis*) are mixed, generalist feeders that graze during summer and browse during winter.

eastern shrubland types (Plate 8). Roux and Vorster (1983) also report a change in the shape and size of these shrublands. This is especially noticeable in the Western and Central Karoo. Today the springbok (*Antidorcas marsupialis*) represents the single most important indigenous herbivore in the karroid shrublands of southern Africa (Plate 9). A. A. Gubb and R. Liversidge (personal communication) have some data from the Kalahari Thornveld, which was invaded by karroid shrubs, and the northeastern False Upper Karoo Veld Type that show that springbok are extremely adaptable and utilize what is most readily available irrespective of the habitat. These small antelope are generalist feeders using a wide variety of species. They are fairly nonselective (unlike their domestic counterparts) but are mainly grazers during summer and browsers during winter. Before the onset of farming with domestic animals, game of the Central and Southern Karoo migrated freely into the Western Karoo winter rainfall area with its better climate and covering of winter annuals, thus practicing summer and winter habitat selection. This was especially noticeable during times of drought stress (Cronwright-Schreiner, 1925).

Although there is competition between springbok and sheep (Liversidge, 1972), this is somewhat reduced because springbok eat a high diversity of species (Gubb and Liversidge, 1981). As with sheep, springbok are largely grazers during summer and browsers during winter. Thus vegetation that is in a poor, degraded state, with its subsequent lowered species diversity, could be expected to lead to an increase in competition between springbok and sheep. An economic alternative to domestic live-stock production in these semiarid shrubland areas has not yet been found (Downing, 1978). Game, or mixed game and domestic stock ranching, has yet to be sufficiently scientifically and economically explored as an impor-tant food and protein resource (Puzo, 1978).

Concerning allelopathic tendencies, data of Squires and Trollope (1979) indicate that the unpalatable species *Chrysocoma tenuifolia* inhibits grass and forb growth in its immediate vicinity. Apparently the allelopathic substance accumulates on the leaves during winter and is washed off with the spring rains to coincide with the stage of maximum growth and germination of the grasses and forbs. In some areas, particularly on the eastern fringes of the Karoo, where there is a tendency for shrub en-croachment into degraded grassland, this species is one of the most ag-gressive invaders, especially on sandy-loam soils.

Some Karoo plants are known to be extremely poisonous, for example, *Geigeria africana* (Nursey, 1970).[3] In parts of the Karoo, stock losses over the last 100 years have been fairly severe as a result of the increase of *Geigeria* in overgrazed range. However, with good management it is possible to avoid stock losses.

Other problem plants are nonindigenous, invasive species (Stirton, 1978), notably *Opuntia imbricata* (Plate 10), *O. aurantiaca,* and *O. ficus-indica* (Plate 11). Many of the exotic problem plants were initially introduced as fodder plants to breach droughts (Roux *et al.,* 1981), for example, *Atriplex* spp., *Opuntia* spp., and *Prosopis* spp. Perhaps the most problematic plant today is *Prosopis glandulosa* (Plate 12), a South Amer-ican legume that has in the past been extensively planted for use of its palatable and nutritious pods (van der Merwe, 1978). Today there is evidence to suggest that this species is capable of converting much productive land into unproductive thicket (Woods, 1977a,b). In addition *Nicotiana glauca* is a problem along dry stream courses. With the degrada-tion of the surrounding vegetation, the environment is suited to invasion by these exotics (see Fig. 8). Biological control has been successful to a considerable degree (Annecke and Neser, 1977; Annecke and Moran, 1978; Moran, 1980), especially in the dry southeast (Annecke *et al.,* 1969).

---

[3] Other known examples of plants that have resulted in stock poisoning are *Urginea* spp., *Cotyledon* spp., *Senecio* spp., *Moraea* spp., *Tribulus terrestris, Kalanchoë* spp., and *Tyleco-don* spp. (Vorster and Roux, 1983).

Plate 10. *Opuntia imbricata* (Haw.) DC.

Plate 11. *Opuntia ficus-indica* (L.) Mill.

Plate 12. *Prosopis glandulosa* Torrey.

Periodic outbreaks of the Karoo caterpillar (*Loxostege frustalis*), the brown locust (*Locustana pardalina*), and termites (*Hototermes mossambicus, Microhodotermes viator,* and *Trinervitermes trinervoides*) often result in large areas being reduced to bare soil and stubble. The Karoo caterpillar outbreaks are due to the encroachment of the host plants, karroid shrubs, especially *Pentzia* spp. (Möhr, 1983). Termites are not the primary cause of veld deterioration and are seldom, if ever, a problem on well-managed farms.

VIII. Conservation

In South Africa, shrublands occupy 339,700 km², and only 552 km² fall into permanently conserved areas in the form of National Parks and Provincial Nature Reserves (Edwards, 1974; Huntley, 1978). Of this minimal amount, 428 km² represent "false" karroid shrublands, which were formerly grasslands and savannas and only recently invaded by dwarf shrubland elements (Acocks, 1953, in Huntley, 1978). Of the 21 shrubland veld types recognized by Acocks (1953) only 9 have permanent conservation areas present in them, none of which is considered adequate in terms of extent, diversity, and ecological viability (Edwards, 1974; Huntley, 1978). A number of Karoo species are either extinct or endangered (Hall *et al.*, 1980).

Figures for the rate of karroid shrubland expansion into the grasslands of the east vary from 1 to 4 km per year, which is alarming. The most worrying factor is undoubtedly that the technology to prevent this desertification is available, for example, by practicing better range management (Acocks, 1966) or by implementing radical range improvement schemes using such species as *Osteospermum sinuatum* (Joubert and van Breda, 1976), yet there is little effective implementation by the authorities. Currently the Karoo areas are suffering one of the worst droughts in recorded history. Because major change occurs when overutilization of the vegetation coincides with a drought, the future for the South African dwarf shrublands is bleak.

Acknowledgments

Our thanks to Richard Cowling for helpful, critical comments on the draft. We also thank the South African Council for Scientific and Industrial Research (E.J.M.) for partial financial support and the Botanical Research Institute, Department of Agriculture, and McGregor Museum, Kimberley, for supplying a number of the photographs.

References

Acocks, J. P. H. (1953). Veld types of South Africa. *Mem. Bot. Surv. S. Afr.* **28**, 1–192.
Acocks, J. P. H. (1955). Agriculture in relation to a changing vegetation. *S. Afr. J. Sci.* **49**(3–4), 155–164.
Acocks, J. P. H. (1966). Non-selective grazing as a means of veld reclamation. *Proc.— Grassl. Soc. South. Afr.* **1**, 33–39.
Acocks, J. P. H. (1976). The invasion came from the north. *Afr. Wildl.* **30**(3), 17–23.
Adamson, R. S. (1938). "The Vegetation of South Africa." British Empire Vegetation Committee, London.
Annecke, D. P., and Moran, V. C. (1978). Critical review of biological pest control in South Africa. 2. The prickly pear, *Opuntia ficus–indica* (L.) Miller. *J. Entomol. Soc. South. Afr.* **41**(2), 161–188.
Annecke, D. P., and Neser, S. (1977). On the biological control of some Cape pest plants. *Proc. Natl. Weeds Conf. S. Afr., 2nd, 1977*, pp. 303–319.
Annecke, D. P., Karny, M., and Burger, W. A. (1969). Improved biological control of the

prickly pear, *Opuntia megacantha* Salin-Dyck, in South Africa through the use of insecticide. *Phytophylactica* **1**, 9–13.

Anonymous (1951). "Report on the Desert Encroachment Committee." Government Printer, Pretoria.

Anonymous (1978). A world plan of action to combat the spread of deserts. UNEP. *SACCAP Action News* **4**(1), 21–24.

Axelrod, D. I., and Raven, P. H. (1978). Late Cretaceous and Tertiary vegetation history of Africa. In "Biogeography and Ecology of Southern Africa" (M. J. A. Werger, ed.), pp. 77–130. Junk, The Hague.

Bosch, O. J. H. (1983). "Plant Growth and Utilization Processes in the Karoo Biome," Karoo Biome Proj. Workshop, University of the Orange Free State, Bloemfontein (unpublished).

Boucher, C., and Moll, E. J. (1981). South African Mediterranean shrublands. *In* "Mediterranean-Type Shrublands: Ecosystems of the World" (F. di Castri, D. W. Goodall, and R. L. Specht, eds.), Vol. 11, pp. 233–248. Elsevier, Amsterdam.

Burchell, W. S. (1822–1824). "Travels in the Interior of Southern Africa," 2 vols. Paternoster Row, London.

Buttner, E. E. (1961–1964). Food value of some Karoo shrubs. *Merino Breeders J.* **23**(3), **23**(4), **25**(1), **25**(3), **26**(1), **26**(2): Short notes on selected species.

Buttner, E. E. (1965). Feeding value of salt bushes. *Merino Breeders J.* **27**(3), 17–19.

Campbell, B. M., Cowling, R. M., Bond, W., and Kruger, F. J. (1981). "Structural Characterization of Vegetation in the Fynbos Biome," S. Afr. Nat. Sci. Programmes Rep. No. 52, C.S.I.R., Pretoria.

Cattrick, A. (1957). "Spoor of Blood." H. Timmins, Cape Town.

Compton, R. H. (1929). The vegetation of the Karoo. *J. Bot. Soc. S. Afr.* **15**, 13–21.

Cowling, R. M. (1983). Vegetation studies—The Humansdorp region of the Fynbos biome. Ph. D. Thesis, University of Cape Town (unpublished).

Cronwright-Schreiner, S. C. (1925). "The Migratory Springbucks of South Africa." T. Fisher Unwin Ltd., London.

de Klerk, J. C. (1947). Weivelde van die suidelike Vrystaat 'n eeu gelede en vandag. *Boerd. S. Afr.* 347–354.

Downing, B. H. (1978). Environmental consequences of agricultural expansion in South Africa since 1850. *S. Afr. J. Sci.* **74**, 420–422.

Edwards, D. (1974). Survey to determine the adequacy of existing conserved areas in relation to vegetation types. A preliminary report. *Koedoe* **17**, 2–37.

Goldblatt, P. (1978). An analysis of the flora of southern Africa: Its characteristics, relationships and origins. *Ann. Mo. Bot. Gard.* **65**, 369–436.

Gubb, A. A., and Liversidge, R. (1981). "Vegetation Availability and Its Use by Springbok." McGregor Museum, Kimberley (unpublished data).

Hall, A. V., de Winter, M., de Winter, B., and van Oosterhout, S. A. M. (1980). "Threatened Plants of Southern Africa," S. Afr. Nat. Sci. Programmes Rep. No. 45.

Hamilton, G. N. G., and Cooke, H. B. S. (1960). "Geology for South African Students." Central News Agency, South Africa.

Henrici, M. (1935). Fodder plants of the Broken Veld. *Sci. Bull.—S. Afr., Dep. Agric. Tech. Serv.* **142**.

Henrici, M. (1939). Germination of Karoo bush seeds. Part II. *S. Afr. J. Sci.* **36**, 212–219.

Hugo, W. J. (1968). "The Small Stock Industry in South Africa." Government Printer, Pretoria.

Huntley, B. J. (1978). Ecosystem conservation in southern Africa. *In* "Biogeography and Ecology of Southern Africa" (M. J. A. Werger, ed.), pp. 1333–1384. Junk, The Hague.

Isaac, W. E., and Gershill, B. (1935). The organic matter content and carbon–nitrogen ratios of some semi-arid soils of the Cape Province. *Trans. R. Soc. S. Afr.* **23**, 245–254.

Jarman, N. G., and Bosch, O. (1973). The identification and mapping of extensive secondary invasive and degraded ecological types (test site D). *In* "To Assess the Value of Satellite Imagery in Resource Evaluation on a National Scale" (O. G. Malan, ed.), pp. 77–80. C.S.I.R., Pretoria.

Joubert, J. G. V., and van Breda, P. A. B. (1976). "Bitou (*Osteospermum sinuatum*) Has the Properties for the Medical Improvement of the Veld of the Little Karoo," Leafl. No. 56. Dept. of Agricultural Technical Services, Pretoria.

Levyns, M. R. (1950). The relations of the Cape and Karoo floras near Ladismith, Cape. *Trans. R. Soc. S. Afr.* **32**(3), 235–246.

Liversidge, R. (1972). Grasses grazed by springbok and sheep. *Proc.—Grassl. Soc. South. Afr.* **7**, 32–38.

Louw, G. N. (1969). The nutritive value of natural grazings in South Africa. *Proc. S. Afr. Soc. Anim. Prod.* **8**, 57–61.

Louw, G. N., Steenkamp, C. W. P., and Steenkamp, E. L. (1968a). Chemiese samestelling van die vernaamste plantspesies in die Noorsveld. *Teg. Meded.—S.-Afr., Dep. Landbou-Teg. Dienste* **77**.

Louw, G. N., Steenkamp, C. W. P., and Steenkamp, E. L. (1968b). Chemiese samestelling van die vernaamste plantspesies in die Westelike Bergkaroo en die distrik Fraserburg. *Teg. Meded.—S.-Afr., Dep. Landbou-Teg. Dienste* **78**.

Louw, G. N., Steenkamp, C. W. P., and Steenkamp, E. L. (1968c). Chemiese samestelling van die vernaamste plantspesies in die Dorre, Skyn-dorre, Skyn-sukkulente en Sentrale Bo Karoo. *Teg. Meded.—S.-Afr., Dep. Landbou-Teg. Dienste* **79**.

McNaughton, J. G. (1967). The Acocks–Howell grazing system. *Angora Goat Mohair J.* **9**(1), 19–25.

McNaughton, J. G. (1969). Symposium on non-selective grazing. *Angora Goat Mohair J.* **11**(1), 27–31.

Möhr, J. D. (1983). "The Karoo Caterpillar *Loxostege frustalis* Zeller (*Lepidoptera: Pyralidae*) of the Karoo Biome," Karoo Biome Proj. Workshop, University of the Orange Free State, Bloemfontein (unpublished).

Moll, E. J., and White, F. (1978). The Indian Ocean coastal belt. *In* "Biogeography and Ecology of Southern Africa" (M. J. A. Werger, ed.), pp. 561–598. Junk, The Hague.

Moran, V. C. (1980). Interactions between phytophagous insects and their *Opuntia* hosts. *Ecol. Entomol.* **5**, 153–164.

Nagel, J. F. (1956). Fog precipitation on Table Mountain. *Q. J. R. Meteorol. Soc.* **82**, 452–460.

Nagel, J. F. (1962). Fog precipitation measurements of Africa's southwest coast. *Notos* **11**, 51–60.

Nursey, W. R. E. (1970). Management of *Geigeria* infested veld in Griqualand West. *Proc.—Grassl. Soc. South. Afr.* **5**, 42–49.

Pratt, D. J., and Gwynne, M. D. (1977). "Rangeland Management and Ecology in East Africa." Hoddes & Stoughton, London.

Puzo, B. (1978). Patterns of man–land relations. *In* "Biogeography and Ecology of Southern Africa" (M. J. A. Werger, ed.), pp. 1051–1112. Junk, The Hague.

Roberts, B. R. (1969). Application of veld management in South Africa—An analysis of progress. *Proc.—Grassl. Soc. South. Afr.* **4**, 92–98.

Roux, P. W. (1967). Die onmiddellike uitwerking van intensiewe beweiding op gemengde Karooveld. *Handel.—Weidingsver. Suidlike Afr.* **2**, 83–90.

Roux, P. W. (1979). "Die veld as Voedingsbron vir die klein vee bedryf," Symp. oor die klein vee bedryf. Universiteit van die Oranje-Vrystaat, Bloemfontein.

Roux, P. W., and Vorster, M. (1983). "Vegetation Change in the Karoo," Karoo Biome Proj. Workshop, University of the Orange Free State, Bloemfontein (unpublished).

Roux, P. W., Vorster, M., Zeeman, P. J. L., and Wentzel, D. (1981). Stock production in the Karoo region. *Proc. — Grassl. Soc. South. Afr.* **16**, 29–35.

Rutherford, M. C. (1978). Primary production ecology in southern Africa. *In* "Biogeography and Ecology of Southern Africa" (M. J. A. Werger, ed.), pp. 621–660. Junk, The Hague.

Schulze, R. E., and McGee, O. S. (1978). Climatic indices and classifications in relation to the biogeography of southern Africa. *In* "Biogeography and Ecology of Southern Africa" (M. J. A. Werger, ed.), pp. 19–52. Junk, The Hague.

Scott, J. D., and van Breda, N. G. (1938). Preliminary studies of the root systems of *Pentzia incana* on the Worcester Veld Reserve. *S. Afr. J. Sci.* **35**, 280–287.

Shaw, J. (1875). On the changes going on in the vegetation of South Africa through the introduction of the merino sheep. *J. Linn. Soc. London* **14**, 202–208.

Skead, C. J. (1980). "Historical Mammal Incidence in the Cape Province," Vol. 1. Dept. of Nature & Environmental Conservation of the Provincial Administration of the Cape of Good Hope, Cape Town.

Squires, V. R., and Trollope, W. S. W. (1979). Allelopathy in the Karoo shrub *Chrysocoma tenuifolia. S. Afr. J. Sci.* **75**(2), 88–89.

Steenkamp, C. W. P., and Hayward, F. C. (1979). Chemiese samestelling van die vernaamste plantspesies in die suid-sentrale sektor van die Groot Eskarpement. *Teg. Meded. — S.-Afr., Dep. Landbou-Teg. Dienste* **149.**

Stirton, C. H., ed. (1978). "Plant Invaders." Dept. of Nature & Environmental Conservation, ABC Press (Pty) Ltd., Cape Town.

Talbot, W. J. (1961). Land utilization in the arid regions of Southern Africa. Part I. South Africa. *Arid Zone Res.* **17**, 299–338.

Theron, G. K., Schweickerdt, H. G., and van der Schijff, H. P. (1968). Anatomiese studie van *Plinthus karooicus* Verdoom. *Tydskr. Natuurwet.* **81**, 69–104.

Tyson, R. D. (1978). Rainfall changes over South Africa during the period of meterological record. *In* "Biogeography and Ecology of Southern Africa" (M. J. A. Werger, ed.), pp. 55–69. Junk, The Hague.

U. N. Conference on Desertification (1977). "Status of Desertification in the Hot Arid Regions: Climate Aridity Index Map." FAO Rome.

van der Merwe, F. J. (1978). Gee muskietboom regte plek. *Landbouweekblad,* September 22, pp. 44–45.

Van Rensburg, W. L. J. (1983). "Die plantoutekologie van die Karoo," Karoo Biome Proj. Workshop, University of the Orange Free State, Bloemfontein (unpublished).

Venter, H. J. T., and Theron, G. K. (1983). "Phytogeography and Phytosociology of the Karoo," Karoo Biome Proj. Workshop., University of the Orange Free State, Bloemfontein (unpublished).

von M. Harmse, H. J. (1978). Schematic soil map of southern Africa south of latitude 16°30′ S. *In* "Biogeography and Ecology of Southern Africa" (M. J. A. Werger, ed.), pp. 71–75. Junk, The Hague.

Vorster, M., and Roux, P. W. (1983). Veld of the Karoo areas. *Proc. — Grassl. Soc. South. Afr.* **18.**

Walter, H. (1979). "Vegetation of the Earth: And Ecological Systems of the Geobiosphere." 2nd ed. Springer-Verlag, New York.

Werger, M. J. A. (1973a). "Phytosociology of the Upper Orange River Valley, South Africa." V & R, Pretoria.

Werger, M. J. A. (1973b). Notes on the phytogeographical affinities of the sourthen Kalahari. *Bothalia* **11**, 177–180.

Werger, M. J. A. (1978). The Karoo–Namib region. *In* "Biogeography and Ecology of Southern Africa" (M. J. A. Werger, ed.), pp. 231–299. Junk, The Hague.

Werger, M. J. A., and Coetzee, B. J. (1978). The Sudano–Zambezian region. *In* "Biogeography and Ecology of Southern Africa" (M. J. A. Werger, ed.), pp. 301–462. Junk, The Hague.

White, F. (1965). The savanna-woodlands of the Zambezian and Sudanian domains. *Webbia* **19,** 651–681.

White, F. (1971). The taxonomic and ecological basis of chorology. *Mitt. Bot. Staatssamml. Muench.* **10,** 91–112.

Woods, D. (1977a). Mesquite—Tough enemy alien. *Veld & Flora* **63**(1), 3.

Woods, D. (1977b). Once more: Mesquite. *Veld & Flora* **63**(3), 7.

This chapter was accepted for publication in 1983.

7

Shrublands of the Indian Subcontinent

K. M. M. Dakshini

I. Introduction

Shrubs form an important component of the various vegetation types found throughout the Indian subcontinent. Although India has an otherwise rich flora, the number of shrubby taxa may not be more than one-fiftieth of the total species represented. However, shrubs are conspicuously present in almost all landforms in varying densities and diversities. India, in general, has a "woodland climate" and closed pure shrub formations are rare, although in transitional areas, because of topography or edaphic, biotic, or localized atmospheric influences, shrubs are common. In the majority of such habitats, "shrubwood" is most often the vegetational cover. Interestingly, shrubwood areas and human habitations have been closely related. Typical woodlands are not generally inhabited, whereas other areas are densely populated. Further, such a cohabitation has resulted, indirectly and unknowingly, in workable ecological relationships among the shrubs and the populace. The dependence on various shrubs for day-to-day basic requirements and social customs, especially in arid and semiarid and marginal forest areas in India, is rather interesting (Dakshini, 1972, 1985). In spite of their common occurrence and multiple uses, shrubs, have been ignored or considered a problem and their potentials (economic, social, and cultural) are yet to be evaluated.

II. Climate, Soil Types, and General Distributional Patterns of Shrubs

India covers a land area of approximately 3,287,000 km^2 and stretches between latitudes 8°04' and 37°06' North and longitudes 68°07' and 97°25' East (Fig. 1) [Food and Agriculture Organization (FAO), 1981]. Within this geographically complex domain, a variety of soil types and climatic conditions are found. Black soils, mountain soils, alluvial soils, red loam

Figure 1. Distribution of vegetation types on the Indian subcontinent. (Adapted from Champion and Seth, 1963).

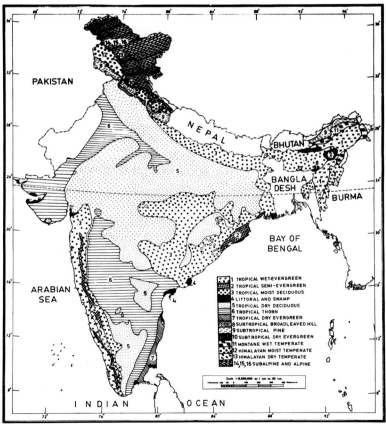

soils, mixed red and black soils, laterites, and gray and brown soils are some of the predominant soil types found in the country (Raychaudhuri *et al.*, 1963). Further, within each of these types, physical or chemical variations are often observed. The climatic characteristic of India is the "tropical monsoon type" with four seasons: the northeast and southwest monsoon seasons (December–March and June–September, respectively), the transitional hot weather (April–May), and the transitional period of the retreating southwest monsoon (October–November) (Spate and Learmonth, 1967). Total amount and distribution of rainfall are important for the growth and development of a range of diverse vegetational types. However, the Himalayas play an important role in controlling the direction of moisture-laden winds and vary the pattern (over 200 cm in Assam to about 12–25 cm in Rajasthan) of rainfall throughout the country (Krishnan, 1977). The yearly rainfall pattern of the peninsula generally has only one maximum, while the extra-peninsular and Indo-Gangetic plain have two maxima. In a large part of the country, the major peak of rainfall is attained during July. In the southeastern and northern parts of the country, this peak is noted in August, and during October southeast of Madras and during July in the northwestern regions and Kashmir. The second peak is recorded during the month of February. Additionally, the amount of precipitation varies with latitude, longitude, and altitude (Agroclimatic Atlas of India, 1978). Thus, the amount of rain received and the overall pattern of rainfall vary seasonally as well as spatially. Local climatic conditions, especially rainfall patterns are also affected by the presence of other mountainous ranges such as the Eastern and Western Ghats, Vindhyas and Satpuras, and the Aravallis. Topographic aspect and wind velocity further influence variations in climatic regimes. Interestingly, the quantity and pattern of rainfall illustrate a close correspondence with the vegetation types represented throughout the length and breadth of the country (Champion and Seth, 1963).

The optimum and characteristic vegetation of this country is thus represented by "tropical evergreen forest," which is a multitiered vegetational stand with broad-leaved evergreen trees (Champion and Seth, 1963; Puri *et al.*, 1983). In this type, the canopy is dense and closed, and the perennial ground cover is very scanty, and though shrubs are present (sparse in the southern counterpart), they do not form a dense cover. However, with gradual desiccation due to a general reduction in precipitation, the height and density of the trees as well as the number of tiers of vegetation decrease, and the canopy opens up with the consequent increase in the perennial plant ground cover (especially shrubs). A relatively poor representation of shrubs in semievergreen types as compared with the tropical thorn forest type substantiates such a reciprocal relationship between the type of tree canopy and the pattern of shrub representation. Furthermore, as climatic stresses increase because of low temperature and high wind velocity at higher elevations, in addition to low rainfall, the tree canopy is opened up and shrubs form an important constituent of the vegetation of such areas. Thus, in the extrapeninsular region, the density of shrubs increases from east to west as well as with altitude. The varying climatic and topographic features combine to sustain diverse vegetation types (Fig. 1) ranging from typical tropical wet evergreen types to subalpine and alpine types. In Table I, data pertaining to location in the country, climatic, rock, and soil types, and general features of each of these vegetational types (Champion and Seth, 1963) are summarized.

Wherever climatic influence, especially rainfall, is not the stress-causing factor, biotic influences, like clearing of the forests, lopping, grazing, and edaphic degradation associated with erosion, control shrub appearance and multiplication. In recent years, therefore, the area covered by shrubs has increased even under types 1, 2, 9, etc. In such habitats, shrubs, on a large scale, represent deflected successional trend or secondary succession and more often lead to disclimaxes (Puri *et al.*, 1983).

III. Shrubs of Different Regions

Climate, especially rainfall pattern, seems to be the most important factor in maintaining the shrubby cover, although shrubs in general occupy different geological formations, soil types, and climatic regimes (Table I). These variables bring about not only regional differences in ecological and physiological conditions but the pattern of shrub occurrence as well. The difference in the shrubby tier in the southern and the northern counterparts of the tropical evergreen type (type 1, Table I) can be explained on this basis. Further, using a similar argument, the existence of various shrubby taxa within different vegetation complexes in the country can be visualized.

In the following paragraphs, some of the characteristic shrubs represented in different regions of India (Champion and Seth, 1963; Collett, 1971; Cooke, 1958; Dakshini, 1972, 1985; Duthie, 1960; Gamble, 1957; Kachroo *et al.*, 1977; Puri *et al.*, 1983; Saldanha and Nicolson, 1976) are enumerated to illustrate not only the diversity of shrubby taxa but also their distributional pattern. Wherever a type is represented in both southern (peninsular) and northern (extrapeninsular and Indo-Gangetic plain) regions, the taxa are listed separately for those two counterparts under that type.

In general, the number of shrubs represented in northern regions is higher than that in southern regions. Further, in comparison to other types, shrubs abound under types 3, 5, 6, 7, and 10, as well as have higher diversity and densities. In types 1, 2, 9, and 11, both density and diversity of shrubs are lower. On the other hand, under types 13, 14, 15, and 16, though the diversity is poor, density may be highest among all other types. However, the typical shrub formations in India are represented under types 6, 10, 15, and 16 and cover about 7 million ha and are extensively distributed throughout the dry peninsular India and in Goa and states in the west (FAO, 1981).

The general ecological features shared by shrubs inhabiting different climatic zones can be summarized as follows.

Tropical: Evergreen; sparsely distributed; mostly in open areas or on the outer fringes of the forest or habitats under extensive biotic interference, both artificial and natural; 2–3 m high, with good vegetative growth. Flowering and seeding poor.

Subtropical: Diversity of shrubs highest; forming conspicuous vegetative cover of the landscape. Evergreen, semievergreen, xerophytic, thorny, clump-forming; 1–3 m high; but low stature types abound. Vegetative growth medium to slow; flowering and seeding and general regeneration good; very susceptible to fire; grazing helps regeneration.

Temperate: Evergreen, with thick leathery leaves, not commonly clump forming; 1–3 m high. Vegetative growth medium to good. Flowering and seeding profuse and regeneration average, but more under protection; withstand grazing and lopping.

Sub-alpine and alpine: Evergreen; low statured; denser when sheltered. Flowering good, seeding and regeneration relatively poor.

The sixteen main vegetation types with their principal shrub species are listed below.

Type 1.   Tropical wet evergreen
   South: *Actephila excelsa, Callicarpa lanata, Canthium dicoccum, Euphorbia epiphylloides, Evodea glabra, Flacourtia montana, Strobilanthus* spp.
   North: *Clausena indica, Croton joufra, Melastoma malabathricum, Osbeckia crinita, Schumannianthus virgatus, Psychotria dalzellii.*
Type 2.   Tropical semi evergreen
   South: *Buettneria andamanensis, Clinogyne grandis, Ixora malabarica.*
   North: *Adhatoda vasica, Antidesma diandrum, Buddleja asiatica, Clerodendrum nutans, Coffea benghalensis, Desmodium laxiflorum, Holarrhena antidysenterica, Indigofera pulchella, Leea edgeworthii, Wendlandia thyrsoidea, Woodfordia fruiticosa.*

Table I. Distribution and general features of physiognomy, climate, and soils of different vegetation types

		Climate				
		Mean annual temperature (°C)	Mean maximum temperature (°C)	Mean minimum temperature	Annual rainfall (mm)	Number of dry months
1.	Tropical wet evergreen	22–27	27–31	18.25	2000–6500	2–4
2.	Tropical semi evergreen	24–27	28–31	19–24	2000–2500	4–6
3.	Tropical moist deciduous	21–27	27–43	10–23	1000–2000	4–8
4.	Tropical littoral and swamp	26–28	28–32	21–25	450–3000	6–9
5.	Tropical dry deciduous	23–27	24–35	17–23	900–1300	5–8
6.	Tropical thorn	24–26	31–34	15–22	250–950	6–10
7.	Tropical dry evergreen	27–28	32–34	22–24	700–1300	4–6
8.	Montane subtropical broad-leaved	15–24	20–27	12.5–17	1000–6000	0–8
9.	Montane subtropical pine	15–24	19–23	11–15	1000–3000	2–7
10.	Montane subtropical dry evergreen	20–24	18–28	9–17	500–1000	3–7
11.	Montane wet temperate	11.5–18	14.5–21.5	8.5–15	1000–6000	0–5
12.	Montane Himalayan moist temperate	12–16	16–20	6–11.5	400–3000	2–5
13.	Montane Himalayan dry temperate	5–17	12–23	−1–11.5	95–800	4–11
14.	Montane subalpine	2–6	9–14	−5–2	50–700	6–12
15.	Montane moist alpine	2–7	8–14	−6–2	Mostly snowfall, total precipitation 200–2000	3–5
16.	Dry alpine scrub	2–7	8–13	−5––2	Mostly snowfall, total precipitation 30–400	4–9

Rock and soil type	Statewise distribution	General physiognomy
Crystalline gneiss, granite, tertiary sandstone. Red tropical soils.	Assam, Bengal, Kerala, Maharashtra, Mysore, Tamilnadu	Canopy 45 m or even higher; extremely dense; in southern counterpart, storys not distinct and with very poor undergrowth; northern region with distinct tiers of vegetation, and the conspicuous shrubs.
Crystalline or metamorphic. Tropical red soils or alluvial soils.	Assam, Goa, Maharashtra, Orissa, West Bengal	Canopy 25–35 m high, less dense than true evergreen type; shrubs poorly developed.
Coarse-grained sandstone. Sandy alluvial to red or black cotton soils.	Andamans, Bihar, Kerala, Madhya Pradesh, Madras, Mysore, Orissa, Uttar Pradesh	Irregular top story of deciduous trees, 40 m or more in height; shrubby evergreen or semievergreen undergrowth very well developed.
Gneiss. Sandy alluvium with high humus, silt or loamy clay.	Andamans, Andhra Pradesh, Gujarat, Kerala, Maharashtra, Mysore, Orissa, Tamilnadu	Canopy 10–25 m high; scattered small evergreen trees with fewer deciduous trees; numerous shrub species present and cover conspicuous areas.
Crystalline and sedimentary rocks. Alluvial, sandy, and lateritic clayey soils.	Andhra, Bihar, Jammu and Kashmir, Madhya Pradesh, Maharashtra, Mysore, Orissa, Punjab, Rajasthan, Uttar Pradesh	Canopy 13–25 m high, closed; second tier poorly defined; shrubby undergrowth usually well developed.
Laterite. Alluvial or eolian shallow, dry, or hard alkaline soils.	Andhra Pradesh, Gujarat, Haryana, Madhya Pradesh, Maharashtra, Mysore, Punjab, Rajasthan, Tamilnadu, Uttar Pradesh	Open low forest 6–9 m high, with thorny hardwood species predominating; small trees or shrubs (usually xerophytic) constitute the poorly defined lower story; shrub density high.
Mostly laterite. Predominantly sandy soils.	Andhra Pradesh, Tamilnadu	Low forest, 9–12 m high, consisting of mostly small coriaceous-leaved evergreens with a closed canopy; several species of spiny shrubs present; not much differentiation between top tree canopy and shrub canopy; areas under shrubs conspicuous.
Basaltic traps, gneisses, and granite. Brown earth soils and/or lateritic soils.	Kerala, Madhya Pradesh, Maharashtra, Mysore, Rajasthan, Tamilnadu	Open canopy with evergreen or dry deciduous species; middle tier of medium-sized trees generally recognizable; shrubby undergrowth.well developed.
Quartzite, mica schist, limestone. Sandy or reddish clay; podsol.	Arunachal Pradesh, Assam, Orissa, West Bengal	Generally pure association of pines; shrubs absent or very poorly developed.
Sedimentary rocks, sandstone, marls, and lime stone. Shallow and dry soils.	Assam, Punjab, Uttar Pradesh	Low 5–8 m scrub forest of small-leaved evergreens; thorny shrub species dominating.
Crystalline, mostly gneissic. Reddish or yellow clayey to sandy loam or black soils rich in humus.	Assam, Bengal, Jammu and Kashmir, Kerala, Mizoram, Punjab, Tamilnadu	Low 4–7 m to medium 10–25 m high; canopy closed; evergreen forest with poorly defined storys; underwood shrubby development only in open areas.
Gneisses and schists extending over quartzites, granites, limestone, and shales. In general, soils are loamy, sometimes rich in humus.	Assam, Bengal, Jammu and Kashmir, Punjab, Uttar Pradesh	Open forest 30–50 m high; well developed deciduous shrubby undergrowth.
Gneisses and schists extending over quartzites, granites, limestone, and shales. In general soils are loamy, sometimes rich in humus.	Himachal Pradesh, Jammu and Kashmir, Punjab, Uttar Pradesh	Open formations with conifers predominating; well-developed xerophytic shrubs, sometimes forming continuous cover.
Schists, quartzites, gneisses. Gravelly soils.	All along Himalayas from Kashmir to the eastern border of the north east frontier area, India	Dominated by small trees and or large shrubs with a few patches of conifers.
Schists, quartzites, gneisses. Gravelly soils.	All along the length of Himalayas	Low open canopy; shrubs common and conspicuous.
Schists, quartzites, gneisses. Gravelly sandy soils.	Along the length of Himalayas extending into Himachal Pradesh, Kashmir, Punjab, and Uttar Pradesh	Low open canopy; dense xerophytic shrubs very conspicuous.

Type 3.   Tropical moist deciduous

South: *Atlantia monophylla, Barleria cristata, Callicarpa lanata, Canthium gracilipes, Grewia tenax, Gymnosporia spinosa, Helicteres isora, Melanthesa rhamnoides, Murraya paniculata, Petalidium barlerioides, Pogostemon plectranthoides, Randia dumetorum.*

North: *Adhatoda vasica, Allophylus cobbe, Ardisia solanacea, Atylosia crassa, Berberis asiatica, Boehmeria platyphylla, Cipadessa fruiticosa, Colebrookia oppositifolia, Daedalacanthus nervosus, Desmodium floribundum, Embelia ribes, Fluggea obovata, Gardenia gummifera, Helicteres isora, Ixora coccinea, Moghania chappar, Randia longispina, Ruellia beddomei, Strobilanthus coloratus, Wendlandia thyrsoidea, Woodfordia fruiticosa.*

Type 4.   Littoral and swamp

Caesalpinia bonduc, Clerodendrum inerme, Colubrina asiatica, Desmodium umbellatum, Heritiera littoralis, Hibiscus tiliaceus, Ixora brunnensis, Sophora tomentosa.

Type 5.   Tropical dry deciduous

South: *Adhatoda vasica, Dodonaea viscosa, Euphorbia* spp., *Flacourtia indica, Gardenia resinifera, Grewia hirsuta, Gymnosporia spinosa, Helicteres isora, Holarrhena antidysenterica, Indigofera pulchella, Nyctanthes arbor-tristis, Osyris peltata, Securinega leucopyrus, Strobilanthes* spp., *Vitex negundo, Woodfordia fruiticosa, Zizyphus nummularia.*

North: *Adhatoda vasica, Balanites aegyptiaca, Barleria prionites, Calotropis procera, Capparis decidua, Carissa spinarum, Eranthemun purpurascens, Helicteres isora, Helinus lanceolatus, Holarrhena antidysenterica, Indigofera pulchella, Ixora arborea, Justicia betonica, Moghania chappar, M. semialata, Murraya koenigii, Nyctanthes arbor-tristis, Petalidium barlerioides, Sarcostemma acidum.*

Type 6.   Tropical thorn

South: *Barleria buxifolia, Canthium dicoccum, Carissa spinarum, Dichrostachys cinerea, Euphorbia tirucalli, Flacourtia indica, Gardenia gummifera, Grewia tiliaefolia, Gymnosporia montana, Mimosa hamata, Opuntia dillenii, Randia dumetorum, Securinega leucopyrus, Zizyphus mauritiana.*

North: *Arthrocnemum indicum, Balanites aegyptiaca, Barleria prionites, Calligonum polygonoides, Calotropis procera, Capparis decidua, C. sepiaria, Crotalaria burhia, Euphorbia neriifolia, Fagonia cretica, Grewia tenax, Limonia acidissima, Hesperethusa crenulata, Indigofera argentea, Mimosa rubicaulis, Salsola* spp., *Sarcostemma parviflora, Suaeda* spp., *Zizyphus nummularia.*

Type 7.   Tropical dry evergreen
Dodonaea viscosa, Flacourtia montana, Randia dumetorum.

Type 8.   Subtropical broad-leaved
South: *Canthium dicoccum, Capparis grandiflora, Gaultheria fragrantissima, Maytenus emarginata, Memecylon edule, Pavetta indica, Scutia indica, Zizyphus rugosa.*

North: *Aechmanthera tomentosa, Boehmeria rugulosa, Cudrania javanensis, Daphne cannabina, Debregeasia velutina, Eurya japonica, Flacourtia indica, Leea crispa, Morinda angustifolia, Myrsine semiserrata, Phlogacanthus* spp., *Pittosporum humile, Psychotria dalzelli, Rubus* spp., *Viburnum* spp.

Type 9.   Subtropical pine
Aechmanthera tomentosa, Berberis lycium, Colebrookia oppositifolia, Dodonaea viscosa, Moghania chappar, Indigofera dosua, Inula cappa, Lespedza sericea, Myrsine africana, Rubus spp., *Viburnum cordifolium*

Type 10.   Subtropical dry evergreen
Adhatoda vasica, Dodonaea viscosa, Punica granatum.

Type 11.   Montane wet temperate
South   *Berberis tinctoria, Gaulheria fragrantissima, Hypericum mysorense, Mahonia nepalensis, Psychotria canarensis, Strobilanthus* spp., *Vaccinium leschenaultii.*

North: *Daphne cannabina, Rubus* spp., *Viburnum* spp.

Type 12.   Himalayan moist temperate
Berberis asiatica, Boenninghausenia albiflora, Buxus sempervirens, Daphne oleoides, Desmodium tiliaefolium, Deutzia corymbosa, Indigofera gerardiana, Leptodermis lanceolata, Lonicera angustifolia, Myrsine africana, Prinsepia utilis, Rubus ellipticus, Sarcococca pruniformis, Skimmia laureola, Spiraea parvifolia, Strobilanthus dalhousianus, Viburnum cotinifolium, Wikstroemia canescens.

Type 13.   Himalayan dry temperate
Abelia triflora, Artemisia maritima, A. vulgaris, Astragalus spp., *Caragana gerardiana, Ephedra gerardiana, Juniperus communis, J. macropoda, J. wallichiana, Myricaria elegans, M. germanica, Plectranthus rugosus, Prunus jacquemontii, Rhododendron anthopogon, Ribes grossularia, Roylea elegans, Salix viminalis, Sophora mollis.*

Type 14.   Subalpine
Berberis uliana, Cassiope fastigiata, Cotoneaster integerrima, Juniperus wallichiana, J. recurva, Haloxylon thomsonii, Ribes glaciale, Rhododendron campanulatum, R. lepidotum, Salix caesia, Spiraea spp.

Type 15.   Moist alpine
Astragalus cicerfolius, Berberis zabeliana, Cotoneaster spp., *Gaultheria*

trichophylla, Lonicera parviflora, Mahonia nepalensis, Polygonum tortuosum, Rhododendron anthopogon, R. lepidotum, R. setosum, R. thomsonii, Salix spp., *Sophora alopecuroides, Spiraea* spp., *Syringa emodi, Viburnum nervosum.*

Type 16.   Dry alpine

Artemisia maritima, Caragana cuneata, Eurotia ceratoides, Juniperus communis, J. macropoda, J. wallichiana, Potentilla fruiticosa, Sophora moorcroftiana.

Variations of Main Vegetation Types

Besides these typical formations, there are various degradational stages of climax-type forests resulting from extensive biotic interference brought about by damage to vegetational cover, deterioration of topographies, soil structure, and microclimate conditions. Such formations are limited and occur only in areas with difficult climatic and edaphic conditions.

In India approximately 600 shrubs belonging to 45 families (angiosperms and gymnosperms) and 160 genera are represented. In general, the ratio of genera to species is low. *Euphorbia, Ixora, Indigofera, Rubus, Viburnum, Leptodermis, Salix, Spiraea* and *Juniperus*, however, are some of the larger shrub genera. Interestingly, most shrub genera inhabiting higher temperate and alpine regions have good species representation incontrast to those restricted to tropical and subtropical regions.

IV. Utilization and Potential

Diversity of habitats creates a condition of high adaptive and selective potentials in plants. In shrubs, this phenomenon is marked since on one hand they are perennial and on the other they have to occupy diverse niches in more ecologically dynamic habitats in the transitional zones. For example, *Adhatoda vasica, Carissa spinarum,* and *Desmodium tiliaefolium* are represented in vegetational types 2 to 8 and to survive they have to adjust to diverse conditions under these types. Adjustments include variation in densities, height, seed production, and, accumulation of secondary metabolites. For example, Nanda (1969) identified differences in weight of the pulp and titratable acid number (TAN) in *Zizyphus nummularia* plants collected from sandy and rocky habitats under semiarid environments. Dakshini and Sabina (1981) have shown the modifications in the life cycle strategies in *Pluchea lanceolata* inhabiting diverse habitats. Interestingly, because of such modifications in the responses of plants, humans dependent on the shrubs around them change their pattern of usage of the same plant in different areas. Thus, in regions with vegetation types 2 and 3, *Adhatoda vasica* leaves are used for poultice, fomentation of swellings, and for ripening the fruits, but in regions 6, 7, and 8, this plant is used for fuel purposes and its leaves for curing the cough and even as a browse for animals. There are no scientific data to explain these variations in usages but such instances of diverse uses of the same plant species are rather common in India.

In the predominantly pastoral life of societies in India, a social structure has evolved whereby dependence of human beings on the vegetational cover, especially the perennial plants—shrubs and trees—is traditional and unique. In Table II some of the important shrub species from different

Table II. Uses of shrub species in India

Species	Plant part used	Remarks
1. Edible		
Acacia concinna	Tender leaves	Acidic leaves used for making chutney
Antidesma diandrum	Fruit	Acidic purple pisiform fruit
Ardisia griffithii	Flowers	Eaten cooked, sweet in taste
A. solanacea	Leaves	Young fleshy leaves eaten as salad
Atlantia monophylla	Fruit	Lime-sized fruits are pickled
Berberis asiatica	Berries	As dried berries
Calligonum polygonoides	Flowers	Eaten cooked or made into bread
Canthium parviflorum	Leaves, fruit	Eaten in curries, sweetish, yellow fruits
Capparis decidua	Flowers, buds, berries	As vegetable or pickle. Ripe red berries edible raw
C. spinosa	Leaves, buds	Eaten as greens, buds as condiments
Carissa congesta	Berries	Purple black, sweet in taste and eaten raw
Cissus repens	Shoots, leaves	Young fleshy shoots and leaves, acidic in taste, are eaten raw or cooked
Crataegus oxycantha	Fruit	Acidic fruits made into preserves
Cudrania javanensis	Fruit, leaves	Leaves for making chutney
Debregeasia hypoleuca	Fruit	Yellow, sweetish pulp taken raw
Embelia nagushia	Leaves, shoots	Tender shoots and leaves eaten cooked
Flacourtia indica	Berries	Consumed raw, good for making jellies, jams, and tarts
Flemingia macrophylla	Pods	As vegetable
Gaultheria fragrantissima	Berries	Small black succulent, sweet pulp
Indigofera pulchella	Flowers	Pink flowers used as vegetable
Leea indica	Fruit and tender shoots	As vegetable
Lonicera angustifolia	Fruit	Raw or for jam

(continues)

Table II. (*Continued*)

Species	Plant part used	Remarks
Mahonia napalensis	Berries	Dark purple, subacidic in taste
Murraya koenigii	Leaves	Used to give flavor to curries
Myrsine africana	Fruit	Red fruits are eaten
Pentatropis spiralis	Tubers	Sweet tubers are eaten raw or cooked
Periploca aphylla	Flower buds	Sweet in taste, eaten raw or cooked
Picrasma quassioides	Fruit	Ripe fruits are eaten
Prunus tomentosa	Fruit	Juicy pulp is edible
Randia dumetorum	Fruit	Fresh ripe fruit roasted and eaten
Rubus spp.	Berries	One of the excellent wild edible fruits, eaten raw or made into preserves
Rodetia amherstiana	Young shoots, berries	Fried and eaten, bright red berries are edible
Skimmia laureola	Leaves	In curries as flavoring agent
Vaccinium serratum	Flowers	Sour in taste, for curries
Viburnum corylifolium	Berries	Eaten raw or pickled
Woodfordia fruiticosa	Flowers	In preparing cool drinks
Zizyphus nummularia	Fruit	Eaten raw or powdered and eaten with some sugar

2. Livestock fodder

Abelia trifolia
Aerva javanica
Alhagi camelorum
A. pseudo-alhagi
Atriplex nummularia
Calligonum polygonoides
Calotropis procera
Calycarpa macrophylla
Cotoneaster vulgaris
Colebrookia oppositifolia
Crotalaria burhia
C. medicagenia
Desmodium pulchellum
Ephedra vulgaris
Farsetia jacquemontii
Flemingia congesta
Flacourtia ramontchii
F. sepiaria

Grewia tiliaefolia
Helicteres isora
Hibiscus sabdariffa
Holarrhena antidysenterica
Indigofera gerardiana
Ixora parviflora
Kochia indica
Maytenus emarginata
Mimosa hamata
Nyctanthus arbor-tristis
Opuntia dillenii
O. elatior
Randia dumetorum
Rhus mysorensis
Sericostoma pauciflorum
Tephrosia purpurea
Thespesia lampas
Wendlandia exerta
Woodfordia fruiticosa

3. Scarcity and famine food
Allophylus cobbe
Aloe vera
Alysicarpus rugosus

Table II.   (*Continued*)

Antidesma diandrum	*Murraya koenigii*
Asystasia coromandeliana	*Opuntia dillenii*
Buettneria herbacea	*O. elatior*
Calligonum polygonoides	*Randia uliginosa*
Canthium dicoccum	*Rhus mysorensis*
Carissa carandus	*Rivea hypocrateriformis*
C. spinarum	*Securinega leucopyrus*
Cassia sophera	*Sesbania aegyptiaca*
Embelia robusta	*Tephrosia purpurea*
Grewia tiliaefolia	*Zizyphus nummularia*
Indigofera cordifolia	
Leea macrophylla	
Leptadenia reticulata	

Species	Plant part used	Remarks
4. Medicinal		
Adhatoda vasica	Leaves, root	Coughs, chronic bronchitis, asthma
Agave americana	Leaves, root	Juice of leaves and root have resolvent and alterative properties; syphilis, conjuctivitis, gonorrhea
Andrographis paniculata	Leaves	For irregular stools; loss of appetite; febrifuge; tonic alternative and anthelmintic
Artemisia vulgaris	Plant	Tonic; febrifuge; nervous and spasmodic affections; in liver diseases
Astragalus hamosus	Pods, plant	Emollient and demulcent; laxative; headaches; also used in catarrhal affections
Balanites aegyptiaca	Seeds, fruits, bark, plant	In gout and colic; as an anthelmintic and purgative; juice as fish poison; for dermatosis; urinary diseases and for rejuvenation
B. roxburghii	Seeds, fruits, bark, leaves	Unripe fruit and bark as anthelmintic; expectorant; purgative
Baliospermum indicum	Seeds, leaves	Purgative; asthma
Barleria cristata	Seeds, root, leaves	Antidote for snake bite; swellings, cough
B. prionites	Leaves, stem, root	Catarrhal affections; boils; toothache; paste of leaves in hot poultices; stem bark to cure stiffness of limbs
Berberis lycium	Root	Febrifuge; chronic ophthalmia; as general appetizer
Caesalpinia bonduc	Seeds	As a tonic; ash for application to ulcers; gum boils; in intermittent fever
Callicarpa arborea	Bark	For cutaneous diseases
C. macrophylla	Leaves	Heated leaves applied to rheumatic joints

(*continues*)

Table II.   (*Continued*)

Species	Plant part used	Remarks
Calotropis gigantea	Bark, flowers	Alterative; tonic; diaphoretic; dysentery; diarrhea; chronic rheumatism
C. procera	Bark, leaves roots	Dysentery; rheumatism; for toothache
Capparis decidua	Leaves, bark, fruit, root	Boils and swelling; diaphoretic; cough; asthma cardiac troubles; rheumatism
Cassia alata	Leaves, root	For skin diseases
Coriaria nepalensis	Leaves	Used to adulterate senna; act as powerful poison
Cressa cretica	Leaves, root, seeds	Tonic; aphrodisiac; expectorant and as antibilious agent
Crotalaria burhia	Branches, leaves	Coolant
C. medicagenia	Plant	Tonic
Croton joufra	Seeds, leaves, root, bark	Leaves applied as poultice to sprains; seeds purgative; bark for chronic enlargements of liver
Daphne oleoides	Root, berries	Purgative; berries are eaten to induce nausea
Desmodium tiliaefolium	Root	Carminative; tonic and diuretic used in bilious complaints
Dichrostachys cinerea	Root, stem	Astringent; in rheumatism; for diseases of the eye
Dodonaea viscosa	Leaves, stem, bark	Febrifuge; purgative; leaves for fomentations; wood carminative
Embelia ribes	Seeds	Anthelmintic; alterative and tonic; for removing tapeworms
Ephedra gerardiana	Stem, root	For heart ailments
Euphorbia caducifolia	Young branches	Smoke from burning of young twigs inhaled to cure asthma
Flacourtia sepiaria	Root, bark, leaves	For snake bite; liniment in gout and rhueumatism
Flemingia macrophylla	Pods	Anthelmintic; for external application to ulcers and swellings
Gardenia gummifera	Gum	For cleaning foul ulcers; antispasmodic; carminative antiseptic
Grewia tenax	Wood, stem	Cough; pain in the sides
Haloxylon recurvum	Plant	Intestinal ulcers
Helicteres isora	Fruit	For stomach complaints
Holarrhena antidysenterica	Bark of stem and root, seeds	Antidysenteric; seed oil as astringent; febrifuge and anthelmintic
Indigofera pulchella	Root	Decoction used for cough; powder for pain in chest
I. tinctoria	Leaves, stem	Dried powder sprinkled over foul ulcers for cleaning
Jasminum multiflorum	Leaves, roots	Skin diseases
Kochia indica	Plant	Cardiac stimulant
Laportia crenulata	Seeds	Ash used for application on wounds

Table II. (*Continued*)

Species	Plant part used	Remarks
Lepidagathis cristata	Plant	As tonic; to cure itchy affections of skin
Mimosa rubicaulis	Leaves, fruit, root	Applied to burns; for piles and powdered root for weakness
Myrsine africana	Fruit	Powerful cathartic; dropsy, collic; laxative
Nardostachys jatamansi	Root	Antispasmodic, epilepsy
Nyctanthes arbor-tristis	Leaves	Fresh juice with honey for fever; rheumatism; diabetes
Opuntia elatior	Fruits, leaves	Antibiotic; for whooping cough; as purgative; for ophthalmic ailments
Pavetta indica	Root	Diuretic given in dropsy; purgative
Prinsepia utilis	Young twigs, seeds	Pain in joints; rheumatism
Punica granatum	Root, bark	Astringent
Randia dumetorum	Fruit	Fish poison
Rhododendron anthopogon	Leaves	Aromatic, having stimulant properties; headache and nausea
R. campanulatum	Leaves, dried twigs	Mixed with tobacco and used as snuff for cold and hemicrania; dried twigs used for chronic fevers
Roylea elegans	Leaves	Bitter tonic and febrifuge
Sarcostemma acidum	Stem, root, plant	Alterative; cooling agent
Securinega leucopyrus	Leaves, plant	To destroy worms in sores; fish poison
Sesbania aegyptiaca	Seeds	Stimulant
Strobilanthus auriculatus	Leaves	Pounded leaves are rubbed on the body during cold stage of intermittent fever
Tephrosia purpurea	Leaves, seeds	Astringent; tonic
Vitex negundo	Root, fruit	Diuretic; skin diseases
Withania somnifera	Seeds	Aphrodisiac and diuretic
Woodfordia fruiticosa	Flowers	Astringent; tonic in affection of mucous membrane and bilious complaints
Zizyphus nummularia	Leaves, fruits, root	Scabies; boils; old wounds and ulcers; bilious affections

5. Fuel (as a major use)

Adhatoda vasica	*Grewia tenax*
Aerva persica	*Haloxylon recurvum*
Balanites aegyptiaca	*Leptadenia pyrotechnica*
Calotropis procera	*Nyctanthes arbor-tristis*
Capparis decidua	*Rhododendron campanulatum*
Carissa spinarum	*Randia dumetorum*
Caragana cuneata	*Zizyphus nummularia*
Euphorbia neriifolia	

(*continues*)

Table II. *(Continued)*

Species	Remarks
6. Fibers	
Abutilon indicum	Fiber from stem
Agave sisalana	Fiber from leaves
Boehmeria macrophylla	Fiber from stem
B. nivea	Cordage fiber
Calotropis gigantea	Stem fiber usually for making ropes
C. procera	Cordage and ropes from stem fiber, floss from seeds for stuffing pillows and for textile
Crotalaria burhia	Fiber from stem
Daphne oleoides	Fiber from stem, for making paper
Dabregeasia valutina	Fiber from stem
Desmodium tiliaefolium	Bark fiber for making paper
Laportea crenulata	Fiber for cordage and manufacture of coarse cloth by Assam tribes
Leptadenia pyrotechnica	Fiber from stem for rope making
Opuntia elatior	A coarse fiber from the stem
Schumannianthus virgatus	Stem fiber used for making hats, table mats, straw braid; also used in paper making
Sida cordifolia	Yield excellent fiber
Tephrosia falciformis	Fiber from stem
Villebrunea frutescens	Fiber from stem, cordage fiber
Vitex negundo	Fiber from stem
Wikstroemia virgata	Fiber from stem, for making paper
7. Gums and resins	
Calotropis gigantea	*Jatropha curcas*
C. procera	*Punica granatum*
Cryptostegia grandiflora	*Sesbania aculeata*
8. Miscellaneous	
Binders of shifting sand dunes:	*Calligonum polygonoides, Crotalaria burhia, Zizyphus nummularia*
Utilization of low-lying water-logged areas:	*Leea macrophylla, Randia uliginosa*
Thatching purposes:	*Calotropis gigantia, C. procera, Capparis decidua, C. spinosa, Leptadenia pyrotechnica, Salix tetrasperma*
Hedge plants:	*Calligonum polygonoides, Euphorbia* spp., *Leptadenia pyrotechnica, Mimosa rubicaulis, Ribs grossularia, Rubus lasiocarpus, Zizyphus nummularia*
Agricultural implements:	*Salix daphnoides, Randia dumetorum*
Religious ceremonies:	*Barleria prionites, Boswellia serrata, Capparis decidua, Clerodendrum viscosum, Commiphora wightii, Daphne oleoides, Jasminum multiflorum, J. humile, Nyctanthes arbor-tristis, Spiraea bella*
Gunpowder charcoal:	*Colebrookia oppositaefolia, Mimosa rubicaulis*
Cloth washing:	*Balanites aegyptiaca, Haloxylon recurvum, Suaeda maritima*
Boat, oars, etc.:	*Capparis decidua, Heritiera littoralis, Thespesia populnea*

parts of the country have been grouped according to their uses (Atkinson, 1980; Bhandari and Govil, 1978; Central Arid Zone Research Institute, 1972, 1974, 1976, 1979; Charak, 1975; Chopra et al., 1956; Dakshini, 1972, 1985; Gupta and Dutta, 1967; Kaul, 1970; Kirtikar and Basu, 1935; Sharma and Tiagi, 1979; Singh and Arora, 1978; Watt, 1971; Wealth of India, 1948–1976) with a view to high-lighting the significance of the potentials of some of the shrubs.

V. Problems and Prospects

Shrubs in India thus occupy diverse habitats, and their distribution extends from the highest mountains to seashores and deserts. Even where grasses do not succeed, shrubs survive successfully and sustain biota through their continuous and reliable productivities and nutritive qualities. Besides giving protection and sheltering of soil cover and their overall important role in ecosystem functioning in disturbed and degraded habitats, shrubs beautify the landscape. Paradoxically, in India the axe of unrbanization, industrialization, river-valley projects, road construction, agricultural development, and population pressures falls first on the shrubby cover and large-scale destruction of innumerable shrubs and shrub-woods has taken place since independence. Foresters have neglected shrubs, builders have hated them, and conservationists do not attach any significance to this important constituent of the vegetational cover. Increased mountaineering and trekking in the Himalayas along with other activities have caused a general massacre of shrubs and denudation of large areas, especially in remote high altitudes where regeneration is very poor. Plantation crops have been preferred over shrubs without understanding the ecology of the area and this has resulted in unmanageable social and economical problems. Further, with the predominantly pastoral nature of the country, shrubs have been the main source of firewood and fodder, especially for the people inhabiting regions along the forest margins and at high altitudes. However, with the enforcement of new settlements and colonization schemes and other developmental and recreational projects, this vital source of livelihood has become scarce and is affecting the general economy of the community.

In India, shifting cultivation is practiced in 12 states where some 2.7 million people are involved and the annual area under shifting cultivation is over 1 million ha. (FAO, 1981). The general effect of such cultivation is to replace the original vegetational stands by secondary forests dominated by diverse but productive shrubs. Earlier, under low population pressure and plenty of available land, the fallow periods were very long and hence the ecological damage to the substratum was minimal and productivity was maintained for a long time. However, at present because of rapid population growth, construction work, and activities related to development, available land areas have shrunk considerably, leading indirectly to a shortening of the fallow period. This has resulted in permanent damage to the substratum and disappearance of many economically important shrubs.

Another major problem that is also intricately related, although indirectly, to vegetation in general and shrubs in particular is the migration of workers from the villages to the urban areas for better job opportunities. Such a movement leaves behind the old or differentially infirm or invalid people who have to depend solely on nearby available shrubs and other undergrowth for fuel purposes. This brings about rapid disappearance of the plant cover and the consequent degradation of the habitat. The irreparable loss of the renewable resources, of both plants and soil, affects the economy of the villages. Yet another grave problem related to shrubwood disappearance is the threat to the existing life-style of various tribes inhabiting such regions. By and large, each tribe is a closed society with its own sociocultural life that has evolved with the natural surroundings. Religion, culture, ethics, food habits, treatment of ailments, and even folklore of these tribes are very intimately related to native plants (Jain, 1981). Many of these tribespeople use locally available plants or plant parts as treatments for fertility, birth control, diabetes, and hypertension. These societies do not welcome any outside interference and are very possessive of their unique and rich culture.

The foregoing account has shown how shrubs and shrublands are interrelated to the general sociocultural system. The diverse usage of shrubs, the pattern of life-style, and society are interwoven intricately and have evolved over the years. However, this dynamic phenomenon is generally not appreciated. The wide distribution and diversity of shrubs through the country exhibit the potential of a valuable renewable resource available for economic harnessing. The immediate need, as pointed out by Dakshini (1972), is to know the shrubs and the large potential they hold for human society in general. Since little is known about the patterns of distribution, regeneration potential, survival mechanisms, and economic usages of most of the shrubs represented in India, detailed investigations along these lines are urgently required as each of the shrub species found in this country has some degree of potential. However, because of their dominance in a region or wider distribution in several vegetation types, many species seem to be more ecologically successful and useful than others. Therefore, priority should be given to species such as those listed in Table III for assessment of potential.

Table III. List of regionwide selected shrub species

Species	Distributed in types	Species	Distributed in types
Melastoma malabathricum	1–2	*Balanites aegyptiaca*	5–7
Psychotria dalzellii	1–2	*Calotropis procera*	5–7
Schumannianthus virgatus	1–2	*Canthium dicoccum*	5–7
Leea edgeworthii	1–3	*Euphorbia nivulia*	5–7
Osbeckia crinita	1–3	*Flacourtia indica*	5–7
Thespesia lampas	1–4	*Gardenia resinifera*	5–7
Moghania bracteosa	1–7	*Grewia tenax*	5–7
Glycosmis pentaphylla	1–8	*Leptadenia pyrotechnica*	5–7
Strobilanthus atropurpureus	1–9	*Lycium europaeum*	
Clerodendrum viscosum	2–4	*Mimosa rubicaulis*	5–7
Wendlandia thyrsoidea	2–6	*Pavetta indica*	5–7
Woodfordia fruiticosa	2–7	*Scurinega leucopyrus*	5–7
Adhatoda vasica	2–8	*Tephrosia purpurea*	5–7
Carissa spinarum	2–8	*Vitex negundo*	5–7
Desmodium tiliaefolium	2–8	*Dodonaea viscosa*	5–8
Petalidium barlarioides	3–5	*Fagonia cretica*	5–8
Capparis decidua	3–7	*Ribes grossularia*	8–10
C. separia	3–7	*Roylea elegans*	8–10
Helicteres isora	3–7	*Rubus elipticus*	8–10
Pogostemon benghalensis	3–7	*R. lasiocarpus*	8–10
Randia dumetorum	3–7	*Salix angustifolia*	8–10
Nyctanthes arbor-tristis	4–5	*Spiraea parvifolia*	8–15
Strobilanthus dalhousianus	8–12	*Juniperus communis*	10–14
Berberis asiatica	9–10	*Lonicera angustifolia*	10–14
Deutzia corymbosa	10–12	*Mahonia nepalensis*	10–14
Cotoneaster acuminata	10–14		

Acknowledgments

I am most grateful to Shri S. K. Gupta and Miss E. Roshini Nayar for their help in preparing this manuscript.

References

Agroclimatic Atlas of India (1978). pp. 1–41. "Agroclimatic Atlas of India," India Meterol. Dep., Div. Agric. Meteorol., Pune, India.

Atkinson, E. T. (1980). "The Economic Botany of the Himalayas" (reprinted ed.). Cosmo Publications, New Delhi, India.

Bhandari, D. S., and Govil, H. N. (1978). Evaluation of fodder tree leaves for sheep and goat in semi-arid areas of Rajasthan. *J. Nucl. Agric. Biol.* **7**(3); 110–113.

Central Arid Zone Research Institute (1972). "Annual Report." CAZRI, Jodhpur, India.
Central Arid Zone Research Institute (1974). "Basic Resources of Bikaner District (Rajasthan)." CAZRI, Jodhpur, India.
Central Arid Zone Research Institute (1976). "Annual Report." CAZRI, Jodhpur, India.
Central Arid Zone Research Institute (1979). "25 Years of Arid Zone Research (1952–1977)." CAZRI, Jodhpur, India.
Champion, H. G., and Seth, S. K. (1963). "A Revised Survey of the Forest Types of India." Mem. F. R. I. Coll., Dehradun, India.
Charak (Maharishi) (1975). In "Charaksamhita " (J. D. Vidyalankar, ed.) Parts 1 and 2. Motilal Banarsidas (Delhi), India.
Chopra, R. N., Nayar, S. L., and Chopra, I. C. (1956). "Glossary of Indian Medicinal Plants." C. S. I. R., New Delhi.
Collett, H. (1971). "Flora Simlensis" (reprint ed.). Bishen Singh Mahendra Pal Singh, Dehradun, India.
Cooke, T. (1958). "The Flora of the Presidency of Bombay" (reprint ed.) 3 vols. Botanical Survey of India, Calcutta.
Dakshini, K. M. M. (1972). Indian subcontinent. In "Wildland Shrubs: Their Biology and Utilization" (C. M. McKell, J. P. Blaisdell, and J. R. Goodin, eds.), USDA For. Serv. Gen. Tech. Rep. INT-1, pp. 3–15. Utah State University, Logan.
Dakshini, K. M. M. (1985). Indian subcontinent. In "Plant Resources of Arid and Semiarid Lands" (J. R. Goodin and D. K. Northington, eds.), pp. 69–128. Academic Press, New York.
Dakshini, K. M. M., and Sabina, C. A. (1981). Ecological strategies of the weed *Pluchea lanceolata* (DC) C. B. Clarke (Asteraceae). Proc. Indian Natl. Sci. Acad. *Part, B* **47**(6); 907–911.
Duthie, J. F. (1960). "Flora of Upper Gangetic Plain and of the Adjacent Siwalick and Sub-Himalayan Tracts" (reprint ed.), 3 vols. Botanical Survey of India, Calcutta.
Food and Agriculture Organization (FAO) (1981). "Tropical Forest Resources Assessment Project: Forest Resources of Tropical Asia." FAO/UN, Rome.
Gamble, J. S. (1957). "Flora of the Presidency of Madras" (reprint ed.), 3 vols. Botanical Survey of India, Calcutta.
Gupta, R. K., and Dutta, B. K. (1967). Vernacular names of the useful plants of N. W. Indian arid regions. *J. Agric. Bot. Appl.* **14**, 401–453.
Jain, S. K. (1981). "Glimpses of Indian Ethnobotany." Oxford and IBH Pub. Co., New Delhi.
Kachroo, P., Sapru, B. L., and Kumar, U. (1977). "Flora of Ladakh: An Ecological and Taxonomical Appraisal." Bishen Singh Mahendra Pal Singh, Dehra Dun, India.
Kaul, R. N. (1970). "Afforestation in Arid Zones." Junk, The Hague.
Kirtikar, K. R., and Basu, B. D. (1935). "Indian Medicinal Plants," 4 vols. L. M. Basu, Allahabad, India.
Krishnan, A. (1977). A climatic analysis of the arid zone of north-western India. In "Desertification and Its Control" (P. L. Jaiswal, ed.), pp. 42–57. I.C.A.R., New Delhi, India.
Nanda, P. C. (1969). Inter-relationship of habitat to acid metabolism in *Zizyphus nummularia* (Burm. f.) W & A. *Ann. Arid Zone* **8**; 85–91.
Puri, G. S., Meher-Homji, V. M., Gupta, R. K., and Puri, S. (1983). "Indian Forest Ecology," Vol 1. Oxford and IBH Publ. Co., New Delhi, India.
Raychaudhuri, S. P., Aggarwal, R. R., Dutta-Biswas, N. R., Gupta, S. P., and Thomas, P. K. (1963). "Soils of India," I.C.A.R., New Delhi, India.
Saldanha, C. J., and Nicolson, D. H. (1976). "Flora of Hassan District. Karnataka, India." Amerind Publ. Co. Pvt. Ltd., New Delhi, India.

8

Shrublands of the USSR in Asia

Horst Paetzold

I. Introduction

The continent of Asia, situated between 50° and about 180° East, 75° North, and 10° South, occupies a greater area than any other continent. With the exception of the islands of Indonesia south of the equator, this continent consists of a compact land mass with high mountains (e.g., the Himalayas) and vast plains; it stretches from subtropical regions in Southeast Asia to the arctic zones of Siberia on the coast of the northern polar sea.

The huge area north of the high mountains is characterized by a harsh continental climate with long, cold winters and short but hot summers. This climate, with its severe conditions for human life and domestic animals, is the reason for the late settlement of these regions and for the low population density.

In this chapter, the regions of the USSR with shrub vegetation are of particular interest, that is, the vast arid plains of eastern Europe, the region north and east of the Caspian Sea, and the immense plains and southern mountains between the Aral Sea and the Mongolian steppes.

The zones of vegetation from north to south fall into the following broad divisions:

- Arctic zones   (tundra)
- Woody zones   (taiga)
- Steppe zones
- Desert zones
- High mountain zones

Agricultural utilization in the USSR, corresponding to these zones, is shown in Fig. 1.

In this general survey, shrublands receiving the greatest emphasis are semideserts and deserts, but some mention will also be made of the relevant features of steppes in order to give an all-around understanding of these regions. The arid regions of Southwest Asia and the Near East will be excluded, because they are dealt with by Dakshini (India), Le Houérou (North Africa), and Zhao and Liu (China) in other chapters.

Figure 1.   Zones of vegetation in USSR. (From Goldmanns Grosser Weltatlas, 1955.)

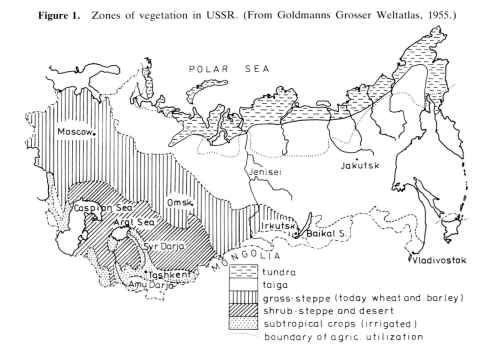

II. The Steppes of Eurasia

A. Climate and Vegetation

To the south of the woody zones (the boreal forests of Siberia) extends the vast steppe zone, which begins in the west on both sides of the Caspian Sea (and the mouth of the Volga), continues along the 50th parallel in an easterly direction, covering the Kazakh SSR and parts of southern Mongolia, and reaches far into the northern provinces of the People's Republic of China. It includes the area between 40° and 120° East and accounts for 156 million ha of the territory of the USSR (Weigand and Paetzold, 1978). The climate is characterized by cold winters and warm summers with average annual temperatures of 4–5°C in eastern Europe and 2–3°C in Siberia. Precipitation decreases from eastern Europe with a maximum of 250–420 mm annually in Kazakhstan, with a peak in summer. Nearly 40% of precipitation is snow. Rainfall is sufficient for the growth of grasses and herbs, but there is little water that is not consumed by the thick layers of roots. The lack of water in the subsoil explains the paucity of woody plants. Only beside riverbeds and on lower sites are there any woody species like *Amygdalus nana, Spiraea hypericifolia,* and *Caragana fintex* (Walter, 1968).

There is no clear boundary from north to south between woody vegetation and steppe. First there are mixed vegetation types: deciduous woods and meadow-steppes. The woods remain on the shallow soils (*Quercus* spp. in the northwest, *Betula* spp. in the northeast of this region), while the meadow-steppes occupy the fertile black soils (chernozem). These "woody steppes" have a loose canopy, so there is sufficient light for the development of grass vegetation below the trees.

Research work into the question of competition between woody plants (trees, shrubs) and grasses has been done in the past and present by many scientists. Long-term experiments in Russia have been the precondition for the future utilization of steppes in the Soviet Union and for the decision whether steppes should be plow up or managed for grazing, including the planting of trees and shrubs for shelter. Water competition seems to be the main limiting factor besides the wind. The typical vegetation of steppes with grasses and herbs needs less water per unit area of land than a woody (deciduous) vegetation. Only by periodically controlling the grass cover is it possible to grow trees and shrubs in the steppes of eastern Europe and Asia. This has been put into practice in recent decades in the USSR by planting shelter belts. The most adapted genera were *Quercus, Ulmus, Fraxinus,* and *Acer* as well as *Robinia pseudoacacia, Morus alba, Gleditschia triacanthus,* and *Caragana arborescens.*

Nevertheless, the aspects of the northern "woody steppes" (between the boreal woods and true steppes) are not comparable with the dry savannas of Africa. The savannas of western Africa, for example, represent a secondary vegetation, a fire-shrub climax under the influences of humans and domestic animals (Franke and Paetzold, 1986). The fire-resistant species survive, resulting in a mixture of trees, shrubs, and grasses. Water and fire are the limiting factors of growth together with the influence of grazing by cattle and wild animals.

In the temperature-cold regions of Asia, precipitation is low, temperatures are low, influence from grazing of game is low, fire impacts are lacking, and the influence of humans has been low until recent settlement. Domestic animals were introduced in the 19th and 20th centuries and have had only recent impacts on vegetation.

The change from woody steppe to steppe is also influenced by soils. Podsolic soils are widespread in the woody steppes (in the subsoil on layers of black soils). Farther to the east, peat soils occur, and with a higher degree of aridity. Farther to the south, first signs of salinity appear.

True steppes include a typical grass plant cover over deep black and fertile soils. With a decrease in precipitation, chestnut soils exist in connection with the degradation of black soils up to types with the character of solonetz. This is the beginning of semideserts, the true "shrublands."

To survey the most important types the discussion will center on "meadow-steppes" and "stipa-steppes," following the classification by Walter (1968).

B. Meadow-Steppes

In eastern Europe the vegetation of meadow-steppes occupies the area north and east of the Black Sea, the plains south of the Ukraine, and parts of western Siberia. The black chernozem soil reaches a depth of up to 150 cm with a humus content of 5% in the upper layers. Root depth of grasses is 100 cm, of herbs 200 cm and more. From west to east, precipitation decreases from 420 to 350 mm. The good quality of soil with its high water-holding capacity has led to the transformation of this steppe into arable land. This process began at the end of the 17th century and has now almost reached completion. At present over 90% of former meadow-steppes have been plowed. Wheat and barley are cultivated but in eastern Europe also maize and sunflowers. They make a considerable contribution to human nutrition.

The Soviet government has been careful to maintain typical areas of vegetation types of meadow-steppes in several parts of the area to study flora, soil development, and fauna. The number of plant species in the reservation near Kursk is about 200, of which 180 are herbs and legumes and about 20 species are grasses.

C. Stipa-Steppes

With increasing dryness farther south, the number of species diminishes. Xerophytic grasses become dominant, and the deep chernozem soils change to chestnut soils. With yearly precipitation between 220 and 320 mm, the boundary of field cropping is reached. Most areas of stipa-steppes have been plowed in the 20th century but in more arid zones, plains of steppes exist even today. There shrubs are found in addition to grasses and herbs. This steppe is characterized by three grasses: *Stipa lessingiana, S. ucrainica,* and *Festuca sulcata,* with their flower stage at the end of May. In this period the highest quantity of phytomass is produced. In June, grasses ripen and only herbs are still in flower stage. The visual aspect of steppe is one of dryness at the end of June. Rains in the autumn bring a new regrowth and a later flowering stage for some species, for example, *Artemisia austriaca* and *Linosyris villosa.*

Forage production in its true sense exists only between the end of April and the end of June. Hoofed mammals have fresh fodder in this short period; for the balance of the year they find only dry grasses, herbs, and a few shrubs.

D. Productivity and Utilization of Steppes in Eurasia

As far as the utilization of the natural vegetation of steppes by grazing animals is concerned, the "yield" of shoots and stems above the soil is the main criterion for humans in evaluating grazing areas. Also of importance is the forage supply throughout the year. But the reciprocal action between soil and vegetation over long periods is certainly of equal importance in maintaining soil fertility by the accumulation of organic matter from root growth. Soviet research deals with aspects of both the quantity and quality of phytomass production above and beneath the surface of the soil. Results from Rodin and Basilevich (1965) from arid regions in eastern Europe and western Siberia show some interesting contrasts in production of phyto-mass as a whole (divided into shoots and underground organs) and yearly phytomass production (Table I). The composition of these six plant communities consists mainly of grasses, legumes, and herbs. In the sixth type (steppe semidesert) in the Altai region, *Artemisia* spp. are widespread. In these dry zones the quantity of roots and underground organs is much higher than the phytomass of aerial shoots. The percentage of

Table I. Productivity of six plant communities in eastern Europe and Siberia

	East Europe		West Siberia and Altai			
	Meadow-steppe	Dry steppe	Meadow-steppe	Moderate dry steppe	Dry steppe	Dry steppe to semidesert
Phytomass (tons/ha)	23.7	22.0	23.0	24.6	21.0	9.8
Shoots	3.7 (16%)[a]	2.0 (9%)	8.0 (35%)	4.5 (18%)	3.0 (14%)	1.4 (14%)
Underground organs	20.0 (84%)	20.0 (91%)	15.0 (65%)	20.1 (82%)	18.0 (86%)	8.4 (86%)
Yearly production (tons/ha)	10.4 (44%)[b]	8.7 (40%)	13.0 (57%)	11.2 (46%)	9.0 (43%)	4.2 (43%)
Shoots	3.7 (36%)	2.0 (23%)	8.0 (62%)	4.5 (40%)	3.0 (33%)	1.4 (33%)
Underground organs	6.7 (64%)	6.7 (77%)	5.0 (38%)	6.7 (60%)	6.0 (67%)	2.8 (67%)

Source: Rodin and Basilevich (1965).

[a] Percentage of phytomass in shoots and underground organs for each steppe type.

[b] Percentage of yearly production of phytomass, shoots, and underground organs.

underground organic matter increases with the aridity and yearly production of underground phytomasss amounts to 40 to 57% of total phytomass. Only the areal parts of plants are of interest for forage production. Quantities from 1.4 tons/ha (steppe semidesert) to 8 tons/ha mentioned in Table I represent the total annual production. Certainly only a part of yearly shoot production will be grazed or eliminated. In previous experiments, Larin (1958) published data of yields (hay) in steppes with 0.65–1.0 tons/ha per year. Assuming this is the "grazing yield" for steppes, three to four hectares would be necessary for the nutrition of one animal-unit per year.

III. Semideserts and Deserts in Asia

The arid zones of the USSR comprise about 455 million ha, divided into three types:

- Steppes   156 million ha
- Semideserts   123 million ha
- Deserts   176 million ha

Most of this vast area is utilized for grazing. Only 5 million ha of steppe are mown regularly for hay production (Sinkovski, 1980). The semideserts and deserts are situated to the east of the Caspian Sea in the Soviet Socialist Republic of Turkmenia, Uzbekistan, Tajikistan, Kirgizia, and the southern parts of Kazakhstan.

The climate is characterized by the continental influence of Middle Asia. The difference in monthly temperatures in Kazakhstan is −10°C in January up to 27°C in July. Precipitation varies from 100 to 185 mm per year. Semideserts have less than 250 mm, but deserts have less than 140 mm per year. Evaporation in summer in the Asiatic deserts ranges up to 1400 mm compared with 4000 to 6000 mm in the Sahara of Africa (Franke and Paetzold, 1986). The unproductive water loss is smaller in the colder deserts of Asia that have a harsher winter period. Precipitation in these zones is distributed over the whole year; in the southern regions winter rain is dominant, snow in winter and early spring being a favorable source of water for the growth of plants in spring. Humidity is low in summer with 20 to 30% combined with high soil temperature up to 70°C. Sandstorms occur in summer and form sandhills and shifting sand dunes in many regions between the Caspian Sea and the southern parts of the People's Republic of Mongolia.

Soils in semideserts and deserts include alluvial sandy types or sandy soils as a result of a long period of mineralization, which causes the formation of dunes by the influence of wind. But in some regions loess soils are also found as well as argillaceous soils, gypseous sierozem soils (e.g., in southwestern Kazakhstan), and types of solonchak. A high level of groundwater favors salinity, especially on silty and argillaceous soils.

Stress-resistant vegetation has developed over long periods of time under the influence of climate and soil. The following general types are to be distinguished (Walter, 1968):

- on sand   = psammophyte vegetation
- on loess and clay   = ephemeral vegetation
- on gypseous soils   = a specific gypseous vegetation
- on argillaceous soils = halophytes

The change from steppe to semidesert is characterized by a decrease of gramineous species and herbs and an increase of xerophytic semishrubs and shrubs. The plant cover is low; barren soil is widespread, but a "compressed vegetation" is observed in old riverbeds or local depressions. The possibilities for erosion by wind and water are evident.

All these factors influence utilization. Without artificial irrigation only grazing is possible, especially for sheep, goats, and camels. The lower boundary of dryland farming without irrigation is characterized by about 250 mm precipitation per year, a quantity seldom occurring in semideserts. Nevertheless, on slopes and in depressions with additional influx of water, rain-fed agriculture is pursued on small plots, just as it is carried on by some seminomadic tribes in North Africa.

Before man entered and settled in these vast areas, hoofed mammals in large herds populated the steppes and semideserts. These were first and foremost antelopes (e.g., *Gazella subgutturosa, Saiga tatarica*), the wild horses (*Equus hemionus*), called "kuban," and wild sheep (*Ovis orientalis areal*). In ancient times a natural balance between plant growth and the life of wild animals was common, influenced also by predators, which reduced the rodents and ensured the selection of hoofed mammals. With the appearance of humans (in the nonirrigated areas) there began:

- a decline in the number of predators
- an increase in the number of rodents (especially *Rhombius opimus*)
- a concentration of sheep and goats in the vicinity of wells
- overgrazing and deterioration of soil
- the cutting of shrubs for fuel
- a decrease in vegetal cover
- a disturbance of the ecological balance

The governments of different Union Republics in these regions began (with the aid of scientific research) to restore the plant cover, to plan and to build huge canals for irrigation, using the water of northern rivers for the semideserts and deserts in Middle Asia, and to plan and implement the management of grazing systems in the nonirrigated areas.

Middle Asia

The Soviet Republics of Middle Asia (Kazakhstan, Turkestan, Uzbekistan, Tajikistan, and Kirgizia) were ancient semicolonial regions before 1917. After the changeover to socialistic systems, natural resources were utilized to build up industry and agriculture and to solve the energy problems by development of hydroelectric schemes. In the field of agriculture two main aims were pursued:

- Maintenance or restoration of the vegetation in all arid zones.
- Extension of irrigated areas to foster crop cultivation.

In this chapter only the first of these is described. The initial success in safeguarding the vegetation was the settlement of nomads, thus avoiding uncontrolled grazing and overgrazing. The second step was implementation of grazing management in all state farms (Sovkhoz) and collective farms (Kolkoz).

1. Sandy Deserts

A survey of the predominant types of vegetation in Middle Asia is shown in Fig. 2. The Kara-Kum desert (meaning black sand) is in the Turkmen SSR

Figure 2. Types of vegetation in Middle Asia. (From Walter, 1968.)

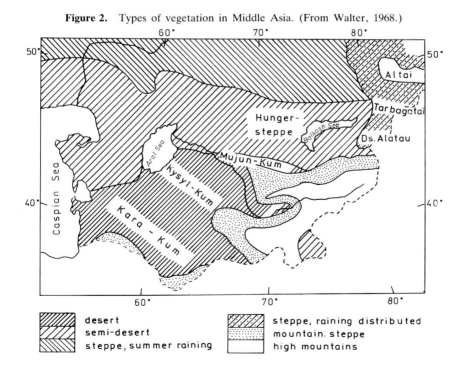

located west of Amu-Darja and the Kysyl-Kum desert (meaning white sand). The Kara-Kum is also located in the Uzbek SSR between Amu-Darja and Syr-Darja and extends from the Aral Sea to the foothills of the Pamirs in the Tajik SSR. To the northwest of Syr-Darja, the Betpak-Dalaa ("hunger steppe") occupies the area between the Aral Sea and Balkash Sea in the south of Kazakhstan. Farther north lie the steppes.

Winter temperatures in the northern regions (Kazakhstan) in January are −5° to −8°C but the average in Uzbekistan is +1° to +3°C. In Uzbekistan it is possible to cultivate cotton, tea, rice, citrus fruits, and maize in the oases. These zones are represented by the deserts of Kara-Kum and Kysyl-Kum. The sandy soil facilitates the penetration of water into the upper layers of soil and is the reason for relatively good plant growth, especially in the spring. Precipitation ranges from 150 to 200 mm per year but surface evaporation is low since the sandy surface reduces capillarity. Not until spring does the growth of ephemerals begin, such as species of *Carex, Cruciferae,* Chenopodiaceae, and Leguminosae. New growth of perennial herbs and shrubs then follows. Among these shrubs, species of *Calligonum, Eremosparton, Ammodendron,* and *Haloxylon* are widespread. Rodlike shoots with a small leaf surface are the reason for the low rate of transpiration. Among the Chenopodiaceae, *Haloxylon aphyllum* (black Saksaul) and *H. persicum* (white Saksaul) are characteristic plants of the sandy deserts and are of great importance in maintaining vegetation and a forage supply for sheep. They reach 2.5 to 4 m in height after 5 to 7 years of growth and are well adapted for growing in shelter belts.

With the beginning of the warm period in summer the upper layers of soil dry out and the ephemerals disappear. The roots of shrubs reach the deeper layers of soil down to two or more meters, thus guaranteeing the requirement of water over the year. In general, the shoots remain green during summer. In longer dry periods shrubs like *Haloxyon* and *Calligonum* shed their small leaves, thus reducing transpiration. The shed leaves represent an additional forage supply during autumn and winter for sheep, which often remain outside if the winter is not too severe.

A special vegetation has developed on the dunes under the influence of sandstorms and is in danger of being overwhelmed by sand. One particular example are the *Aristida* spp. Their underground organs have the ability to continue growth under new layers of sand, building up new layers of root system as the deposition of sand increases. *Carex physodes* also grows on sand. The quantity of underground biomass amounts to 19 tons/ha; on the other hand, the shoots above the surface produce only 3 tons/ha Walter, 1968). When the upper layers of soil have dried out, the shoots of *C. physodes* do not perish, but may recommence growth after rain.

In the sandy deserts there are about 300 different plant species, of which shrubs constitute 48% (Nechajeva, 1974). During a visit to Uzbekistan the author had the opportunity to identify the following species in the semishrub pasture of the Norata District: *Haloxylon aphyllum, Aellenia subaphylla, Alhagi pseudalhagi, Artemisia diffusa, Ceratocarpus utriculosus, Kochia prostrata, Salsola orientalis, Tanacetum umbellifolium, Aegilops orientalis, Poa bulbosa,* and *Stipa hohenhaekeriana.* The ecological variability of *Haloxylon aphyllum* is considerably greater than that of *H. persicum,* especially concerning salt tolerance. A high level of groundwater favors the growth of *Tamarix* spp. as in Iraq. The danger of salinity is much greater on clay and silty soils than on the soil of the sandy deserts.

2. Salt Deserts

In lowlands and depressions without flow-off and along rivers, salt deserts are found where high groundwater levels persist. The soils are rich in clay and chlorides. In extreme cases there are plains without any vegetation, like the chotts in North Africa; in Middle Asia they are called "Schorys." On shallow depressions with temporary inundations, similar accumulations of salt have developed in the upper layers, called "Takyr," which are distributed along the Amu-Darja and on the foothills of the Kopet Dao Mountains near Achshabad in the Turkmen SSR. Around those Takyrs is found a typical flora of halophytes, including *Halocnemum strobilaceum,* species of *Salicornia, Halostachys,* and *Kalidium,* and *Halopeplis pigmata,* which have a high tolerance to salinity. On the periphery of these locations *Haloxylon aphyllum, Seidlitzia,* and *Artemisia* spp. appear. The yearly phytomass has been estimated by Rodin (quoted by Walter, 1968) as being about 100 kg in the center, 300 kg in the middle, and 1200 kg/ha on the periphery of the Takyr (mainly *Artemisia* spp.). These shrubs are a valuable supply of forage for camels, sheep, goats, and asses, on account of their high mineral content (Table II).

The salt deserts are of importance for animals because they furnish a continuous forage supply over the year. Grazing animals seem to prefer *Artemisia maritima.* Salt deserts are not as extensive as other desert types in Asia, but they occur between the steppes in the north down to the southern mountains of the Himalayas and Pamirs and provide habitat for millions of sheep and other hoofed mammals. Since the level of groundwater is high and virtually nothing can be done to change it, this valuable flora of halophytes will continue to be an important component of the vegetation cover.

3. Gypseous Deserts

On higher plains lacking the influence of groundwater, gypseous deserts have developed in some areas (see Fig. 3). Although they do not occupy

Table II.   Halophytes and their mineral content

	Ashes (% DM)[a]		Ashes (% DM)
Chloride halophytes		Sulfate halophytes	
Salicornia europaea	33	*Salsola rigida*	15.5
Salsola turcomanica	24.5	*Karliana caspia*	16.5
Halocnemum		*Halocnemis mollissima*	14.5
strobilaceum	31.5	*Salsola dendroides*	21
Halostachys belangeriana	31		
Kalidium caspicum	32.5		
Anabasis aphylla	18		
Alkali halophytes		Halophytes with secretion of salt	
Suaeda microphylla	35	*Tamarix laxa*	16
Haloxylon aphyllum	22.5	*T. ramosissima*	14.5
Anabasis salsa	22.5	*Aeluropus litoralis*	6–11

Source: Rodin, cited in Walter (1968).
[a]DM = dry matter.

Figure 3.   Deserts of Central Asia. (From Walter, 1968.)

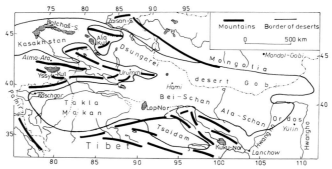

large areas, such as in the southeastern part of Kazakhstan, they deserve mention. The soil surface has an encrusted structure and the layers beneath the surface are loose, but in the subsoil at a depth of 40 to 80 cm there are firm layers with a high content of $CaSO_4$, which inhibit the penetration of roots and the exchange of water and air. The yearly precipitation is between 150 and 240 mm (Prjanishnikov and Alimajev, 1980).

Plants grow in a similar way to those in the "Hamada," the stone deserts of North Africa, which also supports only sparse vegetation in the depressions. Many species have small leaves or spines to reduce transpiration. Typical species of the gypseous deserts in Asia are *Noaea spinosissima*,

Sisymbrium subspinescens, and *Araphasis* spp. and succulent halophytes like species of *Frankenia, Statice,* and *Reaumuria.* In addition, some Capparideae and Rutaceae with high volatile essential oils supplement the vegetation. A few plants have a high nutritional value, for example, the annual Chenopodiaceae, *Ceratocarpus arenarius,* which produces 0.5 tons dry matter (DM)/ha during summer and supplies good forage for Karakul sheep.

4. Ephemeral Deserts

On loamy soils without salinity in the southern parts of Kazakhstan, near the foothills of mountains and in the "hunger-steppe," ephemeral deserts predominate. The vegetation period begins in March and ends in the middle of May. In this short time, rapid growth with a considerable production of phytomass can be observed. The dominant species are *Carex hostii* and *Poa bulbosa.* In addition many types with perennial rhizomes or bulbs have spread out, for example, species of *Ranunculus, Bunias, Halophyllum, Erantis, Tulipa,* and *Geranium.* Grasses like *Bromus, Phleum,* and *Agropyron* complete the vegetation, reaching only 20 cm in height, but less in dry years. In spring an almost closed canopy of plants covers the desert, but the process of drying begins early. Nevertheless, 0.2 to 0.4 tones DM/ha per year are produced in this short period (Korovia, quoted by Walter, 1968). In some places the ephemeral species are mown, providing hay for winter feeding.

5. Measures for the Utilization and Management of Shrublands

In the 1920s and 1930s and after the Second World War, systematic research began in order to utilize the arid regions for the benefit of society. In the All-Union Institute for Karakul Breeding in Tashkent/Uzbekistan, valuable research has been carried out since 1925. This research is directed mainly toward breeding Karakul sheep and planning effective utilization by developing grazing systems to ensure the continuous supply of forage.

Shrubs furnish forage almost year-round. From spring to the end of summer, *Calligonum* spp. are available, and *Artemisia* spp. are utilized from spring to late summer. Forage supply is abundant from the end of winter until the beginning of summer by perennial grasses. Ephemerals such as crucifers, poppies, and legumes are grazed principally in spring.

Actual forage production varies considerably depending on plant cover and type of vegetation. Nechajeva (1974) records the yearly yields of the main types of vegetation where bushes and shrubs are the main components in forage supply (Table III). Perhaps 60–65% of the potential yield can be utilized by browsing sheep or goats. Using this value, the following

Table III.   Yearly yields in arid zones of Middle Asia

	Tons DM/ha	Variation
Bushes (*Haloxylon*, etc.)	1.9	0.9–3.3
Dwarf shrubs (*Astragalus*, etc.)	4.0	0.7–10.0
Perennial grasses (*Carex*, etc.)	—	0.7–2.0
Winter annuals (*Bromus, Eremopyrum*, etc.)	0.5	0.1–0.8
Summer annuals (*Gamanthus*, etc.)	0.6	0.06–3.0

Source: Nechajeva (1980).

usable yearly yields were estimated by Nechajeva (1980):

- Shrub pastures   0.30–0.92 ton DM/ha
- Semishrub pastures   0.22–1.05 tons DM/ha
- Herbaceous pastures   0.13–1.23 tons DM/ha

Sinkovski (1980) estimates yields from herbaceous deserts at 0.15 to 0.40 ton DM/ha, and Djackov *et al.* (1974) figure the carrying capacity of arid pastures in the Uzbek SSR to be from 2 to 20 ha per sheep. This great variation in carrying capacity demonstrates the heterogeneity of phytocoenosis in the deserts of Middle Asia. Not all species are grazed or browsed, for some of them, like *Anabasis salsa, Hordeum leporinum,* and *Psoralea* spp., are rejected by sheep (Gajeskaja, 1958).

To avoid future degradation of desert pastures and to regenerate plant cover where overgrazing has occured, the following measures are recommended:

1. Development of watering places.
2. Planting of shelter belts.
3. Sod-seeding of grasses or shrubs.
4. Provision of water and fertilizers.
5. Establishment of specialized state or collective farms for sheep.
6. Elaboration of grazing systems for each vegetation types.
7. Production of fodder reserves for times of shortage.

The points mentioned above will be taken up briefly.

The problem of developing watering places can be illustrated from experience in the Uzbek SSR, which has a grazing area of about 32 million ha. Because of the lack of water only 5 million ha were used in a seminomadic way up to 1917. Sheep and goats had to make daily journeys of 10 km and more from the wells to grazing places. In the vicinity of wells the flora was completely degraded. By 1980 an area of 20 million ha had been opened up by the drilling of new wells, drawing from a water level between 20 to 40 m under the surface. Now the grazing area around the wells covers a 1- to 4-km radius. The remaining 7 million ha will be developed in the next 10 years.

In other Soviet Republics of Middle Asia similar programs have been implemented, thus improving the output of skins, wool, and mutton. Sometimes artesian water is also available, for example, in Kazakhstan, where some wells have a capacity of about 5000 m^3/sec (Weigand and Paetzold, 1978).

Shelter belt plantings have been used to prevent erosion, to improve microclimate, and to ensure better conditions for wintering Karakul sheep. The most important shrubs in this respect are *Haloxylon aphyllum*, *Calligonum*, and *Ephedra* spp. planted or sown after plowing on flat furrows (Franke and Paetzold, 1986). The young seedlings have to be protected from grazing or browsing during the following 3 to 4 years. These shelter belts reach a height of 2.5 to 4 m and favor the growth of valuable herbs and grasses such as *Stipa* and *Aegilops* spp. Forage supply was increased as a result of planting shelter belt shrubs for browsing use during the winter. In the Uzbek SSR more than 120,000 ha of semidesert have been protected by shelter belts in this way and further expansion has been planned according to Sinkovski (1980).

Sod-seeding experiments with forage plants and shrubs have been more successful in Middle Asia than in North Africa. As early as 1956, Larin published a list of nearly 500 species chosen after initial experiments for sod-seeding or planting. The greatest interest should be paid to shrubs. In the past, the percentage of shrubs decreased, because shrubs were used for fuel. The cutting and uprooting of shrubs for this purpose was common practice. Near the villages, along migration routes, and in the neighborhood of watering points, many woody species were destroyed to provide firewood and charcoal. Le Houérou (1969) calculated that in North Africa an average of 1 kg wood per person per day for fuel is necessary to supply firewood. In this way, 0.5 to 1 ha of woody vegetation per person is destroyed each year.

Common genera used for fuel are *Calligonum*, *Haloxylon*, *Astragalus*, *Ephedra*, *Acontholimon*, *Ziziphyus*, and *Cousinia*. A comparison of the situation in North Africa or the Near East with that in the Soviet Republics of Middle Asia leads to the conclusion that less damage has been caused by cutting and overgrazing in Asia on account of the shorter period of human influence and the lower population density. Nevertheless, sod-seeding is necessary to restore former plant density. Soviet scientists in the All-Union Institute for Karakul Breeding in Tashkent have tested about 260 species from 29 botanical families for their adaptation to sod-seeding over the last 20 years (Djackov *et al.*, 1974). These experiments have been successful,

Table IV. Influence of depth of seeding on yield (tons dry matter/ha) and seed of *Kochia prostrata*

Seed depth (cm)	Year 1 DM	Year 1 Seed	Year 2 DM	Year 2 Seed	Year 3 DM	Year 3 Seed	Total DM	Total Seed	Average DM	Average Seed
0.	3.1	0.40	3.7	0.44	4.0	0.40	10.8	1.24	3.6	0.41
0.5	3.1	0.42	3.9	0.44	4.1	0.41	11.1	1.27	3.7	0.42
1.0	2.5	0.38	3.2	0.42	2.9	0.39	8.6	1.19	2.9	0.40
1.5	1.7	0.29	2.1	0.36	1.8	0.36	5.6	1.01	1.9	0.33

Source: Waljan (1972).

especially for species from the genera *Haloxylon, Calligonum, Kochia, Ephedra, Artemisia, Astragalus, Glycyrrhiza, Salsola, Aellenia,* and *Isatis* (Sinkovski, 1980).

From the point of view of forage supply in the dry season or summer, sod-seeding of *Kochia prostrata* var. *subcanescens,* var. *villosissima,* and var. *canescene* has proved to be very successful. Concerning the depth of seed in its influence on yield of dry matter and yield of seed, the experiments of Waljan (1972) shown in Table IV are relevant. Plants of *Kochia prostrata* varieties are characterized by a longevity of 10 and more years and high salt tolerance. They are deep rooting and withstand cutting and grazing. The shoots remain green in summer and furnish valuable fodder. Results concerning quantity of seed and regrowth in relation to time of cutting are given in Table V. *Kochia prostrata* may be sown in

Table V. Yield and regrowth from *Kochia prostrata* in dependence of quantity of seed and time of cutting

Seed (kg/ha)	Date of first cut	Yield (tons/ha) GM[a]	Yield (tons/ha) DM	Date of second cut	Yield (tons/ha) GM	Yield (tons/ha) DM	Yield total GM	Yield total DM
1.7	June 20	0.9	0.23	Oct. 18	2.0	0.90	2.9	1.1
	July 20	2.1	0.62	Oct. 18	1.2	0.54	3.3	1.4
3.4	June 20	1.4	0.36	Oct. 18	3.1	1.31	4.5	1.6
	July 20	3.0	0.38	Oct. 18	1.9	0.86	4.9	1.7
5.2	June 20	1.9	0.46	Oct. 18	4.0	1.70	5.9	2.1
	July 20	4.1	1.23	Oct. 18	2.5	1.09	6.6	2.3
6.8	June 20	2.0	0.52	Oct. 18	4.5	1.94	6.5	2.4
	July 20	4.4	1.30	Oct. 18	2.7	1.19	7.1	2.4

Source: Waljan (1972).
[a] GM = green matter.

spring by sod-seeding or after plowing to have 30,000 to 40,000 plants per hectare. Fertilization with phosphorus is necessary, and alternating utilization every year between mowing and grazing is recommended. Cutting twice per year is usual. The nutrient content of *K. prostrata* amounts to 17.6 to 26.4% crude protein, 2.3 to 3.0% calcium, and 0.32 to 0.37% phosphorus in dry matter with a digestibility of 58 to 77% in the dry matter (Waljan, 1972).

In the southern regions of Kazakhstan, similar experiments with sod-seeding have been carried out. A comparison between pure seeding of only one species and mixed seeding of semishrubs with grasses has been undertaken by Prjanishnikov and Alimajev (1980) over a 5-year period (Table VI). In general, the seed mixtures yield more than the single-species stands. Experiments in southern Kazakhstan, with an annual precipitation of about 225 mm, also demonstrated the possibility of sod-seeding on gypseous sierozem soils with root depths in the case of *S. orientalis* and *E. ceratoides* of up to 2 m and a penetration of the gypsum horizon with layers between 40 to 80 cm under the surface. Sod-seeding in association with control of the original plant cover and strip-seeding are recommended for sandy and loamy soils, after contour plowing. Instead of a long period of protection from 10 to 15 years as was previously considered necessary, seeding of adapted species accelerates the process of plant recovery as much as 2 years.

Table VI. Dry matter yields of pure and mixed stands of semishrubs in flower stage (1971–1975)

Single-species seeding	Mean yield over 5 years (ton/ha)	Seed mixtures	Mean yield over 5 years (ton/ha)
Kochia prostrata	0.68	*K. prostrata + S. orientalis*	0.90
Salsola orientalis	0.68	*K. prostrata + C. lessingii*	0.67
Eurotia ceratoides	0.75	*K. prostrata + E. ceratoides*	0.94
Camphorosma lessingii	0.47	*K. prostrata + A. terrae-albae*	0.57
Artemisia terrae-albae	0.38	*K. prostrata + S. orientalis + E. ceratoides*	0.97
		K. prostrata + S. orientalis + C. lessingii	0.91
		K. prostrata + S. orientalis + A. terrae-albae	0.72
Control:	0.13	*K. prostrata + C. lessingii + A. terrae-albae + S. orientalis*	0.81
Artemisia + ephemeral vegetation			
		K. prostrata + C. lessingii + A. terrae-albae + S. orientalis + E. ceratoides	0.92

Source: Prjanishnikov and Alimajew (1980).

On soils with salinity (solonetz), similar experiments have been carried out, especially with legumes and grasses. Genera with high salt tolerance are *Melilotus, Medicago, Agropyron, Bromus, Elymus,* and *Hordeum* (Baitkanov, 1980). Pure stands or mixtures, seeded after plowing, yielded an average of 0.5 to 2.3 tons hay/ha yearly over a period of 15 to 20 years. *Elymus junceus* (Russian wild rye) has shown a high aptitude for productivity under grazing management.

In the ephemeral deserts, near the foothills of the Kopet Dag mountain in Turkmen SSR, the restoration of plant cover has been achieved by seeding *Haloxylon persicum, H. aphyllum, Salsola paletzkiana, S. richteri, Aellenia subaphylla, Artemisia badhysi, A. turanica, Calligonum rubens, Kochia prostrata,* and *Astragalus agameticus* (Prikhodko and Prikhodko, 1980). Formerly the degraded vegetation yielded 0.3 to 0.4 ton/ha and after establishment of the new plant cover, yields from 1.5 to 4.5 tons DM/ha were achieved.

The problem of seeding or sod-seeding of adapted species in the arid zones of Middle Asia to restore the vegetation has been solved experimentally. Today many Kolkhoz and Sovkhoz possess areas with improved plant cover, in this way rendering possible an effective output of vegetation. Thus, Karakul breeding in Middle Asia has gained new opportunities for development and the vegetation is also protected for the future.

Water and fertilization in combination are most effective in arid zones where sufficient water is available, as in oases. In addition to irrigated crops there are plains or slopes in Middle Asia with very small inclination (0.001 to 0.002%), where temporary flooding with water, stored behind local dams, is practiced. This is called "Liman irrigation." It requires a great deal of water but little labor and energy. In this way *Medicago sativa* is cultivated with a nutrient supply of 90 kg phosphorus per hectare, yielding 4 to 5 tons DM/ha, which is five to seven times more than the natural vegetation (Franke and Paetzold, 1986).

Even without Liman irrigation, strip-seeding or planting of shrubs and grasses demands additional nutrients. In Uzbekistan, mixed stands of shrubs and grasses yielded three times more by means of a yearly addition of 60 kg nitrogen and 30 kg phosphorus, thus demonstrating the efficiency of fertilizing shrubs, especially in the early stages of development. A mixture of 90% shrubs with 10% grasses is recommended.

Establishment of specialized farms for sheep is a result of research in order to get higher utilization of arid regions. Specialized farms have been founded since the 1930s in the different republics of Middle Asia, the main locale for breeding of Karakul sheep. Shegal and Machmudov (1974) describe a typical collective farm in Uzbekistan, not far from Samarkand, with an area of 123,000 ha. Of the agricultural area, 92,000 ha are semi-desert (grazing land), 18,000 ha are under irrigation producing cotton and lucerne, and the rest is given over to vineyards and gardens. On 4000 ha seed production of *Kochia prostrata* has been developed for use on the farm and for export. The livestock consists of 63,000 sheep, 2700 cattle, 1500 goats, 23 horses and mules, and 23 camels. By seeding and sod-seeding, the forage supply can be increased considerably. After restoration of the vegetation, 1.5 ha per sheep are sufficient for year-round grazing. Wool, meat, milk, cotton, and fruits are the main products of this kolkhoz. The construction of sheds for sheep has led to better conditions for wintering as well as increasing the supply of hay and concentrates for times of scarcity. Thus, 1.74 lambs per ewe per year are produced under the improved practices.

Similar farms have been founded in all arid regions of Middle Asia. Specialization differs, for example, in the mountainous regions of Kirgizia, horse-breeding farms are common with a grazing system of transhumance. In dry periods the herds wander to the higher and cooler regions to find more humid conditions and available forage. In general, long-term scientific research in the past has paid off and the ancient "poor regions" of Middle Asia are now characterized by remarkable prosperity of the population.

Elaboration of grazing systems was obviously necessary to replace the ancient seminomadic utilization of semideserts with its element of uncertainty. An adequate forage supply was by no means guaranteed, especially in winters with long periods of snow, when sheep losses were common. The first step was to determine the area sufficient for a flock of a certain size to be grazed throughout the year. Specifically, the size of the grazing unit must correspond to the yield of the flora. This grazing unit was divided into 6 to 10 paddocks to allow rotational grazing. To provide a varied forage supply, some paddocks were improved by additional seeding or sod-seeding for producing fodder at different times of the year. In this way, special parts of the grazing unit that are best adapted for spring, summer, autumn, or winter grazing can be used accordingly. Sometimes parts of the area were allowed to rest under protection for one season to produce seeds of valuable species and to improve the regeneration of plant vigor.

Information about the relative proportions of different plant families that constitute the forage intake of sheep can show the relative value of plant types for grazing. The results of experiments by Nechajeva (1980) on grazing areas in the Kara-Kum desert, with the main components being *Carex physodes* and *Haloxylon persicum,* show an increase of three times more shrub in sheep diet in the winter than in the summer (Table VII). Herbage intake thus forms the basis of grazing, but the proportion of shrubs increases especially in winter to nearly 50% of the daily intake. In

Table VII. Daily forage intake of Karakul sheep on unimproved grazing areas of the Kara-Kum

	Spring		Summer		Autumn		Winter	
	kg	%	kg	%	kg	%	kg	%
Herbage	1.8	75	2.0	87	1.6	67	1.3	52
Shrubs	0.6	25	0.3	13	0.8	33	1.2	48
Total	2.4	100	2.3	100	2.4	100	2.5	100

Source: Nechajeva (1980).

spring and summer the shoots and sprouts of *Astragalus* and *Calligonum* spp. predominate for browsing, and in autumn and winter forage supply is furnished by *Salsola* and *Haloxylon* spp. It is also of importance that a high proportion of yearly herbage growth is grazed (73 to 88%), while the proportion for the browsing of shrubs is much lower, amounting to 9 to 22% (Nechajeva, 1980). These figures refer to sheep, but when shrubs are browsed by camels or goats, the proportion of intake is much higher. Dimitrijeva *et al.* (1974) summarized some of the important attributes of shrubs in Middle Asia that are suited for livestock grazing (Table VIII).

In former times, seminomadic grazing was common with summer migration to mountainous regions. Now a rotational grazing system has been introduced also on unimproved areas with a moderate stocking rate of 3 ha per sheep. In this rotational system the grazing time per paddock is 7 days, which maintains plant cover as well as ensuring animal output. Higher stocking rates had a detrimental influence on the composition of vegetation as well as on yield (Zhambakin and Moldabekova, 1974). Longer periods of rest between short grazing times must be provided for each paddock to guarantee regrowth or seed production.

The optimum size of flocks is considered to be 600 sheep. Grazing time is in the morning (6 to 10 A.M.), followed by a rest period near the well until 3 P.M. and a second grazing time lasting until the evening (Franke and Paetzold, 1986). In winter, stabling is recommended, though some herds remain within the shelter belts for protection against wind and snow. At this time of the year additional reserves of fodder are useful.

The production of fodder reserves is a main task in arid zones. On farms with irrigation they are gained by producing hay from lucerne or concentrates (cotton meal, maize, etc.). On sheep farms without irrigation the lack of forage in winter can be avoided by:

• the browsing of shrubs
• the grazing of dry grasses in the field

Table VIII. Additional information for important shrubs in Middle Asia adapted for forage supply for sheep, goats, and camels

Species	Soils	Seed (kg/ha)	Growth height (m)	Utilization	Time of forage supply	Yield (tons DM/yr)	Nutritive value	Remarks
Alhagi pseudoalhagi (M. B.) Desv.	Alluvial sands, gray-brown earths, chestnut, solonchak	Planting	1.0	Hay, browse, fuel, bees	Spring	1–3	High carotene, vitamin C	Especially for hay making, silage with grasses
Artemisia badgysi Krasch et Lincz	Sand solenetz	Seed or plant in spring	0.3–0.5	Grazing, hay (May–June)	Autumn, winter, spring	0.4–0.5	High in protein, fat	Important for winter grazing
Artemisia lercheana Web.	Chernozem, chestnut, solonetz	Seed or plant	0.1–0.3	Grazing, hay (June)	Autumn, winter	0.2–0.4	High Ca, P	Hay making with grasses
Artemisia pauciflora Web.	Chestnut, solonetz	Seed or plant	0.1–0.3	Grazing, hay	Spring autumn	0.3–0.4	High in protein, fat	Refused by cattle
Calligonum caput-medusae Schrenk.	Sand	Seed 3–5 or plant in autumn	2	Grazing, brows	Spring, summer (fruits in autumn/winter)	1.0–1.5	High protein	Resistant to cover by sand
Eurotia ceratoides (L.) C.A.M.	Sand, also in Pamir Mtns.	Seed 25–30 (also sod-seed) in spring	0.4–1	Grazing, hay, fuel	Year-round	0.8–1.0	High protein	Salt tolerant

(*continues*)

Table VIII. (Continued)

Species	Soils	Seed (kg/ha)	Growth height (m)	Utilization	Time of forage supply	Yield (tons DM/yr)	Nutritive value	Remarks
Haloxylon aphyllum (Minkw.) Iljin	Chernozem, gray-brown earths, sands	Seed 5 in Dec.	4–8	Browse, fuel, dune fixation	Autumn, winter (camels year-round)	0.5–1.5	High Ca	Shelter belt, low in P
Haloxylon persicum Bge.	Sandy hills	Seed 5 in Dec.	3–5	Browse, fuel, dune fixation	Autumn, winter (camels year-round)	0.3–0.5	High protein	Common for fuel
Kochia prostrata (L.) Schraeb.	All soils, incl. solonetz	Seed 4–8 in autumn	0.2–0.5	Grazing, cutting	Year-round	1.0–2.5 (seed 0.1)	Very high protein, carotene vitamin B	Deep rooted, green in summer, important forage
Salsola richteri Karel.	Sand	Seed 10 or plant	2.5–3	Browse, dune fixation	Spring, autumn (camels year-round)	0.4–0.8	High protein, minerals	Deep rooted, salt and drought resistant
Salsola rigida Poll.	Sandy, gray earths, solonetz	Seed 5–8 in Dec.	0.2–0.8	Grazing, browse	Spring, autumn, winter (camels year-round)	0.3–0.5	High protein	Drought- and salt-resilient
Salsola subaphylla C.A.M.	Sand, gray-brown earths, solonetz	Seed 5–10 in spring or autumn	0.3–1.2	Grazing, browse	Summer, autumn, winter (camels year-round)	0.2–0.4	High vitamins	Seeds damaged by insects and rodents

Source: Dimitrijeva *et al.* (1974).

- producing hay by mowing the natural vegetation
- the seeding and utilization of special low shrubs like *Kochia prostrata*

Haloxylon and *Salsola* spp. are typical plants for browsing in winter. The winter grazing of protected areas is common, with *Poa, Stipa*, and *Bromus* spp. being the mainstay of grazing if the snow is not too high. The mowing of natural vegetation can be done if previously favorable conditions existed for plant growth. In USSR about 5 million ha are utilized in this way for the production of hay. On flat plains with groundwater influence, it is common to cultivate additional forage crops like winter-rye, sorghum, maize, or *Lathyrus* spp. for reserves in winter. Last but not least, the residues of cotton and sunflower can serve as reserve feed. Every farm has to discover for itself the best ways of maintaining a forage supply in relation to existing natural and economic conditions.

IV. Management of Shrublands in Asia/USSR in the Past, Present, and Future

Only one-third of the agricultural surface of the world is useful arable cropland and two-thirds is used for grazing. The intensive utilization of arid land for grazing produces only one-tenth of the food needed for humanity. In the USSR the increasing population on one hand and the severe damage caused by the Second World War on the other led to plowing campaigns in the 1950s. From 1950 to 1965 in Kazakhstan, 42 million ha of steppes were plowed up, and by 1957 the yearly production of wheat in this SSR had increased to 28 million tons (1943; 2.1 million tons). By including grasses in rotation, the soil fertility is maintained.

There remain huge plains where precipitation is less than 250 mm per year, which are suited for grazing. In the past, these shrublands were damaged by unsystematic grazing in the neighborhood of villages or wells. Overgrazing and the cutting of shrubs for fuel led to local desertification. But farther away from human settlements the flora was unused, or only partially used by nomadic tribes. The most spectacular plan for these arid regions in the USSR involves irrigation projects in which waters of the northern rivers are to be diverted to the deserts in the south. Many projects have already been realized, as in Uzbek SSR, and others are under construction.

For the vast regions without irrigation, shrublands provide the foundation for specialized collective or state farms for animal production. Only a few smaller regions still await inclusion in this process. Based on the results of scientific research, nomadic utilization has been eliminated in recent decades. The maintenance of ecological equilibrium will be facilitated by the following measures:

- Protection of shrubs offset by the provision of fuels to prevent cutting shrubs for heating purposes.
- Planting of shrubs for shelter belts and reserve forage.
- Sod-seeding of adapted xerophytic species.
- Installation of wells to facilitate management of shrublands throughout the year.
- Introduction of rotational grazing systems in accord with the phenology of the natural flora.
- Production of fodder reserves (hay, concentrates) for times of scarcity.
- Protection of game by special laws.

The ecological borderline between arable and grazing land must be respected. An increase in plowing land will only be possible by an extension of irrigation. All measures must be planned in accordance with the natural factors in each region to protect flora and fauna and to guarantee a high living standard for society.

References

Baitkanov, K. A. (1980). Improvement of solonetz soils in Kazakhstan for the cultivation of grassland plants. *Int. Grassl. Cong.* [Proc.], 13th, 1977, pp. 599–601.

Dimitrijeva, W., Iglovikov, W. G., Konjushjov, N. S., and Ramenskaja, W. M. (1974). "Pflanzen der Wiesen und Weiden." Edition Kolos, Moscow (in Russian).

Djackov, I. N., Shamsutdinow, S. Sh., and Tsalbash, L. S. (1974). The All-Union Research Institute for Karakul Sheep Breeding, Tashkent (in Russian).

Franke, G., and Paetzold, H. (1986). "Nutzpflanzen der Tropen und Subtropen. III. Grassland und Feldfutterbau." 2nd ed. Hirzel, Leipzig.

Gajevskaja, L. S. (1958). Plants of the Karakul Sheep Pastures in Middle Asia. Uzbek. Akad. Agric. Sci. (in Russian).

Larin, W. (1956). Meadow and Pasture Farming. Selkhozgiz, Moscow-Leningrad (in Russia).

Larin, W. (1958). Besonderheiten der Graslandwirtschaft in der USSR. Stand der Erfassung von Wiesen und Weiden. Int. Grunlandtagung, Berlin, D.A.L.

Le Houérou, H. N. (1969). North Africa: past, present and future. *In* "Arid Lands in Transition," pp. 227–278. Am. Assoc. Adr. Sci., Washington, D.C.

Nechajeva, N. T. (1974). Phytomass structure and yields of Middle Asian desert pastures in relation to plant composition. *Proc. Int. Grassl. Congr. 12th, 1974*, pp. 102–115.

Nechajeva, N. T. (1980). Use of ecosystems in the arid zone of the USSR for pasture farming. *Int. Grassl. Congr. [Proc.], 13th, 1977*, pp. 577–579.

Prikhodko, S. Ya., and Prikhodko, N. D. (1980). Establishment and permanent use of cultivated pastures in the foothill regions of Turkmenia. *Int. Grassl. Congr. [Proc.], 13th, 1977*, pp. 603–605.

Prjanishnikov, S. N., and Alimajev, I. I. (1980). Biological conditions for yield increase of desert pastures on gypseous sierozem soils in southeastern Kazakhstan. *Int. Grassl. Congr.* [*Proc.*] *13th, 1977,* pp. 585–587.

Rodin, L. E., and Basilevich, N. J. (1965). Dynamics of the Organic Matter and Biological Turnover on Ash elements and Nitrogen in the Main Types of the World Vegetation. Acad. Sci. Leningrad (in Russian).

Shegal, W. J., and Machmudov, M. (1974). Der Sowjos Ergacha Dshumanbul Ogla. Min. Landw. USSR, Tashkent (in Russian).

Sinkovski, L. (1980). Main trends in improving natural grazing areas in arid regions of the USSR. *Int. Grassl. Congr.* [*Proc.*], *13th, 1977,* pp. 581–583.

Waljan, G. A. (1972). Die Radmelde (*Kochia prostrata*) und ihre Kultur in Kirgisien. Min. Landw, USSR. Frunse (in Russian).

Walter, H. (1968). Die Vegetation der Erde. *In* "Oko-physiologischer Betrachtung," Vol. II. Fischer, Jena.

Weigand, M., and Paetzold, H. (1978). Probleme, Methoden und Ergebnisse bei der Erschliessung von ariden Gebieten, dargestellt am Beispiel der mittalasiatischen Sowjet-Republiken. Dipl. Arbeit, W.P. Univ. Rostock.

Zhambakin, Sh. A., and Moldabekova, K. M. (1974). The utilization of desert pastures by rotational grazing. *Proc. Int. Grassl. Congr., 12th, 1974,* pp. 591–595.

9

Shrublands of China

Zhao Songqiao
Liu Huaxun

I. Introduction

Because of China's vast territory, mountainous topography, dominantly temperate and subtropical climates, and absence of Quaternary continental glaciation, its plant resources are quite rich and varied. Diverse species of shrubs, with their physiological and morphological advantages that allow adjustment to different habitats, are distributed very widely in China.

The Biology and Utilization of Shrubs
225

II. Distribution of Vegetation Zones and Shrublands in China

The horizontal distribution of China's vegetation zones changes generally from south to north and from east to west according to changes in temperature and moisture conditions (Fullard, 1968). Three vegetation realms and 17 vegetation zones are identified in Table I and Fig. 1. Shrubs are the main components in the horizontal vegetation zones of I.1, II.2, II.3, II.4, II.5, III.2, III.3, and III.4.

Vertical zonation of vegetation, chiefly due to aerial differentiation in elevation and consequently the redistribution of temperature and moisture conditions, is most distinct on the lofty Tibetan Plateau and its surrounding high mountains. Vertical zonation in China might first of all be divided into

Table I. Three vegetation realms and 17 vegetation zones of China

Vegetation realms		Vegetation zones
I. Eastern humid forests	I.1	Cool-temperate needle-leaved forest
	I.2	Temperate mixed needle- and broad-leaved forest
	I.3	Warm-temperate deciduous broad-leaved forest
	I.4	Northern subtropical mixed evergreen and deciduous broad-leaved forest
	I.5	Middle subtropical evergreen broad-leaved forest
	I.6	Southern subtropical evergreen broad-leaved forest
	I.7	Tropical monsoon forest and rain forest
	I.8	South China Sea islands coral-reef evergreen dwarf forest and shrub
II. Northwestern arid steppes and deserts	II.1	Temperate forest-steppe
	II.2	Temperate steppe
	II.3	Temperate desert-steppe
	II.4	Temperate desert
	II.5	Warm-temperate desert
III. Frigid Tibetan Plateau	III.1	Cool-temperate mountain needle-leaved forest
	III.2	Alpine shrub-meadow
	III.3	Alpine meadow and steppe
	III.4	Alpine desert

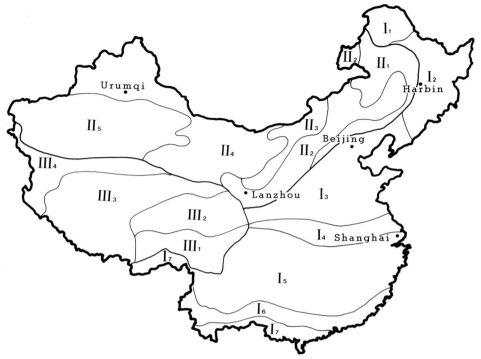

Figure 1. Map of China showing 3 vegetation realms and 17 vegetation zones.

two structural zones, maritime and continental. The maritime type of vertical vegetation zonation, distributed mainly in the eastern forest realm, is dominated by forests and patches of alpine meadow and dwarf shrubs on the upper layers. The continental type of vertical vegetation zonation exists mainly in the northwestern arid steppes and desert realms, as well as the northwestern frigid Tibetan Plateau vegetation realm (Walker, 1982).

Besides these two "primary" or zonal vegetations, shrubs grow and survive in many harsh environments, such as habitats too salty, windy, or sterile for trees. Shrubs are also extensively distributed as secondary growth in different forest zones. After continuous, excessive deforestation or forest fires, trees have been unable to reestablish themselves and shrublands or grasslands now dominate instead. The human impact on China's vegetation has been particularly strong since the beginning of agriculture about 7000 years ago and, as a result, secondary shrublands are widespread in areas that would otherwise be forested in humid eastern

China. However, under good management degraded shrublands could soon be turned into forest again with the exception of some very harsh environments, such as bare limestone rocks.

III. Main Shrubland Types in China

Based on their ecological and morphological features, the shrublands of China can be classified into 4 types and 10 subtypes (Table II).

A. *Alpine Shrublands*

The cold-hardy shrubs of alpine shrublands are widely distributed on high mountains. Their habitat generally has a mean temperature for the coldest month below $-30°C$ and for the warmest month below $10°C$. Annual precipitation ranges from 400 to 800 mm. Owing to continuous low temperature, the shrubs suffer from physiological drought. They are thus generally dwarfed, sometimes forming the so-called "cushion vegetation" (Fig. 2). Three shrubland subtypes are identified.

Table II.   Shrubland types of China

Shrubland types		Shrubland subtypes
Alpine	I.1	Alpine evergreen needle-leaved shrubs
	I.2	Alpine deciduous broad-leaved shrubs
	I.3	Alpine evergreen broad-leaved shrubs
Temperate shrublands	II.1	Temperate deciduous broad-leaved shrubs
	II.2	Temperate evergreen broad-leaved shrubs
	II.3	Temperate fleshy shrubs
Subtropical shrublands	III.1	Subtropical deciduous broad-leaved shrubs
	III.2	Subtropical evergreen broad-leaved shrubs
Tropical shrublands	IV.1	Tropical evergreen broad-leaved shrubs
	IV.2	Tropical fleshy shrubs

Figure 2. Alpine shrub-meadow of cushion vegetation at the source of the Yellow River, northeastern Tibetan Plateau.

1. Alpine Evergreen Needle-Leaved Shrubs

Coexisting with alpine meadow, alpine evergreen needle-leaved shrublands are extensively distributed on the southeastern portions of the Tibetan Plateau and its surrounding high mountains immediately below the snow line. The elevation here is between 3200 and 5500 m. The main shrub species include *Sabina squamata, S. pingii* var. *wilsonii,* and *S. wallichian.* On the Tian-Shan and Altay mountains, the predominant species are *Sabina pseudosabina* and *Juniperrus sibirica,* along with *Rhododendron* spp. and *Cassiope* spp.

2. Alpine Deciduous Broad-Leaved Shrubs

Alpine deciduous broad-leaved, shrubs are mostly distributed at elevations between 3000 and 5000 m. The main shrub species on the arid Tibetan Plateau proper include *Artemisia* spp., *Ajamia tibetica,* and *Ceratoides compacta.* On the humid high mountains, such as on northern Great Hinggan and western Qin-ling mountains, the main species include *Betula rotundifolia, Salix oritrepla, S. eupularis, Caragana jubata,* and *Myricaria prostrata.*

3. Alpine Evergreen Broad-Leaved Shrubs

Found on the eastern Tibetan Plateau and its marginal mountains, alpine evergreen broad-leaved shrubs are rather drought- and cold-resistant and generally have thick, leathery leaves. The main shrubs are *Rhododendron* species, including *R. fastigiatum, R. capitatum, R. thymifolium,* and *R. oreodoxa,* and *Cassiope fastigiata.* There are many *Sinarundnaria* spp., the so-called "Arrow-bamboo," which are the staple food for the panda.

B. Temperate Shrublands

Temperate shrublands are widely scattered on low and middle mountains of temperate, humid eastern China as well as on extensive deserts and desert-steppes of northwestern arid China. There are also a few evergreen shrubs species that might represent the relics of ancient Tertiary and Quaternary subtropical vegetation. Annual precipitation decreases from more than 750 mm in the east to less than 50 mm in the west; correspondingly, the vegetation changes from forest to steppe, then to desert. Three shrubland subtypes are identified.

1. Temperate Deciduous Broad-Leaved Shrubs

Temperate deciduous broad-leaved shrubs exist mostly in temperate, humid eastern China as secondary vegetation after deforestation. In the deserts and desert-steppes of arid northwestern China, this type is the long-established primary vegetation, although its coverage is very sparse. According to changing moisture conditions, the main species make a significant change from east to west. In the humid east, mesophytes dominate, such as *Corylus* spp., *Spiraea* spp., *Prunus* spp., *Lespedeza* spp., *Abelia biflora, Lonicera* spp., *Vitex chinensis, Zisyphus jujuba* var. *spinosa, Rosa* spp., *Cotoneaster* spp., *Rubus* spp., *Sorbus* spp., *Berberis* spp., and *Ribes* spp. In the semiarid areas, shrubs are generally drought-tolerant, such as *Caragana* spp. (Fig. 3), *Sophora* spp., *Caryopteris* spp., *Ajania* spp., and *Hippophae rhamnoides.* In the arid deserts, the sparse, scattered shrubs are generally drought-resistant and salt-tolerant. Here, the main shrub species are usually determined by surface materials of their habitats. In the sandy desert (shamo), the main shrub species include *Tamarix* spp. (Fig. 4), *Nitraria* spp. (Fig. 5), *Calligonum* spp. (Fig. 6), and *Haloxylon* spp. (Fig. 7). In the gravel and stony desert (gobi), *Gymnocarpus xanthoxylon* (Fig. 8), *Zygophyllum xanthoxylon* (Fig. 9), *Sympegma regelii,* and *Iljnia regil* predominate. Shrubs commonly seen on the saline silt and clay plains are *Salsola* spp. (Fig. 10) and *Reaumuria mongolica.*

Figure 3. *Caragana stenophylla* in the plains of Inner Mongolia.

Figure 4. *Tamarix* spp. in flower along the lower reaches of the Tarim River.

Figure 5. *Nitraria sibirica*, the "desert cherry" in the Hexi Corridor.

Figure 6. *Calligonum mongolicum* in the western Mongolian Plateau.

Figure 7.   *Haloxylon ammodendron* in the Junggar Basin.

Figure 8.   *Zygophyllum xanthoxylon* in the western Mongolian Plateau.

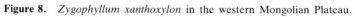

Figure 9. *Gynmocarpus przewalskii* in the western Mongolian Plateau.

Figure 10. *Salsola* spp. in the Ningxia Plain.

2. Temperate Evergreen Broad-Leaved Shrubs

Temperate evergreen broad-leaved shrubs, can be divided into two groups. The mesophytes, generally with leathery leaves, are distributed on middle mountains in temperate, humid eastern China, with *Vaccinum vitis-idaea* and *Rhododendron micranthum* as dominant species. The xerophytes exist mainly on temperate desert plains, with *Ammopiptanthus* spp. (*A. mongolicus, A. nanua*) and *Ephedra przewalskii* dominating.

3. Temperate Fleshy Shrubs

Temperate fleshy shrubs are scattered mainly on saline plains in the temperate deserts and desert-steppes. Their stems and leaves are generally fleshy and include *Kalidium* spp. (*K. gracile, K. folliatum, K. caspicum*), *Halostachys belungeria, Halocnemum strobilaceum,* and *Lycium ruthenicum.*

C. Subtropical Shrublands

Mainly evergreen, subtropical shrublands are distributed on subtropical low mountains and hills. They become the chief secondary vegetation after continuous deforestation. A small number of them are deciduous, which is relevant to a lower temperature, to a limestone environment, or to a hot, dry valley. Generally, the mean temperature of the coldest month of the habitat ranges from 0° to 15°C, while the frost-free season lasts from 250 to 350 days, and the average annual precipitation totals between 1000 and 2000 mm. Two subtypes are identified.

1. Subtropical Deciduous Broad-Leaved Shrubs

Subtropical deciduous broad-leaved shrubs can be further divided into two groups. The first type is represented mainly by mesophytes that grow in the northern subtropical zone or in limestone areas, where, because of a lower temperature or physiological drought, they shed their leaves in winter. The main species include *Lindera glausa, Quercus fabri, Castanea sequinii,* and *Rhus chinensis* in an acid-soil environment. *Coriaria sinica, Vitex negundo, Caesalpinia sepiaria,* and *Zanthoxylum simulans* appear on karst topography. The second group is drought-tolerant and is distributed mainly in dry hot valleys. Some of the main species include *Phyllanthus emblica, Sophora vicifolia, Sageratia pycnophylla,* and *Leptodermie oblonga.*

2. Subtropical Evergreen Broad-Leaved Shrubs

Subtropical evergreen broad-leaved shrubs are chiefly distributed on middle and low mountains in humid subtropical environments. The shrub species are very numerous and varied, including members of the following genera: *Loropetalum, Rhododendron, Vaccinum, Rhodomyrtus, Baeckea, Helicteres, Microcos, Smilax, Melastoma, Aporosa, Glochidion, Breymia, Macaranga, Dodoneae, Camellia, Ternstroemia, Eurya, Gordenia,* and *Ilex*. On limestone mountains, this subtype is usually mixed with III.1 subtype, and is characterized by many species of the genera *Myrsine, Berberis, Pistacia, Alchornea, Psidium, Desmos, Zanthoxylum, Pyracantha, Bauhimia, Callicarpa,* and *Viburnum*.

D. Tropical Shrublands

Tropical shrublands are restricted to humid, tropical mountains or southern subtropical dry, hot valleys. Their habitat is characterized by a coldest month mean temperature of 18°C and a year-round growing season. Two subtypes are identified.

1. Tropical Evergreen Broad-Leaved Shrubs

Tropical evergreen broad-leaved shrubs can be divided into two groups. One group includes drought-tolerant, evergreen, thorny species, mainly distributed on tropical coastal beaches. Commonly seen shrub species are *Pandanus tectorius, Atalantia buxifolia, Flacoustia indica, Scolopia chinensis, Phoenix hanceana, Phyllochlamys toxoides, Streblus asper,* and *Bambusa flexuosa*. Another group has mangroves as its main component and flourishes along the saline tropical and southern subtropical coasts from the southern tip of the Hainan Island (about 18° N, the so-called "edge of the earth") up to the northern Fujian coast (27°20′ N). Shrubs present include *Kandelia candel, Rhizophora apiculata, R. mucronata, Brugiera sexangula, B. conjugata, Avicennia marina, Aegceras corniculatum,* and *Acanthus ilicifolius*.

2. Tropical Fleshy Shrubs

Two groups are also recognized in the tropical fleshy shrubs. One group includes drought-resistant, fleshy, thorny shrubs, scattered chiefly in dry, hot valleys or along sandy coastal beaches. The main species are *Opuntia dillenii* and *Euphorbia royleana*. Another group includes salt-tolerant, fleshy, evergreen broad-leaved shrubs, which grow chiefly on the coral reefs of South China Sea islands. *Scaevola service, Messerschmiedia argentia, Perphis acidula,* and *Clerodendron inerme* are the main species. These shrubs create a beautiful greenish or silvery-greenish cover on the coral reefs.

IV. Uses of Shrublands in China

China has a very long and uninterrupted historical record. According to recent archaeological excavations verified by ^{14}C dating, agriculture was developed in China more than 7000 years ago. Consequently, the Chinese have a very long and well-developed tradition for using shrublands. The shrubs are used mostly for pasturing and fuel, but also for food, medicine, and industrial raw materials. Recently, cultivation of some economically valuable shrubs has been conducted on a large scale. Examples are the famous medicine-shrub "gou-chi" (*Lycium chinense*, Fig. 11) in the arid lands and the all-important tea (*Camellia sinensis*) and "You-cha" or "oil-tea" (*Camellia oleifera*) in the humid subtropics. New uses of shrubs for environmental protection and transformation of desertified land are also receiving considerable attention.

A. Human Food and Beverage

Many shrubs contain a high percentage of starch or sugar, or stimulants in their fruits, seeds, stems, or roots. The following shrubs are commonly used in China:

1. Tea or "cha": A subtropical, evergreen, broad-leaved shrub cultivated from antiquity in China and now also in India, Sri Lanka, Japan, Indonesia, and other countries. Its leaves, leaf buds, and internodes are prepared and cured for the market by several recognized methods to produce green tea, black tea, brick tea, etc. It is the most important aromatic beverage in China.
2. *Corylus heterophylla* and *C. mandschurica:* Two temperate, deciduous, broad-leaved shrubs of the same genus, with seeds containing 20% starch. They also contain tannin in leaves (6–14%) and in bark (9.4%).
3. *Castanea seguinii:* A subtropical, deciduous, broad-leaved shrub, with seeds containing 60–70% starch.
4. *Quercus fabra:* A subtropical, deciduous, broad-leaved shrub, with seeds containing 30% starch.
5. *Rosa hugonis* and *R. omeiensis:* Two subtropical, deciduous, broad-leaved shrubs, with edible fruits that can also be used to brew wine.
6. *Ostryopsis davidiana:* A temperate, deciduous, broad-leaved shrub, with edible seeds.
7. *Rubus corchorifolius:* A temperate, deciduous, broad-leaved shrub, with edible fruits that can also be used to make jam or brew wine.

8. *Hippophae rhamnoides:* A temperate, deciduous, broad-leaved shrub, with edible fruits used to make jam or wine.
9. *Zizyphus jujuba* var. *spinosas:* A temperate, deciduous, broad-leaved shrub, with fruits that contain 6% sugar and seeds containing 24% starch.
10. *Vaccimium bracteatum:* A subtropical, evergreen, broad-leaved shrub, with fruits containing 20% sugar.
11. *Vaccimium uliginosum* and *V. vitis-idaea:* Two temperate, evergreen, broad-leaved shrubs, with fruits to brew wine and make jam. Their seeds also contain 30% of an industrial-used oil as well as 11 to 19% tannin.
12. *Smilax glabra* and *S. japonica:* Two subtropical, evergreen, broad-leaved shrubs, whose stems and roots contain about 70% starch.
13. *Nitraria sibirica* (Fig. 5) and *N. tangytorum:* These two shrubs are called by the Chinese name "white thorn" because of their whitish color and thorny stem. They are widely distributed in temperate deserts and desert-steppes. The fruits are edible and colorful, and are called "desert cherries."

B. Oil and Fat

The following shrubs are widely used for oil and fat (partly edible):
1. *Lindera glauca:* A subtropical, deciduous, broad-leaved shrub, with nuts containing 42% of an industrial-used oil. It also contains 1% aromatic oil in its leaves.
2. *Lespedeza bicolor:* A temperate, deciduous, broad-leaved shrub, with seeds containing 11% of an industrial-used oil. It is widely distributed in north China and northeast China.
3. *Camellia oleifera* (with white flowers) and *C. reticulata* (with red flowers): These two well-known subtropical evergreen "you-cha" shrubs are widely cultivated in south China and southwest China, chiefly on foothills and terraced mountain slopes. Their seeds contain about 70% edible oil and have a delicious taste. They are now the most important edible oil in Yunnan, Hunan, and other southern provinces.
4. *Vitex negundo:* A subtropical, evergreen, broad-leaved shrub or small tree, with seeds containing 20% of an oil used for industrial purposes.
5. *Vitex chinensis:* This temperate, deciduous, broad-leaved shrub is widely distributed in north China and northeast China. Its seeds contain 16% of an oil used for industrial purposes. The stems and leaves also contain from 0.5 to 0.7% of an aromatic oil.

6. *Zanthoxylum bungeanum* and *Z. schinifolium:* These two subtropical, evergreen, broad-leaved shrubs are mostly cultivated for their seeds, which contain 24 to 31% of an edible oil that is also useful for industrial purposes.

7. *Rhus chinensis:* A subtropical, deciduous, broad-leaved shrub or small tree, with seeds containing 20 to 25% of an oil for industrial uses. The whole plant is also rich in tannin.

8. *Phyllanthus emblica:* A subtropical, deciduous, broad-leaved shrub or small tree, with seeds containing 16% of an industrial-quality oil. The bark, leaves, and fruits contain tannin.

9. *Lonicera maackii:* A temperate, deciduous, broad-leaved shrub that may grow as tall as 5 m. It is locally called "gold-silver wood" and produces seeds containing up to 36% of an oil for industrial use.

10. *Prunus armeniaca* L. var. *ansu:* A temperate, deciduous, broad-leaved shrub or small tree, widely distributed in north China and northeast China. The plants are mainly located on dry, sunny slopes and produce seeds containing nearly 50% of an oil useful for industrial and medical use.

11. *Capparis spinosa:* A temperate, deciduous, drought-tolerant shrubby vine, distributed mainly in arid northwest China, which produces seeds containing 35% of an oil for industrial use.

C. Aromatic Compounds

Many shrubs have flowers, fruits, seeds, stems, or leaves that contain valuable aromatic compounds that are widely used in different industries. The following aromatic shrubs are commonly used in China:

1. *Rosa rugosa:* A temperate, deciduous, broad-leaved shrub with flowers containing 0.03% of high-quality aromatic oil. It grows wild in north China and south China.

2. *Sabina pingii* and *Juniperus sibirica:* These two alpine, evergreen, needle-leaved shrubs grow near the forest line on mountains of northeast China and northwest China. They contain aromatic oil in stems, leaves, and roots.

3. *Continus coggygria:* A subtropical, deciduous, broad-leaved shrub, with aromatic oil in the leaves.

4. *Rhododendron dahuricum:* A deciduous, broad-leaved shrub, distributed mainly under cool-temperate needle-leaved forest. It contains about 0.94 ml/100 g of an aromatic oil in leaves.

5. *Rhododendron fastigiatum:* An alpine, evergreen, dwarf shrub distributed mainly in the Tibetan Plateau and its surrounding high mountains. It contains about 0.53% aromatic oil in its leaves.

6. *Thymus mongolicus:* This temperate, deciduous, dwarf shrub contains about 0.6% aromatic oil in stems and leaves.
7. *Zanthoxylum planipinum:* This subtropical, semievergreen, broad-leaved shrub is distributed mainly in sites of karst topography. It contains 0.02 to 0.08% aromatic oil in its stems and leaves and 0.24 to 0.79% in fruits.
8. *Gaultheria yunnanensis:* Plants of this subtropical, evergreen, dwarf shrub are distributed mainly in the high mountains of southwest China. Stems and leaves contains 0.5 to 0.85% aromatic oil.
9. *Gavdenia jasminoides:* A subtropical, evergreen, broad-leaved shrub distributed in remote wild mountains. Its beautiful flowers contain 0.4 to 0.5% aromatic oil. It has now been widely planted in many subtropical gardens.

D. Tannin Extract

In addition to the species mentioned above, the following shrubs are commonly used as a source for extracting tannin, an important industrial raw material:

1. Yellow-flowered willow (*Salix caprea*): A temperate, deciduous shrub or tree that contains 9.4% tannin in its leaves.
2. *Rhododendron simsii:* A subtropical, semievergreen, broad-leaved shrub distributed widely in low mountain areas. Stems and leaves are rich in tannin.
3. *Rhodomyrtus tomentosa:* A subtropical, small shrub, with 12.8% tannin in leaves and branches as well as 20% in bark and roots.

E. Fibers

Many shrubs have branches, stems, and leaves usable for fabricating baskets and other kitchen utensils, and for making pulp and artificial plates. They include *Caragana microphylla* and *C. stenophylla* (Fig. 3), *Amorpha fruticosa, Bauhinia hupehena, Periploca sepium, Lespedeza bicolor, Sinarundnaria* spp., and *Dapline* spp.

F. Medicines

The Chinese pharmacy has used many kinds of shrubs for medicinal purpose since ancient times. Probably the most important use is the fruits

Figure 11. The valuable medicine shrub *Lycium chinense* with ripening fruits on a state farm in the Qaidam Basin.

of "gou-chi," which grows wild in temperate desert and desert-steppe environments and is now widely planted in many gardens and farms, including the state farms in the extremely harsh Qaidam Basin (Fig. 11). The Ningxia Hui Autonomous Region is famous for its "gou-chi" production, a considerable part of which has been exported to Southeast Asia and other countries.

Other shrubs used for medicine include the seeds of *Prunus armeniaca* and *Zizyphus spinosus,* the fruits of *Forsythia suspense* and *Vitex negundo,* the flowers of *Lonicera japonica,* and the leaves of *Rhododendron vitis-idaea.*

G. Grazing

Practically every shrub can be browsed. In arid northwestern China and on the frigid Tibetan Plateau, where shrubs are a major and primary vegetation component, they are important feed plants. In the harsh, extremely arid deserts, camels and goats feed exclusively on shrubs, Consequently, most of China's shrublands have been grazed for thousands of years and are still heavily grazed.

H. Fuel

Another important use of shrublands is for fuel. Especially in China's extensive mountain environments and in arid northwestern China, as well as the frigid Tibetan Plateau, different kinds of shrubs rank as major fuel sources. Some shrubs in arid lands, such as *Haloxylon ammodendron* (Fig. 7), are particularly famous for their high quality as fuel, and are thus intensively exploited. They have been removed in excessive amounts recently. Most of China's shrublands suffer from overexploitation as fuel.

Figure 12. *Hedysarum scoparium* in the Hexi Corridor. (Note the *Poplar* trees in the background used as windbreaks.)

Now, plans for planting "fuel-forests" of shrubs and small trees have been put in practice in many provinces.

I. Environmental Protection and Transformation

Recently, shelter-belts composed of trees and shrubs have been planted to protect farms, pastures, settlements, and highways in northwest China and north China. The famous "Green Great Wall," more than 5000 km in length, is being built in north China and northwest China. As an effective measure to fix active sand dunes and to combat soil erosion, large patches of shrublands have been established around the sandy deserts and on the Loess Plateau. For example, to control shifting sands, *Hedysarum scoparium* (Fig. 12), *Haloxylon ammodendron* (Fig. 7), *Tamarix* spp. (Fig. 4), *Calligonum mongolicum,* and many other psammophytes are planted inside the checkerboards on sand dunes in the Hexi Corridor and the Nigxia Plain (Zhu and Liu, 1979). The most famous results have been obtained at the Minqin Desert Research Station and the Sha-po-tau Railway Sand-Control Station. On the southeastern Ordos Plateau, where desertification has been very serious during the last 1000 years, *Artemisia ordosica* (Fig. 13) and other psammophytes have recently been planted for the same purpose. In addition, people in many localities are planting shrubs and trees to improve environmental quality.

Figure 13. *Artemisia ordosica* in the northwestern Ordos Plateau.

V. Problems and Prospects

The most pressing current problem for China's shrublands is their protection. As a whole, they have been overused and misused, especially in harsh arid environments (Dahl and McKell, 1987). It is easy to cut down a shrub, yet it is very difficult for it to regrow or for a new plant to establish. A long time is usually needed, and sometimes a plant is unable to regrow. The shrubland ecosystem is also very fragile, and removal of sand-fixing and soil-conserving shrubs can lead quickly to accelerated sand-shifting and soil-eroding hazards (Zhao and Xing, 1982). For example, the ruthless cutting of *Haloxylon* spp. and other shrubs in the Gurbantungut Desert of the Jungger Basin during the so-called Cultural Revolution period (1966–1975) caused the percentage of shifting sands in the desert to increase from about 3% to more than 10% (Zhu and Liu, 1979).

China's shrublands need to be improved. Many areas should be sown or planted to supplement existing vegetation. New shrub species should be introduced, especially those with positive economic value. In addition, new technologies for improving shrublands, such as inoculation with mycorrhizae, tissue culture production of elite biotypes, and genetic engineering to improve economically valuable products, should be introduced and adopted as soon as possible.

An overall scheme for the management of shrubland utilization is needed. For example, instead of simply gathering, cutting, and exploiting, they should be conservatively "harvested" and kept continually in efficient production. New uses of shrubs, such as in land rehabilitation and reclamation of mining areas conducted on a large scale in the United States, West Germany, and other developed countries, should be practiced in China.

Shrublands should be developed according to geographic features of soil and topographic suitability. In humid eastern China, nearly all shrubs exist as either secondary growth or cultivated crops. With a few exceptions (such as in the karst areas), forests should be mainly restored, while shrubby species useful for food, oil, and other economic crops should be included as much as possible. In the mountain environment, where the so-called "vertical agriculture" constitutes the major land use pattern, shrubby crops will be a major component of the vegetation on foothills and lower gentle slopes. In arid northwestern China, shrubs are generally much better adapted than tree or grasses to adjust and to survive the desert and desert-steppe environments. Here they should be firmly established as zonal vegetation and, in planting shelter belts, shrubs should be given equal priority with drought-tolerant trees. On the frigid Tibetan Plateau, shrubs can be established as zonal vegetation on upper areas of high mountains.

Shrublands, because of their economic uses, need to be modernized in the near future. In humid eastern China, population pressure results in a reduction of shrublands in area and in density, but they could be increased greatly in quality. In contrast, in arid northwestern China and on the frigid Tibetan Plateau, shrublands should be managed as principal components of zonal vegetation and greatly improved both in quantity and in quality.

References

Dahl, B., and McKell, C. M. (1987). Use and abuse of China's arid lands. *Rangeland J.* (in press).

Fullard, H. (1968). "China in Maps." George Phillip & Son, London.

Walker, A. S. (1982). Deserts of China. *Am. Sci.* **70**(4), 366–376.

Zhao, S., and Xing, J. M. (1982). Origin and development of the Shamo (sandy deserts) and the Gobi (stony deserts) of China. *Striae* **17**, 79–91.

Zhu, Z., and Liu, S. (1979). "The Prevention and Control of Deserts and Desertification in China." Lanzhou Institute of Desert Research, Chinese Academy of Sciences.

II

Environmental Influences and Plant Responses

The natural environment of shrubs is often unfavorable in that it limits individual plant growth as well as inhibits the productivity of plant communities. Community structure and density are markedly influenced by total and seasonal distribution of rainfall and by temperature patterns.

Plant responses to adverse environmental influences are manifested in ecological strategies that include clumping of plant density into islands (with open space between clumps for conservation of soil moisture), seasonal sequencing of variable species in growth activity (which reduces direct competition for scarce ecosystem resources), modification of plant morphology (to improve the effectivity of thermal exchange and to reduce evapotranspiration), and reduction of total biomass (to assure that reproduction occurs).

Under intense herbivory, successional species replacement and dominance may occur as the less palatable species occupy available space vacated by palatable ones removed by grazing.

Many shrubs are able to survive in stressed environments because of their relatively small stature, unique structural features, reproductive vigor, and ability to restrict herbivory through the presence of secondary metabolites and structural defences such as spines and stout twig ends.

10

Shrubs as a Growth Form

G. Orshan

I. Introduction

It is generally accepted that shrubs are plants with lignified stems not developing a distinct main trunk. The stems branch from their basal part above or below the soil surface. This is a more generalized definition than

Du Rietz's (1931) and includes dwarf shrubs, half-shrubs, and cushion plants. Since such a general definition covers plants differing from each other in their size, physiognomy, architecture, and structure, it is the aim of the present chapter to examine and suggest ways of describing and characterizing the great diversity of forms and growth habits of the shrubs as a group.

In various growth form systems, shrubs were divided and classified according to different characters such as plant height (Lindman, 1914; Warming, 1909, 1916; Skottsberg, 1921; Drude, 1928; Du Rietz, 1931), extent of stem lignification (Lindman, 1914; Warming, 1916; Drude, 1928; Rubel, 1930; Du Rietz, 1931), stem consistency (Warming, 1916; Drude, 1928; Du Rietz, 1931), plant mobility (Lindman, 1914; Warming, 1909, 1916; Skottsberg 1921; Drude, 1928; Du Rietz, 1931), bud protection (Rubel, 1930), spinescence (Reiter, 1885; Drude, 1928), and seasonality (Reiter, 1885; Drude, 1928; Rubel, 1930).

Practically all growth form systems known so far are hierarchic with the hierarchy based on different characters in each of them. The character upon which the first subdivision is made had obviously been considered to be more important than the characters determining the following subdivisions. However, the reasons for choosing a certain hierarchic order of characters are not clear in most cases. Generally they seem to depend on the aim of studying and classifying growth forms and the goals toward which these studies should lead.

Apart from clearly expressing the diversity of plant structure and architecture as an objective for itself, the study of plant growth forms is also aimed at obtaining a better insight into the effect of environmental factors in the past and present on plant structure and into plant adaptations to the environmental complex.

One should admit that we know relatively little of what the adaptive values are of the different growth form characters and in most cases we know even less as to how these characters interact in affecting plant adaptation to the environment. It is thus evident that all hierarchic growth form systems express the personal outlook of their authors and the objectives they tried to achieve by the aid of these systems.

To avoid this subjective predetermination of the relative importance of the growth form characters it had been suggested by the author (Orshan, 1983) to use the monocharacter approach in studying plant growth forms. According to this approach several growth form types are defined for each character forming a monocharacter growth form system, for example Raunkiaer's main life-form types that are based on the location of the renewal buds. In the same way parallel growth form systems, each of them based on one character only (e.g., plant height, life duration of leaves, leaf consistency, and others), have been defined. The characters were selected to be mutually exclusive by definition.

Each species can then be characterized in parallel by a series of monocharacter growth form types, based on different characters. When the monocharacter types are determined for each of the species of vegetation units of different ranks in different localities, the data could be analyzed in the following ways:

1. Determine the distribution of each of the monocharacter growth form types within each of the vegetation units and/or territories examined as compared to each other.
2. Determine and compare the distribution of combinations of two or more monocharacter growth form types of different vegetation units and territories.
3. Choose polycharacter growth form types, the distribution of which will be tested along ecological gradients as a first step in determining a polycharacter growth form system or systems that will hopefully better represent plant adaptation to various environmental stresses on one hand, and better describe the physiognomy of plants and plant communities on the other.

In the following an attempt will be made to apply the monocharacter growth form types approach to shrubs. The parallel monocharacter types that are supposed to be more suitable for shrubs are:

- Plant height
- Stem consistency
- Location of renewal buds
- Nature of organs periodically shed
- Life duration of assimilating organs
- Seasonality of assimilating organs
- Leaf size
- Leaf consistency

Each of them will be described in detail and the result of using them to analyze the shrub components of a few selected plant communities in Israel and South Africa will be discussed.

II. Description of Monocharacter Growth Forms

A. *Plant Height*

Plant height was used by several authors (Lindman, 1914; Warming, 1909, 1916; Skottsberg, 1921; Drude, 1928; Du Rietz, 1931) to subdivide shrubs into several classes. Orshan (1983) defined plant height as the maximal height the plant attains under optimal ecological conditions in the field during the seasons of its maximal growth activity. For example, the height of half shrubs is that when the annual parts of their shoots attain their maximal length.

Du Rietz (1931) suggested 0.05, 0.25, 0.8, 2, and 8 m as values delimiting different height classes and terms like high–ordinary–tall and dwarf–low dwarf–very low dwarf shrubs are determined on the basis of these values. Orshan (1983) suggested the values of 0.10, 0.25, 0.50, 1.0, 2, 5, and 10 m as determining height classes. For shrubs it is generally suggested to apply the following names to the height classes listed below:

- Tall shrubs > 5.0 m
- High shrubs   2–5 m
- Low shrubs   0.5–2 m
- Dwarf shrubs < 0.5 m

B. Stem Consistency

Stem consistency is defined according to the degree of lignification and succulence. A lignified stem is one that under field conditions, remains alive and lignified for more than one growing season. Since by definition shrubs are plants with at least part of their branches lignified, the following lignification types apply to shrubs:

1. Holoxyles—Plants with all their branches lignified.
2. Hemixyles—Plants with part of their branches nonlignified. One should point out that these could not necessarily be the upper branches or the upper parts of the branches (see Section II, D).

Apart from the above types, the following should be added.

3. Stem succulents—Plants with nonlignified succulent stems, for example, *Opuntia* spp.
4. Ligno-stem succulents—Plants with lignified stems that have a succulent sheath, for example, *Carnegia gigantea*.
5. Articulate plants—Ligno-succulent plants with a succulent sheath interrupted in the nodes, for example, *Anabasis articulata*.

C. Location of Renewal Buds

Location of renewal buds is the character upon which the well-known Raunkiaer's (1904) life-form system is based. Shrubs are generally either chamaephytes or phanerophytes, although they might also be hemicryptophytes or even geophytes.

Raunkiaer (1904) introduced the term perennating buds and suggested that their location on the plants best represents the capability of the plant to survive the unfavorable season. Others (e.g., Du Rietz, 1931; Braun-Blanquet, 1964; Mueller-Dombois and Ellenberg, 1974) replaced the term perennating buds by the term renewal buds, that is, the buds from which new organs and foliage develop after an unfavorable season. One should point out that these two terms are not necessarily identical, especially for chamaephytic shrubs and half-shrubs, which dominate certain hot deserts and steppes. Most of their renewal buds do not pass the unfavorable summer season as buds but as partly active brachyblasts from which the inflorescence-bearing dolichoblasts develop in the following spring (Orshan, 1964). Under such circumstances the term perennating buds loses its meaning and therefore it is suggested to adopt the term renewal buds.

Let renewal buds, therefore, be defined as buds from which vegetative shoots (bearing or not bearing flowers and fruits) develop and that periodically and rhythmically replace older ones.

One should point out that the words "periodically and rhythmically" and not "seasonally" were used here since the life duration of the organs being replaced may exceed one season in certain cases. The life-forms according to Raunkiaer (1904) that might be relevant to shrubs are:

1. Cryptophytes—Plants whose renewal buds are located in the ground or in water.
2. Hemicryptophytes—Plants whose renewal buds are located at the soil surface.
3. Chamaephytes—Plants whose renewal buds are not higher than 25 cm above ground.
4. Phanerophytes—Plants with renewal buds borne on shoots projecting into the air higher than 25 cm above ground.

In addition to these types, there are plants that have more than one type of renewal bud. The organs developing from them replace older ones at different time intervals. It is suggested to classify these plants as amphiphytes, which should be subdivided according to the location of the different types of renewal buds:

• Hemi-chamaephytes (e.g., *Brachypodium ramosum*, *Ononis antiquorum*)
• Geo-chamaephytes (e.g., *Asparagus cappensis*)
• Geo-phanerophytes (e.g., *Rubus* spp., certain mallee *Eucalyptus* species)

D. Shedding Types

The nature of organs periodically shed was suggested by Orshan (1953) to better represent plant adaptation to the unfavorable season in arid environments than the location of the renewal buds.

Here again the word "periodically" and not "seasonally" is used since the life duration of the organs periodically shed is not necessarily always one growing season or part of it. The types proposed that are relevant to shrubs are:

1. Shoot shedders—Plants periodically shedding their whole shoot, for example, geophytes and hemicryptophytes.
2. Branch shedders—Plants periodically shedding part of their branches.
3. Leaf shedders—Plants periodically shedding only their leaves and inflorescence.

Orshan (1983) distinguished between basipetal branch shedders and acropetal ones. The half-shrubs (Du Rietz, 1931) belong to the basipetal branch shedders since their upper branches die back to a certain height. There are many shrubs and even trees, however, that are acropetal branch shedders. A good example might be *Anthospermum aethiopicum* (Orshan, 1988) growing in the Cape Peninsula of South Africa. It has two types of branches—dolichoblasts that elongate rapidly mainly at the beginning of the growing season and partial brachyblasts that develop at the axils of the leaves of the dolichoblasts.

Although the plant is characterized by apical growth and generally bears inflorescence, not all the dolichoblasts continue to elongate in subsequent seasons. Most of them with their fruit-bearing brachyblasts die in their second year and are shed in their fourth or sometimes fifth year in an acropetal direction.

Acropetal branch shedders are common in South Africa (e.g., *Berzelia langninosa, Elytropappus rhinocerotis, Anthospermum aethiopicum,* and many others) and Australia (e.g., many *Eucalyptus* species, *Melaleuca* spp., and many others). One should point out that *Calluna vulgaris, Erica arborea, Erica tetralix,* and other Ericaceae that are components of European heaths belong to this type (Gimingham, 1972).

E. Life Duration of Assimilating Organs

Life duration of a leaf is the time during which the leaf stays green and intact. Leaves that stay intact dead (of so-called semideciduous plants, e.g., *Quercus pyrenaica*) are considered to be dead.

Life duration of a green stem is the time the stem stays green. Stems losing their green color after less than 3 months are not considered to be green stems. When a plant bears both leaves and green stems their life duration should be accounted for separately.

It is evident that the life span of leaves is not uniform for all plants. For some *Quercus* species (e.g., *Quercus calliprinos, Q. ilex*), some of the leaves live longer than the others although they look identical in shape and structure. It is suggested to consider in such cases the life span of the majority of the leaves, stating also the maximal leaf life span for the species. Certain plants like biseasonally dimorphic chamaephytes (Orshan, 1964) have more than one type of leaves that generally develop in different seasons. It is suggested that the life span of each of these be stated separately. If this is impossible, the life span of the longest-living leaves should be accounted for.

Since the leaves of many evergreen trees and shrubs last slightly more than a year, with the old leaves being shed only after the newly grown ones have already been developed, the time ranges for the suggested types are as follows:

- < 6 months
- 6–14 months
- 14–26 months
- 26–38 months
- 38–50 months

F. Seasonality of Assimilating Organs

Seasonality is defined by the seasons in which plants bear photosynthesizing and transporting organs. A plant is considered to be active even when the greater part of its green body has been shed so long as it bears green leaves and/or green stems.

It is suggested to delimit the summer season as March–August in the Northern Hemisphere and as September–February in the Southern Hemisphere, while the winter will be delimited as September–February and March–August, respectively. An early starting summer was chosen because the intensive growing season starts rather early in Mediterranean-type countries immediately with the rise in temperature in spring.

The subdivision of the year into two seasons is proposed only because a more detailed subdivision will result in a great number of activity season types that will be difficult to determine and later to interpret. Eventually when the life cycles of plants have been studied in detail, the activity seasons of different leaf and branch types can be recorded by month and analyzed accordingly.

The following are the four seasonality types proposed:

1. Evergreen—Plants bearing green organs year-round. They might shed most of their leaves in winter or summer but are considered to be evergreens as long as part of their green body remains intact year-round.
2. Winter deciduous—Plants shedding their green organs only in winter or in part of it.
3. Summer deciduous—Plants shedding all their green organs only in summer or in part of it.
4. Biseasonal—Plants bearing green organs in parts of both seasons or during the whole of one season and part of the other.

G. Leaf Size

Raunkiaer's (1934) leaf size classes are followed but three more were added to better represent leaf size diversity of Mediterranean-type ecosystems. The classes are:

- Subleptophyll ≤ 0.10 cm
- Leptophyll   0.10–0.25 cm
- Nanophyll   0.25–2.25 cm
- Nano-microphyll   2.25–12.25 cm
- Microphyll   12.25–20.25 cm
- Micro-mesophyll   20.25–56.25 cm
- Mesophyll   56.25–180.25 cm
- Macrophyll   180.25–1640.25 cm
- Megaphyll   >1640.25 cm

H. Leaf Consistency

Six types of leaf consistency are suggested. The boundaries between them are not sharp and although it may be difficult sometimes to determine them accurately under marginal situations in the field, the author's experience showed reasonably good agreement between his field determinations and some quantitative parameters cited below, determined in the laboratory by R. L. Specht. The types proposed are:

- Malacophyll
- Semisclerophyll
- Sclerophyll
- Semisucculent
- Water-succulent
- Resin-succulent

The boundaries between malacophylls, semisclerophylls, and sclerophylls should be defined by numerical values to be determined from the ratio

$$\frac{\text{Leaf area}}{\text{Leaf dry weight}}$$

The boundaries between the water-succulents and semisucculents and the other types should be defined by numerical values to be determined from the ratio

$$\frac{\text{Leaf volume}}{\text{Leaf dry weight}}$$

Semisucculents are water semisucculents. It is relatively easy to define the resin-succulents in the field.

III. Monocharacter Growth Form Spectra of Selected Mediterranean-Type Shrub Communities in Israel and South Africa

The monocharacter growth forms mentioned above were used to characterize shrub plant communities in Mediterranean-type ecosystems of Israel and South Africa. In the following, only the distribution of the monocharacter growth form types will be presented.

In Israel the shrub components of three maquis plant associations in the Upper Galilee and of three desert shrub associations in the Negev were analyzed. The analysis is based on phytosociological tables that sum up vegetation records made in 500-m^2 quadrats by Rabinovich-Vin (1979) in the Upper Galilee and in 100-m^2 quadrats by Danin (1970) in the Negev. Altogether, 30 vegetation records with 48 shrub species were made in the Galilee and 65 records containing 52 species in the Negev. The annual amount of rainfall in the Galilee is 750–1000 mm and in the Negev 80–150 mm.

In South Africa the work was carried out recently in collaboration with A. Le Roux. Here only preliminary data are presented. A more detailed account of the growth form analysis there will be published at a later date.

Since plant communities in South Africa were not studied in the same detail as in Israel, a few sample plant records were taken in three major vegetation types that were considered subjectively to represent them well. The following vegetation types (Acocks, 1953) were examined in the winter rainfall part of South Africa with a Mediterranean-type climate.

1. Orange River Broken Veld—Five records were taken with 62 shrub species.
2. Succulent Karoo—Two records were taken with 31 shrub species.
3. Mountain Fynbos—Three records were taken in Jonkershoeck with 43 shrub species.

The annual rainfall of the Orange River Broken Veld and the Succulent Karoo is of the same order of magnitude as that of the Negev. The amount of rainfall in the Jonkershoeck Fynbos site is higher than that of the Upper Galilee.

Tables I–VIII show the distribution of the single monocharacter growth form types as percentages of the number of species present without taking into account their relative cover.

A. Plant Height—Table I shows that in both South Africa and Israel plant heeight decreases with decreasing average annual rainfall and in both countries is of more or less the same order of magnitude under parallel conditions.

B. Stem Consistency—It is evident (Table II) that the percentages of holoxyles are higher in South Africa than in Israel and in both countries they increase with the increase of annual rainfall. The percentages of hemixyles are, on the other hand, markedly higher in Israel than in South Africa and in both countries they decrease with increasing rainfall. Stem succulents are altogether absent in Israel and in the Fynbos sites recorded in South Africa, while articulate plants appear in both countries in the more arid habitats only.

C. Location of Renewal Buds—When one compares the spectra of Raunkiaer's life-form types based on the location of the renewal buds in both countries it is evident (Table III) that for parallel habitats they are

Table I.   Distribution in percentage of presence of shrub height classes in selected plant communities of winter rainfall areas of Israel and South Africa

Vegetation type	Plant height (cm.)						
	< 10	10–25	25–50	50–100	100–200	200–500	500–1000
Israel							
Desert shrubland		12	53	33	2		
Mediterranean maquis		4	38	28	28	2	
South Africa							
Orange River Broken Veld	14	12	40	24	5	4	1
Succulent Karoo	13	18	36	30	3		
Mountain Fynbos			7	13	36	25	19

Table II. Distribution in percentage of presence of shrub stem consistency types in selected plant communities of winter rainfall areas of Israel and South Africa

	Stem consistency type			
Vegetation type	Holoxyle	Hemixyle	Stem succulent	Articulate
Israel				
Desert shrubland	8	86		6
Mediterranean maquis	44	56		
South Africa				
Orange River Broken Veld	46	36	15	3
Succulent Karoo	63	30	7	
Mountain Fynbos	89	11		

surprisingly similar, with percentage of phanerophytes lower and that of chamaephytes higher in more arid habitats.

D. Shedding Types—Table IV presents the growth from spectra based on the nature of the organs periodically shed. One may neglect the shoot shedders with their low representation, which hardly may be considered as typical shrubs, although they have lignified stems persisting for a few growing seasons, and concentrate on leaf and branch shedders. It is evident that the situation in Israel is altogether different from that of South Africa. Leaf shedders are absent from the desert shrub communities of Israel and are well represented in the maquis communities. In South Africa, on the other hand, their percentages increase with increasing aridity. Similar opposite trends can be noted for total branch shedders, with their percentages increasing with increasing aridity in Israel and decreasing in South Africa.

Table III. Distribution in percentage of presence of shrub renewal bud location types (Raunkiaer's main life-form types) in selected plant communities of winter rainfall areas of Israel and South Africa

	Renewal bud location type			
Vegetation	Cryptophyte	Hemicryptophyte	Chamaephtye	Phanerophyte
Israel				
Desert shrubland	2	4	86	8
Mediterranean maquis		12	48	40
South Africa				
Orange River Broken Veld	1	6	79	14
Succulent Karoo	6	5	79	10
Mountain Fynbos	2		45	53

Table IV. Distribution in percentage of presence of shrub shedding types in selected plant communities of winter rainfall areas of Israel and South Africa

Vegetation type	Shoot shedders	Basipetal branch shedders	Acropetal branch shedders	Total branch shedders	Leaf shedders
Israel					
Desert shrubland	6	94		94	
Mediterranean maquis	12	44	2	46	42
South Africa					
Orange River					
Broken Veld	3	38	3	41	56
Succulent Karoo	7	34	10	44	49
Mountain Fynbos	2	16	59	75	23

It had been suggested (Orshan, 1953, 1964) that basipetal branch shedding is an attribute of plant adaptation to drought, since it contributes to the reduction of the transpiring body of the plant in the critical summer season. In fact the percentages of basipetal branch shedders increase also in South Africa with increasing aridity. It turns out that acropetal branch shedders, the branches of which die and are eventually regularly shed after more than one growing season, are similar to leaf shedders, since this type of branch shedding does not directly contribute to seasonal reduction of the transpiring body of the plant. In fact, their percentages markedly decrease with increasing aridity.

E. Life Duration of Assimilating Organs—Apart from a trend to longer life duration of assimilating organs in South Africa as compared to Israel, no conciliation between aridity and the life span of assimilating organs can be noticed in Israel, while in South Africa the average longevity of the organs in the Fynbos is clearly higher than that in the other sites (Table V). This may be attributed to the lower nutrient contents of the rock and soil types in the Fynbos habitats.

F. Seasonality—Table VI shows that summer deciduous plants are altogether absent in Israel and winter deciduous ones are absent in South Africa and in the arid sites of Israel. The percentages of evergreen plants as well as those of the summer shedders seem not to be affected by aridity. The above facts may suggest that in Mediterranean-type ecosystems seasonality is determined to a greater extent by the evolutionary past of the taxa than by recent adaptations to the environment. It is suggested that the winter deciduous plants invaded the Mediterranean Basin from the adjacent Irano-Turanian and Euro-Siberian regions with their severe winter.

Table V. Distribution in percentage of presence of shrub types of life duration of assimilating organs in selected plant communities of winter rainfall areas of Israel and South Africa

Vegetation type	Life duration of assimilating organs (months)			
	<6	6–14	14–26	26–38
Israel				
Desert shrubland	4	81	15	
Mediterranean maquis	4	87	9	
South Africa				
Orange River				
Broken Veld	11	61	28	
Succulent Karoo	3	70	27	
Mountain Fynbos		56	27	17

Such adjacent regions do not exist in South Africa. Even the evergreenness is not in full harmony with the Mediterranean climate, which is characterized by a relatively dry and hot summer.

G. Leaf Size—As seen from Table VII, it is evident that in Israel leaf size tends to decrease in arid habitats and the range of leaf size values of the maquis is markedly higher than that of the desert shrubland. In South Africa, on the other hand, the average leaf size of the more humid Fynbos is markedly lower than that of the more arid communities.

When one compares sites of similar amounts of rainfall in the two countries, the leaf size of the Fynbos components is markedly smaller than that of the maquis ones. In the more arid sites leaf size in the Negev does not exceed 2.25 cm, whereas in South Africa higher size classes are also

Table VI. Distribution in percentage of presence of shrub seasonality types in selected plant communities of winter rainfall areas of Israel and South Africa

Vegetation type	Seasonality type			
	Evergreen	Winter shedders	Summer shedders	Biseasonal
Israel				
Desert shrubland	98			2
Mediterranean maquis	73	21		6
South Africa				
Orange River				
Broken Veld	59		40	1
Succulent Karoo	66		34	
Mountain Fynbos	64		36	

Table VII.   Distribution in percentage of presence of shrub leaf size classes in selected plant communities of winter rainfall areas of Israel and South Africa

Vegetation type	Leaf Size (cm^2)					
	<0.10	0.10–0.25	0.25–2.25	2.25–12.25	12.25–20.25	20.25–50.25
Israel						
Desert shrubland	2	19	79			
Mediterranean maquis		4	52	40	2	2
South Africa						
Orange River						
Broken Veld	11	21	38	26	4	
Succulent Karoo	10	10	45	35		
Mountain Fynbos	32	14	25	25	4	

represented. However, when one compares the percentages of leaves exceeding 0.25 cm^2, the values are 79% for the Negev shrubland and 68 and 80% for the Orange River Broken Veld and the Succulent Karoo, respectively (Table VII).

H. Leaf Consistency—A glance at Table VIII shows similar trends in the distribution of leaf consistency types in Israel and South Africa. Leaf succulents are altogether missing in the more humid sites and play an important role in the more arid ones. The percentage of succulents and semisucculents in the Negev of Israel is 38, whereas in the Orange River Broken Veld and the Succulent Karoo they amount to 67 and 88%, respectively. On the other hand, the percentages of sclerophylls and semisclerophylls put together exceed 50 in the Fynbos and the maquis.

IV. Conclusions

The data presented above may serve as an example of some advantages of describing shrubs by the use of the monocharacter growth form approach.

Detailed descriptions of single species and their monocharacter growth form types were not presented here. In fact, a matrix of monocharacter growth form types against species could be prepared for regions of various sizes, put on computer, and serve as a basis for describing and analyzing single-site plant communities and whole ecosystems within the relevant region. Morever, monocharacter growth form types based on additional characters, such as canopy dimension and density, leaf color, morphology of underground stems, regeneration types, life duration of plant, and others (Orshan, 1983, 1986), could also be used.

Table VIII. Distribution in percentage of presence of shrub leaf consistency types in selected plant communities of winter rainfall areas of Israel and South Africa

Vegetation type	Leaf consistency type					
	Malacophyll	Semisclerophyll	Sclerophyll	Semisucculent	Water-succulent	Resin-succulent
Israel						
Desert shrubland	42	8	8	13	23	2
Mediterranean maquis	46	25	29			
South Africa						
Orange River						
Broken Veld	28	1	4	16	51	
Succulent Karoo	10		3	16	72	
Mountain Fynbos	43	24	33			

Some of the results of distribution of the single-character growth form types presented turn out to be interesting. The high frequency of basipetal branch shedding in Israel and in the Mediterranean Basin in general against a higher percentage of acropetal branch shedding in the Fynbos (Table IV), which is also characteristic of many Australian shrubs, is interesting. Acropetal branch shedding seems to be characteristic to the Southern Hemisphere. It would be interesting to find out whether this will also hold true for South America. As mentioned above, basipetal branch shedding seems to be an adaptation to drought or to low temperatures.

The fact that succulent leaves are absent altogether in the more humid parts, in both Israel and South Africa, is interesting. It may be related to accumulation of salts in the upper soil layers under average annual rainfall values lower than 250–300 mm, which, under Mediterranean conditions, does not allow a full recharge and leaching of the soil profile every year.

From these examples it is evident that analyses of shrub growth forms by the aid of independent single characters do not explain facts but help in pointing out problems to be looked into and serve as objects of research.

References

Acocks, J. P. (1953). "Veld types of South Africa" *Bot. Sur. Mem.* No. 28. Dep. of Agric., Union of South Africa, Pretoria.

Braun-Blanquet, J. G. F. (1964). "Pflanzensoziologie. Grundlagen der Vegetationskunde." Springer-Verlag, New York.

Danin, A. (1970). A phytosociological ecological study of the northern Negev of Israel. Ph.D. Thesis, Hebrew University of Jerusalem (in Hebrew, with English summary).

Drude, O. (1928). "Pflanzengeographische Ökologie—Abderhalden's Handbuch der biologischen Arbeitsmethoden," Sect. XI, Part 4. Berlin.

Du Rietz, G. E. (1931). Life forms of terrestrial flowering plants. *Acta Phytogeogr. Suec.* **3**.

Gimingham, C. (1972). "Ecology of Heathlands." Chapman & Hall, London.

Lindman, C. A. M. (1914). Några bidrag till pågan: Buske eller träd? *K. Vetenskapsakad. Arsb.* **12**. Upsala.

Mueller-Dombois, D., and Ellenberg, H. (1974). "Aims and Methods of Vegetation Ecology." Wiley, New York.

Orshan, G. (1953). Notes on the application of Raunkiaer's life forms in arid regions. *Palest. J. Bot., Jerusalem Ser.* **6**, 120-122.

Orshan, G. (1964). Seasonal dimorphism of desert and Mediterranean chamaephytes and their significance as a factor in their water economy. *In* "Water in Relation to Plants" (A. J. Rutter and F. H. Whitehead, eds.), pp. 206-222. Blackwell, Oxford.

Orshan, G. (1983). Monocharacter growth form types as a tool in an analytic synthetic study of growth forms in Mediterranean type ecosystems. Proc. Int. *Workship Mediterr. Ecologia Mediterranea* **8**, 159–171.

Orshan G. (1986). Plant form as describing vegetation and expressing adaptation to environment. *Annali di Botanica (Roma)* **44**, 8–38.

Orshan G., ed. (1988). Plant Phenomorphological Studies in Mediterranean-Type Ecosystems, C. South Africa. (A. Le Roux, P. Perry, and X. L. Kyriacam). Junk, the Hague. (In press).

Rabinovich-Vin, A. (1979). Influences of parent rock on soil properties and composition of vegetation in the Galilee. Ph.D. Thesis, Hebrew University of Jerusalem (in Hebrew, with English summary).

Raunkiaer, C. (1904). Om biologiske Typermed Hensyn til Plantermes Tilpasning til at overlere ugunstige Aarstider. *Bot. Tiddss.* **26.**

Raunkiaer, C. (1934). "The Life Forms of Plants and Statistical Plant Geography." Oxford Univ. Press (Clarendon), London and New York.

Reiter, H. (1885). "Die Consolidation der Physiognomik. Als Versuch einer Okologie der Gewächse." Graz.

Rubel, E. (1930). "Pflanzengeselschaften der Erde." Bern-Berlin.

Skottsberg, C., ed. (1921). "The Phanerograms of Juan Fernandez Islands: The Natural History of Juan Fernandez and Easter Islands," Vol. II. Uppsala.

Warming, E. (1909). "Oecology of Plants." Oxford Univ. Press (Clarendon), London and New York.

Warming, E. (1916). Bemaerkninger om Livesform og Standplada. *Forh. Skand. Naturf. Mote* **16** [(German translation by H. Ganis in *Engler's Bot. Jahrb.* **56** (1920)].

11

Shrub Palatability

Cyrus M. McKell

I. Introduction

Palatability is an important biological feature of shrubs regarding their acceptability to animals for feed. The evidence of differences in animal preference for some shrub species and not for others is obvious when examining the differential amount of grazing use sustained by various plants in a mixed shrub community. Not only are there palatability differences among shrubs but also among shrubs, grasses, and forbs in general. Through repeated observations of animals in their choice of plant species for feed it may be possible to see differences in preference that appear to be the result of changes in the nature of the plants caused by maturation. Understanding the reasons for animal preferences for some shrubs and not for others is important for many reasons, particularly in managing livestock and wildlife in relation to sustaining the shrublands they occupy. Failure to recognize the signs of overutilization of key shrub species can result in significant deterioration of the shrubland plant community with serious long-term consequences both to ecosystem functioning and to animal populations.

   The fact that animals select one plant species and even an individual plant out of a group of plants suggests that inherent differences exist among the array of species present and that selection is generally a repeatable phenomenon and not a random process. The Range Term Glossary Committee (1964) defines selectivity as the grazing of certain plant species to the exclusion of others. Thus, if animals are selecting one plant in preference to others, we assume that it is more palatable or desirable than the one not selected. Heady (1975) pointed out that selectivity refers to animal reactions and that palatability refers to plant characteristics. His reason for separating the two concepts was to aid in analysis and understanding. However, in understanding the biology and utilization of shrubs it is necessary to keep in mind the interaction of both animal and plant factors. Further, the condition of the plant community must be considered as Chapline and Forsling (1923) advised in making a grazing reconnaissance. They wrote that palatability was the degree to which herbage within easy reach of stock is grazed when the range is properly utilized under the best practicable management. Even though ranges and wildlife habitats may not be in good condition and may not reflect a situation considered to be the result of proper utilization, the fact remains that differences in preferability among plant species will continue to exist, and the relative desirability in relation to other species will remain.

Palatability is not an absolute and unchangeable character of a shrub although a plant may appear to be so noxious or undesirable that no animal will attempt to browse it. Any hierarchical list of species in a given area or vegetation type would certainly change if others in the list were removed or the factors responsible for their desirability to a browsing animal were to change. Under intense grazing pressure, various unpalatable and distinctly inferior species have been shown to be well utilized. As a veteran rancher once commented on a range field day, "any differences in shrub palatability will disappear when animals are starving." Vegetation changes resulting from grazing may be more correlated with both intensity of use as well as actual palatability.

In dealing with the palatability problem in shrubs we are at a disadvantage because of the paucity of scientific data available. Marten (1970) may have been right when he stated that "we have too often been content to show palatability differences and assume that they have biological or economic significance without testing the validity of the assumption." In contrast to forage grasses or forbs such as alfalfa (*Medicago sativa*), we know very little about shrub palatability. However, in addition to this lack of knowledge, shrub utilization is also hampered by a general bias that shrubs are generally unpalatable and not worth the effort. Plummer (1972) suggested that more emphasis be given to improvement of palatability in ecotopes of sagebrush (*Artemisia tridentata*) than to its widespread elimination, as was a priority in the western United States in the 1940s and 1950s.

Figure 1. Many factors serve to influence palatability and animal selection in a complex plant community.

Research and observations by Plummer and his colleagues (Hanks *et al.,* 1975; Welch *et al.,* 1981; McArthur, 1984) as well as by others in the western United States (Stutz and Carlson, 1985; Monsen and Davis, 1985) have shown that considerable diversity exists within shrub species and among species for palatability to wildlife and domestic livestock. This diversity provides the basis for selection and genetic improvement and also for grazing management. In discussing palatability of shrubs, the distinction must be made as to whether individual plants or the species in general are the point of reference.

To make progress in both management of shrublands and genetic improvement of shrubs having desirable characteristics, considerable work must be done. Progress in both of these important areas requires a better understanding of the many factors that influence palatability and selectivity by browsing animals (Fig. 1).

II. Factors Affecting Palatability

Factors affecting shrub palatability include plant-related characteristics as well as those related to animal behavior in which a combination of plant and animal factors interact. Also, some of the plant and animal factors operate in a hierarchical manner, whereby a plant factor may affect animal choices to a moderate degree but an animal factor such as experience will determine further intensity of utilization. In many instances of intense shrub utilization, a combination of factors, sometimes operating over time, determines the amount of herbage removed from a plant and thus serves as visual evidence for what will be interpreted as the palatability of a shrub species or individual plant in a group of plants.

A. Plant Factors

According to Marten (1970) palatability has been observed to be positively correlated, negatively correlated, and uncorrelated with numerous plant characteristics, including chemical composition, morphology, succulence, and disease. In most cases the characterization of palatability involves several factors that cannot be separated in their influence on the attractiveness of a species. Even though the various palatability factors cannot be separated in nature, for clarity in understanding and presentation they will be treated in the following discussion as separate variables.

1. Physical Attributes

As a general rule animals appear to prefer species (or individual plants within species) that are relatively succulent (Dayton, 1931) and have leaves that are large and thin. These features are not emphasized by most desert shrubs, however, because they are in contradiction to anatomical characteristics that are needed for resistance to drought, high temperature, and intense sunlight common to arid areas. Many leaf and stem characteristics have evolved that appear to restrict or deter browsing. Spines, stout twig ends, coarse texture, extreme pubescence, papery touch, and development of a dense stem canopy when browsed are some of the main attributes of less palatable shrub species. However, there are many examples of shrub species that are relatively palatable that have less than ideal features (Wilson, 1977). Fourwing saltbush (*Atriplex canescens*), a species of the desert rangelands of the western United States, has relatively small linear gray leaves, pubescent hairs with salt-containing vesicles at the tips, and a habit of forming stout dead twig ends when browsed. Yet the palatability of this shrub is generally rated as good by range managers (Chapline and Whyte, 1947; Goodin, 1979; Otsyina, 1983; Otsyina *et al.,* 1982, 1984).

In East Africa, Pratt and Gwynne (1977) describe more than 50 small trees and shrubs that are important browse and fodder species, most of which have spines and thorns. Animal use may involve seeds and pods as well as leaves of *Acacia* species, which are well known for their stout and often recurved thorns. Various animal species have developed special

Figure 2. Small thorns of *Caragana microphylla* are sufficiently effective at restricting browsing to protect the plant from elimination and yet allow it to be used as an important winter feed for livestock in Inner Mongolia.

adaptations to cope with adverse plant characters, such as the giraffe with their specialized mouthparts and tall stature, which allow them to utilize tall shrub and tree species that are not available to less well adapted animals.

The small thorns of *Caragana microphylla,* a low shrub of Inner Mongolian rangelands (Fig. 2), may not completely deter grazing but appear to sufficiently restrict browsing to protect the species from elimination under intense use. This shrub provides year-round forage, but is especially useful for stress season feed.

2. Chemical Constituents

Many studies have attempted to relate chemical content to shrub palatability with mixed success. Generally, crude protein correlates positively most frequently with high palatability, although total nutritive value correlates more consistently, according to Cook *et al.* (1951), who investigated sheep nutrition on winter ranges in the Great Basin of the western United States. Sugars have been shown to be an influence in diet selection (Arnold and Hill, 1972) and can serve as a preliminary guide in identifying potentially useful species. Five types of substances have been used to elicit taste

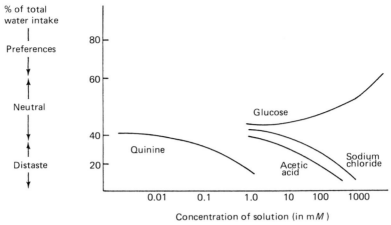

Figure 3.   Taste responses of sheep to solutions of pure chemicals. (From Harborne, 1982.)

perceptions in sheep: sodium chloride (saltiness), sucrose or glucose (sweetness), citric or acetic acids (sourness), quinine (bitterness), and tannic acid (astringency). These chemicals can generally be detected at fairly low concentrations but, with the exception of sugars, an increase in concentration will cause rejection of the food source (Fig. 3). Harborne (1982) pointed out that larger differences in response are noted among species of animals such as goats, cattle, and sheep than among animals of the same species. Cattle appear to be the most sensitive to the tests of chemicals and sheep the least.

Data from a particular laboratory analysis such as total nitrogen, crude fiber, or nitrogen-free extract do not always agree with palatability observations. Much has been speculated about the "nutritional wisdom" of animals in making a selection of feed that is of a high nutritional quality (Zahoric and Houpt, 1977). However, there are too many exceptions for selection based on nutritional wisdom for it to be universally true. Arnold and Hill (1972) pointed out that cues from taste and smell experiences by animals are physically and molecularly based and that animals cannot discriminate on the conveniently analyzable fractions used in the laboratory. An excellent case in point is the experience with *Artemisia tridentata,* which in the winter has a crude protein content of over 11% (Welch and McArthur, 1979) and on this basis should be an excellent winter feed source for wildlife and lifestock. However, *A, tridentata* is of limited palatability to most animals. The low palatability appears to be related to a high monoterpenoid content (Hanks *et al.,* 1971; Welch *et al.,* 1981). Nagy *et al.* (1964) demonstrated that the essential oils of *A. tridentata* reduced rumen bacterial fermentation and appetite in deer and cattle. From the concentrated work done on *A. tridentata* a pattern for development now seems clear that involves selecting highly productive ecotypes that are high in crude protein but low in monoterpenoids (McArthur *et al.*, 1985).

Key examples of aversive chemical influence on palatability show that the influence is related to the presence of secondary products of metabolism that are aversive or toxic to browsing animals. However, detailed knowledge, especially for shrubs, is largely unavailable (Harborne, 1982). Evolutionary theory holds that these chemicals have been selected for and retained in the plant's biological system because of their survival value. In some cases the level of toxicity may not be critical if animals consume certain parts of plants only in moderate quantities, or along with other species or in seasons when levels of the toxic compounds are low. Harborne (1982) and Rosenthal and Janzen (1979) mention some of the secondary plant chemicals that influence herbivore grazing. These chemicals include sugars, organic acids, tannins, coumarins, cyanogenic glycosides, essential oils, isoflavinoids, and alkaloids. Not all these chemicals are found in shrubs used for feed by browsing animals and field evidence of these compounds reducing herbivore feeding activity is limited. In contrast to the relative speed and accuracy of chemical identification in the laboratory, verification of animal aversion is difficult and often speculative.

A recent review of the various secondary plant metabolites and their interaction with herbivores was edited by Rosenthal and Janzen (1979). Their book describes some of the various ways that animals are able to utilize plant species within the constraints posed by the presence of secondary plant metabolites. Some of the major secondary compounds influencing plant palatability generally have a negative effect on taste and smell. Many secondary compounds are variously toxic to animals depending on the amounts ingested (Kingsbury, 1964) or consumed in unique combination with other plant species. However, some of the toxic materials may not act as feeding deterrents because their action is expressed only after ingestion and they do not signal in advance their high toxicity. Only a few examples of research on how chemicals influence shrub palatability and subsequent selection by browsing animals have been reported (Table I).

3. Availability

Availability of plant material is related to the physical nature of the plant and the plant community. In dense shrub stands such as *Adenostema fasciculatum* (chamise) of California, animal accessibility is restricted by the density of stems (Heady, 1975). Whatever succulent herbage exists, either as twig ends or new growth of plants, is generally not available to

Table I.   Secondary compounds found in shrub species that have a negative influence on palatability

Type of compound	Species of shrub	Reference
Essential oils	*Artemisia* spp.	Nagy *et al.* (1964); Welch *et al.* (1981)
Saponins	*Atriplex* spp.	C. M. McKell, M. Balandrin, and E. S. Wurtele (unpublished data, 1985)
Phenolics	*Quercus* spp.	Longhurst *et al.* (1968)
Essential oils	*Juniper* spp.	Smith (1950)
Phenolic resins	*Larrea* spp.	Rhoades and Cates (1976)
Sesquiterpenes	*Myoporum deserti*	Park and Sutherland (1967)

game animals or livestock. Herbage availability also decreases as a result of plant growth response to intense utilization. A dense, hedged plant form develops in which the outer perimeter of the shrub canopy presents a mass of stout and dead twig ends, thus restricting access to the new growth inside the canopy. An example of this is *Purshia tridentata* (bitterbrush), a shrub very palatable to deer in the desert mountains of the Great Basin of the western United States.

Another example of restricted availability, but not generally caused by intense browsing, is the normal habit of *Coleogyne ramosissima*, which exhibits stout protruding terminal twigs that repress growth of new lateral stems. A sufficient number of the terminal twigs die back to give the shrub a spinescent canopy. Bowns (1973) pointed out that winter removal of the spinescent twigs stimulated spring growth of basal and axillary buds that increased the palatability of the shrub as well as its general productivity. The presence of dense spines such as those of various *Acacia* species (Pratt and Gwynne, 1977) may be considered as a means of reducing availability of herbage in addition to their generally considered function of protection (Fig. 4).

Although not a direct characteristic of palatability, plant availability is an important feature of animal selectivity and is a problem to shrubland management. In some cases, fire (Heady, 1975) or browsing may help open up the plant canopy with a corresponding increase in productivity because of the stimulation of growth, whereas in other cases excess browsing may create a hedged plant canopy that has internal productivity but reduced availability to the browsing animal.

4. Abundance

Some species vary in their palatability to certain animal species because of the degree of abundance they may have in a plant community. The reason for the increased palatability is believed to be because a low proportion of

Figure 4. The presence of spines not only deters browsing but, in effect, reduces the availability of the plant for animal use.

an otherwise mundane browse species provides a uniqueness and desirability not found under general circumstances. For example, in eastern Oregon *Chrysothamnus viscidiflorus* (green rabbitbrush) is considered to be relatively unpalatable and is generally abundant, occupying space made available when excess grazing and other disturbance offer it an opportunity for seedling establishment. Yet 700 km to the east in the area of the U.S. Sheep Experiment Station at Dubois, Idaho, the same species of shrub is observed to be moderately palatable and browsed by sheep in their normal selection of feed. However, the presence of "chemical races" or intraspecific chemical variation cannot be ruled out. Cook (1962) observed that on desert rangelands an increase in the proportion of a palatable species led to an increase in its use. However, when the abundance of a less palatable species increased, the degree of utilization decreased.

Experimental evidence to validate abundance as being a factor in shrub palatability is lacking and only observations of a circumstantial nature or those provided by experienced resource managers are available to give confidence that abundance has any influence on animal diet choice. Changes in botanical composition over time in a shrubland community under intense grazing use will result in a different proportion of the total plant population being held by a particular shrub species. This may change the relative preference for a given species because of its abundance.

However, the problem is not so easily solved because other factors related to desirability also change and the real cause may not be related to abundance as much as to other factors such as a seasonally related factor.

5. Seasonality

Closely related to abundance, and sometimes confounded with it, is the effect that seasonal changes in chemical and physical characteristics have on palatability. In rating 77 shrub species for their suitability for restoring big-game range in Utah, Plummer *et al.* (1968) rated each one for its palatable early spring growth and for palatable summer growth. Average palatability was higher in the summer. Species composition changes occur as a result of new plants becoming established during the growing season and the succulent new growth of stems and leaves matures to tissues with less water, more fiber, and generally rougher texture. In general, grasses and forbs are higher in palatability than shrubs in the early part of the growing season. In the chenopod shrublands of Australia, saltbushes are preferred to a higher degree in early autumn than in late winter when annual species become a large proportion of sheep diets (Squires, 1981). Holmgren and Hutchings (1972) considered seasonal palatability to be an important character in rating various shrub species for their usefulness as early, mid, and late winter livestock feed. Successional changes in desert shrub rangelands during a 30-year period of research on desert rangelands were attributed to differences in the seasonal palatabilities of *Artemisia nova,* which is consistently palatable, *Artemisia spinescens,* which is palatable only in late winter, and *Ceratoides lanata,* which varies from year to year in palatability.

In East Africa, Pratt and Gwynne (1977) reported that most indigenous livestock make more use of the foliage of shrubs and trees during times of herbage deficiency than they do when grass is plentiful and high in nutritive value. Heady (1975) assembled a comparison of preferences shown for various animal species during each of the seasons for grasses, forbs, and shrubs in locations of western North America. Generally, cattle selected more browse in the winter and spring than in other seasons. In contrast, sheep in Texas emphasized browse in their diet in summer and fall. Mule deer selected browse in excess of 50% in each season of the year, shifting to 94% in the winter.

6. Breeding for Palatability

Considerable variability exists within species for the various factors that contribute to palatability (Voigt, 1975). In forage grass breeding, a common practice is to turn livestock into field test plots and allow them free choice to select the most palatable accessions. In selecting for palatability in shrubs, selection is being done naturally under field conditions by browsing animals. As a basis for selecting fodder shrub species of useful palatability in Kenya (McKell and Ibrahim, 1979), information was obtained directly from field observations of shrubs that were intensely browsed. Another source of information was responses to questions asked of herders of sheep and goats regarding the plants most preferred by their animals at various times of the year.

Otsyina (1983) conducted a grazing study with five shrubs as a source of late fall supplemental feed. Subsequently, over 700 individual plants of *Atriplex canescens* were classified as to the degree of browse intensity they had received during the preceding 2 years. Even though all shrubs and grasses in the study enclosures were subjected to a high intensity of grazing pressure, only one-third of the *Atriplex* plants were intensely browsed, one-third were browsed to an intermediate degree, and less than one-third were lightly browsed. Preliminary laboratory analysis of saponin content from representative samples of each of the three populations indicate that saponin content is one-third higher in the least palatable plants than in the ones browsed intensely (C. M. McKell, M. Balandrin, and E. S. Wurtele, unpublished data, 1985). New techniques in tissue culture (Wurtele *et al.*, 1987) are now becoming available to propagate plants of unique and valuable characteristics such as high palatability. Mass propagation without changing other genetically important features makes it possible to accelerate the development of palatable biotypes of important browse species. However, selecting for plants with high palatability poses a real challenge to the shrub geneticist because of the multiple factors involved in animal selectivity, the cost of research with animals, and the lack of a clear understanding of factors causing palatability differences.

B. Animal Factors

1. Overview

Physical and chemical features of shrubs can elicit selective behavior by a browsing animal on the basis of the animal's senses of taste, smell, touch, and sight. Many of the present patterns of tolerance to toxic chemicals and preferences for plants of various characteristics have their origin in the evolutionary past. Swain (1978) discussed a few examples of changes in the morphology, anatomy, and physiology of plant defensive mechanisms and the equivalent changes in animals that have taken place in the past 400 million years. Diversity in the nature of plant chemical constituents and animal behavior provides a continual driving force in plant–animal coevolution. Just how animals respond to the stimuli they receive from contact with a shrub of potential browse value depends on several animal-related factors. For a clear understanding of the true palatability value of a shrub, the factors related to animal behavior must be considered separate from plant features to avoid concluding that the observed degree of animal use actually represents the true palatability of a shrub. Three aspects of animal behavior are important: experience, age, and species.

2. Experience

Various studies as well as general observations indicate that the previous exposure of animals to given shrub species will influence the degree of use regardless of the nutritional value or desirability as a feed (Arnold and Maller, 1977). In contrast, Longhurst *et al.* (1968) showed that preferences were inherited, based on a study with pen-fed fawn deer. Squires (1981) speculates that cattle select feed to minimize unpleasant and maximize pleasant olfactory and other sensations. According to Freeland and Janzen (1974) and Arnold and Maller (1977), animal preferences are formed on the basis of experiences and subsequent consequences gained by consuming certain species. These experiences carry over to subsequent encounters with the same or similar species. Provenza and Malechek (1984) imported goats from Texas to southern Utah for use in a browse study on *Coleognye ramosissima,* a species that is considerably different from the kinds of shrubs the goats were accustomed to browsing in Texas. Early results in diet selection suggested that the choices the goats made in their utilization of plant parts and shrub species were conditioned by their previous grazing experience with shrub species common to west Texas. Only after the goats had adjusted to the particular roughness of the local shrub did their choice of browse materials reflect a more accurate picture of *Coleogyne* palatability. In emergency situations such as drought or deep coverage by snow, when usual sources of animal feed become short in supply or unavailable, animals are forced to shift to alternate species regardless of experience.

Efforts to domesticate wildlife species may also involve shifting them to browse species of higher abundance under managed conditions. Limited success in domesticating the eland (*Taurotragus oryx*) of East Africa in game ranches has involved introducing this species to a browse of somewhat different composition than present on typical eland habitat (Taylor, 1968). Of particular interest is the success in shifting the eland to utilize *Lantana camera,* a shrub species introduced from Australia that now has escaped control in Kenya and is a pest according to Renee Haller, ranch manager of the Bambouri Cement Company near Mombassa, Kenya.

3. Age of Animals

Given the fact that animal behavior in making diet selections is based on experience gained in actual contact and utilization of browse species, young animals would obviously have less capability to make "informed" choices of desirable browse species than mature animals. Leuthold (1971) observed that feeding habits of three African game species are formed on the basis of both inheritance and learning. Young impala (*Aepyceros melampus*), gerenuk (*Litocranius walleri*), and lesser kudu (*Tragelaphus imberbis*) learn from older members in the herd. Provensa and Malechek (1986) found that young angora goats learned to browse by associating with their mothers and made similar choices of the nutritious plant parts they selected from the available browse material. The young kids had to spend proportionately more time foraging than their mothers because of their higher nutritional requirements to sustain rapid growth.

In a 2-year grazing study, Otsyina (1983) used 9-month-old lambs previously raised on alfalfa pellets the first year of the study and seasoned 3-year-old ewes with desert shrubland grazing experience the second year. The sheep were allowed to graze on grassland interplanted with shrubs. The inexperienced lambs required an adjustment period of over 1 week to "discover" the fourwing saltbush in the pastures, whereas the experienced sheep began utilizing these shrubs almost immediately. During the same number of days, the experienced animals utilized a significantly higher quantity of shrub feed than did the inexperienced animals. From these limited results no sweeping conclusions can be drawn because of several confounding factors such as different years and weather conditions and different pasture conditions from one year to the next. However, it is clear that the age of the animals and their experience gained with age must be considered in assessing animal choice as an indication of shrub palatability.

4. Animal Species

From the numerous references cited previously, the evidence is strong that various animal species differ significantly in their preferences for feed. Whereas sheep, goats, and camels appear to have a high preference for shrubs in their diets, cattle and horses will choose grasses and forbs during the main grazing season. The list of animals and their feed preferences compiled by Heady (1975) is instructive because it provides a basis for grazing management on rangelands where there are multiple animal species, both domestic and wildlife, using the diverse composition of the plant community. Changes in the species of browsing animal can cause drastic ecological changes in plant species composition as Howard (1967) reported from his observations in New Zealand. The forage species there evolved without being exposed to foraging herbivores, and with the introduction of livestock and deer from Europe and North America animal numbers increased greatly and damaged much of the native vegetation. The diverse range of feed preferences and seasonal shift in palatability of shrubs and other forage species form the basis for grazing systems that can make optimum use of the spectrum of productivity available from shrublands around the world.

III. Summary

Many factors influence the desirability or palatability of shrubs for herbivores. These factors involve physical and chemical characteristics that convey desirability or cause aversion. Other plant-related factors may also influence the degree of animal utilization such as availability, abundance, and seasonal changes brought about by trends in environmental influences.

Plant breeders attempting to breed for high palatability to encourage animal use or develop plant materials with low palatability to protect them from overuse by animals have a difficult task. The interrelationships among various plant factors may cover up or compensate for key factors determining palatability. However, observing animal choices under field conditions may help identify those plants or species with the greatest net palatability in spite of the confounding interactions.

Selection of shrubs by animals is conditioned by behavioral patterns related to the familiarity or experience with browsing shrubs. Age and species of animals also make a difference in preference choices. Various writers point to the observed relationships between plants and animals that appear to have coevolved over millenia. From these relationships, scientists and resource managers must develop management practices to utilize shrub resources, often using subjective animal selection observations and meager chemical and physical data that imply palatability.

References

Arnold, G. W., and Hill, J. L. (1972). Chemical factors affecting selection of food plants by ruminants. *In* "Phytochemical Ecology" Q. B. Harborne, ed. pp. 77–101. Academic Press, New York.

Arnold, G. W., and Maller, R. A. (1977). Effects of nutritional experience in early and adult life on the performance and dietary habits of sheep. *Appl. Anim. Ethol.* **3,** 5–20.

Bowns, J. E. (1973). An autecological study of blackbrush (*Coleogyne ramosissima* Torr.) in southwestern Utah. Ph. D. Dissertation, Utah State University, Logan.

Chapline, W. R., and Forsling, C. L. (1923). "Instructions for Grazing Reconnaissance on National Forests," For. Serv. Manual. USDA, Washington, DC.

Chapline, W. R., and Whyte, R. O. (1947). The use and misuse of shrubs and trees as fodder in the United States. "The Use and Misuse of Shrubs and Trees as Fodder," Jt. Publ. No. 10, pp. 157–176. Imp. Agric. Bur., Aberystwith, Wales.

Cook, C. W. (1962). An evaluation of some common factors affecting utilization of desert range species. *J. Range Manage.* **15,** 333–338.

Cook, C. W., Stoddart, L. A., and Harris, L. E. (1951). Measuring consumption and digestibility of winter range plants by sheep. *J. Range Manage.* **4,** 335–336.

Dayton, W. A. (1931). Important western browse plants. *Misc. Publ. — U.S., Dep. Agric.* **101.**

Freeland, W. J., and Janzen; D. H. (1974). Strategies in herbivory by mammals, the role of secondary compounds. *Am. Nat.* **108,** 269–289.

Goodin, J. R. (1979). The forage potential of *Atriplex canescens. In* "Arid Land Plant Resources" (J. R. Goodin and D. R. Nortington, eds.), pp. 418–424. Texas Tech Univ. Press, Lubbock.

Hanks, D. L., Brunner, J. R., Christensen, D. R., and Plummer, A. P. (1971). Paper chromatography for determining palatability differences in various strains of big sagebrush. *USDA For. Serv. Res. Pap. INT* **INT–101.**

Hanks, D. L. McArthur, E. D., Plummer, A. P., and Blauer, A. C. (1975). Chromatographic recognition of some unpalatable subspecies of rubber rabbitbrush in and around Utah. *J. Range Manage.* **28,** 144–148.

Harborne J. B. (1982). "Introduction to Ecological Biochemistry," 2nd ed. Academic Press, New York.

Heady, H. F. (1975). "Rangeland Management." McGraw-Hill, New York.

Holmgren, R. C., and Hutchings, S. S. (1972). Salt desert shrub response to grazing use. *In* "Wildland Shrubs: Their Biology and Utilization" (C. M. McKell, J. P. Blaisdell, and J. R. Goodin, eds.), USDA For. Serv. Gen. Tech. Rep. INT–1 pp. 153–164. Utah State University, Logan.

Howard, W. E. (1967). Ecological changes in New Zealand due to introduced mammals. ICUN 10th Technical Meeting, Lucern, Switzerland *ICUN Publ.* [N. S.] **9,** 219–240.

Kingsbury, J. M. (1964). "Poisonous Plants of the United States and Canada." Prentice-Hall, Englewood Cliffs, New Jersey.

Leuthold, W. (1971). A note on the formation of food habits in young antelopes. *J. Afr. Wildl. J.* **9,** 154–156.

Longhurst, W. M. Oh, H. K., Jones M. B., and Kepner, R. E. (1968). A basis for the palatability of deer forage plants. *Trans. North Amr. Wildl. Nat. Resour. Conf.* **33,** 181–192.

McArthur, E. D. (1984). Natural diversity of western range shrubs. *In* "Natural Diversity in Forest Ecosystems" J. L. Cooley, and J. H. Cooley, (eds.), pp. 183–200. Inst. Ecol., University of Georgia, Athens.

McArthur, E. D., Welch, B., and Nelson, D. L. (1985). Developing improved cultivars of sagebrushes and other composite shrubs. *Proc. Sel. Pap., 38th Annu. Meet., Soc. Range Manage.,* pp. 188–196.

McKell, C. M., and Ibrahim, K. M. (1979). "Some Fodder Shrubs of Kenya," Proc. Annu. Meet. Soc. Range Manage., Casper, Wyoming. Soc. Range Manage., Denver, Colorado.

Marten, G. C. (1970). Measurement and significance of forage palatability. *In* "Forage Quality, Evaluation and Utilization," pp. D1–D55. Nebraska Center for Continuing Education, Lincoln.

Monsen, S. B., and Davis, J. N. (1985). Progress in the improvement of selected western North American rosaceous shrubs. *Proc. Sel. Pap., 38th Annu. Meet., Soc. Range Manage.,* pp. 201–209.

Nagy, J. G., Steinhoff, H. W., and Ward, G. M. (1964). Effects of essential oils of sagebrush on deer rumen microbial function. *J. Wildl. Manage.* **28,** 785–790.

Otsyina, R. M. (1983). Evaluation of fourwing saltbush (*Atriplex canescens*) and other shrubs as supplements to crested wheatgrass (*Agropyron desertorum*) for sheep in fall and winter. Ph. D. Dissertation, Utah State University, Logan.

Otsyina, R. M., McKell, C. M., and Van Epps, G. A. (1982). Use of range shrubs to meet nutritional requirements of sheep grazing on crested wheatgrass during fall and early winter. *J. Range Manage.* **35,** 751–753

Otsyina, R. M., McKell, C. M., Malechek, J. M., and Van Epps, G. A. (1984). Potential of *Atriplex* and other chenopod shrubs for increasing range productivity and fall and winter grazing use. *USDA For. Serv. Gen. Tech. Rep. INT* **INT–72,** 215–219.

Park, R. J., and Sutherland, M. D. (1967). *Aust. J. Chem.* **22,** 495–496.

Plummer, A. P. (1972). Selection. *In* "Wildland Shrubs: Their Biology and Utilization" (C. M. McKell, J. P. Blaisdell, and J. R. Goodin, eds.), USDA For. Serv. Gen. Tech. Rep. INT–1, Utah State University, Logan.

Plummer, A. P., Christensen, D. R., and Monsen, S. B. (1968). Restoring big-game range in Utah. *Utah Div. Fish Game Pub/***68–3.**

Pratt, D. J., and Gwynne, M. D. (1977). "Rangeland Management and Ecology in East Africa." Hodder & Stoughton, London.

Provenza, F. D., and Malechek, J. C. (1984). Diet selection by domestic goats in relation to blackbrush twig chemistry *J. Appl. Ecol.* **21,** 831–841.

Provenza F. D., and Malechek, J. C. (1986). A comparison of food selection and foraging behavior in juvenile and adult goats. *Appl. Anim. Behav. Sci.* **16,** 49–61.

Range Term Glossary Committee (1964). "A Glossary of Terms Used in Range Management." Am. Soc. Range Manage., Denver, Colorado.

Rhoades, D. F., and Cates, R. G. (1976). Towards a general theory of plant antiherbivore chemistry. *Recent Adv. Phytochem.* **10;** 168–213.

Rosenthal, G. A., and Janzen, D. H., Janzen, eds. (1979). "Herbivores: Their Interaction with Secondary Plant Metabolites." Academic Press, New York.

Smith, A. D. (1950). Inquiries into differential consumption of juniper by mule deer. *Utah Fish Game Bull.* **9,** 4.

Squires, V. L. (1981). "Livestock Management in the Arid Zone." Inkata Press, Melbourne.

Stutz, H. C., and Carlson, J. B. (1985). Genetic improvement of saltbush (*Atriplex*) and other chenopods. *Proc. Sel. Pap. 38th Annu. Meet., Soc. Range Manage.,* pp. 197–200.

Swain, T. (1978). Plant and animal coevolution: A synoptic view of the Paleozoic and Mesozoic. *In* "Biochemical Aspects of Plant and Animal Covolution" (J. B. Harborne ed.), pp. 1–19. Academic Press, New York.

Taylor, C. E. (1968). The minimum water requirements of some East African bovids. *Symp. Zool. Soc. London* **21,** 195–206.

Voigt, P. W. (1975). Improving palatability of range plants, *In* "Improved Range Plants" (R. S. Campbell and H. Herbel, eds.), Range Symp. Ser. No. 1, pp. 23–49. Soc. Range Manage., Denver, Colorado.

Welch, B. L., and McArthur, E. D. (1979). Variation in winter levels of crude protein among *Artemisia tridentata* subspecies grown in a uniform garden. *J. Range Manage.* **32,** 467–469.

Welch, B. L., McArthur, E. D., and Davis, J. N. (1981). Differential preferences of wintering mule deer for accessions of big sagebrush and for black sagebrush. *J. Range Manage.* **34,** 409–411.

Wilson, A. D. (1977). The digestibility and voluntary intake of the leaves of trees and shrubs by sheep and goats. *Aust. J. Agric. Res.* **28,** 501–508.

Wurtele, E. S., Garton, Steven, Young, Donald, Balandrin, Manuel F., and McKell, Cyrus M. (1987). Propagation of an elite high biomass-producing genotype of *Atriplex canescens* by axillary enhancement. *Biomass* **12,** 281–291.

Zahoric, D. M., and Houpt, K. A. (1977). The concept of nutritional wisdom: Applicability of laboratory learning models to large herbivores. *In* "Learning Mechanisms in Food Selection" (L. M. Bartker, M. Best, and M. Domjan, eds), pp 45–671. Baylor Univ. Press, Waco, Texas.

12

Spatial Pattern–Functional Interactions in Shrub-Dominated Plant Communities

Neil E. West

I. Introduction

Most traditional studies in shrub ecology have focused on autecology. Autecological studies deal with the response of sets of individual plants to environmental factors. This may be done either in controlled environments of the laboratory, growth chamber, or greenhouse or under partially or uncontrolled conditions in the field where relevant environmental features are monitored over time. What is found in autecological investigations usually has limitations because many factors (e.g., competition, herbivory, parasitism) operative in the field environment are excluded from consideration. Thus, to more fully understand what is happening in the vegetation, we need to combine information learned from autecological and lower levels with results obtained in community and ecosystem contexts.

The Biology and Utilization of Shrubs

Community- and ecosystem-level ecology have traditionally relied on assessment of natural or unintentional experiments in the field. The modern trend is, however, toward more manipulative experiments in which replicates of entire communities or ecosystems have some experimental or management-style treatment done to the entire system. For example, herbicide treatments, prescribed burning, grazing, etc., may be done on entire plots and the results compared to the situation concurrently measured on untreated "control" plots. Species or functional groups can be added or subtracted to evaluate their role in the community. Data are usually averaged over what are assumed to be internally homogeneous conditions. Vegetation data have often been restricted to two-dimensional parameters, for example, cover, density, or even phytomass measurements taken without consideration of height and depth variation. If one-time measurements are done, the temporal variability is also ignored.

The classical approaches described above have given us initial impressions of the ways shrubs individually and collectively respond to natural and human-altered conditions. The demands for better understanding to enhance productivity of shrublands to help feed, clothe, shelter, and otherwise provide for expanding human populations have, however, encouraged the scientific community to look more closely at the internal variation in plant communities.

The following reviews our current understanding of how spatial patterns, mostly at the scale of relatively small units of landscape, interact with various functional attributes of shrub-dominated ecosystems. Some opportunities for further research and application are also noted.

II. Definitions

All biological phenomena have to be carefully defined by temporal and spatial scales (Osmund *et al.,* 1980). Responses at given scales can be only partially explained by understanding phenomena at lower scales. At each scale, unique properties are evident (McIntosh, 1980). In this chapter the focus is on community- and ecosystem-level phenomena for which only partial explanations are available if only physiological, autecological, or population-level understanding is used.

Only some structural characteristics of communities and ecosystems are intimately related with spatial organization of shrubs. Similarly, the interplay of spatial patterns with only certain functional attributes of ecosystems is considered. The bulk of these attributes center around energy flow and nutrient and water cycles.

Spatial patterns are far more complicated than any density, frequency, or cover data summaries can ever express. The prime character involved is that of dispersion. Dispersion deals with the spatial arrangement of individuals in relation to their neighbors. Definition of dispersion pattern requires examination of two associated attributes—intensity and scale (Pielou, 1974).

Basically, intensity deals with deviation from random arrangement of individuals over a given space or volume. Since random location of individuals in a community is rarely found in nature, most of the problems arise in expressing the departure from randomness. The simplest nonrandom dispersion pattern is regular, for example, grape vines in a vineyard. Natural shrublands sometimes approach this type of pattern, particularly in hot deserts (Phillips and MacMahon, 1981). The other extreme is aggregated. Since it is physically impossible for all plants to occupy precisely the same spot of ground, the most usual pattern is somewhere between regularity and total aggregation.

The average distance between neighboring individuals or clusters is defined as the scale of dispersion (Pielou, 1974). Since the average may be deceptive, we should ideally know the statistical distribution of the interplant or intercluster distances.

Plants have three concomitant causes for dispersion pattern: morphological, sociological, and environmental (Kershaw, 1973). Some plants are inevitably aggregated because of the way they grow and reproduce. This is particularly true of shrubs because their form is usually defined as a woody plant for which individuals have multiple stems emerging from the ground surface. Individual shrubs may or may not be aggregated depending on how they are spaced in relation to their neighbors.

Natural plant communities usually show aggregated dispersions at scales dependent on the morphological features of the component species and the degree of sociological interaction through competition and other antagonistic or mutualistic processes. Dispersion pattern is also altered by environmental patterns as disparate as changes in soil depth, soil texture or chemistry, selective herbivory, mechanical harvest, fire history, etc.

Any real community usually has very complex dispersion patterns in which one has to deal with compound descriptions. For instance, individual stems may be regularly dispersed at the motte scale, but the mottes or clusters could be random or regular at the next highest scale. Each species, and often each size class, has its own dispersion pattern (e.g., Phillips and MacMahon, 1981). The dispersion pattern of the entire community may be quite different from that of its component species.

The existing techniques for quantifying dispersion are burdened with inherent biases (Goodall and West, 1979). A suite of methods must be used to define even the simplest patterns. Compound patterns are just beginning to be dealt with conceptually (Pielou, 1974). More adequate sampling methods and quantitative descriptions remain to be developed. Because much of the older literature describes dispersion patterns with biased methods and often incomplete analyses, care is necessary in interpreting the results. We are also barely getting started in relating dispersion patterns to functional processes. Most of the following should be viewed more as hypotheses for which experimental tests should be designed rather than well-established relationships.

III. Interactions of Spatial Patterns with Ecosystem Functions

A. *Primary Production*

Net primary production is the accumulation of phytomass via photosynthesis. In shrublands the increment to wood and evergreen leaves usually makes this a multiyear process. The common textbook assumption is that plants of a given age should be dispersed regularly so as to divide the space and resources equally (MacArthur and Connell, 1966). As a cohort of plants ages and as individuals grow, there is thinning due to intraspecific competition. The average interplant distance for mature plants is also at least partially a function of the relative favorableness of the site.

The above is a simplistic view influenced by our better understanding of much more internally homogeneous agronomic systems. It also assumes that after limits set by climate and soil fertility, competition is the most important organizing process. Although there are plenty of data showing competition between shrubs and herbaceous understory (e.g., Frischknecht, 1963; Hull and Klomp, 1974; Rittenhouse and Sneva, 1976), the trade-offs are not always linear (Scifres *et al.,* 1982).

Evidence is beginning to accumulate from more stressful environments that shrubs may help increase total productivity of the community. For instance, Halvorson and Patten (1975), Tiedemann and Klemmedson (1973), Patten (1978), and Barth and Klemmedson (1978) have shown that much greater growth of herbaceous species occurs under tall Sonoran Desert shrubs (*Cercidium* and *Prosopis*) than in the relatively bare interspaces. Garcia-Moya and McKell (1970), Wells (1967), and Romney *et al.* (1979) have demonstrated similar phenomena for smaller Mohave Desert shrubs (*Larrea, Coleogyne, Thamnosa,* etc.). Romney *et al.* (1978) have pointed out how the primary production in the "islands" of fertility under shrubs may be as high as in more mesic systems. The main difference

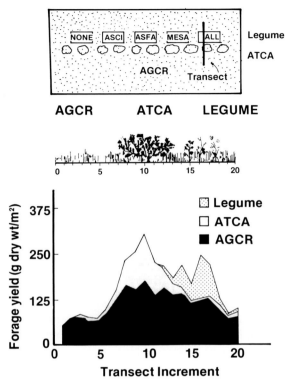

Figure 1. (top) Diagram of one replication of an experimental planting to test grass–legume–shrub interactions near Nephi, Utah. None = no legumes, ASCI = *Astragalus cicer,* ASFA = *Astragalus falcatus,* MESA = *Medicago sativa,* ALL = mixture of the three legumes, ATCA = *Atriplex canescens* and AGCR = *Agropyron cristatum.* (middle) Vertical profile of vegetation across a typical transect sampled in 20 increments. (bottom) Forage yields of the three legumes, *Atriplex canescens,* and *Agropyron cristatum.* (From Rumbaugh *et al.,* 1982.)

is that the desert has relatively little of its total land surface that is capable of high production and the overall average is low. Rumbaugh *et al.* (1982) recently found more than twice as much grass forage in close proximity to *Atriplex canescens* as in a nearby shrub-free grass stand (Fig. 1). Furthermore, protein concentration, protein yield, and rates of regrowth of the grasses were also greater in the neighborhood of the shrubs. Frischknecht (1963) also found that crested wheatgrass (*Agropyron cristatum*) productivity was enhanced by the presence of some rubber rabbitbrush (*Chrysothamnus nauseosus*). It is possible that shrubs favorably alter microenvironments such that enhanced moisture infiltration, soil moisture holding capacity, and nutrient cycling, as well as moderated wind and temperatures, occur. The reduction of livestock grazing under shrubs may also be involved (Bailey, 1970), that is, plant defense guilds are formed (McNaughton, 1978). These processes will now be detailed further.

B. Water Budgets

Specht (1957), Slatyer (1965), and Qashu (1970), in widely different kinds of shrub-dominated ecosystems, have shown greater infiltration (Table I) and storage of soil moisture (Fig. 2) directly under shrubs than in adjacent interspace areas lacking shrubs. Some of the difference is due to stem flow, such as in *Acacia aneura* (Slatyer, 1965), which funnels a remarkably high proportion of rainfall to its stem bases. Some of this greater infiltration is due to more animal holes, decayed root channels, higher soil organic matter, and aggregate stability of fine soil particles under shrub canopies than in interspaces. Also, dissipation of raindrop energy by stems and foliage of shrubs reduces compaction under the shrub cover leading to lower bulk densities, which additionally facilitate better infiltration (Branson *et al.*, 1981). Interception is of varying influence depending on species and type of storms (Hamilton and Rowe, 1949; West and Gifford, 1976; Tromble, 1983). In general, light rain and snowfalls are intercepted more. If these kinds of input are relatively frequent, net input is reduced more under shrubs compared to interspaces.

Differences in water input around shrubs compared to interspaces do not necessarily lead to significant intraspecific competition as Fonteyn and Mahall (1981) have recently demonstrated for a Mohave Desert shrub community. The creation of regular dispersion in *Larrea tridentata* caused

Table I. Mean soil infiltration rates measured at three distances from shrub stems in two areas of Silver Bell Valley, near Tucson, Arizona, in August, 1968.

Area	Shrub species	Infiltration rate (cm/min)			
		Stems	Drip line	Interspace	F
I	*Cercidium microphyllum*	0.644	0.357	0.260	7.03[a]
	Larrea tridentata	0.401	0.212	0.094	10.51[a]
	Both species	0.522	0.285	0.177	7.09[a]
II	*Larrea tridentata*	0.520	0.480	0.197	47.58[b]

Source: Qashu (1970).

[a] .05 = 6.94 for 2, 4 degrees of freedom.

[b] .01 = 18.00 for 2, 4 degrees of freedom.

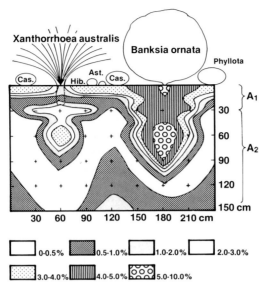

Figure 2. Soil-moisture pattern observed in deep sandy soil under South Australian heathland vegetation following a 25-mm rain in one day (20 March 1965). Soil water potential was near wilting point prior to the rain. Cas = *Casurina pusilla*, Hib = *Hibbertia stricta*, Ast = *Astrotoma conostephoides*, and *Phyllota pleurandroides*. (From Specht, 1981.)

by competition for water sounds logical, but some investigators have not been able to quantitatively demonstrate the assumed regular dispersion in the field (Barbour, 1981).

Bowns and West (1973) have shown how the depth to the petrocalcic horizon (caliche) is about twice as great under individual *Coleogyne ramosissima* as in the interspaces. Wallace and Romney (1972) also noted cupped depressions in the caliche under this and other Mohave Desert shrubs. This probably leads to greater soil moisture storage and root concentration directly under and around the shrubs. This patterning indicates that differential erosion–aggradation, infiltration, growth, and soil genesis have been occuring in the same microsites for considerable time.

Not all shrubs produce positive feedback for continuance of their present dispersion patterns. Some shrubs have chemicals in their foliage or litter that lead to hydrophobic soil surfaces (Qashu and Evans, 1969; DeBano, 1981). Buildup of such litter results in less infiltration of water and may thus lead to xerification of sites rather than edification or amelioration.

Several studies have shown that differences in height and density of shrubs can influence the redistribution of snow, which in turn influences soil moisture budgets (Connaughton, 1935; Hutchison, 1965; Wilken, 1967; Sturges and Taylor, 1981; Sturges, 1983; West and Caldwell, 1983), moderates temperatures, and influences phenology and productivity.

The shrubs may also intercept snowflakes, preventing some from reaching the ground and allowing faster sublimation. Shrubs also emit longwave radiation, thus creating a zone of relatively rapid melting directly adjacent to the shrubs. The most important influence is, however, that shrubs form obstacles to drifting snow particles. Since wind speed is reduced approximately a third to one-half of the free stream, turned 180°, and made very turbulent in the lee (wake) of an obstacle, preferential deposition of snow occurs there, just as a sand shadow forms behind an obstacle. This region, called the "cavity" by some, extends downstream from the obstacle for about two obstacle heights. About ten obstacle heights downwind, the airflow regains its laminar flow in the original direction and speed. Formulae are available for computing the volume of drifts likely (Hinds, 1970). Diameters and heights of the shrub are leading predictive parameters although increasing porosity of the shrubs can greatly complicate prediction. In dense stands of shrubs the reduced ablation of the snow particles due to the reduced movement near the ground (Parmenter and MacMahon, 1983) means that more snow will be left on the ground than if a smoother surface existed.

By combining knowledge of water content of the snow and rooting patterns one could conceivably model effectiveness for enhancing soil moisture. Few data are presently available for validating such models and measuring the effectiveness of shrubs in this role in modifying environments. Observation and intuition lead us to believe that these phenomena may be, however, quite important in certain circumstances, particularly in years of below average precipitation.

As with other phenomena it is difficult to ascribe cause and effect. Shrubs neither solely respond to external environment nor solely create their own environment. They do some of both, making categorization of allogenic and autogenic causes of succession arbitrary (White, 1979). For instance, the interaction with snow mentioned above could lead to a feedback loop of shrubs creating enhanced snow deposition that leads to better shrub growth that leads to more snow deposition.

C. Nutrient Cycling

Hydrological and nutrient cycles are intimately connected (Cowling, 1978). Once primary production has been segregated into patches of high (undershrub) and low (interspace) long-term response, it naturally follows that nutrient cycling will be anisotropic. As phytomass becomes concentrated, so will nutrients. As shrubs or shrub patches accumulate litter under their canopies so also do pools of minerals collect there.

The literature is replete with soil nutrient concentration and some content data showing how shrubs accumulate nutrients around them (Rickard, 1965; Garcia-Moya and McKell, 1970; Sharma and Tongway, 1973; Tiedemann and Klemmedson, 1973; Bowns and West, 1973; Charley and West, 1975; Charley, 1977; Barth and Klemmedson, 1978; Fairchild and Brotherson, 1980; West, 1981; Binkley *et al.*, 1982). Although fewer studies of metabolic activity levels have been done, all show decided spatial patterns (Cowling, 1969; Sharma, 1973; Charley and West, 1977).

These spatial patterns occur because of (a) absorption of nutrients by roots that extend beyond the crown area of the plants (a common situation in arid to semiarid environments), (b) absorption of nutrients by roots in lower soil and substrata, (c) fixation of nutrients by the plant or associated symbiotic organisms (especially nitrogen, see Fig. 3), (d) net import of nutrients by fauna that use the plants for nesting, resting, roosting, or

Figure 3. Percentage total soil nitrogen concentration beneath an average-size *Prosopis juliflora* shrub, Santa Rita Experimental Range, Arizona, as a function of canopy distance and soil depth. (From West and Klemmedson, 1978.)

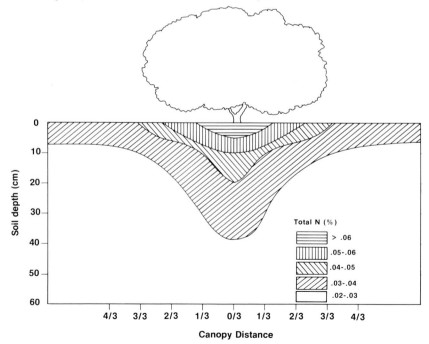

feeding and burrow around them (West, 1981), and (e) deposition of litter and soil due to movement by wind and water. Where inputs exceed outputs, net accumulations of phytomass, soils, and nutrient pools result.

The effectiveness of individual shrubs in affecting change in spatial organization of nutrient cycles varies tremendously by species and even size classes within species (Barth and Klemmedson, 1982). Data to allow comparisons between species or communities are just now starting to accumulate and any generalizations are probably premature.

D. Soil Erosion

The same features of the shrub dispersion pattern that link with energy, water, and nutrient budgets lead to differential erosion since both wind- and water-induced erosion are affected by the density and spatial arrangements of shrubs.

Marshall (1970, 1971) and Wooding *et al.* (1973) have shown that when shrubs are more than about six diameters apart, the nutrient-rich surface soil can easily be lost. In wind-prone areas this can leave smooth, hard soil surfaces called "scalds" (Beadle, 1948). This process is natural in very xeric environments, but in less severe environments it can be triggered by shrub destruction via burning, excessive grazing, vehicular damage, etc. Natural self-healing of this situation is almost undetectably slow, although mechanical disturbance of the surface in conjunction with a seed supply and adequate rains can overcome the "scalding" in some instances (Cunningham *et al.,* 1976). Shrubs may become established and distribution of nutrients may improve during periods of wetter climate, and both survive drought by mutual support. Damage to the shrubs may trigger changes that cannot be reversed without a return to the earlier climate (Westoby, 1979–1980).

The spatial distribution of shrubs is also intimately connected to stability of sand dune systems. Examples of this phenomenon are found on every continent. Removal of shrubs and other cover allows the sands to begin moving. Seedlings establishing on mobile dunes are liable to have either their roots exposed or their shoots buried. The damage may extend out from the original "blowout" area, as even established plants on what had been areas between or outside the dunes are overwhelmed. The existence of fossil dunes now fixed by vegetation shows that vegetation can reestablish on dunes given time and appropriate weather. The healing process can be shortened by management that stops movement of the surface sand (Herbel, 1984).

Wind predominates as an erosive agent in extremely arid regions

(Marshall, 1973). Water erosion becomes especially severe in semiarid regions (Branson *et al.*, 1981). Wind and water act together on any area having bared soil, that is, lacking vegetal cover and/or litter. Shrubs, because of their roots that are generally deeper and thicker than those of herbaceous species, are important in resisting soil movement. For instance, the roots of shrubs in the chaparral regions of the world usually go deep into the profile, even into cracks of bedrock. When the aboveground portions of the community are periodically destroyed by fire, the roots are slow to decompose. This, plus root sprouting, gives the burned community a few years to recover soil stability, reducing the chance of land slumps and slides (Ziemer, 1981; Wells, 1981).

E. Ecosystem Development

As has already been implied, ecosystems are far from static. Some of the most interesting and economically important phenomena are centered on the dynamics of vegetation and soils. Directional vegetation change is the classic type of succession. Because vegetation composition doesn't change without affecting microclimates and soils, ecosystem development is a term that more accurately depicts what goes on. Vegetation contributes more than 98% of the biomass in most ecosystems. If shrubs dominate, they automatically have a key role in successional and developmental trajectories.

Shrubs often serve as the nucleus of successional change and ecosystem development. As shrubs grow up into the wind in arid to semiarid areas, they catch eolian material. As fines and litter collect around and to the lee of shrub bases, the soils and microclimates become more hospitable for other plants (Batanouny and Batanouny, 1968). Shrubs thus often become, like the grit starting a pearl, the nucleus for a whole sere (sequence of plant community changes in succession) (Vasek and Lund, 1980). As many individual shrubs or their clumps develop, the whole landscape can become stabilized. Thus, grasslands that have been destroyed may recover first with desert shrubs and then gradually recover their original grasses as the soils stop moving between the shrub hummocks (Herbel, 1973). Shrubs can also serve as "nurse plants" for woodland development. Under woody *Artemisia* and associated shrubs is where most of the *Pinus* and *Juniperus* seedlings for the expanding pinyon–juniper woodlands get started (West *et al.*, 1975).

We now know that not all successions are directional with a single, stable end point. Watt (1947) pointed out a cyclic pattern in heathland where the ericaceous shrub *Calluna vulgaris* plays a vital role (Fig. 4). Yeaton (1978) showed how *Larrea tridentata* served as a nurse plant for *Opuntia*

Figure 4. Profile of the four phases in the *Calluna* cycle in an English moorland. I. Pioneer: establishment and early growth of *Calluna*—open patches, with many plant species. Years 0–6. II. Building: maximum cover for *Calluna* with vigorous flowering—few associated plants. Years 7–15. III. Mature: gaps begin in *Calluna* canopy and more species invade the area. Years 14–25. IV. Degenerate: central branches of *Calluna* die, lichens and bryophytes very common. Years 20–30. (After Watt, 1955.)

leptocaulis in the Chihuahuan Desert. When the *Opuntia* eventually died, the *Larrea* recolonized the spot of original occupation and the cycle repeated. Such cyclic patterns are probably more common than we presently think. It takes the right set of circumstances to be able to decipher such successions.

Another way that shrubs influence succession is by their flammability. There may even be evolutionary selection for flammability (Mutch, 1970). Some of the same chemicals making shrubs more flammable also contribute to the allelochemical means of interference competition and hydrophobic soils. These interconnections seem to be common to chaparral and heathlands in several parts of the world (Gill and Groves, 1981).

Periodic fire leads to perpetuation of certain kinds of shrubs and shrublands. This appears to be the case in the California chaparral, where succession would appear to lead to tree dominance (Hanes, 1977; Vogl, 1982), given enough time between fires. Among the shrubs, the ones that sprout from roots or have seed germination stimulated by hot temperatures are most abundant in chaparral. The decline in productivity with age of the stand correlates with maximum fuel load buildup (Rundel and Parsons, 1979), and thus probability of reburning. Reburning releases mineral nutrients and stimulates nitrogen fixation by free-fixers (Rundel 1983). Humans want to live in such environments, but have failed to recognize the importance of fire in the self-renewal process. Fire control has led to buildup of so much fuel that fires are now usually catastrophic (Agee, 1977).

F. Animal Interactions

Animals both influence and are influenced by spatial arrangements of shrubs. Some ways that animals influence shrub distributions are via pollination, seed planting, and herbivory. We must also include indirect means, such as when one animal influences the abundance of predators (Gessaman and MacMahon, 1984).

Different kinds of animals contribute and respond to vegetation structure in various ways. For instance, Feinsinger (1976) has shown that the most competitive species of hummingbird dominates the resource-rich clumps and nectar-bearing flowers on shrubs (*Homelia, Cuphea, Justicea*) of the Caribbean islands. The dominant hummingbird's aggressiveness modifies the distribution and abundance of all other hummingbirds in the guild. Since the various islands have differing plants and hummingbirds, varied community structure results. The shrubs probably have evolved differing flower structure and nectar production to compete for the hummingbird's time and pollination services. Clusters of shrubs are also likely to be produced by these coevolutionary pressures.

Davidson and Morton (1981) have shown that ants select certain chenopod shrubs in Australia because of their seed morphology. The ants carry the seeds to their nests; some germinate and differential establishment results.

West (1968) has shown that small rodents, by caching *Purshia tridentata* seeds, cause most of this shrub, at least on pumice soils in central Oregon, to be multistemmed, as well as multi-individual clusters. Sherman and Chilcote (1972) have gone on to show how caching is concentrated in litter-free areas. Rodents are very effective at detecting caches and consuming shrub seeds or seedlings (Evans *et al.*, 1983). This must be taken into account in any revegetation effort. What few seedlings of *Larrea* that survive in interspaces may be due to rodent caching (Sheps, 1973). Rodents cache seeds of many other shrubs in the western United States and Mexico. These caches are now often raided by humans to get stock of seed for research and revegetation (Everett and Kulla, 1976). Although we know that the distribution and abundance of many shrubs are probably significantly affected by animal pollination and seed dispersal, there are probably many other ways that small animals affect shrub dispersion that remain to be described.

Does shrub dispersion pattern change with successional status? West and Goodall (1986) examined fenceline contrasts and haloseres in salt desert shrublands in western Utah. They found that most of the shrub species and the communities as a whole maintained clusters of aggregated individuals regardless of successional status. This they attributed to the importance of the "islands of fertility." Norton and Bermant (1977) have shown that although shrub seedlings occasionally germinate in the infertile interspaces, the only ones that survive occur on microsites where shrub clusters presently or recently grew.

Small-scale structure of shrublands also affects animals. Action and co-action are not so easily separated in the field. That is, it is often hard to distinguish where the animals' effects on the plants leave off and the plants' effects on the animals begin.

The importance of "edge" and pattern interspersion is often cited in the wildlife management literature. Both wildlife professionals and hunters believe that the most game animals are to be found where there is maximum "edge" between differing vegetation types. The more the physiognomic contrast, the better it supposedly is for large animals. Hirst (1975) gives an example of the kinds of sophistication that can be incorporated into correlational studies. Although Romesburg (1981) says the evidence of this sort is all intuitive and regards this as no more that a hypothesis, it could be experimentally tested.

Zoologists working on basic aspects of animal–vegetation relationships have concentrated on the vertical variation in vegetation as it affects animal distribution. Much of the work in this area has been done with birds. Cody (1975), following the ideas of MacArthur and MacArthur (1961), has shown that much of the difference in bird species diversity between areas is correlated to foliage height diversity, that is, the kinds of different foliage and their vertical positioning. His samples from shrublands on three continents show similar patterns.

Others have applied this approach to numerous shrublands, of which the work of Vander Wall (1980) and Vander Wall and MacMahon (1984) is illustrative. They showed that bird species diversity was significantly correlated with foliage height diversity ($r = 0.93, p < .05$) and physiognomic cover diversity ($r = 0.85$, $p < .05$) for changing desert shrublands on several bajadas in the Sonoran Desert of Arizona. There were also changes in bird diversity correlated with changes in vegetation structure over latitudinal gradients within that desert region. Vegetation structure as it affects habitat for prey, nesting sites, escape cover from predators, thermal protection, and more is probably involved.

Although relatively few correlational studies and even fewer manipulative studies have been done, mammals have also been found to respond to differences in large-scale vegetation structure. Although correlations do not necessarily represent a cause–effect relationship, the combined results of studies in shrublands such as those of Allred and Beck (1963), Rosenzweig and Winakur (1969), Brown (1973), Rosenzweig *et al.* (1975), Montgomery (1976), Hafner (1977), and Feldhamer (1979) imply that rodents can integrate certain vegetational attributes in their selection of habitat. Brown *et al.* (1972) have shown that density of a small mammal population may be related to density of a shrublike plant. MacMahon (1976), employing a functional group (= guild) analysis to North American desert mammal communities, found, however, that vertical and horizontal foliage complexity do not correlate well with small mammal functional diversity.

Additional studies employing a variety of perturbations of shrubland architecture (Taylor, 1963; Rosenzweig, 1973; Price, 1978; Holbrook, 1979; LoBue and Darnell, 1959; McGee, 1982; Gashwiler, 1970; Van Horne, 1981; Johnson and Hansen, 1967) have shown that rodent abundances and distributions can be impacted by drastic changes in vegetation. What changes in vegetation attributes cause rodents to select suitable habitat is less well known. Parmenter and MacMahon (1983) have shown that removal of sagebrush from a sagebrush steppe in southwestern Wyoming did not alter the abundance of most resident rodent species because the abundance of major food resources (herbaceous vegetation, soil-seed reserves, and ground-dwelling arthropods) was not affected by shrub removal. The "cover" provided by the shrubs was not important to mammals in that context. Rather, shrubs may be important to rodents in the long term by providing "safe sites" for growth of herbaceous vegetation, thereby enhancing the potential rodent food resources. The importance of shrubs for animal food and cover may be quite different in other contexts, however.

Pianka (1975) correlated the diversity of lizards of desert regions with many variables, including shrub-community characteristics. He found that the patterns were much more complicated than for small mammals and thus are difficult to generalize.

The importance of large-scale vegetation patterns on invertebrates has been relatively little studied, especially in shrublands. What little that has been done is intriguing. For instance, Hatley and MacMahon (1980) found that manipulations of *Artemisia tridentata* resulted in changes in number of spider species, spider guilds, and guild importance values. The numbers of spider species and guilds in the shrubs with branches bound together with twine were significantly higher than those of shrubs that were clipped or controls. Spider species diversity and guilds were positively correlated with indicators of shrub volume and shrub foliage diversity. This suggests that structurally more complex shrubs can support a higher species diversity. Robinson's (1981) later experimental work confirmed this.

J. A. MacMahon (personal correspondence) has observed that certain spiders in the Mohave Desert are concentrated at certain heights between shrubs of certain sizes and spacing. These animals have exacting requirements for web building related to temperature profiles and prey habits. Larmuth (1979) describes some of these temperature patterns. Close observations in other shrublands are bound to yield other interesting correspondences of invertebrate distribution to vegetation structure.

Although most of the literature deals with small, wild animals, there is good reason to believe that larger wild and domestic animals could respond to shrubland patterning also. Iskander (1973) noted that the level of sheep

utilization on individual bitterbrush (*Purshia tridentata*) shrubs was negatively influenced by the proximity of individual sagebrush plants. The
average critical distance, for this influence, was about 56 cm. He also
observed that sheep tended to graze and trample all the vegetation
surrounding the taller shrubs on mountain brushland in Utah. These
phenomena are intriguing and deserving of much more research in other
shrublands.

IV. Implications of Shrub Spatial Patterns for Inventory, Wildland Management, Habitat Manipulation, and Ecosystem Restoration

How should our current understanding of spatial patterns in shrublands
and their interactions with ecosystem functions influence our efforts to
inventory, manage, manipulate, and restore wildlands where shrubs
dominate?

As seen from the foregoing examples, shrublands are far from
homogeneous on a microscale. Especially in semiarid to arid environments, shrubs are usually found in clumps associated with patches of more
favorable soil. Those inventorying various features of these environments
and biotic communities should be very cognizant of this spatial
variability. Sample sizes, shapes, numbers, and spatial placement should
provide for including all parts of the mosaics in proportion to their
occurrence. For instance, although it is easier to dig samples into the soil of
the interspaces, the values of almost all conceivable variables will be
different than those found under the shrub canopies. Different sampling
strategies will lead to different levels of statistical reliability (Moore *et al.*,
1967).

If one radically changes the anisotropic structure of most shrublands,
such as by plowing, a more homogeneous environment should result, but
the productivity could be lowered because the soil nutrients would
disperse across a largely less fertile landscape. It thus seems logical to
either work with the existing structure or mimic it in reconstruction efforts.

Some of the disappointments in range reseeding may be due to disruption of the patchwork of anisotropic soil features via heavy mechanical
alterations. Clearing away of brush skeletons may be inimical to survival
of desirable native and seeded species. Indeed, Herbel (1973) found that
grass establishment was much more successful when the skeletons of
creosote bush (*Larrea tridentata*) were replaced following root plowing and
seeding. Rather than doing any cutting or plowing it may be better to kill

the brush, but let the carcasses stay in place. Reseeding could then occur over the top, if aerial seeding or appropriate ground equipment is used (e.g., rangeland drill).

For more drastically disturbed lands such as roadsides and strip mines, more rapid revegetation may be facilitated by initially planting shrubs in clusters. The shrubs could then catch snow and soil fines and provide perches and hiding places for animals. Litter and nutrient cycling would be concentrated in such patches, accelerating soil development. This idea is currently being tested by the author and his colleagues on a recontoured coal strip mine in southwestern Wyoming.

Because different kinds and sizes of brush patches have differing susceptibility to fire, we could use this understanding to either help control fires or in planning prescribed burning. Since wildlife seem to thrive best on patchy landscapes, we should strive to create patchiness where homogeneity now prevails. This could be done by mosaic application of cutting, herbicides, or prescribed burning. Sufficient management control and technology are available to effect this, if desired. Pelleted herbicides and helitorches allow us to pinpoint the treatments where we want them. After we have developed more of a complex mosaic of different species and size classes, we should have enhanced wildlife use, as well as reduced chances of far-reaching conflagrations.

Since the patchwork of shrubs on several scales will probably influence livestock behavior, we might as well begin testing this also. Shrubs with grass are known to provide better nutritional balance during the nongrowing season in subtropical and temperate regions. Furthermore, it has been demonstrated in some contexts that grass production can be enhanced by some scattered shrubs. Where reseeding takes place in what were originally shrub steppe environments, conversions to grass monocultures are difficult to maintain. Perhaps we should be less worried about keeping out the brush entirely.

We run much greater risk of insect and pathogen outbreaks in grass monocultures. Shrubs provide habitat for important insect predators. For instance, Ostlie (1979) has shown how insect diversity is much higher and population levels of the major grass herbivores, leafhoppers, and black grass bugs are lower where shrubs are intermixed with seeded grasses. Since insects can acount for up to 10 times as much herbivory as livestock in such vegetation (Haws, 1978), maintenance of shrub-free areas may be economically counterproductive. We need to better define at what relative densities such synergism is optimum. Experiments on clustering of shrubs at several scales are needed to see if mimicking nature might be worthwhile for accelerating recovery and enhancing overall productivity and stability.

V. Conclusions

To fully understand shrublands, one has to look at spatial patterns within communities and over landscapes at several scales. Averages taken across areas considered to be internally homogeneous can be deceptive since rates of functional processes can vary greatly over small distances in space and over short time frames. Although there is much more to find out about such patterns, we can already use some of the information to improve inventories, better plan other studies, and develop more effective ways of harvesting, maintaining, and restoring ecosystems in which shrubs have a role.

References

Agee, J. K., ed. (1977). "Fire and Fuel Management Problems in Mediterranean Climate Ecosystems: Research Priorities and Programs" MAB Tech. Note 11. UNESCO, Paris.

Allred, D. M., and Beck, D. E. (1963). Ecological distribution of some rodents at the Nevada atomic test site. *Ecology* **44**, 211–214.

Bailey, A. W. (1970). Barrier effect of the shrub *Elaeagnus commutata* on grazing cattle and forage production in central Alberta. *J. Range Manage.* **23**, 248–251.

Barbour, M. G. (1981). Plant–plant interactions. *In* "Aridland Ecosystems: Structure, Functioning and Management" (D. W. Goodall and R. A. Perry, eds.), Vol. 2, pp. 38-49. Cambridge Univ. Press, London and New York.

Barth, R. C., and Klemmedson, J. O. (1978). Shrub-induced spatial patterns of dry matter, nitrogen and organic carbon. *Soil Sci. Soc. Am. J.* **42**, 804–809.

Barth, R. C., and Klemmedson, J. O. (1982). Amount and distribution of dry matter, nitrogen, and organic carbon in soil–plant systems of mesquite and palo verde. *J. Range Manage.* **35**, 412–418.

Batanouny, K. H., and Batanouny, M. H. (1968). Formation of phytogenic hillocks. I. Plants forming phytogenic hillocks. *Acta Bot. Acad. Sci. Hung.* **14**, 243–252.

Beadle, N. C. W. (1948). "The Vegetation and Pastures of Western New South Wales with Special Reference to Soil Erosion." Government Printer, Sydney.

Binkley, D., Cromack, K., Jr., and Fredricksen, R. L. (1982). Nitrogen accretion and availability in some snowbrush ecosystems. *For. Sci.* **28**, 720–724.

Bowns, J. E., and West, N. E. (1973). Blackbrush (*Coleogyne ramosissima* Torr.) on southwestern Utah rangelands. *Utah Agric. Exp. Stn., Res. Rep.* **27**.

Branson, F. A., Gifford, G. F., Renard, K. G., and Hadley, R. F. (1981). "Rangeland Hydrology" 2nd ed. Kendall/Hunt Publ., Dubuque, Iowa.

Brown, J. H. (1973). Species diversity of seed-eating desert rodents in sand dune habitats. *Ecology* **54**, 775–787.

Brown, J. H., Lieberman, G. A., and Dengler, W. F. (1972). Woodrats and cholla: Dependence of a small mammal population on the density of cacti. *Ecology* **53**, 310–313.

Charley, J. L. (1977). Mineral cycling in rangeland ecosystems. *In* "Rangeland Plant

Physiology" (R. E. Sosebee, ed.), Range Sci. Ser. No. 4, pp. 215–256. Soc. Range Manage., Denver, Colorado.

Charley, J. L., and West, N. E. (1975). Plant-induced soil chemical patterns in some shrub dominated semi-desert ecosystems in Utah. *J. Ecol.* **63,** 945–963.

Charley, J. L., and West, N. E. (1977). Micropatterns of nitrogen mineralization activity in soils of some shrub-dominated semi-desert ecosystems in Utah. *Soil Biol. Biochem.* **9,** 357–365.

Cody, M. L. (1975). Towards a theory of continental species diversities: Bird distributions over Mediterranean habitat gradients. *In* "Ecology and Evolution of Communities" (M. L. Cody and J. Diamond, eds.), pp. 214–157. Harvard Univ. Press, Cambridge, Massachusetts.

Connaughton, C. A. (1935). The accumulation and rate of melting of snow as influenced by vegetation. *J. For.* **33,** 564–569.

Cowling, S. W. (1969). A study of vegetation activity patterns in a semi-arid environment. Ph.D. Dissertation. University of New England, Armidale, New South Wales, Australia.

Cowling, S. W. (1978). Coupling of nutrient to water flows in rangeland ecosystems. *In* "Studies of the Australian Arid Zone. III. Water in Rangelands" (K. H. W. Howes, ed.) pp. 110–121. C.S.I.R.O., Melbourne, Australia.

Cunningham, G. W., Walker, J. P., and Green, D. R. (1976). "Rehabilitation of Arid Lands: Ten years of Research at Cobar, N.S.W., 1964–1974" Soil Conservation Service of New South Wales, Australia.

Davidson, D. W., and Morton, S. R. (1981). Competition for dispersal in ant-dispersed plants. *Science* **213,** 1259–1261.

DeBano, L. F. (1981). Water repellant soils: A state-of-the-art. *USDA For. Serv. Gen. Tech. Rep. PSW* **PSW-46.**

Evans, R. A., Young, J. A., Cluff, G. J., and McAdoo, J. K. (1983). Dynamics of antelope bitterbrush seed caches. *USDA For. Serv. Gen. Tech. Rep. INT* **INT-152,** 195–202.

Everett, R. L., and Kulla, A. W. (1976). Rodent cache seedlings of shrub species in the Southwest. *Tree Planters Notes* **27**(3), 11–12.

Fairchild, J. A., and Brotherson, J. D. (1980). Microhabitat relationships of six major shrubs in Navajo National Monument, Arizona. *J. Range Manage.* **33,** 150–156.

Feinsinger, P. (1976). Organization of a tropical guild of nectarivorous birds. *Ecol. Monogr.* **46,** 257–291.

Feldhamer, G. A. (1979). Vegetative and edaphic factors affecting abundance and distribution of small mammals in southeastern Oregon. *Great Basin Nat.* **39,** 207–218.

Fonteyn, P. J., and Mahall, B. E. (1981). An experimental analysis of structure in a desert plant community. *J. Ecol.* **69,** 883–986.

Frischknecht, N. C. (1963). Contrasting effects of big sagebrush and rubber rabbitbrush on production of crested wheatgrass. *J. Range Manage.* **16,** 70–74.

Gracia–Moya, E., and McKell, C. M. (1970). Contribution of shrubs to the nitrogen economy of a desert wash plant community. *Ecology* **51,** 81–88.

Gashwiler, J. S. (1970). Plant and mammal changes on a clearcut in west-central Oregon. *Ecology* **51,** 1018–1026.

Gessaman, J. A., and MacMahon, J. A. (1984). Mammals in ecosystems: Their effects on the composition and production of vegetation. *Acta Zool. Fenn.* **172,** 11–18.

Gill, A. M., and Groves, R. H. (1981). Fire regimes in heathlands and their plant ecological effects. *In* "Heathlands and Related Shrublands: Quantitative Studies" (R. L. Specht, ed.), Ecosystems of the World, Vol. 9B, pp. 61–84.

Goodall, D. W., and West, N. E. (1979). Comparison of techniques for assessing dispersion patterns. *Vegetatio* **40**, 15–27.

Hafner, M. S. (1977). Density and diversity in Mojave Desert rodent and shrub communities. *J. Anim. Ecol.* **46**, 925–938.

Halvorson, W. L., and Patten, D. T. (1975). Productivity and flowering of winter ephemerals in relation to Sonoran Desert shrubs. *Am. Midl. Nat.* **93**, 311–319.

Hamilton, E. L., and Rowe, P. B. (1949). "Rainfall Interception by Chaparral in California." California Department of Natural Resources, Div. For., Sacramento.

Hanes, T. L. (1977). Succession after fire in the chaparral of southern California. *Ecol. Monog.* **41**, 27–52.

Hatley, C. L., and MacMahon, J. A. (1980). Spider community organization: Seasonal variation and the role of vegetation architecture. *Environ. Entomol.* **9**, 632–639.

Haws, B. A. (co-ord.) (1978). "Economic Impacts of *Labops hesperuis* on Production of High Quality Range Grasses," Final report to Four Corners Regional Commission. Utah Agric. Exp. St., Logan.

Herbel, C. H. (1973). Some developments related to seeding western rangelands. *In* "Range Research and Range Problems," Spec. Publ. No. 3, pp. 75–80. Crop Sci. Soc. Am., Madison, Wisconsin.

Herbel, C. H. (1984). Successional patterns and productivity potentials of the range vegetation in the warm, arid portions of the southwestern United States. *In* "Developing Strategies for Rangelands." pp. 1333–1365. Westview Press, Boulder, Colorado.

Hinds, T. (1970). Snowdrifting. *Proc. Abiotic Spec. Meet., 1970,* pp. 27–30.

Hirst, S. M. (1975). Ungulate–habitat relationships in a South African woodland/savanna ecosystem. *Wildl. Monogr.* **44**, 1–60.

Holbrook, S. J. (1979). Habitat utilization, competitive interactions, and coexistence of three species of cricetine rodents in east-central Arizona. *Ecology* **60**, 758–769.

Hull, A. C., and Klomp, G. J. (1974). Yield of crested wheatgrass under four densities of big sagebrush in southern Idaho. *U.S., Dept. Agric., Tech. Bull.* **1438.**

Hutchison, B. A. (1965). Snow accumulation and disappearance influenced by big sagebrush. *USDA For. Serv. Res. Note RM* **RM-46.**

Iskander, F. D. (1973). Factors affecting feeding habits of sheep grazing foothill ranges of northern Utah. Ph. D. Dissertation, Utah State University, Logan (unpublished).

Johnson, D. R., and Hansen, R. M. (1967). Effects of range treatments with 2,4-D on rodent populations. *J. Wildl. Manage.* **33**, 125–132.

Kershaw, K. A. (1973). "Quantitative and Dynamic Plant Ecology," 2nd ed. Edward Arnold, London.

Larmuth, J. (1979). Aspects of plant habitat as a thermal refuge of desert insects. *J. Arid Environ.* **2**, 323–327.

LoBue, J., and Darnell, R. M. (1959). Effect of habitat disturbance on a small mammal population. *J. Mammal.* **40**, 425–437.

MacArthur, R. H., and Connell, J. (1966). "The Biology of Populations." Wiley, New York.

MacArthur, R. H., and MacArthur, J. W. (1961). On bird species diversity. *Ecology* **42**, 594–598.

McGee, J. M. (1982). Small mammal populations in an unburned and early fire successional sagebrush community. *J. Range Manage.* **35**, 177–179.

McIntosh, R. P. (1980). The background and some current problems of theoretical ecology. *Synthese* **43**, 195–255.

MacMahon, J. A. (1976). Species and guild similarity of North American desert mammal faunas: A functional analysis of communities. *In* "Evolution of Desert Biota" (D. W. Goodall, ed.), pp. 133–148. Univ. of Texas Press, Austin.

McNaughton, S. J. (1978). Serengeti ungulates: Feeding selectivity influences the effectiveness of plant defense guilds. *Science* **199**, 806–807.

Marshall, J. K. (1970). Assessing the protective role of shrub-dominated rangeland vegetation against soil erosion by wind. *Proc. Int. Grassl. Cong., 11th, 1969,* pp. 19–23.

Marshall, J. K. (1971). Drag measurements in roughness arrays of varying density and distribution. *Agric. Meteorol.* **8**, 269–292.

Marshall, J. K. (1973). Drought, land use and soil erosion. *In* "Drought" (J. V. Lovett, ed.), pp. 55–77. Angus & Robertson, Sydney, Australia.

Montgomery, S. J. (1976). Rodent–habitat relationships in Great Basin Desert shrub communities. M. S. Thesis, Utah State University, Logan (unpublished).

Moore, A. W., Russell, J. S., and Coaldrake, J. E. (1967). Dry matter and nutrient content of a subtropical semi-arid forest of *Acacia harpophylla* F. Muell. (Brigalow). *Aust. J. Bot.* **15**, 11–24.

Mutch, R. W. (1970). Wildland fires and ecosystems—An hypothesis. *Ecology* **51**, 1046–1051.

Norton, B. E., and Bermant, D. J. (1977). Plant replacement and population interactions of perennials in salt desert shrub vegetation. Oral presentation at annual meetings of the Ecological Society of America, Lansing, Michigan.

Osmund, C. B., Bjorkman, O., and Anderson, D. J. (1980). "Physiological Processes in Plant Ecology. Studies of the Genus *Atriplex*." Springer-Verlag, New York.

Ostlie, K. R. (1979). Abundance and dispersal of *Labops hesperius* in relation to vegetation. M.S. Thesis, Utah State University, Logan (unpublished).

Parmenter, R. R., and MacMahon, J. A. (1983). Factors determining the abundance and distribution of rodents in a shrub-steppe ecosystem: The role of shrubs. *Oecologia* **59**, 145–156.

Patten, D. C. (1978). Productivity and production efficiency of an upper Sonoran Desert ephemeral community. *Am. J. Bot.* **65**, 891–895.

Phillips, D. L., and MacMahon, J. A. (1981). Competition and spacing patterns in desert shrubs. *J. Ecol.* **69**, 97–115.

Pianka, E. R. (1975). Niche relations of desert lizards. *In* "Ecology and Evolution of Communities" (M. L. Cody and J. M. Diamond, eds.), pp. 292–314. Harvard Univ. Press, Cambridge, Massachusetts.

Pielou, E. C. (1974). "Population and Community Ecology: Principles and Methods." Gordon & Breach, New York.

Price, M. V. (1978). The role of microhabitat in structuring desert rodent communities. *Ecology* **59**, 910–921.

Qashu, H. K. (1970). Infiltration and runoff. *In* "Report on Abiotic Specialist Meeting, Tucson, Arizona," pp. 20–26. US/IBP Desert Biome, Utah State University, Logan.

Qashu, H. K., and Evans, D. D. (1969). Water repellency of soils. *Prog. Agric. Ariz.* **21**(6), 9–11.

Rickard, W. H. (1965). The influence of greasewood on soil moisture and soil chemistry. *Northwest Sci.* **39**, 36–42.

Rittenhouse, L. R., and Sneva, F. A. (1976). Expressing the competitive relationship between Wyoming big sagebrush and crested wheatgrass. *J. Range Manage.* **29**, 326–327.

Robinson, J. V. (1981). The effect of architectural variation in habitat on a spider community: An experimental field study. *Ecology* **62**, 73–80.

Romesburg, H. C. (1981). Wildlife science: Gaining reliable knowledge. *J. Wildl. Manage.* **45**, 293–313.

Romney, E. M., Wallace, A., and Hunter, R. B. (1978). Plant response to nitrogen fertilization in the northern Mohave Desert and its relationship to water manipulation. *In* "Nitrogen in Desert Ecosystems" (N. E. West and J. Skujins, eds.), pp. 232–243. Dowden, Hutchinson & Ross, Stroudsburg, Pennsylvania.

Romney, E. M., Wallace, A., Kaaz, H., Hale, V. Q., and Childress, J. D. (1979). Effect of shrubs on redistribution of mineral nutrients in zones near roots in the Mojave Desert. *Range Sci. Dep. Sci. Ser. (Colo. State Univ.)* **26,** 303–310.

Rosenzweig, M. L. (1973). Habitat selection experiments with a pair of coexisting heteromyid rodent species. *Ecology* **54,** 111–117.

Rosenzweig, M. L., and Winakur, J. (1969). Population ecology of desert rodent communities: Habitats and environmental complexity. *Ecology* **50,** 558–572.

Rosenzweig, M. L., Smigel, B., and Kraft, A. (1975). Patterns of food, space and diversity. *In* "Rodents in Desert Environments" (J. Prakash and P. R. Gosh, eds.), pp. 241–268. Junk, The Hague.

Rumbaugh, M. D., Johnson, D. A., and Van Epps, G. A. (1982). Forage yield and quality in a Great Basin shrub, grass, and legume pasture experiment. *J. Range Manage.* **35,** 604–609.

Rundel, P. W. (1983). The impact of fire on nutrient cycles. *In* "Mediterranean-Type Ecosystems: The Role of Nutrients" (F. J. Kruger, ed.). pp. 192–207. Springer-Verlag, New York.

Rundel, P. W., and Parsons, D. J. (1979). Structural changes in chamise (*Adenostoma fasciculatum*) along a fire-reduced age gradient. *J. Range Manage.* **32,** 462–466.

Scifres, C. J., Mutz, J. L., Whitson, R. E., and Drawe, D. L. (1982). Interrelationships of Huisache canopy cover with range forage on the coastal prairie. *J. Range Manage.* **35,** 558–562.

Sharma, M. L. (1973). Soil physical and physico-chemical variablility induced by *Atriplex nummularia*. *J. Range Manage.* **26,** 426–430.

Sharma, M. L., and Tongway, D. J. (1973). Plant-induced soil salinity patterns in two saltbush (*Atriplex* spp.) communities. *J. Range Manage.* **26,** 121–125.

Sheps, L. O. (1973). Survival of *Larrea tridentata* S.&M. seedlings in Death Valley National Monument, California. *Isr. J. Bot.* **22,** 8–17.

Sherman, R. J., and Chilcote, W. W. (1972). Spatial and chronological patterns of *Purshia tridentata* as influenced by ponderosa pine. *Ecology* **53,** 294–298.

Slatyer, R. O. (1965). Measurements of precipitation interception by an arid zone plant community (*Acacia aneura* F. Muell). *In* "Proceedings of the Montpellier Symposium. Methodology of Plant Eco-physiology," pp. 181–192., UNESCO, Paris.

Specht, R. L. (1957). Dark Island heath (Ninety-mile Plain, South Australia). IV. Soil moisture patterns produced by rainfall interception and stem flow. *Aust. J. Bot.* **5,** 137–150.

Specht, R. L. (1981). The water relations of heathlands: Morphological adaptations to drought. *In* "Heathlands and Related Shrublands: Quantitative Studies" (R. L. Specht, ed.), Ecosystems of the World, Vol. 9B, pp. 123–129. Elsevier, Amsterdam.

Sturges, D. L. (1983). Shelterbelt establishment and growth at a windswept Wyoming rangeland site. *USDA For. Serv. Res. Pap. RM* **RM-243.**

Sturges, D. L., and Taylor, R. D. (1981). Management of blowing snow on sagebrush rangelands. *J. Soil Water Conserv.* **36,** 287–292.

Taylor, R. J. (1963). Vertical distribution of *Peromyscus leucopus* and *P. gossypinnus* under experimental conditions. *Southwest. Nat.* **8,** 107–115.

Tiedemann, A. R., and Klemmedson, J. O. (1973). Effect of mesquite on physical and chemical properties of the soil. *J. Range Manage.* **26,** 27–29.

Tromble, J. M. (1983). Interception of rainfall by tarbush. *J. Range Manage.* **36,** 525–526.

Vander Wall, S. B. (1980). The structure of Sonoran Desert bird communities: Effects of vegetation structure and precipitation. Ph.D. Dissertation, Utah State University, Logan.

Vander Wall, S. B., and MacMahon, J. A. (1984). Avian distribution patterns along a Sonoran Desert bajada. *J. Arid Environ.* **7,** 59–64.

Van Horne, B. (1981). Demography of *Peromyscus manipulatus* populations in seral stages of coastal coniferous forest in southeastern Alaska. *Can. J. Zool.* **59,** 1045-1061.

Vasek, F. C., and Lund, L. J. (1980). Soil characteristics associated with a primary succession on a Mojave Desert dry lake. *Ecology* **61,** 1013–1018.

Vogl. R. J. (1982). Chaparral succession. *USDA For. Serv. Gen. Tech. Rep. PSW* **PSW-158,** 81–85.

Wallace, A., and Romney, E. M. (1972). "Radioecology and Ecophysiology of Desert Plants at the Nevada Test Site." Lab. Nucl. Med. Radiat. Biol., UCLA TID 25954. University of California, Los Angeles.

Watt, A. S. (1947). Pattern and process in the plant community. *J. Ecol.* **35,** 1–22.

Watt, A. S. (1955). Bracken versus heather, a study in plant sociology. *J. Ecol.* **43,** 490–506.

Wells, K. F. (1967). Aspects of shrub–herb productivity in an arid environment. M.S. Thesis, University of California, Berkeley.

Wells, W. G. (1981). Some effects of brush fires on erosion processes in coastal southern California. *IAHS Publ.* **132,** 305–341.

West, N. E. (1968). Rodent-influenced establishment of ponderosa pine and bitterbrush seedlings in central Oregon. *Ecology* **49,** 1009–1011.

West, N. E. (1981). Nutrient cycling in desert ecosystems. *In* "Arid Land Ecosystems: Structure, Functioning, and Management" (D. W. Goodall and R. A. Perry, eds.), Vol. 2, pp. 301–324. Cambridge Univ. Press, London and New York.

West, N. E., and Caldwell, M. M. (1983). Snow as a factor in salt desert shrub vegetation patterns in Curlew Valley, Utah. *Am. Midl. Nat.* **109,** 376–379.

West, N. E., Gifford, G. F. (1976). Rainfall interception by cool-desert shrubs. *J. Range Manage.* **29,** 171–172.

West, N. E., and Goodall, D. W. (1986). Dispersion patterns in relation to successional status of salt desert shrub-vegetation. *Abstracta Botanica* **10,** 187–201.

West, N. E., and Klemmedson, J. O. (1978). Structural distribution of nitrogen in desert ecosystems. *In* "Nitrogen in Desert Ecosystems," (N. E. West and J. S. Skujins, eds.), pp. 1–16. Dowden, Hutchinson & Ross, Stroudsburg, Pennsylvania.

West, N. E., Rea, K. H., and Tausch, R. J. (1975). Basic synecological relationships in juniper–pinyon woodlands. *In* "The Pinyon–Juniper Ecosystem: A Symposium" (G. F. Gifford and F. E. Busby, eds.), 41–53. Utah State University, Logan.

Westoby, M. (1979–1980). Elements of a theory of vegetation dynamics in arid rangelands. *Isr. J. Bot.* **28,** 169–194.

White, P. S. (1979). Pattern, process, and natural disturbance in vegetation. *Bot. Rev.* **45,** 229–299.

Wilken, G. C. (1967). Snow accumulation in a manzanita brush field in the Sierra Nevada. *Water Resour. Res.* **3,** 409–422.

Wooding, R. A., Bradley, E. F., and Marshall, J. K. (1973). Drag due to regular arrays of roughness elements of varying geometry. *Boundary-Layer Meteorol.* **5,** 285–308.

Yeaton, R. I. (1978). A cyclical relationship between *Larrea tridentata* and *Opuntia leptocaulis* in the northern Chihuahuan Desert. *J. Ecol.* **66,** 651–656.

Ziemer, R. R. (1981). Roots and stability of forested slopes. *IAHS Publ.* **132,** 343–361.

13

The Role of Shrubs in Plant Community Diversity

Cyrus M. McKell

I. The Role of Shrubs in Plant Community Diversity

The importance of shrubs to community diversity can be justified on the basis that they broaden the sources of productivity, increase opportunities for multiple use, and extend ecological stability. Because community diversity is derived from various sources, each of these sources adds a degree of stability to the plant community. However, there is no satisfactory determinant as to the amount of each diversity source needed to assure adequate community stability or the need for additional species in the community.

A. *Sources of Community Diversity*

Not all sources of diversity may function to the same degree. According to Harper (1977) community diversity is derived from five sources:

1. Somatic Polymorphism

Somatic polymorphism within the genotype of a species provides for different expressions of root, stem, leaf, and flower size and display according to the space available. Plants in a monoculture tend to emphasize diversity within the same morphological features. West and Rea (1979) working in native sagebrush–grass communities observed that community stability is achieved more by plant plasticity than by shifts in age class distribution although pulses of establishment occur in favorable years.

2. Age Distribution

Age distribution grouping occurs in response to cyclic periods of suitable temporal conditions for germination and establishment. Early seedlings may have a greater opportunity for growth than later ones of the same or different species although a few may be found in an even-aged stand. Distribution of ages within a stand may be one of the elements of diversity that permits or denies the chance of recovery after stress.

3. Genetic Variants within a Species

Genetic variants within a species provide plants that can respond to the range of conditions within sites as well as those found over a spectrum of geographic locations. Species with great genetic diversity may be expected to include genetic combinations capable of resisting stresses as well as those responding to favorable conditions in given habitats. Continued natural selection under such conditions leads to ecotype development. Fourwing saltbush (*Atriplex canescens*) is an example of a genetic complex possessing wide variability as well as extensive stress tolerance. Stutz declared that fourwing saltbush is probably the most variable species in western North America and is a rapidly evolving species (Stutz and Carlson, 1985). Even so, the diversity of individual species is not as wide as the sum of all plant diversities in a mixed community.

4. Diversity of Microsites within the Habitat

Diversity of microsites within the habitat is a nonplant function that is important to community diversity and provides an opportunity for a range of genetic and somatic variants to establish and persist. The safe site concept described by Harper (1977) and elaborated for rangeland conditions by Eckert *et al.* (1978) is a recognition of microsite variability that provides an opportunity for seedling establishment, following disturbance or artificial seeding. Once a stand is established, further seedling recruitment is very limited. Within a fully stocked stand (Hyder and Sneva, 1956), most if not all safe sites have been taken or modified. Competition from mature plants is extreme during critical stress periods when growth of new seedlings is most likely to be impacted.

5. Diversity of Growth Forms

Diversity of growth forms consisting of generic and family diversity in morphology and community composition provide for a stratification of the vegetal cover as well as the distribution of roots. With such diversity, many different plant species can be accommodated in their use of light, nutrients, water, heat, etc., for optimum growth over the maximum seasonal periods of favorability. A forage grass monoculture lacks the height, distribution of leaves and roots, and phenological range that a mixed plant community of shrubs, forbs, and grasses can display. However, physiological efficiency and concentration of biomass productivity in a short favorable season may help to compensate for the deficiency in life-form diversity.

B. Ways in Which Shrubs Cope with Community Diversity

For plants to cope with the above elements or sources of diversity, various species maintain their diversity (to avoid a losing battle of competition) with other species by specializing. Inasmuch as the resources needed by plants are distributed in space as well as time, various diversity specializations are necessary for plants to compete or survive.

Many of the favored grass species used for seeding depleted rangelands have unique biological features and are excellent range forage plants. However, this information should be evaluated in relation to the ways that a mix of grasses and shrubs can provide sufficient diversity to effectively use common-pool resources.

1. Diversity in Relation to the Use of Different Resources

Some species become specialized in their use of pool resources such as development of exclusive mycorrhizal relationships to increase phosphorus uptake. Call and McKell (1982) reported differences in mycorrhizal inoculation response among various shrub species as an indication of their ability to colonize new sites. Many rangeland species vary in their requirements for soil nutrients, and as Harris and Wilson (1970) showed, an annual species such as *Taeniatherum caput-medusae* with a high capacity to respond to nitrogen can dominate a perennial species such as *Agropyron spicatum*. Field observations indicate that seedlings of the annual species grow considerably faster than the perennial seedlings. Generally, shrubs show less response to nitrogen than grasses and are poor competitors with grass under intense management.

2. Use of Lateral Heterogeneity of Microsites

The observation of clumped plant distribution in arid and semiarid ecosystems suggests a favorability created by one species for others associated with it. Rumbaugh *et al.* (1981) reported that fourwing saltbush created a more favorable habitat for production of forage by crested wheatgrass than when the crested wheatgrass was grown alone. Garcia-Moya and McKell (1970) used the term "islands of fertility" to describe the more favorable soil nitrogen status under shrubs in a desert environment than in the open spaces between shrubs. Charley (1972) also noted this soil fertility phenomenon in his work in the Great Basin.

3. Use of Vertical Heterogeneity of Environments

The canopy of shrubs offers considerable protection for understory species that lack vigor and height. Such protection may be against intense grazing or cold temperature but also carries with it the risks of competition for soil moisture, sunlight, and possibly allelopathic substances. Rumbaugh *et al.* (1981) described a favorable influence of the fourwing saltbush canopy on crested wheatgrass and concluded that a synergistic condition was created for the grass by the shrub.

4. Use of Resources Temporally

A group of species with diverse phenological schedules can make greater use of common-pool resources than a monoculture that concentrates its demands for resources according to a single schedule. For example, Fernandez and Caldwell (1975) pointed out that considerable diversity exists in the time that maximum demands are made by the root systems of the three main subspecies of *Artemisia tridentata* ssp. *tridentata*. The continued root activity of these shrubs at a time when grass is dormant suggests that a temporal stratification of activity exists that involves but minimal shrub grass competition during fall months. Mohammad's (1979) comparison of *Agropyron cristatum* and *Atriplex canescens* responses to typical fall temperatures showed a higher level of root activity of the shrub than the grass at a day–night alternating temperature in the range 7°–11°C, typical of conditions during early fall months when grasses have reached maturity.

In each of the sources of community diversity described above as well as the various ways that species cope to survive in a diverse community, it seems clear that a monospecific community of a seeded grass lacks sufficient diversity to achieve long-term stability or to exploit all environmental resources effectively.

II. Need for Diversity in Seeded Grass Monocultures

The need or use of diversity in seeded grass monocultures may not be perceived with equal understanding among range managers. The reason for this is their perception of the role shrubs play in the use of rangelands. If a range area is used principally for spring and summer grazing of livestock, a seeded grass monoculture may be a suitable vegetal cover. However, a combination of grass and shrubs would be the best for use of the range for wildlife habitat.

Even though management of rangelands in the United States is mandated to be on a multiple use basis (Public Land Law Review Commission, 1970), some vegetation types may be more advantageously managed for a particular use than another because of the type of vegetation, topography, and other factors. The composition of the vegetation in a management unit is a big factor in determining optimum use(s). In general, a diverse vegetation composition is more amenable to multiple uses. Rumbaugh *et al.* (1981) concluded that combinations of shrubs and forbs with a perennial grass could extend the grazing season and provide a forage resource less susceptible to attacks by various insects and disease than monocultures of the grass.

Extensive areas seeded in the past to a grass monoculture or areas perceived at present to be appropriate for a range improvement or land reclamation project involving seeding should be carefully considered in relation to the place that shrubs could fill in enhancing their future use. The major uses of rangelands are for grazing, wildlife, watershed, and recreation, and each of these uses has a particular requirement for shrubs.

III. Shrubs Increase Opportunities for Multiple Use

Many shrubs possess unique characteristics that can give added dimension to the uses that may be traditionally required of rangelands or that may be planned under improved management systems.

A. *Grazing Use*

Five main feed criteria must be considered in evaluating the suitability of forage species for rangeland grazing. They are nutritional quality, palatability, digestibility, quantity, and seasonal availability. A commonly used grass for improving the grazing capacity of rangelands in the western United States is crested wheatgrass (*Agropyron cristatum*), which does an excellent job of meeting the first four conditions, but in the fifth criterion its nutritional quality is low in the postmaturity stage (Otsyina *et al.*, 1982; Cook, 1972). The best time for grazing use of crested wheatgrass is in the spring and early summer when livestock are in transition from winter grazing on the desert to summer grazing in the mountains or to remain on crested wheatgrass pastures in the valleys and foothills.

Well-adapted legume species are not available for rangeland seedings in many western U.S. rangeland sites and as a result, including shrubs as a protein source in crested wheatgrass monocultures has been suggested as a way to improve the quality of fall and winter forage (Monson, 1980; Otsyina *et al.*, 1982). Rumbaugh *et al.* (1981) reported the production of crude protein in August to be over ten times greater in plots containing fourwing saltbush (*Atriplex canescens*) and crested wheatgrass as compared with crested wheatgrass alone. In an October–November grazing study at the Nephi Field Station in central Utah with fistulated sheep on pastures planted to either crested wheatgrass alone or to crested wheatgrass plus fourwing saltbush, Otsyina (1983) found that the diet of sheep on a grass/shrub pasture was adequate in digestible protein to sustain gestation, while those on the grass alone pasture were deficient. The conclusions reached from these studies are that shrubs interplanted into crested wheatgrass monoculture plantings could provide adequate feed quality as well as extend the grazing season. Concern for the effect of grazing on regrowth on the shrub must be registered. Inasmuch as many shrubs are not fully dormant in the winter, intensive grazing must be approached carefully until further research is done. Observations of the shrubs following the grazing study at the Nephi Field Station indicated that shrubs are variable in their regrowth.

B. Wildlife Habitat

Because shrubs are used by wildlife for feed, escape cover, and thermal protection, they are a critical component of wildlife habitat. Each species of wildlife has its own set of requirements for plant species in the habitat (Institute for Land Rehabilitation, 1978) for nourishment, survival, and reproduction. Wildlife habitat requirements often overlap, as would be expected where many species are present. Thus, diversity is the main element of habitat quality to meet as many animal species needs as possible. Areas of rangeland dominated by sagebrush that have been converted to crested wheatgrass can still be suitable sagegrouse habitat if areas of sagebrush are left or if some brush reinvasion occurs. In his analysis of quality sagegrouse habitat Phillips (1972) reported that sagebrush density of 2000 plants per acre was optimum for food and cover. Sagebrush stands between 5 and 10% canopy cover afford the best conditions for growth of understory grasses and forbs. Deer habitat can be enhanced by a mosaic of seeded grassland and shrub canopy as long as the openings are not any larger than 0.4 to 0.8 km wide (Institute for Land Rehabilitation, 1978). Welch and McArthur (1979) identified several sagebrush accessions that meet protein requirements for winter deer feed. They pointed to the feasibility of using sagebrush and other shrubs for game range improvement. This follows earlier advice by Plummer *et al.* (1968).

C. Watershed

Adequate vegetal cover of the soil is one of the most critical aspects of a functioning watershed. Watershed condition can be measured in terms of minimal sediment yield and optimal water infiltration and yield. Loss of understory vegetation will increase soil erosion (Branson *et al.*, 1973). Because deep percolation enhances watershed yield, any means to control shrubs might be construed as a means to increase waterflow. However, another force comes into play—the overall stability of the soil mantle. Experience in 1983 and 1984 with intense spring runoff coming from a near-record depth of snow in the mountains of the Wasatch Front of central Utah bears out the need for deep soil stability. Slopes that were the most stable were those where shrub roots permeated the saturated soil to the geologic parent material. A diverse cover of both deep-rooted shrubs and relatively shallow grass is the best answer according to long-term watershed studies conducted by the U.S. Forest Service on mountain plots of the Davis County Watershed in central Utah.

D. Surface Mining

Surface mining is only a temporary land use that by law (U.S. Congress, 1977) must be ameliorated by replacement of spoil and topsoil and seeded to a diverse and productive plant cover. Prevention of erosion and restoration of productivity are two key functions that justify the reclamation costs that often range upward from $2500 per acre. Although regulations give priority to native species in the seeding mix, crested wheatgrass is frequently included with western wheatgrass (*Agropyron smithii*), fourwing saltbush, and sagebrush in seed mixtures. Stringent rules promulgated by the Office of Surface Mining require careful monitoring of species diversity to assure that ecological stability results from seeding operations.

E. Recreational Use

Recreational use of rangelands includes many diverse activities as well as diverse value judgments concerning environmental quality. How much a diverse vegetation adds to the recreation experience is not known. Questionnaires on attitudes tend to show that pristine-looking landscape rates higher in environmental quality perceptions than disturbed areas—the greater the disturbance the lower the recreational experience. Whether shrubs growing in a seeded grass monoculture would raise the quality of experience of recreation visitors to the rangelands is doubtful, but if a mixed grass–shrub planting improved the habitat for wildlife, the recreational opportunity would be considerably increased.

IV. Ways to Establish Shrubs to Achieve Diversity in a Seeded Grass Monoculture

Inclusion of shrub seeds in a seeding mix is the best way to assure their presence in the resulting stand (Plummer *et al.*, 1968). Large numbers of shrub seeds are being seeded in the Intermountain West today as contrasted with 10 years ago. Fourwing saltbush is especially favored as a species for seeding areas to be reclaimed from surface mining. Rangeland seedings for grazing also appear to be including palatable shrubs. Dependable supplies and improvement of techniques must be given much of the credit for this (R. Stewart, personal communication, 1983).

Shrubs seeded directly into existing crested wheatgrass stands face extreme odds for establishment (Hyder and Sneva, 1956). The dense concentration of roots near the surface precludes shrub seedling root growth into moist soil. Van Epps and McKell (1977) reported success in shrub establishment by disking out three rows of crested wheatgrass and seeding in the open space thus created. No shrub seedlings were found in the space adjacent to the crested wheatgrass—thus indicating an area of high risk. Transplanting container-grown plantlets provides a means for establishing shrubs in an existing grass stand. Thousands of shrub seedlings were hand planted to diversify crested wheatgrass pastures at the Nephi Station in readiness for a grazing study (Otsyina, 1983) (Fig. 1). This same technique has been used to establish shrubs in reclamation study sites in the Uinta Basin in eastern Utah, where rainfall averages below 175 mm

Figure 1. A planting of container-grown shrubs in an existing crested wheatgrass stand. Nephi Field Station, central Utah, U.S.A.

(Institute for Land Rehabilitation, 1978). Millions of container-grown shrubs have been transplanted in reclamation sites on a routine basis.

V. Crested Wheatgrass Plantings: An Example of Needed Diversity

In the 1930s there was widespread recognition that because of intense and unregulated grazing, the western rangelands were in a deteriorated condition and getting worse. Observers at that time reasoned that overgrazing had caused sagebrush (*Artemisia tridentata* Nutt.) and other shrubs to invade the depleted grasslands (Cottam and Stewart, 1940). The report of the Secretary of Agriculture to the U.S. Senate (1936) called for research "to develop low cost methods and suitable species for 'seeding or transplanting' on 38 million acres of rangelands now so badly depleted that reasonably rapid natural revegetation appears improbable."

Ecologically, what had happened in the sagebrush–bunchgrass range was that livestock grazing selectively reduced the diversity of the ecosystem by removing most of the grasses and palatable forbs, leaving sagebrush to dominate (Ellison, 1960). This conclusion was validated by several studies in the sagebrush region (Tisdale and Hironaka, 1981; Vale, 1975). From studies of primary succession on volcanic deposits in southern Idaho, Eggler (1941) concluded that the sagebrush–grass region is ecologically stable and that sagebrush is an integral part of the regional climax vegetation.

Nevertheless, remedial action appeared to be necessary in the late 1930s and 1940s as mountain ranges serving a dual purpose as watersheds and grazing lands depleted of their valuable plant cover of grass and litter failed to hold the short-duration intense summer rains and rapid spring runoff. The result was mud and rock flows into small communities along the Wasatch Front and other Mountain West towns. Research efforts to find appropriate species and methods for range improvement resulted in the highly successful formula of brush control and drill-seeding with crested wheatgrass. As early as the mid-1930s crested wheatgrass was suggested as a possible choice for seeding rangelands drier than the Wasatch Plateau, location of the U.S. Forest Service Great Basin Experimental Station (Keck, 1972).

Brush control, vegetation type conversions, range improvement projects, and watershed protection projects sponsored by the U.S. Forest Service and the Bureau of Land Management resulted in over 4 million acres (1,600,000 ha) of foothill and desert rangeland in the 250- to 400-mm rainfall zone being seeded to crested wheatgrass as a principal species (Valentine *et al.*, 1963; Robertson, 1947). In some locations other *Agropyron* species were seeded because they were better suited for site conditions (Plummer *et al.*, 1968). Mixtures of a few species or single-species stands were observed to be easier to manage under grazing use than diverse, multiple-species stands (Cook, 1966).

Reinvasion of sagebrush and other shrubs into a crested wheatgrass seeding appears to be a function of the relative openness of some of the monospecific stands (Cook and Lewis, 1963; Rittenhouse and Sneva, 1976). Blaisdell (1949) observed that the degree of competition between sagebrush and crested wheatgrass seedlings depended largely on their relative ages. According to Frischknecht and Bleak (1957), new crested wheatgrass stands are more vulnerable to invasion of shrub seedlings than old ones. Goodwin (1956) observed sagebrush reinvasion by seed dispersal and seedling establishment from the perimeter of crested wheatgrass plantings on several seeding projects in the Great Basin. The greatest incidence of sagebrush seedlings was near the perimeter of the seeded area and in places where the crested wheatgrass stand was thin. Wasser (1982) noted that the greatest stand longevity occurred when species used in seeding were of similar palatability and phenology.

Good management of seeded stands of crested wheatgrass to minimize sagebrush reinvasion was cited as necessary to keep the stand intact long enough for grazing to pay for seeding costs. Hubbard (1956), in his work with *Purshia tridentata* seedlings, concluded that wheatgrass is as severe a competitor as native vegetation. The gradual increase in sagebrush canopy cover is a prime factor in reducing stand productivity (Frischknecht, 1963; Rittenhouse and Sneva, 1976). From an evaluation of 48 study sites, Shown *et al.* (1969) concluded that the most stable seedings of crested wheatgrass were those located in sites where annual precipitation exceeded 10 inches (250 mm) and on soils with medium moisture-holding capacity. Site unsuitability for crested wheatgrass was a large factor in seedling reinvasion by various species of sagebrush, rabbitbrush (*Chrysothamnus*) species, and halophytes.

Whether a closed community (Robertson and Pearse, 1945) exists or not in a crested wheatgrass monoculture has an important bearing on its long-term stability and longevity. Unless a stand of crested wheatgrass effectively utilizes all factors of the environment at its various phenological stages to restrict reinvasion, it cannot be considered closed. Given the various ways that shrubs can contribute to community diversity and thus increase the stability of the system (Fig. 2), they may be expected to gradually reestablish in the grass monoculture on the sites less favorable to grass.

Figure 2.   Shrubs contribute to community diversity and increase stability of the ecosystem.

VI. Summary

Plant community diversity is based on five major sources: somatic polymorphism, age distribution, genetic diversity, diverse microsites, and diversity in plant growth forms. Shrubs contribute to these sources of diversity but also compete with other plant growth forms in an ecosystem by using common-pool resources at different times and in diverse spatial locations.

In an extensively managed ecosystem, such as a rangeland seeded to a grass monoculture, selected shrub species may be useful to provide added ecosystem stability by balancing the use of common-pool resources and closing the plant community against invasion of undesirable species. Concurrently the presence of desirable shrubs may expand opportunities for multiple-use management.

Lessons learned from seeding crested wheatgrass as a monoculture subsequent to control of sagebrush on overgrazed rangeland in the western United States can help in the management of shrub-dominated ecosystems in other world locations.

References

Blaisdell, M. P. (1949). Competition between sagebrush seedlings and reseeded grasses. *Ecology* **30**, 512–519.

Branson, F. A., Gifford, G. F., and Owen, J. R. (eds.). (1973). "Rangeland Hydrology," Range Sci. Ser. No. 1. Soc. Range Manage., Denver, Colorado.

Call, C. A., and McKell, C. M. (1982). Vesicular-arbuscular mycorrhizae—A natural revegetation strategy for disposed processed oil shale. *Reclam. Reveg. Res.* **1**, 337–347.

Charley, J. L. (1972). The rule of shrubs in nutrient cycling. *In* "Wildland Shrubs: Their Biology and Utilization" (C. M. McKell, J.P. Blaisdell, and J. R. Goodin, eds.), USDA For. Serv. Gen. Tech. Rep. INT-1, pp. 182–203. Utah State University, Logan.

Cook, C. W. (1966). Development and use of foothill ranges in Utah. *Bull.—Utah Agric. Exp. Stn.* **461.**

Cook. C. W. (1972). Comparative nutritive values of forbs, grasses, and shrubs, *In* "Wildland Shrubs: Their Biology and Utilization" (C. M. McKell, J. P. Blaisdell, and J. R. Goodin, eds.), USDA For. Serv. Gen. Tech. Rep. INT-1, pp. 303–318. Utah State University, Logan.

Cook, C. W., and Lewis, C. E. (1963). Competition between sagebrush and seeded grasses on foothill ranges in Utah. *J. Range Manage.* **16**, 245–250.

Cottam, W. P., and Stewart, G. (1940). Plant succession as a result of grazing and of meadow desiccation by erosion since settlement in 1862. *J. For.* **38**, 613–626.

Eckert, R. E., Jr., Wood, M. K., Blackburn, W. H., Peterson, F. F., Stevens, J. L., and Meurisse, M. S. (1978). Effects of surface soil morphology on improvement and management of some arid and semi-arid rangelands. *Proc. Int. Rangeland Congr., 1st,* pp. 299–302.

Eggler, W. A. (1941). Primary succession of volcanic deposits in southern Idaho. *Ecol. Monogr.* **3**, 277–298.

Ellison, L. (1960). Influence of grazing on plant succession of rangelands. *Bot. Rev.* **26**, 1–28.

Fernandez, O. A., and Caldwell, M. M. (1975). Phenology and dynamics of root growth of three semi-desert shrubs under field conditions. *J. Ecol.* **63**, 703–714.

Frischknecht, N. C. (1963). Contrasting effects of big sagebrush and rubber rabbitbrush on production of crested wheatgrass. *J. Range Manage.* **16**, 70–74.

Frischknecht, N. C., and Bleak, A. T. (1957). Encroachment of big sagebrush on seeded range in northeastern Nevada. *J. Range Manage.* **10**, 165–170.

Garcia-Moya, E., and McKell, C. M. (1970). Contribution of shrubs to the nitrogen economy of a desert-wash plant community. *Ecology* **51**, 81–88.

Goodwin, D. L. (1956). Autecological studies of *Artemisia tridentata* Nutt. Ph.D. Dissertation, Washington State University, Pullman.

Harper, J. L. (1977). "Population Biology of Plants." Academic Press, New York.

Harris, G. A., and Wilson, A. M. (1970). Competition for moisture among seedlings of annual and perennial grasses as influenced by root elongation at low temperature. *Ecology* **51**, 530–534.

Hubbard, R. L. (1956). Bitterbrush seedlings destroyed by cutworms and wireworms. *U.S., For. Serv., Pac. Southwest For. Range Exp. Stn., Res. Note* **114**.

Hyder, D. N., and Sneva, F. A. (1956). Herbage response to sagebrush spraying. *J. Range Manage.* **15**, 211–215.

Institute for Land Rehabilitation (1978). "Rehabilitation of Western Wildlife Habitat: A Review." USDI Fish Wildl. Serv., Off. Biol. Serv., Washington, D.C.

Institute for Land Rehabilitation (1979). Selection, propagation, and field establishment of native plant species in disturbed arid lands. *Bull. — Utah Agric. Exp. Stn.* **500**.

Keck, W. (1972). Great Basin station—60 years of progress in range and watershed research. *USDA For. Serv. Res. Pap. INT.* **INT-118**.

Mohammed, N. (1979). Water use efficiency and fall growth of crested wheatgrass and fourwing saltbush. Ph.D. Dissertation, Utah State University, Logan.

Monson, S. B. (1980). Interseeding fourwing saltbush (*Atriplex canescens* Pursh. Nutt.) with crested wheatgrass (*Agropyron desertorum* Schult.) on southern Idaho rangelands. *Abstr. 33rd Annu. Meet., Soc. Range Manage.*, p. 51.

Otsyina, R. H. (1983). Evaluation of fourwing saltbush (*Atriplex canescens*) and other shrubs as supplements to cured crested wheatgrass (*Agropyron desertorum*) for sheep in fall and winter. Ph.D. Dissertation, Utah State University, Logan.

Otsyina, R. H. McKell, C. M., and Van Epps, G. (1982). Use of range shrubs to meet nutrient requirements of sheep grazing on crested wheatgrass during fall and early winter. *J. Range Manage.* **35**, 751–753.

Phillips, T. A. (1972). Information concerning sagebrush stand density and its effect on sage grouse habitat. *USDA For. Range Improve. Notes.* **17**, 3–9.

Plummer, A. P., Christensen, D. R., and Monsen, S. B. (1968). Restoring big game range in Utah, *Utah Div. Fish Game Publ.* **68-3**.

Public Land Law Review Commission (1970). "One Third of the Nation's Land; A Report to the President and to the Congress by the Public Land Law Review Commission." U.S. Govt. Printing Office, Washington, D.C.

Rittenhouse, L. R., and Sneva, F. A. (1976). Expressing the competitive relationship between Wyoming big sagebrush and crested wheatgrass. *J. Range Manage.* **29**, 326–327.

Robertson, J. H. (1947). Responses of range grasses to different intensities of competition with sagebrush (*Artemisia tridentata*). *Ecology* **28**, 1–16.

Robertson, J. H., and Pearse, K. C. (1945). Artificial reseeding and the closed community. *Northwest Sci.* **19,** 58–66.

Rumbaugh, M. D., Johnson, D. A., and Van Epps. G. A. (1981). Forage diversity increases yield and quality. *Utah Sci.* **42**(3), 114–117.

Shown, L. M., Miller, R. F., and Branson, F. A. (1969). Sagebrush conversion to grassland as affected by precipitation soil and cultural practices. *J. Range Manage.* **22,** 303–311.

Stutz, H. C., and Carlson, J. R. (1985). Genetic improvement of saltbush (*Atriplex*) and other chenopods. *Proc. Sel. Pap., 38th Annu. Meet., Soc. Range Manage.*

Tisdale, E. W., and Hironaka, M. (1981). The sagebrush–grass region: A review of the ecological literature. *Univ. Idaho, For. Wildl. Range Exp. Stn., Bull.* **33.**

U. S. Congress (1977). The Surface Mining Control and Reclamation Act of 1977. 91 Stat. 445-91 Stat. 532. U.S. Govt. Printing Office, Washington, D.C.

U.S. Senate (1936). "The Western Range. A Report of the U.S. Secretary of Agriculture in Response to Senate Resolution No. 289. A Report on the Western Range—A Great but Neglected Natural Resource." Doc. No. 199. U.S. Govt. Printing Office, Washington, D.C.

Vale, T. R. (1975). Pre-settlement vegetation in the sagebrush–grass area of the Intermountain West. *J. Range Manage,* **28,** 32–36.

Valentine, J. F., Cook, C. W., and Stoddart, L. A. (1963). Range seeding in Utah. *Utah State Univ., Ext. Circ.* **307.**

Van Epps, G. A., and McKell, C. M. (1977). Shrubs plus grass for livestock forage: A possibility. *Utah Sci.* **38,** 75–78.

Wasser, C. (1982). Ecology and culture of selected species useful in revegetating disturbed lands in the West. *U.S., Fish Wildl Serv., off. Biol. Serv. [Tech. Rep.] FWS/OBS* **FWS/OBS/82-56.**

Welch, B. L., and McArthur, E. D. (1979). Variation in winter levels of crude protein among *Artemisia tridentata* subspecies grown in a uniform garden. *J. Range Manage.* **32,** 467–469.

West, N. E., and Rea, K. H. (1979). Plant demographic studies in sagebrush–grass communities of southeastern Idaho. *Ecology* **60,** 376–388.

III

Genetic Variability in Shrubs

In this section authors discuss the range of genetic diversity for important traits and how these may vary in different habitats.

Clearly obvious to a trained observer is the wide range of genetic variability in most shrubs species and subspecies. Because of their relatively low economic value there has been little study of their genetic diversity.

Given the wide diversity present in shrubs it is easy to see how ecotypic variants develop in response to unique environmental conditions in different sites. New and useful genotypes can be selected from the diverse genetic variability available in shrub populations to increase the level of palatability, seed and biomass production, and usefulness for conservation and land stabilization.

14

Evolution of Shrubs

Howard C. Stutz

I. Introduction

The tempo of evolution is a fairly accurate reflection of habitat stability. In rapidly changing environments evolution is rapid; in stable environments it is slow. Some species have remained unchanged for millions of years; they occupy habitats that have also remained relatively unchanged for that same long period. Other species are only a few years old; they are in newly formed habitats.

Because many shrub species live in rapidly changing environments, they are among the most rapidly evolving species on earth, The shrublands of western North America are particularly unstable and contain numerous new species. In part, these shrublands consist of vast areas that became available for plant habitation only in the last 10,000–12,000 years following the demise of old Lake Bonneville, Lake Lahontan, and other Pleistocene lakes. As these lakes dried up, some of the species growing nearby moved in, but in many cases new species filled the extensive available valleys. Many of the salty and alkaline bottomlands became occupied by new species different from those that occupied the long ribbons of gravels, loams, and clays along the valley sides. Because these exposed areas were so uniform and expansive, each newly formed species often spread unimpeded for many miles.

Southward, beyond the Pleistocene lakes, dramatic climatic changes accompanied the retreat of the northern glaciers resulting in major plant migrations, latitudinally, longitudinally, and altitudinally that oftimes promoted rapid evolution. Not only were many new species formed during these explosive environmental perturbations, but many also became extinct.

Because the last major glaciation was only a few thousand years ago, this explosive evolution still continues and can sometimes be witnessed in process.

Although new species of grasses, forbs, and trees have also arisen in these new evolutionary frontiers, new species of shrubs are more conspicuous. This is true probably because much of western North America is ecologically "shrubland" and also because these shrublands are the areas that have experienced the most dramatic post-Pleistocene ecological changes and have thereby provided many opportunities for new shrub species to succeed. Whereas most species of trees, forbs, and grasses appear to have accomodated the post-Pleistocene ecological changes by simply shifting their distributions altitudinally or latitudinally, many shrubs have exploited the available sites with new taxa. These are *new* shrub sites, provided by the demise of formerly extensive lakes, not just habitats that became climatologically shifted. Consequently, *new* shrub species were invited; and they came.

II. The Shrub Habit

The habit of shrubiness is something of a marvel. Halfway between a tree and an herb, shrubs have advantages of both.

The woodiness of shrubs provides a distinct advantage in energy economy. Using the same "plumbing" system year after year is much less costly than rebuilding new ones each year, as herbaceous plants must do. Woodiness must also be counted an advantage in providing reduced palatability to herbivores. In addition, because woody growth is cumulative, it permits shrubs to tower above most herbaceous plants with which they grow and thus obtain an advantage in harvesting sunlight. Also, under severe stress, shrubs may continue to reproduce with a minimal amount of new growth, whereas herbs may be totally unsuccessful under similar stress because of the extensive growth usually required before the onset of flowering. Furthermore, many shrubs, in contrast to herbs and most trees, are capable of harvesting solar energy even in winter months because of chlorophyll contained in the bark of overwintering stems.

Compared with trees, shrubs have an advantage under drought conditions because of their shorter stature and therefore reduced transpiration costs. Shorter stature is probably also a significant advantage to shrubs, over trees, because they are less susceptible to damage from winds and storms and fires. Interception of water and snow by aboveground stems of woody plants is often a disadvantage in dry climates because much of the moisture caught by the aerial stems evaporates before it reaches the ground. This is more severe with trees than with shrubs, though both are probably disadvantaged by it. Much compensation for this disadvantage is provided to shrubs that grow in climates where a large portion of the annual precipitation is deposited as snow. In such climates the perennial, aerial stems may intercept drifting snow to the extent that there may be as much as ten times more moisture around each shrub than elsewhere.

Shrubiness is such a remarkably adaptive design that one may wonder why more plants have not adopted it.

III. The Challenge

Life on earth is a severe challenge—an ever-changing challenge. No two spots on earth are ever identical, and no spot on earth ever remains the same from moment to moment! Living organisms are able to accommodate this challenge in two different ways: via plasticity and via genetic flexibility.

A. Plasticity

Plasticity is the capacity of a genotype, or an individual organism, to express itself in various ways. Because of the continual changes that occur at every spot on earth, no organism can survive, even for a moment, without plasticity. Every living organism must endure continual changes in temperature, light, atmospheric composition, and all other aspects of the environment. Long-lived organisms usually have more plasticity than short-lived organisms, simply because the longer an organism lives on earth, the more changes it will experience. Also, organisms living in environments that undergo elaborate changes, regardless of the time interval, must have more plasticity than those that occupy more stable environments.

Roots, stems, leaves, flowers, and all other specialized plant tissues are plastic in their development. Because all cells and all tissues of an individual organism have exactly the same genotype, their differences are due solely to different expressions of that genotype in different environments. One set of conditions may promote the development of cotyledons; later, other conditions may cause cells of this same genotype to develop into leaves or flowers.

In nature, natural selection always selects for reduced plasticity. Therefore in stable, predictable environments where natural selection is cumulatively most effective, organisms are conspicuously less plastic than organisms that occupy fluctuating, unpredictable habitats.

In temperate climates shrubs are probably the most plastic of all plants (Table I). Trees and herbaceous plants generally occupy much more predictable environments than do shrubs so have lower levels of plasticity. Herbaceous plants escape some of the environmental fluctuations by becoming dormant during a part of each year. Although the long life span of trees demands extensive plasticity to accommodate the fluctuations in environmental assaults that occur over the span of many years, trees usually require less plasticity than do shrubs. This is because many of the challenges imposed on trees recur rhythmically and predictably year in and year out, resulting in an overall habitat predictability that exceeds that found in the habitats occupied by shrubs. Many 50-year-old trees have lived but 1 year, 50 times.

Shrubs are also usually much more plastic than annuals simply because their longer life span exposes them to more environmental variables. Some authors have suggested that annuals growing in deserts occupy less predictable habitats than perennials because the times and amounts of precipitation they receive are highly sporadic, whereas perennials growing along watercourses are assured a more predictable water supply. However, fluctuations in timing and amounts of rainshowers in these deserts are insignificant compared with the battery of attending predictable impacts

Table I.   Relative levels of plasticity and flexibility in trees, shrubs, perennial herbs, and annuals

	Niche width	Life span	Plasticity	Flexibility
Trees	Moderate	Long	Moderate	Moderate
Shrubs	Wide	Moderate	High	High
P. herbs	Moderate	Moderate	Moderate	Moderate
Annuals	Narrow	Short	Low	Low

they bring. When it rains, the annuals are assured a supply of water that will last them throughout their entire life. All events and situations attending their subsequent rapid germination, growth, and reproduction are therefore highly predictable. Whether it be in June, August, or September, whether it be a 2-inch storm or a 6-inch storm, whether it be associated with wind or calm, all is insignificant in comparison with the single most important boon—water—water sufficient to permit the numerous physiological sequences that lead ultimately to successful reproduction.

Thus because they have comparatively longer life spans, shrubs are usually much more plastic than annuals; and because they occupy more unpredictable changing habitats, they are more plastic than trees, in spite of their shorter life span.

B. *Flexibility*

Shrubs are also among the most flexible of all species (Table I). Genetic flexibility permits species to adjust to environmental fluctuations that exceed those that can be accommodated by plasticity. In geologic time as conditions become hotter or colder, drier or wetter, as spring frosts occur earlier or later, or as migration takes them into areas having different exposures, soils, or competitors, successful species must change genetically. Highly flexible species may make the adjustment easily, whereas more inflexible species, unable to make the adjustment, become extinct. Such evolutionary adjustment continually brings forth new species and eliminates others. It is usually most rapid in unstable changing environments (Stebbins, 1950).

This sensitive evolutionary response to environmental change is usually so perspicuous that it can be read in either direction: (1) rapid evolution is evidence of unstable habitats, or (2) in unstable habitats there will be rapid evolution. Rapid evolution has been described in many North American shrub species, including *Purshia tridentata, Cercocarpus ledifolius, Atriplex canescens, Artemisia tridentata, Chrysothamnus nauseosus,* and *Quercus gambelii*. They all frequent unstable habitats.

In the St. Lawrence River Valley in Eastern North America, where agriculture brought extensive disturbances to a previously somewhat stable habitat, there resulted an unprecedented eruption of numerous new taxa of hawthorns (*Crataegus*) (Brown, 1910). In 1857 there were only 12 described species and 2 varieties of hawthorns in all the United States east of the Mississippi River. By 1901 there were 31 species; by 1903 there were 185; and by 1955 there were more than 1200 named species! Although most taxonomists would dispute the validity of many of these species, the

Table II.   Sexuality of chenopod shrubs in Australia and in western North America

	Australia			North America		
	Bisexual	Monoecious	Dioecious	Bisexual	Monoecious	Dioecious
No. of species	81	0	8	3	6	31

variety nevertheless testifies to the extensive genetic variation that the increase in habitat variation promoted.

The shrublands of western North America are somewhat comparable. They too have been severely altered by recent human settlement. Fires, herbicides, droves of cattle, sheep, burros and horses, highways, recreation areas, and strip mines have all contributed to an explosion of ecological perturbations. Added to these extensive human-caused disturbances are the dramatically altered geology and climate that attended the disappearance of Pleistocene lakes and glaciers. Consequently, almost the entire shrubland landscape of western North America is new and inviting. Novel opportunities still abound and will be accommodated by those taxa that have sufficient flexibility to generate new, corresponding adaptive genotypes.

In more stable environments, the tempo of evolution is much slower. In many of the shrublands of Australia, for instance, where changes in climate during and after the Pleistocene were less dramatic than they were in western North America, evolution has been correspondingly less spectacular. This is reflected in differences in stability of the chenopod shrubs in these areas. As shown in Table II, chenopod shrubs in Australia have responded to the long history of predictability by abandoning meaningful sexuality. Today more than 90% of the chenopod shrub species in Australia are bisexual. Because they have perfect flowers, sexual outcrossing is not required. Natural selection (predictable environments) has thus been phenomenally successful in reducing their genetic flexibility. In contrast, in the explosively changing habitats of western North America, almost all the chenopod shrubs are dioecious. In the absence of predictability, natural selection is less effective and flexibility is high.

IV. The Origin of Species

The sculpturing of genetic variation to create new species can happen in several ways. Generally these avenues can be grouped into four major categories:

- *Mutations,* including new mutations, as well as those that have already accumulated within a species.

- *Hybridization,* particularly intertaxon hybridization, which brings together contrasting batteries of adaptive genes into one pool from which new combinations can be extracted.
- *Autopolyploidy,* which provides multiple doses of a genome.
- *Allopolyploidy,* which provides combinations of different genomes in various dosages.

Each of these evolutionary strategies has been effective and conspicuous in the evolution of shrubs in western North America. In some cases the process has been sufficiently rapid to yield new species of shrubs in historical times.

A. Mutations

Every species on earth possesses genetic variation. Ultimately all this variation comes from gene mutations. Some genes mutate much more frequently than others, but in almost every living organism some genes will mutate. In most sexually reproducing populations at least one out of every ten individuals will have a mutant gene not present in either of its parents. Most of these mutations accumulate, and after long periods of time may be present in phenomenally large amounts.

New mutations are preponderantly deleterious in their effects, but because most are recessive, they do not express their harmful effects immediately. Thus, almost all diploid organisms contain many mutant genes, each of which would be harmful, and in many cases lethal, if expressed. Fortunately some *combinations* of these recessive mutants are often less deleterious than each is by itself. Furthermore, that which is deleterious in one environment is sometimes beneficial in another. Hence the vast stores of genetic variation that most species contain, although largely immediately deleterious, provide the assurance of new opportunities for success under different circumstances.

In mountain mahogany (*Cercocarpus*), mutations have been responsible for the origin of new species capable of occupying dry habitats not tolerated by their ancestors. In leather-leaf mountain mahogany (*C. ledifolius*), any one plant may have leaves that vary in shape and size from large spatulate leaves, 3 cm long by 1 cm wide, to small, needle-shaped leaves less than $\frac{1}{2}$ cm long and 1–2 mm wide (Fig. 1). This variation, because it is all within one plant, is due entirely to plasticity. However, because plasticity itself is genetically determined and may therefore be different from plant to plant, some *C. ledifolius* plants show more intra-plant variation (plasticity) than others. Plants growing at the periphery of populations usually show the most plastic variation, because they are nearest their limits of adaptiveness where environmental stresses they endure are most extreme and variable. In such areas it is not

Figure 1.   Variation in leaves taken from a single plant of *Cercocarpus ledifolius.*

uncommon to find individual plants that produce leaves in the hot dry summer that are less than one-fifth the size of leaves produced during the cooler and moister spring or early summer.

In places where moisture stress is severe and fluctuates rapidly, plants that produce mostly smaller leaves, even when growing conditions are ideal, will be more successful in the long run than plants that produce large leaves during favorable growing conditions but subsequently suffer from excessive transpiration during ensuing months of drought. Under such circumstances, plants that produce smaller leaves even under the best of conditions are the most successful. Perpetual selection for such reduced plasticity for this attribute has produced the species *Cercocarpus intricatus* (Needle-leaf mountain mahogany) which now grows on dry limestone cliffs throughout much of Utah. When it is grown even in the best of garden conditions, with abundant available water, it still produces only small, narrow, needlelike leaves, evidence that in its evolutionary history it gave up much of the plasticity of its progenitors. Because *C. intricatus* is limited to xeric, limestone outcrops in Utah and the borders of the immediately surrounding states, it is probably of fairly recent origin and will likely spread to other areas in western America where similar habitats exist.

This acquisition of genetic control of attributes that begin as portions of the array of plastic characteristics is termed "genetic assimilation." It is the most common way species arise from stores of mutations. It is clean and economical. As environmental assaults promote alterations in phenotypes, those alterations which are beneficial may be gently increased in incidence by genetic assimilation without drastic alteration of an already proven battery of adaptive qualities. To do it any other way—such as by sudden, dramatic macromutations—is much more risky and therefore much less likely.

B. Hybridization

Although spontaneous mutations provide species with abundant variation, they can never do it as fast or as effectively as does interspecific hybridization. Interspecific hybridization not only immediately provides great quantities of genetic variation, but the variation is of high quality. Because selection has already screened out the least fit of the genetic variables in both contributing parents, the hybrids inherit only the best of both. The resulting rich, top-quality genetic pools may therefore be, and frequently are, sources of numerous, new, superior combinations.

1. *Purshia tridentata* (bitterbrush) × *Cowania stansburyana* (cliffrose)

These two species, belonging to different genera in the rose family, differ by many, many genes. They apparently evolved independently for thousands of years and have just recently come together in the Intermountain Area of western North America. Upon contact they have hybridized promiscuously (Stutz and Thomas, 1964).

Bitterbrush grows mostly on the west side of the Continental Divide from British Columbia on the north to southern Utah, Nevada, and California on the south. Cliffrose begins in northern Utah, on the north, and extends southward, on dry exposed hillsides, into north-central Mexico. Almost the entire state of Utah is thus an overlap area of both species (Fig. 2). Although bitterbrush usually flowers earlier in the season than cliffrose, the two often hybridize where they meet along ridges that separate north-facing and south-facing slopes. In such areas, cliffrose plants growing on south-facing slopes are sufficiently advanced in flowering time to permit them to cross with bitterbrush plants growing on contiguous north-facing slopes.

Such opportunities for hybridization are very common throughout Utah. The hybrids are fertile and produce offspring of almost every imaginable combination. Some are F_2 segregants, but most are products derived from backcrossing of hybrids onto bitterbrush. The resulting genetic introgression

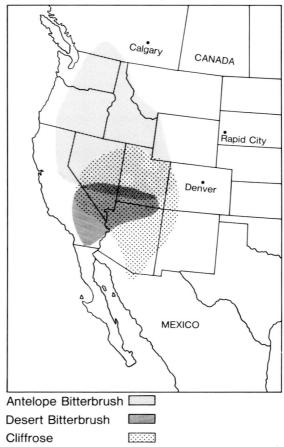

Figure 2. Geographic distribution of *Purshia tridentata, Cowania stansburyana,* and the hybrid derivative *Purshia glandulosa.*

of cliffrose genes into bitterbrush immediately increases the genetic variation of bitterbrush far beyond that which could ever have occurred by mutations alone.

So common is such hybridization and introgression in these species that nowhere in the entire state of Utah is there a bitterbrush population that does not contain cliffrose genes. North of Utah, beyond the range of cliffrose, bitterbrush is also "contaminated." As might be expected, those bitterbrush populations that are close to northern Utah, where the northernmost populations of cliffrose grow, are much richer in cliffrose genes than are populations farther north in Idaho, Oregon, and Washington. Nevertheless, every one of these northern populations that has been examined shows evidence of the presence of at least a few cliffrose genes. The principal promoter of this extensive introgressional flow of cliffrose genes into northern populations of bitterbrush appears to be the lowered palatability to herbivores that cliffrose genes provide. Under strong grazing pressures by sheep and cattle, bitterbrush plants that contain cliffrose genes are differentially spared.

South of Utah, beyond the geographic limits of *Purshia tridentata,* products of this remarkable hybrid have produced a new species, *Purshia glandulosa* (desert bitterbrush). This species, which is a particular combination of bitterbrush and cliffrose genes, is successful on dry, steep slopes in southern Utah, northern Arizona, southern Nevada, and southern California. Although each population is made up of plants having the specific attributes that characterize them as *P. glandulosa,* and that have caused them to stabilize as a new adaptive species, most populations contain a few plants with other traits. These are apparently attributes that have been carried along fortuitously into one population or another, without becoming stabilized.

2. *Atriplex canescens* (fourwing) × *A. tridentata* (saltsage)

Fourwing and saltsage are among the many saltbush species that spread rapidly into the Great Basin after the Pleistocene lakes dried up about 12,000 years ago. Saltsage came in from the north and fourwing from the south (Stutz *et al.,* 1979).

Saltsage is a low-growing (20–50 cm) half-shrub that often spreads asexually by underground rootsprouting. It grows almost exclusively in lake-bottom clays in the valleys formerly covered by Lake Bonneville. It is apparently all hexaploid ($2n = 54$ chromosomes) (see below in the discussion of polyploids) except for a few scattered diploid populations ($2n = 18$ chromosomes) that extend into Montana, and two small tetraploid ($2n = 36$ chromosomes) populations, one near Kemmerer, Wyoming, and one in west-central Utah.

Fourwing saltbush usually grows to more than a meter in height, is woody throughout, and seldom shows any rootsprouting. As it spread to the north, and saltsage spread to the south, they met and hybridized (Fig. 3). Although the fourwing plants are tetraploid and the saltsage plants are hexaploid, the resulting pentaploid hybrids are partially fertile and have produced many peculiar offspring, some of which are remarkably adaptive.

One rather recent derivative from these hybrids now occupies an area of about 80 acres near Grantsville, Utah. Another derivative grows along the freeway between Salt Lake City and Wendover, Utah. Another, not yet at all stabilized, is common along the Reese River in northern Nevada, and

Figure 3.   *Atriplex canescens* × *A. tridentata* hybrid. A, *A. tridentata*; B, *A. canescens*; C, F_1 hybrid. Some of the other plants are seedlings from C.

another is just now becoming established near Topaz Mountain in west-central Utah. Most of these entities are still genetically rich and have not yet stabilized as distinct taxa. However, because many kinds of habitats are available in the Great Basin valleys, some of these populations will prob-ably eventually yield new distinct species from among their numerous genetic combinations.

C. Autopolyploidy

Occasional accidents occur during cell division in many organisms, result-ing in cells having multiple sets of chromosomes. These "polyploid" cells may exist alongside normal diploid cells in the same tissue or may grow into tissue that is entirely polyploid. In plants, particularly in perennial plants, polyploid cells may grow into reproductive structures and produce polyploid sex cells. Upon self-fertilization, these may yield offspring in which all cells are polyploid. Because such polyploid plants are composed of cells containing multiple doses of the same genome, they are referred to as *auto*-polyploids, to distinguish them from *allo*-polyploids, which have combinations of different genomes.

Autopolyploids may also be produced from the union of unreduced gametes, or from the fertilization of an egg by more than one sperm.

Almost always, newly formed autopolyploids have reduced fertility and are therefore usually unsuccessful. However, in some species, there are sufficient compensating advantages attending newly formed autopolyploids to promote their survival. This is particularly true in shrubs. Indeed, autoploidy is more common in shrubs than in any other kind of plant.

In fourwing saltbush (*Atriplex canescens*), autopolyploids are much more common than are diploids. In the Great Basin, diploid fourwing is confined to a tiny sand dune island (Little Sahara Sand Dunes) near Delta, Utah. Most other populations in the Great Basin are tetraploid, including those that surround the sand dunes occupied by the diploids. In the dune area none of the tetraploid plants grow on the dunes and none of the diploids come off the dunes! Elsewhere throughout western America, hexaploid populations of fourwing grow in heavy clay soils. This sharp sensing of different habitats by plants having different chromosome levels is indicative of the very delicate genetic control of ecological adaptation found in many shrub species.

Among the characteristics that distinguish the chromosome races of fourwing, differences in stature are perhaps the most conspicuous. Diploids are routinely the largest, then tetraploids, then hexaploids. The gigas diploid growing on the sand dunes in central Utah grows nearly twice as fast as polyploids and may attain a mature stature several times as great.

Decrease in stature with increase in chromosome number is also present in shrubby forms of sagebrush (*Artemisia*), rabbitbrush (*Chrysothamnus*), and several other species of *Atriplex*. In Rush Valley, Utah, diploid shadscale (*A. confertifolia*) has an average dry-weight biomass more than three times that of tetraploids in the same valley.

In contrast to shrubs, an increase in chromosome number in herbaceous plants usually results in an increase in stature. Reduced stature in shrubs resulting from polyploidy may, therefore, actually be a consequence of the woody habit. This, in turn, may be a reflection of a modification in rate and amounts of cellulose deposition during cell division. Because polyploidy commonly reduces the tempo of cell division by prolonging the intervals between DNA replications, it may be that some of the polyploid cells in shrubby plants begin to form secondary walls during these intervals and may thus preclude the opportunity for further cell division. Also, deposition of cellulose in or near the sluggish meristems of polyploids may reduce the rate and amount of cell elongation over that which occurs in cells of diploids.

Whatever the cause, the reduced stature of polyploid shrubs appears to be adaptive in the environments they occupy. Reduced stature apparently

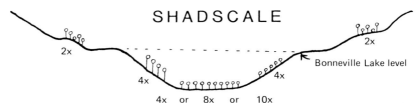

Figure 4. Distribution of chromosome races of shadscale (*Atriplex confertifolia*) in the valleys of the Great Basin. Diploids (2*x*) are variable and grow with several other species. Tetraploids (4*x*) are uniform but each population is different. They grow in monocultures.

increases drought tolerance and frost tolerance and decreases palatability to herbivores. It may be because of such attending advantages—and other less conspicuous advantages—that autopolyploid races of shrubs are so common. Some occur as small populations, uniquely adapted to specific local sites; others form large, extensive populations covering entire valleys. The tetraploid form of creosote bush (*Larrea tridentata*) dominates thousands of acres in the Sonoran Desert of northern Mexico. Extensive stands of hexaploid creosote are common in the more xeric Mojave Desert, whereas the diploids are reportedly confined almost exclusively to the Chihuahuan Desert (Yang, 1970).

Because of the way autoploid races originate, each is genetically uniform. This is particularly conspicuous in areas where the habitat to which a polyploid race is adaptive is extensive. In western North America, the recent sudden exposure of large valleys that had been buried under water for thousands of years provides many such extensive uniform tracts. Many of them have become occupied by vast monocultures of shrubby polyploids such as sagebrush, saltbush, rabbitbrush, and greasewood that show very little between-plant variation.

Although polyploid populations of a species are genetically uniform within, they usually differ significantly from each other because of separate origins. As illustrated in Fig. 4, diploid races of shadscale (*Atriplex confertifolia*) grow in the Great Basin above the Pleistocene lake levels. Although they are genetically highly heterogeneous, they have yielded a variety of purebred tetraploids. Higher chromosome levels (octoploid, decaploid), derived from tetraploids, also occur in purebred monocultures in some of the valley bottoms.

D. Allopolyploidy

Evidence for the origin of new species by allopolyploidy is found in many groups of plants. Some authors estimate that nearly half of all species of flowering plants on earth today arose as allopolyploids. Most of them are shrubs or perennial herbs.

In contrast to autopolyploids, allopolyploids contain *different* genomes; they always come from interspecific hybrids. In some instances allopolyploids are derived by doubling the chromosome number in hybrids that contain one genome from each of two separate species *viz*:

plants: species A × species B $\longrightarrow$ hybrid $\longrightarrow$ allopolyploid
genomes: AA   ×   BB $\longrightarrow$ AB $\longrightarrow$ AABB

Allopolyploids may also originate from unreduced gametes as follows:

plants: species A (diploid) × species B (autopolyploid)
genomes: AA   × BBBB
gametes: AA (unreduced)   × BB $\longrightarrow$ AABB (allopolyploid)

Regardless of their origin, such allopolyploids are "double diploids"— composites of both contributing parents. Because they come from two already successful parents, it is not surprising that the sum of these two "success stories" is often supersuccessful. Such extended heterosis is probably the principal reason why allopolyploid plants are phenomenally common.

The relative scarcity of polyploidy among animals, trees, and annual plants is not because it does not occur in them nor because there is an absence of attending heterosis, but rather because their biology does not permit it. Animals have two principal biological blockades to allopolyploidy: (1) the unlikelihood that cells that undergo chromosome doubling will become reproductive and (2) the unlikelihood of the simultaneous production of an allopolyploid male and an allopolyploid female from the same hybrid parentage. Animals having delicate gene-dosage regulations of sex determination might also have difficulty with fertility even if they were able to circumvent the other obstacles.

For some of the same reasons, allopolyploidy is rare in annual plants and trees. As with animals, the proportion of reproductive tissue in each individual is very small, so that even when hybrids are produced and the accident of polyploidy ensues, it is rare that any derived polyploid cells are present in reproductive structures. In contrast, because of their "immortal" meristems, shrubs and herbaceous perennial plants experience repeated regeneration of plant parts, so that polyploid tissue has a much higher probability of becoming reproductive.

Dioecious plants, like animals, are seldom allopolyploids, simply because of the extremely low probability of the simultaneous occurrence of both a male and a female polyploid hybrid. Consequently, the thousands of polyploid species on earth are mostly shrubs or herbaceous perennials in which male and female sex cells are produced on the same plant. Although the requirements are rather specific, when they are met, a sterile hybrid is suddenly transformed into a marvelous new species genetically unique and reproductively isolated from all other species.

When an allopolyploid plant species proves to be successful, it is not uncommon for the event to happen again, involving a third species:

(1) species   A   × species B ⟶ hybrid ⟶ allopolyploid
    genomes: AA   BB   AB   AABB

(2) allopolyploid × species C ⟶ hybrid ⟶ allopolyploid
    genomes: AABB CC   ABC   AABBCC

This appears to be the way cultivated wheat evolved, being composed of three separate genomes. Some allopolyploid species appear to have been formed from the union of even more genomes.

When allopolyploids come from unreduced gametes they are often derived from hybrids produced by parents, at least one of which is already a polyploid:

parents: AAAA (autopolyploid)   × BB (diploid) ⟶
                                                        AAB hybrid

gametes: AAB (unreduced from hybrid) × B ⟶
                                                        AABB (allopolyploid)

Such an event appears to have been involved in the origin of *Atriplex canescens* var. *laciniata*. This taxon is clearly an allopolyploid derived from *A. canescens* × *A. polycarpa* hybrids (Fig. 5). Both *A. canescens* and *A. polycarpa* occur as autopolyploid races and hybridize readily upon contact in nature. Since hybrids can occur between these species at different chromosome levels, *A. canescens* var. *laciniata* may have originated more than once, by different routes. Because tetraploid chromosome races are most abundant in both species, they are probably the most common immediate ancestors. If so, then high chromosome numbers in *A. canescens* var. *laciniata* were most likely attained by repeated backcrossing via unreduced gametes (u.g.) onto tetraploid parents; viz:

$4x$ *A. canescens* (AAAA) × $4x$ *A. polycarpa* (BBBB) ⟶ $4x$ AABB
AABB (u.g.)   × $4x$ *A. can.* (AAAA) ⟶ $6x$ AAAABB
AAAABB (u.g.)   × $4x$ *A. poly.* (BBBB) ⟶
                                              $8x$ AAAABBBB
AAAABBBB (u.g.)   × $4x$ *A. can.* (AAAA) ⟶
                              $10x$ AAAAAABBBB (*laciniata*)
AAAAAABBBB (u.g.) × $4x$ *A. poly.* (BBBB) ⟶
                              $12x$ AAAAAABBBBBB (*laciniata*)

Large populations at the $10x$ chromosome level (*laciniata*) occur throughout southeastern California from Barstow to El Centro and

Figure 5. *Atriplex canescens* var. *lacinata* ($2n = 108$ chromosomes) in the middle, and its two progenitors: *A. canescens* ($2n = 36$ chromosomes) on the left and *A. polycarpa* ($2n = 36$ chromosomes) on the right.

northern Baja California. Large populations at the $12x$ chromosome level (also *laciniata*) occur in coastal sand dunes of northwestern Sonora, Mexico.

No populations of *laciniata* have been found at the $6x$ or $8x$ levels. This may mean they have not found a suitable ecological niche to which they are uniquely adapted, or merely that they have not yet been discovered. In any case, *A. canescens* var. *laciniata* appears to have originated over and over again.

In some places introgression into *laciniata* from other species has apparently contributed enriching genes that have provided local advantages. For instance, around the Salton Sea, California, *laciniata* has obviously been enriched by *A. linearis* and may have even been independently derived in that area from *A. linearis* $\times$ *A. polycarpa*, much as it has been from *A. canescens* $\times$ *A. polycarpa* in other areas.

V. Summary

Although the evolutionary process in shrubs has been described and exemplified by the four principal avenues for speciation—mutations, recombinations, autopolyploidy, and allopolyploidy—most species originate by a combination of these processes. Mutations are occurring repeatedly in all species; sexual reproduction optimizes introgression of these variables in natural populations; and polyploidy, when available, fixes, momentarily (in evolutionary time frames), superb combinations for unique situations. Although the shrub habit preferentially favors some of these processes more than others, they are all available, and independently and collectively contribute to an unusually effective evolutionary sensing of the numerous challenges that accompany the rapidly changing habitats that shrubs occupy.

References

Brown, H. B. (1910). The genus *Crataegus,* with some theories concerning the origin of its species. *Bull. Torrey, Bot. Club* **37;** 251–260.

Stebbins, G. L. (1950). "Variation and Evolution in Plants." Columbia Univ. Press, New York.

Stutz, H.C., and Thomas, L.K. (1964). Hybridization and introgression in *Cowania* and *Purshia. Evolution (Lawrence, Kans.)* **18,** 183–195.

Stutz, H.C., Pope, C. L., and Sanderson, S. C. (1979). Evolutionary studies of *Atriplex:* Adaptive products from the natural hybrid $6N$ *A. tridentata* $\times$ $4N$ *A. canescens. Am. J. Bot.* **66,** 1181–1193.

Yang, T. W. (1970). Major chromosome races of *Larrea divaricata* in North America. *J. Ariz. Acad. Sci.* **6,** 41–45.

15

Breeding Systems in Shrubs

E. Durant McArthur

I. Introduction

Shrubs do not comprise a cohesive phylogenetic unit, and thus any treatment of their breeding systems will not be an examination of an integral cohesive data set (Stebbins, 1972, 1975). Angiosperms exhibit a diverse array of breeding systems (Grant, 1975); moreover, the shrubby habit is common among many angiosperm families (Table I). The primitive angiosperms are now believed to have been shrubs (Cronquist, 1968; Stebbins, 1972, 1974, 1975). Present-day shrubs, however, need not be ancient as the shrubby habit has not only been maintained (e.g., Ehrendorfer *et al.*, 1979), but has also been derived from arboreal and herbaceous progenitors (Stebbins, 1974, 1975; McArthur and Plummer, 1978). In many large vegetation types of the world, single life-forms prevail in the upper layer of dominant plants, for example, forests and grasslands. Shrubs, however, occur in many different vegetation types including some

Table I. A sample of shrubs considered as crop plants

Crop[a]	Scientific name	Family	Chromosome number		Vegetative reproduction		Pollination	
			x	2n	Possible	Natural	Agent	Type
Tea	*Camellia sinensis*	Camilliaceae	15	2x	Yes	—	Insect	Cross
Hazel	*Corylus avellana*	Corylaceae	14	2x	Yes	—	Wind	Cross
Blueberries	*Vaccinium* spp.	Ericaceae	12	2–6x	Yes	Yes	Insect	Cross
Cassava	*Manihot esculenta*	Euphorbiaceae	18	2x	Yes	—	—	Cross
Currants and gooseberries	*Ribes* spp.	Grossulariaceae	8	2x	Yes	Yes	Insect	Self and cross
Wattles	*Acacia* spp.	Leguminosae	13	2–4x	Yes	—	Insect	Cross
Roselle	*Hibiscus sabdariffa*	Malvaceae	18	2–4x		—	Insect	Self
Guava	*Psidium guajava*	Myrtaceae	11	2–3x	Yes	—	Insect	Cross
Pomegranate	*Punica granatum*	Punicaceae	8,9	2x	Yes	—	Insect	—
Raspberries and blackberries	*Rubus* spp.	Rosaceae	7	2–12x	Yes	Yes	Insect	Cross
Coffees	*Coffea* spp.	Rubiaceae	11	2–4x	Yes	—	Insect	Cross and self
Peppers	*Capsicum* spp.	Solanaceae	12	2x	—	—	Insect	Self

[a] This sample consists of the 12 shrubs listed among the 168 crop plants treated by Simmonds (1976).

types in which they are dominants. In this chapter, I examine conditions that promote the dominance of shrubs and the effect those conditions have on shrub breeding systems. I follow Grant (1975) in treatment of breeding systems, that is, breeding systems are those processes and systems that regulate genetic recombination or affect the ecology of recombination.

II. Shrub Distribution and Dominance

Shrubs occur in many vegetation types but are dominants, for the most part, only in those habitats that place plants under considerable stress. Stebbins (1972, 1975) suggested three primary, often interacting, factors that promote shrubby habits: drought or aridity, nutrient-poor soils, and fire. He also listed additional stress factors that may be interactive that contribute to the shrubby habit: shade, poor soil aeration, winter cold, short growing season, and wind.

Most of these conditions are best met in arid continental climates (McKell *et al.,* 1972). For example, in the conterminous United States, shrubs are distributed widely but are dominants from a continental-scale perspective only in the arid and semiarid west (McArthur, 1984). Table II is an analysis of shrub importance as determined from Küchler's (1964) map and manual. Significant dominance of shrubs is gained only in Küchler's western shrublands and western shrub and grasslands. Shrubs as subdominants (Küchler's other components) are important to a greater or lesser degree in all vegetative types (Table II). As a further illustration, consider Wyoming, whose continental semiarid climate makes it essentially shrub country (Weaver, 1980). Nearly half of Wyoming's land area (45.8% or 11,560,000 ha) is dominated by shrubby vegetation (Küchler, 1964; McArthur, 1981).

Shreve (1942), in his treatise on North American deserts, made the point that many life-forms contribute to the dominants of desert vegetations as compared to other great vegetation types of the world. He provides 25 life-form dominants from diverse ephemerals to woody plants of various kinds. It is noteworthy that in the stressful desert situation, the four life-forms outnumbering all the others include one succulent, two shrub, and one shrubby tree life-forms. On the desert plains the vegetative stands are often simple, consisting of one or a few dominant species. However, nearby sites with only slightly more precipitation and physical relief form patchy, mosaic vegetational patterns (Shreve, 1942; McArthur *et al.,* 1978b). Efficient shrub breeding systems must be of adaptive utility in both uniform and patchy vegetation patterns for the species that are successful in both environments (Harper, 1977).

Table II. Dominant and subdominant shrub species occurrence in the conterminous United States

Vegetative type	N	Dominant species			Subdominant species[a]				Insect pollination index[b]	
			Shrubs			Shrubs		All Shrubs		
		$\bar{x} \pm se$	$\bar{x}$	%	$\bar{x} \pm se$	$\bar{x}$	%	$(\bar{x} \pm se)$	All species	Shrub species
Western needleleaf forests	24	2.3 ± 0.2	0.04	1.7	10.0 ± 1.1	3.9	39.0	3.9 ± 0.6	21	68
Western broadleaf forests	3	1.3 ± 0.3	0	0	10.0 ± 2.3	3.7	37.0	3.7 ± 1.8	42	67
Western broadleaf and needleleaf forests	5	5.6 ± 0.7	0.2	3.6	16.4 ± 3.0	7.6	46.3	7.8 ± 2.1	39	80
Western shrublands	13	2.7 ± 0.6	1.9	70.4	13.6 ± 1.9	8.7	63.9	10.6 ± 1.7	60	62
Western grasslands	8	3.6 ± 0.8	0	0	11.6 ± 2.0	1.6	13.8	1.6 ± 0.6	21	70
Western shrubs and grasslands	6	3.2 ± 0.4	1.3	40.6	17.0 ± 2.5	3.8	22.4	5.2 ± 1.0	38	67
Central and eastern grasslands	17	2.9 ± 0.3	0	0	14.2 ± 1.4	1.4	9.8	1.4 ± 0.4	21	45
Central and eastern grasslands and forests	15	3.4 ± 0.5	0	0	17.2 ± 2.5	1.7	9.9	1.7 ± 0.3	29	64
Eastern needleleaf forests	5	2.4 ± 0.2	0	0	6.8 ± 0.8	2.0	29.4	2.0 ± 0.7	20	50
Eastern broadleaf forests	8	3.1 ± 0.7	0	0	14.9 ± 2.1	1.1	7.4	1.1 ± 0.7	35	75
Eastern broadleaf and needleleaf forests	11	4.0 ± 0.5	0.09	2.2	13.4 ± 2.3	1.9	14.2	2.0 ± 0.4	29	55
Total $\bar{x}$	115 —	— 3.1 ± 0.5	— 0.3	— 9.7	— 13.2 ± 1.9	— 3.4	— 25.8	— 3.7 ± 0.9	— 31	— 65

Source: Data from Küchler (1964). He listed 116 vegetative types including one for barren desert.

[a] Listed by Küchler (1964) as other species.

[b] Index determined by

$$\frac{\text{insect pollination types} + 0.5x \text{ combination (wind and insect) pollination types}}{\text{total vegetation types}}$$

based on dominant and subdominant plant species.

III. Chromosome Systems

The importance of gene linkage systems in plants and their functions is elucidated in several excellent books (e.g., Darlington, 1963; Stebbins, 1971; Grant, 1975). Shrubs exhibit variations in chromosome number, size, and structure as do other plants.

A. *Basic Chromosome Number*

Herbaceous perennial plants (Solbrig, 1972) and woody plants (Stebbins, 1971) have higher basic chromosome numbers than annual plants. Grant (1975) listed the basic modal chromosome numbers, that is, not repeated by polyploidy, as $x = 7$ for monocotyledons, $x = 7–9$ for herbaceous dicotyledons, and $x = 11–14$ for woody dicotyledons. The shrub crop plant sample (Table I) appears to be representative for woody plant basic chromosome numbers ($\bar{x}$ for $x = 12.3$, for mode $x = 12$). The basic chromosome numbers impact recombination and variation in that a greater number of recombined progeny arise from plants with higher x than with lower x. The rule is that an organism with the haploid number n ($=x$) heterozygous for a single gene pair on a chromosome pair can produce 2^n genetically different gametes. Looking only at those conditions (one heterozygotic gene per chromosome pair) and taking modal chromosome numbers for plant classes, the possible chromosome combinations in the gametes are:

$$2^7 = 128 \text{ for average monocotyledons}$$
$$2^8 = 256 \text{ for average herbaceous dicotyledons}$$
$$2^{12.5} = 5793 \text{ for average woody dicotyledons}$$

So, generally, the woody dicotyledons including shrubs have high populational variation and genetic recombination per generation. Polyploidy cuts the exponential growth down for reasons discussed later (Section III,B).

Solbrig (1972) made a comparative study for two families on the occurrence of haploid (n) chromosome numbers. For the comparisons in Table III, I assumed that $n < 9$ were diploids, $9 < n < 18$ were tetraploids, and $n > 18$ were polyploids greater than tetraploids. Although the woody dicotyledons' x is $11–14$, those numbers are thought to represent an ancient polyploid increase from $x = 6$ and $x = 7$ (Stebbins, 1971). Furthermore, some shrubs are derived from herbaceous ancestry (e.g., chenopods and *Artemisia*) (Stebbins, 1974; McArthur *et al.*, 1981), so treating $n > 9$ as polyploid state is reasonable. The n numbers in Table III show a trend of basic chromosome number increase with the perennial growth habit over the annual growth habit. Shrubs (and trees and legumes) continue

Table III. Occurrence of haploid chromosome numbers in the legume and composite families

Family chromosome number	Annual herbs		Perennial herbs		Shrubs		Trees		Totals	
	Species	%	Species	%	Species	%	Species	%	Species	%
Leguminosae										
$n = 5$–9	171	67	324	59	31	19	8	15	534	52
$n = 10$–18	55	22	175	32	69	42	36	67	335	33
$n > 18$	29	11	46	8	65	39	10	19	150	15
	255		545		165		54		1019	
Compositae										
$n = 2$–9	401	53	778	33	133	36	—	—	1312	37
$n = 10$–18	310	41	792	33	149	40	—	—	1251	36
$n > 18$	49	6	810	34	92	25	—	—	951	27
	760		2330		374				3514	

Source: Data from Solbrig (1972).

the trend to the *2x* level but are not as well represented at the higher polyploid levels as are perennial herbs. Chi-square analysis of chromosome number distribution (Table IV) shows that shrubs in the legume–composite sample are overrepresented at the $n = 10$–18 (+17%) and $n > 18$ (+20%) groups.

B. Polyploidy

Polyploidy is a common phenomenon throughout angiosperm families (Stebbins, 1971; Lewis, 1980). It reaches its most common expression in herbaceous perennials (Stebbins, 1971) and is also common in shrubs (Tables I and III) (Solbrig, 1972). It is the easiest mechanism available for

Table IV. Chi-square contingency test of base chromosome number distribution in the legume and composite families

	Number of species					
	Annuals		Perennial herbs		Shrubs	
Base number	Observed	Expected	Observed	Expected	Observed	Expected
5–9	572	417.8	1112	1208.3	164	221.9
10–18	365	330.5	967	1013.4	218	186.9
>18	78	246.7	856	713.3	156	131.0

Source: Data from Table III.
Note: df = 4, $\chi^2 = 237$, $p < .01$.

increasing chromosome numbers and provides the additional recombination that accompanies an increase in chromosome number as previously discussed (Section III,A). However, polyploidy does not increase recombination in the same way that a single chromosome increase (aneuploidy) does. Contrariwise, because of tetrasomic inheritance in tetraploids and analogous inheritance in higher polyploids, the recessive segregates are much lower than for diploids (Solbrig, 1972; Grant, 1975). To illustrate a simple case, the diploid that is Aa will have a chromosome segregation of 1A : 1a and an F_2 phenotypic ratio of 3A– : 1aa. For the duplex heterozygote, AAaa, the chromosome segregation would be 1AA : 4Aa; 1aa with a resulting F_2 phenotypic ratio of 35A–––: 1aaaa. Dosage effects, chromatid segregation, and crossing-over complicate the situation, but the illustration shows that polyploids, especially autopolyploids, reduce the segregating phenotypic variation from the expected results based on chromosome number alone. Most polyploids are not strict autopolyploids, so the gain in variation from increased chromosome number is intermediate between what could be expected from the chromosome number increase and the reduction from tetrasomic or higher inheritance. Hamrick *et al.* (1979) show that the percentage of polymorphic loci goes from 35.5 to 37.4 to 41.4 for plants with $x = 5$–10, $x = 11$–15, and $x > 15$, respectively. Naturally occurring autopolyploids have enough genic differentiation within their genomes that variation is abundant and tetrasomic inheritance is reduced (e.g., McArthur *et al.*, 1981).

Polyploidy has the advantage of stabilizing new gene combinations gained by hybridization of disparate taxa, which may be adaptive in changing environments, that is, adaptive gene combinations may be captured and more easily maintained. Like other plants, shrubs have successfully used this technique.

Long-lived perennials may have exploited polyploid processes more than annuals because in successive generations their environments change more than the environments of annual plants. Long-lived perennials apparently have a substantially higher polymorphic loci frequently than annuals, biennials, or short-lived perennials (Hamrick *et al.*, 1979) that may be correlated with a polyploid state. In their initial stages, polyploids depend on especially favorable combinations of circumstances for survival and perpetuation. Once they have become successful, they may be as competitive and aggressive as related diploids. Long life and vegetative reproduction are, therefore, advantages of polyploids (Randell, 1970; Stebbins, 1971; Sternberg, 1976). Woody colonizers with high polyploidy include dog roses (*Rosa* sect. *Canina*), the hawthorns (*Crataegus*), and brambles (*Rubus*). Possibly the three most successful shrub species in North America form polyploid series: the sagebrushes (subgenus *Tridentatae* of

Artemisia) (McArthur *et al.*, 1981), the creosote bush (*Larrea tridentata*) (Yang, 1970), and the saltbushes (*Atriplex* species) (Stutz and Sanderson, 1979, 1983; Dunford, 1984, 1985).

IV. Pollination and Breeding Systems

The transport of pollen (pollination system) and the regulation of gene flow (breeding system) of shrubs are systems derived more along phylogenetic lines than along growth form lines. Nevertheless, the forces that promote development of growth forms also have an impact on pollination and breeding systems. Shrubs occur in many habitats but reach dominant status usually in stressful situations (Section II). One of the most common of the stress situations favoring the shrubby habit is that of aridity, of which Barlow (1981) gave some general suggestions on the Australian arid zone flora that may have some applicability to many shrubby floras:

> ... a shift towards self-compatibility in the eremean flora [has been noted].
> ... The unpredictable environment of the arid zone has had a second effect in addition to restricting the diversity of pollinators and pollination syndromes. The second effect is a shift to self-compatibility as a 'fail-safe' reproductive system countering pollinator unpredictability, even though the species involved are generally adapted for outbreeding.

In this latter connection it should be noted that perfect flowers are found among normally dioecious saltbushes (*Atriplex* spp.) of American and Australian arid zones—possible "fail-safe" strategies.

A. *Pollination Systems*

Pollen transport for shrubs is accomplished by wind (anemophily) and by animals (zoophily), generally insects (entomophily). For land plants in general, entomophily is the commonest method for the largest number of species (Faegri and van der Pijl, 1966). However, in the arid regions where shrubs are most important and often occur in large populations, the majority of the species are wind pollinated (Ostler and Harper, 1978; Freeman *et al.*, 1980). Wind-pollinated species decrease in abundance whereas insect-pollinated species increase along a species diversity gradient (Ostler and Harper, 1978). Most grasses and temperate zone dominant trees are wind pollinated. Plants that depend on insect pollination may deviate from the promiscuous pattern of wind pollination to specific pollination patterns depending on flower–insect fidelities (Faegri and van der Pijl, 1966; Grant, 1975).

Shrubs include large representations of both insect- and wind-pollinated members. Environmental conditions and the phylogenetic stock of the shrub both play an important role in the kind of pollination a shrub species will have. Table II reveals some interesting patterns of pollination types for important shrubs in the conterminous United States. Shrub species have a higher incidence of insect pollination than all important species in each of the 11 general vegetative types. In every case except the western shrublands, the Insect Pollination Index (IPI) is substantially greater than the "all species" IPI ($x = 2.3$, range $= 1.6–3.3$). In the western shrublands the indexes are virtually the same. This is probably because shrubs make up the preponderance of the important species in western shrublands and because many of the subdominants are insect-pollinated forbs (the "all species" IPI is highest for western shrublands).

Of the 25 shrubs recognized by Küchler (1964) as being important in the conterminous United States, 13 are insect pollinated and 11 are wind pollinated (Table V). This is a higher proportion of wind pollination than might be expected. The presumably random sample of Table I is overwhelmingly insect pollinated. The high incidence of wind pollination in Table V may be attributable to the reason Barlow (1981) outlined, that is, the shift to smaller flowers brought on by the arid conditions that predominate at the growing sites of many of the listed shrubs. Wind-pollinated species growing with each other often have flowering phases offset from one another (Everett *et al.,* 1980); where wind-pollinated species grow with insect-pollinated species, they often flower out of phase with the entomophilous species (Mosquin, 1971; Mooney, 1977). Some shrub species form huge monocultures or near monocultures. Many of these species have small flowers and pollinate during periods of predictable prevailing wind. Insect pollination is favored when the species mix is rich with simultaneously flowering shrubs as in the cases of chaparral (Table V) (Mooney, 1977) and Australian popular boxlands (Hodgkinson, 1979).

Environmental influences are important in determining wind and insect pollination. Phyletic lines, however, have an overriding influence—all *Artemisias* are wind pollinated and legumes are insect pollinated. Environment and genetics interact, then, to provide a shrub flora adapting to environmental conditions as well and as rapidly as genetic constraints allow.

B. Breeding Systems

Regulation of gene flow in angiosperms and hence in shrubs is controlled by many diverse systems that may promote or even enforce outbreeding or inbreeding. Between the extremes lies the intermediate condition of mixed outbreeding and inbreeding. Many species have adopted the mixed strategy

Table V. Pollination of the most important shrubs in the conterminous United States

Species	Vegetative type	Site pollination mode		Other dominant species	Site partitioning[b]					
		Species	Site[a]		N	G	F	S	C	T
Acacia rigidula	Mesquite–*Acacia* savanna	Insect	Mixed	3	21	67	—	19	5	10
Adenostoma fasciculatum	Chaparral	Insect	Insect	2	28	—	—	96	4	—
Ambrosia dumosa	Creosote bush–bursage	Wind	Mixed	1	18	6	—	56	22	17
Arctostaphylos patula	Montane chaparral	Insect	Mixed	2	12	—	—	67	—	33
Arctostaphylos spp.[c]	Chaparral	Insect	Insect	2	28	—	—	96	4	—
Artemisia filifolia	Galleta–three awn shrub-steppe	Wind	Wind	3	24	29	38	33	—	—
Artemisia filifolia	Sandsage–bluestem prairie	Wind	Wind	3	15	80	7	7	7	—
Artemisia tridentata	Juniper steppe woodland	Wind	Wind	0	11	36	27	27	—	9
Artemisia tridentata	Great Basin sagebrush	Wind	Wind	1	12	8	33	58	—	—
Artemisia tridentata	Sagebrush steppe	Wind	Wind	3	14	43	29	29	—	—
Artemisia tridentata	Wheatgrass–needlegrass shrub-steppe	Wind	Wind	3	13	46	—	54	—	—
Atriplex concertifolia	Saltbush–greasewood	Wind	Wind	1	12	8	17	75	—	—
Castanopsis sempervirens	Montane chaparral	Wind	Mixed	2	12	—	—	67	—	33
Ceanothus cordulatus	Montane chaparral	Insect	Mixed	2	12	—	—	67	—	33
Ceanothus spp.[c]	Chaparral	Insect	Insect	2	28	—	—	96	4	—
Cercidium microphyllum	Pale Verde–cactus	Insect	Insect	1	28	—	—	57	29	14
Cercocarpus ledifolius	Oak–juniper–mountain mahogany woodland	Mixed	Mixed	5	36	8	—	64	11	17
Cercocarpus ledifolius	Mountain mahogany–oak scrub	Mixed	Mixed	1	16	—	—	94	—	6
Coleogyne ramosissima	Blackbrush	Wind	Wind	0	5	20	—	80	—	—

Species	Vegetation type				N	G	F	S	C	T
Ephedra viridis	Galleta–three awn shrub-steppe	Wind	Wind	3	24	29	38	33	—	—
Eriogonum fasciculatum	Coastal sagebrush	Insect	Insect	2	11	—	—	100	00	00
Eriogonum fasciculatum	Coastal sagebrush–oakwoods	Insect	Wind	9	29	—	—	62	27	38
Flourensia cernua	Creosote bush–tarbush	Wind(?)	Mixed	1	22	18	—	50	24	5
Flourensia cernua	Trans-Pecos shrub savanna	Wind(?)	Mixed	1	17	41	—	29	24	6
Ilex glabra	Pocosin	Insect	Mixed	1	8[d]	—	—	25	—	75
Larrea tridentata	Creosote bush	Insect	Insect	0	6	—	—	100	—	—
Larrea tridentata	Creosote bush–bursage	Insect	Mixed	1	18	6	—	56	22	17
Larrea tridentata	Creosote bush–tarbush	Insect	Mixed	1	22	18	—	50	27	5
Larrea tridentata	Ceniza shrub	Insect	Mixed	2	11	27	—	36	18	18
Larrea tridentata	Grama–tobosa shrub-steppe	Insect	Mixed	2	29	55	14	17	10	3
Larrea tridentata	Trans-Pecos shrub savanna	Insect	Mixed	2	17	41	—	29	23	6
Leucophyllum frutescens	Ceniza shrub	Insect	Mixed	1	11	27	—	36	18	18
Quercus gambelii	Mountain mahogany–oak scrub	Wind	Mixed	1	16	—	—	94	—	6
Quercus mohriana	Shinnery	Wind	Wind	1	21	43	5	29	5	19
Salvia apiana	Coastal sagebrush	Insect	Insect	9	11	—	—	100	—	—
Salvia apiana	Coastal sagebrush–oakwoods	Insect	Insect	2	29	—	—	62	—	38
Salvia mellifera	Coastal sagebrush	Insect	Insect	9	11	—	—	100	—	—
Salvia mellifera	Coastal sagebrush–oakwoods	Insect	Mixed	2	29	—	—	62	—	38
Sarcobatus vermiculatus	Saltbush–greasewood	Wind	Wind	1	12	8	17	75	—	—

Source: Data from Küchler (1964). Important shrubs are those listed by Küchler. Shrub/tree determinations were after Küchler (1964) and the Bailey Hortorium Staff (1976).

[a] Site pollination mode was determined by: (1) If all dominants are a particular mode, then that is the site mode unless Küchler's (1964) other species are very strongly the other pollination mode; then it is considered mixed. (2) If dominants are of mixed mode then the site mode is considered mixed.

[b] Symbols: N, number of species considered including dominants and other important species (Küchler, 1964); G, % grass species; F, % forb species; S, % shrub species; C, % succulent species; T, % tree species. Because of rounding percent totals may not always equal 100.

[c] Includes several species.

[d] Disallowing *Sphagnum* spp.

Table VI. Breeding system characteristics of 12 successful western North American shrub complexes

Shrub complex	Chromosome numbers		Hybridization	Compatibility	Pollination		Fruit dispersal	Vegetative reproduction	References
	x	Chromosome races			Mode	Type			
Manzanitas—*Arctostaphylos* spp. (Ericaceae)	13	2x–4x	Interspecific is quite common	Outcrossing	Insect	Drupe	Animals	In some species	U.S. Department of Agriculture (1937); Wells (1968, 1969)
Sagebrushes—subgenus *Tridentatae* of *Artemisia* (Compositae)	9	2x–8x	Limited amount of intra- and interspecific	Outcrossing, limited amount of selfing	Wind	Small achene	Wind not specialized	In some species	Daubenmire (1975); McArthur *et al.* (1979a, 1981); Welch and McArthur (1979); Barker (1981)
Saltbushes—*Atriplex* spp. (Chenopodiaceae)	9	2x–12x	Wide interspecific, possible intergeneric	Outcrossing	Wind	Winged and sculptured utricle	Wind but quite heavy	In some species	Blauer *et al.* (1976); Stutz and Sanderson (1979), 1983); Stutz *et al.* (1979); Dunford (1984, 1985); McArthur *et al.* (1986)
Buckbrushes—*Ceanothus* spp. (Rhamnaceae)	12	2x	Intrasectional is common	Outcrossing, limited selfing in some species	Insect	Small 3-lobed capsule	Birds, rodents	In some species	Nobs (1963); Sampson and Jesperson (1963); Raven (1977)
Mountain mahoganies—*Cercocarpus* spp. (Rosaceae)	9[a]	2x	Interspecific is quite common	Outcrossing, limited amount of selfing	Wind (and insect?)	Plumed achene	Rodents, wind	In some species	Pyrah (1964); Stutz (1974); Blauer *et al.* (1975); McArthur and Sanderson (1985)

Common name	x	Ploidy	Hybridization	Breeding system	Pollination	Fruit type	Dispersal		References
Rabbitbrushes—*Chrysothamnus* spp. (Compositae)	9	2x–6x	Common intraspecific, limited specific, and intergeneric	Mostly self but some outcrossing	Insect	Pappus-bearing achene	Wind	In some species	Anderson (1971); Anderson and Reveal (1966); McArthur *et al.* (1978a); Anderson (1986)
Blackbrush—*Coleogyne ramosissima* (Rosaceae)	8	2x	—	Unknown	Wind	Achene	Rodents	No	Bowns and West (1976); J. E. Bowns (personal communication); McArthur and Sanderson (1985)
Cliffrose and bitterbrush—*Cowania* and *Purshia* (Rosaceae)	9	2x	Intergeneric is common	Self-incompatible	Insect	Plumed and nonplumed achenes	Rodents, wind	In some *Purshia* ecotypes	Stutz and Thomas (1964); Blauer *et al.* (1975); McArthur *et al.* (1983)
Mormon tea or joint fir—*Ephedra* spp. (Ephedraceae)	14	2x	Some apparent interspecific	Outcrossing	Wind	Hardened envelope	Rodents	In some species	Cutler (1939); Holmgren and Holmgren (1972); A. Blauer and A. Plummer, personal communication
Bursage—*Ambrosia* spp. (Compositae)	18	2x–8x	Intergeneric and interspecific is possible	Mostly outcrossing	Wind	Achene	Animals, wind	No	Payne (1963, 1964)
Creosote bush—*Larrea tridentata* (Zygophyllaceae)	13	2x–6x	Is possible but natural plant distribution makes unlikely	Outcrossing, limited amount of selfing	Insect, hummingbird	Capsule	Rodents, birds	Yes	Yang (1970); Sternberg (1976); Hunziker *et al.* (1977); Simpson *et al.* (1977)
Oakbrush—shrubby *Quercus* (Fagaceae)	12[b]	2x	Interspecific is common	Primarily an outcrosser	Wind	Nut	Rodents	Common	Olson (1974); Bailey Hortorium Staff (1976)

[a] Pyrah lists $x = 6$–9 but Morley (1949), Semple (1974), and McArthur and Sanderson (1985) have found only $x = 9$.

[b] Incompletely known for shrubby *Quercus* but virtually all *Quercus* are $2n = 24$ (Darlington and Wylie, 1956; Federov, 1969).

(Cronquist, 1968; Grant, 1975). Indeed, most angiosperms are predominantly but not exclusively outcrossers. Cronquist (1968) pointed out that a "mixture of crossing and selfing can keep the evolutionary pot boiling nearly as well as outcrossing alone." A single outcrossing event provides the genetic variation for new and different gene combinations for several generations of selfing. The ericaeceous shrubs (*Gaultheria* and *Zenobia*) of the east-central coastal area of the United States provide an example of the intermediate condition. Both are adapted to outcrossing but are also self-fertile (Dorr, 1981; Mirick and Quinn, 1981) as are several of the species listed in Tables I and VI.

There are various separations of male and female functions within plants and among plant genders (Lloyd, 1980a,b). Shrubs have taken full advantage of many of these systems. The same end result, for example, dioecy, can be achieved as a result of several different selective forces (Valdeyron, 1972; Cox, 1981). Shrubs have used dioecy, monoecy, and other floral arrangements to enforce outbreeding and maintain variability (Grant, 1975). More recently, it has been proposed that these diverse breeding systems may be useful in exploiting different niches and thus giving a species a wider and more effective amplitude of adaptation (Freeman *et al.*, 1976, 1980, 1981; Cox, 1981; and others). Niche exploitation is accomplished by the sexual phenotypes being differentially adapted to slightly different habitats and being reinforced by inbreeding.

Dioecy and subdioecy make a significant contribution to the shrub flora. Freeman *et al.* (1980) and McArthur and Sanderson (1984) suggested that woodiness and anemophily may be acting in concert to predispose species toward the dioecious habit.

Some dioecious and subdioecious shrubs have sex ratios that differ from the standard 1 : 1. Saltbushes of the genus *Atriplex* provide one example. These plants may have populations that are biased toward females (McArthur, 1977; Stutz *et al.*, 1979; McArthur and Freeman, 1982) or toward males (Graetz, 1978; Williams *et al.*, 1978). In the female-favoring case, an argument has been made for a genetic-sex-determining mechanism (Fig. 1) that favors female sex expression in ordinary conditions. The proposed mechanism is sensitive to environmental stress and allows a "retreat" from femaleness during stressful environmental periods (drought, cold winters). The genetic system may be reinforced by selection for female offspring by parents in accordance with the local mate competition theory. This theory states that fitness returns from males under some circumstances are less than linearly increasing with the number of males produced (Wilson and Colwell, 1981; McArthur and Freeman, 1982). The male predominant sex ratios of Australian saltbushes result from preferential grazing (Graetz, 1978; Williams *et al.*, 1978). An interesting facet in the

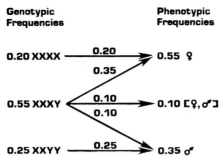

Figure 1. Apportionment of genotypes to observed phenotypes during normal years for tetraploid *Atriplex canescens*. During times of stress, more of the XXXY genotype is expressed as [♀, ♂] and ♂ plants. (From McArthur, 1977.)

dioecious plant problem is in seed-production orchards. Orchards are designed to produce the maximum seed in the space available (McArthur *et al.,* 1978c). Therefore, in the case of *Atriplex canescens,* the ideal situation is to clone constant females (the XXXX genotype of Fig. 1) and place them in an orchard with just enough males to provide adequate pollen (McArthur *et al.,* 1978c; Van Epps, Chapter 25, this volume). The subdioecious floral system of woody *Atriplex* species may be an adaptation to occupy patchy and environmentally contrasting habitats of western North America (Freeman and McArthur, 1982, 1984; Freeman *et al.,* 1984).

Another interesting breeding system is found in *Grayia brandegei,* an endemic western North American chenopod shrub. In this species all plants are monoecious but protogynous and protandrous plants exhibit synchronized and reciprocal flower production, thus ensuring cross-fertilization (Pendleton, 1986).

Gene flow is restricted most generally at the population level by short-distance pollen transport or various kinds of crossing barriers such as temporal separation of flowering time, chromosome arrangement and number, sterility barriers, and pollen vectors (Grant, 1975). However, shrub species differ widely in the amount of intra- and interspecific and even intrageneric hybridization they will tolerate. Table VI gives breeding system parameters of 12 widely distributed western North American shrub complexes.

Breeding systems in shrubs are subject to adaptive change (Baker, 1959). Some of the cultivated crops of Table I have undergone selective pressure for self-compatibility. Randell (1970) pointed out that a group of *Cassia* species in Australia's arid zone had undertaken widespread hybridization, higher polyploidy, and apomictic reproduction in marked contrast to temperate ancestral relatives.

V. Dispersal and Establishment

Shrubs as a group probably have more attractive, succulent, or nutritive fruits than do other life-forms in proportion to their number of species (Harper, 1977). These "berries" or grainlike achenes are often dispersed by birds and small mammals, and this type of seed dispersal often leads to groups of seedlings growing into several intertwining individuals. Other shrub species, including several listed in Table VI, are distributed by wind. Ants and water play lesser roles in shrub seed distribution. In general, dispersal distances are only a few hundred meters, but occasionally wind and birds perform long-distance dispersal. The North American creosote bush (*Larrea tridentata*), for example, is thought to have come from South America via avian assistance (Hunziker *et al.*, 1977). Table VI provides examples of seed dispersal of 12 common western North American shrubs. Reproduction by vegetative means usually results in localized spread except in some aquatic and riparian situations.

Establishment of seedlings in existing stands of their own kind or other vegetation is usually difficult. Shreve (1942), for example, reported that it was not possible to find more than one seedling of *Larrea tridentata* from 2 to 5 years old for every 400 mature plants in a climax *Larrea* community. On the other hand, in disturbance situations, shrub cohorts can rapidly establish. Many successful shrub complexes mix sexual and asexual reproductive means (Table VI).

VI. Marginal Populations

Marginal populations are important in breeding systems development and evolutionary change (Baker, 1959). For example, the *Cassia* case (see Section IV,B) demonstrates that opportunities for changes are abundant in marginal habitats. This is especially true if related taxa occur together in marginal areas such as in *Ceanothus* (Raven, 1977). Differentiated species of *Ceanothus* made a relatively rapid reassortment of genetic material in response to changing climate in a region of changing relief. *Chrysothamnus nauseosus* marginal populations are subject to gall-forming insects in a different way than populations at the center of the species range (McArthur *et al.*, 1979b; Wangberg, 1981; McArthur, 1986). Different subspecies of *Chrysothamnus nauseosus* are associated with different tephritid fly species at the center of the range, but the specificity is not apparent in marginal populations. The different, often more severe, selective pressures on marginal populations restrict variation but often direct remaining variation and consequent evolutionary course along new paths. Paths leading to differentiation and new breeding systems include modification in chromosomal, compatibility, pollination, dispersal, and reproductive attributes.

Acknowledgments

I am grateful to Drs. James E. Bowns, D. Carl Freeman, and Stewart C. Sanderson, and to A. Clyde Blauer and Richard Stevens for stimulating discussions that led to the production of this chapter. Funds from NSF Grant DEB-81-11010 and Pittman-Robertson Project W-82-R facilitated preparation of this chapter.

References

Anderson, L. C. (1971). Additional chromosome numbers in *Chrysothamnus* (Asteraceae). *Bull. Torrey Bot. Club* **98**, 222–225.

Anderson, L. C. (1986). Sympatric subspecies in *Chrysothamnus nauseosus*. *USDA For. Serv. Gen. Tech. Rep. INT* **INT-200**, 98–103.

Anderson, L. C., and Reveal, J. L. (1966). *Chrysothamnus bolanderi,* an intergeneric hybrid. *Madroño* **18**, 225–233.

Bailey, L. H., Hortorium Staff (1976). "Hortus Third." Macmillan, New York.

Baker, H. G. (1959). Reproductive methods as factors in speciation. *Cold Spring Harbor Symp. Quant. Biol.* **24**, 177–191.

Barker, J. R. (1981). Genetic differences between large and small *Artemisia tridentata* plants in contiguous populations. Ph.D. Dissertation, Utah State University, Logan.

Barlow, B. A. (1981). The Australian flora: Its origin and evolution. *In* "Flora of Australia," Vol. 1, pp. 25–75. Australian Government Publishing Service, Canberra.

Blauer, A. C., Plummer, A. P., McArthur, E. D., Stevens, R., and Giunta, B. C. (1975). Characteristics and hybridization of important Intermountain shrubs. I. Rose family. *USDA For. Serv. Res. Pap. INT* **INT-169**, 1–36.

Blauer, A. C., Plummer, A. P., McArthur, E. D., Stevens, R., and Giunta, B. C. (1976). Characteristics and hybridization of important Intermountain shrubs. II. Chenopod family. *USDA For. Serv. Res. Pap. INT* **INT-177**, 1–42.

Bowns, J. E., and West, N. E. (1976). Blackbrush (*Coleogne ramosissima* Torr.) on south-western Utah rangelands. *Utah, Agric. Exp. Stn., Rep.* **27**, 1–27.

Cox, P. A. (1981). Niche partitioning between sexes of dioecious plants. *Am. Nat.* **117**, 295–307.

Cronquist, A. (1968). "The Evolution and Classification of Flowering Plants." Houghton Mifflin, Boston, Massachusetts.

Cutler, H. C. (1939). Monograph of North American species of the genus *Ephedra*. *Ann. Mo. Bot. Gard.* **26**, 373–428.

Darlington, C. D. (1963). "Chromosome Botany and the Origin of Cultivated Plants," 2nd ed. Allen & Unwin, London.

Darlington, C. D., and Wylie, A. P. (1956). "Chromosome Atlas of Flowering Plants." Macmillan, New York.

Daubenmire, R. (1975). Ecology of *Artemisia tridentata* ssp. *tridentata* in the state of Washington. *Northwest Sci.* **49**, 24–35.

Dorr, L. J. (1981). The pollination ecology of *Zenobia* (Ericaceae). *Am. J. Bot.* **68,** 1325–1332.

Dunford, M. P. (1984). Cytotype distribution of *Atriplex canescens* (Chenopodiaceae) of southern New Mexico and adjacent Texas. *Southwest. Nat.* **29,** 223–228.

Dunford, M. P. (1985). A statistical analysis of morphological variation in cytotypes of *Atriplex canescens* (Chenopodiaceae). *Southwest. Nat.* **30,** 377–384.

Ehrendorfer, F., Silberbauer-Gottsberger, I., and Gottsberger, G. (1979). Variation on the population, racial, and species level in the primitive-relic angiosperm genus *Drimys* (Winteraceae) in South America. *Plant Syst. Evol.* **132,** 53–83.

Everett, R. L., Tueller, P. T., Davis, J. B., and Brunner, A. D. (1980). Plant phenology in galleta (*Hilaria jamesii*)–shadscale (*Atriplex confertifolia*) and galleta–sagebrush (*Artemisia tridentata* ssp. *wyomingensis*) associations. *J. Range Manage.* **33,** 446–450.

Faegri, K., and van der Pijl, L. (1966). "The Principles of Pollination Ecology." Pergamon, Oxford.

Federov, A. A. (1969). "Chromosome Numbers of Flowering Plants." Izd. Nauk, Leningrad.

Freeman, D. C., and McArthur, E. D. (1982). A comparison of water stress between males and females of six species of desert shrubs. *For. Sci.* **28,** 304–308.

Freeman, D. C., and McArthur, E. D. (1984). The relative influences of mortality, nonflowering and sex change on the sex ratios of six *Atriplex* species. *Bot. Gaz. (Chicago)* **145,** 385–394.

Freeman, D. C., Klikoff, L. G., and Harper, K. T. (1976). Differential resource utilization by the sexes of dioecious plants. *Science* **193,** 533–579.

Freeman, D. C., Harper, K. T., and Ostler, W. K. (1980). Ecology of plant dioecy in the Intermountain Region of western North America and California. *Oecologia* **44,** 410–417.

Freeman, D. C., McArthur, E. D., Harper, K. T., and Blauer, A. C. (1981). Influence of environment on the floral sex ratio of monoecious plants. *Evolution (Lawrence, Kans.)* **35,** 194–197.

Freeman, D. C., McArthur, E. D., and Harper, K. T. (1984). The adaptative significance of sexual lability in plants using *Atriplex canescens* as the principal example. *Ann. Mo. Bot. Gard.* **71,** 251–263.

Graetz, R. D. (1978). The influence of grazing by sheep on the structure of a saltbush (*Atriplex vesicaria* (Hew. ex Benth.)) population. *Aust. Rangel. J.* **1,** 117–125.

Grant, V. (1975). "Genetics of Flowering Plants." Columbia Univ. Press, New York.

Hamrick, J. L., Linhart, Y. B., and Mitton, J. B. (1979). Relationships between life history characteristics and electrophoretically detectable genetic variation in plants. *Annu. Rev. Ecol. Syst.* **10,** 173–200.

Harper, J. H. (1977). "Population Biology of Plants." Academic Press, London.

Hodgkinson, K. C. (1979). The shrubs of popular box (*Eucalyptus populnea*) lands and their biology. *Aust. Rangl. J.* **1,** 280–293.

Holmgren, A. H., and Holmgren, N. H. (1972). Ephedraceae. *In* "Intermountain Flora" (A. Cronquist, A. H. Holmgren, N. H. Holmgren, and J. L. Reveal, eds.), Vol. I, pp. 244–248. Hafner, New York.

Hunziker, J. H., Palacios, R. A., Poggio, L., Naranjo, C. A., and Yang, T. W. (1977). Geographic distribution, morphology, hybridization, cytogenetics and evolution. *In* "Creosote Bush: Biology and Chemistry of *Larrea* in New World Deserts" (T. J. Mabry, J. H. Hunziker, and D. R. DiFoe, Jr., eds.), pp. 10–47. Dowden, Hutchinson & Ross, Stroudsburg, Pennsylvania.

Küchler, A. W. (1964). Potential natural vegetation of the conterminous United States (map and manual). *Am. Geogr. Soc., Spec. Publ.* **36,** 1–116.

Lewis, W. H. (1980). Polyploidy in angiosperms: Dicotyledons. *In* "Polyploidy: Biological Relevance" (W. H. Lewis, ed.), pp. 241–268. Plenum, New York.

Lloyd, D. G. (1980a). Benefits and handicaps of sexual reproduction. *Evol. Biol.* **13**, 69–111.

Lloyd, D. G. (1980b). Demographic factors and mating patterns in angiosperms. *In* "Demography and Evolution in Plant Populations" (O. T. Solbrig, ed.), pp. 67–88. Blackwell, Oxford.

McArthur, E. D. (1977). Environmentally induced changes of sex expression in *Atriplex canescens. Heredity* **38**, 97–103.

McArthur, E. D. (1981). Shrub selection and adaptation for rehabilitation plantings. *In* "Shrub Establishment on Disturbed Arid and Semi-arid Lands" (V. H. Stelter, E. D. DePuit, and S. A. Mikol, tech. coords.), pp. 1–8. Wyoming Game and Fish Department, Laramie.

McArthur, E. D. (1984). Natural diversity of western range shrubs. *In* "Natural Diversity in Forest Ecosystems" (J. L. Cooley and J. H. Cooley, eds.), pp. 193–209. Inst. Ecol., University of Georgia, Athens.

McArthur, E. D. (1986). Specificity of galls on *Chrysothamnus nauseosus* subspecies. *USDA For. Serv. Gen. Tech. Rep. INT* **INT-200**, 205–210.

McArthur, E. D., and Freeman, D. C. (1982). Sex expression in *Atriplex canescens:* Genetics and environment. *Bot. Gaz.(Chicago)* **143**, 476–482.

McArthur, E. D., and Plummer, A. P. (1978). Biogeography and management of native western shrubs: A case study, section *Tridentatae* of *Artemisia. Great Basin Nat. Mem.* **2**, 229–243.

McArthur, E. D., and Sanderson, S. C. (1984). Distribution, systematics, and evolution of Chenopodiaceae: An overview. *USDA For. Serv. Gen. Tech. Rep. INT* **INT-172**, 14–24.

McArthur, E. D., and Sanderson, S. C. (1985). A cytotaxonomic contribution to the western North American rosaceous flora. *Madroño* **32**, 24–28.

McArthur, E. D., Hanks, D. L., Plummer, A. P., and Blauer, A. C. (1978a). Contributions to the taxonomy of *Chrysothamnus viscidiflorus* (Asteraeae, Compositae) and other *Chrysothamnus* species using paper chromatography. *J. Range Manage.* **31**, 216–223.

McArthur, E. D., Plummer, A. P., and Davis, J. N. (1978b). Rehabilitation of game range in the salt desert. *In* "Wyoming Shrublands, Proceedings of the Seventh Wyoming Shrub Ecology Workshop" (K. L. Johnson, ed.), pp. 23–50. Agric. Ext. Serv., University of Wyoming, Laramie.

McArthur, E. D., Plummer, A. P., Van Epps, G. A., Freeman, D. C., and Jorgensen, K. R. (1978c). Producing fourwing saltbush seed in seed orchards. *Proc. Int. Rangel. Congr., 1st*, pp. 406–410.

McArthur, E. D., Blauer, A. C., Plummer, A. P., and Stevens, R. (1979a). Characteristics and hybridization of important Intermountain shrubs. III. Sunflower family. *USDA For. Serv. Res. Pap. INT* **INT-220**, 1–82.

McArthur, E. D., Tiernan, C. F., and Welch, B. L. (1979b). Subspecies specificity of gall forms on *Chrysothamnus nauseosus. Great Basin Nat.* **39**, 81–87.

McArthur, E. D., Pope, C. L., and Freeman, D. C. (1981). Chromosomal studies of subgenus *Tridentatae* of *Artemisia:* Evidence for autopolyploidy. *Am. J. Bot.* **68**, 589–605.

McArthur, E. D., Stutz, H. C., and Sanderson, S. C. (1983). Taxonomy, distribution, and cytogenetics of *Purshia, Cowania,* and *Fallugia* (Rosoideae, Rosaceae). *USDA For. Serv. Gen. Tech. Rep. INT* **INT-152**, 4–24.

McArthur, E. D., Sanderson, S. C., and Freeman, D. C. (1986). Isozymes of an autopolyploid shrub, *Atriplex canescens* (Chenopodiaceae). *Great Basin Nat.* **46**, 157–160.

McKell, C. M., Blaisdell, J. P., and Goodin, J. R., eds. (1972). "Wildland Shrubs: Their Biology and Utilization," USDA For. Serv. Gen. Tech. Rep. INT-1.

Mirick, S., and Quinn, J. A. (1981). Some observations on the reproductive biology of *Gaultheria procumbens* (Ericaceae). *Am. J. Bot.* **68,** 1298–1305.

Mooney, H. A. (1977). Southern coastal scrub. *In* "Terrestial Vegetation of California" (M. G. Barbour and J. Major, eds.), pp. 471–489. Wiley, New York.

Morley, T. (1949). Documented chromosome numbers of plants. *Madroño* **10,** 95.

Mosquin, T. (1971). Competition for pollinators as a stimulus for the evolution of flowering plants. *Oikos* **22,** 398–402.

Nobs, M. A. (1963). Experimental studies on species relationships in *Ceanothus. Carnegie Inst. Washington Publ.* **623,** 1–94.

Olson, D. F., Jr. (1974). *Quercus* L. *In* "Seeds of Woody Plants in the United States" (C. S. Schopmeyer, tech. coord.). USDA For. Serv. Agric. Handb. No. 450. U.S. Govt. Printing Office, Washington, D.C.

Ostler, W. K., and Harper, K. T. (1978). Floral ecology in relation to plant species diversity in the Wasatch Mountains of Utah and Idaho. *Ecology* **59,** 848–861.

Payne, W. W. (1963). The morphology of the inflorescence of ragweeds (*Ambrosia–Fransaria:* Compositae). *Am. J. Bot.* **50,** 872–880.

Payne, W. W. (1964). A re-evaluation of the genus *Ambrosia* (Compositae). *J. Arnold Arbor. Harv. Univ.* **45,** 401–438.

Pendleton, R. L. (1986). Studies in plant populations biology: *Grayia brandegei* and *Quercus gambelii.* Ph.D. Dissertation, Wayne State University, Detroit, Michigan.

Pyrah, G. L. (1964). Cytogenetic studies of *Cercocarpus* in Utah. M.S. Thesis, Brigham Young University, Provo, Utah.

Randell, B. R. (1970). Adaptations in the genetic system of Australian arid zone *Cassia* species (Leguminosae, Caesalpinioideae). *Aust. J. Bot.* **18,** 77–97.

Raven, P. H. (1977). The California flora. *In* "Terrestrial Vegetation of California" (M. G. Barbour and J. Major, eds.), pp. 109–137. Wiley, New York.

Sampson, A. W., and Jespersen, B. S. (1963). California range brushlands and browse plants. *Calif., Agric. Exp. Stn., Ext. Serv. Man.* **33,** 1–162.

Semple J. C. (1974). Chromosomes of phanerogams. 4. *Ann. Mo. Bot. Gard.* **61,** 902–903.

Shreve, F. (1942). The desert vegetation of North America. *Bot. Rev.* **8,** 195–246.

Simmonds, N. W., ed. (1976). "Evolution of Crop Plants." Longman Group Ltd., London.

Simpson, B. B., Neff, J. C., and Moldenke, A. R. (1977). Reproductive system of *Larrea. In* "Creosote Bush: Biology and Chemistry of *Larrea* in New World Deserts" (T. J. Mabry, J. N. Hunziker, and D. R. DiFeo, eds.), pp. 92–114. Dowden, Hutchinson & Ross, Stroudsburg, Pennsylvania.

Solbrig, O. T. (1972). Cytology and cytogenetics of shrubs. *In* "Wildland Shrubs: Their Biology and Utilization" (C. M. McKell, J. P. Blaisdell, and J. R. Goodin, eds.), For. Serv. Gen. Tech. Rep. INT-1, pp. 127–137.

Stebbins, G. L. (1971). "Chromosomal Evolution in Higher Plants." Edward Arnold, London.

Stebbins, G. L. (1972). Evolution and diversity of arid-land shrubs. *In* "Wildland Shrubs: Their Biology and Utilization" (C. M. McKell, J. P. Blaisdell, and J. R. Goodin, eds.), USDA For. Serv. Gen. Tech. Rep. INT-1, pp. 111–120.

Stebbins, G. L. (1974). "Flowering Plants: Evolution above the Species Level." Belknap Press, Cambridge, Massachusetts.

Stebbins, G. L. (1975). Shrubs as centers of adaptive radiation and evolution. *In* "Proceedings, Symposium and Workshop on the Occasion of the Dedication of the U.S. Forest

Service Shrub Sciences Laboratory" (H. C. Stutz, ed.), pp. 120–140. Brigham Young University, Provo, Utah.

Sternberg, L. (1976). Growth of *Larrea tridentata. Madrōno* **23**, 408–417.

Stutz, H. C. (1974). Rapid evolution in western shrubs. *Utah Sci.* **35**, 16–20, 33.

Stutz, H. C., and Sanderson, S. C. (1979). The role of polyploidy in the evolution of *Atriplex canescens. In* "Arid Land Plant Resources" (J. R. Goodin and D. K. Northington, eds.), pp. 615–621. Texas Tech. Univ. Press, Lubbock.

Stutz, H. C., and Sanderson, S. C. (1983). Evolutionary studies of *Atriplex:* Chromosome races of *A. confertifolia* (shadscale). *Am. J. Bot.* **70**, 1536–1547.

Stutz, H. C., and Thomas, L. K. (1964). Hybridization and introgression in *Cowania* and *Purshia. Evolution (Lawrence, Kans.)* **18**, 183–195.

Stutz, H. C., Pope, C. L., and Sanderson, S. C. (1979). Evolutionary studies of *Atriplex:* Adaptative products from the natural hybrid, *6N A. tridentata* × *4N A. canescens. Am. J. Bot.* **66**, 1181–1193.

U.S. Department of Agriculture, Forest Service (1937). "Range Plant Handbook," U.S. Govt. Printing Office, Washington, D.C.

Valdeyron, G. (1972). On the development of incompatibility and sex systems in higher plants and their evolutive meaning. *In* "Evolution in Plants" (G. Vida, ed.), pp. 83–91. Akadémiai Kiadó, Budapest.

Wangberg, J. K. (1981). Gall-forming habits of *Aciurina* species (Diptera: Tephritidae) on rabbitbrush (Compositae: *Chrysothamnus* spp.) in Idaho. *J. Kans. Entomol. Soc.* **54**, 711–732.

Weaver, T. (1980). Climates of vegetation types of the northern Rocky Mountains and adjacent plains. *Am. Midl. Nat.* **103**, 392–398.

Welch, B. L., and McArthur, E. D. (1979). Feasibility of improving big sagebrush (*Artemisia tridentata*) for use on mule deer winter ranges. *In* "Arid Land Plant Resources" (J. R. Goodin and D. K. Northington, eds.), pp. 451–473. Texas Tech. Univ. Press, Lubbock.

Wells, P. V. (1968). New taxa, combinations, and chromosome numbers in *Arctostaphylos* (Ericaceae). *Madroño* **19**, 193–210.

Wells, P. V. (1969). The relation between mode of reproduction and extent of speciation of woody genera in the California chaparral. *Evolution (Lawrence, Kans.)* **23**, 264–267.

Williams, D. G., Anderson, D. J., and Slater, K. R. (1978). The influence of sheep on pattern and process in *Atriplex vescicaria* populations from the Riverine Plain of New South Wales. *Aust. J. Bot.* **26**, 381–392.

Wilson, D. S., and Colwell, R. K. (1981). Evolution of sex ratios in structured demes. *Evolution (Lawrence, Kans.)* **35**, 882–897.

Yang, T. W. (1970). Major chromosome races of *Larrea divaricata* in North America. *J. Ariz. Acad. Sci.* **6**, 41–45.

IV

Physiological Adaptation of Shrubs

Chapters in this section discuss the effects of stress on physiological processes of shrubs and describe the kinds of strategies shrubs employ to meet physiological stress.

Through geologic time, shrubs have evolved biological strategies that have improved their survival and reproduction under such stress conditions as drought, temperature extremes, salinity, and adverse soil conditions. Certain shrub species may employ unique systems for enduring or avoiding the effects of stress. For example, in *Atriplex canescens* three mechanisms are reported to deal with high salinity levels. Osmotic adjustment allows cells to accumulate high levels of salts in order to offset or balance the high levels of salts in the adjacent soil. Some ecotypes are known to selectively substitute potassium for sodium and thus reduce the potential for sodium toxicity. Internal levels of salinity can be reduced by the accumulation and subsequent excretion of salt through vessicles on the tips of leaf hairs. Many such examples of stress adaptations have been described for shrubs.

16

Moisture Stress Adaptation in Shrubs

Ronald J. Newton
Joseph R. Goodin

I. Introduction

Water supply to wildland shrubs is an important factor in their growth habit, survival, and distribution. Shrubs have evolved a variety of morphological and physiological mechanisms adapted to water deficits. For example, *Franseria* of the Sonoran Desert experienced a water potential differential of 7.5 MPa in one season (Halvorson and Patten, 1974), indicating significant physiological adaptations to a fluctuating water supply. Our understanding of physiological adaptations in shrubs has been advanced in part because of the recent explosion of knowledge and interest in moisture stress adaptation, particularly in crop plants. The purpose of this review is to present recent information concerning mechanisms of drought resistance that provide the ability of wildland shrubs to maintain productivity and/or survive during periods of low water supply. The classification and generic terms used are those of Turner and co-workers (Jones *et al.*, 1981).

II. Drought Resistance

The term *drought resistance* is used to describe the physiological and biochemical features that contribute positively to the ability of shrubs to survive and reproduce in conditions of limited water availability. Three types of drought resistance have been suggested (Turner, 1979): (1) *drought escape:* the ability of a plant to complete its life cycle before a serious plant water deficit develops; (2) *drought tolerance at high tissue water potential:* the ability of a plant to endure periods of precipitation deficit while maintaining a high tissue water potential; and (3) *drought tolerance at low tissue water potential:* the ability of a plant to endure precipitation deficits at low tissue water potential. This review will include the latter two types of drought resistance: drought tolerance at both high and low tissue water potential. The concept of *water use efficiency* is excluded because it is considered elsewhere.

III. Maintenance of High Tissue Water Potential

The maintenance of high tissue water potential while shrubs are experiencing a soil water deficit or a high evaporative demand can be accomplished by restricting water loss or by maintaining the current water supply. Shrubs can restrict water loss by allowing changes in stomatal conductance, evaporative surface area, and radiation absorbed. This review will briefly consider the last of these, the radiation absorbed. Shrubs can also maintain the water supply by developing an extensive root system. This not only decreases water loss by exposing only a relatively small part of the plant to the atmosphere, but it also provides a high capacity for absorbing water from a large volume of soil. Rooting patterns, root resistances to water flow, and mycorrhizal–root interactions are important physiological factors involved in the maintenance of high tissue water potential in shrubs.

A. *Restricting Water Loss*

Reduction in absorbed radiation

Water loss reduction can be achieved by reducing the amount of absorbed radiation. *Atriplex hymenelytra* leaves have been suggested to be steeply inclined to reduce solar radiation absorption in the middle of the day and increase absorption in the cool, more humid morning (Mooney *et al.,* 1977b). Inclined leaves of *A. hymenelytra* reduced both leaf temperature and transpiration.

Radiation is also reduced by production of hair, wax, or salt on the surface. This increases the reflectance of the leaves. Increased pubescence has been associated with sun leaves (Esau, 1977) and xerophytic conditions (Cunningham and Strain, 1969). Pubescence can significantly influence leaf temperature by altering radiation absorption or thickness of the air boundary next to the leaf (Nobel, 1974). Increases in pubescence of *Encelia farinosa* led to a 30% decrease in leaf absorption of solar radiation according to Smith and Nobel (1977), who concluded that a decreased absorption due to increased pubescence could reduce leaf temperature and hence transpiration without necessarily decreasing photosynthesis.

B. Maintaining the Current Water Supply

1. Rooting Patterns

Root systems possess morphological plasticity that enables them to adapt to extremely variable soil and moisture conditions. Perennial shrubs of dry regions usually have root/shoot ratios above 1 (Caldwell, 1975; Evenari *et al.,* 1975) and part of this increased root mass represents carbon storage rather than absorbing tissue. In shrub communities of the western U.S. Great Basin, root/shoot ratios of 9 have been observed (Caldwell and Fernandez, 1975). Root/shoot ratios increase with lower soil water potential (Dwyer and DeGormo, 1970), and it appears that the ratio changes so as to maintain plant water potential within certain limits (Fischer and Turner, 1978). Increases in root/shoot ratios can be associated with deeper rooting as well as with shallow, widespread root systems (Kummerow, 1980). In the cool desert shrubs of Utah, annual reconstruction of a significant fraction of the lateral root system occurs, and root element extension has been observed under an extreme water potential of −7.0 MPa (Caldwell and Fernandez, 1975). The mechanism by which lowered plant water potential affects root/shoot carbon allocation has not been established, but it is known that factors other than water stress also affect carbon and nutrient partitioning (Kummerow, 1980). The carbon costs of root system maintenance and growth activity are considerable when compared to aboveground growth activity (Caldwell and Fernandez, 1975).

In *Quercus* seedlings, water-stressed roots were altered morphologically, causing them to become long and thin (Osonubi and Davies, 1978). This alteration was associated with lowered osmotic potential and apparent partitioning of assimilates to the root. Presumably, the change in root morphology accompanied by lowered osmotic potential provided an advantage of water absorption from drying soil. However, repeated water stress cycles did not alter root dry weight or root/shoot ratios (Osonubi and Davies, 1978).

Root system distribution of nine perennial species growing in the Mohave Desert, including *Atriplex, Larrea, Lycium, Ambrosia,* and *Krameria,* showed that the root zones were relatively shallow and limited by the depth of penetration of precipitation (Wallace *et al.*, 1980). Roots in the first 10 cm of soil consisted largely of multiple, woody taproots with smaller roots residing in the second 10 cm of soil. Some species have a two-tiered root system. For example, *Artemisia* competes with understory and annual plants for available moisture in the upper 50 cm of soil early in the growing season, but when this supply is exhausted, the deeper-rooted *Artemisia* continues its life cycle using moisture as deep as 2.5 m (Campbell and Harris, 1977). The symmetrical distribution of *Larrea,* first reported to be due to allelochemicals (Went, 1955), has also been shown to be determined by the available water supply (Barbour, 1969; Woodell *et al.*, 1969).

Water potential extremes in *Larrea* are opposite of those observed in most plants. Minimum water potentials were observed at night and maximum water potentials were observed during the day, suggesting that water vapor in the soil, responding to temperature gradients, moved up out of the rooting zone at night and back down into the rooting zone during the day (Syvertsen *et al.*, 1975). The extent to which this phenomenon occurs and its significance for survival of evergreen, perennial shrubs under extreme environmental conditions warrant further investigation.

The proportion of the root biomass that is active in water uptake has not been established. The zone of most rapid water absorption lies behind the meristematic region of the root tip and ahead of where suberization occurs (Chung and Kramer, 1975), but considerable quantities of water are absorbed through suberized portions of roots (Kramer and Bullock, 1966). Apparently the endodermis does not always form an impermeable barrier to water absorption and young roots forming from the pericycle produce gaps in the endodermis for free water movement (Dumbroff and Peirson, 1971; Queen, 1967). Water may move through endodermal cell wall plasmodesmata (Clarkson *et al.*, 1971), suggesting that water absorption may occur at locations that are long distances from woody plant root tips (Kramer and Kozlowski, 1979).

2. Root Resistance

Roots may absorb adequate amounts of moisture from the soil, but hydraulic resistances within the plant must be low enough to conduct water to the location of need in the shoot. The major resistance to water flow in plants occurs in the roots (Kramer, 1969), but water flow in the soil–plant continuum may have a major resistance at the soil–root interface (Weatherley, 1982). Contraction of the roots resulting from hydrostatic tensions in the plant would increase this resistance. Positive feedback mediated by stomata through reduced transpiration may increase root turgor and reduce the soil–root resistance (Weatherley, 1982). Similarly, through control of root resistance, leaf water potential can be influenced and controlled at any given soil and water flux (Fischer and Turner, 1978). Parsons and Kramer (1974) observed a minimum of root resistance at midday and a maximum near midnight, suggesting cyclic control signals from the shoots. Differences in root resistance with variation in transpiration rates have been observed in several woody species (Camacho-B. *et al.*, 1974), and Kaplan and Gale (1972) observed that increased salinity in the growth medium increased root resistance in *Atriplex halimus*.

Root resistance to water flow is due primarily to radial movement (Weatherley, 1982), indicating that the axial component of root resistance is small especially if the vessel diameters are large (Carlquist, 1975). The adaptive value of less axial resistance of a wide xylem element is apparent only when negative xylem tensions are not high; as the xylem element diameter increases, the water columns become subject to cavitation under increased tension (Carlquist, 1975).

Radial resistance of water transfer across the root may occur in either the apoplast or the symplast (Weatherley, 1982) and resistance is dependent on flow rate (Stoker and Weatherley, 1971). Considerable movement of water occurs in the cell walls (Strugger, 1949) and Kramer (1969) has observed less resistance to water flow in unsuberized cell walls as compared to flow across protoplasts. Variations in resistance to flow have been demonstrated between species of sitka spruce (*Picea sitchensis*) (Hellkvist *et al.*, 1974), but the significance of this resistance to drought resistance has not been demonstrated.

3. Mycorrhizal Fungi

Certain groups of soil-borne fungi have symbiotic associations with plant roots and form structures called mycorrhizae. These associations are so wide spread that the nonmycorrhizal plant may be the exception rather than the rule (Gerdemann, 1970). *Larrea* and *Prosopis* have extensive mycorrhizal associations, especially with their tertiary root systems (Staffeldt and Voight, 1975). Shrubs may benefit from mycorrhizae that provide a greatly enlarged absorptive surface in the form of hyphal strands. These strands may extend outward from the root surface allowing additional exploration of soil regions not accessible to roots alone. Mycorrhizae obtain most of their energy from living host roots, and account for approximately 25% of the root/mycorrhizae respiration (Harley, 1971).

Mycorrhizal fungi may enhance drought resistance of shrubs in several ways, most of which may be traced to enhanced absorption of either mineral nutrients or water. In soybeans, Safir *et al.* (1971) found that mycorrhizae (*Glomus mossae*) decreased water flow resistance by 40% and attributed it to enhanced root nutrient status brought about by the fungus. However, mycorrhizae increased water flow resistance in *Pinus* (Sands and Theodorou, 1978). In lemon seedlings (*Citrus*), the effect of mycorrhizae in recovery from water stress was attributed to stomatal regulation rather than reduced root resistance (Levy and Krikun, 1980), suggesting hormonal influence by the fungus.

Survival under drought conditions may be contingent on fungal–host relationships. *Atriplex* grown in a region of less than 250 mm of rainfall and inoculated with *G. mosseae* showed increased survival rates over nonmycorrhizal plants (Aldon, 1975; Call and McKell, 1984). Inoculation of *Chrysothamnus nauseosus* with *G. fasciculatus* also showed increased growth and survival (Lindsey *et al.,* 1977). Increased occurrence of mycorrhizae in the roots of *Larrea* during the summer months (Staffeldt and Voigt, 1975) may be related to its observed drought tolerance. *Atriplex* roots from mycorrhizal transplants grew more actively in soil and processed oil shale than roots from nonmycorrhizal transplants (Call, 1981). The mycorrhizae apparently permitted greater root extension and increased use of available water for enhanced seedling survival.

There are also varying degrees of drought tolerance among species of mycorrhizae (Mexel and Reid, 1973; Theodorou, 1978). Generally, high moisture levels retard mycorrhizal formation (Powell and Sithamparathan, 1977), but certain ectomycorrhizal fungi are adapted to wet soils (Trappe, 1977).

The potential use of mycorrhizal fungi to achieve efficient use of water in arid regions is unknown, but it could be appreciable. Soil moisture must profoundly affect mycorrhizal activity, but a mycorrhizal role in relation to water stress has not been established. More research is needed to establish the beneficial effects of mycorrhizal associations under natural conditions in wildland shrubs. The ecological requirements of mycorrhizae are particularly relevant to improvement of degraded rangelands.

IV. Drought Tolerance at Low Water Potential

A. *Maintenance of Turgor*

Cell turgor has been shown to influence many morphological, physiological, and biochemical processes in plants, including leaf expansion, stomatal aperture, and enzymatic reactions. Results from several laboratories (Green *et al.,* 1971; Hsiao *et al.,* 1976; Meyer and Boyer, 1981) suggest that drought tolerance is associated with the plant's ability to maintain growth during drought. An obvious benefit to shrubs for growth maintenance would be to allow root growth for exploration of additional soil water and maintenance of a population of young, photosynthetically active leaves, even though mature leaves are senescing. The ability of shrubs to maintain growth through maintenance of cell turgor as water potentials decrease can be attributed to low osmotic potential, increased tissue elasticity, and reduced cell size. Because tissue and cell elasticities have been difficult to characterize and cell measurements are cumbersome, most turgor maintenance has been investigated and explained in terms of reduction in osmotic potential.

1. Osmotic Adjustment

Adjustment of osmotic potential in response to water stress is related to the maintenance of a positive turgor potential. Changes in osmotic potential can be brought about by changes in the number of solute osmoles in the symplasm or changes in the volume of water in the symplasm (Hsiao *et al.*, 1976). An increase in solute osmoles may result from the synthesis of organic solutes or the uptake of inorganic salts.

Pressure–volume (PV) curves are a convenient method for examining the magnitude of osmotic adjustment (Richardson and McKell, 1980; Richter *et al.*, 1980; Wenkert *et al.*, 1978), and they are obtained from measurements of water content and total water potential in plant cells, tissues or organs. Boyle's and Van't Hoff's laws produce an equation (πV = constant) that states that the product of osmotic potential and solution volume is a constant for any given amount of osmotically active solutes in an ideal osmotic system (Hinckley *et al.*, 1980). A linear relationship may be obtained by converting relative water content (RWC) to its reciprocal (Richter *et al.*, 1980).

A PV curve (Fig. 1) can be used to estimate three important water relations parameters. First, the potential at which the "straight portion" of the line intercepts the vertical at RWC^{-1} gives the osmotic potential (A_1, A_2, A_3) at full saturation (π). Second, the point where the "curve portion" of the line meets the "straight portion" (B_1, B_2) is the osmotic potential at zero turgor potential (π_0). Third, the intersections of the "straight portion" of the curve with abscissa and ordinate provide an estimate of the "ideality" of a given set of data. The larger the distance of these intersections from the origin (e.g., line 3), the larger is the deviation from an ideal osmotic system (Richter *et al.*, 1980). Differences between PV curves can then be used to demonstrate the existence or absence of osmotic adjustment (Hinckley *et al.*, 1980). For example, a change in the angle between the coordinates and the extrapolated "straight portion" (line 1 vs. line 2) would indicate an addition of solutes to a given amount of vacuolar solution through a lowering of osmotic potentials at both full saturation (A_1 changes to A_2) and zero turgor (B_1 changes to B_2). Wenkert

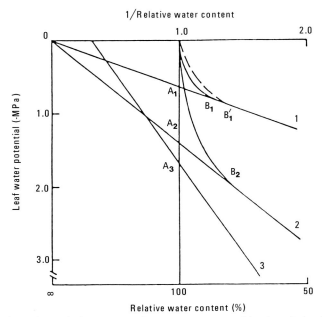

Figure 1. Three theoretical pressure–volume curves expressed by the relationship between water potential and the reciprocal of the relative water content. Curves 1 and 2 follow the "ideal system" by going through the zero point, whereas curve 3 deviates from the ideal. A is the osmotic potential at full saturation; B is the water potential or osmotic potential at the turgor loss point; osmotic adjustment occurs when A_1 changes to A_2 and B_1 changes to B_2; a shift in the turgor loss point from B_1 to B'_1 (dashed line) indicates an increase in cell wall elasticity. (From Hinckley *et al.*, 1980)

et al. (1978) proposed using the difference between the osmotic potentials at full saturation (π, $A_2 - A_1$) and at zero turgor (π, $B_2 - B_1$) to determine osmotic adjustment.

Hinckley *et al.* (1980) studied osmotic adjustment properties in several drought-hardy shrubs including *Cornus, Crateagus, Sorbus,* and *Virburnum.* Osmotic adjustment was relatively small in mature, nonsenescing leaves, except for *Cornus sanguinea.* With *Crataegus monogyna,* drought history or site did not play a role in osmotic adjustment. Poole and Miller (1978) found no appreciable osmotic adjustment in four evergreen shrub species from Chile, and Duhme (1974) found evidence for adjustment in only 5 of 28 species in southern France.

Two woody shrubs, *Larrea* and *Atriplex,* have relatively low osmotic potentials associated with high turgor potentials while experiencing water stress (Monson and Smith, 1982). *Encelia* and *Olneya* exhibited intermediate osmotic potentials and intermediate turgor potentials when subjected to water stress (Monson and Smith, 1982). Osmotic adjustments of about −0.5 MPa occurred in both *Larrea* and *Atriplex* with plant water potential changing by −1.4 MPa for *Atriplex* and −2.6 MPa in *Larrea;* thus, adjustment appeared to be more advantageous to *Atriplex* than *Larrea* (Monson and Smith, 1982). Richardson and McKell (1980) observed osmotic adjustment in *Atriplex* that maintained positive turgor at a water potential of −3.9 MPa.

It is assumed that much of the adjustment in *Atriplex* is also due to sodium chloride, where it accounts for nearly 50% of the osmotic potential (Walter and Stadelmann, 1974). In *Larrea,* the adjustment is probably associated with organic solutes (Saunier *et al.,* 1968), since salt contributes less than 15% to the osmotic potential (Walter and Stadelmann, 1974). Turgor in *Larrea* is only 60% of that in *Atriplex* (Bennert and Mooney, 1979). demonstrating the more dominant role of inorganic solutes in osmotic adjustment in halophytes. Many halophytic species such as *Atriplex* accumulate high solute concentrations regardless of whether or not they are subjected to water stress, and they successfully maintain turgor at low tissue water potentials.

Immature leaves appear to be the most drought-tolerant, and they show a unique capacity for resuming growth after prolonged stress (Runyon, 1934). Young leaves of *Larrea* have been observed to accumulate more calcium (Shreve and Mallery, 1933), resin (Rhoades, 1977), and protein (Duisburg, 1952) than mature leaves. Solute accumulation associated with lowered osmotic potentials may have a significant influence on later responses to subsequent, lower water potentials. *Larrea* plants with the best growth were those that experienced the widest range of osmotic potentials (Runyon, 1934).

In contrast to *Larrea,* true osmotic adjustment occurred with age in *Prosopis,* with mature shoots having lower osmotic potentials than juvenile shoots (Nilsen *et al.,* 1981). This was associated with the capacity of *Prosopis* for recharging its water content from deep groundwater and maintaining turgor and carbon fixation. Indeed, maximal diurnal osmotic changes (0.7 MPa) in other taxa (Bennert and Mooney, 1979) were less than half of those observed by Nilsen *et al.* (1981) in *Prosopis* (1.1 MPa). Similarly, in two evergreen shrubs, *Prunus* and *Ilex,* osmotic potentials of newly emerged leaves were 1 MPa higher than those of mature, overwintered leaves (Karlic and Richter, 1983). These differences were maintained until mature leaves became senescent and osmotic potentials then increased (Fig. 2).

Solute accumulation during water stress assists in maintenance of turgor and high leaf conductance in *Quercus* seedlings (Osonubi and Davies, 1978), mature leaves of *Prosopis* (Nilsen et al., 1981), and several shrubs

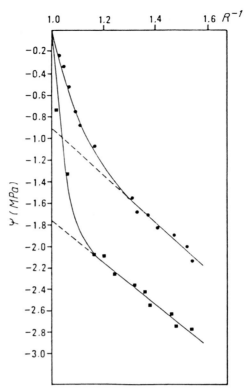

Figure 2. Pressure–volume curves from leaves of *Ilex aquifolium* showing the relationship between water potential and/or osmotic potential with the reciprocal of relative water content (R^{-1}).

(Hinckley *et al.*, 1980). Karlic and Richter (1983) suggest that low osmotic potentials provide more flexibility to leaves during high evaporative demand before they reach the critical water potential where turgor is lost. Indeed, Hinckley *et al.* (1980) have shown in shrubs that a decline of water potentials to a value near the turgor loss point triggers stomatal closure, thus effectively stopping further water potential decline. However, Duhme (1974) found significant changes in threshold water potentials for stomatal closure in only 5 of 28 shrub species studied, and Hinckley *et al.* (1980) found changes in only one species. A very large change of 2.75 MPa in threshold water potential was observed in *Juniperus phoenicea* (Duhme, 1974).

Limited data suggest that shrub roots may make some osmotic adjustment under water stress (Osonubi and Davies, 1978). During a 2-week water stress cycle, *Quercus* seedling roots accumulated carbohydrate and performed the adjustment more effectively than leaves (Osonubi and Davies, 1978). The adjustment was accompanied by increased root length.

The nature of accumulated solutes during osmotic adjustment have not been well characterized in shrubs. Levels of nonstructural carbon pools appear to be low in *Larrea* (Strain, 1969). When water stressed, *Larrea* leaves accumulated phenylalanine and proline, but glucose and sucrose levels were significantly reduced (Saunier *et al.*, 1968). Proline levels increased in *Atriplex* in response to water stress, with higher levels produced in seedlings than in mature plants (Barr, 1979). Glycine-betaine accumulated in water-stressed *Atriplex* and high concentrations were associated with low osmotic potentials in *Acacia* (Wynn Jones and Storey, 1981). The precise roles of betaine compounds in stressed shrubs are yet to be elucidated.

Adaptation of *Larrea* to arid environments may be associated with its soluble, natural components and their possible role in osmotic adjustment. The two most xerophytic species, *L. tridentata* and *L. cunefolia*, contain higher relative amounts of soluble, natural products than those species adapted to more mesic environments (Mabry *et al.*, 1977). Primary components of aqueous, soluble fractions have been shown to be flavonoid glycosides (Mabry *et al.*, 1977).

The data available at the present time indicate that osmotic adjustment may not be a typical mechanism for drought tolerance at low water potentials in woody shrub species. However, more investigations with precise determination on more species are required. The evaluation of osmotic adjustment requires elaborate studies on each species before a final conclusion can be made. More root studies are also needed.

2. Elasticity

When a stress is applied to a cell, a strain results. This strain can be elastic, plastic, or both. An elastic strain occurs if the cell returns to its prestressed shape after the stress is released. In a living plant cell it is the elastic properties of the cell walls that apply the restoring force on the cell sap and thus produce a positive internal turgor pressure (Tyree and Jarvis, 1982). High tissue elasticity contributes to turgor maintenance as tissue water content and water potentials decline.

Elasticity can be measured from the relationship between turgor pressure and cell volume (Steudle *et al.*, 1977), and leaf water potential and relative water content (Hinckley *et al.*, 1980; Noy-Meir and Ginzburg, 1967; Richter *et al.*, 1980). An increase in cell wall elasticity can be determined from the water potential vs. RWC^{-1} relationship (see Fig. 1). A shift in the zero turgor point to higher values of RWC^{-1} (point B_1 to point B_1', line 1) indicates increased elasticity of cell walls and turgor maintenance.

Three perennial, woody species (*Atriplex, Larrea,* and *Olneya*) possess low tissue elasticity when experiencing low water potential and high tissue elasticity when a high water potential exists (Monson and Smith, 1982). This is similar to observations in *Hammada scorparia* (Kappen *et al.,* 1975), but is in contrast with studies on apple (Davies and Lakso, 1979). Apparently increased elasticity in stressed apple leaves influences turgor maintenance more than changes in osmotic potential (Davies and Lakso, 1979). Osmotic adjustments in *Larrea* and *Atriplex* were quite substantial during water stress and apppeared to be more dominant than changes in elasticity (Monson and Smith, 1982). Increased elasticity in response to low water potential occurs principally in expanding tissues (Jones *et al.,* 1981).

Low leaf water potentials caused cell walls to thicken in cotton (Cutler *et al.,* 1977) and this presumably modified their elasticity. The inelastic nature of drought-resistant plants such as *Acacia harpaphylla,* as shown from moisture release curves (Slatyer, 1960), suggests that cell wall structure and thickness contribute to turgor maintenance and Turner (1980) suggests that they may even override contributions arising from osmotic adjustment.

Generalizations about the importance of cell wall elasticity in maintaining turgor pressure in shrubs are limited by the lack of research in this area. Furthermore, the influence of water deficits on tissue elasticity is also modified by changes in cell size as the tissue water potential is reduced. Small cells appear to have more elastic walls than large cells (Steudle *et al.,* 1977).

3. Cell Size

The size of cells is often reduced in plants that have developed under water stress conditions (Evenari *et al.,* 1971; IIjin, 1957). Nobel (1980) observed a 50% increase in the ratio of leaf mesophyll surface area to total leaf area (A^{mes}/A) in the shrub *Encelia farinosa* under water stress conditions. Leaf thickness was not changed; therefore, the increase in A^{mes}/A was due to more mesophyll cells with a smaller size. Cutler *et al.* (1977) measured solutes per cell in leaves of cotton plants grown under stress conditions and found a reduction in both cell size and osmotic potential in the stressed plants. This suggests that the reduced cell size observed in *E. farinosa* during water stress could be associated with reduced osmotic potential. However, as indicated previously (Section IV,A,2), reduced osmotic potentials are not wholly consequent upon small cell size, and tissue elasticity changes could also contribute to the observed changes in osmotic potential.

4. Negative Turgor?

Negative turgor in the sense of tension exists in the xylem, but can leaves of shrubs maintain negative turgor? Substantial negative turgor potentials have been reported for *Acacia* (Slatyer, 1960), *Larrea* (Odening, 1970), and *Artemisia* (Kappen *et al.,* 1972). This is due in part because turgor potential is deduced as the difference between water potential and osmotic potential and because the magnitude of osmotic potential is underestimated (Tyree, 1976). In plots of the reciprocal of leaf water potential vs. relative water content, Tyree (1976) found no evidence for negative turgor in *Acacia aneura* or *Ceratonia siliqua,* nor did he find evidence for a significant matric potential.

B. Desiccation Tolerance

Desiccation tolerance refers to the capacity of protoplasm to withstand extreme desiccation without irreversible injury (Kramer and Kozlowski, 1979). Woody plants such as creosote bush, sagebrush, acacias, and shrubs of the Mediterranean maquis and California chaparral have considerable dehydration tolerancee (Kramer and Kozlowski, 1979). The degree of dehydration varies among species. Almond leaves can be dried to a saturation deficit of 70%, olive to 60%, and fig to 25% before injury occurs (Oppenhiemer, 1932). *Larrea* leaves produced during dry weather can be dried to a saturation deficit of 50% (Runyon, 1936). Tolerance of protoplasm to desiccation was attributed as the reason why post oak survive a level of extreme desiccation that would be fatal to white or red oak (Bourdeau, 1954). However, Levitt (1972) has concluded that the capacity to avoid or postpone desiccation is more important than the capacity for tolerance.

Low osmotic potential has been regarded as an adaptation to water stress (Section IV, A, I) and it is obtained with accumulated sugars in stressed *Quercus* seedlings (Osonubi and Davies, 1978). Sugars are also known to generally protect plant cells against a variety of stress injuries (Url, 1957; Parker, 1972). This protective effect may be due to the association of sugar molecules with membrane structures (Lee-Stadelmann and Stadelmann, 1979), whereby they may replace water removed by dehydration. It is also possible that sugar may serve as an energy source in extending cell viability or protecting proteins (Klotz, 1958) in the cytoplasm (Lee-Stadelmann and Stadelmann, 1979). Sugars appear to accumulate in the cytoplasm and not the vacuole (Levitt, 1972) and may exert beneficial effects for membranes and cytoplasmic proteins.

Considerable changes in membrane permeability in drought-tolerant cells (Lee-Stadelmann and Stadelmann, 1976) suggest that hormonal regulation is involved in membrane permeability (Livne and Vaadia, 1972). Cytokinin accumulation in stressed plants is thought to be involved in protoplasmic drought tolerance (Lee-Stadelmann and Stadelmann, 1979). Resistance of fine, protoplasmic structures to drought stress has been shown in the photosynthetic apparatus of creosote bush produced in a dry habitat compared to a less resistant apparatus in a moist habitat (Mooney *et al.*, 1977a).

V. Summary

This chapter has briefly reviewed physiological adaptations and responses by shrubs that contribute to drought resistance. For more discussion on photosynthetic and water-use responses to water deficits, the reader is referred elsewhere in this volume. There is much more to be learned about the effects of water stress on shrub physiological processes, particularly regarding the importance of osmotic adjustment and protoplasmic tolerance to desiccation. The various forms of solutes and their accumulation may reflect major changes in metabolic patterns or solute translocation. Changes in metabolism and translocation may also reflect a redirection toward desiccation tolerance. For example, sugar accumulation resulting from reduced metabolism and translocation could provide desiccation tolerance to protoplasm by its association with dehydrated membranes. Walter and Stadelmann (1974) have shown that xeromorphic shrubs have a significant capacity for solute accumulation. In addition to their osmotic properties, these solutes may have a more subtle, biochemical significance that has not been previously recognized.

References

Aldon, E. F. (1975). Endomycorrhizae enhance survival and growth of fourwing saltbush on coal mine spills. *U.S., For. Serv., Res. Note RM* **RM–294.**
Barbour, M. G. (1969). Age and space distribution of the desert shrub *Larrea divaricata. Ecology* **50,** 679–685.
Barr, M. L. (1979). Drought stress and proline levels in native xeric plants. *Plant Physiol.* **63,** Suppl., 139.
Bennert, W. H., and Mooney, H. A. (1979). The water relations of some desert plants in Death Valley, California. *Flora (Jena)* **168,** 405–427.
Bourdeau, P. F. (1954). Oak seedling ecology determining segregation of species in Piedmont oak–hickory forests. *Ecol. Monogr.* **24,** 297–320.
Caldwell, M. M. (1975). Primary production of grazing lands. *In* "Photosynthesis and Productivity in Different Environments, IBP3" (J. P. Cooper, ed.), pp. 41–73. Cambridge Univ. Press, London and New York.

Caldwell, M. M., and Fernandez, O. A. (1975). Dynamics of Great Basin shrub root systems. *In* "Environmental Physiology of Desert Organisms" (N. F. Hadley, ed.), pp. 38–51. Dowden, Hutchison & Ross, Stroudsburg, Pennsylvania.

Call, C. A. (1981). Effects of endomycorrhizae on the establishment and growth of native shrubs on paraho processed oil shale and disturbed native soil. Ph.D. Dissertation, Utah State University, Logan.

Call, C. A., and McKell, C. M. (1984). Field establishment of fourwing saltbush in processed oil shale and disturbed native soil as influenced by V A Mycorrhizae. *Great Basin Nat.* **44** (2), 363–371.

Camacho-B., S. E., Hall, A. E., and Kaufman, M. R. (1974). Efficiency and regulation of water transport in some woody and herbaceous species. *Plant Physiol.* **54**, 169–172.

Campbell, G. S., and Harris, G. A. (1977). Water relations and water use patterns for *Artemisia tridentata* Nutt. in wet and dry years. *Ecology* **58**, 652–659.

Carlquist, S. (1975). "Ecological Strategies of Xylem Evolution." Univ. of California Press, Berkeley.

Chung, H. H., and Kramer, P. J. (1975). Absorption of water and ^{32}P through suberized and unsuberized roots of loblolly pine. *Can. J. For. Res.* **5**, 229–235.

Clarkson, D. T., Robards, A. W., and Sanderson, J. (1971). The tertiary endodermis in barley roots: Fine structure in relation to radial transport of ions and water. *Planta* **96**, 292–305.

Cunningham, G. L., and Strain, B. R. (1969). An ecological significance of seasonal leaf variability in a desert shrub. *Ecology* **50**, 400–408.

Cutler, J. M., Rains, D. W., and Loomis, R. S. (1977). The importance of cell size in water relations of plants. *Plant Physiol.* **40**, 255–260.

Davies, F. S., and Lakso, A. N. (1979). Diurnal and seasonal changes in leaf water potential components and elastic properties in response to water stress in apple trees. *Physiol. Plant.* **46**, 109–114.

Duhme, F. (1974). Die kennzeichnung der okologischen Konstitution von Geholzen im Hinblick auf den Wasserhausalt. *Diss. Bot.* **28**, 1–43.

Duisburg, P. C. (1952). Some relationships between xerophytism and the content of resin, nordihydroquaiaretic acid, and protein of *Larrea divaricata* Cav. *Plant Physiol.* **27**, 69–77.

Dumbroff, E. B., and Peirson, D. R. (1971). Probable sites for passive movement of ions across the endodermis. *Can. J. Bot.* **49**, 35–35.

Dwyer, D. D., and DeGormo, H. C. (1970). Greenhouse productivity and water-use efficiency of selected desert shrubs and grasses under four soil-moisture levels. *N. M., Agric. Exp. Stn., Bull.* **570**, 1–15.

Esau, K. (1977). "Anatomy of Seed Plants." Wiley, New York.

Evenari, M., Shanan, L., and Tadmor, N. (1971). "The Negev: The Challenge of a Desert." Harvard Univ. Press, Cambridge, Massachusetts.

Evenari, M., Schulze, E. D., Kappen, L., Buuschbom, U., and Lange, O. L. (1975). Adaptive mechanisms in desert plants. *In* "Physiological Adaptation to the Environment" (F. J. Vernberg, ed.), pp. 111–129. Intext Educ. Publishers, New York.

Fischer, R. A., and Turner, N. C. (1978). Plant productivity in the arid and semiarid zones. *Annu. Rev. Plant Physiol.* **29**, 277–317.

Gerdemann, J. W. (1970). The significance of vesicular-arbuscular mycorrhizae on plant nutrition. *In* "Root Diseases of Soil-Borne Plant Pathogens" (T. A. Tousso, R. V. Bega, and P. E. Nelson, eds.) pp. 125–129. Univ. of California Press. Berkeley.

Green, P. B., Erickson, R. O., and Buggy, J. (1971). Metabolic and physical control of cell elongation rate. *Plant Physiol.* **47**, 423–430.

Halvorson, W. L., and Patten, D. T. (1974). Seasonal water potential changes in Sonoran Desert shrubs in relation to topography. *Ecology* **55**, 173–177.

Harley, J. L. (1971). Fungi in ecosystems. *J. Appl. Ecol.* **8**, 627–642.

Hellkvist, J., Richards, G. P., and Jarvis, P. G. (1974). Vertical gradients of water potential and tissue water relations in sitka spruce trees measured with the pressure chamber. *J. Appl. Ecol.* **11**, 637–668.

Hinckley, T. M., Duhme, F., Hinckley, A. R., and Richter, H. (1980). Water relations of drought hardy shrubs: Osmotic potential and stomatal reactivity. *Plant, Cell Environ.* **3**, 131–140.

Hsiao, T. C., Acevedo, E., Fereres, E., and Henderson, D. W. (1976). Stress metabolism: Water stress, growth, and osmotic adjustment. *Philos. Trans. R. Soc. London, Ser. B* **273**, 479–500.

Iljin, W. A. (1957). Drought resistance in plants and physiological processes. *Annu. Rev. Plant Physiol.* **8**, 257–274.

Jones, M. M., Turner, N. C., and Osmond, C. B. (1981). Mechanism of drought resistance *In* "The Physiology and Biochemistry of Drought Resistance in Plants" (L. G. Paleg and D. Aspinall, eds.), pp. 15–37. Academic Press, New York.

Kaplan, A., and Gale, J. (1972). Effect of sodium chloride salinity on the water balance of *Atriplex halimus. Aust. J. Biol. Sci.* **25**, 895–903.

Kappen, L., Lange, O. L., Schulze, E.-D., Evenari, M., and Buschbom, U. (1972). Extreme water stress and photosynthetic activity of the desert plant *Artemisia herba-alba* Asso. *Oecologia* **10**, 177–182.

Kappen, L., Oertli, J. J., Lange, O. L., Schulze, E. D., Evenari, M., and Buschbom, U. (1975). Seasonal and diurnal courses of water relations of the arids-active plant *Hammada scoparia* in the Negev Desert. *Oecologia* **21**, 175–192.

Karlic, H., and Richter, H. (1983). Developmental effects on leaf water relations of two evergreen shrubs (*Prunus laurocerasus* L. and *Ilex aquifolium* L.). *Flora (Jena)* **173**, 143–150.

Klotz, I. M. (1958). Protein hydration and behavior. *Science* **128**, 815–822.

Kramer, P. J. (1969). "Plant and Soil Water Relationships: A Modern Synthesis." McGraw-Hill, New York.

Kramer, P. J., and Bullock, H. C. (1966). Seasonal variations in the proportions of suberized and unsuberized roots of trees in relation to the absorption of water. *Am. J. Bot.* **53**, 200–204.

Kramer, P. J., and Kozlowski, T. T. (1979). "Physiology of Woody Plants." Academic Press, New York.

Kummerow, J. (1980). Adaptation of roots in water-stressed native vegetation. *In* "Adaptation of Plants to Water and High Temperature Stress" (N. C. Turner and P. J. Kramer, eds.), pp. 57–73. Wiley, New York.

Lee-Stadelmann, O. Y., and Stadelmann, E. J. (1979). Drought tolerance and protoplasmic qualities in mesophytic higher plants. *In* "Arid Land Plant Resources" (J. R. Goodin and D. K. Northington, eds.), pp. 501–528. Texas Tech Univ. Press, Lubbock.

Levitt, J. (1972). "Responses of Plants to Environmental Stresses." Academic Press, New York.

Levy, Y., and Krikun, J. (1980). Effect of vesicular-arbuscular mycorrhiza on *Citrus jambhiri* water relations. *New Phytol.* **85**, 25–31.

Lindsey, D. L., Cress, W. A., and Aldon, E. F. (1977). The effects of endomycorrhizae on growth of rabbit brush, fourwing saltbush, and corn in coal mine spoil material. *U.S. For. Serv., Res. Note RM* **RM–343.**

Livne, A., and Vaadia, Y. (1972). Water deficits and hormone relation. *In* "Water Deficits and Plant Growth" (T. T. Kozlowski, ed.), Vol. 3, pp. 255–275. Academic Press, New York.

Mabry, T. J., Difeo, D. R., Sakibara, M., Bohnstedt, C. F., and Seigler, D. (1977). The natural products chemistry of *Larrea*. *In* "Creosote Bush: Biology and Chemistry of *Larrea* in New World Deserts" (T. J. Mabry, J. H. Hunziker, and D. R. DiFoe, Jr., eds.), pp. 115–134. Dowden, Hutchinson & Ross, Stroudsburg, Pennsylvania.

Mexel, J., and Reid, C. P. P. (1973). The growth of selected mycorrhizal fungi in response to induced water stress. *Can. J. Bot.* **51**, 1579–1588.

Meyer, R. F., and Boyer, J. S. (1981). Osmoregulation, solute distribution, and growth in soybean seedlings having low water potentials. *Planta* **151**, 482–489.

Monson, R. K., and Smith, S. D. (1982). Seasonal water potential components of Sonoran Desert plants. *Ecology* **63**, 113–123.

Mooney, H. A., Bjorkman, O., and Collatz, G. J. (1977a). Photosynthetic acclimation to temperature and water stress in the desert shrub *Larrea divaricata*. *Year Book — Carnegie Inst. Washington* **76**, 328–335.

Mooney, H. A., Ehleringer, J., and Bjorkman, O. (1977b). The energy balance of leaves of the evergreen desert shrub *Atriplex hymenelytra*. *Oecologia* **29**, 301–310.

Nilsen, E. T., Rundel, P. W., and Sharifi, M. R. (1981). Summer water relations of the desert phreatophyte *Prosopis glandulosa* in the Sonoran Desert of Southern California. *Oecologia* **50**, 271–276.

Nobel, P. S. (1974). "Introduction to Biophysical Plant Physiology." W. H. Freeman, San Francisco.

Nobel, P. S. (1980). Leaf anatomy and water use efficiency. *In* "Adaption of plants to Water and High Temperature Stress" (N. C. Turner and P. J. Kramer, eds.), pp. 43–55. Wiley, New York.

Noy-Meir I., and Ginzburg, B. Z. (1967). An analysis of the water potential isotherm in plant tissue. *Aust. J. Biol Sci.* **20**, 695–721.

Odening, W. R. (1970). The effect of decreasing water potential on net CO_2 exchange of intact woody desert shrubs. Ph.D. Dissertation, Duke University, Durham, North Carolina.

Oppenhiemer, H. R. (1932). Zur Kenntnis der hochsomerlichen Wazzerbilanz mediterranean Geholze. *Ber. Dtsch. Bot. Ges.* **50**, 185–243.

Osonubi, O., and Davies, W. J. (1978). Solute accumulation in leaves and roots of woody plants subjected to water stress. *Oecologia* **32**, 323–332.

Parker, J. (1972). Protoplasmic resistance to water deficits. *In* "Water Deficits and Plant Growth" (T. T. Kozlowski, ed.), Vol. 3, pp. 125–176. Academic Press, New York.

Parsons, L. R., and Kramer, P. J. (1974). Diurnal cycling in root resistance to water movement. *Physiol. Plant.* **30**, 19–23.

Poole, D. K., and Miller, P. C. (1978). Water related characteristics of some evergreen sclerophyll shrubs in central Chile. *Oecol. Plant.* **13**, 289–299.

Powell, C. L., and Sithamparanathan, J. (1977). Mycorrhizae in hill country soils. IV. Infection rate in grass and legume species by indigenous mycorrhizal fungi under field conditions. *N. Z. J. Agric. Res.* **20**, 489–494.

Queen, W. H. (1967). Radial movement of water and ^{32}P through suberized and unsuberized roots of grape. Ph.D. Dissertation, Duke University, Durham, North Carolina.

Rhoades, D. F. (1977). The antiherbivore chemistry of *Larrea*. *In* "Creosote Bush: Biology and Chemistry of *Larrea* in New World Deserts" (T. J. Mabry, J. H. Hunziker, and D. R. DiFeo, Jr., eds.). pp. 135–175. Dowden, Hutchinson & Ross, Stroudsburg, Pennsylvania.

Richardson, S. G., and McKell, C. M. (1980). Water relations of *Atriplex canescens* as affected by the salinity and moisture percentage of processed oil shale. *Agron. J.* **72**, 946–950.

Richter, H., Duhme, F., Glatzel, G., Hinckley, T. M., and Karlic, H. (1980). Some limitations and applications of the pressure–volume curve technique in ecophysiological research. *In* "Plants and Their Atmospheric Environment" (J. Grace, E. D. Ford, and P. G. Jarvis, eds.), pp. 263–272. Blackwell, Oxford.

Runyon, E. H. (1934). The organization of the creosote bush with respect to drought. *Ecology* **15**, 128–138.

Runyon, E. H. (1936). Ratio of water content to dry weight in leaves of the creosote bush. *Bot. Gaz. (Chicago)* **97**, 518–533.

Safir, G. R., Boyer, J. S., and Gerdeman, J. W. (1971). Mycorrhizal enhancement of water transport in soybean. *Science* **172**, 581–585.

Sands, R., and Theodorou, C. (1978). Water uptake by mycorrhizae roots of radiata pine seedlings. *Aust. J. Plant Physiol.* **5**, 301–309.

Saunier, R. E., Hull, H. M., and Ehrenreich, J. H. (1968). Aspects of drought tolerance in creosotebush (*Larrea divaricata*). *Plant Physiol.* **43**, 695–721.

Shreve, F., and Mallery, T. D. (1933). The relation of caliche to desert plants. *Soil Sci.* **35**, 99–113.

Smith, W. K., and Nobel, P. S. (1977). Influences of seasonal changes in leaf morphology on water-use efficiency for three desert broadleaf shrubs. *Ecology* **58**, 1033–1043.

Slatyer, R. O. (1960). Aspects of the tissue water relationships of an important arid zone species (*Acacia aneura* F. Meull.) in comparison with two mesophytes. *Bull. Res. Counc. Isr.* **82**, 159–168.

Staffeldt, E. E., and Voight, K. B. (1975). Mycorrhizae of desert plants. *Desert Biome Res. Memo.* **75–37**, 1–7.

Steudle, E., Zimmerman, U., and Lüttge, U. (1977). Effect of turgor pressure and cell size on the wall elasticity of plant cells. *Plant Physiol.* **59**, 285–289.

Stoker, R., and Weatherley, P. E. (1971). The influence of the root system on the relationship between the rate of transpiration and depression of leaf water potential. *New Phytol.* **70**, 547–554.

Strain, B. R. (1969). Seasonal adaptations in photosynthesis and respiration in four desert shrubs growing *in situ*. *Ecology* **50**, 511–513.

Strugger, S. (1949). "Prakticum der Zell- und Gewebephysiologie der Planzer." Springer-Verlag, Berlin and New York.

Syvertsen, J. P., Cunningham, G. L., and Feather, T. V. (1975). Anomalous diurnal patterns of stem xylem water potentials in *Larrea tridentata*. *Ecology* **56**, 1423–1428.

Theodorou, C. (1978). Soil moisture and the mycorrhizal association of *Pinus radiata* D. Don. *Soil Biol. Biochem.* **10**, 33–37.

Trappe, J. M. (1977). Selection of fungi for ectomycorrhizal inoculation in nurseries. *Annu. Rev. Phytopathol.* **15**, 203–222.

Turner, N. C. (1979). Drought resistance and adaptation to water deficits in crop plants. *In* "Stress Physiology in Crop Plants" (H. Mussel and R. C. Staples, eds.), pp. 343–372.

Turner N. C. (1980). Drought resistance and adaptation to water deficits in crop plants. *In* "Adaptation of Plants to Water and High Temperature Stress" (N. C. Turner and P. J. Kramer, eds.), pp. 43–372. Wiley, New York.

Turner, N. C., and Jones, M. M. (1980). Turgor maintenance by osmotic adjustment: A review and evaluation. *In* "Adaptation of Plants to Water and High Temperature Stress" (N. C. Turner and P. J. Kramer, eds.) pp. 87–103. Wiley, New York.

Tyree, M. T. (1976). Negative turgor pressure in plant cells: Fact or fallacy? *Can. J. Bot.* **54**, 2738–2746.

Tyree, M. T., and Jarvis, P. G. (1982). Water in tissues and cells. *In* "Physiological Plant Ecology. II. Water Relations and Carbon Assimilation" (O. L. Lange, P. S. Nobel, C. B. Osmond, and H. Ziegler eds.), Vol. 12B, pp. 35–77. Springer-Verlag, Berlin.

Url, W. (1957). Zur Kenntris der Todeszoner im konzentrations gest uften Resistenzversuch. *Physiol. Plant.* **10,** 318–327.

Wallace, A., Romney, E. M., and Cha, J. W. (1980). Depth distribution of roots of some perennial plants in the Nevada test site area of the Mojave Desert. *Great Basin Nat. Mem.* **4,** 201–207.

Walter, H., and Stadelmann, E. (1974). A new approach to water relations of desert plants. *In* "Desert Biology" (G. W. Brown, ed.), Vol. 2, pp. 213–310. Academic Press, New York.

Weatherly, P. E. (1982). Water uptake and flow in roots. *In* "Physiological Plant Ecology, II. Encylopedia of Plant Physiology" (O. L. Lange, P. S. Nobel, C. B. Osmond, and H. Ziegler, eds.), Vol. 12B, pp. 79–108. Springer-Verlag, Berlin.

Wenkert, W., Lemon, E. R., and Sinclair, T. R. (1978). Water content–potential relationship in soybean: Changes in component potentials for mature and immature leaves under field conditions. *Ann. Bot. (London)* [N. S.] **42,** 295–307.

Went, F. W. (1955). The ecology of desert plants. *Sci. Am.* **192,** 68–75.

Woodell, S. R. J., Mooney, H. A., and Hill, A. J. (1969). The behavior of *Larrea divaricata* (creosote bush) in response to rainfall in California. *J. Ecol.* **57,** 37–44.

Wynn Jones, R. G., and Storey, R. (1981). Betaines. *In* "The Physiology and Biochemistry of Drought Resistance in Plants" (L. G. Paleg and D. Aspinall, eds.), pp. 171–204. Academic Press, New York.

17

Temperature Stress Adaptation

Ronald J. Newton
Joseph R. Goodin

I. Introduction

Shrubs do not constitute either a taxonomic or an evolutionary category, and their evolution from either trees or herbs probably occurred many times during the evolutionary history of flowering plants (Stebbins, 1972). Shrubs exemplify a great plasticity in response to temperature extremes that has been largely responsible for their survival as a life-form. They reach their most northerly distribution in the arctic tundra, where temperatures lower than −50°C are experienced (Billings, 1964), and they are found in Death Valley, California, where they are subjected to a temperature of over 50°C (Bjorkman et al., 1980).

Many physiological processes in plants are influenced by temperature, including respiration, cell enlargement, division, and photosynthesis; therefore temperature is a major factor in determining how a shrub functions. Shrub temperature, as in any plant, is determined by its total environment and the principle of the conservation of energy applies whereby the energy balance of a shrub exists in an environment with many energy fluxes. The energy input minus the energy output is equal to the energy storage (Nobel, 1983). The various contributions to the energy balance of a shrub are as follows:

absorbed solar irradiation, absorbed infrared irradiation from surroundings	emitted infrared radiation, heat convection, heat conduction, heat loss accompanying water evaporation	photosynthesis, other metabolism, shrub temperature changes
Energy into shrub −	Energy out of shrub	= Energy storage by shrub

Solar and infrared irradiation, heat conduction and convection, and transpiration all contribute to the shrub temperature and/or energy storage. Although very little energy is stored (or released) in the form of leaf temperature changes in terms of the total energy budget (Nobel, 1983), extreme leaf temperature changes have great consequences on shrub physiological processes such as photosynthesis, enzyme activity, and growth rates.

Shrub temperature is an important parameter of the energy budget because the direction and magnitude of heat exchange that comes from irradiational and transpirational cooling are all dictated by a combination of temperature and atmospheric conditions. Shrubs must, in effect, balance their energy budget by balancing transpiration against their temperature. Shrub transpiration and temperature are known to be functions of air temperature, irradiation, wind speed, relative humidity, leaf dimensions, and diffusive resistance.

Extremes in air temperature are referred to as *heat* and *cold*. They impair the vital functions of shrubs and limit their distribution. Hot and cold air temperatures expose shrubs to unfavorable conditions and "trigger" physiological responses within their tissues. These physiological mechanisms of resistance in response to extreme temperatures enable shrubs to maintain productivity and/or survive. The purpose of this review is to present recent information concerning these physiological mechanisms. The terminology used in this review follows that suggested by Levitt (1980).

II. Resistance to Temperature Stress

The term *temperature resistance* is used to describe physiological and biochemical processes that contribute to the capacity of shrubs to survive and reproduce while subjected to extremes in temperature. Two types of temperature stress resistance have been described by Levitt (1980) (see Fig. 1). They are *avoidance* and *tolerance*. Avoidance of extreme temperature stress is the process of preventing or decreasing the penetration of the stress into the tissues; it is accomplished by the shrub whereby thermodynamic equilibrium is avoided with the temperature extremes. The shrub is able to exclude the temperature stress, by means of a physical, chemical, or metabolic barrier that insulates the cells from temperature extremes.

A shrub may also be resistant to temperature stress even though the stress enters its tissues. This resistance is called *tolerance*. Tolerance is made possible because of the ability of tissues to come to thermodynamic equilibrium with the stress without suffering injury.

Cold resistance comprises two components: *chilling* and *freezing*. *Chilling resistance* deals with plant response to low temperatures above the tissue freezing point and *freezing resistance* concerns plant responses below the freezing point. *Heat resistance* is considered to occur when plants withstand temperatures at 15°C and above (Levitt, 1980).

At very high air temperatures, shrub temperatures may be considerably lower than that of the air. In this way shrubs may exhibit *high-temperature avoidance*. When shrubs survive in spite of their internal temperatures being above that of air, they are considered to possess *high-temperature tolerance*.

Adaptive changes to chilling and frost temperatures, in terms of both survival and metabolic efficiency, are termed *acclimation* or *hardening* (Levitt, 1980).

III. Responses to Chilling Temperature

Shrubs from temperate climates routinely survive exposure to chilling temperatures and, therefore, are fully resistant to chilling. Shrubs from tropical and semitropical climates, on the other hand, are variable in their chilling resistance. Only a few studies on chilling resistance in shrubs have been conducted. Sellschop and Salmon (1928) demonstrated a direct sensitivity to chilling temperature in *Gossypium* after 12 hours. In contrast, *Coffea* leaves showed rapid discoloration when plants were subjected to temperatures of 3°C for 6 hours (Franco, 1958). Less direct visual injuries observed after several days of chilling exposure were noted in *Eranthemum* and *Boehmeria* (Molisch, 1897).

Symptoms of chilling vary with the tissue involved. During seed hydration in *Gossypium,* the radicle tip aborted, and during seedling growth, chilling temperatures resulted in damage to the root cortex (Christiansen, 1963). Subsequent studies showed that injury during seed hydration could

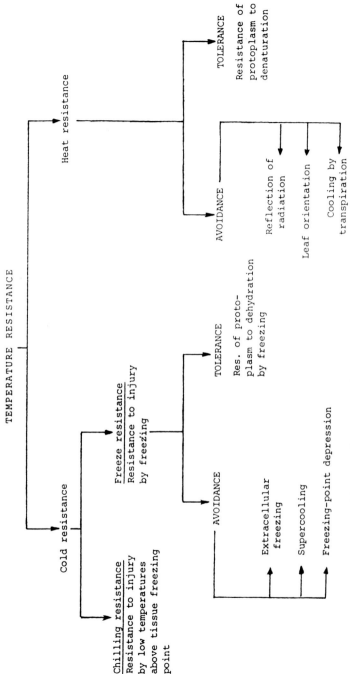

Figure 1. Components of temperature resistance (After Levitt, 1980.)

be avoided if the seed had first been allowed a brief hydration at elevated temperature before chilling (Christiansen, 1967). Furthermore, chilling injury during seed hydration showed cultivar variation, suggesting heritable control (Christiansen, 1969).

Chilling temperatures of 5°C caused wilting in light-grown *Gossypium* seedlings (McWilliam *et al.*, 1982). The 5°C temperature appeared to reduce hydraulic conductivity of the root membranes and stomatal control in leaves. Subsequently, reduced water flow and continued transpiration (because of slow stomatal closure) resulted in a rapid decline of leaf water potential. The deleterious effects of low temperature on root hydraulic conductivity appear to be ameliorated by abscisic acid (Markhart, 1984). Abscisic acid has been shown to prevent chilling injury in *Gossypium* (Rikin *et al.*, 1979).

The direct, primary effect of chilling appears to be on membrane-associated enzyme systems (Lyons *et al.*, 1979). In addition, chilling also affects membrane proteins, cytoskeletal proteins, and soluble enzyme systems (Graham and Patterson, 1982). These events appear to cause metabolic imbalances and solute leakage leading to injury. Chilling decreased RNA, protein, lipid-soluble phosphate, ATP, and other nucleotides in *Gossypium* seedlings (Guinn, 1971; Stewart and Guinn, 1969, 1971). In herbaceous plants soluble proteins generally increase at low temperatures (Kacperska-Palacz, 1978), but this has not been documented in shrubs.

Many of the effects of temperature on enzymes probably relate to their activity as determined by the maximum rate, V_{max}, and the affinity constant, K_m. Furthermore, although most enzyme systems are stable at low temperatures, some are inactivated by chilling. The photosynthetic enzyme PEP carboxylase is sensitive to low temperatures and the K_m of several temperate alpine and temperate plants is low at temperatures ranging from 10° to 1.5°C according to Graham *et al.* (1979). However, the kinetics of carbon assimilation through the intermediates of the C_4 pathway are not disrupted at low temperatures in both warm- and cool-desert species of *Atriplex* (Caldwell *et al.*, 1977), suggesting that PEP carboxylase activity in these shrubs is not affected by low temperatures.

Sudden drops in temperature appear to cause physical changes in mitochondrial lipids and subsequent changes in respiration (Graham and Patterson, 1982). These can be determined by plotting respiratory activity as a function of the reciprocal of the absolute temperature and observing a "break" or discontinuity in the Arrhenius plot (Lyons and Raison, 1970). Respiration of *Cornus stolonifera* callus using this method showed chilling injury below 13°C, but not in isolated mitochondria (Yoshida and Tagawa, 1979). This suggests that mitochondrial respiration is not the limiting factor in response to chilling temperatures and that other forms of respiration are equally important. The cyanide (CN)-insensitive alternate pathway accounted for a major part of the mitochondrial respiration in *C. stolonifera* callus, and in the presence of SHAM (salicylhydroxamic acid), which is an inhibitor of this pathway, a discontinuity in the Arrhenius plot was obtained. This suggests that the alternate CN-insensitive pathway is very important in this shrub when exposed to chilling temperatures and it may also reflect cold-induced membrane reorganization or adaptation.

IV. Responses to Freezing Temperature

Temperature stresses during late spring and early fall frosts, low midwinter minima, and rapid temperature changes cause various types of injury that are associated directly or indirectly with freezing water in shrub tissues. These include sunscald on thin-barked species, winterburn to evergreen foliage, blackheart and frost cracking in xylem, blossom kill, and death of vegetative shoots, buds, and bark (Burke *et al.*, 1976). Freezing resistance changes markedly with season and stage of development. For example, many cold-tolerant shrubs of the Rocky Mountain West are especially susceptible to freezing temperatures during the seedling stage (Wasser, 1982). Also, cold-tolerant woody-plant species can survive $-196°C$ during winter dormancy but may be killed at $-3°C$ during active spring growth (Burke *et al.*, 1976). A common winter injury is the killing of flower buds, whereas leaf buds usually survive freezing temperatures.

Injury to shrub roots can be quite common in colder regions of the world. Young roots can be lost to low temperatures without severe adverse effects on shoots (Havis, 1976). Killing of secondary, mature roots results in reduced top growth. *Ilex* sp. had 50% of the root system killed at $-6°$ to $-9°C$, whereas *Rhododendron* sp. roots generally were not killed until temperatures of $-12°$ to $-18°C$ were reached (Havis, 1976).

The temperature at which shrubs are killed by freezing also depends on their physiological state and the degree of preconditioning or hardening.

Resistance to Freezing

Direct injury due to freezing can occur only as a result of intracellular freezing. When plant cells freeze and ice forms inside the living protoplasm, this disrupts the integrity of the cell and causes death. Shrubs have evolved several mechanisms for resisting freezing temperatures. For convenience, these can be classified into *avoidance* and *tolerance* mechanisms (Levitt, 1980).

1. Avoidance

Many deciduous shrubs avoid freezing in some, but not all, of their tissues by *supercooling* to low temperatures (Burke *et al.*, 1976). For example, deep supercooling to −41°C occurs in dormant winter buds of *Rhododendron kosterianum* Schneid (George *et al.*, 1974) with only slight supercooling of −2° to −6°C occurring in stems. Supercooling to low temperatures without freezing probably occurs because of a lack of nucleating substances necessary for ice initiation and ice growth in the tissues (Burke *et al.*, 1976). In the absence of nucleating substances, pure water can supercool to −38°C. Bud tissues and xylem parenchyma cells apparently lack ice nucleating substances and they supercool to temperatures around −40°C. When ice nucleation does occur in cells that have been supercooled, freezing is probably intracellular and lethal (Burke *et al.*, 1976). In addition to the absence of nucleators, small cell size, low moisture content, and the presence of antinucleators (freezing inhibitors) also contribute to the capacity of the tissue to supercool to low temperatures before freezing (Levitt, 1980). George (1983) hypothesizes that xylem cell wall porosity contributes to deep supercooling and freezing avoidance.

It appears that *supercooling resistance* to freezing, particularly in buds and xylem parenchyma cells, governs the northern distribution of shrubs (such as *Rhododendron kosterianum*) just as it does with 47 tree species native to the eastern deciduous forest of North America (George *et al.*, 1974). Furthermore, data suggest that shrub species of the boreal forest of North America (such as *Cornus stolonifera*) have no supercooling mechanisms (George *et al.*, 1974) and can survive freezing to −196°C, which extends their range to the arctic zones. At these low temperatures, all the freezable water is frozen extracellularly (Sakai and Yoshida, 1967). Therefore, *avoidance of intracellular freezing* by freezing extracellularly is a second mechanism by which shrubs can survive freezing temperatures. Since there is no extracellular space in xylem parenchyma cells, supercooling may be the only resistance mechanism available to this tissue. Supercooling of xylem parenchyma is also favored by the small size of their protoplasts (because of thick cell walls) and their low water content (Levitt, 1980).

Shrubs may also avoid freezing by *maintaining the freezing point of their cells below that of their environment.* Shrubs with high solute concentrations, particularly halophilic shrubs, have large freezing point depressions. Osmotic potentials in *Atriplex confertifolia* of −20 to −200 bars (Harris, 1934) could theoretically lower the freezing point by approximately 1.5° to 16°C, whereas −30 to −73 bars of osmotic potential in *Artemisia tridentata* (Harris, 1934) would lower it by 2.5° to 6°C. Although solute accumulation may not provide complete freezing avoidance, in combination with other resistance factors it may be very important.

In some tissues, shrub cells have little or no water for freezing (seeds, pollen, fall-hardened buds) and therefore avoid freezing.

2. Tolerance

Because of piercing of membranes by internal ice crystals, which is lethal, tolerance of intracellular freezing is not available to shrubs; therefore, tolerance to freezing is accomplished extracellularly. This is, in effect, a form of drought tolerance because removal of water from cells to extracellular ice imposes a desiccation stress on protoplasm. However, damage cannot be attributed solely to desiccation, but most likely includes lipid-phase separations and/or chilling injury.

In midwinter, hardy shrubs can survive extreme dehydration when freezable water crystallizes extracellularly. *Cornus stolonifera* tolerates extreme temperatures of −196°C when fully acclimated by freezing extracellularly (George *et al.*, 1974). Other woody species of *Betula, Salix,* and *Populus* tolerate extreme low temperatures also by extracellular freezing (George *et al.*, 1974). The unfreezable (bound) water fraction in winter stems of such species is about 30% of the total water in the tissue, but the relationship between bound water and acclimation is not clear (Burke *et al.*, 1974).

Dehydration due to extracellular freezing causes injury to cells through protein denaturation. Membranes and enzymes become less functional and membrane-mediated phosphorylation is disrupted (Burke *et al.*, 1976).

V. Acclimation (Hardening) to Low Temperature

Acclimation or hardening results in a lowering of the temperature at which the shrub is damaged or killed by chilling/freezing temperatures. For example, cowberry (*Vaccinium vitis idea*) is killed at −2°C in the unhardened state and at −22°C when hardened, and *Rhododendron* species survive freezing temperatures at nearly −30°C when hardened (Ulmer, 1937). The degree of acclimation is determined by the developmental stage of the shrub interacting with several environmental factors. Hardy woody-plant species (*Betula, Populus,* and *Salix*) develop maximum hardiness in the winter and thus acclimate in response to low temperatures, but light, water, and mineral nutrients also have a role (Levitt, 1980). The suppression of short-day cold acclimation in *Cornus stolonifera* by interruption of dark periods with red light (Williams *et al.*, 1972) indicates a relationship between acclimation, photoperiod, and development. McKenzie *et al.* (1974) indicate that cold acclimation in this species is phytochrome mediated. Acclimation in *Pyracantha* was not controlled by red irradiation. Water stress for 7 days lowered the freezing tolerance temperature in *C. stolonifera* from $-3°$ to $-11°C$ (Chen *et al.*, 1975, 1977).

According to Weiser (1970), woody plants typically undergo three sequential stages in acclimation to cold. They are: (1) cessation of growth and metabolic changes that condition the plant to respond to low temperature during the next stage; (2) induction by freezing or near-freezing temperatures; and (3) triggering of changes by very low temperatures ($-30°$ to $-50°C$). Stage 1 is influenced by decreasing day length and possibly translocatable, hardiness-promoting factors (Weiser, 1970). Stage 2 includes changes in sugars, proteins, amino acids, and organic acids. The final stage appears to be a physical process involving the binding of water.

During cold acclimation, RNA and proteins increased in frost-resistant Korean boxwood (*Buxus microphylla*) but DNA changed very little and ribonuclease decreased (Gusta and Weiser, 1972). Ribosome patterns in cold-hardened and nonhardened tissues of black locust seedlings (*Robinia pseudoacacia*) were different (Bixby and Brown, 1975). In this species, there was also a general increase in phospholipids during acclimation that was associated with cell membrane proliferation (Siminovitch *et al.*, 1975).

The need for light and photosynthesis during cold acclimation is presumably related to sugar accumulation. Sugars are also partly derived from starch hydrolysis (Kramer and Kozlowski, 1979) and protect against freezing injury (Levitt, 1980) as well as depress the freezing point. The kinds of sugar that accumulate vary among species, but sucrose is most common (Kramer and Kozlowski, 1979).

VI. Responses to High Temperature

Death Valley, California, is one of the hottest environments on earth, where air temperatures reach over $50°C$. Typical shrub species native to Death Valley, (*Atriplex hymenelytra, Atriplex lentiformis, Larrea divaricata,* and *Tidestroma oblongifolia*) are physiologically adapted to high temperatures (Bjorkman *et al.*, 1980). While the native *Atriplex* species survived, *A. glabriuscula* and *A. sabulosa* from cooler habitats died when planted in Death Valley even though they were supplied with ample water (Bjorkman *et al.*, 1973). The lethality of high temperatures was due in part to injury to chloroplasts and disruption of photosynthetic processes (Bjorkman *et al.*, 1980).

A. Heat Stress Injury

A well-established heat injury in woody plants is bark burn of thin-barked species (Huber, 1935). The injury is thought to be due to overheating of the cambium, where temperatures of 55°C have been recorded (Levitt, 1980). Because temperatures of small leaves are closer to the air temperature than are large leaf temperatures, heat injury to larger leaves is first evident. Great danger of heat injury also occurs when soil is exposed to irradiation, reaching temperatures of over 60°C. A serious injury to seedlings of woody plants is the killing of a narrow strip of bark at the soil level (Munch, 1913, 1914). Young *Coffea* plants developed such an injury and died when subjected to soil temperatures exceeding 50°C (Franco, 1961). Ingram and Buchanan (1984) have established lethal temperatures for citrus rootstocks.

A complicating factor in heat stress injury is the sudden change of liquid water to vapor at temperatures that are not found under natural conditions. This will produce indirect stress injury, some of which is due to dehydration.

A result of heat stress often experienced by shrubs is growth inhibition (Levitt, 1980). The native *Atriplex* species (*A. hymenelytra* and *A. lentiformis*) of Death Valley have low periods of growth during the hotter times of the year. This is not due simply to water stress, because another shrub native to the same environment, *Tidestroma oblongifolia,* maintains its highest growth rates during the hottest part of the growing season (Bjorkman *et al.,* 1975). In these cases, inhibited growth is not a result of injury, which is often the case with more heat-susceptible shrubs.

B. Resistance to Heat Stress

The intense absorption of radiant energy by leaves and other plant parts usually results in a temperature higher than that of the transparent air. The term *avoidance* in the case of a heat-resistant plant does not necessarily mean that the plant temperature is lower than that of the air, but it simply means that the temperature is lower than that of a control, less-avoiding plant under the same environmental conditions (Levitt, 1980).

Heat tolerance is the ability of the organism to survive heat stress within its tissues. Lange and Lange (1963) found that avoidance was the main basis for heat resistance in woody plants characterized by mesomorphic leaf structure with a high transpiration rate and low heat tolerance. Hard-leaved, or sclerophyll, woody plants have a low transpiration rate and low heat avoidance, but they also have high heat tolerance.

1. Avoidance

Avoidance of heat by shrubs is accomplished by decreased respiration, decreased absorption of irradiation, and transpirational cooling. Of these three, the latter two appear to be the most important. Decreased absorption of irradiation can be brought about by leaf movements and reflectance.

Mooney *et al.* (1977) showed that vertically inclined leaves of *Atriplex hymenelytra* reduce absorbed irradiation in the middle of the day and increase it during the cooler, early morning and late afternoon. A leaf angle of 70° reduced the leaf temperature by 2 to 30 C° compared to a leaf angle of 0°.

Absorbed radiation is also reduced by the presence of hairs, surface wax, or salt, all of which increase leaf reflectance. Plants growing in arid habitats tend to have more hairs (pubescence) than those found in more mesic environments (Ehleringer, 1980). Hairs on the suffrutescent shrub *Encelia* result in decreased absorption of irradiation (Ehleringer, 1980). Pubescence in *E. farinosa* reduces absorptance by increasing leaf reflectance. A change in leaf absorptance from 50 to 15% by hairs is estimated to reduce midday leaf temperature by 5 C° with air temperature at 40°C (Ehleringer, 1980).

Increased reflectance in *Atriplex hymenelytra* is associated with high salt content in the leaves as well as leaf dehydration (Mooney *et al.*, 1977). This reflectance reduced leaf temperature 5 C° in horizontal leaves and 4 C° in steeply inclined leaves.

Several investigators have proposed that pubescence will increase the boundary layer resistance, modify diffusion of heat and mass transfer, and thus modify transpiration. Estimates of increase of boundary layer resistance for the heavily pubescent *Encelia farinosa* leaf indicate that hairs will have only a small effect on transpiration under natural conditions (Ehleringer, 1980). Therefore, it appears that leaf temperature, as affected by pubescence, is modified more by reflectance phenomena than by transpiration modifications.

Large leaves absorb more irradiation than small leaves and attain higher temperatures (Nobel, 1983). In Death Valley the area of *Atriplex hymenelytra* leaves produced during the cool season averaged over 5 cm^2, whereas those produced during the hot season were 2 to 3 cm^2 per leaf (Mooney *et al.*, 1977). Shrubs of the Mediterranean zone shed larger winter leaves and produce smaller leaves with the onset of the dry season, which provides them with a smaller absorbing surface and consequently a lower leaf temperature (Evenari *et al.*, 1971).

Transpirational cooling plays a relatively strong role in modifying leaf temperatures (Gates, 1963). Gates measured temperatures of 48°C in sunlit leaves of *Quercus macrocarpa* at an air temperature of 28°C, whereas shade leaves were 1.5 C° lower than the air temperature. He concluded that transpirational cooling was most important in this species with convection as a relatively inefficient process in temperature modification. Lange (1959) observed pronounced lowering of leaf temperatures of several woody species (*Acacia, Tamarix*) at air temperatures of 40°C and higher. The air temperatures were 5 to 10 C° above the heat-killing temperature.

In *Atriplex hymenelytra*, leaves oriented at a 70° angle had temperatures to 43° to 47°C and transpiration of 2.5 to 3.0 $\mu g/cm^2/sec$. These data suggest a strong correlation between transpiration and leaf temperature.

2. Tolerance

Heat tolerance varies from season to season and depends on environmental factors (temperature, light, moisture, nutrients) and on shrub characteristics. Seasonal cycles in heat tolerance have been observed in *Erica tetralix* with maxima during the summer and winter (Lange, 1965). A rise in heat tolerance of over 6 C° was shown during the summer with a maximum temperature of about 50°C reached before 50% of the leaves were killed. Young leaves of shrubs appear to be less heat tolerant than older ones. Young leaves of *Ilex aquifolium* had a heat-killing point of 46°C, whereas an older leaf was killed at 48°C (Lange, 1965).

The evergreen shrubs *Larrea divaricata* and *Atriplex hymenelytra* tolerate air temperatures of over 40°C for several months out of the year, thus starvation is prevented by continued photosynthesis. According to Mooney *et al.* (1978), photosynthetic rates in *L. divaricata* leaves with leaf temperatures at 40°C were similar to those at 20°C, indicating great heat tolerance of this species native to Death Valley. The acclimation to high temperature has been attributed to the increased stability of key components of the photosynthetic apparatus.

Although photosynthesis continues in these desert shrubs at high temperatures, injury due to starvation is also prevented by shrub adaptation with lower dark respiration rates in the summer compared to winter when both are measured at 25°C (Strain, 1969). This high compensation point associated with high temperatures is a well-demonstrated acclimation mechanism possessed by C_4 shrubs that allows them to continue to grow rapidly when exposed to high temperatures.

Metabolic adaptations are also developed during acclimation. *Atriplex lentiformis* plants from desert habitats have higher CO_2 uptake rates than those grown at lower temperatures. At low temperatures, the differences were associated with levels of RUDP carboxylase activity (Pearcy, 1977).

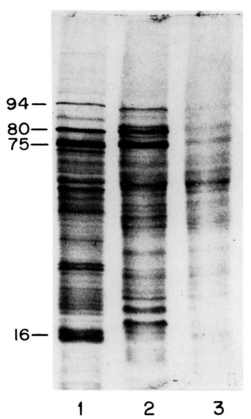

94—
80—
75—

16—

1   2   3

Figure 2. Autoradiogram of [^{35}S]methionine-labeled extracts after sodium dodecyl sulfate (SDS)–polyacrylamide (12.5–20% gradient) electrophoresis. Lane 1: Soybean seedlings transferred from 25° to 40°C for 30 min followed by 60 min at 40°C with [^{35}S]methionine. Lane 2: Vegetative shoots from 8-day-old jojoba seedlings grown at 25°C, transferred to 40°C for 30 min, followed by 90 min at 40°C with [^{35}S]methionine. Lane 3: Vegetative shoots of jojoba seedlings labeled at 25°C for 90 min with [^{35}S]methionine. The figures on the left are the molecular weights (in thousands) of the major soybean heat-shock proteins. (From M. Altschuler, C.-M. Xiao, and J. P. Mascarenhas, unpublished results.)

At higher temperatures, differences were due to decreased respiration rates and increased heat stability of the photosynthetic apparatus (Pearcy, 1977). Leaf lipids were also more saturated at higher temperatures (Pearcy, 1978).

Recently, it has been shown that heat-shock induces the production of proteins (HSP) whose exact function is unknown, but that are presumed to help the organism cope with altered biochemical demands of the elevated

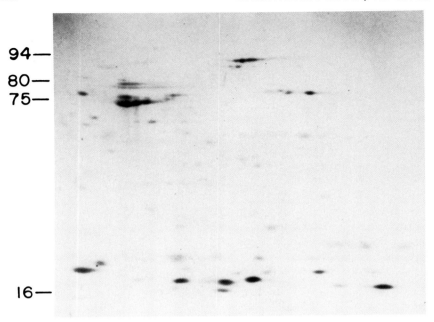

Figure 3.   Analysis of proteins synthesized by vegetative shoots of jojoba seedlings grown at 25°C, transferred to 40°C for 30 min, followed by labeling with [^{35}S]methionine for 90 min at 40°C. Autoradiogram of two-dimensional gel with the acidic end shown to the left. The isoelectric focusing gel contained pH 5–8 ampholytes and the second dimension was SDS, 12.5–20% polyacrylamide gradient gel. The numbers at the left are the molecular weights (in thousands) of the major soybean heat-shock proteins. (From M. Altschuler, C.-M. Xiao, and J. P. Mascarenhas, unpublished results.)

temperatures (Ashburner and Bonner, 1979). Raising the temperature from 25° to 37°C results in a rapid induction of mRNA synthesis within 1 hr. Additionally, the synthesis of most other mRNA's is suppressed. Heat-shock proteins were observed in *Jojoba* seedlings (M. Altschuler, C. M. Xiao, and J. P. Mascarenhas, unpublished results) when temperatures were elevated to 40°C for 2 hr (Figs. 2 and 3). Several new proteins were found with molecular weights of 75,000 to 94,000 and slightly above 16,000. When compared to soybean, new proteins in *Jojoba* were smaller in molecular weight (slightly larger than 16,000) (Fig. 2).

VII. Summary

There is an abundance of information concerning physiological responses to temperature in a few, select number of genera; for example, *Cornus*,

Atriplex, and *Larrea.* For a fuller understanding of temperature stress response mechanisms in shrubs, more studies are required on other species. Much can be learned about physiological tolerance responses to temperature change, particularly in regard to stress proteins and the role of membranes. Solutes that accumulate during temperature stress are suggested to have a protective function on cell membranes. Membrane stability is very sensitive to changes in temperature; these stability changes may be the process by which shrub physiological changes are mediated in response to environmental temperature fluctuations. The capacity of shrubs to respond to temperature extremes has been responsible for their evolutionary success and wide distribution over the earth.

References

Ashburner, M., and Bonner, K. K. (1979). The induction of gene activity in *Drosophila* by heat shock. *Cell (Cambridge, Mass.)* **17,** 241–254.

Billings, W. D. (1964). "Plants and the Ecosystem." Wadsworth, Belmont, California.

Bixby, J. A., and Brown, G. N. (1975). Ribosomal changes during induction of cold hardiness in black locust seedings. *Plant Physiol.* **56,** 617–621.

Bjorkman, O., Nobs, M., Berry, J., Mooney, H. A., Nicholson, F., and Catanzaro, B. (1973). Physiological adaptation to diverse environments: Approaches and facilities to study plant responses to contrasting thermal and water regimes. *Year Book—Carnegie Inst. Washington* **74,** 748–767.

Bjorkman, O., Mooney, H. A., and Ehleringer, J. (1975). Photosynthetic responses of plants from habitats with contrasting thermal environments. *Year Book—Carnegie Inst. Washington* **74,** 743–748.

Bjorkman, O., Badger, M. R., and Armond, P. A. (1980). Response and adaptation of photosynthesis to high temperatures. *In* "Adaptation of Plants to Water and High Temperature Stress" (N. C. Turner and P. J. Kramer, eds.), pp. 233–249. Wiley, New York.

Burke, M. J., Bryant, R. G., and Weiser C. J. (1974). Nuclear magnetic reasonance of water in cold acclimating red osier dogwood stem. *Plant Physiol.* **54,** 392–398.

Burke, M. J., Gusta, L. V., Quamme, H. A., Weiser, C. J., and Li, P. H. (1976). Freezing and injury in plants *Annu. Rev. Plant Physiol.* **27,** 507–528.

Caldwell, M. M., Osmond, C. B., and Nott, D. (1977). C_4 pathway photosynthesis at low temperature in cold-tolerant *Atriplex* species. *Plant Physiol.* **60,** 157–164.

Chen, P. M., Li, P. H., and Weiser, C. J. (1975). Induction of frost hardiness in red-osier dogwood stems by water stress. *HortScience* **10,** 372–374.

Chen, P. M., Li, P. H., and Burke, M. J. (1977). Induction of frost hardiness in stem cortical tissues of *Cornus stolonifera* Michx. by water stress. I. Unfrozen water in cortical tissues and water status in plants and soil. *Plant Physiol.* **59,** 236–239.

Christiansen, M. N. (1963). Influence of chilling upon seedling development of cotton. *Plant Physiol.* **38,** 520–522.

Christiansen, M. N. (1967). Periods of sensitivity to chilling in germinating cotton. *Plant Physiol.* **42,** 431–433.

Christiansen, M. N. (1969). Exudation by cotton seedling radicles at low temperature. *Proc. Natl. Cotton Counc. Beltwide Cotton Prod. Res. Conf.*, January 7–8, pp. 127–130.

Ehleringer, J. (1980). Leaf morphology and reflectance in relation to water and temperature stress. *In* "Adaptation of Plants to Water and High Temperature Stress" (N. C. Turner and P. J. Kramer, eds.), pp. 233–249. Wiley, New York.

Evenari, M., Shanan, L., and Tadmor, N. (1971). "The Negev: The Challenge of a Desert." Harvard Univ. Press, Cambridge, Massachusetts.

Franco, C. M. (1961). Lesao do colo cafeeiro, causada pelo calor. *Bragentia* **20,** 645–652.

Gates, D. M. (1963). Leaf temperature and energy exchange. *Arch. Meteorol., Geophys. Bioklimatol., Ser. B* **12,** 321–326.

George, M. F. (1983). Freezing avoidance by deep supercooling in woody plant xylem: Preliminary data on the importance of cell wall porosity. *In* "Current Topics in Plant Biochemistry and Physiology" (D. D. Randall, D. G. Blevins, R. L. Larson, and B. J. Rapp, eds.), Vol. 2, pp. 84–95. Univ. of Missouri Press, Columbia.

George, M. F., Burke, M. J., Pellet, H. M., and Johnson, A. G. (1974). Low temperature exotherms and woody plant distribution. *HortScience* **9,** 519–522.

Graham, D., and Patterson, B. D. (1982). Responses of plants to low, non-freezing temperatures: Proteins, metabolism, and acclimation. *Annu. Rev. Plant Physiol.* **33,** 347–372.

Graham, D., Hockley, D. G., and Patterson, B. D. (1979). Temperature effects on phosphoenol pyruvate carboxylase from chilling-sensitive and chilling-resistant plants. *In* "Low Temperature Stress in Crop Plants: The Role of the Membrane" (J. M. Lyons, D. Graham, and J. K. Raison, eds.), pp. 453–461. Academic Press, New York.

Guinn, G. (1971). Changing sugar, starch, RNA, protein and liquid soluble phosphate in leaves of cotton at low temperatures. *Crop Sci.* **11,** 262–265.

Gusta, L. V., and Weiser, C. J. (1972). Nucleic acid and protein charges in relation to cold acclimation and freezing injury of Korean boxwood leaves. *Plant Physiol.* **49,** 91–96.

Harris, J. A. (1934). "The Physico-chemical properties of Plant Saps in Relation to Phytogeography. Data on Native Vegetation in Its Natural Environment," pp. 65–70. Univ. of Minnesota Press, Minneapolis.

Havis, J. R. (1976). Root hardiness of woody ornamentals. *HortScience* **11**(4), 385–386.

Huber, H. (1935). Der Warmehaushalt der Pflanzen. *Naturwiss. 2. Forst-Landwirtsch.* **17,** 148.

Ingram, D. L., and Buchanan, D. W. (1984). Lethal high temperatures for roots of three citrus rootstocks. *HortScience* **109,** 189–193.

Kacperska-Palacz, A. (1978). Mechanisms of cold acclimation in herbaceous plants. *In* "Plant Cold Hardiness and Freezing Stress: Mechanisms and Crop Implications" (P. H. Li and A. Sakai, eds.), Vol. 1, pp. 1399–152. Academic Press, New York.

Kramer, P. J., and Kozlowski, T. T. (1979). "Physiology of Woody Plants." Academic Press, New York.

Lange, O. L. (1959). Untersuchungen uber Warmehaushalt und Hitzeresistenz mauteranis-cher Wusten- und Sarannenpflanzen. *Flora (Jena)* **147,** 595–651.

Lange, O. L. (1965). The heat resistance of plants, its determination and variability. *In* "Methodology of Plant Ecophysiology" (F. Eckhardt, ed.), pp. 399–405. UNESCO, Paris.

Lange, O. L., and Lange, R. (1963). Untersuchungen uber Blattemperaturen, Transpiration und Hitzeresistenz an Pflanzen mediterraner Standorte (Costa brava, Spanien). *Flora (Jena)* **153,** 387–425.

Larcher, W. (1975). "Physiological Plant Ecology." Springer-Verlag, New York.

Levitt, J. (1980). "Responses of Plants to Environmental Stresses" 2nd ed. Academic Press, New York.

Li, P. H., and Weiser, C. J. (1967). Evaluation of extraction and assay methods for nucleic acids from red osier dogwood and RNA, DNA, and protein changes during cold acclimation. *Proc. Am. Soc. Hortic. Sci.* **91**, 716–727.

Lyons, J. M., and Raison, J. K. (1970). Oxidative activity of mitochondria isolated from plant tissues sensitive and resistant to chilling injury. *Plant Physiol.* **45**, 386–389.

Lyons, J. M., Raison, J. K., and Steponkus, P. L. (1979). The plant membrane in response to low temperature. *In* "Low Temperature Stress in Crop Plants: The Role of the Membrane" (J. M. Lyons, D. Graham, and J. K. Raison, eds.), pp. 1–24. Academic Press. New York.

McKenzie, J. S., Weiser, C. J., and Li, P. H. (1974). Effects of red and far-red light on the initiation of cold acclimation in *Cornus stolonifera* Michx. *Plant Physiol.* **53** 783–789.

McWilliam, J. R., Kramer, P. J., and Musser, R. L. (1982). Temperature-induced water stress in chilling-sensitive plants. *Aust. J. Plant Physiol.* **9**, 343–352.

Markhart, A. H. (1984). Amelioration of chilling-induced water stress by abscisic acid-induced changes in root hydraulic conductance. *Plant Physiol.* **74**, 81–83.

Mooney, H. A., Ehleringer, J., and Bjorkman, O. (1977). The energy balance of leaves of the evergreen desert shrub *Atriplex hymenelytra*. *Oecologia* **29**, 301–310.

Mooney, H. A., Bjorkman, O., and Collatz, G. J. (1978). Photosynthetic acclimation to temperature in the desert shrub, *Larrea divaricata*. I. Carbon dioxide exchange characteristics of intact leaves. *Plant Physiol.* **61**, 406–410.

Munch, E. (1913). Hitzeschaden an Waldpflanzen. *Naturwiss. Z. Forst.- Landwirtsch.* **12**, 169–188.

Munch, E. (1914). Nochmals Hitzeschaden an Waldpflanzen. *Naturwiss. Z. Forst.- Landwirtsch.* **12**, 169–188.

Nobel, P. S. (1983). "Biophysical Plant Physiology and Ecology." Freeman, San Francisco, California.

Pearcy, R. W. (1977). Acclimation of photosynthetic and respiratory carbon dioxide exchange to growth temperature in *Atriplex lentiformis* (Torr.) Wats. *Plant Physiol.* **59**, 795–799.

Pearcy, R. W. (1978). Effect of growth temperature on the fatty acid composition of the leaf lipids in *Atriplex lentiformis* (Torr.) Wats. *Plant Physiol.* **61**, 484–486.

Pearcy, R. W., Berry, J. A., and Fork, D. C. (1977). Effects of growth temperature on the termal stability of the photosynthetic apparatus of *Atriplex lentiformis* (Torr.) Wats. *Plant Physiol.* **59**, 873–878.

Rikin, A., Atsmon, D., and Gitler, C. (1979). Chilling injury in cotton (*Gossypium hirsutum* L.): Prevention by abscisic acid. *Plant Cell Physiol.* **20**, 1537–1546.

Sakai, A., and Yoshida, S. (1967). Survival of plant tissue at super-low temperature. VI. Effects of cooling and rewarming rates on survival. *Plant Physiol.* **42**, 1695–1701.

Siminovitch, D., Singh, J., and de la Roche, I. A. (1975). Studies on membranes in plant cells resistant to extreme freezing. I. Augmentation of phospholipids and membrane substance without changes in unsaturation of fatty acids in hardening of black locust bark. *Cryobiology* **12**, 144–153.

Stebbins, G. L. (1972). Evolution and diversity of arid-land shrubs. *In* "Wildland Shrubs: Their Biology and Utilization" (C. M. McKell, J. P. Blaisdell, and J. R. Goodin, eds.), USDA For. Serv. Gen. Tech. Rep. INT-I, pp. 111–120. Utah State University, Logan.

Stewart, J. McD., and Guinn, G. (1969). Chilling injury and changes in adenosine triphosphate of cotton seedlings. *Plant Physiol.* **44**, 605–608.

Stewart, J. McD., and Guinn, G. (1971). Chilling injury and nucleotide changes in young cotton plants. *Plant Physiol.* **47**, 166–170.

Strain, B. R. (1969). Seasonal adaptations in photosynthesis and respiration in four desert shrubs growing *in situ*. *Ecology* **50**, 511–513.

Ulmer, W. (1937). Ober den Jahresgang der Frosharte einiger immergruner Arten der alpinen Stufe, sowie der Zirbe and Fichte. Unter Berucksichtigung von osmotischen Wert, Zuckerspiegel and Wassergehalt. *Jahrb. Wiss. Bot.* **84,** 553–592.

Wasser, C. H. (1982). Ecology and culture of selected species useful in revegetating disturbed lands in the west. *U.S., Fish Wildl. Serv., Off. Biol. Serv. [Tech. Rep.] FWS/OBS* **FWS/OBS-82/56.**

Weiser, C. J. (1970). Cold resistance and injury in woody plants. *Science* **169,** 1269–1278.

Williams, B. J., Pellet, N. E., and Klein, R. M. (1972). Phytochrome control of growth cessation and initiation of cold acclimation in selected woody plants. *Plant Physiol.* **50,** 262–265.

Yoshida, S., and Tagawa, F. (1979). Alternation of the respiratory function in chill sensitive callus due to low temperature stress. I. Involvement of the alternate pathway. *Plant Cell Physiol.* **20,** 1243–1250.

V

Multiple Uses of Shrubs

To the uninformed observer shrubs may seem to have little economic value. However, in the following chapters the value of shrubs for many uses is described. Research literature is discussed and data are presented to illustrate the nutritional value of shrubs for livestock fodder, to show the importance of shrubs for escape cover and thermal protection of wildlife, to outline new concepts for using shrubs to control soil erosion and rehabilitate drastically disturbed lands, and to utilize stress tolerant native shrubs to provide aesthetic appeal for landscapes, but with lower maintenance costs than required by traditional landscape species.

Although not of direct economic value, shrubs support vital ecosystem functions by cycling nutrients, adding organic matter to the soil, modifying environmental temperatures, and serving as hosts for beneficial and nonbeneficial insects. As increased understanding of the biology of shrubs is gained it will be possible to improve the management of their important ecosystem functions.

18

Nutritive Value of Shrubs

Bruce L. Welch

I. Introduction

The primary driving force of all animals is the necessity to find the right kind of food and enough of it (Elton, 1938, in Van Dersal, 1938). Food is the burning question in animal populations, and the survival and activities of animals are dependent upon the questions of food supply. Dietz (1972) declared: "To many animals, shrubs are food—sometimes their only food; thus the nutritional values of shrubs is of major importance to man and of all importance to the animals consuming them."

To appreciate the nutritive value of shrubs, one needs to know the nutrient requirements of range animals and how these requirements are expressed. These nutrient needs include dry matter intake, energy, protein, minerals, and vitamins. In a general manner, the seasonal nutrient content of shrubs, grasses, and forbs must be considered. Seasonal effects on the nutritive value of specific shrub species are different among shrub species. Given that differences exist in nutritive quality it appears that the feasibility of selecting and breeding for superior nutrient content in shrubs is high. Finally, to make the best use of shrubs high in nutritive value, management systems are needed that optimize shrub use (McKell, 1980).

Two morphological characteristics set shrubs apart from grasses and forbs: a deep and extensive root system and a rigid and tall stature. A deep, extensive root system allows shrubs to draw water from a greater soil volume than can grasses and forbs. This makes shrubs a more dependable forage source during both seasonal and extended drought. A taller and rigid stature makes shrubs more available for consumption during periods of deep snow or when grasses have been destroyed.

II. Nutrient Needs of Range Animals

The quantity of nutrients needed by animals varies according to species, age, size, and activity (National Academy of Sciences, 1975; Maynard *et al.*, 1979). Qualitatively, nutrient needs of animals can be put into five classes: dry matter, energy-producing compounds, protein, minerals, and vitamins.

A. Dry Matter

Intake of dry matter by animals varies according to species, weight, and activity of the animal. Greatest consumption of dry matter, as a proportion of liveweight, occurs with lactation, followed by growth, gestation, and maintenance. The amount of dry matter consumed is of considerable importance to range managers calculating carrying capacity. Dry matter intake of selected animals is given in Table I.

B. Energy-Producing Compounds

Energy-producing compounds are the single largest class of nutrients needed by animals (Dietz, 1972; National Academy of Sciences, 1975). Energy is needed to drive the various physiological processes of the body and to provide movement and heat. Energy can be derived from a variety of compounds, including sugars, fats, pectins, starch, and protein, and in the case of ruminants and others with fermentation abilities, indirectly

Table I. Nutritive requirements of selected range animals

	Dry matter[a] (lb)	*In vitro* digestion[b] (%)	Crude protein[c] (%)	Calcium[c] (%)	Phosphorus[c] (%)	Carotene[d] (mg/kg)
Sheep						
Maintenance						
110[e]	2.2	50	8.9	0.30	0.28	1.9
132	2.4	50	8.9	0.28	0.26	2.0
154	2.6	50	8.9	0.27	0.25	2.2
176	2.9	50	8.9	0.25	0.24	2.3
Last 6 weeks of gestation						
110	3.7	53	9.3	0.24	0.23	3.6
132	4.2	53	9.3	0.23	0.22	3.9
154	4.6	53	9.3	0.21	0.20	4.2
176	4.8	53	9.3	0.21	0.20	4.5
Lactation						
110	3.7	60	11.0	0.52	0.37	2.6
132	4.2	60	11.0	0.50	0.36	2.9
154	4.6	60	11.0	0.48	0.34	3.1
176	6.6	60	11.0	0.48	0.34	3.3
Growth						
66	2.7	56	10.0	0.45	0.25	1.5
88	3.1	56	9.5	0.44	0.24	1.8
110	3.3	56	9.5	0.42	0.23	2.1
132	3.3	56	9.5	0.43	0.24	2.5
Cattle						
Maintenance						
881	13.4	50	5.9	0.18	0.18	4.1
1102	15.9	50	5.9	0.18	0.18	4.1
1323	18.3	50	5.9	0.18	0.18	4.1
Gestation						
881	16.5	50	5.9	0.18	0.18	4.1
1102	19.0	50	5.9	0.18	0.18	4.1
1323	21.4	50	5.9	0.18	0.18	4.1
Lactation						
881	23.8	53	9.2	0.42	0.38	5.7
1102	26.0	53	9.2	0.39	0.36	5.7
1323	28.4	53	9.2	0.36	0.34	5.7
Growth						
661	19.4	57	10.2	0.31	0.26	3.2
881	24.3	57	10.2	0.21	0.21	3.2
1323	26.5	56	8.8	0.18	0.18	3.2
Horses						
Maintenance	16.4	50	8.5	0.30	0.20	2.4
Gestation	16.4	53	11.0	0.50	0.35	5.0
Lactation	21.5	56	14.0	0.50	0.35	4.1
Growth	13.2	58	16.0	0.70	0.50	2.9

(*Continues*)

Table I.   (*Continued*)

	Dry matter[a] (lb)	*In vitro* digestion[b] (%)	Crude protein[c] (%)	Calcium[c] (%)	Phosphorus[c] (%)	Carotene[d] (mg/kg)
Horses (*Continued*)						
Work						
Light	—	53	8.5	0.30	0.20	2.4
Moderate	—	57	8.5	0.30	0.20	2.4
Intense	—	58	8.5	0.30	0.20	2.4
Deer						
Maintenance	2.2	50	7.5	0.30	0.25	—
Gestation	2.5	53	9.0	0.30	0.25	—
Lactation	3.0	60	10.0	0.48	0.48	—
Growth	—	56	16.0	0.38	0.27	—
Elk						
Maintenance	9.6	50	—	—	—	—
Small range animals (rabbits, squirrels, foxes)						
Maintenance	—	—	22.0	0.30	0.30	8.7
Gestation	—	—	38.0	0.40	0.40	8.7
Lactation	—	—	46.0	0.60	0.60	8.7
Growth	—	—	35.0	0.40	0.40	8.7
Range birds (grouse, pheasant, quail, turkey)						
Maintenance	—	—	12.0	0.50	0.25	5.9
Breeding	—	—	14.0	2.25	0.35	5.9
Growth	—	—	20.0	0.75	0.38	5.9

Source: From Halls (1970) and National Academy of Sciences (1975, 1976, 1977, 1978, 1982, 1984). Some data are averages derived from several sources.

[a] Dry matter intake is expressed as pounds per day per head.

[b] Energy is expressed as a percentage of dry matter digested by *in vitro* means. Unfortunately, the total digestible nutrients content or amount of metabolizable energy is unknown for many range forages. More information is expressed as *in vitro* digestibility. Maintenance was set at 50% *in vitro* digestibility, with other activities adjusted accordingly (Ammann *et al.*, 1973).

[c] Crude protein, calcium, and phosphorus are expressed as a percentage of dry matter.

[d] Carotene is expressed as mg/kg of dry matter.

[e] Weight of the range animals.

from cellulose and hemicellulose (Dietz, 1972; National Academy of Sciences, 1975; Maynard *et al.*, 1979).

The energy needs of animals are expressed in several forms such as total digestible nutrients (TDN) and metabolizable energy (Maynard *et al.*, 1979). TDN requirements of an animal are expressed as kilograms per animal per day or as a percentage of the diet. Metabolizable energy requirements of an animal are expressed as megacalories per animal per day or as megacalories per kilogram of dry matter.

Energy needs of animals vary according to weight and activity of the animal. Larger animals require more kilograms of TDN per day for a given activity than do smaller animals. A lactating female requires more kilo-grams of TDN per day than a nonlactating female of similar weight. On a constant weight basis, lactation requires more energy than any other activity. In descending order of energy needs, lactation is followed by fattening, growth, gestation, and maintenance. Unfortunately, the TDN content or amount of metabolizable energy is unknown for many forages. Table I expresses the energy requirements of animals in terms of *in vitro* digestibility. Maintenance requirement was set at 50% *in vitro* digestibility with all other activities adjusted accordingly (Ammann *et al.,* 1973).

C. Protein

Animal protein makes up a large, chemically related, but physiologically diverse, group of compounds. Protein is the major organic compound of the organs and soft tissues of the body and in other structures including hemoglobin, cytochromes, and membranes. Enzymes are another func-tionally important group of protein compounds.

Because proteins are involved in so many bodily functions, the animal body needs a liberal and continuous supply. As with energy, the protein requirements of an animal vary according to species, weight, and activity (Table I). For ruminants and other animals that have fermentation-type digestive systems (horses, rabbits, burros, etc.), the quality of the protein is not important—only the quantity. The protein requirement of an ani-mal is expressed as grams per day of digestible protein or as a percent-age of digestible protein in the diet. Protein requirement may also be expressed as grams per day of crude or total protein or as a percentage of crude or total protein in the diet. As with energy, the greater the weight of the animal, the higher are the protein needs, assuming that body activity is held constant. Protein needs for the various animal activities with body weight held constant are in the same order as for energy.

D. Minerals

Of approximately 15 elements essential for the health of animals, 7 are considered major: sodium, chlorine, calcium, phosphorus, magnesium, potassium, and sulfur. The remaining 8 are classified as trace elements: iodine, iron, copper, molybdenum, cobalt, manganese, zinc, and selenium. These essential mineral elements constitute the major components of bones and teeth, maintain osmotic relations and acid–base equilibrium, play an important role in regulating enzymatic systems and muscular contraction, and are constituents of most organic compounds. They are also important in energy transfer (Ensminger and Olentine, 1978; Maynard *et al.,* 1979).

Under most conditions, calcium and phosphorus are the mineral elements of major concern. Animal needs for calcium and phosphorus are expressed as grams per day per animal or as a percentage of the diet (Table I). Larger animals under similar body activity need greater amounts of calcium and phosphorus than do smaller animals. With size held constant, lactating animals require the most calcium and phosphorus, followed by growth, fattening, gestation, and maintenance.

E. Vitamins

Vitamins are organic compounds that the body needs in relatively small amounts. Vitamins are unrelated chemically but function as metabolic regulators (Maynard *et al.*, 1979). For animals capable of supporting microbial fermentation, only vitamin A is of major concern. Vitamin A combines with a specific protein of the eye to produce visual purple. In addition to visual purple, vitamin A plays an important role in normal development of bones, in the normal power of disease resistance, and in maintaining healthy epithelium tissues. Vitamin A is manufactured in the liver from the plant precursor carotene. Therefore, the vitamin A requirement is expressed in terms of carotene as either milligrams per animal per day or milligrams per kilogram of dry matter (Table I). With size held constant, a lactating animal requires the most carotene, followed by fattening, growth, gestation, and maintenance.

III. Nutritive Value of Shrubs

The nutritive value of shrubs continues to receive worldwide attention (McKell, 1975, 1980) as evidenced in the following papers published in symposium proceedings, journals, and other outlets: western United States—Smith (1950), Cook (1972), Dietz (1972), Harris (1972), Tueller (1979), Welch (1983); Chile—Benjamin (1980); Australia—Wilson and Harrington (1980); West Africa—Le Houérou (1980); Nigeria—Mecha and Adegbolia (1980); and many more.

A. Comparison of Shrubs to Other Forage Types

Comparative seasonal nutritive value of shrubs, forbs, and grasses has been graphically presented in terms of stage of growth by Cook (1972) and in terms of date by Tueller (1979). Cook (1972) used four stages of plant growth—vegetative, anthesis, fruiting, and maturing—to compare the general nutritive value of shrubs, forbs, and grasses for meeting the lactation and gestation requirements of large ruminants. At the vegetative stage all forage classes greatly exceed the lactation requirement for energy, protein, phosphorus, and carotene. A high nutritive content continues until the anthesis growth stage. At anthesis, shrubs are still well above the lactation requirement, and furnish higher amounts of protein, phosphorus, and carotene than do forbs and grasses. At this stage, all forage classes exceed the energy requirement for lactation, with shrubs and forbs dropping rapidly. At the fruiting stage, shrubs furnish higher amounts, still above the lactation requirement of protein, phosphorus, and carotene. Protein and phosphorus levels in grass at anthesis have dropped below the gestation and probably below the maintenance requirements. Energy content of forbs and grasses still meets the lactation requirement, while shrub energy content is just above the gestation requirement. At the mature stage, shrubs furnish higher (at or above the gestation requirement) amounts of protein, phosphorus, and carotene than do forbs and grasses. Protein and carotene content of forbs and grasses fall below gestation and probably below the maintenance requirements. Forbs supply enough phosphorus to meet the gestation requirement. Grasses do not. Cook (1972) showed that at the mature stage, grasses contain enough energy to meet the lactation requirement. It appears that these values for grasses are too high. This statement is based on the data given in Table III that clearly show that energy levels of dormant grass are at or slightly above the maintenance requirement. Energy levels in shrubs are not high enough to meet the gestation requirement.

Tueller (1979) compared the nutritive value of shrubs and grasses over seasons. Some of his data are given in Table II. The shrubs *Artemisia tridentata* and *Purshia tridentata* and the unknown grass crude protein peaked in the spring vegetative stage and then decreased, reaching the lowest level during the winter or dormant season (December mature stage and perhaps beyond).

Table II. Seasonal variation of crude protein for *Artemisia tridentata*, *Purshia tridentata*, and an unknown Nevada grass

Month/year	Big sagebrush	Bitterbrush	Grass
June 1968	11.8	13.4	13.4
July 1968	12.7	12.8	7.8
September 1968	11.8	9.7	9.6
December 1968	10.5	7.5	2.7
March 1969	14.0	9.9	3.4
May 1969	15.0	11.3	21.3

Source: Data from Tueller (1979).

One other comparison needs to be made among shrubs, forbs, and grasses. During drought or other conditions (deep snow) shrubs provide a more dependable source of forage for wildlife and livestock when forbs or grasses are either absent or unavailable (Dietz, 1972; McKell, 1975). Medin and Anderson (1979) indicated that some shrub species such as *A. tridentata* provide more forage during drought than do others such as *P. tridentata*.

In general, shrubs provide higher dormant or winter levels of protein, phosphorus, and carotene than do forbs and grasses. Dormant shrubs can meet the protein, phosphorus, and carotene gestation requirements of large ruminants and are a more dependable forage source during drought and other conditions than are grasses and forbs.

B. Seasonal and Interspecies Variability

Nutritive value of shrubs, as with other types of forage, varies according to stage of growth. Stage of growth is linked closely to yearly variation in temperature and rainfall. In most of the temperate zones of the world, seasonal variation is marked by large changes in temperature and rainfall. In other parts of the world, the changes are more defined in terms of wet and dry periods. Regardless of the mechanism, these periods can have profound effects on the nutritive value of certain species of shrubs such as *P. tridentata,* whereas other species such as *A. tridentata* show less variation among seasons (Table II).

Nutritive value of shrubs, forbs, and grasses vary considerably between the three main seasons: winter (dormant or dry period), spring (beginning of growing season or the wet period), and summer, initiation of senescence (beginning of the dry period) (Tables III, IV, and V). Duration of the various seasons was set according to the following dates: winter, December 21 to March 21; summer, June 21 to September 21; and spring, March 21 to June 21. The most difficult data to interpret are from the spring. During the spring, some range plants may still be dormant and technically in a winter stage or starting new growth. Unfortunately, initiation of new growth is not calendar dependent and may vary by 3 to 4 weeks. Data given for spring season were for initial growth. Because the data in these three tables are means of studies from various locations, they should be used to draw general conclusions only.

1. Winter (Dormant or Dry Period)

During the winter dormant or dry period, the nutritive needs of range animals, especially wild range animals, drop to maintenance levels. Correspondingly, the nutritive content of range plants drops in many cases below maintenance levels. Grasses lead this trend in every category except energy and are followed by forbs, with shrubs showing the least amount of decline. Table III contains three exceptions to the rule that winter grasses contain more energy than shrubs. These three exceptions are *A. tridentata, A. nova,* and *Cercocarpus ledifolius.* Their *in vitro* digestibilities were 57.8, 53.7, and 49.1% of dry matter, respectively. These three shrub species have one characteristic in common: they are nondeciduous. Other nondeciduous shrub species such as *Ceratoides lanata, Atriplex canescens,* and *Juniperus osteosperma* are lower in energy than are *Artemisia tridentata, Artemisia nova, Cercocarpus ledifolius,* and many grasses.

Atriplex canescens, however, deserves special note. Although the *A. canescens* nutritive value is not impressive in Table III (38.3% in *vitro* digestibility and 8.9% protein), Ostyina *et al.* (1982) reported fall (September to December in the western United States) crude protein content at 15% with much higher energy values. *Atriplex canescens* slowly loses the majority of its leaves, which reduces its nutritive value from midwinter to midspring. During the fall, *A. canescens* can supply greater amounts of protein, phosphorus, and perhaps energy than can most shrubs. Another shrub that may perform similarly to *A. canescens* is *Purshia tridentata.*

Although shrubs in general exceed the protein, phosphorus, and carotene levels of grasses and forbs in the winter or dormant period, it is evident in Table III that the nutritive values of some shrub species exceed others. *In vitro* digestibility for the shrub species listed in Table III ranged from 23.5% for *Purshia tridentata* to a high of 57.8% for *Artemisia tridentata.* The same was true for crude protein. *Quercus gambelii* contained the lowest crude protein at 5.3% and *A. tridentata* the highest at 11.7%. Phosphorus content ranged from a low of 0.11% for *Ceratoides lanata* to a high of 0.18% for *A. tridentata, A. nova,* and *Juniperus osteosperma.* Good range management should ensure that palatable shrubs high in nutritive value are protected and allowed to flourish.

Fall regrowth of grasses, exemplified by *Agropyron desertorum,* provides excellent winter forage for wintering range animals. However, regrowth cannot constitute the mainstay of a winter range program because regrowth is dependent on rainfall, which does not occur each fall, and because in certain areas of the world snow can render the regrowth unavailable. From a winter nutritive point of view, *Artemisia tridentata* is superior to all the other shrub species and forage types listed in Table III in amount of nutrients and in many cases in amount of biomass produced. This range plant species has been and continues to be much maligned because of its general characteristic of being unpalatable to cattle grazing spring and summer ranges. Not only is *A. tridentata* a superior winter forage plant in its adapted areas, but it is a more dependable source of forage during drought (Medin and Anderson, 1979).

Table III. Winter nutritive values of selected range plants

Species	In vitro digestibility (%)	Crude protein (%)	Phosphorus (%)	Carotene (mg/kg)
Shrubs				
Purshia tridentata	23.5	7.6	0.14	—
Artemisia tridentata	57.8	11.7	0.18	8.0
Artemisia nova	53.7	9.9	0.18	8.0
Ceratoides lanata	43.5	10.0	0.11	16.8
Cercocarpus ledifolius	49.1	10.1	—	—
Atriplex canescens	38.3	8.9	—	3.1
Quercus gambelii	26.6	5.3	—	—
Chrysothamnus viscidiflorus	36.0	5.9	0.15	—
Cercocarpus montanus	26.5	7.8	0.13	—
Chrysothamnus nauseosus	44.4	7.8	0.14	—
Juniperus osteosperma	44.1	6.6	0.18	—
Forbs				
Balsamorhiza sagittata	—	3.6	0.06	—
Helianthella uniflora	—	2.8	0.17	—
Sanguisorba minor	—	6.6	—	—
Grasses				
Agropyron spicatum	45.5	3.2	0.05	0.22
Agropyron smithii	50.2	3.8	0.07	0.20
Sitanion hystrix	42.0	4.3	0.07	1.10
Agropyron desertorum	43.7	3.5	0.07	0.20
Agropyron desertorum (fall regrowth)	50.6	15.0	0.39	432.00
Hilaria jamesii	48.2	4.6	0.08	0.40
Festuca idahoensis	46.1	3.8	0.08	—
Oryzopsis hymenoides	50.5	3.1	0.06	0.44
Phalaris arundinaceae	—	7.8	0.14	—
Stipa comata	46.6	3.7	0.07	0.40
Poa secunda	—	4.2	—	—
Sporobolus cryptandrus	53.2	4.1	0.07	0.50
Bromus inermis	47.0	4.1	0.12	—

Note: Data are expressed as a percentage of dry matter, except carotene, which is expressed as mg/kg of dry matter.

References for Tables III, IV, and V:

Baker, D. L., and Hansen, D. R. (1985). Comparative digestion of grass in mule deer and elk. *J. Wildl. Manage.* **49,** 77–79.

Bissell, H. D., Harris, B., Strong, H., and James, F. (1955). The digestibility of certain natural and artificial food eaten by deer in California. *Calif. Fish Game* **41,** 57–78.

Cook, C. W., Harris, L. E. (1950). The nutritive content of the grazing sheep's diet on summer and winter ranges of Utah. *Bull—Utah Agric. Exp. Stn.* **342.**

Davis, A. M. (1981). The oxalate, tanin, crude fiber, and crude protein composition of young plants of some *Atriplex* species. *J. Range Manage.* **34,** 329–331.

Dietz, D. R., Udall, R. H., and Yeager, L. E. (1962). Chemical composition and digestibility by mule deer of selected forage species, Cache La Poudre Range, Colorado. *Tech. Publ.—Colo Div. Game, Fish Parks* **14.**

Erdman, J. A., and Ebens, R. J. (1979). Element content of crested wheatgrass grown on reclaimed coal spoils and on soils nearby. *J. Range Manage.* **32,** 159–161.

(*Continues*)

Table III. References for Tables III, IV, and V (*Continued*)

Everett, R. L., and Sharrow, S. H. (1985). Response of grass species to tree harvesting in single-leaf pinyon–Utah juniper stands. *USDA For. Serv. Res. Pap. INT* **INT-334.**

Hart, R. H., Waggoner, J. W., Jr., Clark, D. H., Kaltenbunch, C. C., Hager, J. A., and Marshall, M. B. (1983). Beef cattle performance on crested wheatgrass plus native range vs native range alone. *J. Range Manage.* **36,** 38–40.

Hart, R. H., Abdalla, O. M., Clark, D. H., Marshall, M. B., Hamid, M. H., Hager, J. A., Waggoner, J. W., Jr. (1983). Quality of forage and cattle diets on the Wyoming high plains. *J. Range Manage.* **36,** 46–51.

Hickman, O. E. (1975). Seasonal trends in the nutritive content of important range forage species near Silver Lake, OR. *USDA For. Serv. Res. Pap. PNW* **PNW-187.**

Hobbs, N. T., Baker, D. L., Ellis, J. E., and Swift, D. M. (1981). Composition and quality of elk winter diets in Colorado. *J. Wildl. Manage.* **45,** 156–177.

Hobbs, N. T., Baker, D. L., and Gill, R. B. (1983). Comparative nutritional ecology of montane ungulates during winter. *J. Wildl. Manage.* **47,** 1–16.

Holter, J. B., Hayes, H. H., and Smith, S. H. (1979). Protein requirement of yearling white-tailed deer. *J. Wildl. Manage.* **43,** 872–879.

Kufeld, R. C., Stevens, M. S., and Bowden, D. C. (1981). Winter variation in nutrient and fiber content and *in vitro* digestibility of Gambel oak (*Quercus gambellii*) and big sagebrush (*Artemisia tridentata*) from diversified sites in Colorado. *J. Range Manage.* **34,** 149–151.

Mould, E. D., And Robins, L. (1982). Digestive capabilities in elk compared to white-tailed deer. *J. Wildl. Manage.* **46,** 22–29.

National Academy of Sciences (1958). Composition of cereal grains and forages. *N.A.S.–N.R.C., Publ.* **585.**

National Academy of Sciences (1964). "Nutrient Requirements of Sheep." Publ. No. 5. National Research Council, Washington, D.C.

Otsyina, R. M., McKell, C. M., and Van Epps, G. A. (1982). Use of range shrubs to meet nutrient requirements of sheep grazing on crested wheatgrass during fall and early winter. *J. Range Manage.* **35,** 751–753.

Pederson, J. C., and Harper, K. T. (1979). Chemical composition of some important plants of southeastern Utah summer ranges related to mule deer reproduction. *Great Basin Nat.* **39,** 122–128.

Pederson, J. C., and Welch, B. L. (1982). Effects of monoterpenoid exposure on ability of rumen inocula to digest a set of forages. *J. Range Manage.* **35,** 500–502.

Rowland, M. M., Alldredge, A. W., Ellis, J. E., Weber, B. J., and White, G. C. (1983). Comparative winter diets of elk in New Mexico. *J. Wildl. Manage.* **47,** 924–932.

Samuel, M. J., Rauzi, F., and Hart, R. H. (1980). Nitrogen fertilization of range: Yield, protein, content, and cattle behavior. *J. Range Manage.* **33,** 119–121.

Sheehy, D. P. (1975). Relative palatability of seven *Artemisia* taxa to mule deer and sheep. M. S. Thesis, Oregon State University, Eugene.

Short, H. L. (1981). Nutrition and metabolism. *In* "Mule and Black-tailed Deer of North America" (Wallmo, O. C. ed.), pp. 99–127. Univ. of Nebraska Press, Lincoln.

Smith, A. D. (1952). Digestibility of some native forages for mule deer. *J. Wildl. Manage.* **16,** 309–312.

Smith, A. D. (1957). Nutritive value of some browse plants in winter. *J. Range Manage.* **10,** 162–164.

Tueller, P. T. (1979). "Food Habits and Nutrition of Mule Deer on Nevada Ranges." University of Nevada-Reno, Reno.

Urness, P. J., Smith, A. D., and Watkins, R. K. (1977). Comparison of *in vivo* and *in vitro* dry matter digestibility of mule deer forages. *J. Range Manage.* **30,** 119–121.

Urness, P. J., Austin, D. D., and Fierro, L. C. (1983). Nutritional value of crested wheatgrass for wintering mule deer. *J. Range Manage.* **36,** 225–226.

Van Dersal, W. R. (1938). Utilization of woody plants as food by wildlife. *Trans. North Am. Wildl. Conf.* **3,** 768–775.

Wallmo, O. C., Carpenter, L. H., Regelin, W. L., Gill, R. B., and Baker, D. L. (1977). Evaluation of deer habitat on a nutritional basis. *J. Range Manage.* **30,** 122–127.

Ward, A. L. (1971). *In vitro* digestibility of elk winter forage in southern Wyoming. *J. Range Manage.* **35,** 681–685.

Tables III. References for Tables III, IV, and V (*Continued*)

Welch, B. L. (1978). Relationships of soil salinity, ash, and crude protein in *Atriplex canescens*. *J. Range Manage.* **31**, 132–133.

Welch, B. L., and Monsen, S. B. (1984). Winter nutritive value of accessions of fourwing saltbush (*Atriplex canescens* [Pursh] Nutt.) grown in a uniform garden. *USDA For. Serv. Gen. Tech. Rep. INT* **INT-172**, 138–144.

Welch, B. L., Monsen, S. B., and Shaw, N. L. (1983). Nutritive value of antelope and desert bitterbrush, stansbury cliffrose, and apache-plume. *USDA For. Serv. Gen. Tech. Rep. INT* **INT-152**, 173–185.

Williams, W., Bailey, A. W., Mclean, A., and Kalnin, C. (1981). Effects of fall slipping or burning on the distribution of chemical constituents in bluebunch wheatgrass in spring. *J. Range Manage.* **34**, 267–268.

2. Spring (Initiation of Growth, Starting of Wet Period)

Spring is when the energy, protein, phosphorus, and carotene requirements of range animals are highest because females are lactating and young are growing rapidly. Nutritive values of plants are also highest at this time (Table IV), but plants are low in biomass production until mid to late spring. Grasses, however, greatly exceed shrubs for their *in vitro* digestibility, which ranges from 60 to 75% as compared to shrubs at 50 to 60%. This is also true for forbs; their digestibility ranges from 70 to 85%. Forb protein content is about 25% in comparison to grasses at about 17% and shrubs at about 14%. Phosphorus content is about the same for grasses, forbs, and shrubs. In the spring, management emphasis should be placed on grass and forb production, reserving shrubs as backup for periods of drought.

3. Summer (Initiation of Senescence, Starting of Dry Period)

During the summer, animal needs for energy, protein, phosphorus, and carotene are lower than during the spring. The nutritive value of range forages starts to decline, with the grasses declining more rapidly than forbs and shrubs (Table V). During this period, digestibility of grass declines from 60 to 75% to 50 to 60%. Protein levels in grasses also decline from about 17% to about 10%, whereas protein in shrubs drops 1% to about 13% and in forbs to about 17%. Phosphorus content is highest in shrubs, with forbs and grasses about the same. The information given in Table V illustrates the importance of having a mixture of palatable grasses, forbs, and shrubs available for animal consumption during the summer.

C. Intraspecies Variability

Some shrub species contain higher levels of winter crude protein than do others (Table III). This is also true for accessions within shrub species, not only for crude protein but also for *in vitro* digestibility, productivity, and preference. Research on *A. tridentata* serves as an example for selecting and breeding shrubs for superior nutrient content.

Table IV. Spring nutritive values of selected range plants

Species	*In vitro* digestibility (%)	Crude protein (%)	Phosphorus (%)	Carotene (mg/kg)
Shrubs				
Purshia tridentata	49.1	12.4	0.19	—
Artemisia tridentata	58.1	12.6	0.25	—
Ceratoides lanata	—	21.0	—	—
Cercocarpus ledifolius	—	9.9	—	—
Atriplex canescens	—	14.1	—	—
Chrysothamnus viscidiflorus	—	22.6	0.46	—
Chrysothamnus nauseosus	—	20.7	0.45	—
Juniperus osteosperma	49.0	6.2	0.15	—
Forbs				
Medicago sativa	86.8	28.5	0.37	372.0
Vicia americana	71.3	21.2	—	—
Balsamorhiza sagittata	—	28.8	0.43	—
Sphaeralcea grossulariaefolia	69.7	19.7	—	—
Helianthella uniflora	—	20.0	0.40	—
Sanguisorba minor	—	17.4	—	—
Grasses				
Agropyron spicatum	60.6	17.0	0.30	414.0
Agropyron smithii	77.2	17.6	0.45	185.0
Sitanion hystrix	72.3	18.5	0.24	—
Agropyron desertorum	73.6	23.7	0.36	452.0
Agropyron cristatum	72.6	11.3	—	—
Festuca idahoensis	—	14.0	0.30	92.0
Oryzopsis hymenoides	76.1	15.9	—	—
Agropyron intermedium	74.3	8.2	—	—
Stipa comata	64.4	12.0	0.18	—
Phalaris arundinocea	—	16.2	0.40	—
Poa secunda	62.2	17.3	0.33	—
Sporobolus cryptandrus	—	15.1	0.25	—
Bromus inermis	—	23.5	0.47	493.0

Notes: Data are expressed as a percentage of dry matter, except carotene, which is expressed as mg/kg of dry matter. See references, Table III.

Preference is an important characteristic because the more preferred plants are the ones more likely to be eaten in higher amounts. During winter digestibility trials, Smith (1950) noted that mule deer (*Odocoileus hemionus hemionus*) showed definite aversion to individual *A. tridentata* plants. Subsequently, others have observed this winter differential preference of deer for certain populations and individual plants of *A. tridentata* (Welch *et al.*, 1981). Welch and McArthur (1986) reported differential preference of wintering *O. h. hemionus* for accessions of *A. tridentata* grown in a common garden. Preference, as measured by the percentage of current year's growth eaten, ranged from 28.3 to 57.5%. One accession

Table V.   Summer nutritive values of selected range plants

Species	In vitro digestibility (%)	Crude protein (%)	Phosphorus (%)	Carotene (mg/kg)
Shrubs	—	13.1	0.22	—
Purshia tridentata	—	13.2	0.40	—
Artemisia tridentata	—	13.6	—	—
Ceratoides lanata	—	12.2	0.23	—
Cercocarpus ledifolius	47.1	12.0	—	—
Atriplex canescens	—	15.8	—	—
Quercus gambelii (leaves)	—	12.1	0.35	—
Chrysothamnus viscidiflorus	—	12.8	0.38	—
Chrysothamnus nauseosus	—	8.1	0.21	—
Juniperus osteosperma				
Forbs				
Medicago sativa	—	17.8	0.28	109.0
Vicia americana	—	17.6	0.20	—
Balsamorhiza sagittata	—	17.0	0.26	—
Helianthella uniflora	—	12.4	0.31	—
Sanguisorba minor	—	9.8	—	—
Grasses				
Agropyron spicatum	—	14.5	0.23	77.0
Agropyron smithii	—	11.8	—	117.0
Sitanion hystrix	59.7	8.0	0.17	1.1
Agropyron desertorum	51.0	12.1	0.23	153.0
Agropyron cristatum	—	—	0.13	—
Hilaria jamesii	—	7.7	0.09	0.4
Festuca idahoensis	54.0	9.5	0.18	34.0
Stipa comata	—	6.5	0.10	0.4
Phalaris arundinocea	—	12.4	0.20	—
Poa secunda	—	9.4	0.17	43.0
Sporobolus cryptandrus	—	5.7	0.10	0.4
Bromus inermis	60.6	11.0	0.28	103.0

Notes: Data are expressed as a percentage of dry matter, except carotene, which is expressed as mg/kg of dry matter. See references, Table III.

named Hobble Creek was significantly preferred over the other 20 accessions tested.

Domestic sheep also showed a strong differential preference for accessions of *A. tridentata* grown in a common garden. Welch *et al.* (1987) found that preference ranged from 0.0 to 98.3% for current year's growth eaten. Unlike *O. h. hemionus*, domestic sheep preferred 7 out of 21 accessions. Two accessions received no use. The Hobble Creek accession was among the 7 preferred accessions. Unlike the *O. h. hemionus* study, domestic sheep were given free access to high-quality alfalfa hay and 0.75 lb of rolled barley per head per day. The sheep were not forced to eat *A. tridentata*.

Differential preference for certain accessions of *A. tridentata* has been demonstrated for wintering pygmy rabbits (*Brachylagus idahoensis*) (White *et al.*, 1982) and sage grouse (*Centrocercus urophasianus*) (Remington, 1983). Many other observations indicate that other shrub species have variants that elicit differential preference.

Artemisia tridentata also varies significantly in other traits such as productivity, crude protein, and *in vitro* digestibility. McArthur and Welch (1982) reported that productivity, as characterized by length of stem leader, ranged from 15.3 to 41.4 cm per year among 21 accessions grown in a common garden. The most productive accession, named Dove Creek, was among the least preferred by *O. h. hemionus* and domestic sheep. This was also true for other nutritive values. Midwinter crude protein content for the 21 accessions varied from 10.0 to 16.0% (Welch and McArthur, 1979). Dove Creek contained the highest midwinter crude protein at 16.0%. Hobble Creek crude protein was 11.0%. Midwinter *in vitro* digestibility for 10 accessions ranged from 44.6 to 64.8% (Welch and Pederson, 1981). Dove Creek was next to the most digestible at 64.6%. Hobble Creek digestibility was 52.6%.

The possibility exists that the high preference for the Hobble Creek accession could be combined with the high nutritive value of the Dove Creek accession to produce a superior cultivator of shrub not found in nature. Crosses between the two accessions have been made, and hybrid plants are being evaluated (Noller and McArthur, 1986). Many shrub species other than *A. tridentata* have been observed to have significant variability in nutritive value. These include *Atriplex canescens* (Welch and Monsen, 1984), *Purshia tridentata* (Welch *et al.*, 1983), *Artemisia nova* (Behan and Welch, 1985, 1986), *Kochia prostrata* (Davis and Welch, 1984; Welch and Davis, 1984), and *Juniperus osteosperma* (Bunderson *et al.*, 1986). Opportunities exist worldwide for breeding and selecting programs to develop nutritionally superior cultivars of shrubs.

IV. Optimizing Shrub Use

With so much of the arid and semiarid regions of the world dominated by shrubs, it is reasonable that efforts should be given to optimize the use of shrubs for animal feed in management systems.

A. Managing Cattle to Utilize Shrubs

An example of livestock management to optimize shrub use was reported by Zimmerman (1980), who owns and operates a cattle ranch in central

Nevada in the United States. The rangelands used for grazing have some grass but are basically shrub (browse) ranges. This makes the cattle "browse cattle—not grass cattle," according to Zimmerman. Cattle eat different kinds of shrubs, forbs, and some grasses, plus *Salix* spp. and *Populus tremuloides* leaves—all of which are indigenous to the ranch. Shrub species eaten include *Ceratoides lanata*, *Artemisia spinescens*, *Atriplex canescens*, *Tetradymia* spp., *Purshia tridentata*, *Ephedra* spp., *Coleogyne* spp., and *Chrysothamnus* spp. Cows, calves, and steers do not receive any nutrient supplements. Steer calves at weaning age are moved to meadowlands for 2 months for finishing. Two key items make the Zimmerman ranch operations successful—the genetic makeup of the cattle and appropriate grazing management. The cattle are a multiple cross among Brahman, Santa Gertrudis, Charbray, and Hereford, which results in tough cattle that can adapt and survive on the open range year-round. Grazing management is a rest and rotation system. Some of the pastures are totally rested every other year and used differently after rest. Sometimes the livestock (cattle) are permitted to eat all the forage and other times they are allowed only 30, 40, 50, 60, or 70% usage. It all depends on what management determines that a certain pasture needs. Cattle distribution is controlled by placement of water.

Because the cattle are also somewhat selective eaters, long rest periods and dispersed number of cattle duplicate the natural system and foster success for the operation (Zimmerman, 1980; Platou and Tueller, 1985).

B. Overgrazing and Reduction of Preferred Shrubs

Although much has been written about the effects of overgrazing, a few points should be made regarding the loss of preferred shrubs from a population. In general, overgrazing reduces preferred forage species. This can also happen within a population of shrubs. Welch *et al.* (1987) observed preferences of domestic sheep for certain accessions of *Artemisia tridentata*. They noted a marked tendency for sheep to remove significant (60 to 70%) amounts of the current year's growth from the most-preferred accessions before removing even small amounts from less-preferred accessions. Assuming this is typical grazing behavior, preferred *A. tridentata* plants may be lost in areas subject to repeated grazing. Shepherd (1971) reported that 10 years of heavy clipping (80%) of the current year growth of *A. tridentata* after the growing season had no effect on the long-term production of vegetative biomass. R. L. Rodriguez and B. L. Welch (data unpublished) found similar results between *A. tridentata* plants heavily grazed by wintering *O. h. hemionus* and those protected from grazing. However, they observed two additional situations not reported by Shepherd (1971). First, heavily grazed plants showed a higher mortality, and second, seed production of heavily grazed plants was greatly reduced, almost to zero. These two factors could combine to reduce the number of preferred individual plants in a stand of *A. tridentata* and thus lower the overall preference of the stand.

Eventually a stand could become dominated by the least preferred individuals from the original stand. The key to survival of palatable species and preferred genotypes in most shrub-dominated ecosystems is a sufficient rest period between grazing periods (Platou and Tueller, 1985). If this management practice is followed, stands of shrubs containing high numbers of preferred individuals can be maintained. Conversely, stands containing high numbers of less-preferred individuals will have to be renovated or managed to allow the establishment and persistence of preferred genotypes.

V. Summary

The deep-rooted nature of shrubs gives them the advantage of extracting moisture from greater depths in the soil. This characteristic allows shrubs to remain green and to produce a more dependable food source during drought. Also, shrubs are usually taller and more rigid than grasses and forbs. These two characteristics allow shrubs to be available to consuming animals when grasses and forbs are dormant or unavailable during winter.

During the winter or dormant seasons, shrub forage is higher in crude protein, phosphorus, and carotene than grasses and forbs. However, with the exception of certain nondeciduous shrubs, shrubs are lower in energy than are grasses and forbs.

Significant variation in nutritive value exists in shrub species. These variations are expressed for many nutritive characteristics such as productivity, preference, *in vitro* digestibility, and the level of certain nutrients including crude protein, phosphorus, and carotene. Research results indicate that selection and breeding programs can result in the development of nutritionally superior cultivars of shrubs.

As with other forage types, proper management of shrub stands is essential for optimum shrub use. Overgrazing results in a loss of preferred individuals. The key factor in shrub management is adequate rest between grazing periods. Strains of cattle can be developed that will do well on shrub-dominated ranges.

References

Ammann, A. P., Cowan, R. L., Mothershead, C. L., and Baumgardt, B. R. (1973). Dry matter and energy intake in relation to digestibility in white-tailed deer. *J. Wildl. Manage.* **37**, 195–201.

Baker, D. L., and Hansen, D. R. (1985). Comparative digestion of grass in mule deer and elk. *J. Wildl. Manage.* **49**, 77–79.

Behan, B., and Welch, B. L. (1985). Black sagebrush; mule deer winter preference and monoterpenoid content. *J. Range Manage.* **38**, 278–280.

Behan, B., and Welch, B. L. (1986). Winter nutritive content of seven accessions of black sagebrush grown on a uniform garden. *Great Basin Nat.* **46**, 161–165.

Benjamin, R. W. (1980). The use of forage shrubs in the Norte Chico region of Chile. *In* "Browse in Africa: The Current State of Knowledge" (H. N. Le Houérou, ed.), pp. 299–302. International Livestock Centre for Africa, Addis Ababa, Ethiopia.

Bunderson, E. D., Welch, B. L., and Weber, D. J. (1986). *In vitro* digestibility of *Juniperus osteosperma* (Torr.) Little from 17 Utah sites. *For. Sci.* **32**, 834–840.

Cook, C. W. (1972). Comparative nutritive values of forbs, grasses, and shrubs. *In* "Wildland Shrubs: Their Biology and Utilization" (C. M. McKell, J. P. Blaisdell, and J. R. Goodin, eds.), USDA For. Serv. Gen. Tech. Rep. INT-1, pp. 303–310. Utah State University, Logan.

Davis, J. N., and Welch, B. L. (1984). Seasonal variation in crude protein content of *Kochia prostrata* (L.) Schrad. *USDA For. Serv. Gen. Tech. Rep. INT* **INT-172**, 145–149.

Dietz, D. R. (1972). Nutritive value of shrubs. *In* "Wildland Shrubs: Their Biology and Utilization" (C. M. McKell, J. P. Blaisdell, and J. R. Goodin, eds.), USDA For. Serv. Gen. Tech. Rep. INT-1, pp. 289–302. Utah State University, Logan.

Elton, (1938). *In* Van Dersal, W. R. 1938. Utilization of woody plants as food by wildlife. *North Am. Wildl. Cont. Trans.* **3**, 768–775.

Ensminger, M. E., and Olentine, C. G., Jr. (1978). "Feeds and Nutrition—abridged." Ensminger Publ. Co., Clovis, California

Halls, L. K. (1970). Nutrient requirement of livestock and game. p. 10–18. *Misc. Publ.— U.S., Dep. Agric.* **1147.**

Harris, L. E. (1972). Physiological problems in animal use of shrubs as forage. *In* "Wildland Shrubs: Their Biology and Utilization" (C. M. McKell, J. P. Blaisdell, and J. R. Goodin, eds.), USDA For. Serv. Gen. Tech. Rep. INT-1, pp. 319–330.

Le Houérou, H. N. (1980). Chemical composition and nutritive value of browse in West Africa. *In* "Browse in Africa: The Current State of Knowledge" (H. N. Le Houérou, ed.), pp. 261–264. International Livestock Centre for Africa, Addis Ababa, Ethiopia.

McArthur, E. D., and Welch, B. L. (1982). Growth rate differences among big sagebrush (*Artemisia tridentata*) accessions and subspecies. *J. Range Manage.* **35**, 396–401.

McKell, C. M. (1975). Shrubs—A neglected resource of arid lands. *Science* **187**, 803–809.

McKell, C. M. (1980). Multiple use of fodder trees and shrubs—A worldwide perspective. *In* "Browse in Africa: The Current State of Knowledge" (H. N. Le Houérou, ed.), pp. 141–149. International Livestock Centre for Africa, Addis Ababa, Ethiopia.

Maynard, L. A., Loosli, J. K., Hintz, H. F., and Warner, R. G. (1979). "Animal Nutrition," 7th ed. McGraw-Hill, New York.

Mecha, I., and Adegbolia, T. A. (1980). Chemical composition of some southern Nigeria forage eaten by goats. *In* "Browse in Africa: The Current State of Knowledge" (H. N. Le Houérou, ed.), pp. 303–306. International Livestock Centre for Africa, Addis Ababa, Ethiopia.

Medin, D. E., and Anderson, A. E. (1979). "Modeling the Dynamics of a Colorado Mule Deer Population," Wildl. Manage. No. 68. Wildlife Society, Washington, D.C.

National Academy of Sciences (1975). "Nutrient Requirements of Sheep." 5th rev. ed., Publ. No. 5. National Research Council, Washington, D.C.

National Academy of Sciences (1976). "Nutrient Requirements of Beef Cattle," 5th rev. ed., Publ. No. 4. National Research Council, Washington, D.C.

National Academy of Sciences (1977). "Nutrient Requirements of Rabbits," 2nd rev. ed., Publ. No. 9. National Research Council, Washington, D.C.

National Academy of Sciences (1978). "Nutrient Requirements of Horses," 4th rev. ed., Publ. No. 6. National Research Council, Washington, D.C.

National Academy of Sciences (1982). "Nutrient Requirements of Mink and Foxes," 2nd rev. ed., Publ. No. 7. National Research Council, Washington, D.C.

National Academy of Sciences (1984). "Nutrient Requirements of Poultry," 8th rev. ed., Publ. No. 8. National Research Council, Washington, D.C.

Noller, G. L., and McArthur, E. D. (1986). Establishment and initial results from a sagebrush (*Artemisia tridentata*) mass selection garden. *USDA For. Serv. Gen. Tech. Rep. INT* **INT-200,** 104–107.

Otsyina, R. M, McKell, C. M., and Van Epps, G. A. (1982). Use of range shrubs to meet nutrient requirements of sheep grazing on crested wheatgrass during fall and early winter. *J. Range Manage.* **35,** 751–753.

Platou, K. A., and Tueller, P. T. (1985). Evolutionary implications for grazing management systems. *Rangelands* **7,** 57–61.

Remington, T. E. (1983). Food selection, nutrition, and energy reserves of sage grouse during winter, North Park, Colorado. M. S. Thesis, Colorado State University, Fort Collins.

Shepherd, H. R. (1971). Effects of clipping on key browse species in southwestern Colorado. *Tech. Publ.—Colo., Div. Game, Fish Parks* **28.**

Smith, A. D. (1950). Sagebrush as winter feed for mule deer. *J. Wildl. Manage.* **14,** 285–289.

Tueller, P. T. (1979). "Food Habits and Nutrition of Mule Deer on Nevada Ranges." University of Nevada-Reno, Reno.

Van Dersal, W. R. (1938). Utilization of woody plants as food by wildlife. *Trans. North Am. Wildl. Conf.* **3,** 768–775.

Welch, B. L. (1983). Big sagebrush: Nutrition, selection, and controversy. *In* "Proceedings, of the First Utah Shrub Ecology Workshop" (K. L. Johnson, ed.), pp. 21–33. Utah State University, Logan.

Welch, B. L., and Davis, J. N. (1984). *In vitro* digestibility of *Kochia prostrata* (L.) Schrad. *Great Basin Nat.* **44,** 296–298.

Welch, B. L., and McArthur, E. D. (1979). Variation in winter levels of crude protein among *Artemisia tridentata* subspecies grown in a uniform garden. *J. Range Manage.* **32,** 467–469.

Welch, B. L., and McArthur, E. D. (1986). Wintering mule deer preference for 21 accessions of big sagebrush. *Great Basin Nat.* **46,** 281–286.

Welch, B. L., and Monsen, S. B. (1984). Winter nutritive value of accessions of four wing saltbush (*Atriplex canescens* [Pursh] Nutt.) grown in a uniform garden. *USDA For. Serv. Gen. Tech. Rep. INT* **INT-172,** 138–144.

Welch, B. L., and Pederson, J. C. (1981). *In vitro* digestibility among accessions of big sagebrush by wild mule deer and its relationship to monoterpenoid content. *J. Range Manage.* **34,** 497–500.

Welch, B. L., McArthur, E. D., and Davis, J. N. (1981). Differential preference of wintering mule deer for accessions of big sagebrush and for black sagebrush. *J. Range Manage.* **34,** 409–411.

Welch, B. L., Pederson, J. C., and Clary, W. P. (1983). Ability of different rumen inocula to digest range forages. *J. Wildl. Manage.* **47,** 873–878.

Welch, B. L., McArthur, E. D., and Rodriguez, R. L. (1987). Variation in utilization of big sagebrush accessions by wintering sheep. *J. Range Manage.* **40,** 113–115.

White, S. M., Flinders, J. T., Welch, B. L. (1982). Preference of pygmy rabbit (*Brachylagus idahoensis*) for various populations of big sagebrush (*Artemisia tridentata*). *J Range Manage.* **35,** 724–726.

Wilson, A. D., and Harrington, G. N. (1980). Nutritive value of Australian browse plants. *In* "Browse in Africa: The Current State of Knowledge" (H. N. Le Houérou, ed.), pp. 291–297. International Livestock Centre for Africa, Addis Ababa, Ethiopia.

Zimmerman, E. A. (1980). Desert ranching in central Nevada. *Rangelands* **2,** 184–186.

19

Fodder Shrubs for Range Improvement: The Syrian Experience

Omar Draz*

I. Introduction

Of Syria's 18,500,000 ha of total land area, the steppe covers around 10,859,000 ha or about 58% of the area in a rainfall zone of 250 mm or less per year. This resource supplies the country with about 80% of the feed requirement for its 8 million sheep. A large percentage of this sheep and goat population is owned by merchants and urban citizens and is shepherded by Bedouins together with their own flocks. Sheep graze on

---

* Deceased. For reprints, write to Agricultural Research Center, Crops Research Institute, Forage Section, Cairo University, Giza, Egypt.

The Biology and Utilization of Shrubs

the ranges of the steppe, mostly along the traditional eastward or south-ward–northward migration routes corresponding with annual rainy and dry seasons.

Erratic and uncertain rainfall and years of drought occur at intervals of about 5 to 8 years and result in wide fluctuations in sheep numbers from one season to another. Over 40% of the population was lost during a series of unfavorable seasons (1958 to 1960).

A. Historical Aspects of Overgrazing and Degradation of Syrian Rangelands

Several authors have described the thick vegetative cover that used to dominate all Syrian rangeland. Emberger (1956) indicated that Syria was entirely forested except in areas of saline soils. He also referred to the wealth of grasses and legumes that once were dominant throughout the country and that have been replaced by less productive species. Evidence by Pearce (1970) indicated that climatic fluctuations were responsible for deterioration of the natural vegetation in the Middle East, suggesting that for the past 4000 years, the climate of the area has fluctuated around a mean that closely resembles that of the present (Butzer, 1961; Bobek, 1968; Thalen, 1979).

As a result of overgrazing in the absence of control measures, the more platable subshrubs, perennial grasses, and legumes, such as *Salsola vermic-late, S. lancifolia, Stipa barbata, Astragalus* spp., and *Onobrychis* spp., formerly common in the Syrian steppe, were replaced by less palatable plants such as *Noea mucronata, Peganum harmala*, and several spiny shrubs of very low forage value. Where *Poa sinaica* was once the dominant species, overgrazing has brought about an increase in *Carex stenopylla*, a less productive species.

In the mountain ranges and high rainfed areas of the northern Jezireh and along the coastal plains, some of the best forage grasses, legumes, and forbs have been eliminated from large areas and replaced by weeds and spiny plants such as *Poterium spinosum*. On much of the high rainfed mountain ranges little remains except barren eroded rocks. The traditional seasonal migration of flocks, which formerly gave the range some rest and a chance to recuperate, has been disrupted by modern transport of animals and water.

Plowing of the original natural vegetative cover has completely destroyed a number of valuable plant associations such as *Poa sinaica, P. bulbosa, Stipa barbata,* and *S. lagascae,* and these have been replaced by less productive annuals such as *Hordeum murinum* and *Stipa capensis,* which are not reliable forage during drought years or dry seasons.

Under Syrian conditions, reestablishment of the natural vegetative cover after plowing is a slow process. In many cases, unplatable shrubs, such as *Anabasis syriaca*, have become the dominant species on previously plowed rangeland.

Degradation of the plant cover has intensified wind and water erosion, causing a decrease in soil fertility (including a marked loss of organic matter). This is usually accompanied by a subsequent downward trend in both long-term water-retaining capacity and total production in forage or grain yield.

Cutting of trees and shrubs for firewood, where these formerly were common, has also increased soil erosion with a subsequent decrease in soil fertility and productivity. The animal population has thus been deprived of an important source of forage during certain seasons of the year. Palatable subshrubs, shrubs, and trees such as *Salsola vermiculata, S. lancifolia, Haloxylon articulatum,* and *Quercus* spp. are rated highly both as firewood and as feed.

Feed reserves to carry animals through critical periods (such as dry seasons and drought) have not been adequate. Until recently, very little feed concentrate was utilized. Although the country has for decades been producing large quantities of barley and other concentrated feed, proper systems for utilization of such feeds have been developed only lately through a UNDP/FAO project (SYR/68/011). More than 90% of the cottonseed cake produced in Syria had previously been exported; but at the present time, export of feed is prohibited.

Although about one-third of the steppe ranges (including the most fertile parts) have been plowed for grain production, no substitute for forage production in the higher rainfed or irrigated areas was made available with the result that more animals were forced to graze areas of lower productivity.

The present dichotomy of animal and plant production systems predominating over the region could be considered a continuation of the age-old struggle between herder and farmer. It has even been intensified lately in Syria through a number of intervening factors such as the Syrian Legislative Decree No. 65 of 1966, which required an annual seasonal movement of sheep and goats out of the cultivated areas into the steppe ranges until the cropping season in the cultivated areas was over. This decree was passed to stop herds from trespassing in the fields. Until recently, no action of a similar nature was considered to stop plowing. This bias in favor of crop production prevented proper utilization of large areas of the traditionally fallowed land (in rotation with wheat) for fodder production, and thus precluded integration of animal production into the agricultural system.

Sheep and goat raising on the range has been carried out under a system of free uncontrolled grazing practices. In the past, traditional rights of use had been recognized and were claimed by most tribes on certain range sites, with enough support from the previous Tribal Act and related traditional laws (ourf). Most recent governments of the region have considered the steppe (perhaps for political or internal security reasons) as state- or government-owned land open to free grazing by all. The abrogation of previous tribal grazing rights without compensation of a practical substitute opened the gate for the destructive "mashaa" system of free uncontrolled grazing, which has been defined by Hardin (1968) as a "tragedy of the commons."

Previously, the Bedouin had been powerful enough not only to protect their range resources, but also to enforce tribute from settlements for the protection of their crops by avoiding trespassing. Now, with a sedentary settled population predominant, some other type of integration is needed to ensure proper utilization of complementary forage resources.

B. Traditional Role of Shrubs in Range Uses

Shrubs used to constitute a high percentage of the native vegetative cover in the plant associations of Syrian range sites mentioned above. Many of these species are of economic value for either fodder, fuel, or timber. Among the main useful species are: *Salsola vermiculate, S. lancifolia, Atriplex leucoclada, A. halimus, Noea mucronata, Salsola inermis, Artemisia herba-alba, Achillea* spp., *Astragalus* spp., *Onobrychis olivieri, Erodium cicutarium, Tamarix articulata, Pistacia palistyina,* and *Rhamnus palistina.*

C. Development of the Concept of Fodder Shrub Plantations in Syria

Reasons for the deteriorating conditions of Syrian rangelands have been essentially social and governed by political, military, and economic factors that are mostly beyond the control of the Bedouins living under modern conditions imposed on their traditional life-style. Instability of modern life and the abandonment of the traditional grazing rights in the ecologically fragile arid and semiarid environment increase the pressure of overgrazing, cutting of woody plants as firewood, and plowing of marginal areas for precarious grain production. Consequently most areas that once formed the best grazing lands have deteriorated and are now considered as "human-made deserts" (see Fig. 1).

Against this background, the Syrian experience in range improvement is based on a broad approach that tackles the different problems simul-

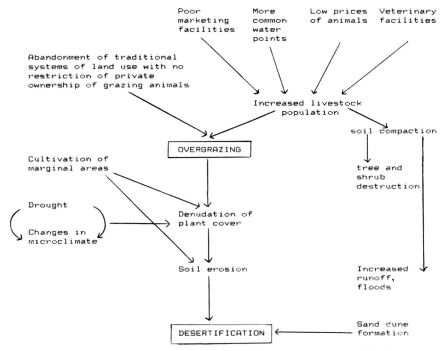

Figure 1. Interaction of factors leading to overgrazing and desertification.

taneously by utilizing different inputs. A schematic development and organization program of Syria is shown in Table I, which briefly outlines the different phases and activities incorporated.

A new approach utilizing an ancient grazing system was tried. The "Hema system" of grazing in the form of a range cooperative was found acceptable to the Bedouins while also meeting the technical requirements of government administrators. This has become a model for sound management leading to improved socioeconomic conditions for the Bedouins. Of particular importance was the discovery that certain incentives encouraged the Bedouins to accept the recommended management practices and ensured their full participation and involvement in the program from the beginning.

Establishment of the first Hema cooperative paved the way for development of the Syrian National Range and Steppe Development Program. This included establishment of government Hema centers, fattening cooperatives, legislation for control on plowing of the steppe, and integration of animal production in the agricultural system. Revival of the ancient Hema system in a cooperative form reversed the belief of most recent regional

Table I. Schematic development and organization of SYR/68/011 project and related complementary activities

I INITIATION PHASE

	Government Policy	Establishment of Executive Agency
Inclusion within National Agricultural Development Plan	Development of rangeland and forage crop production, and stabilization of nomadic sheep husbandry Integration and development of plant and animal production	Establishment of Steppe, Range, and Sheep Department

II PLANNING PHASE

Problem Analysis

- Increasing human population and food requirement causing shortage in food and feed production
- Most land is grazing area (Mediterranean climate with long dry summers and drought seasons)
- Depletion of the range through overgrazing, uprooting of plants and plowing of marginal lands
- Valuable natural perennial vegetation destroyed and wildlife mostly eradicated
- Traditional communal rights of use stopped with no compensation or substitute
- Trampling, erosion, loss of water causing expanded desertification
- Seasonal starvation of animals
- Inadequate legislation and absence of incentives for proper land use and grazing management
- Lack of organized marketing arrangements
- Dichotomy or lack of integration between agricultural and grazing resources
- Very little feed reserve
- Improper economic interrelationship between sheep and the range
- Lack of trained personnel in range management

Outline of a National Master Plan

Technical Assistance	Predevelopment Surveys	Training Schemes	Finance and Legislation	Support Services
UN/FAO TA Bilateral TA Est. ACSAD Est. of International regional research program	Ecological and phyto-geographical surveys Experimental testing for plant introduction Management surveys Preparation of development programs	UN fellowships Agricultural Colleges Training Arab Forestry and Range Management Institute, Lattakia Special courses In-service training Bilateral assistance	Government funds UNDP/FAO/WFP/NFRF World Bank Bilateral assistance Legislation Establishment of Project Planning Follow-up Committee and NFRF Executive Board Establishment of National Feed Policy Committee	Water development program Cooperative program Introduction of forage crops into the rotation Advisory assistance to related complementary activities and projects

III ACTION PHASE

Establishment of Development Units

	Range and sheep hema cooperatives	Fattening cooperatives	Dairy cattle cooperatives feed requirements	Integration of livestock into the farming system through introduction of forage crops in rotation	NFRF and its Executive Board	Legislation (controlled grazing, control on plowing)
Est. SRSD Range and Sheep Govt. Centers for Extension, Education and Training						
Fellowships						Water development (dams, wells, and cisterns)
College training						Wildlife and game protection
Arab Forestry and Range Management Institute, Lattakia						Research program
			Specialized Cooperative Union of Project Cooperatives			
Bedouin Training Center, Esseriyeh	Marketing facilities through cooperatives	Establishment of General Feed Organization and building up of government feed reserve	Intensification of agricultural production plan, development of irrigation projects, and integration of plants and animal production.			

SUPPORTING PROGRAMS

Planning and Follow-up Committee	UNDP/FAO SYR/68/011	Stabilization of Nomadic Sheep Husbandry, WFP (002) project	Integration of Animal Production into the Agricultural System, WFP (272) project		Animal Production WFP (2018) project	Dam construction WFP (269) project
				WFP (2164) Jolan Resettlement project		Farmers' Union

World Bank Loan Agreement
FRG and US bilateral aid
NE/FAO Government Cooperatives Program
Plans for Cooperative Program with EMASAR, ACSAD, ICARDA and other regional and interregional programs (started, in preparation, or under discussion)

governments that all the steppe ranges should be kept as government-owned land and common free range. The program reintroduced the concept of controlled grazing management to replace the former destructive systems.

The success achieved by a series of hema cooperatives in the vicinity of Wadi El-Azib Range Station, where conservation practices have been demonstrated since 1959, suggested the opportunity to establish similar centers for training purposes in other locations. Subsequently, ten similar centers were established that covered a total land area of 124,460 ha. The grazing sheep population in seven of these centers in 1985 was 18,000 awasi sheep, which are also utilized in a sheep breeding and improvement program in cooperation with ACSAD (Arab Centre for Semi-Arid and Arid Zone Development).

II. The Shrub Plantation Program

A. *Developing the Plan*

As indicated earlier, the Syrian National Range and Steppe Development Program incorporated a special project for shrub plantations that has had a fair amount of success. This includes:

1. Establishment (during 1968–1972) of observation test plots for adaptation of range and forage crops in areas representing different ecological conditions along the Syrian steppe. *Atriplex nummularia* proved to be adapted to most of these steppe range sites.
2. Implementation of the Syrian program, through a World Food Program, became a model for projects of this type. A series of interrelated actions were initiated to stabilize and develop nomadic sheep husbandry. Project achievement, including the formation of *Atriplex* plantations, has been far above the targets stipulated (Draz, 1980).

   So far about 15,000 ha of palatable drought-resistant shrubs have been planted. The present Government Five-Year Development Plan aims at the production of 45 million seedlings for planting 45,000 ha. Establishment of 270 Hema cooperatives in 9 Mahafazat incorporating 33,608 members has made the concept of fodder shrub reserves a national reality.

   Further, establishment of ten Government Range and Sheep centers for training, extension, and research purposes has made possible the establishment of ten nurseries for production of palatable shrubs for transplantation.
3. Conservation of rangeland through prohibition of plowing and cultivation in the steppe lands has become a part of the National Range

and Steppe Development Program through Legislative Decree No. 140 of 1971, which was endorsed by the Syrian Parliament through Law 13 of 1973, "Prohibition of Ploughing and Cultivation of Rangelands within the Steppe Regions."

4. Development of the water resources through restoration of rainwater systems, digging of surface and deep wells, and establishment of surface dams has made it possible to meet the watering requirements of transplants during establishment stages whenever necessary.

5. Other activities such as establishment of fattening cooperatives, animal health programs, and training programs for research and extension have directly or indirectly supported the Shrub Plantation Program.

6. Not the least in importance has been the technical assistance of UNDP/FAO through Project SYR/68/011, which made it possible to obtain World Food Program assistance and support and consequently the establishment of the National Feed Reserve Program (NFRP).

7. The NFRP has become an important factor in the Syrian range development program. It has also become powerful enough to be recognized by the World Bank to qualify for a loan of U.S. $17.5 million. The loan was used to support program activities, mostly to provide credit to members of Hema Range Cooperatives or Fattening Cooperatives. This was a historical landmark for the Bedouins as they have been deprived of government and banking credit facilities, their rangelands have been considered to be government-owned, and their nomadic flocks have not been of any recognized lending value to financial organizations. The system initiated and developed by the project through NFRF has now solved these problems.

B. Selection of Species

Early experimental introduction of *Atriplex* spp. started in 1959 during the political union between Syria and Egypt as the United Arab Republic (1958 to 1961) (Draz, 1960). This work was started at Deir El Hgar Experimental Dairy Farm. Upon returning to Syria as an FAO Range Management Expert during 1967, Draz noticed about 20 *Atriplex* shrubs growing in the same nursery together with many other introduced grasses, possibly planted by van der Veen (1962, 1966). Plants of *A. nummularia* were outstanding in growth. One single shrub was 3 m high and covered about 15 m^2 surface area. Subsequently this species also showed promise in transplant success under conditions of the eight observation test plots.

Fifteen exotic dryland palatable shrubs including five varieties of *A. canescens* were included in experimental trials at two forestry nurseries near Damascus from 1973 to 1980. One *A. canescens* ecotype (FAO Accession No. 32261) showed good growth features and adaptability to a number of range sites. Lack of available seeds of this variety and low vegetative reproduction have hindered or limited expansion of *A. canescens* compared with *A. nummularia.*

Plants grown from locally produced seeds of the American variety demonstrated a high cold tolerance and snow resistance during a very cold winter season. Because of a favorable comparison with *A. nummularia* from the Mediterranean Southern Australian climate, interest has shifted toward the American variety of *A. canescens.*

Colutea aleppica (Syn. *C. istria*), a native leguminous shrub that grows up to 3 m in height, was observed by Draz (1975) in Jordan steppe ranges along the road to Petra. The native habitat of this shrub extends from Turkey to Syria and spreads southward to Jordan and Mount Sinai. Seeds were collected by Draz and planted in Syria and Jordan and lately in the northern Sinai in shrub nurseries. The species has been included in observation plots in comparison with other shrubs and appears to be well suited to cold mountain ranges.

Under the protection given to exotic shrub plantations, a number of native shrubs and perennial grasses have shown rapid natural regeneration within the introduced shrub stands. Outstanding among these were *Salsola vermiculata* (Syn. *S. villosa*) and *Atriplex leucoclada,* with the result that they are now being used in the production of seedlings in the Shrub Plantation Program. This is shown in data relative to seedling production during 1982–1983 in the ten specialized project nurseries that have been established for this purpose, as shown below:

Species	Origin	No. of seedling transplants
Atriplex canescens	American	3,619,000
A. nummularia	Australian	1,670,000
A. halimus	Tunis, Jordan	1,196,000
A. californiana	American	680,000
Salsola vermiculata	Syrian	500,000
A. leucoclada	Syrian	260,000
Tamarix sp.	Syrian	40,000
A. lentiformis	American	39,000
Medicago arborea	Southern Europe	18,000
Other different trees, shrubs, and horticultural species		1,193,000
		9,221,000

ACSAD has contributed to the supply of seeds for three exotic *Atriplex* species from its nurseries, one at Wadi El-Azib Government Range and

Sheep Station and the other at Muslemieh near Aleppo (in cooperation with the University of Aleppo). Many experts and consultants from different international, regional, and bilateral organizations have also contributed to the planning and organization of this Shrub Plantation Program through their suggestions, criticism, donations of equipment, genetic resources, and training facilities.

C. Forage Values

Analyses for digestibility (both *in vivo* and *in vitro*) have been carried out in many countries of the Middle East on native and introduced shrubs that are likely to be tried under Syrian steppe conditions. In addition, nutritional values have been reported in the international literature, particularly from the United States and Australia. During the initiation of the UNDP/FAO/SYR/68/011 Project the research program was limited to the development program that emphasized experimental plant introductions with the principal emphasis on perennial shrub plantations. The attraction of shrubs to the Bedouin community was their rate of growth, drought resistance, salt tolerance, and volume of feed produced during the dry season. Under dry season conditions, quantity, palatability, and ability to establish plants were higher objectives than feed quality and comparative nutritional value. Fortunately the first successful shrub species in the experimental shrub plantation program filled most of the nutritional requirements.

At a later stage of project development, Draz (1978) prepared a note on a "National Development-Oriented Research Program in the Field of Range Management and Forage Crops Production." A high committee chaired by the Minister of Agriculture, plus members representing concerned national, regional, and international organizations, evaluated *Atriplex* spp. for their grazing use to fulfill the requirements of the World Bank Loan Agreement with the Syrian Government in support of the National Range and Steppe Development Program. The assessment was very favorable.

In 1985, some of the research programs of the Shrub Plantation program include:

1. Investigate the best time for transplantation of seedlings in ten Government Range and Sheep Centers (GRSC).
2. Establishment of shrub plantations in 4-m bands of three rows of *Atriplex* along contour lines for interplanting of barley between the rows; seven GRSC are cooperating in this program.
3. Reseeding trials in five GRSC. Positive results have already been obtained in reseeding of *Salsola vermiculata, Atriplex halimus,* and

A. leucoclada with the result that a Seed Production Center has been established at Kasr El Heir (near Palmyra) for annual production of these species (Samman, 1985).

Observations and accumulated data show clearly to Bedouins and responsible officials that the program of shrub plantations is highly efficient in filling certain gaps in sheep feeding in the Syrian steppe. Under Hassakeh conditions in North Jezireh (280 mm rainfall average), 3-year-old *Atriplex nummularia* shrubs, partially grazed in the first and second years, produced in the third year a biomass of about 10 tons/ha of green edible leaves and twigs (Draz, 1980). Average production under 150 mm precipitation along the Syrian steppe in suitable areas could be estimated at around 1 ton of edible leaves and twigs per hectare. This should be enough to supply vitamin, mineral, and protein requirements during part of the dry season through the massive palatable green feed it produces. The deficiency of carbohydrate content in *Atriplex* as an energy source to livestock could be supplemented through careful management and protection of the native annual and perennial grazing biomass growing between rows in the shrub plantations.

D. Local Involvement

The system adopted in the Syrian Shrub Plantation Program has been based on demonstrating the results of the experimental work with large-scale plots among the different GRSC to stimulate interest of the local people. Specialized cooperatives offering free shrub transplants to Bedouins or farmers who would agree to grow, maintain,, and properly utilize these plants made it possible to launch a successful shrub introduction program. Through the direct involvement of the people, about 2800 ha have been planted to shrubs under the initial plan. Subsequently an expansion program to cover 45,000 ha has been planned through the NFRP incentives and credit facilities.

A model cash flow of credit facilities through the NFRP to members of the specialized cooperatives is shown in Fig. 2; this has been modified often to fit with prevailing ecological and social conditions in different parts of the Syrian steppe.

E. Consequences of Protection and Management during Establishment

Prior to launching the UNDP/FA/SYR/68/011 Project, Syria endeavored to develop its range and sheep resources on a sound scientific basis.

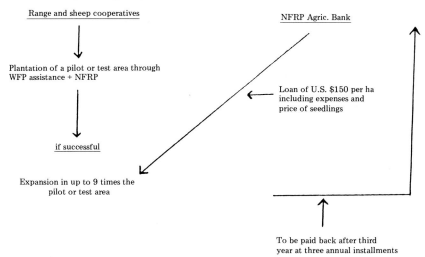

Figure 2. Model cash flow for plantation of fodder shrubs through NFRP.

Warehouses were built at selected key points within the Syrian steppe for storage and distribution of feed reserves. A program of digging wells and developing surface water was launched. A fuel oil stove specially suited to Bedouin requirements to minimize their need for shrubs and woody plants as firewood was produced and distributed to Bedouins on easy terms. Although World Food Program assistance included emergency feed stocks, it did not materially improve the precarious situation of the rangeland along the Syrian steppe. World Food Program assistance in feed might have even supported an increase in sheep population during the drought years of 1964–1966. At the same time measures to develop and maintain controlled grazing on the steppe were incomplete. Restriction of plowing of the steppe was not being enforced, and water resources were misused. Sheep fattening for effective offtake from the range had been very limited up to this time. Most of these defects were handled carefully as the Project SYR/68/011 developed along a broad front.

Under a Hema system of management, cooperative shrub plantations have been of great help in the reallocation and restoration of grazing rights to vast rangeland areas that had previously been abrogated and canceled during the last few decades.

The large volume of biomass from the growth of the selected shrubs provides enough useful green feed reserves to livestock during the autumn and early winter seasons when very little feed is available on the range. This grazing system helped to restore the traditional nomadic and transhumance grazing systems that represented a highly rational adaptation of

Bedouin life in the severe and adverse Syrian steppe environment. Most of the nomadic and seminomadic groups used to start their eastward and/or southward migration to their traditional rangelands during the autumn season, when they made use of the dominant shrubs. The availability of fodder from shrubs gives the nomads a chance to use the annual and perennial regrowth of grasses and legumes that germinate under favorable conditions created by winter and spring rainfall. During the summer when water for the flocks becomes the essential element for survival in these regions, the Bedouin groups return to the cultivated areas to graze or eat grain stubble and then to move to the cotton fields during early autumn, thus completing a grazing cycle. This cycle has been described extensively by Masri and Sankari (1978).

The reintroduction of the Shrub Plantation Program also provides soil protection and helps to regenerate the natural plant cover, *Salsola verminculata, Atriplex leucoclada,* and *Stipa barbata* in many areas.

III. Integration of Fodder Shrub Use with Total Range Use and Livestock Production

A. *Social Benefits*

Probably one of the main social benefits obtained from the broad approach of the Syrian program (which supported the Shrub Plantation Program as one of its main projects) has been the revival and modernization of traditional systems of grazing management to overcome overgrazing and misuse of vegetation. The establishment of Hema cooperatives has proven to be acceptable to both Bedouins and government officials. This has made it possible to extend several services to the Bedouin communities such as credit facilities, veterinary assistance, training, and systems for storage and distribution of concentrated feed reserves. This in turn reestablished the cooperative unity of a demarcated and registered area of grazing land in replacement of tribal usufruct. This was supported by the government in the Legislative Decree No. 10 of 1971.

B. *Integration of Fattening Programs with Livestock Grazing*

Increasing fodder production (including browse from shrubs) helps to supply more lambs, at a young age, to lamb fattening enterprises. Meanwhile, these enterprises, through about 50 fattening cooperatives, mostly located along the marginal fringes of the Syrian steppe, have promoted planting of fodder shrubs. The Syrian Prime Minister's Office has passed regulations that specify that land used for private cultivation is limited to a maximum of 45 ha. The following restrictions apply:

* No more than 70% of each property may be used for barley production.
* 30% should be planted to palatable shrubs.

Under irrigation from wells (the compulsory limit is 14 ha per well), the following should be planted:

* 4 ha for summer crops
* 8 ha for winter crops
* 2 ha for plantations of palatable shrubs

During 1983, about 50 fattening cooperatives in 9 Mohafazat (provinces) comprising around 6400 members fattened approximately 1,742,999 head of sheep. The management and financing of these cooperatives constitute only one part of the picture; the availability of sheep for purchase depends on the production of healthy sheep properly fed on the range.

References

Bobek, H. (1968). "History of Iran," Vol. 1. Cambridge Univ. Press, London and New York.

Butzer, K. W. (1961). Climatic change in arid regions since the Pliocene. *Arid Zone.* **17,** 31–56.

Draz, Or. (1960). "Report to the Syrian Government on Range Management and Fodder Development for Sheep Production" (in Arabic).

Draz, Or. (1975). "Rangeland Development in Saudia Arabia". Univ. of Riyadh Press (in Arabic).

Draz, Or. (1978). Revival of the Hema system of range reserves as a basis for the Syrian Range Development Program. *Proc. Int. Rangel. Congr., 1st,* pp. 100–105.

Draz, Or. (1980). "Final Report to Syrian Arab Republic on Syrian Rangeland Development and Sheep Fattening Program and National Feed Revolving Fund," UNDP/FAO/SYR 68/011 Proj.

Emberger, L. (1956). "Report of Mission to the Middle East." Letter addressed to Omar Draz containing an extract of original unmodified report. Inst. Bot. Univ. Montpellier, Montpellier, France.

Hardin, G. (1968). The tragedy of the commons. *Science* **162,** 1243–1248.

Masri, M., and Sankari, M. (1978). "Cycle of Cattle Grazing Movement in Utilizing Rangeland and Stubble-fields in Syria." Report to Syrian Government.

Pearce, C. K. (1970). Grazing in the Middle East: Past, present, and future. *J. Range Manage.* **24,** 13–16.

Samman, (1985). "Report of Seed Production Center, Kasr-El Heir. Annual Production of Seeds for the Syrian Rangeland Development Programme." Damascus, Syria.

Thalen, D. C. P. (1979). "Ecology and Utilization of Desert Shrub Rangelands in Iraq." Junk, The Hague.

van der Veen, J. P. H. (1962). Some aspects of land use for livestock production in southwest Asia with particular reference to Iraq. *Land Econ.* **38,** 356–369.

van der Veen, J. P. H. (1966). "Range Management and Fodder Development. Report to the Government of Syria," Proj. FAO/TA 2351 Pl TA/43.

20

Shrubs as Habitats for Wildlife

Philip J. Urness

I. Introduction

Shrubs, and trees whose canopies occupy the shrub layer (about 1–3 m) because of youth or site conditions, contribute significantly to habitat values for a broad spectrum of wildlife species. Woody plants provide food or feeding sites, security, and breeding areas for vertebrate and invertebrate animals above and below ground. The relative importance of shrubs as a group to the ecology of particular species can vary from casual facultative associations to ones that are strongly obligatory. Habitat in the latter context is more than space to occupy, rather it is truly a niche that encompasses satisfaction of life requirements in total.

Recognition of these complex relationships only makes the task of reducing them to useful discussion in a brief review more difficult. However, it is of interest to contrast the quite disparaging assessment of the role shrubs play in forage resources of both domestic and wild ungulates by Wilson (1969) with the optimistic general view in the proceedings of the 1971 symposium at Utah State University (McKell *et al.*, 1972).

The thrust of this review is the increasing attention that has been paid, during the past decade since Robinette's (1972) paper in the 1971 symposium, to concepts of wildlife "cover" and where shrubs appear to fit into them. At this juncture such concepts are not well defined, even for the more common North American ungulates, and should be considered working hypotheses.

II. Shrubs as Protection from Weather

A. Cold Climates

Thermal cover has been viewed rather broadly as seasonal or diurnal shifts in animal distribution to vegetational types, topographic features, and elevations that afford relief from the high energetic costs of tempering extremes of cold or heat, high wind (chill factor), and driving precipitation. In effect, a homeotherm attempts to maintain itself in a thermal-neutral environment (Moen, 1973, pp. 286–296). More recent papers by Black *et al.* (1976) and Thomas *et al.* (1979) have given very specific definitions of thermal cover for deer (*Odocoileus* spp.) and elk (*Cervus elaphus*) on spring–summer ranges in coniferous forests of the Pacific Northwest. These guidelines were based in part on distributions of animals observed for long periods (Pedersen *et al.*, 1980; Leckenby, 1984). Winter cover needs were said to be more critical, yet guidelines were not forthcoming because of potentially severe "consequences of error" and the need to alter cover only after careful study at the local or stand level. Although these authors emphasized the preliminary nature of their guidelines, managers have tended to proceed on the assumption that the relationships are generally applicable and have incorporated them into timber management plans on an interregional scale (Cole, 1983, Smith and Long, 1987).

Peek *et al.* (1982) reasonably questioned the specific thermal guidelines of Thomas *et al.* (1979) on the basis that requirements for deer and elk have not been quantified. The former's view of the distribution of animals in the Blue Mountain example was an expression of habitat preference rather than absolute need (the theoretical versus real basis for current thermal cover designs was also recently pointed out by Severson and Medina, 1983). Stark exceptions to the Thomas *et al.* model are exemplified by an apparently successful elk population in shrub–grass steppe at the Hanford Reserve in the Columbia Basin Desert (Rickard *et al.*, 1977) and red deer on islands, barren of trees or tall shrubs, with harsh climates in Scotland (Clutton-Brock *et al.*, 1982; Clutton-Brock and Albon, 1983), where topography provides some shelter from cold winds.

The role of shrubs in thermal cover considerations is important because they moderate wind force near the ground and thus increase the effectiveness of tree canopies. Shrubs also make more open habitats (e.g., shrub–grass steppe) usable (Leckenby *et al.*, 1982). However, shrub stands alone appear to be intermediate in value as winter habitats for deer in eastern Oregon since weather severity indexes there are higher than in juniper woodland but lower than in open grasslands (Fig. 1; Leckenby, 1977, 1978; Bright, 1978) of the cold desert. Neff (1980) found large clearings created by chaining juniper woodland in northern Arizona to be used extensively by deer in mild weather if Gambel oak (*Quercus gambelii*) sprouts formed shrubby thickets with good lateral cover. Such clearings were unused during winter storms, indicating that shrubs alone (especially deciduous ones) are often less attractive habitats if denser cover is available. These shrub stands can, however, make other cover types more valuable by providing feed resources that forest cover frequently lacks (Terrel and Spillett, 1975).

Vegetation types in mountainous western North America usually split on ridgelines such that timbered north-facing slopes have sparse understories and deep snow, while south- and west-facing slopes have less forest cover and snow, but more food for wild ungulates in the form of browse plants. Low winter sun angle from the south periodically melts snow and/or winds tend to deposit snow on cold north exposures. Thus, winter ungulate distribution is usually concentrated on south- and west-oriented slopes despite the lower cover values there (Loveless, 1967). Areas of normally deep snow (e.g., coastal Alaska and western Canada) may eliminate availability of even tall shrubs unless old-growth conifer forests are retained to intercept snow (Hanley, 1984). Wallmo and Gill (1971) graphically expressed the difficulty deer have in coping with deep snow in the high central valleys of Colorado. Populations fluctuate widely with oscillations in winter severity despite dense shrub stands.

Evidence of the negative impacts of shrub removal on habitat values of a shrub-dependent bird, the sage grouse (*Centrocercus urophasianus*), while not invariable, is overwhelming (Braun *et al.*, 1977; Heady and Bartolome, 1977). Widespread control of sagebrush with fire, herbicides, and mechanical means (usually followed by seeding of crested wheatgrass *Agropyron desertorum* or *A. cristatum*) has generally been inimical to sage grouse from both food resource and cover standpoints. October to May diets of this bird are nearly 100% big sagebrush leaves and wintering areas selected are preponderantly those with canopy coverage in excess of 20%, generally in lowland sites at times many kilometers from the breeding complex (Beck, 1977; Autenrieth, 1981). Snow depth is a critical factor in winter survival of sage grouse; depths above 30 cm are not uncommon and can

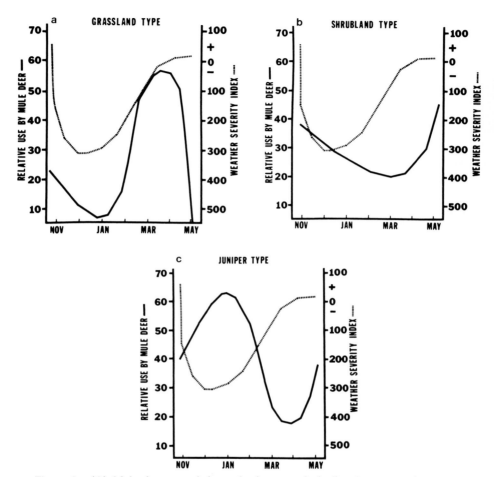

Figure 1. (A) Mule deer occupied grassland types principally when young forage was available and effective temperature was least stressful (weather severity index averaged less than −150). The WSI was constructed from temperature, wind, and snow measures to approximate effective temperature and consequent heat losses of deer. Relative use as calculated was (deer per acre in type/total deer per acre all types) × 100. (B) Mule deer occupied shrubland types principally when these stands provided the best forage and effective temperatures increased the need for cover (weather severity index averaged greater than −150). (C) Mule deer occupied juniper types when woodlands provided protection from stressful effective temperatures (weather severity index averaged greater than −200). (From Leckenby, 1978.)

blanket most sagebrush plants, making only the tallest available for food or cover. Tall sagebrush stands are indicators of deep soils and high potential for grass production and are most likely to be selected for control treatments. That there has been a strong direct correlation between sagebrush control and sage grouse declines in most areas of the bird's habitat in the western United States is undeniable; the degree of cause and effect, however, is a hotly debated question (Vale, 1974).

B. Hot Climates

At the opposite end of the spectrum are shrub values for shade and food resources for browsers and other wildlife in hot environments. Successional dynamics from grasslands to woodlands or shrublands and back to grassland in semiarid and arid regions are recognized worldwide as the result of oscillations in fire, grazing, and browsing, or a combination. The consequences of this cycle for shrub-dependent wildlife can be extreme. Several case studies continents apart illustrate the point.

An excellent explanation of this process as it applies to the Serengeti and other parks in East Africa was written by Norton-Griffiths (1979). In this scenario woodland and bush-thicket types in the Serengeti declined in the 1960s and 1970s, especially in the northern section, as a consequence of increased fire frequency and browsing impacts on short regenerating trees and shrubs by giraffe (*Giraffa camelopardalis*), elephant (*Loxodonta africana*), and rhinoceros (*Diceros bicornis*). Shifts toward grassland were strong until the elimination of rinderpest (a viral disease affecting ruminants) allowed irruptions in populations of grazers, particularly wildebeest (*Connochaetes taurinus*) and buffalo (*Syncerus caffer*). Greatly increased offtake of primary production by these expanded herds reduced fuel loading and fires declined.

Recovery of trees and shrubs can be predicted but the population responses of browsing animals are not known sufficiently well to say with certainty how they will affect long-term trends. If they are resource limited and die before reducing shrub-tree resources through overutilization, then their population levels would track the woodland/grassland cycle with a short lag time. If, however, they do not die before overutilization of woody plants occurs, then they could trap the system in permanent grassland. Flexible feeders like elephant that can do reasonably well on either grass or browse are the critical factor in this process (Wing and Buss, 1970). Allowing all possible random events that intervene to dampen oscillations in a middle condition of maximum vegetal diversity would be desirable according to Norton-Griffiths, to negate extremes in either grassland or woodland dominance and grazer/browser population fluctuations over time for a more stable and resilient system. In a park situation there is merit in managing species populations not only to head off possible extinction of rare species but also to assure diversity of species to provide greater opportunities for visitors to experience a richer fauna (i.e., seeing a few rare woodland or bush-thicket forms has greater utility than seeing a thousand more wildebeest).

On managed rangelands the purposeful inclusion of grazers and browsers can maintain stability of plant species composition or drive succession in desired directions as well as maximize offtake of animal products and assure the flexibility of a diversified operation (Pratt and Gwynne, 1977). This can be accomplished by integrating domestic and wild ungulates or more readily managed domesticated "wild" ungulates such as eland (*Taurotragus oryx*). Native animals appear to be more heat tolerant, disease resistant, and nutritionally less constrained on native vegetation, especially shrubs in the dry season, than domestic breeds.

The dry season is a severe test of ruminants. A study of abusive grazing predominantly of grasses and forbs in India by domestic livestock, cattle (*Bos indicus*), and buffalo (*Bubalus bubalis*) in the Gir Forest in Giujarat state revealed the relatively low adaptability of these animals contrasted to six species of antelope and deer (Berwick, 1976). Whereas cattle and buffalo required expensive supplementation to maintain a low level of production during the dry season, native ungulates (almost exclusively browsers) remained fat because of greater forage quality of browse leaves versus grass. Concern for the continued welfare of these wild ungulates was, therefore, not based on competition for limited forage resources that they scarcely shared with livestock but rather on the tremendous soil erosion and incipient collapse of the system as a result of excessive use of the understory vegetation.

White-tailed deer and other shrub-adapted wildlife were apparently rare in the presettlement arid grasslands of central and south Texas (Teer *et al.,* 1965). Heavy livestock grazing and greatly curtailed fire frequency resulting from reduced fuel loading had, by 1900, shifted succession to a strong shrub or low tree dominance of oaks (*Quercus* spp.), mesquite (*Prosopis glandulosa*), and many other woody plants and succulents. Provision of browse resources, shade during the hot summers, and security cover allowed deer population increases to very high densities by the 1940s. Herbicide spraying of dense brush in strips caused short-term evacuation of treated pastures but posttreatment growth of forbs and shrubs resulted in an increase in deer use (Tanner *et al.,* 1978). Tall woody plant cover was reduced temporarily but effective screening cover at deer height was not affected. A return to "normal" deer densities occurred in a year and population effects were negligible. High ambient temperatures forced movement of white-tailed deer out of open grassland and upland types but not out of brush-savanna in Oklahoma (Ockenfels and Bissonette, 1984). Most moved to riparian habitats, where heavier cover and cooler temperatures prevailed. Steuter and Wright (1980) showed a direct correlation between deer density and thorn scrub cover in the Rio Grande Plains of south Texas. Cover of less than 43% had a maximum deer density of 1.4/40.5 ha, cover between 43 and 60% had 3.3 deer/40.5 ha, and cover from 69 to 97% had 7.5 deer/40.5 ha.

Mule deer occupy the more wooded sites in open desert and grassland (Wallmo, 1973). These animals and other species of wildlife also prospered with increased woody plant dominance on overgrazed and unburned desert grassland and prairie types; included in this group were peccary (*Tayassu tajacu*), wild turkey (*Meleagris gallopavo*), and several species of quail. Indeed, Wallmo stated that cover dependence in a hot climate for scaled and Gambel quail (*Lophortyx gambelii*) is absolute. Scaled quail (*Callipepla squamota*) make use of shortgrass prairie communities in Oklahoma, Texas, New Mexico, and Colorado only where human-made cover is developed for shade during the hot period. Burning of mesquite–tobosa grass (*Hilaria mutica*) communities for shrub reduction to increase livestock forage was detrimental to bobwhite quail (*Colinus virginianus*) because it was too frequent for shrubs to attain adequate size to provide necessary shade (Renwald *et al.*, 1978). Retention of unburned patches of larger shrubs eliminated that problem.

Davies (1973) described the need for homeotherms to cope seasonally with heat and cold stress in Australian shrublands. They did this via avoidance (e.g., seeking thermal-neutral refuges such as caves), concentration on optimal or "best available" habitat such as run-on areas of precipitation accumulation and better food availability, and migration to better habitats. Because of low relief and rather monotonous mulga (*Acacia aneura*) shrublands, shifts were horizontal in residual species and shrubs were important as shade in a very hot, dry climate. Permanent artificial water sources are much more abundant on managed stations, thus reducing wildlife concentrations in drought periods.

These examples illustrate the importance of woody plants as weather-protecting elements of contemporary wildlife habitats ranging from extremes of nonessential enhancement to apparent requirements. General statements are of limited utility in this area; each situation must be assessed on its own merits. One cannot shrug off the conclusion that diverse habitats, with all vegetation classes including shrubs present at some degree, offer more diverse faunal associations and, thus, more interesting environments for human enjoyment and well-being (Dealy *et al.*, 1981).

III. Shrubs as Protection from Harassment

Those who work and play in areas whose large predator complement has largely or entirely been lost are at an interpretative disadvantage compared to those who regularly experience more "natural" ecosystems. This is especially true when evaluating importance of cover for protection from harassment, lethal or otherwise, in terms of the energetic cost of existence and what that means for survival and productivity of many wildlife species.

The lack of predatory shaping of animal behavior may have long-term impacts that we as yet have not attempted to assess (Bertram, 1979; Geist, 1981). Yet Clutton-Brock *et al.* (1982) described pre- and postpartum behavior of red deer hinds in Scotland as innate antipredator tactics in environments where mammalian predators have long been absent. Moreover, tractable "wild" ungulates such as mule deer raised from birth by bottle feeding in predator-free pens still exhibit lifelong anxiety toward other animals in their environment (i.e., horses, dogs), even at considerable distances. These deer can readily be put into panicky flight without overt threats (Olson-Rutz and Urness, 1987).

A balance in prey behavior regarding cover must be struck between great vulnerability to predation in very dense cover versus the need for some degree of screening to minimize frequency of being seen and chased (Bertram, 1979). Presence of different types of predatory modes of attack in the Serengeti, for example, between cats and hyenas or wild dogs, makes natural selection for ungulate escape mechanisms at best a compromise. This is true for the individual's selection of habitats and, thus, cover as well. Where cover, predators, and prey are in good balance, the latter may be maintained in more healthy and productive condition by predators keeping prey populations at levels where food resources are not limiting as in the Gir Forest of India (Berwick, 1976).

Substitution of hunting strictly by human predators is viewed by some to compensate for loss of other mammalian predators. However, the influence of regulated hunting as we now know it in late twentieth-century North America is scarcely applicable since it tends to have a narrow time frame and occurs at times when energy costs are relatively low (fall) and animal condition is high. Still, the sheer numbers of hunters, increasingly restricted cover amounts, and ubiquity of mechanized access to coverts often impose an intensity of harassment that makes security cover management a major concern for wildlife biologists (Thomas *et al.,* 1979; Lyon, 1979; Leckenby *et al.,* 1982; Skovlin, 1982; Severson and Medina, 1983).

Behavioral exclusion of many species from vast areas of otherwise usable habitat often occurs, at least temporarily, with intense harassment and/or where cover is marginal. Shrub communities with modest cover densities and height are more subject to negative impacts than forested types; yet combinations of shrubs, topographic features of the landscape, and distance from the cause of disturbance can compensate for sparse cover in some situations (Severson, 1981; Leckenby *et al.*, 1982). Prairie deer are most vulnerable to hunting mortality and excessive exploitation because of inadequate security cover and the limited value of topography alone (Swenson, 1982). Management agencies need to be more sensitive to this issue than they have been generally. Patchy cover, if suitable for security, can be effective even if inadequate for feeding activity because *night* is itself security cover (Darr and Klebenow, 1975; Terrel and Spillett, 1975; Skogland and Mølmen, 1980), especially where large mammalian predators are scarce or absent.

Closely related wildlife species often differ radically in response to security cover as exemplified by white-tailed and mule deer in northern temperate forest/shrub (Keay and Peek, 1980) as well as arid shrubland types (Teer *et al.*, 1965). White-tailed deer occupy much denser cover areas than mule deer by preference and, where they are sympatric, shifts in cover conditions can cause similar changes in relative abundance between the two species. White-tailed deer in Texas and Arizona (Fig. 2) occur in more mesic woodland and chaparral types, whereas mule deer occupy the drier desert shrub communities (Wallmo, 1973); the latter seldom, if ever, reach densities half as great as those of white-tailed deer in the best habitats. Hiding strategy is much more developed in adult white-tailed deer than in mule deer; the latter have relatively high tolerance for disturbance compared to white-tailed deer and, thus, to open habitats (Geist, 1981). As fawns, both species are "hiders."

Security from harassment is important to wildlife in both cold and hot environments because the energetic costs of escape behavior are additive to climatic stress (Moen, 1973). Ability of shrubs to buffer various harassment agents is probably weak unless stands are also tall, dense, rocky, and steep. Winter survival of deer in areas of deep snow and cold temperatures is to a great extent dependent on energy-conservation tactics centered around minimizing activity. Given freedom from harassment, wild ungulates often become "standing hibernators," restricting energy demand in recognition that winter foods generally have low energy yields and serve only to slow the process of fat catabolism (Mautz, 1978). An example of severe population impact on elk from snowmobile activity was cited by Anderson and Scherzinger (1975) in central Oregon. However, Bergerud *et al.* (1984) found no apparent increase in mortality in caribou (*Rangifer tarandus*) in Alaska and Canada due to harassment except as new roads facilitated hunter access (a view strongly challenged by Klein and White, 1984; Whitten and Cameron, 1984; Miller and Gunn, 1985).

Figure 2. (A) Arizona chaparral of dense tall shrubs occupied primarily by Coues white-tailed deer (*Odocoileus virginianus couesi*). There is sympatry with desert mule deer at the chaparral–desert ecotone. (B) Sonoran Desert shrub type in central Arizona occupied by desert mule deer (*Odocoileus hemionus crooki*).

If, then, cover values of shrublands to minimize harassment are adequate only in the tall, dense types, more open or short types will need frequent managerial intervention to prevent excessive impacts on hunted wildlife populations and where entrepreneurial and recreational activities present a threat of cumulative encounters (Wolfe, 1978). The subtlety of this process is lost on people untrained to observe it; most see single events and view them as generally benign, but it is the additive effect of often repeated events that becomes critical. Complexity and inconsistency of cover–predator–prey relationships over space and time are even more difficult to interpret as evidenced by volatile debates among trained professionals. Consequently, hope for ready cover designs for species or entire suites of species is a forlorn one indeed and, despite appeals for ecosystem approaches to land and wildlife management, it is unlikely to be forthcoming outside large nature preserves or parks, if there. Elsewhere, dominant or favored-species management will continue to be emphasized, with perhaps a somewhat greater sensitivity exhibited toward a larger faunal array than was true in the past. Social and legal constraints, if not economic and biological ones, will dictate this (Gilbert, 1978).

IV. Shrub Stands as Breeding Complexes

Shrubs likely have their greatest cover values as habitat elements affecting the reproductive process: from dancing or nesting sites of sage grouse and other birds to fawning or calving areas for deer, antelope, elk, and other ungulates. While adults of various wildlife species have mobility or escape options to avoid weather and enemies, neonates and hatchlings do not. Thus, they are far more vulnerable to both and cover at or near the location where independent life begins is critically important for the individual as well as the population. That more open shrublands are frequently selected for this activity appears to be a compromise in many species between greater surveillance capability against predators versus more exposure to weather.

The importance of the fawning area in "hider" species in allowing for proper establishment of bonding between neonate and dam is well recognized in ungulates (Cowan, 1974) and likely is most critical for species in which the new fawn or calf hides apart from its mother for extended periods up to several weeks or even months (e.g., some African antelopes, *Antilocapra, Odocoileus,* and others). Bonding of the dam on the young may occur in a few minutes or several hours, but bonding of young on the dam can be extended over a long period. Tolerance to disturbance factors at this time varies among species; harassment can have severe effects on neonate survival and later effectiveness in the population.

Selection of calving sites by Rocky Mountain elk have disproportionately been reported as open sagebrush and grass or other shrubland types when dense conifer stands occur in the immediate area (Altmann, 1952; Boyd, 1978; Thomas *et al.*, 1979; Skovlin, 1982). Ward (1973) indicated little change in cow–calf behavior in this regard, even when sagebrush was heavily reduced by herbicidal treatment in Wyoming. Thus, openness of habitat for calving may be relatively unimportant so long as escape cover is close by. Abundance of high-quality forb and grass forage to support the high energetic demands of lactation may be more significant than shrub cover per se in a robust species like elk that can readily defend young against most predators. Whereas Ward (1973) and Altmann (1952) suggested considerable fidelity to the same calving areas in succeeding years, Houston (1982) reported elk exhibiting great year-to-year variation in calving location.

Deer, being smaller and less capable of fending off predator attacks on neonates, use somewhat denser fawning cover (Fielder and McKay, 1984). Also, they go to greater behavioral lengths to avoid predator contacts (e.g., stronger hider reflex, separation of fawns of multiple births, fawns selecting bed sites away from last contact with the doe, etc.) (Lent, 1974; Marchinton and Hirth, 1984). White-tailed deer defend fawning "territories" by aggressively excluding other deer, even members of the family group, for up to a month postpartum. This tends to disperse fawning over the entire habitat and reduce predatory losses as well as assuring exclusive feeding sites to support lactation (Nelson and Mech, 1981; Ozoga *et al.*, 1982). Similar behavior has been reported for black-tailed deer by Taber and Dasmann (1958) (Fig. 3) and Miller (1974). Thomas *et al.* (1979) described mule deer fawning habitat as being shrubs and low trees, but under an open tree overstory (approximately 50% canopy closure), in the Blue Mountains of northeastern Oregon.

Pronghorn antelope (*Antilocapra americana*) have a close affinity to shrublands generally, but to sagebrush–grass steppe particularly (Sundstrom *et al.*, 1973), in regions of greatest abundance today. Yet there appears to be a threshold of shrub height and density above which habitat values decline and opening up of taller dense stands via fire or other means has resulted in restoration of antelope use (Yoakum, 1980). Greater vulnerability of antelope fawns to predation in taller portions of shrub communities such as drainage channels in desert types (Beale and Smith, 1973; Smith and Beale, 1980) likely dictates that fawning and hiding of neonates occur in shrubs of low to moderate stature and density in flat or rolling uplands away from drainages, which predators tend to use as hunting pathways. Fichter (1974) worried that loss of sagebrush stands of moderate height (45–60 cm) to herbicidal treatments could have heavy

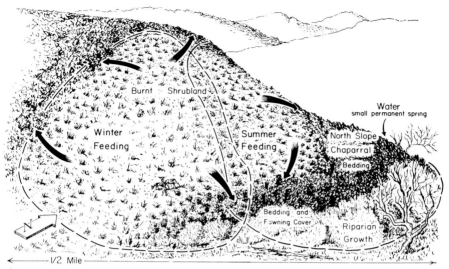

Figure 3. An example of a deer home range in California chaparral. Deer move from one exposure to another according to the season, feeding on warm south-facing slopes in winter and cool north-facing slopes in summer. Temperature variation within a single day will also influence movement. During summer, deer feed on south slopes in the cool night and in deep shady stream bottoms at midday. This sketch shows an area of shrubland (managed chaparral) half a mile in diameter, within which a doe could find her requirements for the entire year and within which she might spend her entire life. (From Taber and Dasmann, 1958.)

impact on antelope fawn survival since it was these types that parturient does sought out. He speculated that neonates imprinted on the birthing habitat for the "move-to-lie-secluded" phase of neonatal development (Autenrieth and Fichter, 1975).

Shrubland breeding complexes of sage grouse have received more research and management attention perhaps than any other single wildland bird species in North America. Despite that concern, it seems to be in retreat nearly everywhere in its range (Autenrieth, 1981). Widespread alteration of sagebrush types, from either wildfires or purposeful reduction to favor grasses as livestock forage, is usually accepted as the primary cause (Klebenow, 1970; Braun *et al.*, 1977; Autenrieth *et al.*, 1982). Breeding, nesting, and early broodrearing all appear to center on the lek or dancing ground as a hub. Most nests are located under the tallest sagebrush available within 2–3 km of the lek. Although broodrearing tends to be in more open types where green forbs and insects are abundant, canopy coverage reduction of sagebrush below 5–10% becomes untenable as habitat. Maturity of early-growth forbs on lowland sites often leads to an upslope migration of broods gradually over the summer to follow the green-feed cycle. Meadows and streamside vegetation bordered by sagebrush become important at this time (Klebenow, 1969). Guidelines for managing breeding-complex habitat have been quite conservative (Braun *et al.*, 1977; Autenrieth *et al.*, 1982) and may overly constrain direct habitat improvement opportunities (Urness, 1979) as demonstrated by the Vale Rangeland Rehabilitation Program (Heady and Bartolome, 1977). Water developments in a formerly dry area plus mixed grass–forb seedings and rejuvenated sagebrush stands likely were the reasons why sage grouse in southeastern Oregon have performed significantly better than elsewhere in eastern Oregon. Despite these differences, however, sage grouse populations are at levels far below those sustained on the Vale district in the 1920s and 1930s.

References

Altmann, M. (1952). Social behavior of elk (*Cervus canadensis nelsoni*) in the Jackson Hole area of Wyoming. *Behaviour* **4**(2), 116–143.

Anderson, E. W., and Scherzinger, R. J. (1975). Improving quality of winter forage for elk by cattle grazing. *J. Range Manage.* **28**(2), 120–125.

Autenrieth, R. E. (1981). Sage grouse management in Idaho. *Idaho Dep. Fish Game, Wildl. Bull.* **9.**

Autenrieth, R. E., and Fichter, E. (1975). On the behavior and socialization of pronghorn fawns. *Wildl. Monogr.* **42.**

Autenrieth, R. E., Molini, W., and Braun, C., eds. (1982). Sage grouse management practices. *West. States Sage Grouse Comm., Tech. Bull.* **1.**

Beale, D. M., and Smith, A. D. (1973). Mortality of pronghorn antelope fawns in western Utah. *J. Wildl. Manage.* **37**(3), 343–352.

Beck T. D. I. (1977). Sage grouse flock characteristics and habitat selection in winter. *J. Wildl. Manage.* **41**(1), 18–26.

Bergerud, A. T., Jakimchuk, R. D., and Carruthers, D. R. (1984). The buffalo of the north: Caribou (*Rangifer tarandus*) and human developments. *Arctic* **37**(1), 7–22.

Bertram, B. C. R. (1979). Serengeti predators and their social systems. *In* "Serengeti: Dynamics of an Ecosystem" (A. R. E. Sinclair and M. Norton-Griffiths, eds.), Chapter 9, pp. 221–248. Univ. of Chicago Press, Chicago, Illinois.

Berwick, S. (1976). The Gir Forest: An endangered ecosystem. *Am. Sci.* **64**(1), 28–40.

Black, H., Scherzinger, R. J., and Thomas, J. W. (1976). Relationships of Rocky Mountain elk and Rocky Mountain mule deer habitat to timber management in the Blue Mountains of Oregon and Washington. *In* "Elk—Logging Roads Symposium Proceedings" (S. R. Hieb, ed.), pp. 11–13. University of Idaho, Moscow.

Boyd, R. J. (1978). American elk. *In* "Big Game of North America: Ecology and Management" (J. L. Schmidt and D. L. Gilbert, eds.), Chapter 2, pp. 11–29. Stackpole Books, Harrisburg, Pennsylvania.

Braun, C. E., Britt, T., and Wallestad, R. O. (1977). Guidelines for maintenance of sage grouse habitats. *Wildl. Soc. Bull.* **5**(3), 99–106.

Bright, L. (1978). Weather stress difference between two levels of juniper canopy cover.

U.S., For. Serv., Pac. Northwest For. Range Exp. Stn., Gen. Tech. Rep. **PNW-74**, 91–95.

Clutton-Brock, T. H., and Albon, S. D. (1983). Climatic variation and body weight of red deer. *J. Wildl. Manage.* **47**(4), 1197–1201.

Clutton-Brock, T. H., Guinness, F. E., and Albon, S. D. (1982). "Red Deer: Behavior and Ecology of Two Sexes." Univ. of Chicago Press, Chicago, Illinois.

Cole, D. M. (1983). Canopy development in lodgepole pine: Implications for wildlife studies and multiple resource management. *USDA For. Serv. Gen. Tech. Rep. INT* **INT-139**.

Cowan, I. M. (1974). Management implication of behaviour in the large herbivorous mammals. *In* "The Behaviour of Ungulates and its Relation to Management" (V. Geist and F. Walther, eds.), pp. 921–934. International Union for Conservation of Nature and Natural Resources, Morges, Switzerland.

Darr, G. W., and Klebenow, D. A. (1975). Deer, brush control, and livestock on the Texas Rolling Plains. *J. Range. Manage.* **28**(2), 115–119.

Davies, S. J. J. F. (1973). Land use by emus and other wildlife species in the arid shrublands of western Australia. *In* "Arid Shrublands: Proceedings of the Third Workshop of the United States/Australia Rangelands Panel" (D. N. Hyder, ed.), pp. 91–98. Society for Range Management, Denver, Colorado.

Dealy, J. E., Leckenby, D. A., and Concannon, D. M. (1981). Wildlife habitats in managed rangelands—The Great Basin of southeastern Oregon: Plant communities and their importance to wildlife. *U.S., For. Serv., Pac., Northwest For. Range Exp. Stn., Gen. Tech. Rep.* **PNW-120**.

Fichter, E. (1974). On the bedding behavior of pronghorn fawns. *In* "The Behaviour of Ungulates and Its Relation to Management" (V. Geist and F. Walther, eds.), pp. 352–355. International Union for Conservation of Nature and Natural Resources, Morges, Switzerland.

Fielder, P. C., and McKay, C. E. (1984). Vegetation types used by mule deer fawns, mid-Columbia River, Washington. *Northwest Sci.* **58**(1), 80–84.

Geist, V. (1981). Behavior: Adaptive strategies in mule deer. *In* "Mule and Black-tailed Deer of North America" (O. C. Wallmo, ed.), Chapter 5, pp. 157–223. Univ. of Nebraska Press, Lincoln.

Gilbert, D. L. (1978). Sociological considerations in management. *In* "Big Game of North America: Ecology and Management" (J. L. Schmidt and D. L. Gilbert, eds.), Chapter 26, pp. 409–416. Stackpole Books, Harrisburg, Pennsylvania.

Hanley, T. A. (1984). Relationships between Sitka black-tailed deer and their habitat. *U.S., For. Serv., Pac., Northwest For. Range Exp. Stn., Gen. Tech. Rep.* **PNW-168**.

Heady, H. F., and Bartolome, J. (1977). The Vale Rangeland Rehabilitation Program: The desert repaired in southeastern Oregon. *U.S. For. Serv., Pac. Northwest For. Range Exp. Stn., Resour. Bull.* **PNW-70**.

Houston, D. B. (1982). "The Northern Yellowstone Elk: Ecology and Management." Macmillan, New York.

Keay, J. A., and Peek, J. M. (1980). Relationships between fires and winter habitat of deer in Idaho. *J. Wildl. Manage.* **44**(2), 372–380.

Klebenow, D. A. (1969). Sage grouse nesting and brood habitat in Idaho. *J. Wildl. Manage.* **33**(3), 649–661.

Klebenow, D. A. (1970). Sage grouse vs. sagebrush control. *J. Range. Manage.* **23**(6), 396–400.

Klein, D. R., and White, R. G. (1984). Letter to the Editor. *Arctic* **37**(3), 293–294.

Leckenby, D. A. (1977). Management of mule deer and their habitat: Applying concepts of behavior, physiology, and microclimate. *Proc. West. Assoc. Fish Game Comm.* **57**, 206–217.

Leckenby, D. A. (1978). Western juniper management for mule deer. *U.S. For. Serv. Pac., Northwest For. Range Exp. Stn., Gen. Tech. Rep.* **PNW-74,** 137–161.

Leckenby, D. A. (1984). Elk use and availability of cover and forage habitat components in the Blue Mountains, northeastern Oregon, 1976–1982. *Oreg. Dep. Fish Wildl., Wildl. Res. Rep.* **14.**

Leckenby, D. A., Sheehy, D. P., Nellis, C. H., Scherzinger, R. J., Luman, I. D., Elmore, W., Lemos, J. C., Doughty, L., and Trainer, C. E. (1982). Wildlife habitats in managed rangelands—The Great Basin of southeastern Oregon: Mule deer. *U.S. For. Serv., Pac., Northwest For. Range Exp. Stn., Gen. Tech. Rep.* **PNW-139.**

Lent, P. C. (1974). Mother–infant relationships in ungulates. *In* "The Behaviour of Ungulates and Its Relation to Management" (V. Geist and F. Walther, eds.), pp. 14–55. International Union for Conservation of Nature and Natural Resources, Morges, Switzerland.

Loveless, C. M. (1967). Ecological characteristics of a mule deer winter range. *Tech. Publ.—Colo., Div. Game, Fish Parks* **20.**

Lyon, L. J. (1979). Habitat effectiveness for elk as influenced by roads and cover. *J. For.* **77,** 658–660.

McKell, C. M., Blaisdell, J. P., and Goodin, J. R. (Techn. eds.) (1972). Wildland shrubs—their biology and utilization. *U.S. For. Serv. Intern. For. Range Exp. Stn. Gen. Tech. Rep.* **INT-1.**

Marchinton, R. L., and Hirth, D. H. (1984). Behavior. *In* "White-tailed Deer: Ecology and Management" (L. K. Halls, ed.), Chapter 6, pp. 129–168. Stackpole Books, Harrisburg, Pennsylvania.

Mautz, W. W. (1978). Nutrition and carrying capacity. *In* "Big Game of North America: Ecology and Management" (J. L. Schmidt and D. L. Gilbert, eds.), Chapter 22, pp. 321–348. Stackpole Books, Harrisburg, Pennsylvania.

Miller, F. L. (1974). Four types of territoriality observed in a herd of black-tailed deer. *In* "The Behaviour of Ungulates and Its Relation to Management" (V. Geist and F. Walther, eds.), pp. 644–660. International Union for Conservation of Nature and Natural Resources, Morges, Switzerland.

Miller, F. L., and Gunn, A. (1985). Letter to the Editor. *Arctic* **38**(2), 154–155.

Moen, A. N. (1973). "Wildlife Ecology, an Analytical Approach." Freeman, San Francisco, California.

Neff, D. J. (1980). "Effects of Watershed Treatments on Deer and Elk Range Use," Fed. Aid Final Rep. W-78-R WP4,J5. Arizona Game and Fish Dept, Phoenix, Arizona.

Nelson, M. E., and Mech, L. D. (1981). Deer social organization and wolf predation in northeastern Minnesota. *Wildl. Monogr.* **77.**

Norton-Griffiths, M. (1979). The influence of grazing, browsing, and fire on the vegetation dynamics of the Serengeti. *In* "Serengeti: Dynamics of an Ecosystem" (A. R. E. Sinclair and M. Norton-Griffiths, eds.), Chapter 13, pp. 310–352. Univ. of Chicago Press, Chicago, Illinois.

Ockenfels, R. A., and Bissonette, J. A. (1984). Temperature-related responses in northcentral Oklahoma white-tailed deer. *In* "Deer in the Southwest: A Workshop" (P. R. Krausman and N. S. Smith, eds.), pp. 64–67. Coop. Wildl. Res. Unit, University of Arizona, Tucson.

Olson-Rutz, K. M., and Urness, P. J. (1987). Comparability of foraging behavior and diet selection of tractable and wild mule deer. Utah Division of Wildlife Resources Pub. **88-3.** Salt Lake City, Utah.

Ozoga, J. J., Verme, L. J., and Bienz, C. S. (1982). Parturition behavior and territoriality in white-tailed deer: Impact on neonatal mortality, *J. Wildl. Manage.* **46**(1), 1–11.

Pedersen, R. J., Adams, A. W., and Skovlin, J. M. (1980). Elk use in an unlogged and logged forest environment. *Oreg. Dep. Fish Wildl., Wildl. Res. Rep.* **9.**

Peek, J. M., Scott, M. D., Nelson, L. J., Pierce, D. J., and Irwin, L. L. (1982). Role of cover in habitat management for big game in northwestern United States. *Trans. North Am. Wildl. Conf.* **47,** 363–373.

Pratt, D. J., and Gwynne, M. D. (1977). "Rangeland Management and Ecology in East Africa." Hodder Stoughton, London.

Renwald, J. D., Wright, H. A., and Flinders, J. T. (1978). Effect of prescribed fire on bobwhite quail habitat in the Rolling Plains of Texas. *J. Range. Manage.* **31** (1), 65–69.

Rickard, W. H., Hedlund, J. D., and Fitzner, R. E. (1977). Elk in the shrubsteppe region of Washington—An authentic record. *Science* **196,** 1009–1010.

Robinette, W. L. (1972). Browse and cover for wildlife. *In* "Wildland Shrubs: Their Biology and Utilization" (C. M. McKell, J. P. Blaisdell, and J. R. Goodin, eds.), USDA For. Serv. Gen. Tech. Rep. INT-1, pp. 69–76. Utah State University, Logan.

Severson, K. E. (1981). Plains habitats. *In* "Mule and Black-tailed Deer of North America" (O. C. Wallmo, ed.), Chapter 12, pp. 459–485. Univ. of Nebraska Press, Lincoln.

Severson, K. E., and Medina, A. L. (1983). Deer and elk habitat management in the Southwest. *J. Range. Manage., Monogr.* **2.**

Skogland, T., and Mølmen, Ø. (1980). Prehistoric and present habitat distribution of wild mountain reindeer at Dovrefjell. *Proc. Int. Reindeer/Caribou Symp., 2nd, 1979,* pp. 130–141.

Skovlin, J. M. (1982). Habitat requirements and evaluations. *In* "Elk of North America: Ecology and Management" (J. W. Thomas and D. E. Toweill, eds.), Chapter 9, pp. 368–413. Stackpole Books, Harrisburg, Pennsylvania.

Smith, A. D., and Beale, D. M. (1980). Pronghorn antelope in Utah: Some research and observations. *Utah Div. Wildl. Resour. Publ.* **80-13.**

Smith, F. W., and Long, J. N. (1987). Elk hiding and thermal cover guidelines in the context of lodgepole pine and stand density. *West. J. Applied For.* **2** (1), 6–10.

Steuter, A. A., and Wright, H. A. (1980). White-tailed deer densities and brush cover on the Rio Grande Plain. *J. Range. Manage.* **33**(5), 328–331.

Sundstrom, C., Hepworth, W. G., and Diem, K. L. (1973). Abundance, distribution and food habits of the pronghorn: A partial characterization of the optimum pronghorn habitat. *Wyo. Game Fish Comm. Bull.* **12.**

Swenson, J. E. (1982). Effects of hunting on habitat use by mule deer on mixed-grass prairie in Montana. *Wildl. Soc. Bull.* **10**(2), 115–120.

Taber, R. J., and Dasmann, R. F. (1958). The black-tailed deer of the chaparral: Its life history and management in the North Coast Range of California. *Calif. Dep. Fish Game Bull.* **8.**

Tanner, G. W., Inglis, J. M., and Blankenship, L. H. (1978). Acute impact of herbicide strip treatment on mixed-brush white-tailed deer habitat on the northern Rio Grande Plain. *J. Range. Manage.* **31**(5), 386–391.

Teer, J. G., Thomas, J. W., and Walker, E. A. (1965). Ecology and management of white-tailed deer in the Llano Basin of Texas. *Wildl. Monogr.* **15.**

Terrel, T. L., and Spillett, J. J. (1975). Pinyon–juniper conversion: Its impact on mule deer and other wildlife. *In* "The Pinyon–Juniper Ecosystem: A Symposium" (G. F. Gifford and F. E. Busby, eds.), pp. 105–119. Utah State University, Logan.

Thomas, J. W., Black, H., Jr., Scherzinger, R. J., and Pedersen, R. J. (1979). Deer and elk. Chapter 8. *U.S., Dep. Agric., Agric. Handb.* **553,** 104–127.

Urness, P. J. (1979). Wildlife habitat manipulation in sagebrush ecosystems. *In* "The Sagebrush Ecosystem: A Symposium," pp. 169–178. Utah State University, Logan.

Vale, T. R. (1974). Sagebrush conversion projects: An element of contemporary environmental change in the western United States. *Biol. Conserv.* **6**(4), 274–284.

Wallmo, O. C. (1973). Important game animals and related recreation in arid shrublands of the United States. *In* "Arid Shrublands: Proceedings of the Third Workshop of the United States/Australian Rangelands Panel" (D. N. Hyder, ed.), pp. 98–108. Society for Range Management, Denver, Colorado.

Wallmo, O. C., and Gill, R. B. (1971). Snow, winter distribution, and population dynamics of mule deer in the central Rocky Mountains. *In* "Proceedings of the Snow and Ice in Relation to Wildlife and Recreation Symposium" (A. O. Haugen, ed.), pp. 1–15. Coop. Wildl. Res. Unit, Iowa State University Ames.

Ward, A. L. (1973). Sagebrush control with herbicides has little effect on elk calving behavior. *U.S., For. Serv., Res. Note RM* **RM-240.**

Whitten, K. R., and Cameron, R. D. (1984). Letter to the Editor. *Arctic* **37**(3), 293.

Wilson, A. D. (1969). A review of browse in the nutrition of grazing animals. *J. Range Manage.* **22** (1), 23–28.

Wing, L. D., and Buss, I. O. (1970). Elephants and forests. *Wildl. Monogr.* **19.**

Wolfe, M. L. (1978). Habitat changes and management. *In* "Big Game of North America: Ecology and Management" (J. L. Schmidt and D. L. Gilbert, eds.), Chapter 23, pp. 349–368. Stackpole Books, Harrisburg, Pennsylvania.

Yoakum, J. (1980). "Habitat Management Guides for the American Pronghorn Antelope." Bureau of Land Management, USDI, Denver, Colorado.

21

Reclamation and Erosion Control Using Shrubs

Dennis J. Hansen

I. Introduction

Vegetation has protected land surfaces for thousands of years. It has modified the local landscape, providing habitat for animals and cycling of nutrients, water, and gases. When this protective cover is destroyed by mining and construction activities, large acreages of soil and underlying geological materials are stripped of all living plants and organic matter. Such drastic disturbances significantly depreciate land values and uses. Productivity of these disturbed lands for wildlife and livestock is usually lost in the short term and significantly reduced in the long term without the implementation of a conscientious reclamation program. The soil is often compacted by vehicles, intermixed, moved to new locations, and left exposed on steep and smooth cut slopes that are subject to erosion.

The energy responsible for erosion of such exposed land is provided by falling rain and flowing runoff water. The kinetic energy of falling rain is normally dissipated by the vegetative cover. In its absence, bare and disturbed soil receives the full force of the energy. It is reported that raindrops strike the ground with a velocity of about 19 miles per hour (Thronson, 1971). Like miniature projectiles, they knock individual soil particles loose and compact the exposed soil surface. This falling rain and flowing runoff provide the energy required to erode large quantities of soil and to transport it farther downstream. One inch of precipitation falling on one acre of exposed soil weighs 110 tons. The energy associated with such masses of water has been responsible for the movement of sediments 20,000 to 40,000 times greater than that from adjacent vegetated areas in an equivalent period of time (Thronson, 1971). These unprotected surfaces may also become the source of dust and other undesirable substances. The impacts of such sediments in the environment eliminate or drastically disturb aquatic life downstream. They may also obstruct stream channels, plug culverts, reservoirs, and flood control structures, and contribute nutrients or pollutants that may threaten the quantity and quality of valuable water supplies.

Conditions produced by such land development activities often result in disturbed earth surfaces that make difficult the reestablishment of a protective mantle of vegetation. Additionally, reestablishment of desirable vegetation may be made more difficult by subsequent changes in the chemistry of the soil and perturbations due to grazing or browsing animals, climatic extremes, invasion of weedy species, fire, and the activities of humans. Disturbed soil surfaces may lack micronutrients, secondary nutrients, or essential plant nutrient elements, principally nitrogen, phosphorus, and potassium in available forms. Some soils may become too alkaline or too acidic or yield toxic elements such as selenium, boron, or total soluble salts. Particle size of the soil may be changed and organic matter reduced or eliminated, thereby decreasing water and nutrient holding capacity and altering soil microbiology, nutrient cycling, and structure of the soil. Such exposed surfaces may have reduced infiltration and encourage flooding and alterations in the watershed of an area. Changes due to disturbance of these surfaces present a challenge for the establishment of most vegetation.

Shrubs often provide effective solutions for revegetating drastically disturbed lands because of the diverse selection pressures that have shaped their evolutionary development. Shrubs have evolved in environments where harsh and adverse environmental conditions are often the rule rather than the exception. Water or the lack of it is frequently a key factor in the distribution of many shrub species. Shrubs appear to be particularly well adapted to fluctuations and variations in soil moisture conditions. For example, MacMahon (1981) has shown that biomes such as the desert and tundra have a greater variability in mean annual precipitation by orders of magnitude than any of the other biomes. Riparian habitats with fluctuating moisture levels also appear to support an abundance of shrub species that predominate the vegetation of these habitats (Hansen, 1977). Such variation in precipitation and soil moisture within these habitats has contributed to the diversity of responses to harsh environmental conditions. On the other hand, biomes dominated by perennial trees, grasses, or forbs typically have rather predictable precipitation events and amounts, thereby eliminating many of the selection pressures that favored such a variety of phenotypic expression and responses to environmental stresses that are often characteristic of drastically disturbed lands.

II. Project Planning

A. *The Use of Shrubs Is Guided by Land Use and Site Conditions*

Land use and reclamation objectives provide the guiding force that steers the reclamation efforts toward their desired destination. When land use or reclamation objectives are glossed over or ignored, subsequent reclamation efforts may be in vain and lead to undesirable economic, legal, and environmental consequences.

Differences in land use objectives for such things as wildlife use, livestock use, watershed, erosion control, or combinations of these uses will greatly influence the types of shrub species that will be ultimately selected to help achieve this use. According to Merkel and Currier (1973), information useful in making land use decisions includes, but is not limited to, the following: land ownership; hydrology; land use zoning; past and current management practices; kinds, extent, and severity of existing land problems and their causes; managing agencies involved; present biotic uses; current resources; climatic data; landform data; geology and soils information; kinds, types, and extent of vegetation present; general public factors to be considered, such as safety, aesthetics, and recreational possibilities; land and cultural improvements, present and needed; kinds and extent of land, water, and air pollutants; possible legal problems present and anticipated; land legislation that may be needed, etc.

B. *Site Conditions as Defined through Baseline Studies and Information*

A knowledge of site conditions helps to determine which reclamation techniques should be used to establish and maintain shrub species selected on the basis of the target land use, while a knowledge of actual reclamation practices will assist in determining the cost-effectiveness of alternative practices. Baseline studies are designed to provide this type of information. The baseline study can provide comprehensive description of physical, floral, and faunal resources of an area to be disturbed, as well as information necessary for three basic reasons: to define potential impacts, to define potential problems in impact mitigation, and to provide a resource data base on which to formulate reclamation objectives and methods, and thus provide a means for subsequent evaluation of reclamation success.

Information assembled during the baseline assessment can be useful in directing subsequent reclamation efforts (Merkel and Currier, 1973). For example, information about the vegetation may be useful in indicating which species might best be suited for the site, or it might indicate correlation with adverse climatic conditions such as excessive winds or snowdrift accumulation. The nature of the soil may determine its ability to function as a growth medium; if good soil material is sparse, salvaging and stockpiling topsoil may be necessary; other soil parameters such as physical and chemical factors might dictate the types of species that will be best suited to the altered site, and its potential erosion. Climatic information may help to assess the need for specialized reclamation techniques such as adequate protection from the wind and mulching requirements. Biotic factors such as the presence of livestock, wildlife, rodents, and insects may be important to know in planning control measures. For example, hay mulches may attract wildlife or livestock in some areas and the use of artificial mulches may retard erosion. Knowing that unusually heavy grazing pressures might occur in the area might be important when selecting species that tolerate such pressures yet provide sufficient erosion control. Baseline information is useful in many ways when developing the reclamation plan.

C. *Selection of Adapted Species of Shrubs*

Selection of adapted shrub species for the reclamation of disturbed lands is a challenging process. Only a few publications provide information on the subject. Cook *et al.* (1974), Plummer *et al.* (1968), Campbell and Herbel (1975), Power *et al.* (1975), Plummer (1977), USDI Fish and Wildlife Service (1977, 1978), Van Epps and McKell (1978), Institute for Land Rehabilitation (1979), Vallentine (1980), and the USDA Forest Service (1979, 1983) mention problems associated with species selection and provide information on the suitability of species for reclamation and erosion control.

Figure 1. A mixture of adapted shrubs, forbs, and grasses stabilizes a slope reclaimed from drastic disturbance.

Successful selection of proper plant materials for reclamation depends on numerous factors. In selecting species, Hanks *et al.* (1971), Plass (1973), Blauer *et al.* (1975, 1976), Van Epps and McKell (1978), McArthur *et al.* (1979), and the USDA Forest Service (1983) point to a high variability among plants within the same species, subspecies, or even biotype. Therefore, Jaynes and Harper (1978) and Van Epps and McKell (1979) stress using species that have demonstrated an ability for establishment on disturbed sites in the vicinity of the disturbed area. Seeds produced by these plants should have a greater chance of success than plant materials selected from other sources and locations (Fig. 1).

A considerable amount of literature has accumulated on general characteristics of shrub species for disturbed site revegetation in the western United States. More familiar publications include Vories and Sims (1977), Eddleman (1977), Long (1981), Thornburg (1982), Wasser (1982), and USDA Forest Service (1983). It is generally agreed that mixtures of plants designated for permanent revegetation should contain species that are well adapted, easy to establish, self-regenerating, useful for proposed land uses, reasonably available for seeding or transplanting, and that comply with legal requirements if so stipulated.

biological processes and to alter soil temperatures; cultivation practices may be used to encourage soil aeration for increased oxygen supply and to stimulate microbial activities; and special pretreatment techniques such as scarification and seed cleaning may help overcome the problems of dormancy.

3. Specialized Seed Coats and Variation in Seed Size

Shrub seed coats and seed size have evolved to facilitate seed dispersal and establishment. Specialized seed coats and variations in seed size from one species to another often create problems in sowing a seed mixture. Fluffy or "trashy" seeds, like those associated with winterfat (*Ceratoides lanata*), often clog drill boxes, hydroseeders, and other broadcast seeders. Because shrubs are often sown in mixtures, seed size may present problems, such as the segregation of certain small seeds so that they are not dispersed evenly during sowing. For drill seeding, differences in seed size often present additional problems of placing seeds at the "optimum" depth for germination during planting; small seeds usually require a shallow planting, while larger seeds require a deeper planting.

Reclamation techniques to help minimize problems associated with specialized seed coats and variable sizes of seed in the seed mixture usually focus on segregating seeds into one or more mixtures of seed that have similar sowing requirements. Segregated seed mixtures may then be sown in different hoppers of a seed drill or may be sown adjacent to or during a second pass over the area to to be seeded. Rice hulls have also been added in various ratios to facilitate the passage of fluffy seeds and to prevent the segregation of small, dense seeds from lighter seeds during broadcast seeding. The use of rice hulls added to shrub mixtures also helps serve as a visual marker that is useful while hand seeding small seeds with a broadcast seeder. Disadvantages of using rice hulls are the added cost and additional handling time that is required.

4. Germination Requirements

There have been relatively few studies conducted to determine the specific germination requirements of shrub species or accessions of seed within a given species. The general physiology of seeds has been reviewed by McDonough (1977). Other better-known references on the subject include Eddleman (1977) and Sabo *et al.* (1979). Eddleman showed significant differences in germination requirements among different accessions of the same species from collections of shrubs in Montana.

Data by Sabo *et al.* (1979) show some rather interesting differences in germination response under moisture stress for shrubs as compared to grasses. Figure 2 shows the germination responses of grasses to a gradient

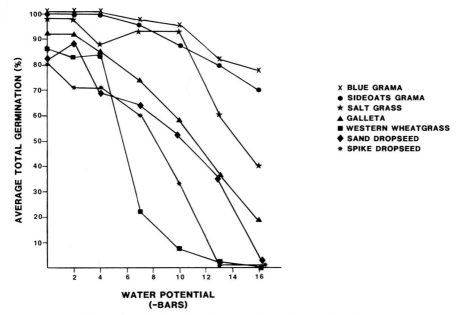

Figure 2. Germination of grass seeds under moisture stress.

of increasing moisture stress. Germination of most of the grass species investigated did not show significant reductions in average total germination until moisture stress exceeded water potential values of −7 bars. Germination of most shrub species (Fig. 3), on the other hand, was significantly reduced with moisture stress levels in excess of only about −3 bars. Many of these same shrub species are capable of tolerating moisture stress levels far in excess of those reported by Sabo *et al.* (1979). These data suggest that while mature shrubs may be very drought tolerant, they are nevertheless very sensitive to moisture stress during germination, even more so than many grass species. Some species of shrubs have apparently undergone selection pressures that favored an opportunistic response to low moisture stress during periods of abundant soil moisture, while other species have evolved protection mechanisms to prevent them from germinating until sufficient moisture and germination conditions are favorable. A knowledge of the sensitivity of many shrub seeds to moisture stress during germination can be useful in selecting reclamation techniques that can encourage successful establishment of shrub species.

Reclamation techniques that favor seed germination of commonly used shrub species sensitive to moisture stress include: water harvesting and water retention techniques; the use of mulches to retain soil moisture and

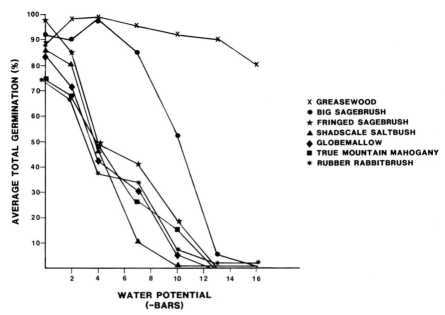

Figure 3. Germination of shrub seeds under moisture stress.

alter soil temperatures (warmer in the spring and cooler in the summer); tillage to reduce compaction of surface crusts and increase soil aeration, which provides the necessary oxygen required for germination; firming of the soil bed after sowing to provide good seed-to-soil contact to permit the capillary flow of moisture from the soil to the seed; and proper covering of the soil to prevent desiccation and loss of seeds to animals. Timing of reclamation activities is often scheduled to optimize the availability of dependable supplies of soil moisture for germination.

A need currently exists to index or categorize seed on the basis of ability to germinate under a specified set of environmental conditions such as moisture stress, temperature, and tolerance to salinity and various levels of soil pH. This information would be extremely valuable in helping to overcome many problems of obtaining consistent response in establishing shrubs from seed. Because of the relatively high cost of such research, it is doubtful that individual users will bear the burden of these costs.

5. Unpredictable Seed Production

The production of viable shrub seed is often controlled by a variety of environmental factors. Weather plays an important role in the development of seed, for when conditions are not favorable, seed production is curtailed or eliminated during that year. Outbreaks of insect pests and untimely frost can also prevent formation and maturation of viable seed. As long as the seed production is dependent on collection from native stands, the dependability of having seed available in any given year is open to the likelihood of seed failure for any of the above-mentioned reasons. Demand for shrub seed with desirable phenotypic traits has stimulated the collection of seed during favorable conditions and its subsequent storage until needed. In some cases, superior germ plasm has been evaluated by plant material centers, increased, and released for propagation and commercial production of seed. Commercial propagation of most shrub seeds is currently rather limited, but is likely to increase as demand for seed increases.

B. Transplanting Shrubs

Transplanting methods can be divided into the following categories: sprigging, planting mature plants, planting bareroot plantlets, and transplanting container-grown plants.

1. Sprigging

Sprigging involves the process of inserting pieces of dormant woody stems or roots into a moist soil and allowing roots to develop from the stem or root into the surrounding soil. It is most often used with shrubs that root readily from stems or other root pieces. Rhizomatous species such as willow (*Salix*), polar (*Populus*), rose (*Rosa*), currant (*Ribes*), and raspberry (*Rubus*) are most commonly used. This technique is typically used for erosion control in riparian and other mesic environments.

Sprigging materials usually involve stem segments of wood from 1 to 3 years in age, ranging from 6 to 12 inches in length. Longer segments tend to desiccate rapidly as they do not absorb sufficient water through the buried end. Wood should only be used in a dormant stage to prevent excessive transpiration through leaves. Sprigging material may also be rooted in moist burlap and stored under cool temperature prior to planting (Hartmann and Kester, 1975).

For sprigging to be successful, materials must be inserted into a continuously moist substrate. To maintain the proper polarity when sprigging, buds should be oriented upward. Failure to plant with the "right side up" usually prevents plant establishment. Exception to this would be when the entire stem or root is buried under a shallow layer of soil. Sprigged materials should be placed with approximately one-third to one-half of their length into the ground to ensure proper water-absorbing area and anchoring. The top of the sprig is usually cut off squarely when collected to mark the proper polarity. It is sometimes treated with grafting paint or dipped in beeswax to prevent loss of moisture. The rooted end is usually cut diagonally to form a tapered end that increases the surface area for moisture absorption. It is often helpful to dip this end in a rooting hormone powder to stimulate rooting and in a fungicide to prevent fungal damage to the sprig.

Wattling is another form of sprigging in which bundles from 8 to 10 inches in diameter, of wood materials with butts alternating, are bound together with twine at 12 to 15-inch intervals and buried in trenches across steep slopes. The wattling bundles are placed horizontal to the surface and are usually anchored by other stems placed vertically in front of and through the bundle to a depth of at least 18 inches. The bundles tend to provide soil erosion control until the individual sprigs sprout to form a living row of shrub materials. Wattling is most successful in moist soil conditions where the soil is subject to severe erosion or scouring.

2. Mature Plant Transplants

Transplanting mature-sized individual shrubs is generally limited to transplanting them from nearby populations onto disturbed areas. Because the deep roots are often severed during excavation, an improper shoot-to-root ratio results and dieback of the topgrowth and often death of the plant are commonly observed. The technique is most successfully used with species of shrubs that tend to sucker and resprout and is least successful with species that do not resprout. Usually the less the root system is damaged and disturbed the greater are the chances of plant survival.

Front-end loaders, tree spades, and similar pieces of equipment are used to transplant larger materials. Smaller materials may be dug with a shovel. The transplanting is usually done when the shrubs are dormant, early in the spring just after the soil thaws and the soil is still moist.

Some shrubs can be effectively transplanted within a soil–root mass and placed into a disturbed area to form "islands" of native seed and root material. This can increase the diversity of indigenous species, which may be impossible to obtain commercially or difficult to establish by seeding. The practice provides centers for dispersal of these species and their associated beneficial microorganisms in the soil mass. The technique of mature plant transplanting is most applicable to large, flat areas of disturbance. The margins of narrow areas are commonly observed to be recolonized by adjacent undisturbed plant material that may provide roots and seed materials to the disturbance.

3. Bareroot Transplant

The main advantage of bareroot plants in comparison with container-grown plants is that bareroot plants are cheaper. Bareroot shrubs are usually larger and have greater caliper than container-grown plants. Bareroot shrubs are usually dug in the spring when they are dormant and must be planted into moist soil. Bareroot plants are usually harder to establish and require greater care in shipping, storage, and planting than container-grown plants. Although they can be held in a dormant state in cold storage for short periods of time, there are limits, usually within a few weeks, as to when the bareroot stock can be lifted and planted. Advanced planning is necessary to ensure the availability of bareroot materials because it usually requires 1 to 2 years to produce a bareroot plant. Survival data comparing bareroot and container-grown plants are varied. Even though bareroot plants are older and have a larger caliper, they do not have the advantages of being planted in a growth medium with a higher water-holding capacity. Van Epps and McKell (1980) indicated that on very harsh sites, success of container-grown plants exceeded that of bareroot plants.

4. Container-Grown Plants

Shrubs grown in containers from seed or cuttings often provide plant material with the greater amount of flexibility when planting compared with bareroot plant material. They can be used later in the season as there is less disturbance to the root system. Although container plants are more expensive than bareroot plants they perform better on extremely harsh sites and are generally more available on short notice. Container-grown plants are available in a variety of sizes. The smaller sizes are often referred to as "tubelings." These plants are usually planted when dormant, although with supplemental water they can be planted while their above-ground shoots are actively growing. Larger container sizes are probably not necessary for most reclamation purposes. On a survival basis, larger container-grown individuals tend to be less cost-effective, although survival success of individual plants may be greater.

Physiological hardening is a necessity for container-grown plants. This requires about 2 to 3 months depending on the season of year. Hardening is the process whereby the plant makes certain physiological and morphological adaptations that make it better able to withstand adverse growing conditions such as heat, cold or drought stress likely to be encountered in the field. The process is initiated at a nursery by reducing the supply of moisture, altering the nutrient balance, reducing the temperature, and increasing the exposure to direct sunlight to approximate ambient conditions that are likely to be experienced at the planting site.

5. Plant Care before Planting

If site conditions are dramatically different from climatic conditions at the nursery it may be advantageous to attempt to site-harden the plants for a

and site conditions.

Planting on steep slopes offers challenges that must be adequately dealt with if plant establishment is to be achieved. Planters should be instructed few weeks or months. However, it should be emphasized that a short period of moisture stress at the planting site a few days before planting will do little to harden the plants, since hardening is a developmental process. Therefore, withholding water from containerized stock in an effort to

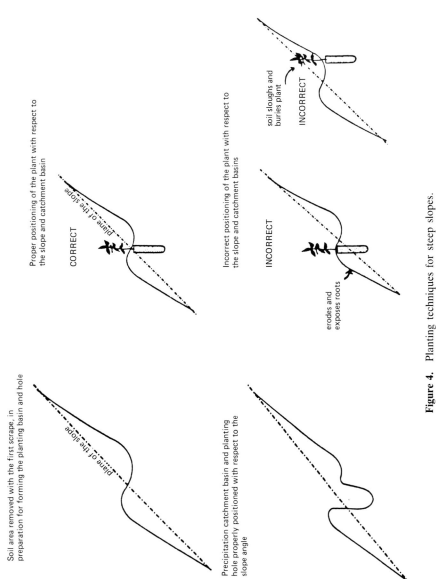

Figure 4. Planting techniques for steep slopes.

to begin at the top of the slope and work across and eventually down the slope. There should be no planters working directly below another planter as sloughing from above may bury lower plants and dislodged rocks may endanger the planter below.

Positioning of the plants on very steep slopes is especially important. Precipitation catchment basins of about one foot in diameter often help to stabilize the slope, increase infiltration, and direct moisture to the plant. Using a hole or shovel, the above-slope area should be scraped to remove excess soil from above the plant that might otherwise slough off and bury the seedling (Fig. 4). Next, a catchment basis is formed and the hole positioned near the outer edge of the lip of the basin. The plant (and in some cases the slow-release fertilizer tablet) is then inserted and covered.

The plant should be positioned near the outer lip of the catchment basin to prevent loss due to burial of the plant or exposure of the root system by erosion. The crown of the root plug should be aligned with the plane of the undisturbed slope. In general, soil positioned above the plane of the slope will erode away with time and leave any root plugs in the eroded area exposed. Depressions or basins below the plane of the slope will eventually fill in by sloughing and surface materials washed from upslope, thereby burying any plants positioned in this area. In short, the plane of the slope will tend to restablished itself with time.

If the soil is not moist at the time of planting, plants should be "watered in" by providing sufficient water per plant. The water helps settle the soil and removes pockets of air that might damage the roots. Costs of planting, replanting, and watering should be evaluated to determine if providing plants with supplemental water is cost-effective. In extremely arid environments it is usually cost-effective. In more mesic areas it is not.

IV. Monitoring Revegetation Efforts and Handling Special Problems

The purpose of a monitoring and maintenance program is to locate, identify, and solve problems before they escalate and become more serious and expensive to correct. Monitoring and corrective maintenance is perhaps the most overlooked part of a reclamation program, yet it has the potential for considerable cost savings. Monitoring should occur during construction to ensure that work is being carried out according to specifications. Correction of improper techniques or miscommunications are far more effective and far less expensive early in the construction activities than after a reclamation project has been in place for several years.

Monitoring need not involve extensive data gathering, but should serve to identify problems so they can be properly addressed. Potential problems likely to be identified during the reclamation process include destruction of plants by wildlife or livestock, premature drying of the site due to a lack of precipitation, damage from traffic by humans unaware of the revegetation efforts, competition from weeds and shrubs growing too densely (Van Epps and McKell. 1983), and erosion caused by failure of erosion control structures.

References

Bauer, A., Berg, W. A., and Gould, W. L. (1978). Correction of nutrient deficiencies and toxicities in strip mined lands in semi-arid and arid regions. *In* "Reclamation of Drastically Disturbed Lands" (F. W. Schaller and P. Sutton, eds.), pp. 451–466. American Society of Agronomy, Crop Science Society of America, Soil Science Society of America, Madison, Wisconsin.

Blauer, A. C., Plummer, A. P., McArthur, E. D., Stevens, R., and Guinta, B. C. (1975). Characteristics and hybridization of important intermountain shrubs. I. Rose family. *USDA For. Serv. Res. INT.* **INT-169.**

Blauer, A. C., Plummer, A. P., McArthur, E. D., Stevens, R., and Guinta, B. C. (1976). Characteristics and hybridization of important intermountain shrubs. II. Chenopod family. *USDA For. Serv. Res. Pap. INT* **INT-177.**

Campbell, R. S., and Herbel, C. H. (1975). "Improved Range Plants," Range Symp. Ser. No. 1. Soc. Range Manage., Denver, Colorado.

Cook, C. W., Hyde, R. M., and Sims, P. L. (1974). Revegetation guidelines for surface mined areas. *Range Sci. Dep. Sci. Ser. Colo. State Univ.* **16.**

DePuit, E. J. (1982). Cool-season perennial grass establishment on Northern Great Plains mined lands: Status of current technology. *Proc. Symp. Surf. Coal Min. Reclam. Northern Great Plains,* pp. P(14)–P(24).

Eddleman, L. E. (1977). Indigenous plants of southeastern Montana. I. Viability and suitability for reclamation in the Fort Union Basin. University of Montana, Missoula.

Hanks, D. L., Brunner, J. R., Christensen, D. R., and Plummer, A. P. (1971). Paper chromatography for determining palatability differences in various strains of big sagebrush. *USDA For. Serv. Res. Pap. INT* **INT-1101.**

Hansen, D. J. (1977). Interrelations of valley vegetation, stream regimen, soils, and solar irradiation along the rock creek in the Uinta Mountains of Utah. Ph.D. Dissertation, University of Michigan, Ann Arbor.

Hartmann, H. T., and Kester, D. E. (1975). "Plant Propagation Principles and Practices," 3rd ed. Prentice-Hall, Englewood Cliffs, New Jersey

Institute for Land Rehabilitation (1979). Propagation and establishment of native plants in disturbed arid lands. *Bull. —Utah Agric. Exp. Stn.* **500.**

Jaynes, R. A., and Harper, K. T. (1978). Patterns of natural revegetation in arid southeastern Utah. *J. Range Manage.* **31**(6), 407–412.

Long. S. G. (1981). "Characteristics of Plants Used in Western Reclamation," 2nd ed. Environmental Research & Technology, Fort Collins, Colorado.

McArthur, E. D., Blauer, A. C., Plummer, A. P., and Stevens, R. (1979). Characteristics and hybridization of important intermountain shrubs. III. Sunflower family. *USDA For. Serv. Res. Pap. INT* **INT-220.**

McDonough, W. T. (1977). Seed physiology. *In* "Rangeland Plant physiology" (R. E. Sosebee, ed.), Range Sci. Ser. No. 4, pp. 155–184. Soc. Range Manage., Denver, Colorado.

MacMahon, J. A. (1981). Succession of ecosystems: A preliminary comparative analysis. *In* "Successional Research and Environmental Pollutant Monitoring Associated with Bioshene Reserves" (M. A. Hemstrom and J. F. Franklin, tech. eds.), pp. 5–26. USDA Forest Service and USDI National Park Service.

Merkel, D. L., and Currier, W. F. (1973). "Critical Area Stabilization in New Mexico," Rep. No. 7. Agric. Res. Serv., USDA, Las Cruces, New Mexico. Recommendations prepared at April 1971 Critical Area Stabilization Workshop. Sponsored by New Mexico Inter-Agency Range Committee.

Monsen, S. B., and Christensen, D. R. (1975). Woody plants for rehabilitating rangelands in the Intermountain region. *Wildland Shrubs Symp. Workshop Proc.* pp. 72–119.

Plass, W. T. (1973). Genetic variability in survival and growth of Virginia pine planted on acid surface-mine spoils. *In* "Ecology and Reclamation of Devastated Land" (R. J. Hutnik and G. Davis, eds.), Vol. 1, pp. 493–507. Gordon & Breach, New York.

Plummer, A. P. (1977). Revegetation of disturbed intermountain area sites. *In* "Reclamation and Use of Disturbed Land in the Southwest" (J. L. Thames, ed.), pp. 302–340. Univ. of Arizona Press, Tucson.

Plummer, A. P., Christensen, D. R., and Monsen, S. B. (1968). Restoring big-game range in Utah. *Utah Div. Fish Game, Publ.* **68–3.**

Power, J. F., Ries, R. E., Sandoval, F. M., and Willis, W. O. (1975). Factors restricting revegetation of strip mine spoils. *In* "Proceedings of the Fort Union Coal Field Symposium" (W. F Clark, ed.), pp. 336–346. Eastern Montana College, Billings.

Sabo, D. G., Jonnson, G. U., Martin, W. C., and Aldon, E. F. (1979). Germination requirements of 19 species of arid land plants. *USDA For. Serv. Res. Pap. RM* **RM-210.**

Stelter, L. H., DePuit, E. J., and Mikol, S., eds. (1981). "Shrub Establishment on Disturbed Arid and Semi-arid Lands. "Wyoming Game and Fish Dept., Sheridan.

Thornburg, A. A. (1982). "Plant Materials for Use on Surface Mined Lands in Arid and Semi-arid Regions," SCS-TP-157/EPA-600/7-79-134. USDA Soil Conserv. Serv., Washington, D.C.

Thronson, R. E. (1971). "Control of Erosion and Sediment Deposition from Construction of Highways and Land Development." Office of Water Programs, U.S. Envir. Prot. Agency, Washington, D.C.

USDA Forest Service. (1979). User guide to vegetation. *USDA For. Serv. Gen. Tech. Rep. INT* **INT-64.**

USDA Forest Service (1983). "Managing Intermountain Rangelands—Improvement of Range and Wildlife Habitats," Proc. Symp.: September 15–17, 1981, Twin Falls, Idaho and June 22–24, 1982, Elko, Nevada, Gen. Tech. Rep. INT-157. Compiled by S. B. Monsen and N. Shaw.

USDI Fish and Wildlife Service (1977). "The Plant Information Network," 4 vols, USDI FWS Rep. FWS/OBS 77/38-39-49-41. USDI/FWS, Washington, D.C.

USDI Fish and Wildlife Service (1978). "Rehabilitation of Western Wildlife Habitat: A Review," Publ. FW/OBS 78-86. USDI/FWS, Washington, D.C.

Vallentine, J. R. (1980). "Range Development and Improvements," 2nd ed. Brigham Young Univ. Press, Provo, Utah.

Van Epps, G. A., and McKell, C. M. (1978). Major criteria and procedures for selecting and establishing range shrubs as rehabilitation of disturbed lands. *Proc. Int. Rangel. Congs., 1st,* pp. 352–354.

Van Epps, G. A, and McKell, C. M. (1980). Revegetation of disturbed sites in the salt desert range of the Intermountain West. *Utah Agric. Exp. Stn. Land Rehab. Ser.* No. 5.

Van Epps, G. A., and McKell, C. M. (1983). Effect of weedy annuals on the survival and growth of transplants under arid conditions. *J. Range Manage.* **36,** 366–369.

Vories, K. C. (1980). Growing Colorado plants from seed: A state of the art. Vol. I. Shrubs. *USDA For. Serv. Gen. Tech. INT* **INT-108.**

Vories, K. C., and Sims, P. L. (1977). The plant information network. Vol. I. A user's guide. *U.S., Fish Wildl. Serv., Off. Biol. Serv.* [*Tech. Rep.*] *FWS/OBS* **FWS/OBS-77/38.**

Wasser, C. H. (1982). Ecology and culture of selected species useful in revegetating disturbed lands in the west. *U.S., Fish Wildl. Serv., Off. Biol. Serv.* [*Tech. Rep.*] *FWS/OBS* **FWS/OBS-82/56.**

22

Use of Shrubs for Fuel

James A. Young
Jerry D. Budy
Raymond A. Evans

I. Introduction

The use of shrubs as a source of energy is a way of life for a large portion of the world's population who reside in less developed countries. This is especially true in those countries that are located in semiarid and arid environments that do not have extensive forests. The overutilization of this resource poses the potential for desertification. In similar environments in developed countries, large amounts of woody biomass have accumulated on many shrub/grass rangelands as a result of past improper grazing. In

The Biology and Utilization of Shrubs

479

these developed countries the accumulations of shrubs have rarely been considered as even a potential fuel source.

In retrospect both problems are governed by the same biological parameters. Shrubs often enjoy a competitive advantage over grasses because the shrubs do not have to renew their meristematic growing points annually. Second, many shrubs have evolved physical or chemical mechanisms that protect them from browsing animals. These mechanisms may be spines and thorns that discourage even voracious goats from feeding or complex biochemicals that repel potential browsers.

Many of the nonpreferred shrubs have been found to inhibit the function of rumen microflora when ingested in large quantities (Nagy *et al.*, 1964; Nagy, 1979). These biochemical protectants are only functional in protecting the shrub when the potential browsers sense their presence, probably by olfactory means (Longhurst *et al.*, 1968). The net result of overgrazing *Artemisia*-dominated rangelands in western North America and central or southwestern Asia is an overabundance of the relatively nonpreferred shrub. In a country like Afghanistan the *Artemisia* shrubs may represent site protection from desertification and loss of site potential. In either Afghanistan or the western United States the overabundance of nonpreferred shrubs must be reduced before a stable mixture of plants, including preferred shrubs, can be established to increase range productivity.

II. Magnitude of the Fuel Problem

A. *Less Developed Countries Depend on Woody Fuel*

It is difficult for residents of developed countries to visualize how serious fuel problems are in the less developed countries. In less developed countries the fuel wood problem translates into the number of hours required to collect the daily fuel requirement. In Nepal it takes a day's journey to collect a family's fuel requirement where a generation ago only 1 or 2 hours were required (Eckholm, 1975). It is estimated that one-half of all the timber cut annually in the world is cut for fuel. Nine-tenths of the people in the poorest countries depend on firewood to prepare their food and the average user burns one ton per year (Eckholm, 1975). The problem is most acute on the Indian subcontinent, the semiarid African fringe of the Sahara Desert, and Latin America, including the Andean upland region, Central America, and the Caribbean. Some of these critical areas are characterized by tropical forests or woodlands, but common denominators for many of the areas are a semiarid environment, lack of commerical forest, and overgrazing.

The disappearance of shrubs in the vicinity of watering points and along migration tracts is seldom entirely due to overgrazing alone, but usually is a result of fuel collection and severe grazing.

Because of the relatively low density of fuel wood and the subsequent cost of transportation, overutilization of fuel wood resources is almost always a local problem. The consequences of overutilization, accelerated erosion, siltation, and desertification rapidly become regional problems. Shortage of fuel wood leads to the substituting of dried animal dung and crop residue for wood. This substitution reduces manure available for crop production. The worldwide use of livestock droppings for fuel instead of fertilizer is thought to lower grain production by 20 millions tons annually, enough food to nourish 100 million people (Smith, 1981).

The continued destruction of woodland habitat in the less developed countries reduces the habitat for some of the world's endangered animal species. The loss of habitat leads to the loss of animals, no matter how willing the governments of these countries are to protect the endangered species.

B. Role of Shrubs in Fuel Requirements

The use of shrubs for fuel in the less developed countries often represents unique cultural adaptation. The collection of shrub fuel is a labor-intensive operation. For a family of five nomadic herdsmen in Afghanistan, the daily fuel requirement is 12 kg of *Artemisia* daily (Casimir *et al.,* 1980). In this culture the collection of fuel is a task for children (Fig. 2). In many cultures, shrubs and small trees are preferred as fuel because the collectors do not have saws, wedges, and heavy equipment to move and split large trunk cross sections (Eckholm, 1981).

C. Mode of Degradation

It seems highly improbable that a nomadic culture living in equilibrium with its environment would suddenly begin to induce rapid desertification through excessive harvesting of shrubs for fuel. If excessive harvesting were practiced for any length of time during the evolving of the culture it would have self-destructed. Since World War II there have been several interacting factors that have contributed to the overharvesting of fuel wood resources. Rapidly growing populations in response to improved health care and disease control or for other reasons have contributed to this increased demand for energy. In the case of shrubs used as fuel in semiarid environments, the forced settlements of nomads may be a major factor in overutilization of renewable energy resources. Stable villages may have many redeeming social features, but biologically they can be the epicenters of excessive grazing and fuel collection. The concentration of grazing animals near villages can break down or override the protective mechanisms that limit preference. In many of the less developed countries in the semiarid zone there is a continuum of browsing animals ranging from cattle, sheep, and goats to camels.

The lopping of shrubs for fuel interacts in two ways with browsing preference. First, the shrubs may not sprout and essentially are removed from the community until seedling establishment recurs. Throughout the Northern Hemisphere this is the case for many woody species of *Artemisia* that characterize semiarid environments (McArthur and Plummer, 1978). Second, the shrub may root or crown sprout following removal of the aerial portion of the plant. The sprouts may be more highly preferred by browsing animals than the mature, woody structures, that were removed. If judicious grazing is not practiced, the sprouts of woody species may be destroyed. The sprouts of some species, species of *Quercus,* for example, have sprouts with polymorphic leaves that provide protection from browsing until the aerial portion of the plant renews itself.

In truly semiarid environments where shrubs are by necessity the energy source, shrubs are often found growing on small mounds. These mounds result from the accumulation of wind-eroded soil particles trapped by the shrubs. A large part of the woody biomass of shrubs growing in such situations is often found at and just below the surface of the mound in the form of a thickened, woody crown. Bedouins in Iraq do not just lop the aerial portion of *Haloxylon salicornicum* shrubs, they also dig out the woody crown. This practice greatly increases shrub mortality compared to simple lopping at the soil level (Thalen, 1979).

Shifting cultivation in the most favorable desert environment can also contribute to the loss of shrubs. The most productive environments for shrub production are often the sites chosen for cereal culture in favorable years (Thalen, 1979). Some of the most valuable shrubs for fuel in Iraq have been virtually eliminated from the flora by prolonged and excessive cultivation (Thalen, 1979). These include *Haloxylon ammondendrow* and *Calligonum comosum.*

III. Charcoal Production

Making charcoal from wood is essentially the process of partially burning the wood. By carbonizing wood through controlled combustion, it is possible to obtain a fairly high-energy-value fuel with a 60% savings in volume and an 80% savings in weight of raw wood (Anonymous, 1943).

The CUSAB kiln (acronym for charcoal from useless shrub and brush) has been developed to rapidly carbonize scrap wood, twigs, branches, and shrubs that cannot be treated by traditional charcoaling methods. The kiln is provided with a vertical row of air ducts that pierce the wall. Looking through these holes, operators can see the wood burning. As charcoaling proceeds up the vertical tank of the kiln, the operator can see the flames change to the red glow of burning charcoal and then can plug up the air ducts as the level of charcoal rises. Garriet (1982) offers innovative designs for earth-covered pit kilns for charcoal production and for portable commercial kilns.

What charcoal production does for the energy supply from renewable resources is to allow utilization by consumers in urban areas and thus to extend resource exploitation for greater distances into the countryside than would be possible without the energy concentration of the carbonizing process. This practice has probably resulted in more excessive exploitation of resources than the increasing demand for extensive but limited use by villagers (Openshaw, 1974).

Systems have evolved for charcoal production that exist in relative equilibrium with renewable resources. Such a system is the utilization of tree prunings from *Quercus ulex* woodlands in Spain for charcoal production. The trees are pruned on a rotational basis to maximize mass production. The prunings, down to branchlets, are converted to charcoal using the earth-covered mound method.

Charcoal production represents a relatively labor-intensive technology that has changed only slightly in thousands of years. Despite its antiquity, charcoal production is the only applicable technology available to enhance the efficiency and reduce the transportation cost of raw wood.

IV. Second-Generation Technology

If the aerial portions of shrubs could be collected, centralized in a limited area, and converted to pellets of uniform size and moisture content, they would represent a highly valuable and usable energy source. Unfortunately, this process results in pellets that cost more to produce per unit of energy than conventional fuels (Smith, 1981). Other potential ways to obtain energy from shrubs include extracting sap that is naturally high in hydrocarbons, converting woody biomass to alcohol, and producing utilizable gas (Brown, 1980; Datta and Dutt, 1981).

In terms of organic matter, wood is approximately 50% cellulose, 20% hemicellulose, and 30% lignin (Abelson, 1982). Lignin can be used as an adhesive, a filter in plastics, and, when pyrolyzed, it forms a superior metallurgical coke. Cellulose can be used directly as cattle feed or converted to glucose by acid hydrolysis or by use of enzymes. The enzyme method gives the highest yields and is becoming less expensive. Glucose derived from wood can be used as food for humans, as a carbon source for microbial formation of protein, or as a feedstock for fermentation processes yielding liquid fuels, chemicals, and pharmaceuticals. Abelson (1982) editorialized that "wood is in the process of resuming its ancient central role, but on a broader scale as science and technology point the way to more effective production and use." It appears logical that these highly technological uses of woody biomass will be economically feasible, first for tree plantations and sometime in the distant future for shrubs.

The processing of hydrocarbons from shrubs is probably best exemplified by guayule (*Psidium guajava*). The potential of culturally specific shrubs for hydrocarbon extraction may be great, but these shrubs probably will be grown on agricultural soils and not collected from native stands. Wood alcohol (methanol) is a potential fuel, although its energy value and corrosive nature limit its application. It is difficult to find examples of conversion of wood from shrubs to methanol. Methanol can be produced by biomass gasification followed by catalytic conversion of synthetic gas. So far, only large methanol plants have been proposed for biomass utilization. For instance, a plant proposed for Brazil that would produce 4 million kg of methanol per day (from 8.4 million kg of dry wood per day) is expected to cost $350 million (Rooker, 1980).

Access to mechanical power is needed in the villages of less developed countries for lift irrigation, plowing, threshing, transportation, and other uses (Datta and Dutt, 1981). Traditionally, people in less developed countries have obtained a major share of their mechanical energy from draft animals. A comparison of the energy efficiency of agricultural production showed that less developed countries use more energy per unit of production than do developed countries. However, developed countries use high-quality, nonrenewable energy sources such as petroleum and natural gas, whereas virtually all the energy used by farmers in less developed countries is derived from crude agricultural residues and other biomass (Makhijani and Poole, 1975).

As petroleum becomes less available and more expensive, farmers in less developed countries cannot improve their efficiency by using conventional internal combustion power sources. Less developed countries poor in fossil fuel must, therefore, seek to increase the energy efficiency of renewable energy resources such as wood (including shrubs), crop residue, dung, and solar radiation (Datta and Dutt, 1981). Given their constraints of capital, the diffuse nature of the resource, and lack of technology and know-how, this will not be an easy task. For example, photovoltaic power (generation of electric energy from sunlight) is not economically feasible with current technology. Wind power and hydropower are site-specific and generally limited to stationary applications. Production of methanol and ethanol from biomass is still energy-inefficient and capital-intensive. Small steam engines have low efficiency. Stirling engines need a major development effort to make them cost-effective (Beale *et al.,* 1980).

In contrast to the problems associated with alternative power sources, the producer gas engine has several advantages (Datta and Dutt, 1980). It is an internal combustion engine that can run on solid fuels such as wood and straw; it has a moderately high efficiency, a low cost, and is easily adaptable to existing internal combustion engines. This proven technology can provide both mobile and stationary power. The gas for producer gas engines is a mixture of several gases, including carbon monoxide, hydrogen, and nitrogen, and is a product of partial combustion of biomass fuels in a series of complex chemical reactions that are only partially understood.

Most of the advanced technological methods of obtaining energy from biomass base their source of raw material on either waste products such as crop residue and wood waste or the products of energy plantations. These plantations usually are high-energy-content crops such as sugarcane or fast-growing trees. Little attention has been devoted to shrub plantations for energy production, a subject we will develop later. Plantations may be feasible in the near future, but eventually the question arises as to the relative value and efficiency of producing direct-consumption food crops versus energy crops. This question of the competition for use of arable land for either food or energy suggests the possibility of growing energy crops on nonarable land such as rangeland.

V. Open-Hearth Efficiency

One of the major reasons for the high per capita consumption of wood in less developed countries is the relative inefficiency of open-hearth cooking. Only 6 to 8% of the energy of wood burned on open hearths for cooking is put to productive use (Smith, 1981). The October 1981 issue of *VITA News* (Anonymous, 1981) contains an assessment of stove design and testing. Most tropical staples, for example, rice, yams, plantains, and sweet potatoes, require relatively large amounts of energy for preparation

(Smith, 1981). Numerous stoves have been designed to alleviate this inefficiency such as the Indian Chulah or the Guatemalan Lorean stoves (Anonymous, 1981). The problem is to develop an efficient stove at low enough cost so it can be acquired and used by individuals in countries with extremely low incomes and no systems for credit purchases.

VI. Developed Countries

A. Historical Perspectives

The residents of developed countries tend to forget that their energy sources in the recent past were based on wood. In 1850, the United States was 91% dependent on wood for energy, by 1900 this had dropped to 25%, and now wood constitutes only 3% of our energy use (Smith, 1981).

In the sagebrush grasslands of the western United States shrubs were used as fuel by American Indians as late as 1900 (Fig. 1). The collection in historic times of woody species of *Artemisia* for fuel is strikingly similar to

Figure 1.   Collection of big sagebrush (*Artemisia tridentata*) shrubs for fuel by American Indians at Wadsworth, Nevada, about 1900, shows adaptation for the use of shrubs for energy in a treeless environment. (Photograph courtesy of Cowles family, Reno, Nevada.)

Figure 2. Collection of dwarf *Artemisia* shrubs for fuel by the sons of Afghan nomads in 1979. Each load represents one family's daily fuel requirement. The biological parameters for governing renewal of the fuel resource are the same in developing and developed countries. (Photograph courtesy of Dr. Michail J. Casimir, Institute für Völkerkunde, University Zu Kölen, West Germany.)

current procedures in central Asia (Fig. 2). The use of *Artemisia* shrubs for fuel was not restricted to American Indians. Extensive areas of big sagebrush (*Artemisia tridentata*) were harvested for fuel for the nineteenth-century mining industry (Budy and Young, 1979). Shrubs were utilized in areas where conifer woodlands did not occur. If conifer woodlands did exist, even woodlands composed of the relatively diminutive trees of single-leaf pinyon (*Pinus monophylla*) and Utah juniper (*Juniperus osteosperma*) were converted to charcoal as an energy source.

B. Present Conditions in North America

Many hectares of rangeland in the western United States, Canada, and Mexico have relatively large accumulations of woody biomass that could potentially serve as an energy source (Young and Evans, 1981). These areas are considered rangelands for domestic and wild animals, watersheds, and recreational areas. Because of successional changes induced by the excessive grazing of domestic livestock and suppression of wildfires, huge amounts of woody material have accumulated on these rangelands at the expense of herbaceous species. In the Intermountain Area this accumulation is represented by species of *Artemisia,* in Texas and New Mexico by species of *Prosopis* (Allred, 1953), and in the Southwest by pinyon–juniper woodlands (Johnson, 1962). A considerable effort has been spent by rangeland managers during the past 30 years at correcting the imbalance of shrubs and grasses by applying mechanical, herbicidal, or prescribed burning treatments to shift the ecological balance in favor of herbaceous species. Depending on the plant community and the amount of woody biomass accumulated, these treatments may have included a destructive disposal of the accumulation of woody material, usually through burning. Where lesser amounts of woody biomass were dealt with, as in the case of spraying brush, the woody material was allowed to decay in place. Superficially these accumulations of woody biomass would appear to be a potential source of energy. What problems are associated with harvesting and utilization of this energy?

C. Sustained Yield

One of the first conflicts that must be faced in an analysis of fuel wood harvest from noncommercial woodlands is the question of sustained yield. Modern forestry is predicated on the basis of sustained yield. In the western United States, there are millions of acres of rangelands with an accumulation of woody biomass. However, the sustained regrowth of such biomass probably is not the most economically or environmentally desirable use of the land. After a century of misuse, large quantities of woody biomass, in respect to the environmental potential, have accumulated. However, the annual increment of usable wood of these shrubs is so small that the sites probably are capable of producing forage, browse, or water of greater value then the fuel potential. Data for economic evaluation of such comparisons are badly needed.

In an analysis of fuel wood harvesting costs and returns, the land manager must consider the capital investment in harvesting, processing, and transporting the product. In the case of many rangeland communities, this cost must be discounted for a one-time-only harvest from each area.

In less developed countries the same constraints should be considered. A degraded shrub community may be the last step before accelerated erosion. Is it desirable to maintain this degraded community or should it be replaced with the most productive community that the site will support? This is another example of how developed and less developed countries may be dealing with different ends of the spectrum in terms of energy and forage resources from rangelands, but the biological and physical parameters that constrain the processes are the same.

D. Harvesting Methodology

In less developed countries there is no question that energy harvesting from rangelands is a labor-intensive operation. In developed countries the cost and availability of labor preclude the use of labor-intensive techniques. The low productivity per unit area is the biological basis of this problem and again operates in both developed and developing countries.

In developed countries the answer to labor problems is to substitute capital for the purchase of machinery for the labor-intensive practices. Agricultural equipment for harvesting forage or grain cannot be substituted for equipment for harvesting shrubs on rangelends. Range managers have found it necessary to develop specialized equipment for range improvement (Young and McKenzie, 1982). Design, development, and testing of this specialized equipment require a major expenditure of a qualified engineering staff with a support budget. Developing and manufacturing range improvement equipment require large amounts of capital for a specific and limited market.

The physical requirements of shrub-harvesting equipment are impressive. This equipment would have to be able to travel over rugged and often rocky topography while cutting, collecting, and transporting bulky shrubs growing in an uneven distribution with varying heights. Once collected the universal problems of fuel wood harvesting must be dealt with. These include reducing the material to pellets of uniform density for fluid handling and, most importantly, uniformly reducing the moisture content. Initial moisture contents probably will average 50%, so it is important to desiccate this material before transporting.

E. Site Conversion

Many of the rangeland sites that contain excessive accumulations of woody biomass were, under pristine conditions, dominated by a mixture of herbaceous species and shrubs. The optimum long-term use of this land, in terms of both usable production and protection of the resource, demands the conversion of the site from solely woody dominance back to a mixture of shrubs, forbs, and grasses. The value of the accumulated woody biomass as an energy source offers a way of paying for the cost of this conversion. However, this means that the energy-harvesting procedure must include site preparation for the revegetation. This site preparation includes control of undesirable woody vegetation that is too small or scattered for energy harvesting, slash disposal, and seedbed preparation. If this woody vegetation were to be harvested for fuel, development of herbaceous and young woody plants would be stimulated because of the site resources released by the removal of the woody biomass. These dynamics, also, may lead to sudden expression of herbaceous weeds that will require suppression if desirable species are to be established.

The removal of woody biomass for energy alters patterns in nutrient cycling on the collection site. Several cycles of such harvesting may reduce the inherent productivity of some sites. However, on sites where pinyon/juniper woodlands have invaded former shrub/grasslands, the accumulations of woody biomass may represent a sink of nutrients that is unavailable for plant growth. Unfavorable carbon–nitrogen ratios of these woodlands inhibit microbial degradation of litter, perpetuating these sinks.

The expression of vegetation dynamics may attract rodents, insects, and wild large herbivores to the fuel wood-harvesting area. This would be especially pronounced if the harvesting area were a small portion of an extensive woodland. Integrated pest management is a continuing necessity in energy harvesting.

A review of the literature of the attempts at reforestation in developing countries finds numerous references to marauding livestock as the main destroyer of planted trees (Smith, 1981). In both developed and developing countries, grazing management is essential for the site improvements to have a chance for successful establishment with the eventual persistence of desirable forage, browse, and/or energy species. This means that, initially, livestock must be excluded to assure seedling establishment. After establishment, the harvested and revegetated site has inherently different forage production from any remaining woodland or rangeland, creating a problem of distribution of grazing animals.

Foresters seem to instinctively distrust grazing animals, probably from bitter experience with animal damage to plantations, but any site conversion must be in harmony with the local culture for it to succeed. Virtually every type of range improvement that involves recruitment of seedlings must encompass a period of rest from use by grazing animals. Regardless of the level of development of national economies, deferment or rest from grazing is a biological fact of life. Rest from grazing is necessary even if prescribed grazing is used to reduce competition with the seedlings. Control of the herdsman and his animals is essential. This involves physical exclusion through fencing or cooperation of the herdsmen, which may be extremely difficult to uniformly obtain and maintain. The success of reforestation in South Korea has been traced to entrusting the program to villagers who understand that the program is for their benefit (Eckholm, 1979).

VII. Choice of Woody Species for Energy Plantations

The recent publication "Firewood Crops—Shrub and Tree Species for Energy Production" lists 35 perspective species for culturing in arid or semiarid environments for energy production (National Academy of Sciences, 1983). Over 50% of these species belong to the family Leguminosae. This reflects the lack of nitrate-nitrogen in the soils of many degraded wildland communities and the prohibitive cost of nitrogen fertilizers in most developing countries. The growth of some of the leguminous trees or shrubs has been shown to favorably influence soil nitrogen levels (Singh and Lal, 1969; Shankar *et al.*, 1976).

A review of the presently available plant material for woody energy crops reveals few true shrubs and fewer yet species adapted to cold desert environments. Other than species of *Haloxylon* or *Tamarix*, which are often phreatophytic, there are species in many shrub genera that are adapted to semiarid sites with severe frost.

VIII. Perspective

We live in a world where there are many inequalities in resource allocations. Nowhere is this more apparent than in fuel wood resources. Despite the gross differences in dependence and use or misuse of this resource, it is vital to remember that the same biological and physical parameters govern renewal of the resources in both the developed and less developed worlds.

References

Abelson, P. H. (1982). Energy and chemicals from trees (Editorial). *Science* **215,** 1349.

Allred, B. W. (1953). Influence of shrub invasion on U.S. rangelands. *Proc. Int.Grassl. Congr., 6th, 1952,* pp. 578–584.

Anonymous (1943). "How to Make Charcoal on the Farm" USDA For. Serv. Washington, D.C.

Anonymous (1981). A burning issue—wood conserving cook stoves. *VITA News, October,* pp. 3–8.

Beale, W. T., Wood, J. G., and Chagnot, B. J. (1980). Stirling engines for developing countries. *Proc. 15th Annu. Intersoc. Energy Convers. Eng. Conf.* p. 1020.

Brown, L. R. (1980). Food or fuel: New competition for the world's cropland. *World Watch Pap.* No. 35.

Budy, J. D. and Young, J. A. (1979). Historical use of Nevada's pinyon–juniper woodlands. *J. For. Hist.* **23,** 113–121.

Casimir, M. J., Winter, R. P., and Glatzer, B. (1980). Nomadism and remote sensing: Animal husbandry and the sagebrush community in a nomad winter area in western Afghanistan. *J. Arid Environ.* **3,** 231–254.

Datta, R., and Dutt, G. S. (1981). Producer gas engines in villages of less developed countries. *Science* **213**, 231–236.

Eckholm, E. (1975). The other energy crisis: Firewood. *World Watch Pap.* No. 1.

Eckholm, E. (1979). Planting for the future: Forestry for human needs. *World Watch Pap.* No. 26.

Eckholm, E. (1981). Introduction. *In* "Firewood Crops: Shrub and Tree Species for Energy Production," pp. 1–7. National Academy of Sciences, Washington, D.C.

Garriet, G. (1982). Four improved charcoal kiln designs. *Energy Bull.* **2**(1), 11-B, 15.

Johnson, T. N., Jr. (1962). One seed juniper invasion of northern Arizona grasslands. *Ecol. Monogr.* **32**, 187–207.

Longhurst, W. M., Oh, H. K., Jones, M. B., and Kepner, R. E. (1968). A basis for the palatability of deer forage plants. *Trans. North Am. Wildl. Nat. Resour. Conf.* **33**, 181–192.

McArthur, E. D., and Plummer, A. P. (1978). Biogeography and management of native western shrubs: A case study, section *Tridentatae* of *Artemisia. Great Basin Nat. Mem.* **2**, 229–243.

Makhijani, A., and Poole, L.A. (1975). "Energy and Agriculture in the Third World." Ballinger, Cambridge, Massachusetts.

Nagy, J. G., Steinroff, H. W., and Ward, G. M. (1964). Effect of essential oils of sagebrush on deer rumen microbial function. *J. Wild. Manage.* **28**, 785–790.

Nagy, J. G. (1979). Wildlife nutrition and the sagebrush ecosystem. *In* "The Sagebrush Ecosystem: A Symposium," pp. 164–168. Utah State University, Logan.

National Academy of Sciences (1983). "Firewood Crops—Shrub and Tree Species for Energy Production," Vol. 2. Report of an *Ad hoc* Panel, Advisory Committee for Technology Innovation, National Academy Press, Washington, D.C.

Openshaw, K. (1974). Wood fuels. The developing world. *New Sci.* **61**, 883–834.

Rooker, J. H. (1980). "Energy from Biomass and Waste." Inst. Gas Technol., Chicago, Illinois.

Shankar, V., Dadhich, N. K., and Saxena, S. K. (1976). Effect of Kherji tree (*Prosopis cineraria* Macbride) on the productivity of range grasses growing in its vicinity. *Forage Res.* **2**, 91–96.

Singh, K. S., and Lal, P. (1969). Effect of Kherji (*Prosopis spicigera* Linn.) and babool (*Acacia arabica*) trees on soil fertility and profile characteristics. *Ann. Arid Zone* **8**, 33–36.

Smith, N. (1981). Wood: An ancient fuel with a new future. *World Watch Pap.* No. 42.

Thalen, D. C. P. (1979). "Ecology and Utilization of Desert Shrub Rangelands in Iraq." Junk, The Hague.

Young, J. A., and Evans, R. A. (1981). Something of value—Energy from wood on rangelands. *Rangelands* **3**, 10–12.

Young, J. A., and McKenzie, D. (1981). Rangeland drill. *Rangelands* **4**, 108–113.

23

Shrubs in the Naturalized Landscape

G. Michael Alder
W. Kent Ostler

I. Introduction

This chapter investigates the use of shrubs in a naturalized landscape. The concept of a naturalized landscape is defined as one that requires no additional inputs, that is, water, fertilizer, herbicides, etc., once it is established. Although the ultimate goal of this concept is no inputs, there exist many stages between this end of the spectrum and that of current landscapes that require constant and significant inputs for the vegetation to persist. This concept of a naturalized landscape is gaining much more acceptance in the field of landscape design. A major key to the success of this concept is the use of plant materials specifically adapted to the environment of interest. Native shrubs with their vast diversity will undoubtedly play a major role in the success of the naturalized landscape.

The Biology and Utilization of Shrubs

493

Color, form, texture, diversity, and organization all characterize the modern landscape, much to the benefit of mankind and our need and desire for aesthetic beauty. As an option among the varied choices available in naturalized landscaping, the use of native shrubs may be an idea whose time has arrived (Cochrane and Brown, 1978; Jones, 1981; Wasowski and Ryan, 1985). Many adaptations of current practices and attitudes must occur, however, to bring widespread use and acceptance (Landscape Architectural Forum, 1980). Commercial and residential landscaping have grown to depend on a matrix of inputs including irrigation, fertilizer, pesticide application, mowing, and pruning. This dependence has developed over generations of time and today's landscapes, at least in the United States, now require annual inputs of billions of dollars for water, materials, and labor. The high cost in time, money, water, and materials has reached such an extreme that alternatives designed to lower landscaping inputs have considerable momentum.

The values placed on more traditional domesticated plants and, probably more importantly, the inadequate supply of native shrubs have severely limited the latter's use as ornamentals (Sutton, 1975). However, during the past 10–20 years we have begun to recognize that native and adapted plants offer opportunities for cost savings in maintenance labor and materials, as well as providing an aesthetic transition to the natural environment. This interest has stimulated a substantial effort in developing propagation and plant production methods to meet the demand for these plant materials (Wasowski and Ryan, 1985; Murphy, 1984; Wasser, 1982; Fulbright et al., 1982; Redente et al., 1982; Vories, 1981). To date there is still a considerable "knowledge gap" between horticulturalists, landscape architects, garden book writers, and nursery owners concerning use and production needs (Sutton, 1975). Several attempts have been made to supply basic ecological and cultural information on a regional basis (Hightshoe and Niemann, 1982; Vories, 1981; Duffield and Jones, 1981; Rowell, 1980; Keith and Giles, 1980; Lenz and Dourley, 1981; Kruckeberg, 1982), however, much of the information on cultural practices, and in particular production techniques, is still relatively unrefined or often unknown.

Hardiness to temperature and climate extremes, lower irrigation requirements, and adaptation to local soils have all proven to be important factors that have influenced higher demand for native and proven adapted plants (Wasowski and Ryan, 1985; Sunset, 1982). This chapter focuses on the role of shrubs in the naturalized landscape, however, many of the principles described also apply to wildflowers, groundcovers, succulents, and trees.

II. The Role of Native Shrubs in Sustaining the Naturalized Landscape

Shrubs are an integral part of landscape design. Their size may vary from low woody groundcovers to shrublike trees that are 15 feet (5 m) or more in height. Also, textures, colors, leaf or branching effects, flowers, and fruits are so diverse that shrubs are considered the most versatile landscaping plant group. This diversity is a major factor in making shrubs so popular and valuable to the landscape architect. In the naturalized landscape, herbaceous plants are generally short-lived and are more adversely affected by climatic extremes than woody plants. Also, trees are often challenging to establish and difficult to maintain in good condition over a long period of time with little or no maintenance input. The major permanent design components of many native plant landscape projects are therefore shrubs or shrublike plants (e.g., bushy cacti and yuccas).

In addition to the diversity of form and function of shrubs, a major factor in their use in the naturalized landscape is their ability to effectively exploit the limited resources of the environment, particularly that of water. Many shrubs have developed adaptations to survive in times of drought, frost, and even fire. Some desert species partially defoliate during drought to manage water loss. Fuzzy leaves to screen sunlight and thickened leaf cuticles to protect against excess water loss are common adaptations to reduce plant water requirements. These water-conserving characteristics have helped to identify and develop a whole new concept in landscaping—xeriscape. Statistics indicate that 44% of the culinary water consumed in the western United States is used to irrigate turf and other landscape areas. The limiting factor to future development in many western cities is available water. Therefore, the xeriscape, a concept of designing landscapes with low water use, including reducing lawn area, using mulches, and planting drought-tolerant shrubs and other plants, as well as other techniques, has become a major emphasis of current landscapers and city governments (Miller, 1985; Wasowski and Ryan, 1985; Fort Worth Water Dept., 1985).

III. Receptivity of the Landscaping Industry to Native Shrubs

Ornamental landscaping from its beginnings has been based on traditional plant materials arising from early European and Oriental gardens and gardening practices. Ornamentals since that time have been improved or selected on the basis of valued characteristics. Horticulturists developed or adapted methods for their routine production. The early fund of information about propagation and culture grew and the skills and materials were refined and passed down. Present-day horticulture is a recognized art and science with an extensive reference literature. However, because of the complex and integrated background required to produce plants on a large scale, the delicate nature of living systems during the growing process, the challenging logistics in moving plants to market, and unpredictable sales, large business entities have not wanted to become involved until recent years. Even so, the bulk of this industry is still a cottage industry that seems adapted to those with the most interest and skill.

The development of large wholesale ornamental nurseries across the United States and in many other countries has made it possible for landscape architects and designers to have a reliable source of adequately sized quality plant material. These nurseries produce large inventories of plants in advance of their sale. However, this stockpile system leaves both the wholesaler and retailer vulnerable to oversupply situations. Hence, both groups are naturally conservative when unique plants are introduced.

Woody plant introduction is a difficult task because (1) the United States lacks a coordinated system to evaluate and promote plants and (2) the time required to breed and evaluate shrubs. These programs take long-term commitments of staff, funds, land, and labor (Creech, 1985). Despite these constraints, some nurseries have taken an interest in native shrubs and have tried to specialize or introduce them on a limited basis. Many of these efforts have remained obscure because of the complexity of finding and growing seed and cuttings. Motivation to use certain types of plant materials comes from the marketplace, yet, when asked, nearly all consumers would like to be able to select from plants that have the hardiness and adaptability of natives especially when they understand the lower requirements of natives for water and fertilizer. The disparity arises because of the time necessary to grow a plant to a marketable size and production runs 2–3 years behind market demands for new species or changes in traditional species.

In the United States during the last decade, renewed interest in natives has stimulated several large wholesale nurseries to produce and stock them on a more consistent basis. As regular sources of these plant materials have developed, landscape architects and designers have begun to include them in their projects. The stimulation from the marketplace has generated more interest in expanding and diversifying supplies and appears to be building an expanded foundation for future growth. This growth pattern may serve as a model in other countries where development of the ornamental nursery industry may be greatly augmented by native shrubs. The critical issue in use of native shrubs by the landscaping industry appears to be availability.

IV. The Increasing Economic Benefits of Landscaping with Native Shrubs

An example of the opportunity for cost reduction and natural efficiency of xeriscape landscaping comes primarily from the arid/semiarid regions of the world, particularly the U.S. Southwest. In these areas, water is a limiting factor and has become the driving force in the movement to find drought-tolerant shrubs, trees, groundcovers, and grasses. The desire for alternatives to traditional, more water-requiring plants has stimulated workshops, papers, books, and articles (Duffield and Jones, 1981; Kelly and Schnadelbach, 1976; Denver Water Dept., 1984).

Several western U.S. cities regulate water for landscape irrigation and penalize offenders who abuse the conservation ordinances. In Albuquerque, New Mexico, a Fugitive Water Ordinance now invokes a misdemeanor penalty for allowing water to run off any landscaped property (City of Albuquerque Bill No. 055, 1979). In Aurora, Colorado, building permits are not issued until a landscape plan showing the heavy use of drought-tolerant plants is submitted to the planning commission. Periodic droughts have caused enough alarm that some concerned individuals have replaced existing landscape plants with natives or those known to be low water users. Sandy City, Utah, is now landscaping its roadsides and median strips with native shrubs such as *Rhus trilobata* (Fig. 1). Irrigation is only used to establish the transplants in the first year. Except for a biannual application of preemergent herbicides and some pruning, these plantings have had no other inputs for 5 years and they have a well-maintained, aesthetic appearance.

Keesen (1984) calculated that by using xeriscape principles millions of gallons of water could be saved. He estimated that for an average-sized, multifamily housing complex with 150,000 square feet of landscaped area, the average water savings per year would be 3,465,000 gallons, a reduction of 66% over conventional irrigation use in typical landscaping. Figuring water cost at $1.20 per thousand gallons, he predicts dollar savings of $4158 for 1 year and, allowing for price increases, $70,000 over a 10-year period.

The top three winners of the 1985 Xeriscape Yard Contest in the Denver area all averaged over 60% reductions in water use (Table I). With the average metropolitan water customer using about 182,000 gallons per year (Denver Water Dept., 1984), this amounts to saving over 110,000 gallons

Figure 1. *Rhus trilobata,* a hardy, dark-green shrub planted on a highway median strip in Sandy, Utah.

Table I. 1985 xeriscape yard contest for Denver area

	Winning residences			Typical area residence
	Ammann 1st	Thompson 2nd	Gabel 3rd	
Total lot (ft^2)	14,380	10,580	9,375	7,500
Structures (ft^2)	3,284	3,914	4,112	2,500
Open space (ft^2)	11,096	8,565	5,263	5,000
Turf (ft^2)	2,250	3,460	3,200	4,000
Buffalo grass (ft^2)	1,800	925	3,200	0
Bluegrass (ft^2)	450	2,535	0	4,000
Plant beds (ft^2)	8,846	5,105	2,063	1,000
Avg. indoor water use ×1000 (gal)	89	116	70	91
Avg. outdoor water use ×1000 (gal)	75	61	22	91
Avg. total water use ×1000 (gal)	164	177	92	182[a]
Avg. outdoor gal/ft^2 of open space	6.75	7.12	4.18	18.20
Per ft^2 outdoor use as % of typical	63%	61%	77%	Typical

[a] The typical Denver metropolitan area water customer uses about 182,000 gallons of water each year (Denver Water Dept., 1984).

per year per person. Water cost will certainly vary by location and availability, but at these rates it represents a substantial savings to the normal property owner.

Further evidence of changes in landscaping practices is in new U.S. highway landscaping programs. Expensive plantings that require irrigation, fertilizer, mowing, and pruning are being abandoned. The Federal Highway Administration has provided funding to study techniques to encourage native species recovery along roads in attempts to reduce maintenance costs (FHWA, 1985). Thus, new methods and materials are being sought and much of the plant materials will come from the natural adjacent environment where they are adapted to low inputs for survival (Dehgan *et al.*, 1977).

V. Essential Components in Utilizing Native Shrubs for Landscaping

The trend toward naturalized landscapes and/or xeriscapes includes new options in the essentials of all landscape efforts: *materials, methods,* and *aesthetics.* The challenge lies in developing resources in each of these areas simultaneously to provide a program that proceeds fast enough to retain the interest of the consumers. All three components are well understood by nursery owners, landscape contractors, landscape architects, and designers when using traditional plants. However, for native or adapted plants the experience base is much smaller and must improve if growth in the use of native shrubs is going to continue.

To relate how native shrubs can provide an option for low-maintenance, low-cost landscaping, a brief discussion follows regarding necessary components to consider in naturalized landscaping.

A. The Landscaped Area as a System

The role of native shrubs in natural plant communities is better understood today than at any time in the past. Plant ecologist, naturalists, taxonomists, and soil scientists, along with many other subdisciplines in botany, range science, and wildlife biology, are continuing to build the information base each year. Much of this information base has come from the reclamation industry in which costs for reestablishing native vegetation have to be minimal because of the tremendous land areas that are being reclaimed. Unfortunately, very little of this information is directly involved in determining the needs for horticulture and landscape design with shrubs. It is through the field experience, and a knowledge of current literature, that an individual with a technical-ecological background can become an important resource in planning the design, describing plant species performance, and suggesting ways to obtain permanence of a project utilizing native shrubs. Much of this information has been obscure to the landscape architect or nursery owner, yet as the interest in native shrubs increases, these people are becoming familiar with that knowledge and are generating their own literature and data on growth and performance of native shrubs. In addition to knowing plant form, function, flowering patterns, etc., the landscape architect is under greater pressure to know the environmental tolerance of native species. Knowledge of soil, precipitation, slope, exposure, elevation, competition, and the effects of microclimate must be integrated to plan an ecologically successful naturalized planting and/or seeding.

Three essential principles should be adhered to in designing a naturalized landscape:

1. Consult with experts on available information and recommendations for the best-adapted plants to use. Even though specialists may lack some experience with landscape uses of native shrubs, this assistance will probably make the difference between success and failure of any naturalized landscape project.
2. Use as much data as possible from the site and environmental setting and on plant tolerances in the design and selection of plants for projects.

3. Obtain the right size of planting stock and high-quality seed, for example, big plants may not adapt as well as small plants on a harsh, low-precipitation/irrigation site.

When these principles, together with appropriate methods, are put into practice, the designer may begin to "design with nature" (McHarg, 1971) or, in other words, develop the landscaped area as a self-regulating system.

B. Choice of Plant Materials

The criteria for species selection need to consider all the physical and environmental parameters of the site and the design aesthetics. Selection criteria will, of course, vary from site to site, however, broad characteristics for selecting species could include:

- tolerance to site stresses, that is, temperature, wind, and drought;
- tolerance to soil conditions, that is, salinity, depth, texture, and water-holding capacity;
- rooting depth and habit, such as deep or spreading;
- special color effects and their season;
- texture of foliage;
- potential of creating hazards, that is, poisonous fruits, irritating pollen, or woodiness (crash hazard);
- palatability—highly palatable species would not be desirable for roadsides, where the attraction of wildlife would be undesirable or a hazard;
- spatial requirements and size at maturity;
- longevity.

An example of the application of the selection criteria is the performance of *Rhus trilobata,* a hardy, dark-green shrub used on a highway median strip-planting in Sandy, Utah (Fig. 1). Annual precipitation is in the range of 13–18 inches with approximately 50% coming during the winter months in the form of snow. Here container-grown plants 8–10 inches tall were planted in a coarse, sandy soil with some gravel at 3-ft spacings. No other species were used. The planting was made in the fall with a 21-g slow-release (20–10–5) fertilizer tablet placed in the bottom of each planting hole. Supplemental irrigation with a tank truck was given twice during the first growing season. No other irrigation or other supplemental fertilizer has been used in 5 years since planting. Natural water harvesting for increased plant survival and growth was achieved by destroying competition with an initial weeding and then broadcasting a preemergence herbicide on the surface of the soil. This herbicide treatment has been repeated every 2 years. Survival has been 90% with growth to closure of the shrub canopy occurring in three growing seasons.

The foregoing example points out some very important elements concerning the future use of *Rhus trilobata* and the application of cultural techniques that are suitable for its establishment. Perhaps the most important point is that few inputs were required to establish this planting. Other factors of importance for future plantings would include the rate of growth and time to canopy closure, the survival rate, soil characteristics that are tolerated, precipitation that is suitable for growth, and cultural practices that aid in establishing this species.

C. Appropriate Cultural Techniques

Although the ideal of the native plant landscape may be to use no extra water or other inputs during establishment, experience has shown that some supplementary assistance is very beneficial and often required, particularly during the establishment period. Since the designer/planner must write specifications for appropriate methods of planting, seeding, and establishment practices, a brief discussion of principles is given to introduce major concepts. The following points are intended to emphasize those factors that may be unique to the use of shrubs in landscaping situations.

1. Seeding

Seeding of shrubs and other native plants should generally follow local practices for sowing. Many woody or perennial natives may require a cold season with freeze–thaw cycles to stimulate seed germination the following spring. Most desert and tropical species have different seed dormancy requirements and should be sown when adequate moisture is available through the germination and establishment periods. Greatest success is achieved when seeding is done immediately preceding the most reliable period of precipitation. In regions with wet winters, fall or early spring is usually the best time to seed or plant to take advantage of natural precipitation and high levels of soil moisture.

2. Container and Bareroot Plants

Most landscape plantings in the United States today utilize container-grown plants. The rationale for using the containerized plant is to provide a low-shock headstart for the plant at a time convenient to the user.

Bareroot nursery plants are easily transported in large volumes and are cheaper than container-grown plants. Since the bareroot transplant has a need to regenerate root hairs and deal with environmental resistance simultaneously, the best conditions must exist for these plants to be used on landscape projects. Where irrigation is planned or annual precipitation is sufficient, bareroot planting remains economical if the quantity and size of plant material desired is available. However, the project may be more difficult to design inasmuch as loss factors may be hard to predict. If timing is critical, container-grown plants remain the best alternative for projects that require long periods of time for installation. Container-grown plants are also best for off-season planting, in areas that have erratic precipitation, and for projects that require a predictable, more aesthetic result after installation.

3. Size of Plant Material and Rate of Seeding

When rapid visual results from intensive landscape projects are required, the largest plants possible are chosen and heavy seeding rates are used. Both of these practices need to be reviewed if efficiency in use of materials and rapid naturalization of the project are to be achieved. Small plants establish quicker and reduced seeding rates have less competitive effects in new seedings. If high-intensity maintenance is to be continued through the first growing season, plant size and seed rates should be carefully planned to avoid large mortality rates when extra maintenance ceases. If native species are treated with traditionally high maintenance inputs, more rapid growth should be expected than when they are growing in nature.

4. Irrigation

In areas where natural precipitation is above 25 inches (500 mm) per year, irrigation may not be necessary except during unusually dry periods. During the first season of establishment, careful site monitoring is essential to determine if supplementary water is necessary to assure survival. In drier areas, temporary irrigation to support establishment may be necessary. Watering cycles need to be gauged carefully so seedlings and transplants do not become water dependent. In colder regions water should be withdrawn before the end of the first growing season so that plants are not exposed to their first frost in a soft and succulent condition. Unless large transplants are used, no irrigation should be required after the first year if appropriate plant materials have been selected.

5. Mulching

The value of mulching is twofold; first it helps maintain more even moisture conditions around transplants or in seedbeds, and second it protects the soil prior to plant establishment. Caution should be used to avoid mulches that may contain foreign seeds or weed seeds that can compete with the species that are being seeded. It is not uncommon for a barley straw mulch to contain 2% seed. If 2 tons of mulch are used per acre, the site is receiving 80 pounds of seed. This is often much more than the seeding rate of the desired species. Mulches sprayed on with seed suspended in the slurry (hydromulched) should be avoided where rainfall is scarce or erratic unless irrigation is planned. Seeding followed by a spray mulch applied on top is more desirable in drier climates.

6. Fertilizer

Initial fertilization of new plants may seem unnecessary if naturalization is the goal; however, in most landscaping situations, a mixing of subsoil layers has occurred during the development of a project. If soils are low in fertility, initial inputs of nitrogen may help both survival and vigor during the establishment phase. Phosphorus is also very important for establishing native shrubs since it enhances root development. It is very important that plants in a naturalized landscape with reduced water inputs have a vigorous root system, but high levels of fertilization are not necessary and may actually be detrimental by encouraging too much shoot growth for the root system to support. Thus, low levels of fertilizers with a low nitrogen to phosphorus ratio are better for native shrubs. Slow-releasing fertilizers are excellent for the generally slower-growing natives, particularly if release of nutrients occurs when plants are actively growing.

7. Maintenance

Naturalized plantings will tend to require much less time for maintenance than the conventional or more formal landscapes. Because of the slower growth of native shrubs and the desire for a more natural form, pruning is greatly reduced. Also, native species are adapted much better to climatic conditions and will experience less breakage and plant death due to unusual weather conditions. In most cases native shrub plantings are better adapted to insect and disease problems and will require less time and money in controlling these important components and keeping plants healthy.

VI. Aesthetics—A Prime Attribute Available with Native Shrubs

The use of native shrubs in landscaping begins with effective design and specification of appropriate materials. Natives provide a broad range of choices to enhance aesthetics. Groupings or associations of plants that imitate natural plant communities add to the quality of natural landscaping. Although the complexities of natural plant communities could never be totally reconstructed, the architect/designer may gain much from the study of dominant plant associations in natural settings. In addition to designing with nature, the landscape architect/designer needs more than plant names and size availability to develop designs. The attributes that are necessary for adequate background on any plant that may be used include:

- Growth form, size, and structure
- Texture of foliage, flowers, stems, or fruits
- Color attributes
- Special soil or drainage requirements
- Range of climatic adaptation
- Maintenance requirements
- Special concerns such as invasive roots
- Longevity under cultivation
- Disease or insect susceptibility under nonnatural conditions
- Genetic variability
- Weediness

Given this information, the landscape planner and designer may still be hesitant to do more than experiment. These experiments are important but may often take years before performance evaluations can be made. Hence there is a dramatic need for demonstration gardens and projects that are accessible to the public for observation (Creech, 1985). Some plantings in botanical gardens and arboreta serve a dual role of answering many of the attribute questions listed above as well as providing the experimental data base needed to give confidence to the designer (Cathay, 1985; Ware, 1985; Ching and Murray, 1985). Unfortunately, many of the species being tested in arboreta are exotics and much more emphasis is needed on the performance of natives.

VII. Overview

An approach for planning and planting naturalized landscapes is based on the general concepts presented in this chapter. The new frontier in landscape design seeks to utilize the best aspects of natural systems. Creating a natural landscape with attention to aesthetics can provide a pleasing and effective environment for people while making efficient use of resources. Society has not demanded natural efficiency in the past but in the future it seems inevitable. When properly used, native shrubs, in combination with trees, herbaceous plants, and grasses, can add to the natural beauty and stability of landscaped systems while potentially reducing overall costs.

References

Cathay, H. M. (1985). National arboretum introductions. *Am. Nurseryman* **161**(9), 53–60.

Ching, F., and Murray, E. (1985). Select ornamentals for southern California. *Am. Nurseryman* **161**(9), 37–41.

Cochrane, T., and Brown, J. (1978). "Landscape Design for the Middle East." RIBA Publ., London.

Creech, J. L. (1985). New introductions face many obstacles. *Am. Nurseryman* **161**(9), 25–28.

Dehgan, B., Tucker, J. M., and Takher, B. S. (1977). "Propagation and Culture of New Species of Drought-Tolerant Plants for Highways," Interim Rep., Jan. 1973–June 1975. Office of Landscape Architecture, California Dept. of Transportation, Sacramento, and Dept. of Botany, U. C. Davis Arboreton, University of California, Davis.

Denver Water Dept. (1984). "Xeriscape—The Future Today," Proc. Symp., 1984. Denver Water Dept., Denver, Colorado.

Duffield, M. R., and Jones, W. D. (1981). "Plants for Dry Climates: How to Select, Grow and Enjoy." H. P. Books, Tucson, Arizona.

Federal Highway Administration (FHWA) (1985). "Accelerated Recovery of Native Vegetation on Roadway Slopes after Construction," Contract No. DTFH 61-85-R–2087. FHWA, Washington, D. C.

Fort Worth Water Dept. (1985). "Fort Worth Area Drought Tolerant and Native Plant Directory." Fort Worth Water Dept., Fort Worth, Texas.

Fulbright, T. E., Redente, E. F., and Hargis, N. E. (1982). "Growing Colorado Plants from Seed: A State of the Art," Vol. 2, FWS/OBS–82/29. VSDI, Fish Wildl. Serv. Off. Biol. Serv., Washington, D. C.

Hightshoe, G. L., and Niemann, R. S. (1982). Plant selection system (PLTSEL): Midwestern and Eastern floristic regions. *Landscape J.* **1**(1), 23–30.

Jones, W. D. (1981). Low-water landscaping: Not just rocks and cacti. *Progressive Agric. Ariz.* **32**(2), 6–11.

Keesen, L. E. (1984). Irrigation to xerigation. *Proc. Symp. Xeriscape—The Future Today, 1984.*

Keith, R.M., and Giles, F. A. (1980). "Dwarf Shrubs for the Midwest." Univ. of Illinois Press, Urbana.

Kelly, K., and Schnadelbach, R. T. (1976). "Landscaping the Saudi Arabian Desert." Falcon Press, Philadelphia, Pennsylvania.

Kruckeberg, A. R. (1982). "Gardening with Native Plants of the Pacific Northwest." Univ. of Washington Press, Seattle.

Landscape Architectural Forum (1980). Design approaches to desert landscaping. *Landscape Architectural Forum, Fall, 1980,* pp. 15–21.

Lenz, L., and Dourley, J. (1981). "California Native Trees and Shrubs for Garden and Environmental Use." Rancho Santa Ana Botanic Garden, Claremont, California.

McHarg, I. (1971). "Design with Nature." Doubleday/Natural History Press, New York.

Miller, G. (1985). Return of the natives. *Tex. Highways,* November 19.

Murphy, P. M. (compiler) (1984). The challenge of producing native plants for the Intermountain area. *Proc. Intermt. Nurseryman's Assoc. Conf., 1983,* Gen. Tech. Rep. INT–168.

Redente, E. F., Ogle, P. R., and Hargis, N. E. (1982). "Growing Colorado Plants from Seed: A State of the Art," Vol. 3, FWS/OBS–82/30. USDI, Fish Wildl. Serv., Off. Biol., Serv., Washington, D. C.

Rowell, R. J. (1980). "Ornamental Flowering Shrubs in Australia." Reed Pty, Ltd., Sydney, Australia.

Sunset (1982). What can natives do for you? *Sunset,* October, pp. 238–241.

Sutton, R. K. (1975). Why native plants aren't used more. *J. Soil Water Conserv.* **30**(5), 240–242.

Vories, K. C. (1981). "Growing Colorado Plants from Seed: A State of the Art," Vol. 1, Gen. Tech. Rep. INT–103. USDA, For. Serv., Washington, D. C.

Ware, G. (1985). Urban trees and shrubs from the Morton Arboretum. *Am. Nurseryman* **161**(9), 42–47.

Wasowski, S., and Ryan, J. (1985). "Landscaping with Native Texas Plants." Texas Monthly Press, Austin.

Wasser, C. H. (1982). "Ecology and Culture of Selected Species Useful in Revegetating Disturbed Lands in the West," FWS/OBS–82/56. USDI, Fish Wildl. Serv., Off. Biol. Serv., Washington, D. C.

VI

Shrub Establishment and Management

To realize the benefits available from using shrubs as described in the previous section, better management practices should be followed. In some situations, it may first be necessary to establish better shrub species to replace the less desirable ones or add desirable ones as a supplement to the existing plant community. In areas where drastic disturbance has occurred through fire, surface mining, or other causes, a new plant community structure must be established consisting of an optimal mix of shrubs, grasses, and herbaceous species.

Chapters in this section provide useful methods for collecting and processing seeds from natural stands or from superior genotypes planted in seed production orchards. Techniques for mass propagation of bareroot or container-grown transplants are described for producing quality plant materials to be available for outplanting at the most favorable seasons. Methods for establishment of shrubs emphasize ways to achieve success under adverse environmental conditions.

Without improved management practices the multiple uses of shrubs cannot be obtained. In the past, many grazing practices have emphasized reduction of shrubs or have ignored shrubs in favor of grasses with the result that undesirable shrubs have increased in density. Management techniques discussed in Chapter 28 focus on ways to obtain optimal use of shrubs in a mixed plant community.

24

Seed Collecting, Processing, and Storage

Claire Gabriel Dunne*

I. Site Adaptability

Most seed is still collected from native stands because wild shrubs have not been brought under cultivation. In the interim, collections from native stands must supply the bulk of seeds required by the market.

A key point in seed collection is the range of adaptation for the species desired, both for planning collecting operations and for predicting the areas where the species would be successful when planted. Unfortunately, the range of adaptability of many species is not adequately known. For example, wild rose (*Rosa woodsii*) is broadly adaptable, whereas fourwing

---

* Author is co-owner of Absaroka Seed Company in Manderson, Wyoming.

saltbush (*Atriplex canescens*) is more site specific. Thus, fourwing saltbush seeds should be collected within the range of adaptation of the site where it is to be used. Even if the species can be purchased from a seed dealer, it may be worth the expense to collect it locally.

II. Preparing for the Harvest

A. *Quantity to Collect*

Collecting enough seed to grow plants in a nursery is easier than gathering enough for direct seeding onto a field site; in the nursery almost every viable seed can be turned into a plant, but thousands of times more seed must be sown on a harsh site to produce the same number of plants. Collecting large quantities of seed near a proposed planting site may be impossible. For example, 100 kg of serviceberries (*Amelanchier alnifolia*) yields only 3 kg of clean seed, so it is unlikely that a site will have a large enough stand nearby to yield the quantity needed.

Good seed is not formed every year: inadequate soil moisture, frost at bloom, or insect attack can ruin a crop. For example, blackbrush (*Coleogyne ramosissima*) collected in southern Utah in 1978, after a wet spring, was the first good crop in 9 years. In 1981, Gambel oak (*Quercus gambelii*) was infested with weevil larvae in Utah, but produced so many good acorns in south-central Colorado that they "rained" into a truck bed driven through the thickets. After checking stands of low rabbitbrush (*Chrysothamnus viscidiflorus*) in four states in 1983, only one small stand was found that produced good seed. Since many wild species set good seed crops only occasionally, stockpiles should be accumulated during good seasons.

B. *Locating Good Stands*

In preparation for a productive collection season, look for large, pure stands of well-spaced, vigorous plants on workable terrain. Avoid collecting from individual plants that may not be cross-pollinated. Learn the noxious weeds in the area and avoid collecting seeds in weed-infested areas.

C. *Timing the Harvest*

As the seed matures check the health of the seed unit; look for frost, insect, and fungus damage. Cut 50 seeds to check their fill; good fruit doesn't always mean good seed. The best reference for seed biology of North American shrubs is "Seeds of Woody Plants in the United States"

(Schopmeyer, 1974). After several seasons, experience will teach recognition of good seed.

Seed ripens 4 or more weeks after flowering. However, seasonal events will vary the collection date of the same stand as much as 2 weeks from year to year. Some seed, such as sagebrush (*Artemisia* spp.), drops soon after ripening, whereas others, such as fourwing saltbush, are retained for months. Capsules of *Ceanothus* spp., and fruit of other species that split open when dry, eject the seed away from the mother plant and must be collected green and covered with screens to dry.

Although most stands need to be checked more than once, some species, such as antelope bitterbrush (*Purshia tridentata*), need constant surveillance. Bitterbrush may look good until almost ripe, then seeds may blacken and shrivel from insect damage the last week. Also, dry winds or rains can cause seed to drop overnight. A bitterbrush crop may be unripe one afternoon and on the ground the next morning. The time approaching seed maturity creates many hazards. Fleshy fruits may be eaten by birds; fluffy seed, such as winterfat (*Ceratoides lanata*), may be lost to the wind; and palatable seed heads may be nipped by livestock.

D. Collecting Mature Seed

For best viability seed should be collected when mature. Fortunately, most species mature at least a week before fleshy fruits drop or dry seed dehisces. Seed of many wildland plants is produced in indeterminate inflorescences; thus, the collector must harvest only the ripe parts of the fruiting head, make several visits to the site, or cut the seed stalks and take them to a warehouse to continue ripening. The first seed to fall naturally from a plant and the last seed hanging on are often substandard and generally should be avoided.

Immature seed often has low viability and a short storage life (Harrington, 1972). Generally, seed should be allowed to pass through the liquid (milk) stage as well as through the congealed (soft dough) stage, and harvested as it is hardening (hard dough stage). When it is necessary to collect unripe fruit, the seed will often mature if part of the stem is taken along with the seed head and dried on screens in a ventilated area. Some species in the rose family (and others) may germinate readily when harvested somewhat green; on the other hand, a mature seed will store longer, but may be dormant and require pretreatment to induce germination (Mirov and Kraebel, 1939).

Seed moisture curves can be developed for each species to predict harvest time. Seed moisture drops from about 60% in immature seed to about 10% in ripe seed, at the rate of about 3% a day (Young *et al.*, 1981).

III. Harvesting

Until seed is cleaned and dried, it should be stored in clean, porous bags or boxes (never airtight plastic). Aeration prevents mold and overheating, which can occur within a few hours. If spread outdoors, cover seed at night as a protection from wind, rain, and dew.

A. Harvesting by Hand

Thousands of kilograms of seed can be collected by flailing, beating, or brushing seed or fruit into a heavy nylon canvas hopper slung across the back. For species such as fourwing saltbush that cling to the branch, a box or tub shoved under the plant will catch hand-stripped seed. Since picking up seed from the ground will increase cleaning costs by adding stones, dirt, weed seed, and pathogens to the seed, spilled seed is best left on the ground.

Seeds of shrubs too tall to beat into hoppers, such as curlleaf mountain mahogany (*Cercocarpus ledifolius*), can be knocked onto tarps spread under the bush. However, care should be taken not to kick weed seeds onto the tarp. Alternately, airborne seeds can be caught downwind of the bush with a fiberglass screen suspended between poles. As it drops from the screen, the seed can be caught in a canvas pocket (Plummer *et al.*, 1968).

B. Harvesting by Machine

Vacuums can harvest small amounts of some species from mixed stands. Vacuums are best suited to small, wind-dispersed seed and are often slower than a collector working with both hands. The U.S. Forest Service Equipment Development Centers in San Dimas, California, and in Missoula, Montana, are designing and testing backpack as well as vehicle-mounted vacuums.

A major difficulty associated with using machines in wildland harvest is finding large, pure, weed-free stands. Small-plot combines developed for agriculture may be used to harvest small areas of grasses or legumes, though they may require modification for each kind of seed (Larson, 1980). Also, they are not built strong enough to withstand the rigors of wildland harvest, such as steep slopes and rough, rocky terrain.

If a combine is used, timing is of the essence; since most native species ripen unevenly, one must choose the best time to catch most of the ripe seed before it falls. A combine will cut the plant stalks, thresh and separate ripe seed from the heads, and discharge most of the green seed with the

Figure 1. Reel-type harvester mounted on the front bumper of a four-wheel-drive vehicle.

plant debris. Alternatively, the stalks can be windrowed and dried, and later picked up and threshed, but such a procedure introduces contaminants. As a third alternative, the stalks can be cut and transported to safety for drying and ripening.

Mechanical seed strippers collect seed without cutting the plant, using flails, beaters, reels, or brushes to strip mature seed from the stalks (Larson, 1980). A tractor-drawn stripper has been used successfully to harvest winterfat from a flat, uniform stand (Plummer *et al.,* 1968). The U.S. Forest Service and the Utah Division of Wildlife Resources in Ephraim, Utah, have jointly developed a reel-type harvester mounted on the front bumper of a four-wheel-drive vehicle. Wood or metal paddles or rods knock ripe seed into a bin as the vehicle drives through wild stands (Fig. 1).

IV. Care of Seed after Harvest

To maintain viability, handle seed gently through all phases of collecting, drying, and processing. For best results pick seed when it is dry, carry it in porous containers, and then continue to dry it by spreading it on tarps or screens. The viability of damp seed can drop overnight. Berries will ferment within a few hours and should be cleaned or spread thinly to dry before the rotting fruit overheats the seed. If seed is to be stored until it can be processed, provide good aeration between bags or throughout bins.

Seed that is too moist or too dry can be easily damaged by harvesting or cleaning machinery (Bass *et al.,* 1961). In addition, high moisture content may cause seed to begin germination or may foster the growth of microorganisms or insects that attack seed. Most seed should be promptly dried to 5–14% moisture content, depending on the species, and kept at that level (Harrington, 1973). To dry seed, a moisture gradient must exist from seed to air, since seed moisture content is a function of relative humidity. Air drying is suitable for first-stage drying of freshly harvested seed, but except in deserts with low relative humidities, heated air must be used to continue drying to a safe level. Drying can be hastened by increasing airflow over the seed or by increasing the seed surface exposed to air, as in a tumbler. If the moisture gradient from the seed coat to the air is steeper than from the seed interior to the seed coat, the seed will dry too fast, damaging it by hardening or cracking the seed coat. The safe range of drying temperatures for most seed is 32–43°C (Brandenburg *et al.,* 1961). Air temperatures should start at the lower end of the range and increase to the upper end only as the moisture content of the seed drops below 10%.

Oven drying is a simple method of measuring moisture content: thoroughly dry a weighed amount of seed at 130°C for 1 hr, reweigh, then calculate the percentage moisture lost.

V. Processing

Careful cleaning is vital to storage success and may influence the choice of planting equipment.

A. Fleshy Fruits

Moist, fleshy fruits should be cleaned within a few hours of collecting to avoid damage to the embryo caused by fermenting and subsequent overheating. If prompt cleaning is impossible, spread the fruits thinly to dry in a ventilated area. Since mushy berries are easier to clean than dry ones, presoaking dried berries overnight (no longer) will aid removal of the flesh in a macerator. A popular small macerator is the Dybvig, available from Melvin Dybvig in Milwaukie, Oregon. The standard model is powered by a variable-speed electric motor, but to clean berries during a lengthy field collection, a gas-powered model with a streamwater pump permits field cleaning and reduces the bulk as much as 98%. The Dybvig gently spins fruits in a stream of water, rubbing off soft tissue. The plate is adjusted close enough to keep the seed in the tank as the fleshy debris is washed under the plate. Large seeds such as chokecherry (*Prunus virginiana*) require little further cleaning other than floating off the empty seed; smaller seeds, such as snowberry (*Symphoricarpos* spp.), must be spread to dry with the bits of pulp that did not wash away. Later, the seed and remaining pulp are run through the Dybvig to rub the dry pulp from the seed, which are then separated on a air-screen cleaner. The Dybvig macerator is also useful for detaching tails from small lots of cliffrose (*Cowania mexicana*) and other species when there is not enough mass to operate a debearder.

B. Dry Fruits

Small seed lots of dried fruits can be processed by crushing them in a cloth bag or by rolling them between rubber-covered blocks, followed by screening and winnowing. Appendages such as husks and awns must be rubbed loose before separating seeds in an air-screen cleaner. For seed lots of at least two bushels a debearder is the safest method, though a variable speed hammermill can be used if closely supervised. While a debearder threshes by tumbling the seeds against each other, a hammermill uses moving steel hammers to flail and trim the seed until small enough to fall through the chosen screen.

A useful machine for cleaning wild seed is the two-screen air cleaner. It is smaller than an agricultural cleaner but large enough to handle a few thousand kilograms efficiently. Seed is fed from a bin onto the top screen, which allows seed to drop through the screen, but carries off (scalps) larger trash. The lower screen is smaller than the seed, allowing dust and smaller trash to fall through. Finally, the seed passes through an air column that blows away chaff and empty seed. Other seed cleaners separate seeds from trash on the basis of shape, color, density, surface texture, terminal velocity, electrical conductivity, and resilience (see Brandenburg, 1968, for a list of manufacturers). For descriptions of machines and methods used in cleaning large quantities see Harmond *et al.* (1968).

VI. Storage

Proper storage is important since most species do not produce abundant crops each year. Storage also preserves a valuable accession for repeated tests. Seed longevity is affected primarily by moisture and secondarily by temperature. Harrington (1973) suggests the following rules-of-thumb:

- Every 1% reduction in seed moisture content doubles its life.
- Every 5°C reduction in seed storage temperature doubles its life.

Most insects and fungi found in stored seed cannot reproduce below 8% moisture and below 4°C (Brandenburg *et al.*, 1961; Henderson and Christensen, 1961). Storage fungi weaken or kill the seed embryo or create heat and moisture, which may kill seeds at 38°C in a few hours (Henderson and Christensen, 1961). The best protection against damage from storage fungi is to store seed in dry, cool, and clean containers.

The shelf life of valuable small lots can be extended in cold storage (0–5°C) or in subzero storage. Although seed will not be damaged by freezing temperatures so long as its moisture content is less than 14%, seeds must be sealed in moisture-proof packages or stored in a dehumidified atmosphere (Harrington, 1973). In general, to store seed until the following season, dry the seed to equilibrium with 65% relative humidity; for 2 to 3 years' storage, dry seed to equilibrium with 45% relative humidity. For long-term storage, seed should be dried to equilibrium with 25% relative humidity, or to 5–6% moisture content, then sealed against moisture (Harrington, 1973).

References

Bass, L. N., Ching, T. M., and Winter, F. L. (1961). Packages that protect seeds. *In* "Seeds: The Yearbook of Agriculture." p. 330, U.S. Dep. Agric., Washington, D. C.

Brandenburg, N. R. (1968). Bibliography of harvesting and processing forage-crop seed, 1949–1964. *U.S. Agric. Res. Serv.,* **ARS 42–135.**

Brandenburg, N. R., Simons, J. W., and Smith, L. L. (1961). The processing of seeds. *In* "Seeds: The Yearbook of Agriculture." p. 295, U.S. Dep. Agric., Washington, D. C.

Harmond, J. E., Brandenburg, N. R., and Klein, L. M. (1968). Mechanical seed cleaning and handling. *U.S. Dep. Agric., Agric. Handb.* **354.**

Harrington, J. F. (1972). Seed storage and longevity. *In* "Seed Biology" (T. T. Kozlowski, ed.), Vol. 3, pp. 145–240. Academic Press, New York.

Harrington, J. F. (1973). Problems of seed storage. *In* "Seed Ecology" (W. Heydecker, ed.), pp. 251–263. Pennsylvania State Univ. Press, University Park.

Henderson, L. S., and Christensen, C. M. (1961). Postharvest control of insects and fungi. *In* "Seeds: The Yearbook of Agriculture." p. 348, U.S. Dep. Agric., Washington, D.C.

Larson, J. E. (1980). "Revegetation Equipment Catalogue." U.S. Forest Service, Missoula Equip. Dev. Cent. Publ., Washington, D.C.

Mirov, N. T., and Kraebel, C. J. (1939). "Collecting and Handling Seed of Wild Plants," For. Publ. No. 5. U.S. Dep. Agric., Washington, D.C.

Plummer, A. P., Christensen, D. R., and Monsen, S. B. (1968). Restoring big game range in Utah. *Utah Div. Fish Game Publ.* **68–3,** 141–173.

Schopmeyer, C. S., ed. (1974). Seeds of woody plants in the United States. *U.S., Dep. Agric., Agric. Handb.* **450.**

Young, J. A., Evans, R. A., Kay, B. L., Owen, R. E., and Budy, J. (1981). Collecting, processing and germinating seeds of western wildland plants" ARM-W-3. U.S. Dep. Agric., Washington, D.C.

25

Seed Production from Plantations

Gordon A. Van Epps

I. Introduction

Seed orchards or plantations established for seed production will become inevitable as the demand for viable shrub seed continues to increase. They will become even more necessary as improved variants are obtained through breeding and selections.

Growing shrubs for their seed, at the present time, is very much in the infancy stage. The much needed technology is still relatively undeveloped. Success will be influenced by the use of sound biological information obtained in these early stages by using many of the systematic principles followed in agronomy, horticulture, and forestry.

The justifications for developing seed orchards are to obtain a reliable seed source of desired species. In addition, there is the probability of breeding and selecting clones possessing genetic traits and attributes in growth, habit, palatability adaptation, and chemical characteristics that are not available in wildland plants or not in the quantities needed.

The Biology and Utilization of Shrubs

519

Interest in shrub seed, other than for improvement of wildlife habitat, is a rather recent phenomenon. This has been mainly brought about in the United States by laws requiring that energy-related disturbed areas must be reclaimed using native plants. In other areas of the world, desertification, lack of woody material for fuel growing in close proximity to the users (National Academy of Sciences, 1980), and the need for livestock browse have generated an increased interest in the value of shrubs. Recent studies in the United States are proving the importance of shrubs in a shrub–grass mixture for improving the quantity and quality of forage produced as compared to a monoculture of grass (Rumbaugh *et al.*, 1981; McKell, 1986). Experimental seed orchards of antelope bitterbrush (Giunta *et al.*, 1977) and of fourwing saltbush (Van Epps and Benson, 1979) have been established to evaluate some of the management problems.

The demand for seed to meet future needs is expected to far surpass the present methods of obtaining them from desired species. This is done through hand collecting from various endemic shrub populations. This high-cost method and the unreliability of seed crops from wildland stands must be overcome if shrubs with desirable qualities are to be planted in sufficient quantities for future range improvement.

In forestry, four general types of woody plant stands, natural or planted, are utilized for seed. These are unclassified stands, classified stands, seed production areas, and seed orchards (Rudolf *et al.*, 1974). A similar type of classification may be applied for obtaining shrub seed, though shrub improvement has not presently advanced to this stage. Genetic control of seed quality is increased as progress is made from unclassified populations to seed orchards.

Unclassified populations are those in which no particular selections are made as to desirability of the parent material, but seeds are harvested from them because they may be high seed producers that are easy to harvest. These are wildland collections that may be composed of various seed sources. Classified populations for seed collecting are those that have been selected because of the desirable attributes of their parents, such as plant size, rate of growth, growth habit, etc. The third category, seed production areas, are improved natural populations where further upgrading for improved seed is obtained through removal of less desirable plants of the desired species, along with some cultural practices such as pruning, removal of other species to lessen competition, and in practicing some pest control measures. The area of improvement may also be protected through fencing. These practices should induce heavier seed production and make seed harvesting more convenient. Seed orchards or plantations are artificial plantings made specifically for seed production. These are plantings made by direct seeding, natural seedlings, or clonal propagules obtained from selected superior parents that have the desired qualities and attributes.

Shrub seed plantations may be established for different reasons depending on use. These may be for improving the quantity and quality of browse on rangelands, as fuel for heating or cooking, for improved wildlife habitat, and for watershed improvement and erosion control. Selections might also be made for use in shelter belts, as snow fences, for ornamentals in landscaping, for extraction of chemicals for industrial uses and medicine, or for nitrogen fixation.

Establishing seed orchards is expensive, especially when considering the years of research and development needed in selecting superior stock and the technology necessary for growing them successfully. In addition, the costs of producing the planting stock and plantation maintenance must be paid until a seed crop is produced. This lag time may be two to several years depending on the species. Also important are the future market demands for the commodity being produced.

II. Choice of Planting Stock

Naturally the primary purpose of seed orchards is to produce seed. Within species, great differences in seed-producing ability between individual plants have been observed and it would generally be assumed that these "plus" seed producers may be selected. However, the need and use of the progeny must be kept in mind, which might give seed-producing ability a lower rating in relation to other attributes. The need for disease- or insect-resistant material or large-statured plants within a species may take priority over high seed production.

The amount of genetic selections obtainable in seed orchards is usually greater than that in endemic seed-producing areas. This is dependent on the intensity of the selection, the heritability of those traits on which selections are based, and the number of generations since making the initial selections. Two species with special attributes for industry that are being grown in seed orchards though for different purposes are jojoba (*Simmondsia chinensis*) for the liquid wax in its seed (Hogan, 1979; Fink and Ehrler, 1979) and guayule (*Parthenium argentatum*) for the rubber content in the plant (Weihe and Glymph, 1979). Shrub selections for browse should include such traits as seedling vigor, palatability, leafiness, leaf retention, high protein, plant habit including height, winter hardiness, pest resistance, and possibly wide adaptation. Welch and McArthur (1979) are assessing the feasibility of crossing big sagebrush (*Artemisia*) subspecies to utilize the high protein content found in some plants with the relative high palatability found in others as improved browse for wildlife. Large-statured forms of big sagebrush (*A. tridentata*) and fourwing salt-bush (*Atriplex canescens*) have been found to contain diploid chromosomes rather than the more general tetraploid. This chromosome trait may exist with other large-statured woody shrubs in which selecting for fuel, snow fence, or other purposes is desirable.

III. Types of Planting Material

First-generation seed orchards have been established from direct seeding, from seedlings, and from vegetative propagules of desired species and seed sources and to a limited extent from selected plants. To limit the problems associated with inbreeding and adaptability from initial endemic seed collections two practices are suggested. First, seeds from the plantation should be harvested within a colony or population, from a single plant showing the desired traits and growing at the site where the progeny will be planted, or from a single plant from a similar site having the same climatic and soil conditions. Second, seeds should be collected from other selected single plants that are in other colonies from different provenances or seed sources with similar site characteristics. The greater the number of seed collections from individual plants obtained from various provenances, the greater is the potential gene pool for the progeny.

Seeds from each single plant can be planted in rows for later provenance identification or they may be mixed and planted depending on species and intensity for later selection. The progeny from establishing a seed orchard by direct seeding using this method should be superior to a typical wild seed collection but the desired traits may or may not be expressed. The same is true with planting seedlings grown from the selected seed. If selections are to be obtained from seedlings then it is suggested that the seeds collected from individual plants be kept separate. These should be planted in separate rows or beds for better control of seedling source. Thinning out of plants exhibiting undesirable traits would be a followup practice as the plants reach equilibrium size.

Seed orchards of dioecious species should not be planted by direct seeding or from seedlings because of the number of non-seed-producing staminate plants. Staminate plants should not necessarily exceed the number needed to ensure adequate pollination of the pistillate plants. These may be planted in rows or interspaced depending on species and method of pollination. Some dioecious species exhibit monoecious and sex reversal characteristics. McArthur *et al.* (1978) recommend using only those plants that are constantly pistillate or staminate in fourwing saltbush seed orchards as they are generally superior in seed production. This same reasoning may hold true for other dioecious species.

Establishing seed orchards by direct seeding or through seedlings may be necessary where adequate technology for growing rooted cuttings is not known. A good procedure for rooting stem cuttings of the genera *Chrysothamnus*, as an example, has not been worked out yet. Plantlets from tissue cultures for the species and selections desired are not always available, but could be developed if necessary.

Vegetative propagation from selected clones exhibiting the desired traits is far superior to establishing seed orchards by direct seeding or from seedlings. Several generations of testing may be eliminated when effective genetic selections are made through vegetative propagation. In some, if not most, cases, plants from various species will mature a seed crop 1 to 2 years earlier than from seeds or seedlings.

Three major methods of vegetative propagation are grafting, rooting of stem cuttings, and plantlets from tissue cultures. The method used will depend on the species, availability of plant material, and the expertise of the personnel. Some species that readily root sprout may be propagated by root cuttings. Fourwing saltbush can be propagated by rooting stem cuttings. These propagules have shown remarkable genetic constancy with the mother clone for the various selected traits (McArthur *et al.*, 1978). Wurtele *et al.* (1987) were successful in tissue culture propagation of *gigas* biotypes of *Atriplex canescens*.

Choosing the proper maturation and the time for obtaining cuttings are still unknowns for many shrub species. There is also the problem of selecting plants within a species that exhibit a high capability to root from cuttings along with all the other desired traits.

Alvarez-Cordero and McKell (1979) found that three factors crucial to the successful rooting of stem cuttings from big sagebrush were stimulation of root production with indole-3-butyric acid (IBA) treatments, preferably in the 2.0% range, collecting cuttings in late winter just prior to dormancy break, and plant selection. Cuttings from this species apparently need to be terminal twigs with intact terminal buds. Fourwing saltbush cuttings root best from selected plants that possess the rooting trait when collected in early summer on current season's growth and treated with IBA at 0.3 to 0.8% concentrations (Richardson *et al.*, 1979). Antelope bitterbrush cuttings obtained from ripened hardwood in early spring at time of leaf formation rooted best when treated with IBA at 0.1% (Nord, 1959). Doran (1957) has described methods for rooting cuttings of nearly 500 plant species.

A technique developed in forestry that could be applied to appropriate shrub species in obtaining more juvenile cuttings is called hedging (Libby,

1979). This consists of pruning the crown of the ortet (cutting clone) to varying degrees depending on species so as to increase the number of new sprouts for stem cuttings.

IV. Orchard Location

There are several pertinent factors that should be considered when selecting a site for a seed orchard. These will naturally vary with the species and even ecotypes within species. Of major consideration are soil characteristics and climate.

In general, orchards should be established in the same general soil conditions and climatic characteristics as the parent plants or ortets. They may be planted south and possibly at a lower elevation to improve conditions at harvest time. One example is fourwing saltbush. Studies have shown that northern ecotypes of this widely adapted species can be grown south in a warmer climate but southern ecotypes will experience winterkill (Fig. 1) if moved north, where they are subjected to more severe climatic conditions (Van Epps, 1975). Most known ecotypes of antelope bitterbrush grow on well-drained soils. If bitterbrush orchards are established on

Figure 1.   A young *Atriplex canescens* plant showing basal sprouting following winterkill of top growth, except for a few stems that were partially protected by snow cover.

heavy soils and then irrigated to increase seed production, many of the plants will become chlorotic and die or will not produce seed. Ecotypes of bitterbrush grow well on both acid and basic soils, however, seed from ecotypes growing on granitic and basaltic soils having an acid reaction have grown poorly on basic sedimentary soils (Plummer *et al.*, 1968). Until more is learned of the fertility needs of shrubs, soil should be selected and maintained at an intermediate level.

A climate favorable to plant growth, flowering, and fruiting should be considered. Air drainage to reduce the potential danger of frost damage to the flowers and fruits should be kept in mind. Species in *Purshia* and especially in *Chrysothamnus* should be grown in areas free from wind during that period when the fruit ripens. Late-maturing species such as most of the *Artemisia* and *Atriplex* should be planted in areas with open winters or where relatively free of snow until the fruit has matured and harvesting can be completed.

Orchards should be established in areas that may be protected from wildlife and livestock damage, from contamination due to undesirable pollen, from flooding, and from various human depredations. Other factors to consider are accessibility, proximity to labor, availability of equipment, and a water source if irrigation is needed.

V. Orchard Design

A productive and manageable orchard should consider such factors as plant spacing to meet plant needs and equipment, pollen flow, the position of pistillate and staminate plants if dioecious, the choice of planting stock, the number of seed sources to include, and the desirability of mixed species. Depending on the species grown, seed orchards may last 5 to 30 years or longer, which behooves great care in the design.

Mature plant size and equipment to be used in various cultural practices and possibly mechanized harvesting as it is developed will indicate spacing needs. Often individual plants from species are selected that exhibit the desired traits when at equilibrium with their indigenous environment and subjected to the various stresses that occur at that site. Upon removal from these stresses, ramets or seedlings from these plants may express their growth and biomass quite differently than shown in the field. This occurs often when progeny are planted in a seed orchard and must be considered in the design and spacing. Seedlings from the same source of fourwing saltbush with an average crown diameter of 3.5 m under stress from spacing have more than doubled this size when allowed to grow uninhibited.

Figure 2. An *Atriplex canescens* seed orchard in a 2.5- by 4-m spacing.

A conservative spacing of fourwing saltbush, depending on ecotype and receiving approximately 32 cm of precipitation, may be 3 × 5 m, which is greater than previously suggested by McArthur *et al.* (1978). A plant area of approximately 20 m^2 (4.5 × 4.5 m) is now being considered for antelope bitterbrush as compared to an earlier spacing of 9 m^2 (2.4 × 2.7 m). These spacings with clean cultivation are still under study and should not be considered as final (Fig. 2). Row widths depend on the type of equipment to be used for various cultural practices and especially for pesticide application. Plant spacing is of prime importance when considering method of seed harvest. Row width may generally be closer for hand harvesting, while with machine harvesting rows must be wide enough for equipment manipulation.

The wind and its prevailing direction during the period of pollination will enter into the orchard design for those species using wind as the pollen carrier. The pollinators must be placed so as to obtain optimum benefits from the pollen and wind. The staminate plants with dioecious species should be located so pollen flow is with wind direction and generally toward pistillate plants. The number of rows of pistillate plants between the staminate rows will depend on the distance of adequate pollen flow and row widths. McArthur *et al.* (1978) have proposed an orchard design for fourwing saltbush consisting of four pistillate rows alternating with a single staminate row, though this may change because of results from future studies.

The choice of planting stock such as direct seeding, seedlings, or clonal material will depend on the species being planted and the previous research in plant selections for the species. One to several generations in selections may have been accomplished in previous work prior to setting out a current seed orchard.

The larger the number of seed sources or provenances from which the propagation material is obtained, the greater is the gene pool that will be expressed in the progeny. If limited to only one source, then problems associated with a narrow adaptation range and inbreeding might occur.

Damage from insects may become a primary factor in successful seed production. It is a relatively unknown category with shrubs but progress is being made in insect identification and in determining their life cycles. A practice, though not tested, to lessen the potential disasterous effect from insects on a shrub monoculture seed orchard would be through species diversity in the orchard. This might include rows of forbs, grasses, or other shrub species between the rows intended for seed harvest to act as alternate insect host plants for parasites and predators. If this or a similar action appeared feasible then the design of the orchard would be such that it would complement rather than interfere with the primary objective of seed production.

VI. Cultural Practices

Seed orchards should be planted on agricultural cropland or land that can be cultivated. Level ground is essential for good equipment operation and maintenance. Smoothed ground is especially needed where the seed crop is harvested off the ground, from tarpaulins, or from netting placed around or under the plants. Vacuum-type harvesting equipment may be developed for harvesting seed off the ground. If this becomes feasible, such as for species of *Pushia* or *Cercocarpus,* then it may be desirable to compact the soil or use a soil sealant to prevent lifting the soil crust during the harvesting operation (Fig. 3).

Surface irrigation systems if used should be installed during land preparation and prior to planting the orchard. Drip and sprinkler irrigation systems could be installed later. Cultivation to control weeds or the use of preemergence chemical sprays should be considered in land preparation.

Figure 3. Adverse lifting of soil crust while vacuuming *Purshia tridentata* seed from the soil surface.

Weed control is a continuous problem whether on dry land or in irrigated orchards. Competition must be controlled on arid sites to conserve soil moisture for the benefit of the planted crop. Weeds may not be as serious in areas of higher precipitation but they generally interfere with harvesting and cause additional labor and often contaminate the seed crop. Hand labor is expensive and should be kept to a minimum. The beneficial use of herbicides with shrubs is relatively unknown other than for use around ornamental nurseries. Most available herbicides are marketed to control shrubs. There are a few, however, used in the ornamental industry that are beneficial, but their effect on seed production is not known. The area under the plants should be kept in a clean mulch condition at least for the first few years following initial planting for the benefit of plant establishment.

Maintaining the orchard in a bare condition depends on a number of factors, including shrub species being grown, moisture availability, soil erosion, and rodent control. Cover crops such as a grass or a legume may be beneficial under certain conditions, especially for erosion control, fertility, and insect diversity. They should be low-growing types. A ground-cover may present problems in causing moisture stress and nutrient tie-up and in creating a better habitat for rodents, so should generally be avoided.

Data are not available pertaining to the effect of supplemental water and fertilizers on seed production but in general may encourage vegetative growth at the expense of seeds. These are areas needing additional study for various species. The effect of pruning on seed production is not known. It may be beneficial to do some shaping of plants through pruning for improving seed harvesting. This latter is especially true in jojoba for mechanical harvesting of seed.

Insects and, in some species, disease may create severe problems. Vegetative- and seed-destroying insects that may concentrate in seed-collecting areas and seed orchards require continued monitoring and pest management (Furniss and Krebill, 1972). A prime example of insect damage was the complete destruction of the potential seed crop on antelope bitterbrush by a new invader, the walnut spanworm (Furniss and Van Epps, 1981). Bees or other beneficial insects, on the other hand, may be considered for inclusion in an orchard for pollination, depending on the species, and the possibility for using insect parasites and predators as a control measure.

VII. Seed Harvesting

Two prerequisites of seed harvesting are a knowledge of species maturity for viable seed and that the fruiting bodies actually contain viable seed. Many shrub seeds are harvested too green to ensure good quality. In many instances seeds are not viable because of insect damage and climatic conditions during floral development and fruit formation.

A few shrubs such as winterfat (*Ceratoides lanata*) (J. Fraiser, data on file at the SCS Plant Material Center, Los Lumas, New Mexico) and fourwing saltbush (probably *A. aptera* rather than *A. canescens*) have been combine harvested (Stroh and Thornburg, 1969). A plantation of prostrate summer cypress (*Kochia prostrata*) has also been combined (R. Stevens, data on file at the Great Basin Experimental Area, Ephraim, Utah). Pure stands of black sagebrush (*A. nova*) could possibly be combined because of their inflorescent growth characteristics. Problems with combining have been excessive clogging and equipment breakage.

Various vacuum- or suction-type experimental units have been used on species of *Artemisia, Atriplex, Cercocarpus, Chrysothamnus, Clematis, Cowania, Halimodendron, Lonicera, Purshia,* and *Sarcobatus* with varying degrees of success (R. Stevens, data on file at the Great Basin Experimental Area, Ephraim, Utah; G. A. Van Epps, data on file at the Snow Field Station, Ephraim, Utah). These have included back pack units and prototypes mounted on a wheelbarrow, tractor, trailer, or truck that

Figure 4. Harvesting *Purshia tridentata* seed from a tractor-mounted and -powered experimental vacuum harvester.

Figure 5. Harvesting *Atriplex canescens* seed with a modified vacuum leaf and cut grass collector.

Figure 6. Collecting *Chrysothamnus nauseosus* seed by knocking the fruit into a hopper.

are in various stages of development (Fig. 4). Some units are modifications of machines developed for other purposes, such as for leaf and trash collecting (Fig. 5). Guayule seeds have been collected using a vacuum insect net, which is a backpack unit.

Seed harvesting during the early stages of seed orchard development will continue to be by hand. This may be done by using hoppers (Fig. 6), with the seed being shaken, stripped, or beat from the plant into a hopper or by other means. Seed from some species may be collected by spreading tarpaulins or net under the plant. The growth habits of shrubs along with the various types of fruiting bodies do not readily lend themselves to any one type of harvesting mechanism. Various types of harvesting equipment will need to be developed to meet the seed-collecting problems associated with the numerous shrub species.

Attention following seed harvest must be given to the handling of seed to prevent spoilage, along with adequate cleaning to preserve viable seed and to eliminate various contaminations such as pulp material, other seeds, and various debris. These steps must be followed by proper storage for each species. The latter includes seed moisture, storage humidity, and temperature for extending the duration of good seed viability. Adequate sanitation in the seed-cleaning and storage facilities along with seed treatment are precautionary management procedures for eliminating or controlling insect damage.

References

Alvarez-Cordero, E., and McKell, C. M. (1979). Stem cutting propagation of big sagebrush (*Artemisia tridentata* Nutt). *J. Range Manage.* **32,** 141–143.

Doran, W. L. (1957). Propagation of woody plants by cuttings. *Mass., Agric. Exp. Stn., Bull.* **491.**

Fink, D. H., and Ehrler, W. L. (1979). Rufonn farming for Jojoba. *In* "Arid Land Plant Resources" (J. R. Goodin, and D. K. Northington, eds.), pp. 212–222. Texas Tech Univ. Press, Lubbock.

Furniss, M. M., and Krebill, R. G. (1972). Insects and diseases of shrubs on western big game ranges. In "Wildland Shrubs: Their Biology and Utilization" (C. M. McKell, J. P. Blaisdell, and J. R. Goodin, eds.), USDA For. Serv. Gen. Tech. Rep. INT-1, pp. 218–226. Utah State University, Logan.

Furniss, M. M., and Van Epps, G. A. (1981). Bionomics and control of the walnut spanworm, *Phigalia plumogeraria* (Hulst), on bitterbrush in Utah. *Great Basin Nat.* **41,** 290–297.

Giunta, B. C., Stevens, R., and Jorgensen, K. (1977). An evaluation of selected cultural *30th* practices in an antelope bitterbrush (*Purshia tridentata*) seed orchard. *Abstr. Pap. 30th Annu. Meet. Soc. Range Manage.* pp. 15.

Hogan, L. (1979). Jojoba—A new crop for arid regions. *In* "New Agricultural Crops" (G. A. Ritchie, ed.), AAAS Sel. Symp. No. 38, pp. 177–203. Westview Press, Boulder, Colorado.

Libby, W. J. (1979). Clonal selection of forest trees. *Calif. Agric.* **33,** 8–9.

McArthur, E. D., Plummer, A. P., Van Epps, G. A., Freeman, D. C., and Jorgensen, K. R. (1978). Producing fourwing saltbush seed in seed orchards. *Proc. 1st Int. Rangel. Congr.,* pp. 406–410.

McKell, C. M. (1986). The role of shrubs in diversifying a crested wheatgrass monoculture. *In* "Crested Wheatgrass: Its Values, Problems and Myths" (K. L. Johnson, ed.), pp. 109–115. Utah State University, Logan.

National Academy of Sciences (1980). "Firewood Crops, Shrub and Tree Species for Energy Production," Report of an *Ad hoc* Panel, addressing Committee for Technology Innovation. National Academy Press, Washington, D.C.

Nord, E. C. (1959). Bitterbrush plants can be propagated from stem cuttings. *U.S., For. Serv., Pac. Southwest For. Rang Exp. Stn. Res. Note* **RN-149,** 1–4.

Plummer, A. P., Christensen, D. R., and Monsen, S. B. (1968). Restoring big game range in Utah. *Utah Div. Fish Game Publ.* **68–3.**

Richardson, S. G., Barker, J. R., Crofts, K. A., and Van Epps, G. A. (1979). Factors affecting root of stem cuttings of salt desert shrubs. *J. Range Manage.* **32,** 280–283.

Rudolf, P. O., Dorman, K. W., Hitt, R. G., and Plummer, A. P. (1974). Production of genetically improved seed. *U.S., Dep. Agric. Hand.* **450,** 53–74.

Rumbaugh, M. D., Johnson, D. A., and Van Epps, G. A. (1981). Forage diversity increases yield and quality. *Utah Sci.* **42,** 114–117.

Stroh, J. R., and Thornburg, A. A. (1969). Culture and mechanical seed harvesting of fourwing saltbush grown under irrigation. *J. Range Manage.* **22,** 60–62.

Van Epps, G. A. (1975). Winter injury to fourwing saltbush. *J. Range Manage.* **28,** 157–158.

Van Epps, G. A., and Benson, B. (1979). Establishing a fourwing saltbush (*Atriplex canescens*) seed orchard on cultivated land. *Abstr. Pap. 32nd Annu. Meet. Soc. Range Manage.* p. 16.

Weihe, D. L., and Glymph, E. M. (1979). Guayule as a commercial source of natural rubber. *In* "Arid Land Plant Resources" (J. R. Goodin and D. K. Northington, eds.), pp. 230–243. Texas Tech Univ. Press, Lubbock.

Welch, B. L., and McArthur, E. D. (1979). Feasibility of improving big sagebrush (*Artemisia tridentata*) for use on mule deer winter ranges. *Arid Land Plant Resour.* pp. 451–473.

Wurtele, E. S., Garton, S., Young, D., Balandrin, M., and Mckell, C. M. (1987). Propagation of an elite high biomass-producing genotype of *Atriplex canescens* by axillary enhancement. *Biomass* **12,** 281–291.

26

Native Shrub Propagation and Nursery Stock Production

G. Michael Alder
W. Kent Ostler

I. Introduction

Techniques for producing native shrubs as nursery stock have lagged behind traditional nursery practices until recently. Hence the availability of adequate materials with suitable size and quality has been a major obstacle to the development of native shrubs in the nursery industry.

The first major work on the production and culture of native shrubs from seed came from the Forest Service in 1948 and was updated by Schopmeyer (1974). Ferguson and Monsen (1974) reviewed the basic types of plant containers, growing media, plant density, disease problems, age and size at planting time, acclimatization of seedlings, and survival data after out-planting on 28 native or adapted shrubs in Idaho. Young *et al.* (1978) and Wasser (1982) described basic collecting, processing, and germinating techniques for seed of numerous western natives. McKell *et al.* (1979)

provide an overview of species, methods of propagation, and establishment, including an individual synopsis of 31 desert species appropriate for revegetating disturbed arid lands. Lohmiller and Young (1972) and Vories (1981) focus on methods of propagation and culture of wildland shrubs. Sabo *et al.* (1979) and SEAM (no date) assembled information on seed dormancy, stratification and germination requirements for over 90 shrub species in the western United States. Landis and Simonich (1984) outlined container plant production methods, materials, equipment, and facilities for woody native plants, while Browse (1979) described seedling production of woody species grown in outdoor nursery beds, primarily in Great Britain.

Much of the knowledge for production of shrubs has been adapted from techniques developed and utilized in the forest seedling industry. Duryea and Landis (1984) devote 30 chapters in their handbook on such topics as developing the bareroot seedling nursery, starting seedlings, managing soil and water, cultural guidelines, harvesting, outplanting, and nursery management, much of which is directly applicable to the production of native shrubs. Similar overviews of containerized forest seedling production systems have been provided by Tinus and McDonald (1979). Tinus *et al.* (1974) and Scarratt *et al.* (1982) edited symposia proceedings that focused on forest seedling production but also included papers on native shrub propagation experiments.

Although these publications provide more detail than space allows here, an overview for producing native shrubs from seed and vegetative methods is presented along with necessary components for producing shrubs in different types of nursery facilities. This is designed to give a perspective to the problems and challenges in the production of native shrubs.

II. Native Shrubs Produced from Seed

The most economical way to produce nursery stock is generally from seed. Other methods utilize asexual means to produce plants but require much more labor, time, and equipment. Major advantages of growing nursery stock from seed are:

- Seed preserves the genetic variability of a selection. Hence, some plants will survive in a variety of sites where stresses or disease incidence are high.
- Plants produced from seed cost less, because of the general low cost of seed and the ease of handling seedlings in the nursery.
- Through storage of seed of desired species, a ready supply of plants may

be produced throughout the year and on short notice. This may not be possible using other techniques for producing native shrubs.

Major disadvantages of producing nursery stock from seed are:

- If a high degree of genetic variability exists, the performance of seedlings for certain uses may be limited, for example, in landscaping where uniformity is desired.
- Dormancy factors may complicate production cycles.
- Seed availability of native shrubs is erratic.

Where seeds of forest and agricultural species are usually available commercially and dormancy requirements are well known, seeds of woody natives usually are not available and techniques to enhance germination are obscure or nonexistent. Therefore, certain constraints should be discussed that relate specifically to the production of native shrubs from seed.

Woody natives usually produce smaller quantities of seed with less predictability than perennial and annual herbaceous plants. Seed crops vary from year to year as a result of climatic variation, insect predation, and other environmental stresses (Heit, 1964). Abundant seed (bumper) crops in the western United States occur only about once each decade. A crop size that allows for collection of seed for producing seeedlings and perhaps some surplus storage may not occur every year. If a steady quantity of seedlings is necessary, erratic native seed production may be a limiting factor unless seed collection and storage are carefully planned. Storage of a variety of native seed from season to season can become complex because of loss of viability over time if proper conditions are not provided. However, cool, dry storage away from insect and rodent pests is the minimum necessary to protect valuable hand-collected seed.

Although several attemps to produce native seed in plantations are currently under way, most woody species are hand collected. The seed vendor should be able to supply seed quality and source information at the time of purchase. The knowledgeable buyer should request the following data in addition to locational (ecological) information: germination, purity, or pure live seed (PLS), which equals purity × germination.

Probably the most complex problem associated with propagation of native or adapted species from seed is the varying degree of dormancy exhibited. Both seed coat and embryo dormancy are found, and sometimes they coincide. These factors are most prominent in species found in temperate climates, with tropical and annual plants generally exhibiting little or no seed dormancy.

Overcoming dormancy is crucial to successful germination. Seed coat dormancy may be either physical (a hard seed coat) or chemical (germination inhibitors are present) (Mayer and Poljakoff-Mayber, 1963). Embryo dormancy may be present in some seeds in combination with seed coat dormancy or by itself. Embryo dormancy is a physiological state or condition that keeps the seed from germinating (Hartmann and Kester, 1975). Both types of dormancy may be overcome through natural processes such as freezing and thawing, fire, or diurnal temperature variations of cold and warm. Artificial methods for breaking dormancy require finding the right combination of treatments (see Table I). The benefit of having seed available at any time for greenhouse production may justify the effort necessary to determine appropriate treatments for breaking dormancy.

Although these factors are all important in producing native shrubs from seed, they are of little or no concern to growers of conventional ornamental species because the seed is readily available and there is an abundance of information on how to germinate the seed. Therefore it is important to realize the special constraints facing startup production.

Because problems relating to individual species and specific germination requirements cannot be described here, the reader is referred to the reference section for more details on particular shrubs.

Table I. Methods used for inducing germination in 80 selected species of woody or perennial plants native or adapted to the western United States

Technique	Number of species
Mechanical scarification plus cold-water soak plus long, natural diurnal temperature stratification	1
Hot-water soak only	1
Gibberellic acid plus cold stratification	1
Cold-water soak only	1
Acid scarification plus warm stratification plus cold stratification	1
Warm stratification then critical germination temperature	2
Hydrogen peroxide plus cold stratification	2
Hot-water soak plus cold stratification	2
Gibberellic acid plus hot-water soak	2
Freezing plus cold stratification	2
Warm-water soak plus cold stratification	3
Thiourea treatment plus cold stratification	3
Acid scarification with cold stratification	3
Potassium nitrate plus cold stratification	4
Acid scarification	5
Long, natural diurnal temperature stratification	8
Cold moist stratification only	17
No pregermination treatment required	22

Source: Data from experiments conducted by Stan Akagi, Seed Specialist, NPI, Salt Lake, City, Utah.

III. Native Shrubs Produced Asexually

Vegetative propagation may be used if germ plasm is limited, if methods for growing plants from seeds cannot be conveniently developed, or if a specific genotype or characteristic is desired that would be lost through seed production. Several alternatives for using asexual propagation of shrubs exist, including rooting of cuttings, tissue culture, budding, grafting, and layering. Major advantages that can be gained from asexual reproduction include:

- Plants are genetically uniform for desirable traits.
- Cultural uniformity can be achieved by starting with similar-sized plantlets or cuttings, or by budding or grafting on similar-aged plants.
- Results can be more predictable than with plants whose seed exhibit complex dormancy factors.

Major disadvantages include:

- Cost per plant produced is generally much higher than from seed.
- Facilities for rooting cuttings or for tissue culture may be quite elaborate and are initially capital intensive.
- Routine production of plants from cuttings usually requires space to maintain stock plants (cuttings taken from plants in the wild may vary considerably from season to season or year to year regarding their ability to root).

A. Rooted Cuttings

Rooting of cuttings of woody plants has been and remains the most common method of asexual propagation used (Doran, 1957). Requirements for collecting and rooting a number of native shrubs have been described in detail by Landis and Simonich (1984), McKell *et al.* (1979), and Lohmiller and Young (1972). Yet for most of the native shrubs there are no data available on best methods for asexual propagation. The general principles of rooting cuttings will apply equally as well to natives as to ornamental shrubs.

1. Facilities: Ideal conditions would include a greenhouse equipped with misting capability and bench bottom heat. Outdoor rooting can also be attempted under partial shade and mist if a greenhouse is not available or practical.
2. Stock plants: The condition of stock plants as sources for cuttings is critical to the success of rooting. Cutting material should be free from

diseases, moderately vigorous, and productive (Hartmann and Kester, 1975). Using container-grown greenhouse stock plants as sources for cuttings can increase percentages of rooting (Richardson *et al.,* 1979).

3. Media: Clean, well-drained rooting media such as sharp sand or mixtures of sand, perlite (expanded mineral), pumice, and/or peat moss have proven to be the most acceptable. Cuttings of many species will root in a wide variety of media, however, some species that are difficult to root can be greatly influenced by the rooting medium (Long, 1932).

4. Cutting size, care, and preparation: The type of cutting and size has a tremendous influence on the successful propagation of a species (Hartmann and Kester, 1975). While techniques have been developed for many ornamental shrubs, propagation techniques for native species are mostly unknown. Some important principles are given. Take the cutting at the appropriate time of year. This is generally during the dormant season in late winter or late fall when energy reserves in the stem are high. Cutting stock should be stored in a cool, humid, but not wet environment and should be planted as soon as possible to prevent wilting. The bottom one-half to one-third of the cutting should be cleaned to remove all leaves, trash, or other parts that might promote the growth of fungi during rooting. Reducing the size of the cutting and its effective leaf surface to slow transpiration loss is important. Experimentation to arrive at the right size cutting and time of collection may be the only way to determine efficiencies in rooting many of the native species.

5. Root-promoting substances: Several commercial preparations of talc or liquids for dipping are available with various combinations of root-promoting substances that enhance both the rate and number of roots produced (Pearse, 1984; Thimann and Behnke-Rogers, 1950). Preparations of indolebutyric acid (IBA) and naphthaleneacetic acid (NAA) in various combinations and percentages are the most common compounds used for promoting rooting (Stoutemyer, 1954; Hartmann and Kester, 1975).

6. Environment: Cuttings are generally best rooted under relatively high light intensity and under high humidity or light mist. A bottom heat temperature of 75–80°F has provided good results (Hartmann and Kester, 1975). Some experimentation will be necessary to find the right optima for various native shrubs.

7. Use of chemicals and fertilizers: The rooting process is generally quite sensitive to chemicals or fertilizers. No chemicals other than root promoters should be used unless absolutely required, for example, a fungicide to prevent root rot. A test should always be conduc-

ted prior to broad application. Labels may not describe how to use the chemical on natives but generally should be followed closely as to dilutions and applicator rates.

Rooted cuttings are usually planted in containers either in the greenhouse or in the field. However, rooted cuttings can be produced in outdoor beds for later shipment as bareroot stock. In greenhouse production systems, cuttings are generally transplanted soon after rooting to avoid slowing of growth that would otherwise occur as a result of the rather inert cutting medias that are low in nutrients.

B. Tissue Culture

Tissue culture has been used to rapidly multiply selected clones of native plants. Although this propagation tool is more commonly applied to ornamental species (George and Sherrington, 1984), selections of *Populus, Salix, Atriplex* spp., *Mahonia* spp., *Kalmia,* and *Arctostaphylos* are among those genera presently being propagated by tissue culture in the United States. The cost factors for developing production systems for tissue culture propagation of woody plants are large enough to limit the application of this tool to only those species with the highest demand or those being produced for research purposes. Multiplication rates far exceed those of conventional asexual propagation methods (Table II). Given the rate of multiplication for *Populus* sp. (3.0) and the time period for that multiplication (3–4 weeks), from 1.6 to 129 million plants can be produced from just one bud in the course of one year. Because of the advantage of being able to produce cloned plants quickly and in large volumes, the future use of tissue culture for propagating native woody plants will become more widespread with increased demand for selected high-value clones.

Table II. Multiplication rates of some shrubs and trees placed in tissue culture on multiplication media

Species	Multiplication time (Weeks)	Average rate of multiplication
Salix sp.	3–4	3.0–4.0
Populus sp.	3–4	3.0
Rosa sp.	3–4	2.5
Vitis sp.	3–4	3.0
Alnus sp.	3–4	3.0–4.0
Mahonia sp.	4–5	1.8

Source: Data courtesy of NPI Tissue Culture Production Laboratory.

C. Budding, Grafting, and Layering

Budding, grafting, and layering have seldom been employed with natives unless for unique uses. An example of budding being used currently to increase a western U.S. native tree is *Acer grandidentatum*. The slow development of an adequate root system on most seedlings of this tree stimulated experiments to bud it onto other maple rootstocks. Compatibility has not been fully tested but increased growth rates that would make the tree a better commercial variety are encouraging. Grafting and layering are seldom used because of the time and labor required for these methods to produce propagules. However, if only one plant of a selection exists, these techniques may be suitable.

IV. Production of Native Shrubs in a Nursery

After a system for producing propagules is developed, that is, by seed or cuttings, etc., options for producing finished planting stock should be chosen. Commonly used nursery production systems with their respective advantages and disadvantages are described below.

A. Bareroot Nursery Production

This type of nursery operation generally consists of preparing, sowing, and mulching outdoor production beds. After seed germination, suitable practices for thinning, irrigation, weeding, and insect and disease control are required to maintain the production system. The final sequence of tasks includes lifting (digging procedures), grading (sorting as to age and size), cold storage, and shipping.

Major advantages of outdoor nurseries include:

- Production follows the natural sequence of the local climate.
- Capital requirements are low except for land and some equipment and ancillary buildings. Hence, large volumes of seedlings can be produced for low cost per plant.
- Production capability is relatively easy to expand.
- Cold storage of lifted seedlings allows for volume production and scheduled handling and shipping.

Major disadvantages of outdoor nurseries include:

- Plants are subject to extreme climatic fluctuations.
- Seedlings must be lifted bareroot, hence loss of root hairs often influences outplanting success.

- Planting of bareroot stock must generally be done in a very short time period at the beginning of the growing season.
- Weeds, diseases, and insects are often more difficult to control than in greenhouses.

The major factors for production in outdoor nursery operations include seedbed characteristics and preparation, sowing, irrigation, weed control, lifting, grading, cold storage, and shipping. Cultural practices for the bareroot nursery are covered in depth by Duryea and Landis (1984).

1. Nursery Siting and Seedbed Production Practices

The seedbed should be located in an area with the longest possible growing season that is compatible with the requirement of the species to be grown. Important characteristics of a site include temperature, frost incidence, light, shelter, water availability, water quality, and drainage. Ideally a light sandy loam is the most suitable soil type for an outdoor nursery bed. Although any seedbed can be improved through the addition of organic matter and other amendments, this may be costly if soils are heavy textured. Another important aspect of the seedbed is soil pH, which can have a significant effect on the production of seedlings. Most shrub species perform best under a near neutral soil pH, even though the ecological conditions of the natural habitat may be on the acid or basic side. Failure to determine optimum soil conditions may result in lost production.

Bed size is usually determined by equipment available and ease of access to thin and weed. Most beds in nurseries in the United States are approximately 4 feet wide and any convenient length.

Because of the critical requirement to control weeds, insects, and diseases, fumigation is often used prior to planting. Residuals from chemicals can have severe effects on new seedlings if proper procedures are not followed.

Seedbed fertility is a very important aspect of plant performance. Although the nutritional needs of native shrubs are a relatively unresearched area, there is valuable information that can be extracted from the forest tree nurseries. A fertile, level, well-worked surface is necessary for seeding to proceed properly.

2. Sowing

The season of sowing or planting will depend on the species being grown. Factors such as seed viability, seed dormancy, precipitation patterns, type of transplant, bareroot or containerized, and availability of irrigation water will influence the best time for planting and sowing.

Precision seeding equipment makes drill seeding of valuable seed the standard method for most bareroot nurseries in the United States. However, broadcast sowing is still a necessary skill if a wide variety of native or adapted species are to be produced. Some very fine seeded plants cannot be drill seeded because they do not have the capability of germinating through a soil cover. Broadcast seeding methods require careful calibration of equipment to avoid over- or underseeding. Density trials should be undertaken at early stages of production to determine optimum spacing between plants of different species.

Various seed coverings have been used. However, to standardize performance, soil and washed sand are the most commonly used. Sanding machines have been successfully developed that will lay a thin covering of sand over small-seeded species. Organic mulches are subsequently used during fallow periods to improve soil tilth.

Because seed is sown in a natural sequence with the local climate, the bareroot nursery does not normally need to develop the expanded methods to treat seed described earlier. However, if off-season planting is desirable, methods for artificially breaking dormancy may be required.

3. Water Quality and Irrigation

Any outdoor facility for the production of nursery stock should provide supplemental irrigation for germinating seeds and optimizing growth. Water quality is an important aspect of the irrigation plan. If water quality is questionable, particularly salinity (Landis, 1982), samples should be analyzed. Methods of water application vary tremendously, but a good design should include equipment that can deliver sufficient water to cover the seedbeds with a gentle undisturbing spray and yet not enough that the percolation rate of the soil is exceeded during irrigation.

4. Weeding and Weed Prevention

Where the outdoor nursery is exposed to the environment, weed seeds continually blow in from adjacent areas (Neill, 1984). Preemergent, postemergent, and contact herbicides may be effective on a broad range of weed seeds, yet they must be used only for those shrub species covered by their registration. Hand weeding may be the only alternative for controlling some weed species, however, this is much more costly than chemical control.

5. Lifting

Although hand methods of digging are traditional, mechanized procedures for mass harvesting of seedlings contribute significantly to efficient, volume operations. Tractor-drawn implements known as lifters are available in several different designs. This task is usually undertaken during the dormant season, as early as possible. It is extremely important that the seedlings be properly hardened prior to lifting.

6. Grading

Size and quality standards have been adopted by nursery stock producers in the forestry industry. These standards have not been universally applied or adapted to all species and their usefulness for shrub species has not been fully documented. Over- or undersized plants often have lower survival rates but the ideal transplant size will vary by species and can only be determined experimentally for each species.

7. Cold Storage

After lifting and grading, bareroot seedlings must be protected from desiccation. Therefore, cold storage facilities with humidification are essential unless quantities of seedlings produced are small enough to be transplanted as they are lifted. Cold storage temperatures and humidities may vary depending on climate, however, a 34°F temperature at 90% humidity is a guideline to be followed in temperate regions.

8. Shipping

Guidelines for shipping bareroot seedlings include careful packing with moist fibrous material (e.g., peat moss, sphagnum moss, wood shavings). Root systems and shoots must be protected from drying and temperature extremes. Shipping should be done early enough to take advantage of seedling dormancy and low stress conditions in the transplant environment.

B. Greenhouse/Shadehouse Production

Production of container-grown plants in the greenhouse or shadehouse includes many of the same functions that are required for producing bareroot plants with some major additions. Because the greenhouse allows for a controlled growing environment, plants produced from a variety of propagation methods and with varied environmental requirements can be grown rapidly with good vigor and survival.

The functions necessary for growing shrubs in containers include scheduling crops, choosing containers, growing media, and planting or sowing (from seed, cuttings, tissue culture, bareroot, or collected wildings). It is also important to maintain control of temperatures, humidity, light, nutrients, irrigation, and pests in the greenhouse, and to condition plants in a shadehouse prior to shipping or outplanting.

Major advantages of greenhouse-grown containerized plants include:

- Year-round production is often possible.
- Control of the plant's environment is possible through the most vulnerable stages of growth and development.

- Container-grown plants allow a wide time period for outplanting (virtually year-round on irrigated projects).
- Survival of containerized plants is usually better than bareroot because of the low shock experienced at transplant.

Major disadvantages of greenhouse-grown containerized plants include:

- Capital cost to initially set up facilities is high.
- Unit costs of production are high.
- Bulk and weight of containerized plants are usually higher than bareroot.

Major considerations for producing containerized native plants in greenhouses are discussed below.

1. Greenhouses/Shadehouses

Reviews of greenhouse design and construction for growing containerized plants have been done by Newland (1974), Ekblad (1973), and Tinus and McDonald (1979). The type and design of the structure will depend on the site where the plants will be grown and the kind of plants being grown. Potential snow weight, peak wind pressures and steadiness, ambient temperatures, and cropping schedules are examples of factors that need to be considered in choosing structures and coverings. Also important is the placement of structures to avoid shading problems or wind stress. Interior design should include consideration of efficient use of space, bench placement, convenient aisles, and adequate headroom.

2. Containers and Growing Media

Numerous types of containers are available from manufacturers and each has advantages for the particular species being grown and the size of the final product. Containers above the half-gallon size are fairly standard. However, there are numerous types and manufacturers of containers for plants that will be used for outplanting, such as in large-scale forestry or reclamation projects. Although containers may vary, some important design components should be considered (Spencer, 1974; Allison, 1974; Van Eerden, 1982). These include:

- Container volume should be sufficient to permit seedlings to be grown to a size and quality desired.
- Containers should protect the stock and root systems in the nursery.
- Roots spiraling within the container should be discouraged.
- Root systems should remain intact and undisturbed when removed from the container or they should not be impeded by the container if it is not removed at planting.

- Container should allow for air pruning of bottom roots to promote secondary root development.
- Bench density should be maximized and flexible so spacing can occur as plants become larger and need more room.
- Root development should be easily inspected.
- A high root/shoot ratio should be encouraged.
- Price should be kept low.

An example of a container that satisfies the above criteria is shown in Fig. 1.

The medium that is used in a container operation can have a tremendous impact on plant growth (Phipps, 1974). Soil-less media are becoming more common in the industry with peat–vermiculite mixtures predominating. The main advantages of a soil-less medium include pest reduction, since much of the material is sterile, the medium is sufficiently porous to permit aeration and rapid root development, shipping costs are low because the medium is lightweight, and it has improved waterholding capacity. Some components of the soil-less mixes may hinder growth of some species, for example, peat moss will tend to reduce soil pH or bark may tie up considerable amounts of nitrogen. Soil-less media also do not have the buffering capacity of most soil media and thus may require careful monitoring and early correction of problems or growth may be reduced. Greenhouse benches may not accommodate all types of containers or trays that hold containers. Planning for materials handling even for small-production operations can avoid later problems and waste.

Figure 1. A Tubepak container system developed at NPI showing some important characteristics of a good container, including vertical corrugations to prevent root spiraling, air pruning of tap roots, and an easy method of inspecting root systems and extraction of the seedlings for planting.

3. Sowing and Planting

Several methods of sowing and planting are successfully used in producing container-grown natives. Only high-quality seed should be used in a nursery operation because it is costly to carry blank containers through the growing cycle in the nursery or to thin excess seedlings from containers. One method to avoid this is to sow presprouted seed. Generally seed with viability less than 50% should not be direct sown into containers (Tinus and McDonald, 1979). The seed or stock plant sources should be identified so that plants produced can be chosen for their suitability to the area where they will be planted. Failure of plantings due to incompatability of the species to a particular environment is not uncommon. Direct-sown, nondormant, or treated seed is usually covered with medium-coarse sand to a depth equal to the diameter of the seed being sown. Presprouted seed that has been sprouted in stratification is also hand sown and sanded. Tissue culture plantlets, plants from seedflats, rooted cuttings, bareroot plants, and wildings may be individually transplanted using adequate care to protect roots from excessive mechanical damage or drying (Landis and Simonich, 1984).

4. Cultural Practices and Production Schedules

Each shrub species has its own requirements for optimum growth in the greenhouse. If a number of species are to be produced together, scheduling for optimal growth may be very difficult. However, individual treatments for species may be possible, and requirements can be studied and more fully met. The two most important controllable factors in the greenhouse are temperature and humidity. However, optimum values for native shrubs are mostly unknown. Recommendations for several native trees are given by Tinus and McDonald (1979). Watering and fertilizing are also important factors in nursery stock production. While watering and fertilizer regimes differ with the type of plant being produced, nutrient levels are generally kept high with application of water-soluble fertilizers in each irrigation except for periodic leaching with clear water. Injection of nutrients into the irrigation water gives the best control of nutrition and is a flexible technique if a change is needed. Since optimal nutrient levels are unknown for most native shrubs, plants should be continually monitored to detect visual dificiency symptoms. Insects, diseases, and weeds should be kept in control with careful monitoring and application of pesticides.

Because many plants are photoperiod sensitive, night-lighting to extend day length may be required for year-round production operations. For most species, full response can be obtained with 400 lux (Arnott, 1979). Light for dormancy control can be on as little as 3% of the time provided no dark period is longer than 30 minutes (Cathay and Campbell, 1977).

Various formats are available to develop a production schedule for a given species. It is important that the production schedule provide the grower with a plan of events that is to occur while the species is in the nursery. Some important features in any schedule should include:

- The complete schedule of the species from seed to maturity including dates that the species is in the greenhouse and lengths of each segment in the growing process.
- Monitoring the condition of the species at critical times during the growing phase, target height, caliper, and other growth measures.
- Location of the species in the greenhouse and space required for each phase of production.
- The environmental controls, that is, temperature, humidity, light, fertilizer, watering, etc., should be designated for optimizing each stage of growth for a species. These should be based on the best available information on the species and should be refined and upgraded as the grower becomes more aware of the species requirements under nursery conditions.

5. Acclimatization

After plants have been judged to be of adequate size, conditioning to outdoor conditions needs to be undertaken. Generally a shadehouse covered with shadescreen or wood lathe can be used to reduce the amount of direct sunlight while exposing plants to other outdoor conditions. Cuticles on leaves and bark on stems thicken as plants begin to function in a more normal growing environment. Also, changing the fertilization rate to decrease nitrogen and increase phosphorus and potassium can encourage hardening (Tinus and McDonald, 1979). The time necessary to accomplish adequate acclimatization varies by species. However, 4 to 8 weeks is a good range for planning purposes.

6. Shipping

A variety of shipping systems have been developed to accomodate various types of container-grown plants. The alternatives include (a) extracting plants from containers and packaging to avoid desiccation, (b) shipping containers and plants in boxes to the field (containers may be disposable or returned for reuse), and (c) shipping plants in greenhouse growing trays.

V. Contract Production of Nursery Stock

Small numbers of nursery stock may well be obtained by contracting with existing nurseries to produce materials from seed or cuttings. Standard horticultural practices should produce good results. Nurseries have trouble with native shrubs when they cannot obtain seed or cutting material, when appropriate cultural practices are not known, or when problems occur in marketing the final product. The alternative of contract production should be considered where the need for plants is erratic or where volumes do not justify initial capital requirements for setting up a nursery.

Private nurseries are accustomed to bidding and competitive pricing, especially for smaller quantities. A lower price per plant may actually be achieved by purchasing plants on a bid basis and employing the plant producer as a consultant rather than by trying to grow plants as an extra project or internal program cost.

VI. Overview

In the past, wildland or native shrub production has been limited and the necessary technology was not developed. As described in the current literature, appropriate methods combined with better equipment and facilities now provide the ability to produce quality nursery-grown native shrubs in a more standardized way.

References

Allison, C. J., Jr. (1974). Design considerations for the RL single cell system. *In* "Proceedings of the North American Containerized Forest Tree Seedling Symposium" (R. W. Tinus, W. I. Stein, and W. E. Balmer, eds.), Great Plains Agri. Counc. Publ.No. 68, pp. 233–236. U.S. Govt. Printing Office, Washington, D. C.

Arnott, J. T. (1979). Effect of light intensity during extended photoperiod or growth of amabilis fir, mountain hemlock, and Engelmann spruce seedlings. *Can. J. For. Res.* **9**(1); 82–89.

Browse, P. D. A. M. (1979). "Hardy Woody Plants from Seed." Grower Books, London.

Cathay, H. M., and Campbell, L. E. (1977). Light frequency and color aid plant growth regulation. *Am. Nurseryman* **153**(19), 16.

Doran, W. L. (1957). Propagation of woody plants by cuttings. *Mass., Agric. Exp. St., Bull.* **491**.

Duryea, M. L., and Landis, T. D. (1984). "Forest Nursery Manual: Production of Bareroot Seedlings." Martinus Nijhoff/Dr. W. Junk Publ., The Hague.

Ekblad, R. B. (1973). "Greenhouses: A Survey of Design and Equipment," pp. 255–259. Proj. Rec. ED and T 2340, USDA For. Serv., Missoula Equip. Dev. Cent., Missoula, Montana.

Ferguson, R. B., and Monsen, S. B. (1974). Research with containerized shrubs and forbs in southern Idaho. *In* "Proceedings of the North American Containerized Forest Tree Seedling Symposium" (R. W. Tinus, W. I. Stein, and W. E. Balmer, eds.), Great Plains Agri. Coun. Publ. No. 68. pp. 349–358. U.S. Govt. Printing Office, Washington, D.C.

George, E. F., and Sherrington, P. D. (1984). "Plant Propagation by Tissue Culture." Exegenetics Ltd., Eversley Basingstoke, Herts, England.

Hartmann, H. D., and Kester, D. E. (1975). "Plant Propagation Principles and Practices," 3rd ed. Prentice-Hall, Englewood Cliffs, New Jersey.

Heit, C. E. (1964). The importance of quality, germinative characteristics and source for successful seed propagation and plant production. *Proc. Int. Plant Propag. Soc.* **14**, 74–85.

Landis, T. D. (1982). Irrigation water quality in free nurseries in the inland West. *In* Proc. 1981 Intermountain Nurserymen's Assoc. Meeting, Aug. 11–13. Can. Dept. Environ. Info. Rept. **NDR-X 241**, pp. 60–67. Edmonton, Alberta, Canada.

Landis, T. D., and Simonich, E. J. (1984). Producing native plants as container seedlings. *In* "The Challenge of Producing Native Plants for the Intermountain Area," Gen. Tech. Rep. INT-168, p 16–25. USDA For. Serv., Ogden, Utah.

Lohmiller, R. G., and Young, W. C. (1972). Propagation of shrubs in the nursery. *In* "Wildland Shrubs: Their Biology and Utilization" (C. M. McKell, J. P. Blaisdell, and J. R. Goodin, eds.), USDA For. Serv. Gen. Tech. Rep. INT-1. Utah State University, Logan.

Long, J. C. (1932). The influence of rooting media on the character of the roots produced by cuttings. *Proc. Am. Soc. Hortic Sci.* **29**, 352–355.

McKell, C. M., Van Epps, G. A., Richardson, S. G., Barker, J. R., Call, C., Alvarez, E., and Crofts, K. A. (1979). Selection, propagation and field establishment of native plant species on disturbed arid lands. *Bull. — Utah, Agric. Exp. St.* **500.**

Mayer, A. M., and Poljakoff-Mayber, A. (1963). "The Germination of Seeds." Macmillan, New York.

Neill, G. B., ed. (1984). "Weed Control in Tree Nurseries," Proc. Workshop; July 17–18, 1984. Agriculture Canada, Prairie Farm Rehabilitation Administration, Indian Head, Saskatchewan, Canada.

Newland, L. C. (1974). Greenhouse design: The choice of components. *In* "Proceedings of the North American Containerized Forest Tree Seedling Symposium" (R. W. Tinus, W. I. Stein, and W. E. Balmer, eds.), Great Plains Agric. Council Publ. No. 68, pp. 255–259. U.S. Govt. Printing Office, Washington D.C.

Pearse, H. L. (1948). Growth substances and their practical importance in horticulture. *Common. Bur. Hortic Plant Crops. (G. B.) Tech. Commun.* **20.**

Phipps, H. M. (1974). Growing media affect size of container-grown red pine. *U. S., For. Serv. Res. Note NC* **NC-165.**

Richardson, S. G., Barker, J. R., Crofts, K. A. and Van Epps, G. A. (1979). Factors affecting rooting of stem cuttings of salt desert shrubs. *J. Range Manage.* **32**(4); 280–283.

Sabo, D. G., Johnson, G. V., Martin W. C., and Aldon, E. F. (1979). Germination requirements of 19 species of arid land plants. *U.S. Rocky Mt. For. Range Exp. Stn., For. Serv. Res. Pap. RM* **RM-210.**

Scarratt, J. B., Glerum, C., and Plexman, C. A. (1982). "Proceedings Canadian Containerized Tree Seedling Symposium." Sept. 14–16, 1981. COJFRC Symp. Proc. D-P-10. Sault Ste. Marie, Ontario, Canada.

SEAM (no date). "Native Shrub Production Project, Coeur D'Alene Nursery." USDA, For. Serv., Inter. For. Range Exp. Stn., Ogden, Utah.

Schopmeyer, C. S., tech. coord. (1974). "Seed of Woody Plants in the United States," Agric. Hand. No. 450. USDA, Washington, D.C.

Spencer, H. A. (1974). To "engineer" the container. *In* "Proceedings of the North American Containerized Forest Tree Seedling Symposium" (R. W. Tinus, W. I. Stein, and W. E. Balmer, eds.), Great Plains Agric. Counc. Publ. No. 68, pp. 229–232. U.S. Govt. Printing Office, Washington, D.C.

Stoutemyer, V. T. (1954). Encouragement of roots by plant regulators. In "Plant Regulators in Agriculture" (H. B. Tukey, ed.). Wiley, New York.

Thimann, K. V., and Behnke-Rogers, J. (1950). "The Use of Auxins in the Rooting of Woody Cuttings." Harvard Forest, M. M. Cabot Foundation, Petersham, Massachusetts.

Tinus, R. W., and McDonald, S. E. (1979). How to grow tree seedlings in containers in greenhouses. USDA For. Gen. Tech. Rep. **RM-6.**

Tinus, R. W., Stein, W. I., and Balmer, W. E. (1974). "Proceedings of the North American Containerized Forest Tree Seedling Symposium." Great Plains Agric. Counc. Publ. No. 68. U.S. Govt. Printing Office, Washington, D.C.

Van Eerden, V. (1982). The fundamentals of container seedling production. In "Proceedings of the Canadian Containerized Tree Symposium" (J. B. Scarratt, C. Glerum, and C. A. Plexman, ed.), pp. 83–90. Dep. Environ., Can. For. Serv., Great Lake For. Res. Cent., Sault Ste. Marie, Ontario.

Vories, K. C. (1981). "Growing Colorado Plants from Seed: A State of the Art," Vol. 1, For. Serv. Gen. Tech. Rep. INT-103. USDA, Washington D. C.

Wasser, C. H. (1982). Ecology and culture of selected species useful in revegetating disturbed lands in the west. U.S., Fish Wildl. Serv., Off. Biol. Serv. [Tech. Rep.] FWSS/OBS **FWS/OBS-82/56.**

Young, J. A., Evans, R. A., Kay, B. L., Owen, R. E., and Jurak, F. L. (1978). "Collecting, Processing and Germinating Seeds of Western Wildland Plants," ARM-W-3. USDA Sci. Educ. Admin., Agric. Rev. Man., Berkeley, California.

27

Forage Shrub Production on Salt-Affected Soils

C. V. Malcolm

I. Introduction

Some salt-tolerant shurbs are capable of growing under very saline conditions. For example, *Atriplex canescens* and *A. cuneata* have their growth reduced to half by 2400 and 3000 mS/m EC_e, respectively (Richardson and McKell, 1980). The prospects of utilizing the superior salt tolerance of certain forage shrubs to give production from saline soils and for which engineering reclamation measures are inappropriate are examined in this chapter.

Under natural conditions salt-affected soils support salt-tolerant shrub vegetation. Large areas of halophytic vegetation are reported to occur in Algeria, Tunisia, Libya, and Egypt (Novikoff, 1957; Le Houérou, 1980), North America (Branson *et al.*, 1967; Ungar, 1972), Australia (Jones, 1966a), and Siberia (Kurkin, 1967). Other areas occur in India (Rolla and Kanodia, 1962), Afghanistan (Pelt *et al.*, 1968), and Saudi Arabia (Zahran,

1982). In addition to naturally salt-affected land, about 53 million ha of the world's irrigated land are also salt-affected (Mudie, 1974). This includes about 30 million ha in Iraq (Boumans et al., 1963), 6 million ha in India (Kanwar, 1969), 5.5 million ha in Pakistan (Schroo, 1967), and lesser amounts in numerous other countries. In addition, substantial areas of land have become salt-affected because of induced hydrological changes. Prime examples are in Texas (Carter and Wiegand, 1965), Western Australia (Henschke, 1980), and North Dakota (Benz et al., 1976). Use of salt-affected soils for unrestricted grazing, subsistence cropping, or intensive fuel gathering results in degradation of the vegetative cover, which may take decades to reverse and may never return to its original condition.

The salt-affected sites available for forage shrub production include degraded natural halophyte areas, salted wastelands associated with irrigation projects, and areas of secondary salinity caused by the hydrological effects of land use changes.

Efforts have been made to return salt-tolerant forage plants to denuded rangelands for many years, especially in the United States and eastern Australia. Extension of the work to salt-affected soils in irrigated and nonirrigated farming areas has been limited.

Various authors have considered using halophytes to produce food (Somers, 1979) and other products (Singh, 1970; Mudie, 1974). Many other benefits are also claimed from growing salt-tolerant plants on salt-affected sites, including reduced soil erosion (Jones, 1966a), pollution control (Hill and Nolhard, 1973), coastal sand stabilization (Le Roux, 1974), improved wildlife habitat (Plummer et al., 1968), vegetation of mine dumps (McKell, 1978), and improved aesthetics.

Revegetating saline areas may reduce salt flow into streams and water storages (Skogerhoe and Walker, 1973), catch snow, give shelter for stock (Shamsoutdinov, 1966), and increase the ecological diversity of otherwise barren areas. Finally, forage shrubs may be grown and used without the substantial energy inputs increasingly demanded by modern agricultural systems.

II. Salt-Tolerant Forage Shrub Resources

The most salt- and waterlogging-tolerant group of forage shrubs are the samphires (or glassworts), which include such genera as *Salicornia, Arthrocnemum, Halocnemum, Halosarcia,* and *Allenrolfea.* They occur on the fringes of saline lakes and marshes, where they may be subject to extremely high salinity levels and to inundation. The flesh of these leafless plants is succulent and extremely salty, but provided good-quality water is available they are eaten to varying degrees by camels, sheep, and goats when other feed is scarce.

The saltbushes, which include such genera as *Atriplex, Chenopodium, Rhagodia,* and *Halimione,* occur on less waterlogged sites than the samphires but are capable of growing on highly saline soils. Many of the woody perennial *Atriplex* spp. possess C_4 metabolism. The saltbushes vary in palatability, but most of them are eaten by grazing animals when feed is scarce and several species are readily grazed. The saltbushes possess characteristically gray leaves due to the development of salt bladders on the leaf surface. Their physiology and ecology have been studied in considerable detail (Osmond *et al.,* 1980).

A third important but not so easily characterized group includes genera such as *Salsola, Kochia, Maireana, Sarcobatus, Suaeda,* and *Enchylaena.* The members of this group develop succulent leaves, in contrast to the succulent stems of the samphires, and in many cases have fruits adapted for wind dispersal. Some members of this group are excellent forage shrubs but others are not readily eaten by animals and contain high oxalate levels.

III. Selecting Forage Shrubs for Salt-Affected Soils

Halophytes under natural conditions are zoned according to the salinity and hydrology of the site. On areas that are intermittently flooded the development of vegetative cover may be cyclical. Relief is important in determining the distribution of salt and water and thereby the zonation of the vegetation in areas with shallow groundwater (Pelt *et al.,* 1968; Ungar, 1972). Relief is also important in influencing the runoff and infiltration of rainfall and the survival of shrubs in dry areas (Jones, 1969). There is a divergence of opinion concerning the importance of salt type in determining plant adaptation to salt-affected sites (Strogonov, 1964; Ungar, 1970). pH was not found to be important in North American inland salt marshes (Ungar, 1972), but the extremes of alkalinity in the Indian subcontinent and acidity on some mine dumps (Hill, 1977) may be important, especially in influencing the solubility of toxic ions.

Salt accumulation in soil depends on the depth to groundwater and the seasonal balance between rainfall and evaporation. Under low rainfall conditions no deep percolation occurs and salts accumulate in the root zone. If groundwater is present, the severity of salting is greater the closer the groundwater is to the surface.

Accumulation of salt at the surface from the saline groundwater is influenced by management, soil, and climatic factors reviewed elsewhere (Malcolm, 1980).

Table I. Salinity levels in soil from beneath halophytic vegetation and other salt-affected sites

Location	Site or species	Depth (cm)	Salinity	Reference
New South Wales	Unponded scalds	0–5	1.0% TDS[a]	Jones (1967a)
	Ponded scalds	0–5	0.25% TDS	Jones (1967a)
Iraq	Salt-affected land in irrigation areas	0–100	1600 mS/m[b]	Boumans et al. (1963)
South Dakota	Salicornia sp.	0–10	4.8% TDS	Ungar (1970)
	Puccinellia sp.	0–10	1.2–4.1% TDS	Ungar (1970)
Southeast Utah	Atriplex corrugata	0–40 approx.	540 to 5140 mS/m	West and Ibrahim (1968)
Western Australia	18 test sites	0–90	1100–4530 mS/m (means)	C. V. Malcolm (unpublished data)
New South Wales	Atriplex spp. and Maireana georgei	0–30	0.40% Cl[−c]	Gates and Muirhead (1967)
		30–60	0.61% Cl[−]	
		60–90	0.39% Cl[−]	
Texas	Lower Rio Grande Valley	0–7.5	1800–11,000 mS/m	Carter and Wiegand (1965)
India	Salt-affected soils	—	830–12,400 mS/m	Kanwar (1969)

[a] Percentage total dissolved solids by conductivity of 1:5 suspension.
[b] Electrical conductivity of saturation extract.
[c] Percentage chloride on dry weight basis by titration of 1:5 suspension.

The climate in areas with salinity problems is in many cases arid to semiarid, for example, Uzbekistan has 108–334 mm annual average rainfall (Shamsutdinov and Korsun, 1968), New South Wales has 350–425 mm (Beadle, 1948), Utah and Nevada have 75–250 mm (Bleak *et al.*, 1965), and Western Australia has down to 300 mm (Malcolm, 1980). Plants must therefore cope with water stress due to both salinity and aridity.

Salinity levels in soils are extremely variable in both time and space (Carter and Wiegand, 1965; Malcolm, 1980) and different methods have been used to express soil salinity. A few selected data in Table I show that the range of conditions encountered by halophytes in their natural environment compares with the salinity of some salt-affected areas.

Selection and use of wildland shrubs has been described as a virgin field, with tremendous variation available for study. It is also a field in which substantial efforts may be made for extremely limited returns. In a 25-year program of selecting plants for the salt desert ranges in the United States, one or two of over 200 species were successful (Plummer, 1966).

In Western Australia a collection of over 900 seed samples of forage plants of reputed salt tolerance has been accumulated (Malcolm *et al.*, 1984). The material has been subjected to a series of testing phases by planting established plants into representative salt-affected sites. In the initial testing a small range of criteria were used to assess adaptation at two salt-affected sites. Criteria included survival, flowering, seed production, and general vigor. Species showing some promise were then planted at 14 regional test sites, where data were obtained on the soil conditions, plant growth, and reproduction. Finally, additional ecotypes were obtained for the most promising species and these were planted in ecotype comparison trials at several sites (see Fig. 1).

The most important aspects of an adequate selection program are:

• A collection of seed samples representing all likely useful plants.
• Test sites that truly represent the problem areas.
• Adequate facilities and methods for test work.
• Meaningful selection criteria.

Forage shrubs have been found in some cases to be closely adapted to particular sites (Plummer *et al.*, 1968; Jefferies *et al.*, 1981), although reciprocal planting between four salt marsh vegetation zones was successful (Stalter and Batson, 1969). Williams (1960) suggested that climax species should be sought but in many cases soil erosion or hydrological changes have altered site conditions to such a degree that climax species are not fully adapted and do not persist (Quinones *et al.*, 1980; Malcolm, 1980).

The use of homoclimes is emphasized by some workers but in the south of Western Australia the two most successful saltbushes (*Atriplex amnicola*

Figure 1. (a) An experiment in Western Australia in which ecotypes of several species of *Atriplex* are being tested as ten single-plant replicates on a saline soil. Note the spreading habit of *A. cinerea* in the foreground. (b) Sheep have heavily grazed *A. cinerea* (prostrate bush) and *A. amnicola* (spreading bushes), leaving *A. nummularia* and *A. bunburyana* virtually untouched.

and *A. undulata*) are not from homoclimes. Moreover, recent testing in Saudi Arabia indicates outstanding growth by *A. amnicola, A. undulata,* and *A. canescens* at El Qatif, although none of these is from a similar climate (S. Z. Hyder, personal communication, 1982). Thus it is advisable to obtain as wide a range of material as possible that offers any chance of success.

A suitable testing site is one that is representative of the problem areas in soil type and climate and of moderate severity with respect to degree of salinity. Vagaries of season will normally vary the ecological amplitude of the plants with respect to severity of the site.

A 4 × 4-m spacing (625 plants per hectare) is used for adaptation testing in 300 to 375-mm rainfall zones in southern Western Australia. Bushes are planted as single plant replicates, using 20 replications to counteract the high variability that characterizes salt-affected soils. Grazing control is essential, and it is helpful to enclose an unplanted buffer zone in which colonization is observed. Observations should be continued for at least 3.5 years but preferably much longer. Where climatic conditions are highly unreliable, differences in survival have been noted between 20 and 30 years on some sites (Judd and Judd, 1976).

Possible selection criteria include survival (for various periods), growth, cold tolerance, flowering and seed production, natural reseeding, grazing value, ion composition, grazing recovery, growth habit, digestibility, resistance to pests or diseases, salt and waterlogging tolerance, drought tolerance, resistance to sand blasting, and palatability.

IV. Factors Affecting Establishment

A. *Environmental Factors*

Natural regeneration of forage shrubs on salt-affected sites may occur with grazing protection but on certain areas periods of stock exclusion of up to 15 years (Cunningham, 1974) failed to produce a plant cover of any sort. Colonization in dry seasons is poor but wet seasons may produce a good cover quickly.

Numerous attempts have been made to achieve a plant cover more quickly by sowing seeds of salt-tolerant forage shrubs. In western New South Wales over the last 30 or so years attempts have been made to establish *Atriplex nummularia, A. vesicaria,* and other species on scalded areas (Jones, 1966a, and many others). No reliable method of establishing a stand of perennial shrubs by direct seeding has been devised despite the use of many furrowing, cultivation, ponding, and other techniques. Attempts at direct seeding in the United States have also had limited success, especially in salt desert shrub areas receiving less than 200 mm annual rainfall.

In the course of experiments many factors have been observed to influence establishment and various sowing methods have been devised to improve results. Plants that are well adapted to the site must be used (Gomm, 1974). Premature deaths of established plants or deterioration of some species with time indicates poor adaptation. Drought, grazing, and attacks by scale insects have been observed to cause death of *Atriplex nummularia* in the Coolabah District of New South Wales, where *A. vesicaria* persisted (Cunningham, 1974). Well-adapted species have been observed in Wyoming to have survived for 15 years (Fisser *et al.*, 1974) and in Utah, 34-year survival charts showed little change of eight major species from the second year after establishment (West, 1979), indicating excellent adaptation. In Western Australia observation of test plantings on salt-affected soils for 12 years revealed marked changes in relative performance of species with time. Species such as *Atriplex halimus, A. canescens,* and *A. lentiformis* performed well in early years but were much poorer than *A. amnicola* by year 9.

In western New South Wales the deterioration of shrubs on some sites has been observed to be due to the formation of hummocks resulting in shedding of water (Cunningham, 1974). The effectiveness of furrows and other structures declines with time, resulting in death of plants due to water shortage.

Water is the most important factor influencing establishment of salt-tolerant forage shrubs on salt-affected soils. The quantity of rainfall or snow, its distribution and seasonal incidence, and the fate of the water when it reaches the ground influence establishment and survival in various ways.

In Western Australia establishment problems may occur in a Mediterranean climate with up to 400 mm annual rainfall. In western New South Wales scald regeneration problems occur in areas receiving less than 425 mm of rainfall of roughly equal summer and winter incidence. In North Africa failure of rangeland seeding occurs where annual rainfall is less than 300 mm. Salt desert shrub areas in the United States receive less than 250 mm annual rainfall.

Summer rainfall is less effective than winter rainfall because of high evaporative loss and the likelihood of reduced germination or death of seedlings due to excessively high soil temperatures (Burbidge, 1945; Wein and West, 1972; McKell *et al.*, 1979). However, in winter, temperatures may be too low for optimum germination (Malcolm *et al.*, 1982) or rainfall may not be sufficient (Springfield, 1969).

Rainfall is needed to leach salt from the soil (Malcolm, 1980) or inhibitors from the sown fruits to provide water for germination by increasing the soil matric potential (Springfield, 1966) and to keep the soil soft for root growth and seedling emergence (Koller *et al.*, 1958). Water may be concentrated to achieve adequate leaching of salt (Jones, 1966b) but concentration of water in depressions causes drowning of seedlings even in arid climates (Frost and Hamilton, 1965; Jones, 1967b; Wein and West, 1971), while sites within a meter may be too dry for seedlings to establish. Soil crusting reduces both the infiltration of water and the emergence of seedlings.

Water must be available in the soil near the seedling for survival and growth. For this to occur on areas of poor infiltration the water must run off some sections and be concentrated and held until it infiltrates. Sloping areas have been found to regenerate poorly because of the lack of infiltration (Stannard and Condon, 1958; Cunningham, 1974).

B. Plant Factors

Seeds of *Atriplex* species are enclosed in bracts that contain water-soluble germination inhibitors, largely sodium chloride and saponin. The seeds plus bracts are referred to as the fruits. Bracts in which seeds have failed to develop are referred to as unfilled.

Seed fill may vary between wide limits: *Atriplex nummularia*, 10 to 84% (Jones, 1968); *A. canescens*, 49 to 93% (Springfield, 1964); and *A. halimus*, 43.5 to 91.5% (Koller *et al.*, 1958). Germination of the enclosed seeds may also vary greatly: 34 to 80% for *A. canescens* (Springfield, 1964) and 2 to 62% for *A. nummularia* (Jones, 1968).

The fruits of *Atriplex* spp. contain water-soluble inhibitors in sufficient amounts to influence or even suppress germination. The possibility of other inhibitors has also been suggested in *A. canescens* (Gerard, 1965) and there is evidence of dormancy in *Halosarcia* spp. (Malcolm, 1964) and *A. repanda* (Cristi and Gasto, 1971; Lailhacar-Kind and Laude, 1975) and an after-ripening requirement in *A. obovata* (Edgar and Springfield, 1977) and *A. canescens* (Springfield, 1970). Germination is improved by bract removal for some *Maireana* spp. (Burbidge, 1946; Malcolm, 1963) and bract removal or scarification improves germination of *A. obovata* (Edgar and Springfield, 1977), *A. canescens* (Gerard, 1965), *A. halimus* (Koller *et al.*, 1958), *A. nummularia* (Jones, 1968), and *A. repanda* (Lailhacar-Kind and Laude, 1975; Cristi and Gasto, 1971). In *A. repanda* both bract removal and piercing of the testa were required.

Milling of *A. nummularia* fruits failed to improve field establishment (Jones, 1968). Benefits from dewinging *A. canescens* fruits include faster germination, easier handling, reduced bulk, and easier burial (Springfield, 1964, 1970). As there are no studies on the function of the wings, it is not clear whether dewinging improves field establishment. In fact slow germination at low temperatures may give hardened seedlings and be advantageous (Springfield, 1964).

Natural wetting and drying cycles are a normal feature of field sites. Five hours of soaking in water was found to remove a substantial proportion of the salt inhibitor in *A. nummularia* fruits but use of milled or leached fruits in pot and field experiments failed to improve establishment of *A. nummularia* (Jones, 1968). Soaking and washing fruits of *A. halimus* for up to 36 hr was beneficial to establishment only if the seed was planted into moist soil, otherwise field sowing was a major problem (Koller *et al.*, 1958).

Soaking fruits of *A. canescens* in water did not appear to improve germination though soaking in sulfuric acid for 40 min increased germination over dewinging (Gerard, 1965). Sulfuric acid treatment for 45 min raised the germination of fruits of *A. repanda* from 0 to 31.2% and was better than using sodium hydroxide, sandpapering, or washing (Cristi and Gasto, 1971).

Fruits of *A. lentiformis* and *A. semibaccata* gave better germination at some constant temperatures after they had been washed in water (Young *et al.*, 1980). However, best germination was obtained with fluctuating temperatures of about 10° to 25° or 10° to 30°C and 10° to 20° or 10° to 25°C for the two species, respectively.

Halophytes differ markedly in their germination response to temperature. In Fig. 2 the marked difference in temperature response between four *Atriplex* spp. and *M. brevifolia* is illustrated. The *Atriplex* spp. all germinate poorly at cold temperatures and respond spectacularly at warmer ranges. Significant differences also occur between species of *Atriplex*. In the case of *A. nummularia* and *A. glauca* an increase in the upper temperature from 8° to 15°C greatly increased germination though it failed to cause a response in *A. lentiformis* and *A. amnicola*. These two species responded when the lower temperature was raised from 4° to 8°C.

Constant temperatures are a poor indicator of field conditions (Malcolm *et al.*, 1982) and optima determined in the absence of water or salinity stress may be misleading. Osmotic stress (induced by mannitol) interacted with temperatures above and below the optima to reduce the germination of fruits of *A. canescens* (Springfield, 1966) and *A. repanda* (Cristi and Gasto, 1971). Salinity interacted with temperatures above and below the optima to reduce the speed of germination of seeds of *M. brevifolia* (Malcolm, 1963). Temperature was also found to interact with salt in reducing the germination of *Halosarcia* sp. (Malcolm, 1964). Temperature optima for germination are also influenced by seed washing (Young *et al.*, 1980) or dewinging (Burbidge, 1945).

Temperatures of the soil in the immediate vicinity of seed placement sites have been found to depart from the optima for seed germination and seedling survival. Soil temperatures in scalds in western New South Wales

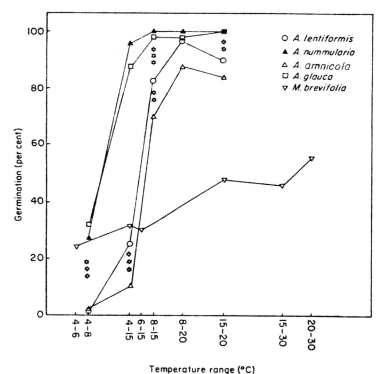

Figure 2. Germination of four *Atriplex* spp. counted on day 8 and *Maireana brevifolia* counted on day 5 (after Malcolm, 1963) at several temperatures. (Temperature ranges are plotted as degree totals, e.g., 8–15°C = 23°C.) ** and *** denote statistical significances at the 1 and 0.1% levels, respectively. (From *Journal of Arid Environments*, vol. 5, p. 186, 1982. Copyright Academic Press, London.)

reached 49°C at about 2 cm on hot days (Jones, 1969) and in Utah temperatures higher than 60°C were reported for the soil surface in July (Wein and West, 1972), thereby exceeding the thermal limit for plant tissue, let alone the optimum temperature for germination. Soil temperature studies in California indicated that the best time for seeding *A. polycarpa* was in early March rather than autumn (Cornelius and Burma, 1970) and the best temperatures for germination of *A. canescens* were found to be in the cooler seasons when water was not optimum (Springfield, 1969). In Western Australia establishment of *M. brevifolia* and two *Atriplex* spp. was increased by spraying the soil with black latex to raise the temperature (Malcolm *et al.*, 1982).

The salt tolerance of many halophytes during the germination stage is low. Reduction of germination by 50% has been shown to occur at 5.8g/liter sodium chloride for *A. halimus* (Mayer and Poljakoff-Mayber,

Table II. Conversion of salt levels affecting germination to salt levels in soils

Water content (%) by weight of dry soil at		Salt content of soil solution[b] at 34 kPa (g Cl⁻/liter)	Salt content of oven-dry soil (% Cl⁻)	Approximate EC_e^c (mS/m)
Saturation[a]	Field capacity[a] (34 kPa)			
12.7	4.6	3.5	0.03	320
12.7	4.6	12	0.09	1100
21.2	12.1	3.5	0.07	510
21.2	12.1	12	0.02	1770
41.4	25.7	3.5	0.15	560
41.4	25.7	12	0.51	1940

[a] The values are for soil from 0 to 7.5 cm at 17 salt-affected sites in Western Australia. Each value is for a composite site sample and those used are the lowest, mean, and highest for the 17 sites.

[b] The values are the highest (12 g/liter) and lowest (3.5 g/liter) causing a 50% reduction in germination during testing of halophytic shrubs in the laboratory, taken here as a soil solution (see text for details).

[c] The conversion factor used on the soil solution at the saturation percentage was EC_{25} mS/m × 6.410 = TDS mg/liter.

1963), 15 to 20 g/liter for *M. brevifolia* (Malcolm, 1963), 12 to 17 g/liter for several *Atriplex* spp., 18 g/liter for *A. polycarpa* (Chatterton and McKell, 1969), and approximately 9 and 20 g/liter for two *Halosarcia* spp. (Malcolm, 1964).

These values are not directly comparable with the salt levels in Table I. In Table II data for soil water retention in Western Australian salt-affected soils have been used to convert the germination data to salt values for soil.

The salt levels in most of the soils reported in Table I are much higher than those required to cause a 50% reduction in germination at optimum temperatures and in the absence of matric potential and seed inhibitor effects. If these other demands for water are added the chance of germination problems occurring due to the combined effects of salt, dryness, temperature, and inhibitors will be seen to be very great. To overcome these barriers to establishment the seeding method must engineer the available water to efficiently overcome the problem.

Once seedlings have emerged they face a new array of problems. For *A. undulata* in Western Australia, 79.3% of viable seeds sown produced an emerged seedling in winter but by late summer survival was only 26.9% (Malcolm *et al.*, 1982). Factors observed to affect seedling survival include submergence, frost, sandblasting, soil burial, insects, rodents or other animals, damping off, drought, salinity, soil erosion, and weed competition. It is not uncommon for field experiments to result in few mature plants and even where plants establish the ratio of viable seeds sown to plants established may be extremely high. In Chile the best treatment gave one plant for each 284 sown fruits of 98% seed fill (Cristi and Gasto, 1971). Thus, there is an urgent need to devise establishment methods to overcome the problems discussed.

V. Field Establishment Methods

A. *Planting Established Plants*

It is possible to avoid the problems of direct seeding by raising plants and placing them in the field. This method is preferred for plant testing, where establishment problems can be studied separately. For purposes such as coastal sand stabilization, mine dump revegetation, or restoration of areas disturbed by development, where the costs can be borne, planting established plants is more reliable.

The acceptability of using plants for establishment depends on the cost. In many countries it is doubtful if plants could be grown and established in the field for less than $0.5 U.S. each, or $555 per hectare (for 3×3-m spacing), which is prohibitive in terms of the expected returns. In countries such as India and Pakistan, where individual farmers have a small area of land and labor is cheap, vegetative propagation, including the use of cuttings from vigorous selected bushes, may be acceptable. However, if the millions of hectares of degraded salt-affected land in the world are to be revegetated at an acceptable cost and in a reasonable time, successful direct seeding methods are essential.

B. *Direct Seeding*

Major differences in soil type, climate, and species requirements will influence the specific direct seeding methods devised for particular problem areas. Seed quality and treatment have already been discussed, and the time of sowing must be determined experimentally for each area after careful consideration of climatic factors and plant requirements.

The most important reason for failures from direct seeding of shrubs in salt-affected areas is ineffective utilization of rainfall. The need to concentrate water has been widely recognized. Measures designed to hold water include basins, pits, furrows, ridges, plowing, checkerboarding, contouring, and ponding. These structures hold water better than a smooth, bare surface but in dispersive soils the benefit is short-lived, maybe 1 to 2 years, and even relatively large structures such as ponding banks may need to be reshaped after a few years to remain effective.

Ponding is suited to flat areas where the slope is between 0.05 and 0.5% and infiltration is low (Jones, 1967a). Ponding is a means of establishing annual cover on bare scalds rather than a preparation for direct seeding of perennial shrubs.

Pitting is best used on medium to heavy soil on flats or gentle slopes (Herbel, 1972). Interrupted contour furrows may be used on more sloping land (Herbel, 1972). However, most of the research on the use of these measures fails to combine a soil-forming action with a precise seed placement, thereby reducing their effectiveness.

Seed placement methods ranging from haphazard spreading of seed on roughened ground to precise placement in a prepared niche (Harris and Leiser, 1979) have been used for seeding shrubs. Placement of seed at a variety of depths or positions has been suggested to give at least some seeds a chance of survival. A common method of seed placement is to place seeds in the bottom of a small pressed furrow (Frost and Hamilton, 1965; Herbel, 1972; Giunta et al., 1975). The press-seeder may be run across basins or pits (Frost and Hamilton, 1965) to improve establishment. Seeds placed high on slopes do not establish because of lack of water, and seedlings from those in depressions in some soil types are drowned (Frost and Hamilton, 1965; Jones, 1967b; Cunningham, 1974). Seedlings are observed to establish at or about the high watermark, and even in dry years the bank base position is superior to the furrow bottom (Jones, 1967b).

The possibility of placing the seeds on the slope of a furrow has been considered (Herbel, 1972) and a machine has been developed for seeding the sides of pits (Frost and Hamilton, 1965). Another machine, referred to as a niche seeder, plows a furrow, forms a small ridge, and presses a seeding niche on the ridge (Malcolm and Allen, 1981). During development of the niche seeder, models were tried in which a niche was pressed on the slope of the furrow. However, the niche eroded into the furrow too readily. In the latest model of the seeder (see Fig. 3a), twin opposed disks form the furrows and bank and a "V" press wheel forms a broad niche on top of the bank. This structure has proved to be more stable. The height of the niche may be varied from below ground level to about 15 cm above ground level to suit the requirements of different sites. Raising the niche above ground level may improve leaching and reduce waterlogging.

Experiments on depth of seeding with A. canescens indicate that as depth is increased beyond about 1 cm, emergence is reduced (Springfield and Bell, 1967) and there is a possibility that only sufficient cover to prevent blowing is best. Shallow sowing is also necessary for A. halimus (Koller et al., 1958), A. vesicaria, and Maireana sedifolia (Burbidge, 1945, 1946) and several chenopods used in Uzbekistan (Shamsutdinov, 1970). Compression of soil over the seed may encourage crusting and reduce emergence (Koller et al., 1958). Burial with a few millimeters of soil was found to give lower establishment than covering the fruits with a black

Figure 3.   (a) The Mallen Niche Seeder making placements of seeds and black latex spray in a prepared raised niche on a saline soil. The machine is being covered by Australian Patent no. 538636 and is in commercial production in Western Australia. (b) Niche created by the Mallen Niche Seeder. The seeds covered with vermiculite and sprayed with black latex are deposited by the machine at 1.5-m intervals in the slightly raised niche. (c) One-year-old stand of *Atriplex undulata* direct seeded with the Mallen Niche Seeder on saline soil in Western Australia.

latex spray for *M. brevifolia, A. amnicola,* and *A. undulata* (Malcolm *et al.,* 1982), and in subsequent experiments a mulch of vermiculite has proved to be superior to soil cover and latex, the best response being obtained for a combination of vermiculite and black latex spray (Malcolm and Swaan, 1985).

Although expensive, mulches may be used in critical sites to improve leaching of salt by rainfall (Malcolm *et al.,* 1980), reduce evaporation from soil (Wiegand *et al.,* 1968), and reduce soil temperature (Herbel, 1972).

Figure 3. (*Continued*)

Sprayed coatings may be used to reduce erosion, increase soil temperature, and reduce water loss (Malcolm *et al.,* 1982). Treatments such as mulch and spray are too expensive to be used as an overall treatment, but their use as a spot treatment has been suggested (Springfield, 1978). The niche seeding machine discussed earlier places seeds at predetermined intervals (adjustable from about 1 to 3 m) in the niche. In the same operation the seed placement is covered with vermiculite mulch and the whole placement is covered with black latex spray (Malcolm and Allen, 1981) (see Fig. 3b). The machine has given improved establishment of chenopod shrubs on salt-affected soils in Western Australia (see Fig. 3c) (Malcolm *et al.,* 1980) and is undergoing commercial development. In some areas it may be preferable to use a white spray to reduce soil temperature (Springfield, 1978). Other treatments that could be incorporated on the spot using the niche seeder include gypsum and pesticides. Costs of establishment using the niche seeder with vermiculite and black latex and seeding at a density of about 2200 plants per hectare have been estimated at less than $120 U.S. per hectare (1986 prices), of which the black latex cost represents about 65%.

Direct seeding results may be greatly improved by selecting ecotypes with a superior ability to establish. Differences in field establishment between selections of *Atriplex amnicola* may exceed 20-fold.

The row spacing determines the areas of bare soil that shed water and may cause erosion (Cunningham, 1974). Damage was reduced in New South Wales by reducing furrow spacing from 10 to 2.5 m. The spacing appropriate to any particular area will depend on the soil and rainfall and the size of the bushes to be sown.

Weed competition must be considered in shrub establishment. Annual plants are frequently more vigorous in the first year than perennials and may seriously compete with the sown species. Weeds may be controlled chemically or some form of mechanical measure may be used to reduce competition (Giunta *et al.,* 1975; Herbel *et al.,* 1973; Herbel, 1972).

Finally, it is essential to control insects or other animals that may attack the young plants. Attacks by red-legged earth mites (*Halotydeus destructor*), Rutherglen bugs (*Nysius vinitor*), and *Lepidopterous* grubs have been observed in Western Australia (Malcolm *et al.,* 1982).

VI. Summary

Millions of hectares of soils too salty for normal crops and pastures lie idle. Salt-tolerant forage shrubs may be grown on these soils. Adaptation trials are needed to determine which shrubs to use in particular areas.

Most halophytic forage shrubs are salt sensitive at germination and many have germination inhibitors and special temperature requirements.

Interactions between temperature, salinity, matric potential, and inhibition require special attention in designing establishment methods.

Direct seeding innovations include special soil-forming techniques to catch and hold water and precision placement of seed. Expensive treatments such as mulches and covering sprays may be used at an acceptable cost if applied as a spot treatment.

References

Beadle, N. C. W. (1948). Studies in wind erosion. Part III. Natural regeneration on scalded surfaces. *J. Soil Conserv. N.S.W.* **4,** 123–134.

Benz, L. C., Sandoval, F. M., Doering, E. J., and Willis, W. O. (1976). Managing saline soils in the Red River Valley of the north. *U.S., Agric. Res. Serv. [Rep.] ARS-NC* **ARS-NC-42.**

Bleak, A. T., Frischknecht, N. C., Plummer, A. P., and Eckert, R. E. (1965). Problems in artificial and natural revegetation of the arid shadscale vegetation zone of Utah and Nevada. *J. Range Manage.* **18,** 59–65.

Boumans, J. H., Hulsbos, W. C., Lindenbergh, H. L. J., and van der Sluis, P. M. (1963). Reclamation of salt affected soils in Iraq—Soil hydrological and agricultural studies. *Publ.—Int. Inst. Land Reclam. Improv.* **11.**

Branson, F. A., Miller, R. F., and McQueen, I. S. (1967). Geographic distribution factors affecting the distribution of salt desert shrubs in the United States. *J. Range Manage.* **20,** 287–296.

Burbidge, N. T. (1945). Germination studies of Australian Chenopodiaceae with special reference to the conditions necessary for regeneration *Atriplex vesicarium* Heward. *Trans. R. Soc. S. Aust.* **69,** 73–85.

Burbidge, N. T. (1946). Germination studies of Australian Chenopodiaceae with special reference to the conditions necessary for regeneration. II. (a) *Kochia sedifolia* F. v. M. (b) *K. pyramidata* Benth (c) *K. georgei* Diels. *Trans. R. Soc. South Aust.* **70,** 110–120.

Carter, D. L., and Wiegand, C. L. (1965). Interspersed salt-affected and unaffected dryland soils of the lower Rio Grande Valley. I. Chemical, physical and mineralogical characteristics. *Soil Sci.* **99,** 256–260.

Chatterton, N. J., and McKell, C. M. (1969). *Atriplex polycarpa.* 1. Germination and growth as affected by sodium chloride in water cultures. *Agron. J.* **61,** 448–450.

Cornelius, D. R., and Burma, G. D. (1970). Seeding and seedbed ridging to improve dry grazing land in central California. *Proc. Int. Grassl. Congr., 11th, 1969,* pp. 107–111.

Cristi, A. A., and Gasto, C. J. (1971). Alteraciones ambientales y del fruto en la germinacion de *Atriplex repanda* Phil. *Fac. Agron. Univ. Chile, Santiago Estac. Exp. Agron. Bol., Tec.* **34,** 25–40.

Cunningham, G. M. (1974). Regeneration of scalded duplex soils in the Coolabah District, New South Wales. *J. Soil Conserv. N.S.W.* **30,** 157–169.

Edgar, R. L., and Springfield, H. W. (1977). Germination characteristics of broadscale: A possible saline–alkaline site stabilizer. *J. Range Manage.* **30,** 296–298.

Fisser, H. G., Mackey, M. H., and Nicholls, J. T. (1974). Contour-furrowing and seeding on nuttall saltbush rangeland of Wyoming. *J. Range Manage.* **27,** 459–462.

Frost, K. R., and Hamilton, L. (1965). Basin forming and reseeding of rangeland. *Trans. ASAE* **8,** 202–203, 207.

Gates, C. T., and Muirhead, W. (1967). Studies of the tolerance of *Atriplex* spp. 1. Environmental characteristics and plant response of *A. vesicaria, A. nummularia* and *A. semibaccate. Aust. J. Exp. Agric. Anim. Husb.* **7,** 39–49.

Gerard, J. B. (1965). Factors and treatments affecting fruit fill, seed germination and seedling emergence of fourwing saltbush (*Atriplex canescens* (Pursh) Nutt.). M.Sc. Thesis, New Mexico State University, Las Cruces.

Giunta, B. C., Christensen, D. R., and Monsen, S. B. (1975). Interseeding shrubs in cheatgrass with a browse seeder-scalper. *J. Range Manage.* **28,** 398–402.

Gomm, F. B. (1974). Forage species for the northern Intermountain Region: A summary of seeding trials. *U.S., Dep. Agric., Tech. Bull.* **1479.**

Harris, R. W., and Leiser, A. T. (1979). Direct seeding woody plants in the landscape. *Univ. Calif., Div. Agric. Sci., Leafl.* **2577.**

Henschke, C. J. (1980). Saltland in statistics. *J. Agric., West. Aust.* [4] **21,** 116–119.

Herbel, C. H. (1972). Using mechanical equipment to modify the seedling environment. *In* "Wildland Shrubs: Their Biology and Utilization" (C. M. McKell, J. P. Blaisdell, and J. R. Goodin, eds.), USDA For. Serv. Gen. Tech. Rep. INT-1, pp. 369–381. Utah State University, Logan.

Herbel, C. H., Abernathy, G. H., Yarbrough, C. C., and Gardner, D. K. (1973). Rootplowing and seeding arid rangelands in the Southwest. *J. Range Manage.* **26,** 193–197.

Hill, J. R. C. (1977). Establishment of vegetation on copper, gold and nickel mining wastes in Rhodesia. *Trans.—Inst. Min. Metall., Sect. A* **86,** A135–A146.

Hill, J. R. C., and Nothard, W. F. (1973). The Rhodesian approach to the vegetating of slime dams. *J. S. Afr. Inst. Min. Metall.* **74,** 197–208.

Jefferies, R. L., Davy, A. J., and Rudmik, T. (1981). Population biology of the salt marsh annual *Salicornia europaea* agg. *J. Ecol.* **69,** 17–31.

Jones, R. M. (1966a). Scald reclamation studies in the Hay District. Part I. Natural reclamation of scalds. *J. Soil Conserv. N.S.W.* **22,** 147–160.

Jones, R. M. (1966b). Scald reclamation studies in the Hay District, N.S.W. Part II. Reclamation by ploughing. *J. Soil Conserv. N.S.W.* **22,** 213–229.

Jones, R. M. (1967a). Scald reclamation studies in the Hay District, N.S.W. Part III. Reclamation by ponding banks. *J. Soil Conserv. N.S.W.* **23,** 3–17.

Jones, R. M. (1967b). Investigations of seedling establishment on a reclaimed scald. *J. Soil Conserv. N.S.W.* **23,** 187–191.

Jones, R. M. (1968). Studies on the stimulation of germination and emergence of old man saltbush (*Atriplex nummularia* Lindl.). *J. Soil Conserv. N.S.W.* **24,** 271–278.

Jones, R. M. (1969). Scald reclamation studies in the Hay District. Part IV. Scald soils: Their properties and changes with reclamation. *J. Soil Conserv. N.S.W.* **25,** 104–120.

Judd, B. I., and Judd, L. W. (1976). Plant survival in the arid southwest 30 years after seeding. *J. Range Manage.* **29,** 248–251.

Kanwar, J. (1969). Salt affected soils in India, their nature and distribution. *Agrokem. Talajtan* **18,** 79–86.

Koller, D., Tadmor, N. H., and Hillel, D. (1958). Experiments in the propagation of *Atriplex halimus* L. for desert pasture and soil conservation. *Ktavim (Engl. Ed.)* **9,** 83–106.

Kurkin, D. A. (1967). The role of autecological, coenitic, human and historical factors in determining the composition of halophytic coenoses in the Baraba forest-steppe. *Byull. Mosk. O-va. Ispyt. Prir., Otd. Biol.* **72,** 68–79.

Lailhacar-Kind, S., and Laude, H. M. (1975). Improvement of seed germination in *Atriplex repanda* Phil. *J. Range Manage.* **28,** 491–494.

Le Houérou, H. N. (1980). Browse in northern Africa. *In* "Browse in Africa: The Current

State of Knowledge" (H. N. Le Houérou, ed.), pp. 55–82. International Livestock Center for Africa, Addis Ababa, Ethiopia.

Le Roux, P. J. (1974). Establishing vegetation in saline soil to stabilise aeolian sand at Walvis Bay, South-West Africa. *For. S. Africa* **15**, 43–46.

McKell, C. M. (1978). Establishment of native plants for the rehabilitation of Paraho processed oil shale in an arid environment. *In* "The Reclamation of Disturbed Arid Lands" (R. A. Wright, ed.), pp. 13–32, Univ. of New Mexico Press, Albuquerque.

McKell, C. M. *et al.* (1979). "Selection, Propagation, and Field Establishment of Native Plant Species in Disturbed Arid Lands." Bull. 500, 49 pp. Utah Agric. Exp. Stn., Logan.

Malcolm, C. V. (1963). An agronomic study of *Kochia brevifolia* R. Br. Univ. of Western Australia M.Sc. (Agric.) Thesis.

Malcolm, C. V. (1964). Effects of salt, temperature and seed scarification on germination of two varieties of *Arthrocnemum halocnemoides*. *J. R. Soc. West. Aust.* **47**, 72–74.

Malcolm, C. V. (1980). Wheatbelt salinity—A review of the salt land problem in south western Australia. *West. Aust., Dep. Agric., Tech. Bull.* **52.**

Malcolm, C. V., and Allen, R. J. (1981). The Mallen Niche Seeder for plant establishment on difficult sites. *Aust. Rangel. J.* **3**, 106–109.

Malcolm, C. V., and Swaan, T. C. (1985). Soil mulches, sprayed coatings and seed washing to aid chenopod establishment on saline soil. *Aust. Rangel. J.* **7**(1), 22–28.

Malcolm, C. V., Swaan, T. C., and Ridings, H. I. (1980). Niche-seeding for broadscale forage shrub establishment on saline soils. *Int. Symp. Salt-Affected Soils*, Karnal, 1980, pp. 539–544.

Malcolm, C. V., Hillman, B. J., Swaan, T. C., Denby, C., Carlson, D., and D'Antuono, M. (1982). Black paint, soil amendment and mulch effects on chenopod establishment in a saline soil. *J. Arid Environ.* **5**, 179–189.

Malcolm, C. V., Clarke, A. J. and Swaan, T. C. (1984). Plant collections for saltland revegetation and soil conservation. *West. Aust., Dep. Agric., Tech. Bull.* **65.**

Mayer, A. M., and Poljakoff-Mayber, A. (1963). "The Germination of Seeds." Pergamon, Oxford.

Mudie, P. J. (1974). The potential economic uses of halophytes. *In* "Ecology of Halophytes" (R. J. Reimold and W. H. Queen, eds.), pp. 565–597. Academic Press, New York.

Novikoff, G. (1957) Les associations halophiles de la Tunisie et leur mise en valeur. *Ann. Serv. Bot. Agron. Tunis.* **30**, 171–179.

Osmond, C. B., Bjorkman, O., and Anderson, D. J. (1980). "Physiological Processes in Plant Ecology: Toward a Synthesis with *Atriplex*." Springer-Verlag, Berlin and New York.

Pelt, J. M., Hayon, J. C., and Younos, M. C. (1968). The flora and vegetation of a halophilous steppe zone on the border of Amou-Daria (Afghanistan). *C.R. Hebd. Seances Acad. Sci., Ser. D* **267**, 505–508.

Plummer, A. P. (1966). Experience in improving salt desert shrub range by artificial planting. *In* "Salt Desert Shrub Symposium." U.S. Dep. Interior B.L.M. Cedar City, Utah.

Plummer, A. P., Christensen, D. R., and Monsen, S. B. (1968). Restoring big game range in Utah. *Utah Div. Fish Game Publ.* **68-3.**

Quinones, F. A., Gould, W. L., Leman, D. J., and Ferraiolo, J. A. (1980). Evaluation of range plants at the San Juan Mine near Farmington. *Res. Rep.—N.M., Agric. Exp. Stn.* **424.**

Richardson, S. G., and McKell, C. M. (1980). Salt tolerance of two saltbush species grown in processed oil shale. *J. Range Manage.* **33**, 460–463.

Rolla, S. R., and Kanodia, K. C. (1962). Studies on the vegetation and flora of Jodhpur Division, Rajasthan State. *Ann. Arid Zone* **1**, 16–46.

Schroo, H. (1967). Notes on the reclamation of salt-affected soils in the Indus Plain of West Pakistan. *Neth. J. Agric. Sci.* **16,** 207–220.

Shamsoutdinov, I. Sh. (1966). The improvement of desert ranges in Uzbekistan. *Proc. Int. Grassl. Congr., 10th, 1966,* pp. 960–962.

Shamsutdinov, Z. (1970). Creation of permanent pastures in the Uzbekistan desert zone. *Proc. Int. Grassl. Congr., 11th, 1969,* pp. 69–71.

Shamsutdinov, Z., and Korsun, V. (1968). Establishment of perennial autumn/winter pastures in semi-desert foothills of Uzbekistan. *Luga Pastbishcha* **2,** 11–13.

Singh, L. B. (1970). Utilisation of saline–alkali soils for agro-industry without prior reclamation. *Econ. Bot.* **24,** 439–442.

Skogerhoe, G. V., and Walker, W. R. (1973). Salt pickup from agricultural lands in the Grand Valley in Colorado. *J. Environ. Qual.* **2,** 377–382.

Somers, G. F. (1979). Natural halophytes as a potential resource for new salt-tolerant crops: Some progress and prospects. *In* "The Biosaline Concept" (A. Hollaender, ed.), pp. 101–115. Plenum, New York.

Springfield, H. W. (1964). Factors affecting germination of fourwing saltbush. *USDA For. Serv. Res. Note RM* **RM-25.**

Springfield, H. W. (1966). Germination of fourwing saltbush seeds at different levels of moisture stress. *Agron. J.* **58,** 149–150.

Springfield, H. W. (1969). Temperatures for germination of fourwing saltbush. *J. Range Manage.* **22,** 49–50.

Springfield, H. W. (1970). Germination characteristics of *Atriplex canescens* seed. *Proc. Int. Grassl. Congr., 11th, 1969,* pp. 586–589.

Springfield, H. W. (1978). Using mulches to establish woody chenopods—An arid land example. *In* "Special Readings in Conservation," FAO Conserv. Guide No. 4. FAO, Rome.

Springfield, H. W., and Bell, D. G. (1967). Depth to seed fourwing saltbush. *J. Range Manage.* **20,** 180–182.

Stalter, R., and Batson, W. T. (1969). Transplantation of salt marsh vegetation, Georgetown, South Carolina. *Ecology* **50,** 1087–1089.

Stannard, M. E., and Condon, R. W. (1958). Studies on Trida regeneration area. *J. Soil Conserv. N.S.W.* **14,** 159–176.

Strogonov, B. P. (1964). "Physiological Basis of Salt Tolerance of Plants (as Affected by Various Types of Salinity)." Acad. Sci. USSR (Inst. Plant Physiol. in K.A. Timiryazeva, Israel Program for Scientific Translations).

Ungar, I. A. (1970). Species soil relationships on sulphate dominated soils of South Dakota. *Am. Midl. Nat.* **83,** 343–357.

Ungar, I. A. (1972). The vegetation of inland saline marshes of North America, north of Mexico. *In* "Grundfagen und methoden in der Pflanzensoziologie (Basic Problems and Methods in Phytosociology)" (E. van der Marel and R. Tüxen, eds.), pp. 397–411.

Wein, R. W., and West, N. E. (1971). Seedling survival on erosion control treatments in a salt desert area. *J. Range Manage.* **24,** 352–357.

Wein, R. W., and West, N. E. (1972). Physical microclimates of erosion control structures in a salt desert area. *J. Appl. Ecol.* **9,** 703–719.

West, N. E. (1979). Survival patterns of major perennials in salt desert shrub communities of south western Utah. *J. Range Manage.* **32,** 442–445.

West, N. E., and Ibrahim, K. I. (1968). Soil-vegetation relationships in the shadscale zone of south eastern Utah. *Ecology* **49,** 445–456.

Wiegand, C. L., Heilman, M. D., and Swanson, W. A. (1968). Sand and cotton bur mulches, bermudagrass seed and bare soil effects. I. Evaporation supression. *Soil Sci. Soc. Am. Proc.* **32,** 276–280.

Williams, O. B. (1960). The selection and establishment of pasture species in a semi-arid environment—An ecological assessment of the problem. *J. Aust. Inst. Agric. Sci.* **26,** 258–265.

Young, J. A., Kay, B. L., George, H., and Evans, R. A. (1980). Germination of three species of *Atriplex. Agron. J.* **72,** 705–709.

Zahran, M. A. (1982). "Vegetation Types of Saudi Arabia." Ministry of Education, King Abdul Aziz University, Jeddah.

28

Management Practices for Shrub-Dominated Lands to Assure Multiple-Use Benefits

Cyrus M. McKell

I. Introduction

The ecological, anatomical, physiological, and genetic features of shrubs confer biological advantages on them to compete successfully with other types of plants such that they often dominate a plant community. Prior to the advent of intensive human use of land resources, the natural interactions of shrubs and other species of plants were conditioned primarily by those natural characteristics that allowed the best-adapted plants to survive and reproduce.

Shrubs are used for many purposes, the principal one being browse for domestic animals and wildlife. However, as the intensity of use increases beyond the natural ability of plants to adjust in a natural community to the impact of use, or to reproduce and reoccupy the space after destructive use has occurred, some kind of management is needed if the desired balance in species composition is to be maintained.

Modern management practices, particularly range improvement strategies for control of undesirable plants, provide tools for manipulation of plant communities where the dominance of undesirable shrub species has reduced the overall capability for productive uses. Some of the most effective means of controlling undesirable shrubs include combinations of control methods followed by seeding species chosen for their ability to provide optimum and stable productivity. Grazing management is also a means of moderating plant competition by distributing the intensity of use among desirable and less desirable or unpalatable species.

II. Historical Aspects of Management Impacts on Shrublands

Shrublands are major vegetation units delineated in the classification of natural vegetation of the various continents of the earth (Küchler, 1964; Walter, 1979; di Castri *et al.*, 1981; Williams, 1979). In arid and semiarid regions, shrublands are the principal vegetation types. Some examples are the chaparral of Mediterranean climates, the Monte in the rain shadow of the Andes Mountains of western Argentina, shrublands of central Asian deserts, and the desert shrub communities of the southwestern desert of the United States and northwestern Mexico. These shrublands and others have one thing in common—they are ecologically very tolerant to stress.

A. *Pristine Conditions under No Management*

Under pristine conditions shrubs and understory grasses and forbs generally maintain a dynamic balance in species composition. However, shifts in composition and dominance of major vegetation components have occurred in the past as a result of geologic and climatic changes. One of the best-documented examples is in the American Southwest, where a gradual shift from a mesic to a xeric climate during the early Tertiary period resulted in the development of a microphyllous geoflora. Dry-tropic shrubs and grasses evolved together in the arid region and share dominance, according to Patton (1982).

In a generalized way, shrubs and grasses are relatively compatible in their codominance of a plant community. The deep root system of shrubs (Phillips, 1962) allows them to exploit the limited precipitation that percolates deeply into the soil, which thus sustains the shrub during periods of moisture deficit. In contrast, grasses have a shallow and highly diffuse root system that intercepts percolating soil moisture during periods of precipitation. When dry periods occur, grasses are able to go into dormancy and escape the adverse effects of drought.

Impacts from animal use have also influenced the evolutionary development of shrubs. In addition to the natural defenses of plants, shrubs and grasses appear to have a degree of latitude for sustaining a moderate amount of defoliation. Indeed, this is the basis for managing grazing at some sustainable level of proper use (Heady, 1975; Stoddart *et al.*, 1975). This level of use is based on the premise that plants have evolved under a tolerable amount of browsing or grazing use (Donart, 1984). Low and Berlin (1984) cited numerous studies that show photosynthesis to be well below the level that is possible and removal of some leaves may well stimulate the remaining leaves to be more efficient. In simulated grazing studies of *Symphoricarpos* and grasses, Willard and McKell (1973) found that a moderate amount of twig removal stimulated shrub regrowth. However, excessive defoliation reduced the vigor of the grasses and caused them to die out after a period of 3 years.

B. Grazing Abuses Result in Shrub Dominance

Resource use and misuse have had a significant impact on the dominance of shrubs in most world locations. A brief look at changes in shrublands in recent times may be helpful to understand some of the major influences causing changes in species composition involving shrubs. When a plant community is subjected to selective grazing pressure, shrub dominance may increase. Lacking some of the vigor and resistance to stress commonly displayed by shrubs, many palatable grasses and forbs may give way in successional replacement to shrubs.

Settlement of the southwestern United States and establishment of livestock ranches and farms in the 1800s and early 1900s took place under a glow of uninformed optimism and encouragement from the government to settle the land (Donart, 1984). Livestock numbers were immense, estimated to be 7.6 million head of cattle in the 11 western states in 1886 according to a report to the U.S. Senate (1936) and far exceeding the capacity of the range to sustain them on a continuing basis. Impacts from the large numbers of grazing animals coupled with periods of cyclic drought and other limiting conditions caused significant changes in plant composition.

In the southwestern desert shrub grassland type, *Prosopis juliflora* increased 50% based on longterm records maintained at the Jornada Experimental Range. The other woody species to show a marked increase was *Larrea tridentata*.

On the Colorado Plateau various species of *Juniperus* increased in density and encroached from hillsides on valley grasslands as a result of intense and selective grazing on the palatable grasses which reduced their ability to compete with juniper seedlings.

One of the most striking changes, however, was in the northern portion of the Great Basin, where species of *Artemisia* and various grasses had maintained a tenuous ecological balance under moderate grazing pressure from wildlife species (Tisdale and Hironaka, 1981). According to Young *et al.* (1984) the ecosystem was not adapted to concentrations of large herbivores, although small numbers of ungulate wildlife had historically made natural use of the available feed. Overgrazing by cattle and sheep selected out the palatable grasses and forbs, leaving the relatively unpalatable *Artemisia* to increase in density where it already existed and to encroach where it did not exist before. Destabilization of the plant community by overgrazing also opened the way for invasion of alien weeds such as the high-oxalate-containing *Halogeton glomeratus* and the annual grass *Bromus tectorum*.

In each of the preceding examples, the shrubs that increased in dominance at the expense of the other species in the plant community were generally unpalatable to livestock and ecologically agressive. Useful productivity for livestock grazing was significantly reduced and soil stability was impaired for optimum watershed functioning. As a result, the woody species became the target of control and replacement efforts. The experience of land managers in the southwestern United States in devising methods to control and manage undesirable shrub dominance has been useful to other areas of the world in designing management plans and improvement programs for shrub-related resource problems.

Under extreme exploitive use, even the most unpalatable shrubs may be eliminated. Thalen (1979) described the devastating soil erosion resulting from overgrazing of palatable shrubs and the removal of the remaining shrubs for fuel in Iraq. He concluded that over extensive areas, natural regeneration of a productive vegetation has become difficult or impossible because of increased runoff, removal of the topsoil, and formation of desert pavement that limits seed germination and establishment. Under this condition, seeds of desirable species are no longer being produced.

C. Fire and Government Protection Policies

Various *Artemisia* species are unable to resprout following fire, a characteristic that makes it possible to control them by conducting planned burns. In contrast, numerous shrubs and tree species have evolved various structures such as dormant buds at the base of the stem or a fire-resistant bark sufficient to protect the cambial layer for a short period of time.

Presently, rather strict managment policies of the public land management agencies in the United States limit the use of fire as a management tool. Box (1984) declared that the policy of quick suppression and or prohibition of using fire as a tool in controlling undesirable woody vegetation has led to an increase in density of shrubs and a large accumulation of fuel, such that the devastation from naturally occurring fires increases severalfold. Two of the objections to control burning are the risk of a burn escaping control and because desirable as well as undesirable species are killed.

Environmental policy has inhibited the use of certain tools of vegetation management in the United States. Restrictive policies regarding the use of chemicals have discouraged the development of new tools to selectively control undesirable vegetation. Often the species receiving the highest priority for control are agressive shrubs such as *Artemisia.* Using selective methods for control of undesirable species as well as establishing productive and useful species like *Atriplex canescens,* considerable improvement in productivity and multiple uses could be obtained.

III. Need for Improved Management

Few arid and semiarid shrublands used for grazing and other multiple purposes are currently producing at optimum levels. With improved management these lands could be more productive and stable. However, increased understanding of available management practices and the biology of shrubs and animals using them is needed. Undoubtedly social changes must also be initiated but these must be worked out in conformity with local customs and values (Gonzalez, 1978). Three major questions must be addressed to ensure the optimum use of shrublands:

- How much intensity of use or kinds of use are possible within the capacity of shrubs to maintain productivity?
- How can undesirable or unpalatable shrubs and other plants be kept from invading or increasing in areas where desired species are under intense use?
- What are the best methods for enhancing the productivity of shrubs to meet multiple requirements while at the same time maintaining a desired balance of shrubs, grasses, and forbs?

A. To Maintain a Balance in Species

Use of shrublands depends to a great degree on the inherent biological constitution of the plants involved. Critical periods of phenological/ physiological development involving germination, establishment, growth, reproduction, and resistance to environmental stress should be understood as a basis for avoiding intensive use at vulnerable times. Low periods of physiological and growth activity must be considered in determining the intensity and timing of plant use. George (1976) showed that continued removal of new growth of *Symphoricarpos oreophilus* depleted carbon reserves to the point that plants died even though a portion of stored carbohydrate was still present but apparently not available for transloca- tion from storage tissues. Experiments in clipping shrubs at various seasons have shown that regrowth can be stimulated as long as growing points are not destroyed. Willard and McKell (1973) found the highest number of new shoots and the greatest survival rate to be associated with a stimulated management schedule resembling rest–rotation grazing. Lopping of shrub or tree stems for emergency feed for sheep in Australia has its limits according to Everist (1969), who advised that cutting should be sufficiently high on the stem to preclude sheep from consuming the subsequent new shoots. Thinning dense stands of *Acacia aneura* increased overall land productivity but excessive thinning reduced land stability.

B. To Manipulate Ecological Succession

Plant control may be approached in different ways depending on environ- mental circumstances and shrub biology. In some cases, control of un- palatable shrubs may be necessary to keep them from increasing in dominance when palatable shrubs and other forage species are under intense grazing pressure (Vallentine, 1980). This situation occurs frequent- ly and is a major reason why great emphasis was placed on *Artemisia tridentata* control—even eradication (Cook, 1958) by plowing and seeding perennial grasses in the 1940–1950 period in the western United States. In other situations control may be less demanding and requires only the manipulation of plant populations to prevent less desirable species from becoming too dominant, such as aerial application of tebuthiuron pellets to sites infested with *Larrea tridentata* and *Flourensia cernua* (Herbel, 1984) or by treating individual plants to deter invading species from becoming established in areas where they are not desired (National Research Council, 1968).

C. To Enhance Ecosystem Capacity to Sustain Use

Often the various uses of shrubs overlap or occur concurrently. The obvious combinations are grazing, wildlife habitat, and protecting the soil surface of watersheds. In countries where fuel is in short supply, shrubs and trees may be cut for use in cooking fires (Thalen, 1979) and charcoal manufac- ture (Kabagambe, 1978), thus removing them from any other uses. To obtain the optimum benefits from shrubs, some form of management is necessary to allocate the consumptive multiple uses while at the same time maintaining the functional or nonconsumptive uses. Many strategies have been developed to enhance the productivity of shrublands, but many of the methods are expensive, are only partially effective, and must be used in combination with other methods. One of the most obvious management strategies is restriction of grazing intensity or time of grazing use.

IV. Improving Shrubland Productivity

Strategies for improving shrubland productivity and use fall into two groups. The first group uses direct methods for controlling undesirable shrubs such as chemicals, fire, biological systems, and mechanical means. The objective is to keep shrubs from dominating more desirable species and make way for plants that can maintain or increase ecosystem productivity. The second group involves replacement of undesirable species and managing animal and human use consistent with the biological requirements of the plants in the system. Many of the main principles and strategies for shrub control and rangeland improvement are discussed by Vallentine (1980), Stoddart *et al.* (1975), and the National Research Council (1984).

A. *Control of Undesirable and Unpalatable Shrubs*

1. Fire

A key element in controlling shrubs with fire is the vulnerability of vital plant parts to damage by high temperatures generated by the combustion of fuel from understory species and the shrubs themselves (Wright, 1984). In East Africa many of the climatic bushland and woodland types would attain thicket status were it not for fire, some naturally occurring and some set by man, as a means of maintaining a balance between shrubs and grasses (Pratt and Gwynne, 1977). Many grasses are able to survive a fire if the duration is short and the amount of fuel is low. Such conditions result in a lower temperature near the ground than in levels above in dense fuel (McKell *et al.*, 1962). In the shrublands of the Great Basin of the western United States, fire has been a qualified success in controlling *Artemisia.* However, problems in stimulating regrowth of undesirable shrubs such as *Chrysothamnus,* the destruction of valuable forage species, the potential liability that could result from a loss of fire control, and public criticism arising from environmental impacts have reduced government management agency plans for including control burns in management operations (Box, 1984).

Shrubs such as chamise (*Adenostema fasiculatum*) have evolved the ability to resprout vigorously after fire and new growth following burning must be treated with an herbicide. Subsequently, the area must be seeded with replacement species to take advantage of the temporary opening of the plant community (Bently, 1967). Often the occurrence of a control burn or a wildfire has the advantage of reducing the density of fuel, which reduces the hazard of a more disastrous fire in the future as well as opening up the area for wildlife (Heady, 1975).

2. Chemicals

Several hormone-type chemicals are effective in controlling shrubs, although the number is considerably less than the types that are available for control of herbaceous species (Table I). Certain features of shrubs make them difficult to control by herbicide application (Vallentine, 1980). Leaves with a thick epidermis or a waxy cuticular layer restrict the entry of herbicides. Dormant buds at the base of stems may initiate regrowth quickly if only the aerial parts are damaged. Periods of low physiological activity depress the effectiveness of chemical action in tissues and restrict translocation to meristematic areas, where herbicidal action is most pronounced (National Research Council, 1968). Deep root systems may preclude uptake of shallowly percolating soil-applied herbicides, but with appropriate herbicide formulations, pellets applied to the soil surface can be effective on a number of species (Morton *et al.,* 1978).

One of the most effective chemicals used in controlling shrubs is 2, 4-dichlorophenoxyacetic acid (2, 4-D), which acts as a plant growth hormone and adversely affects respiration, food reserves, and cell division. Variations in chemical formulation as well as combinations of this herbicide with other chemicals have been the basis for effective control of many undesirable shrubs. Several other chemicals are effective on a wide range of shrubs (Table I). Application rates are generally low with hormone-type chemicals. Selectivity among shrubs, and between shrubs and other broadleaf species, is generally limited to differentiation between dicotyledons and monocotyledons. Often the best selectivity can be obtained by seasonal timing, spray additives such as surfactants, and spot treatments instead of area application.

Time of application is critical for optimum effectiveness and minimum amount of herbicide used. Generally, plants should be in a physiologically active state, which generally means that soil moisture must be favorable for water uptake and translocation. Ambient temperatures should be between 55° and 75°F and be favorable for active plant growth and minimum volatilization of the chemical. Hyder *et al.* (1962) showed how critical timing can be, based on their studies for control of both *Artemisia* and

Table I. Herbicides for application to undesirable shrubs

Common and chemical names	Type and application	Physiological effects	Some typical shrub species controlled
Ammate, ammonium sulfamate	Inorganic translocated spray	Absorbed through foliage or cut surface, cell poison	*Juniperus* spp. *Quercus* spp. *Salix* spp.
Dicamba, 3,6-dichloro-*o*-anisic acid	Auxinlike foliar and soil applied	Suppresses growth like a growth regulator	*Prosopis juliflora* *Rhus trilobata* *Sarcobatus vermiculatus*
2,4-D, (2,4-dichlorophenoxy)acetic acid and derivatives	Phenoxy translocated selective foliar spray	Disrupts respiration, cell division	*Adenostema fasiculatum* *Artemisia tridentata* *Ceanothus cuneatus* *Chrysothamnus* spp. *Quercus* spp.
Garlon, triclophyr[(3,5,6-trichloro-2-pyridinl)oxy]acetic acid	Translocated foliage spray on tree, stems	Auxinlike growth regulator	*Quercus* spp. *Rosa* spp. Root-sprouting spp.
Glyphosate, (Roundup) *N*-(phosphonomethyl)-glycene	Aliphatic translocated broad-spectrum aerial spray	Interferes with amino acid synthesis	*Alnus tenuifolia* *Quercus* spp. *Rosa* spp. *Rubis strigosus*
Picloram, 4-amino-3,5,6-trichloropicolinic acid and in other combinations	Hormone-type absorbed from foliage or by roots from soil	Interferes with hormone systems and growth, chlorosis	*Acacia farnesiana* *Juniperus* spp. *Prosopis juliflora* *Quercus* spp. *Rosa bracteata*
Silvex, 2-(2,4,5-trichlorophenoxy) propionic acid	Phenoxy selective translocated foliar spray	Affects respiration, cell division	*Opuntia* spp. *Prosopis juliflora* *Quercus douglassii* *Tamarix* spp.
Tebuthiuron, *N*-{5-(1,1-dimethyl-ethyl)-1,3,4-thiadiazol-2-yl}-*N,N'*-dimethyl urea	Substituted urea, nonselective translocated soil sterilant	Inhibits photosynthesis, absorbed through roots	*Juniperus osteosperma* *Prosopis juliflora* *Quercus douglassii* *Rosa bracteata* *Larrea tridentata* *Flourensia cernua*

Notes: Many chemicals are not registered for use on shrubs even though they would be biologically effective. Possible reasons are that the market size may not justify the testing required to provide the response data necessary for including a particular species in the licence. Herbicidal activity of the above chemicals may be expected in other world locations for shrubs that are physiologically and ecologically similar.

Chrysothamnus at various times of herbicide application. They found that the optimum herbicide application period for *Chrysothamnus* was more restrictive than the relatively long period for controlling *Artemisia* in mixed stands. Application of 2,4-D at 6.6 kg/ha (3 lb/acre) active ingredient had to be timed for optimum effect on *Chrysothamnus* to preclude controlling only the *Artemisia* and leaving the plant community open for quick proliferation of *Chrysothamnus*.

Individual shrubs and small trees such as *Quercus douglassii* can be controlled by chopping into stems and applying a translocatable chemical full strength to the cut surface. Another method is by distributing pellets of chemicals such as tebuthiuron or picloram to the basal area of shrubs and waiting for the pellets to release their chemical for percolation into the root zone (Morton *et al.*, 1978). Selective area application may allow a thinning action rather than broad-scale control. Depending on the suspectibility of various species to the type of chemical used, such applications may also control other species in the understory of the shrubs.

Chemicals can be judiciously used in conjunction with other shrub control treatments such as spraying 2,4-D to control regrowth from the basal area of species such as *Adenostema fasciculatum* following fire (Leonard and Harvey, 1965). Herbicides can also be used to shift the balance of species by reducing the dominance of undesirable shrubs (Perry *et al.*, 1967) but also instituting grazing management to allow important forage species to regain productivity. After two applications of 2,4-D to Macartney rose in Texas, Hoffman (1968) reported an increase in forage production from 2800 kg/ha to 5400 kg/ha and range carrying capacity increased threefold.

3. Mechanical

The most drastic shrub control strategy is by mechanical means. Mechanical methods involve the use of mechanical force to cut, crush, tear up, dig out, or break off shrub stems and roots (Vallentine, 1980). Equipment may range from an axe to a heavy machine pulled by a crawler tractor (Range Reseeding Equipment Committee, 1965). Many types of mechanical equipment have been developed for shrub control according to the requirements of the situation. Rangeland plows and disks can dig out low shrubs such as *Artemisia* spp. Heavy anchor chains drawn between two crawler tractors can uproot or break off larger shrubs and trees such as *Juniperus* (Phillips, 1977) and mixed shrubs (Scifres and Mutz, 1978). Bulldozers can push over shrub thickets such as mulga in Australia (Everist, 1972) for drought feeding so that sheep can utilize the sprouting stems and the regrowth of grasses. However, as Harrington *et al.* (1984) point out, soil disturbance may allow seedlings of the vigorous shrub species to establish. Heavy brush cutters or root plows have been used on *Prosopis juliflora* (Range Reseeding Equipment Committee, 1965). New shoots from roots and stem bases can be a problem if not treated properly. Resprouting species must be removed from the soil completely as with a root plow or by apply an herbicide to control regrowth (Herbel, 1973).

Some of the disadvantages of using mechanical equipment are obvious. High energy costs in the 1970s and 1980s precluded the use of most heavy equipment because the costs of control exceeded the returns from greater range productivity. Incomplete plant control of target species as well as indiscriminate control of desirable shrubs and forbs create problems for widespread use of mechanical means for multiple-use resource management. Drastic disturbance of soil and vegetation requires that treated areas be seeded to desired species. However, judicious use in choosing small areas to be treated rather than large-scale plant control make it possible to be selective in controlling high-density patches of undesirable shrubs.

4. Biological Agents

Limited success has been achieved in controlling some species using natural biological pests of target species. Absolute specificity is required, however, to avoid having the natural pest turn to alternate hosts and thus eliminate valuable plants.

A demonstrated use of biological control of shrubs is by herding goats on them. Provenza *et al.* (1983) and Merrill and Taylor (1976) showed that goats will consume large portions of shrubs sufficient to reduce them but control cannot be complete without sacrificing goat productivity. The key to any type of biological control is appropriate management of the control organism. Selectivity is necessary because the species that are preferred for retention must be allowed the opportunity to survive and benefit from the reduction in competition. Appropriately conducted grazing management has the opportunity to deal with difference in attractiveness to the grazing animal by scheduling the season, intensity, or type of animal.

B. Range Improvements Enhance Shrubland Productivity

1. Seeding and Planting

Following any one of the previously described control measures, seeding of a mixture of desired species is a necessity (Herbel, 1973). Because of the often indiscriminate control of some species by most control methods, the seed mixture can replace some of the natural diversity as well as introduce adapted species that are highly productive. Seeding provides an opportunity to include shrub species that will contribute stability and diversity as well as useful productivity to the ecosystem (McKell, 1986). Numerous palatable shrub species have been seeded or planted under field conditions for improved productivity and stability. Reports from various world locations indicate that positive results may be expected: Hadri (1980) reported on large-scale plantings of *Acacia cyanophylla, Atriplex canescens, A. halimus,* and *Opuntia* (*Ficus indica*) in Libya, Forti (1971) found that *Atriplex nummularia* plantings in Israel provided necessary fodder in the dry season, Draz (1978) found that planting *Atriplex* in Syria was a valuable adjunct to reestablishment of the traditional Hema grazing system, Otsyina *et al.* (1983) showed that *Atriplex* and other chenopod shrubs provided a valuable supplement for sheep grazing in the fall and winter in the Great Basin of the western United States, Ueckert (1985) advised establishing special-use shrub pastures in south Texas for emergency forage during drought, Malcolm *et al.* (1980) developed a "niche" seeder for establishment of chenopod shrubs in salinized lands in Western Australia, and Olivares and Gasto (1981) showed how *Atriplex repanda* could be used for improved rangeland productivity in Chile. Container-grown plants produced in nurseries have been successfully transplanted to sites where precipitation may be inadequate for dependable establishment from seeds. Subsequent protection of seeded or planted areas has been shown in some cases to create suitable conditions for spontaneous seed production, thus triggering the return of desirable native species (Draz, 1978).

Where plantations of shrubs are to be used for industrial crops such as jojoba (*Simmondsia chinensis*) or guayule (*Parthenium argentatum*), management of the plantation must be on an agricultural basis. Usual practices of land preparation, irrigation, weed control, fertilization, and harvesting must be adapted to the growth form and biological requirements of the shrub crop. Whittaker (1982) reported that jojoba plantations are commonly established by seeding rows 12 to 15 feet apart. The interrow space may be used for short-rotation crops while waiting for the jojoba to begin bearing, which may vary from 3 to 5 years. Although more costly, using transplants developed from rooted cuttings or produced in tissue culture from plants of superior characteristics and known sex is a better way to obtain a plantation of high production potential than by planting genetically variable seeds.

2. Grazing Management

As generally employed, grazing management seeks to regulate the intensity, season, and distribution of grazing use by livestock (Heady, 1975; Stoddart *et al.,* 1975). Considerably less management can be done with wildlife. Many methods have been devised to implement the above objectives and are self-descriptive, that is, season-long management starts at determined dates or stages of plant development and limits the number of animals to be served until the end of the season. A rotation system shifts grazing use to a new pasture or range location on a predetermined schedule. Rest–rotation grazing allows one location to be completely rested for 1 year as heavy grazing use is rotated to other pastures on a schedule. In a high-intensity–low-frequency grazing system (Acocks, 1966) all animals are concentrated in one area for high-intensity use but are subsequently rotated to one pasture area after another. The frequency of animals being returned to the first area is limited until a sufficient period of time has elapsed for plants to recover. In the latter two systems, animal selectivity for the most desired species is reduced because animals are obliged to graze most if not all the species because of high animal density. Shrubs of low palatability are thus utilized to some degree along with the more preferred species and the area does not experience the selective or competitive advantage available in low-intensity grazing.

In spite of the reduction in competitive advantage provided by the grazing system, research has shown that grazing management cannot by itself significantly reduce undesirable shrubs (Donart, 1984). However, grazing management can moderate the impacts of differential palatability and aggressive regrowth common to shrubs that would otherwise become dominant.

3. Combination of Methods

A combination of methods is often the best approach in managing shrublands (Heady, 1975). Some obvious combinations are: controlled burning, seeding, and grazing management; mechanical control of unproductive species, seeding of a mixture of grasses, forbs, and shrubs, and light application of a selective herbicide and grazing management to retard the return of woody species. Innovative combinations of animal types, such as goats (Merrill and Taylor, 1976) to concentrate on rough forages and cattle to concentrate on grassy forages, distribute the grazing impact to a wide range of plant species and help to reduce selective use. As a result, grazing management is most useful for keeping an ecological balance between grasses and shrubs when it is properly applied. Otherwise, selective grazing may increase problems of shrub dominance.

V. Summary

Under pristine conditions a dynamic balance among shrubs, grasses, and forbs may prevail in plant communities. Unregulated and selective grazing by livestock has shifted many plant communities to a situation where aggressive shrubs of low palatability dominate. Good management is the key to maintaining a desired species balance. Drastic range improvement strategies such as burning, application of selective herbicides, or mechanical control of unwanted species may be used to restructure unproductive plant communities where undesirable shrubs dominate and to facilitate subsequent improvement methods. A desirable mixture of species in which palatable shrubs are included should be seeded after any drastic shrub control practice. A combination of management strategies may facilitate maintenance of an effective and productive plant community in which shrubs perform a vital role in meeting multiple-use opportunities.

References

Acocks, J. P. (1966). Non-selective grazing as a means of veldt reclamation. *Proc. — Grassl. Soc. South. Afr.* **1**, 33–39.

Bently J. R. (1967). Conversion of chaparral areas to grassland: Techniques used in California. *U.S., Dep. Agric. Handb.* **328.**

Box, T. W. (1984). Role of land treatments on public and private lands. *In* "Developing Strategies for Rangeland Management," pp. 1397–1419. Nat. Res. Counc. Committee, Westview Press, Boulder, Colorado.

Cook, C. W. (1958). Sagebrush eradication and broadcast seeding. *Utah, Agric. Exp. Stn., Bull.* **408.**

di Castri, F., Goodall, D. W., and Specht, R. L. eds). (1981). "Mediterranean-Type Shrublands," Ecosystems of the World, Vol. 11. Elsevier, Amsterdam.

Donart, G. B. (1984). The history and evolution of western rangelands in relation to woody plant communities. *In* "Developing Strategies for Rangeland Management," pp. 1235–1258. Nat. Res. Counc. Committee, Westview Press, Boulder, Colorado.

Draz, O. (1978). Revival of the Hema system of range reserves as a basis for the Syrian range development program. *Proc. Int. Rangel. Congr., 1st,* pp 100–103.

Everist, S. (1969). Use of fodder trees and shrubs. *Queensl. Dep. Primary Ind., Plant Ind., Leafl.* **1024.**

Everist, S. (1972). Australia. *In* "Wildland Shrubs: Their Biology and Utilization" (C. M. McKell, J. P. Blaisdell, and J. R. Goodin, eds.), USDA For. Serv. Gen. Tech. Rep. INT-1, pp. 16–25. Utah State University, Logan.

Forti, M. (1971). "Introduction of Fodder Shrubs and Their Evaluation for Use in Semiarid Areas of the Northwestern Negev." Div. Life Sci., Negev Inst. Arid Zone Res., Beer Shiva, Israel.

George, M. R. (1976). Distribution of carbon reserves in snowberry (*Symphoricarpos oreophilus*). Ph.D. Dissertation, Utah State University, Logan.

Gonzalez, N., ed. (1978). "Social and Technological Management in Dry Lands," AAAS Sel. Symp. Ser. Westview Press, Boulder, Colorado.

Hadri, H. (1980). The planting of browse species in pastoral improvement projects in Libya. *In* "Browse in Africa: The Current State of Knowledge" pp. 135–137. (H. N. Le Houérou, ed.), International Livestock Center for Africa, Addis Ababa, Ethiopia.

Harrington, G. N., Wilson, A. D., and Young M. D. (1984). "Management of Australia's Rangelands." CSIRO, East Melbourne, Australia.

Heady, H. F. (1975). "Rangeland Management." McGraw-Hill, New York.

Herbel, C. H. (1973). Some developments related to seeding western rangelands. Range research and range problems. *Crop Sci. Soc. Am., Spec. Publ.* **3,** 75–80.

Herbel, C. H. (1984). Successional patterns and productivity potentials of the range vegetation in the warm, arid portions of the southwestern United States. *In* "Developing Strategies for Rangeland Management," pp. 1333–1365. Nat. Res. Counc. Committee, Westview Press, Boulder, Colorado.

Hoffman, G. O. (1968). Range improvement with the use of herbicides. *Abst. Pap., 21st Annu. Meet., ASRM,* pp. 28–29.

Hyder, D. N., Sneva, F. A., and Freed, V. H. (1962). Susceptibility of big sagebrush and green rabbitbrush to 2,4-D as related to certain environmental, phenological, and physiological conditions. *Weeds* **10,** 288–295.

Kabagambe, D. M. (1978). "Aspects of Resource Conservation and Utilization. The Role of Charcoal Industry in the Kenya Economy," Work. Pap. No. 271. Inst. Dev. Stud., University of Nairobi.

Küchler, A. W. (1964). Potential natural vegetation of the conterminous United States (map and manual). *Amer. Geog. Soc., Spec. Publ.* **35.**

Leonard, O. A., and Harvey, W. A. (1965). Chemical control of woody plants. *Bull. —Calif. Agric. Exp. Stn.* **812**

Low, B. S., and Berlin, J. A. (1984). Natural selection and the management of rangelands. *In* "Developing Strategies for Rangeland Managements," pp. 1179–1234. Nat. Res. Counc. Committee, Westview Press, Boulder, Colorado.

McKell, C. M. (1986). Shrubs to diversify a crested wheatgrass rangeland. *In* "Crested Wheatgrass: Its Values, Problems, and Myths" (K. L. Johnson, ed.), pp. 109–117. Utah State University, Logan.

McKell, C. M., Wilson, A. M., and Kay, B. L. (1962). Effective burning of rangelands infested with medusahead. *Weeds* **10,** 125–131.

Malcolm, C. V., Swaan, T. C., and Ridings, H. I. (1980). Niche-seeding for broadscale forage shrub establishment in saline soils. *Int. Symp. Salt-Affected Soils,* pp. 539–544.

Merrill, L. B., and Taylor, C. A. (1976). Take note of the versatile goat. *Rangeman's J.* **3,** 74–76.

Morton, H. L., Lamar Smith, E., Olivera, M., and Hull, H. M. (1978). Soil applied herbicides for brush control in southwestern United States and northeast Brazil. *Proc. Int. Rangel. Congr., 1st,* pp. 647–650.

National Research Council (1968). Weed control. Subcommittee on weeds. *N.A.S.-N.R.C. Publ.* **1597.**

National Research Council (1984). "Developing Strategies for Rangeland Management." Westview Press, Denver, Colorado.

Olivares, A., and Gasto, J. (1981). "*Atriplex repanda.* Organizacion y manejo de ecosistemas con arbustos forrajeras," Cienc. Agric. No. 7. For. Universidad de Chile. Santiago.

Otsyina, R. M., McKell, C. M., Malechek, J. M., and Van Epps, G. A. (1983). Potential of *Atriplex* and other chenopod shrubs to increasing range productivity and fall and winter grazing use. *USDA For. Serv. Gen. Tech. Rep. INT* **INT-172,** p 215–219.

Patton, D. R. (1982). Management applications of biotic community data. *Desert Plants* **4**(1-4), 7–16.

Perry, C. A., McKell, C. M., Goodin, J. R., and Little, T. M. (1967). Chemical control of an old stand of chapparral to increase range productivity. *J. Range Manage.* **20,** 166–169.

Phillips, T. A. (1977). "An Analysis of Some Forest Service Chaining Projects in Region 4, 1954–1975." USDA For. Serv. Ogden, Utah.

Phillips, W. S. (1962). Depth of roots in soil. *Ecology* **44,** 424.

Pratt, D. J., and Gwynne, M. D. (1977). "Rangeland Management and Ecology in East Africa." Hodder & Stoughton, London.

Provenza, F. D., Bowns, J. E., Urness, P. J., Malechek, J. C., and Butcher, J. E. (1983). Biological manipulation of blackbrush by goat browsing. *J. Range Manage.* **27**, 437–443.

Range Reseeding Equipment Committee (1965). "Handbook of Range Seeding Equipment" (rev.). USDA AND USDI, U.S. Govt. Printing Office, Washington, D.C.

Scifres, C. J., and Mutz, J. L. (1978). Herabaceous vegetation changes following applications of tebuthiuron for brush control. *J Range Manage.* **31**, 375–378.

Stoddart, L., Smith, A. D., and Box, T. W. (1975). "Range Management," 3rd ed. McGraw-Hill, New York.

Thalen, D. C. P. (1979). "Ecology and Utilization of Desert Shrub Rangelands in Iraq." Junk, The Hague.

Tisdale, E. W., and Hironaka, M. (1981). The sagebrush–grass region: A review of the ecological literature. *Univ. Idaho, For. Wildl. Range Exp. Stn. Bull* **33.**

Ueckert, D. N. (1985). Use of shrubs for rangeland revegetation. *Proc. Int. Ranchers Roundup Tex. Agric. Ext. Serv., 1985,* pp. 1900–2196.

U.S. Senate (1936). "A Report on the Western Range: A Great but Neglected Natural Resource," U.S. Senate Doc. 199, 74th Congress. U.S. Govt. Printing Office, Washington, D.C.

Vallentine, J. (1980). "Range Development and Improvements," 2nd ed. Brigham Univ. Press, Provo, Utah.

Walter, H. (1979). "Vegetation of the Earth: An Ecological System of the Geo-biosphere," 2nd ed. Springer-Verlag, New York.

Whittaker, C. A. (1982). Considerations in developing a jojoba plantation. *In* "Jojoba and Its Uses, Through 1982," Proc. 5th Intl. Conf. Arid Lands, pp 115–118. Office of Arid Lands, University of Arizona, Tucson.

Willard, E., and McKell, C. M. (1973). Simulated grazing management systems in relation to shrub growth responses. *J. Range Manage.* **26,** 171–174.

Williams, O. B. (1979). Ecosystems of Australia. *In* "Arid Land Ecosystems: Structure, Functioning and Management" (D. W. Goodall and R. A. Perry, eds.), pp. 145–212. Cambridge Univ. Press, London and New York.

Wright, H. A. (1984). Response to successional patterns and productivity potentials of the range vegetation in the warm, arid portions of the southwestern United States. *In* "Developing Strategies for Rangeland Management," pp. 1369. Nat. Res. Counc. Committee, Westview Press, Boulder, Colorado.

Young, J. A., Evans, R. A., and Eckert, R. E., Jr. (1984). Successional patterns and productivity potentials of the sagebrush and salt desert ecosystems. *In* "Developing Strategies for Rangeland Management," pp. 1259–1399. Nat. Res. Counc. Committee, Westview Press, Boulder, Colorado.

VII

Social and Economic Aspects of Shrubs

Throughout the world many people's social customs and adaptations have developed and been influenced by their use of the plants in their surroundings. The first chapter in this section is a case study of the Pokot people of north eastern Kenya, and is but one vignette of many describing the influence of shrubs on people's social customs and everyday existence. Living in a shrub-dominated semiarid region, the Pokot people use shrubs for livestock fodder, construction of shelters and animal enclosures, fuel wood, and many personal needs.

Intensive use of shrubs in traditional societies as well as in more modern cultures is predicated upon economic considerations. Chapter 30 deals with an economic analysis of shrub establishment on a large project basis. Examples of investments on an area basis and returns on investment are provided. Although it is interesting to speculate on the potential outcome of either intensifying a current shrub use or finding new uses, the "bottom line" is economic worth—something of value must be realized in return for the time and expenses invested.

29

The Pokot Way with Thorny Shrubs: A Case Example

Francis Paine Conant

I. Introduction

This chapter looks at the Pokot people in East Africa in relation to their management and use of shrubs. The Pokot are a farming and herding people in northwestern Kenya and place a major focus on use and management of *Acacia miseria* and *A. mellifera*. These shrubs are found widely in the drier parts of Pokotland and are shrubs or trees 25 or 30 feet high with paired, sharply recurved thorns (Dale and Greenway, 1961). They also are widely distributed in semiarid and arid areas in East Africa (Pratt and Gwynne, 1977). At least three strategies can be observed in the Pokot case that are significant for the use and management of these shrubs as well as for survival in dryland areas. Recognition of these strategies might improve the chance of success of development projects aimed at shrubland areas of the African Sahel, and perhaps beyond. Thus far innovation and planned development of traditional peoples in semiarid areas have had almost no success (Bates and Conant, 1981; Goldschmidt, 1982).

The three Pokot strategies are (1) integration of herding and farming subsistence activities, (2) multiple uses of shrubs and their products, and

(3) the active engagement of women as well as men (and children) in the maintenance of rangeland quality. Unless the social arrangements underlying these strategies are recognized, innovations and attempts to develop pastoral peoples in semiarid areas are likely to remain difficult to implement.

The significance of the Pokot case is not that it is representative of all other users of dry shrubland areas, rather, the significance lies in the fact that Pokot traditional values and social arrangements underlying their subsistence strategies are still essentially intact. Some idea of the importance of social arrangements in the use and management of shrubland areas can be gained by looking more closely at the Pokot case. In addition, the wealth of knowledge the Pokot have of their environments is still in force—and available. One of the striking accomplishments of contemporary anthropology has been the development of field techniques for eliciting the knowledge a people have of their surroundings. Pokot understanding of the world around them is communicated using concepts and metaphors quite foreign to Western scientists, but *what* the Pokot know can be of vital importance to scientists and resource managers in trying to understand, for example, processes affecting desertification in shrubland areas.

An important feature of the basic management strategies is the exploitation of areas of mixed vegetation rather than those having uniform potential. This management strategy spans the complete range of environments utilized by the Pokot. The characteristics of the thorny shrubs in Pokotland influence their local uses and management. Multiple uses of shrubs (and other plants) are traditional to the Pokot and their neighbors. In Pokot perceptions, all resources have some value *relative to some other*. Some shrubs are more useful than others; none is a "weed." This perception is important in terms of Pokot management techniques.

II. Shrubland Populations and the Pokot Case

The world's dry, shrubland areas are or have been homeground to representatives of all the major human races, all language families, and cultural patterns ranging from the simplest to the highly complex. Dry shrublands, past and present, have been exploited by combinations of almost every known traditional subsistence system, including gathering and hunting, swidden or shifting cultivation, open-range livestock management, and irrigation farming. Peoples exploiting dry shrublands adjacent to coastal areas or lake systems (two examples, respectively, are Peru and Chad) also have fishing and shellfish gathering as subsistence options integrated with that part of the livelihood gained from shrubland utilization. Major cities, some of great antiquity, continue to exist at the edge or in the midst of shrubland areas, as in the case of Niamey just north of the great bend of the Niger River in West Africa and, in India, the walled cities of Rajistan.

If shrubland areas are equated with arid and semiarid areas (such as the African Sahel or the Sonoran Desert in southwestern United States), then together they account for about one-third of the earth's land surface. Given such large numbers and such great diversity in shrubland populations, why focus on a relatively small group such as the Pokot, in a remote part of Kenya?

The first consideration is that Pokot traditional values and environmental perceptions are still largely intact, thus allowing us the opportunity to understand how a cultural system so different from our own has succeeded in managing a notably difficult and volatile environment. The Pokot survived the colonial period without being displaced from their homeland south of Lake Turkana and east and northeast of Mt. Elgon.

The Pokot have largely succeeded in preserving their traditional "mix" of subsistence strategies: shifting cultivation on the steep slopes of the eastern branch of the Rift Valley escarpment and, on the lowland plains, open-range management of livestock (cattle, goats, sheep, camels, and donkeys). Unlike Masai herders, who were forcibly relocated to southern Kenya and Tanzania, the Pokot herders have been able to maintain exchange relations with their farming kin in the foothills of the escarpment. The surplus of the herds (milk, meat, blood, hide, horns) is exchanged for surplus of the farms (grain, a staple food among the herders for making porridge, beans, cucurbits, spices). The herding population on the Masol Plains in the West Pokot District of Kenya used to number about 25,000 persons of both sexes and all ages, as compared to some 100,000 farmers in the surrounding hills and mountains. Because of recent events the number of herders has been greatly reduced.

The herding and farming populations are by no means separate, as government officials and other outsiders have tended to treat them. Young men from the farming areas may elect to move onto the plains as apprentice herders, seek their fortune as raiders and traders, and only return to the farming area once they have accumulated some wealth in livestock and have access to sufficient land to farm. Some young women "marry out" from the farming areas and into the herding population. Women from farming areas are essential brokers in the exchange of herding for farming surplus produce. Women also are largely responsible for the continuing availability of the staple grains needed in the diet of the herders. Thus the distinction between "farmers" and "herders" as *competing* subsistence economies is by no means shared by the Pokot themselves. Pokot children grow up within a unified culture of shared knowledge of subsistence strategies and many of the same values (Edgerton, 1971).

Variants of this integration of farming and herding subsistence areas are widespread throughout the African Sahel. The mix of subsistence strategy is probably of considerable antiquity and represents a successful adaptation for the exploitation of environmentally fragile areas such as the semiarid shrublands and grasslands of the Sahel. Long-term experience of the area and its multiple environments have resulted in the accumulation of knowledge about the relative value of different forms of plant cover, from grass and shrublands to hardwood forests.

The second consideration is that the Pokot have succeeded in maintaining their exchange strategy of shrubland and farmland produce in spite of quite intensive efforts (especially in the farming area) to get them to adopt more productive ways. How long the traditional system can last is an open question, given the efforts of missionaries, veterinary officers, argonomists, and rangeland managers. The Pokot shrublands and grasslands have figured episodically in projects for roads, wells, dams, airstrips, and tourist lodges by a variety of national and international funding agencies. But despite these attentions some Pokot (especially those living away from administrative centers) have maintained their traditional subsistence and exchange system, which, in effect, integrate low-potential shrubland areas with higher-potential farming areas.

How the Pokot perceive this environment and their role within it involves a good deal more active management of their resources, in particular by women, than is generally acknowledged. This management, of course, depends on a store of acquired knowledge shared by men and women and transmitted from one generation to the next, sometimes in the context of ritual.

III. Pokot and Neighbors: Basic Management Strategies

The Pokot describe three major zones of exploitation (Porter, 1965). One is *masob*, a high and cold area where (and only relatively recently) a few sheep are kept for wool, and there is also some potato cultivation. The *kamass* is the most densely populated zone. It is at middle elevations (generally between 2500 and 1000 m above sea level), with a plant cover ranging from hardwood and bamboo forests at higher elevations to combretum shrubland down lower. The kamass is the prime area for cultivation of grain (sorghum, maize, and finger millet) and also beans and gourds.

The lowland plains, *psigogh*, are used mainly for open-range herding of livestock. Plant cover on the plains ranges from riverine forest and thicket to scattered shrubs and grassland. There is some grain grown on flood plains, and some tobacco grown on dry, higher ground. In the driest parts of the plains gravels are common, the grass is tufted, and *Acacia* spp. dominate the landscape.

For the Pokot it is not so much the differences between the masob, kamass, and psigogh that are so important as it is the way in which each ecozone merges with the other. In terms of usage, the basic Pokot strategy is exploitation of ecozones by utilizing a mix of subsistence techniques rather than reliance on one subsistence technique tailored to a single ecozone. Thus the members of each household (which is the basic unit of production) spread their efforts over several areas and utilize techniques appropriate to farming and herding under a variety of conditions.

This strategy of competence in multiple subsistence efforts rather than specialization in only one of them is clearly reflected in the spatial arrangement of the Pokot residential area or "neighborhood," the *korok*. Not uncommonly the korok includes two of the three major ecozones, and sometimes all three (Conant, 1965). The korok, in effect, is a subsistence system that is neither specifically nor physiographically clearly defined. Physically the korok is an interfluvial area with cultural markers at its upslope and downslope boundaries. As a unit of social space the korok serves as much to integrate subsistence activities as it does to separate them. Much the same is true of the age grade, *pin*. As among many other East African peoples, the Pokot age grades organize men (and among some peoples there may be parallel organizations for women) into groups characterizable as "oldest of the old," "elders," "warriors," and "youths."

Although the details may differ, the basic Pokot strategy of multiple subsistence efforts to take advantage of a variety of landscapes is widely reflected among their near neighbors as well as among more distant peoples. Jie and Turkana (Gulliver, 1955), Karamojong (N. Dyson-Hudson, 1966; R. Dyson-Hudson, 1972), the Sebei (Goldschmidt, 1976), Samburu and Rendille (Spencer, 1973), Nuer (Evans-Pritchard, 1940), and Dinka (Deng, 1972) are all committed to the traditional pattern of multiple subsistence strategies. In this literature, both old and new, there is also ample evidence for the role of women in the use and maintenance of natural resources, as among the Pokot.

IV. Pokot Maintenance of *Acacia* and Grassland

In East Africa it has long been recognized that certain species of *Acacia* are invaders and unless checked, tend to dominate grasses growing on gravelly soil. Active measures are required for the maintenance of a grassy cover if there is to be one. In the absence of such measures, impenetrable thickets develop and the area is all but lost to human use.

The speed and thoroughness with which *Acacia* "takes over" from the grasses was dramatically illustrated when, several hundred Pokot herding families were forced to withdraw from the Masol Plains because of events quite beyond their control—in this case heavily armed and motorized raiders intent on capturing cattle in the Karasuk and West Pokot districts for later slaughter and sale in parts of Uganda facing near-famine conditions. Under traditional conditions, cattle raiding is carried out with a minimum loss of life, with women, children, and the household goats almost always spared. Thus even though all cattle may have been driven off and some men killed, women and the goats remained, and the *Acacia* shrublands remained in check. In the 1970s, anyone standing in the way of the new-style cattle raiders was massacred. In 1974 the Pokot prudently withdrew from the Masol Plains: men, women, children, cattle, and goats fled the area.

Landsat data for before (1973) and after (1978) this withdrawal were used to estimate the change in the mix between grass and shrubs in a 70-km^2 herding area known as Simbol. By 1978 shrubs covered almost 50% of Simbol where before they amounted to about 24%; for the same period the grassy area was reduced from about 38% to 13% (Conant, 1983). Correspondence (1980–1984) with informants indicates that the *Acacia* has continued to spread, but to what extent awaits acquisition and analysis of additional Landsat data.

The withdrawal from the Masol Plains and the subsequent spread of *Acacia* provoked a number of inquiries into what mechanisms in normal times serve to keep the *Acacia* in check. At least four factors seem to be at work. The first is the mixed herds managed by the Pokot in which zebu cattle are outnumbered by goats often by 5 to 1 and sometimes by an even higher ratio. The goats regularly browse on the shoots, seed pods, twigs, leaves, and bark of the *Acacia* shrubs. Pokot women tend to be the managers of the household goats; men are almost always the managers of cattle.

A second factor is the multiple uses the Pokot find for the various kinds of *Acacia* on the plains. Perhaps the most extensive use is of the branches from the smaller trees and stems from the shrubs for building fences around the entire household encampment. In addition, each house or hut within the encampment has its own yard enclosed with *Acacia* fencing; further, there are separate thorn fences to separate mature cattle from goats, and separate byres for calves and kids. Daytime holdings pens sometimes are built outside the encampment area.

A medium-sized household encampment (4 adults, 8 children, and some 40 cattle and 200 goats) requires on the order of 2000 of fencing each year for the main household and an additional one-half kilometer of *Acacia* fencing for each dry-season cattlecamp. The households and camps are rebuilt each season from new materials, if possible (enormous numbers of fleas take over the abandoned household areas, making reuse almost impossible).

A third factor in checking the spread of *Acacia* is the annual firing of the plains. The firing seems to encourage the growth of new grass as much as it kills off new *Acacia* shoots. The Pokot themselves claim the firing has more effect on the grass than the thorn shrubs.

Acacia stems, bark, seeds, and flowers are also variously used as ingredients in infusions for a number of disorders, as a source of fiber for twine and lashings, for gum, and as dye. Log beehives are wedged into the higher branches of *Acacia* trees; both trees and shrubs are nesting areas for a variety of birds, and *Acacia* thickets are refuge areas for small game and fowl hunted by the Pokot. Since each kind of livestock in the Pokot mixed herd has its own feeding habits, it follows that Pokot women, often in charge of the goats, must be aware of the preferences and relative value of the shrubs and other vegetation on which their animals browse. Similarly, men must know the preferences and value of the various grasses preferred by the cattle. To a large extent both women and men share in the knowledge possessed by the other.

Among Pokot, as among other preliterate peoples, ritual is often the context in which knowledge is shared or communicated from older persons to younger, or from one segment of the community to another. One example of this is haruspexy, which is widely practiced in East Africa. The entrails of an animal (for the Pokot, most commonly a goat but occasionally an ox) are closely inspected for (a) the pattern of veining in the intestinal walls and (b) stomach as well as intestinal contents. The haruspex "reads" the veining pattern to arrive at some statement about outside forces ("natural" as well as "supernatural") at work on the animal, on the herd from which it came, and as possibly affecting the owner/manager of the herd. The stomach/intestinal contents are closely examined to determine where the animal was last feeding, what it was feeding on, and on what "mix" of grass, forbs, and shrubs it was relying.

This information is used for a variety of purposes, for example, to estimate where an animal was last feeding (an important consideration in cases involving stolen animals) and to estimate the general "savvy" or shrewdness of the animal's owner/manager. Separate households that are considering going into a herding partnership may each offer up a goat, the entrails of which are read to predict the likely outcome of the partnership by assessing each household's skills in livestock management. Thus divinatory ritual for the Pokot, and very widely for East African peoples, is not simply mumbo jumbo: estimates of environmental quality are involved, as are the feeding habits of different animals and the shrewdness of an individual livestock manager, man or woman.

Much knowledge, of course, is shared outside the context of ritual, as we have seen in the use of shrubs for house and fence building, in strategies for controlling the spread of *Acacia*, and in the preparation of folk medicines. Although the metaphors used by a local people such as the Pokot to communicate their knowledge are likely to be quite different from our own, patience and skill in interviewing are the keys to sharing in local perceptions of the environment and the forces at work within it. Of course not everything a local people "knows" is therefore "right." As in advanced societies, the Pokot have on occasion misinterpreted and misused their own resources; on the whole, though, they have succeeded for many generations in utilizing a fragile and uncertain range of environments. Surely what they have learned in this process is worth knowing. Information gained from informants regarding utilization and changes in natural resources can be a valuable adjunct to interpretation of data obtained through vegetation analysis (Reining, 1978; Conant, 1978, Conant *et al.,* 1983).

V. Summary and Conclusions

Understanding shrub use and management in any society requires more than a list of uses and management techniques. Since shrubs and shrublands constitute a natural resource, understanding must begin with a realization of how a people perceive and experience the wider environment in which the resource is found.

In the case of the Pokot, while the environment can be described in terms of discrete types—masob, kamass, and psigogh, for example—the experience of the environment is seldom in terms of "high cold country" only, or just the "middle slopes for farming," or "lowland grass and bushlands" for herding. For the Pokot the environment and the resources within it constitute a cline in which the areas of transition are as important (or more so) than areas of uniformity. While discrete subsistence techniques exist for each sector, the persons practicing them are integrated by institutions that span the entire range of the environment.

For the Pokot and many other East African peoples one such institution is the neighborhood. The korok, as we have seen, can stretch from highlands to lowlands. The Pokot age grade pin draws on both farmers and herders. Marriage and the affinal kin ties it activates are important in the exchange of surplus products between herding and farming households. Thus the use of any one resource such as shrubs and shrublands involves personal participating in the exploitation of still other resources.

A second consideration is that among these personnel women and not just men are actively engaged in resource utilization and management. In the Pokot case women must be included among the essential actors in the management of thorny shrubs and the maintenance of rangeland quality.

The reason for taking a closer look at the Pokot case is because the people, their values, and their social system are still relatively intact. They constitute a "whole" (in the sense of a functioning) society that is carrying their past experience of dry, shrubland areas into the present and, presumably, into the near future. How much longer this will be the case is difficult to say. Recent events in Pokotland, and throughout the African sahel, give some urgency to understanding traditional techniques of shrubland management before events beyond local control threaten the functioning of the "whole" system.

The conclusion here is that a first step in innovation among shrubland and grassland peoples is to understand their perception of how they and their local resources fit into the world around them. Traditionally oriented peoples like the Pokot do not function in isolation, and to perceive them as doing so, or to treat shrubland as a separate and isolated resource, is to create the conditions for misunderstanding and the likely failure of a planned innovation.

Acknowledgments

The fieldwork and satellite data analyses on which the present article is based were made possible by grants from the National Science Foundation (BNS77–15622 and SER–7914954), the City University of New York (11787E and 13981), and the Wenner-Gren Foundation for Anthropological Research.

References

Bates, D. G., and Conant, F. P. (1981). Livestock and livelihood: A handbook for the 1980's. *In* "The Future of Pastoral Peoples" (J. Galaty, D. Aronson, and P. Salzmann, eds.), pp. 89–100. International Development Center, Ottawa.

Conant, F. P. (1965). Korok: A variable unit of physical and social space among the Pokot of East Africa. *Am. Anthropol.* **67,** 429–434.

Conant, F. P. (1978). Folk taxonomies as an ethnographic method for monitoring desertification. *In* "Handbook on Desertification Indicators" (P. Reining, compiler), pp. 76–78. Am. Assoc. Adv. Sci., Washington, D.C.

Conant, F. P. (1983). Thorns paired, sharply recurved: Cultural controls and rangeland quality in East Africa. *In* "Desertification and Development: Dryland Ecology in Social Perspective" (B. Spooner and H. S. Mann, eds.), pp. 111–122. Academic Press, London.

Conant, F. P., Rogers, P., Baumgardner, M., McKell, C. M., Dasmann, R., and Reining, P., eds. (1983). "Natural Resource Inventories and Baseline Studies: Methods for Developing Countries." Am. Assoc. Adv. Sci., Washington, D.C.

Dale, I. R., and Greenway, P. J. (1961). "Kenya Trees and Shrubs." Hatchard's, London.

Deng, F. M. (1972). "The Dinka of the Sudan." Holt, New York.

Dyson-Hudson, N. (1966). "Karamjong Politics. Oxford Univ. Press (Clarendon), London and New York.

Dyson-Hudson, R. (1972). Pastoralism: Self-image and behavioural reality. *J. Asian Afr. Stud.* **7**(1–2), 30–47.

Edgerton, R. B. (1971). "The Individual in Cultural Adaptation." Univ. of California Press, Berkeley.

Evans-Pritchard, E. E. (1940). "The Nuer." Oxford Univ. Press, London and New York.

Galaty, J., Aronson, D., and Salzmann, P., eds. (1981). "The Future of Pastoral Peoples." International Development Center, Ottawa.

Goldschmidt, W. (1982). Toward an anthropological approach to economic development. *Hum. Organ.* **41**(1), 80–83.

Gulliver, P. (1955). "The Family Herds." Routledge & Kegan Paul, London.

Reining, P., compiler (1978). "Handbook of Desertification Indicators." Am. Assoc. Adv. Sci., Washington, D.C.

Spencer, P. (1973). "Nomads in Alliance." Oxford Univ. Press, London and New York.

30

An Assessment of the Economic Feasibility of Fodder Shrubs Plantation (with Particular Reference to Africa)

Henri N. Le Houérou

I. Introduction

Substantial areas of fodder shrubs have been established in northern Africa, particularly in Tunisia and Libya over the past two decades; similar programs have more recently been initiated in the Near East, notably in Iran, Syria, Egypt, Israel, and the Gulf states. Sizable areas have also been planted in South Africa to fodder cacti and saltbushes (De Kock, 1980). Other species of shrubs and trees ("trubs") are also being planted in the African tropics, particularly *Acacia senegal* in the Republic of Sudan and *Faidherbia albida* in Senegal and other Sahelian countries of West Africa. Furthermore, introduction of phyllodineous acacias (wattles) from Australia has been successfully achieved in Mediterranean Africa beginning about 1870 (Le Houérou and Pontanier, 1987). Approximately 100,000 seedlings per annum were planted in western Libya since 1920, particularly for sand dune stabilization around the city of Tripoli (Leone, 1924). More recently these wattles (*A. saligna, A. cyclops, A. salicina,*

A. victoriae, A. ligulata, and *A. pycnantha*) have also been planted for fodder reserves as part of a drought-evading strategy for stock. Those plantations cover some 200,000 ha north of the Sahara, of which as much as 80% are of *A. saligna (=A. cyanophylla)*. Similar efforts are presently being made in the dry tropics with other species of wattles from north western Australia (*A. holosericea, A. tumida, A. linarioides,* and *A. bivenosa*) (Hamel, 1980).

The cultivation of *Leucaena leucocephala* as a fodder crop or cash crop for meal production in the humid and subhumid tropics is expanding in Malawi, Ethiopia, Ivory Coast, and other countries, as well as Central America, the Caribbean, Australasia, the Far East, and the Pacific islands.

Some scientists and developers have questioned the technical validity, the economic feasibility, or the social acceptability of fodder shrub development endeavors. The technical validity of browse plantations has been discussed in a large number of papers. There is, of course, no overall "yes or no" answer: shrub development may be desirable and necessary or undesirable and unnecessary, according to circumstances. It certainly is a valid solution in many marginal areas of the arid and semiarid zones and in montane regions for both erosion control and as dry season fodder reserves under climates and soils that are unfit for conventional agriculture. The technical validity of fodder shrub plantations may be more questionable in areas of intensive farming, but it is not necessarily so, as shown by the cultivation of *Leucaena* as a cash crop for small farmers in Malawi or in semi-intensive animal production systems in Ivory Coast.

The economic feasibility of browse plantations has apparently not been subject to detailed assessments in Africa, with the exception of antierosion schemes in Tunisia and *Leucaena* intensive cropping in Malawi. A review was published by De Montgolfier-Kouevi and Le Houérou (1980) concerning a number of case studies in tropical Africa. The present attempt is broader in scope both from the geographical viewpoint since it encompasses the continent as a whole and from the methodology viewpoint as it takes three methods of approach instead of one. Many references to those case studies will be made in the present study.

II. Evaluation of Shrubs

Fodder shrubs are essentially planted as supplementary or emergency feed for periods of grazing shortage, that is, in dry season and prolonged droughts, as part of a drought evasion strategy, or in higher elevations or higher latitudes in periods of cold weather when there is no green herbage available. The use of shrubs under such circumstances is justified by the fact that most of them (at least those used in planting programs) remain green throughout most of the dry season and even through abnormally prolonged periods of drought or cold weather. Their protein and carotene content remains fair to high when dried herbage is very low in these nutrients and unable to meet the maintenance requirements of livestock or wildlife. The role of shrubs is thus similar to feed supplementation with nitrogen and vitamin-rich concentrates; some shrub species rich in minerals may even replace salt licks. Browse plantations could therefore be replaced either by these or, partly, by nonprotein nitrogen sources such as urea.

Taking for granted that stock need dry or cold season supplementation, the question is then to determine which type of supplementation is more practical, advantageous, or cheaper: fodder shrub plantations or utilization of concentrates and/or urea (complemented with vitaminic salt licks in the latter case). But it does not merely come down to determining which is cheaper; an overall assessment of shrub utility is more complex as it includes the production of fuelwood, which is often in short supply in Africa and Asia. It also embraces the problems of erosion control, optimal use of marginal land, wildlife management, multiple use of marginal lands, and other aspects that are difficult to quantify in monetary terms. Furthermore, the notions of practicality, social acceptability, and the actual availability of concentrates in local markets may interfere seriously with cost/benefit ratios, particularly in Africa. The main difficulty in the economic assessment of shrub plantations, however, comes from the monetary value (shadow price) that should be ascribed to this type of feed, since this item is usually not an object of trade and marketing (with very few exceptions around main cities and some products such as *Acacia albida* pods, habitually reserved for pet and prestige animals). I have considered three main approaches to this problem.

1. The first approach is to ascribe to shrub feed the same monetary value as the cheapest, most common, and readily available concentrate that would be needed to fulfill the same nutritional role, that is, cereal grains and bran (barley grain in the Mediterranean and millet or sorghum in the dry tropics) and for local agroindustrial by-products such as cotton seed, rice bran, low-grade rice flour, etc. The price of those, however, is usually well above the international price in most African countries.

2. The second approach takes the opposite view: given the price of meat, how much can one afford to pay for protein supplementation from shrubs for:
   (i) Maintenance of body weight,
   (ii) Liveweight gain.

3. The third approach, in contrast with the other two, is an attempt to quantify the market value of browse from fixed opportunity costs of the capital invested.

The first approach is a rather common one used by many authors (LeHouérou and Barghati, 1982). The second approach is quite unusual albeit pragmatic. The third has been used by a few authors (De Montgolfier-Kouevi and Le Houérou, 1980, 1981; Barachette, 1980a, b).

The present assessment is based on a number of concrete case studies of fodder shrub development in various countries such as Tunisia, Senegal, Sudan, Libya, Malawi, Cape Verde Islands, and, for the sake of comparison, data from Chili and Israel were examined as well (De Montgolfier-Kouevi and Le Houérou, 1980, 1981). All monetary data are expressed in U.S. dollars as of 1980.

Costs of establishment include several alternatives, for example, direct sowing versus planting of nursery-grown seedlings, building or not of fences, and metallic fences versus thorn hedges. Production for each species has been estimated using a number of assumptions from low to high yields, according to local ecological conditions and the managerial skill of the users.

As most plantations require total protection from grazing for a few years, the value of the ungrazed fodder produced is added to the actual cost of establishment. The value of wood production is added to the fodder production value in the calculation of cost/benefit ratios, and so is the value of the herbage growing between shrubs from the time these are being browsed. All these elements are used for the calculation of Internal Rates of Return (IRR), which naturally vary with species concerned, with establishment techniques and other inputs, and with yield assumptions and management scenarios.

Thus there is, for each shrub species, a wide array of IRRs, some negative and some highly positive, according to the combination of alternative solutions and inputs that are used for establishment and management and according to yield expectancy.

III. Shadow Prices and Other Problem Subjects

Plantation of fodder trees and shrubs is of undeniable interest in countries where labor is cheap and plentiful, as in many African countries. In addition to producing fuelwood and specific products, such as gum arabic, they provide the livestock with dry season or bridging-up season supplementary feed that is usually rich in protein, minerals, and vitamins; this is of particular value in arid and semiarid zones with long dry seasons. Browse is thus a factor of stability in animal production that does not compete with food crops for land use; quite the opposite, since fodder shrubs and trees are able to grow on marginal lands that are not fit for conventional farming (dunes, steep slopes, stony soils, land prone to flooding, saline soils), they may play an important role in the protection of catchment basins, erosion control, and the struggle against desertification. Some species are amenable to planting in cultivated fields and thus contribute to the maintenance or improvement of soil fertility and to the increase of crop yields owing to the organic matter and nutrients they bring to the topsoil from deep layers of the subsoil and to their smoothing off the microclimatic conditions (Windbreak and screen effects).

For all these reasons the cost of feed from fodder trees and shrubs is lower than the price of most concentrate feeds that could be used to play the same dietetic role in livestock nutrition. The cheapest concentrates such as cereal bran, molasses, and urea are usually not available in sizable quantities away from the areas of production. They are, to a large part, used in dairy production operations in the vicinity of major cities, but the cost of transport would render them prohibitive away from where they are produced. Their contribution to livestock feeding will therefore remain limited in Africa for the foreseeable future, while an enlightened strategy of browse development should be able to contribute not only to better feeding and productivity of livestock but also to the solution of the energy crisis (fuelwood shortage is often acute in the arid, semiarid, and even subhumid zones; in many cities the cost of firewood for a family amounts to 20–30% of the wages of an unskilled laborer), and at the same time it will maintain soil fertility and land productivity. This is why it seemed to be a valuable exercise to assess from the economic viewpoint, on the basis of case studies, the validity of developing fodder shrub plantations.

To carry out this evaluation, I took into account the cost of afforestation, as obtained in actual development schemes, using nursery-grown seedlings. These costs include land preparation, possible soil and water conservation works, clearing, plowing, and weeding between the time of planting and the beginning of the production phase. These costs are closely linked to the cost of labor, which altogether represents about 80% of the overall cost whenever soil preparation is moderately mechanized. The use of heavy machinery does not substantially reduce the costs but it does strongly affect the breakdown of these costs into local currency and hard-currency spending. Neither the salary of technical supervisors nor the rental value of the land has been accounted for. The production value of the land, however, and the way it is affected by the planting program (loss of herbage production for several years because of exclosure) are accounted for. To the normal costs of planting we should add the cost of fencing, as fencing is a mandatory protective measure against trespassing and possible destruction of plantations by hungry, free-wandering stock. Fencing may be done either with barbed wire or other metallic structures, with thorn hedges or spiny branches (*Zeriba, Boma*), or with a combination of these. Metallic fences are usually much more expensive than live hedges or *Zeriba*. But here again, there are substantial differences. The cost of a barbed-wire fence is three times higher in intertropical Africa as compared to northern Africa.[1] The cost of transport is, to a large extent, responsible for this difference. Hedges, on the other hand, ought to be planted at least 2–3 years ahead of time if they are to fulfill their protective role when the plantation is established. A combination of live hedge and *Zeriba* may be ideal as the life span of *Zeriba* is 2–3 years in the tropics (depending on rainfall and termite activity). Fencing is always an important and some-times overriding item in the overall investment costs; therefore we have attempted to systematically single it out in cost and profitability calculations.

Estimating operating costs is somewhat more difficult as the subject is poorly documented; estimates draw largely on a number of assumptions. It has been assumed, for instance, that since this type of operation is a rather extensive one, operating costs are mainly fixed expenses (e.g., patrolling, watchman) that are independent of production, the latter being governed by ecological factors such as aridity, soil type, or socioeconomic factors affecting management. Nonetheless, it was also argued that although fod-der shrubs can theoretically be used without variable operating costs since the feed can be consumed on the spot by the stock, the offtake of wood implies cutting (by hand or mechanically) and transport costs, which are directly linked to the level of output. This approach may have led to some underestimation of operating costs, especially for plantations that were deemed to have the benefit of good management.

In most cases evaluation of production was done on the basis of several yield assumptions so as to take into account various levels of management and various degrees of ecological adaptation of the species concerned to the local conditions. The spectrum of production assumptions selected does correspond to actual field figures obtained in extensive conditions under various ecological and managerial circumstances.

---

[1] $1 U.S. per linear meter of fence ($150 per hectare) in Tunisia versus $3 U.S. per linear meter ($450 per hectare) in Senegal for plantations of about 10 ha in size. Thorn hedges (double rows) would cost about $1 U.S. per linear meter in tropical Africa. However, locally made mesh fence, known as "Ferlo fence" in Senegal, derived from the Australian "cyclone" type, cost only about $2 U.S. per linear meter in 1986; this figure includes the cost of construction in the field (transport and labor) (Le Houérou, 1987).

Estimating the value of production also caused difficulties related to establishing shadow prices for animal feed. Shadow prices have extremely important implications for calculating the Internal Rate of Return that one is trying to estimate. Determining this shadow price is a very complex problem and we found that no overall solution to it can be fully satisfactory. First of all, price of concentrate feed varies greatly from one country to the next and from one year to another. The price ratio between energy and Digestible Crude Protein (DCP) also varies greatly from one country to another, from one concentrate type to another, and from one year to the next. These may induce substantial differences in the calculated IRR from one country to the next and from year to year. I have therefore elected to use regional averages.

The cheapest concentrates are usually available only in limited quantities in limited areas, as mentioned earlier, so these cannot be taken as representative since even if they did become available their price would be considerably higher outside their area of production because of transportation costs. The price of cereal grains thus appears to be a much more significant index than concentrates, since they are available everywhere at prices that are subject to much less variability in time and space than agroindustrial by-products. The cereals used for determining shadow prices are barley grain for North Africa and millet/sorghum grain for intertropical Africa. One kilogram of each of these is equivalent to one Scandinavian Feed Unit (SFU) of Net Energy (NE) and 60 to 80 g of DCP. These concentrates are thus somewhat richer in energy and poorer in protein than browse dry matter (DM), as shown in Table I.

The nutritive value of browse as dry season supplementary feed is thus significantly greater than that in cereals since protein—not energy—is the main limiting factor in the diet in time of nutritional stress. This difference in nutritive value in favor of browse is further enhanced by its relative richness in carotene, while cereal grains have no vitamin A.

Table I. Net energy and digestible crude protein levels

	NE[a] (SFU/kg)[b]	DCP[c] (g/kg)
Cereal grains	1.0 (0.9–1.1)	70 (60–80)
Browse DM	0.8 (0.6–0.9)	90 (70–120)

[a] NE = net energy.
[b] SFU (Scandinavian feed unit) = net energy of 1 kg of barley grain = 0.7 kg TDN (total digestible nutrients), that is, 1.65 to 1.88 Mcal of NE or 2.62 to 2.90 Mcal of ME (metabolizable energy) = 10.95 to 12.12 MJ of ME.
[c] DCP = digestible crude protein.

The average price ratio between energy and protein in concentrates averaged 1 : 1.5 in intertropical Africa between 1975 and 1980 (subject to important local and temporary distortions, as mentioned earlier). The shadow price values used in the present paper are $0.16 U.S. per SFU and $0.24 U.S. per kilogram of DCP; these figures are from the study of statistics on grain prices in Africa.

The second approach to fixing a shadow price to browse is based on average price of meat on the hoof at the producer's level ($0.6 U.S. per kilogram in intertropical Africa for 1980). It is reckoned that 10 SFU and 1 kg of DCP are needed, on the average, to produce 1 kg of liveweight gain every 3 days (these conversion rates are purposely modest, even for African zebus).

Because, on the other hand, the DCP maintenance needs of the average 250-kg Tropical Livestock Unit (TLU) are 160 g ($2.52 g/kg^{0.75}$), maintenance of body weight throughout the 9 months of dry season in the arid and semiarid zones would be $0.160 \times 270 = 43$ kg DCP. These needs are not met in traditional production systems in which body weight losses during the dry season are about 50 kg in adult zebus and 20–40 kg in 2- to 4-year-old animals (Wilson *et al.*, 1983). Furthermore, as the typical African zebu raised within extensive traditional systems reaches the mature weight of 280 kg at the age of 5 years, the average annual overall liveweight gain is thus 280 kg–20 kg (birth weight) ÷ 5 = 52 kg. An adequate feed supply in dry season could double that productivity so that mature size could be reached between 30 to 36 months of age instead of 60 months.

As a consequence of the foregoing, the shadow price of browse, as drawn from liveweight market value could be calculated in two different ways:

(i) Value of maintenance of body weight gained on the range during the rainy season grazing (0.5 to 1.0 kg/day).
(ii) Value of additional liveweight gain carried on through the dry season with supplementary feeding from browse.

In the first case, assuming a 9-month dry season and a zero DCP value of dry grasses, maintenance requirements of 43 kg DCP will be worth a "nonloss" of 50 kg of liveweight valued 50 kg × $0.6 = $30 U.S., or a shadow price of 30 ÷ 43 = $0.70 per kilogram of DCP. Reckoning that average DCP content in browse dry matter is 8.4%. (Le Houérou, 1980c) we thus have a shadow price value of 0.7 ÷ (100/8.4) = $0.06/kg DM. Shadow price would substantially change when the dry season is longer or shorter.

In the dry ecological limit of cattle husbandry, under the 200 mm isohyet, with 10 months of annual dry season we would have the figures

160 g/day × 300 days = 48 kg DCP.

48 kg DCP/yr would thus be needed to prevent a body weight loss of 40 kg gained during the 60 days of rainy season. Hence 48 ÷ 40 = 1.20 kg DCP are needed to maintain each kilogram of body weight. The shadow price is therefore $0.60 ÷ 1.20 kg DCP = $0.50/kg DCP or $0.50 ÷ 100/8.4 = $0.04/kg DM of browse.

In the subhumid zone with 6 months of dry season the figures become

160 g/day × 180 days = 29 kg DCP.

It would be necessary to maintain the 90 kg of body weight gained during the rainy season. Hence 29 ÷ 90 = 0.320 kg DCP are needed to maintain each kilogram of body weight. The shadow price thus becomes

$0.6 ÷ 0.320 = $1.88/kg DCP

or

$1.88 ÷ (100/8.4) = 0.16/kg DM of browse.

The values of $0.04, 0.06, and 0.16 per kilogram DM thus found for browse compare very favorably with the price of *Acacia albida* pods sold on West African markets: $0.21/kg in Senegal ($0.27/kg DM) and $0.125/kg in Mali, in 1980. Browse cut in the bush and sold in cities like Bamako also sells for about the same price per kilogram DM as *Acacia albida* pods, that is, far beyond the shadow prices as calculated above.

In the second case, assuming a daily liveweight gain of 330 g, the DCP requirements would be 1 kg per kilogram of gain (higher gains can hardly be expected without concentrates, given the energy content of the ration, which is assumed to be a combination of dry grass and browse). Under these circumstances the shadow price of DCP would be equal to the price of 1 kg of meat on the hoof ($0.6 U.S.), which is a little lower than in the case of body weight maintenance in arid and semiarid zones.

In conclusion, it appears that the shadow price of DCP as drawn from its value in meat production is two to seven times greater as compared to the value derived from more or less nutritionally equivalent cereal grains. We have reckoned an average DCP shadow price of $0.7/kg when calculated from meat value and $0.24/kg when drawn from cereals, hence an approximate ratio of 3:1.

A third method was also used in trying to determine the monetary value of browse starting from the opportunity cost of the capital invested. Two opportunity costs of capital were selected, based on 10 and 15% interest rates (which are quite high for agricultural operations). Another set of difficulties then arose because fodder shrubs have a dual use objective: fodder and wood (not to speak of unquantifiable uses such as amenities, erosion control, and fertility maintenance). Three assumptions were thus envisaged.

(i) Fodder is a by-product of wood and consequently all investment costs should be ascribed to wood production; the cost price of browse is then the income from wood and fodder that permits one to balance the cash flow with the IRR that has been selected. We have labeled this price the *"marginal cost price"* per SFU.

(ii) One may, on the contrary, assume that the dual-purpose exploitation is equally shared between wood and fodder. This assumption comes down to determining the cost price of fodder, the value of wood being known from its marketable value. But the breakdown of these values is not easy, particularly regarding investments that are made globally for both activities. It could be done *a priori* on an income flow share basis, but this type of breakdown then depends on the shadow price ascribed to browse, which is precisely what we are trying to find out. The problem was solved in sharing in a more or less arbitrary way the various costs between the two activities. It was thus decided that all fixed operating costs would be attributed to fodder production while variable costs (cutting and transport of wood) were attributed to wood production. The cost thus established was labeled *"average cost price."*

(iii) A third possible assumption is that fodder is the main item and wood production is only marginal or negligible as in small shrubs like *Cassia sturtii* or *Atriplex vesicaria;* in some instances there is no wood production at all, such as in *Cactus,* in *Atriplex glauca, A. semibaccata,* and *A. leucodada.* In cases where farmland is used for a fodder shrub plantation, the net value of the alternative common crop is taken into account; this is called the *opportunity cost of the land.* When plantations are established on grazing land, the value of the grazing, based on the shadow price of SFU, is deduced. The latter case results in an overevaluation of the opportunity cost since grazing is, in principle, free. In this method, however, it is assumed that the areas withdrawn from grazing would compel the users to undertake or increase concentrate feeding, or grow fodder crops, in order to replace the temporarily excluded grazing, while retaining the same level of income. This is probably the way it should be in an ideal situation, but such is seldom the case. The common situation is only that the grazing pressure is accentuated on the neighboring ranges; but how to quantify range depletion? On how large an area should additional depletion be spread and shared?

IV. Case Studies

A. *Cactus Plantations in Tunisia*

Cactus, a low-protein, bulk foodstuff, is regarded as an emergency feed and is cultivated as such in Brazil, South Madagascar, South Africa, North Africa, and elsewhere as a part of drought evasion strategies for livestock. Yields may be extremely high given the ecological conditions in which the crop is grown. The ecology of fodder cacti, however, is pretty narrow; they cannot grow in all arid zones. They do not grow in the Sahel, for instance, while they do in East Africa (down to the 300-mm isohyet and maybe less). The main limiting factor is air moisture (Peyre de Fabrègues, 1966). The rule of thumb is that fodder cacti would not grow wherever mean daily air moisture goes beneath 40% for over 1 month continuously (Le Houérou, 1980a).

When planted in adequate ecological conditions, and reasonably well managed, yields are very high, 20 to 100 tons/ha/yr of fresh matter (FM) (3–15 tons DM, 1500–7500 SFU), with a density of 2000 shrubs per hectare (Monjauze and Le Houérou, 1965). Figures of 200–300 tons FM/ha/yr have often been recorded in the literature under particularly good ecological and managerial conditions (use of fertilizers, etc.) in the semiarid and subhumid zones, or under irrigation.

Cattle and sheep may consume up to 15% of their body weight in fresh cacti as long as 1% is provided as dry roughage, straw, or hay (Cordier, 1947; Monjauze and Le Houérou, 1965). Moreover, cactus feeding considerably reduces the drinking water requirement as this feed contains 80 to 90% water. Cactus cladodes (also commonly called joins or pads) may be grazed directly by the stock or cut and carried for pen feeding. Both methods of management have advantages and shortcomings that bear extremely important consequences on the financial aspect of the operation.

- Direct browsing necessitates a very tight control on grazing, otherwise wastage may reach 50% of the fodder produced (cladodes partially eaten and abandoned) and the plantation itself may be destroyed by overbrowsing within a very few months of overstocking (Monjauze and Le Houérou, 1965; De Kock, 1980). The advantage of this type of management is its very low cost and the fact that the grass layer between the shrubs is available to the stock. These two facts result in the much better financial results of this type of management.

- Zero grazing or the cut-and-carry technique bear the opposite consequences. Loss of feed is virtually nil and risk of overutilization is considerably reduced. Overexploitation may occur, however, especially in case of too early harvest in young plantations; this may be very detrimental to the future production potential of the crop. But the zero grazing technique is costly in labor, although the method is amenable to mechanization, and the grazing layer herbage remains unavailable to the stock.

In most cases in Africa the zero grazing management is to be recommended because of insufficient grazing discipline and therefore high risk of destruction. *Investment costs* have been estimated several times in Tunisia; they may be evaluated at $425 U.S. per hectare (from 1980) for plantations and maintenance until the beginning of the exploitation phase at 4 to 5 years of age. To this amount should be added the cost of fencing.

Investment cost may be broken down as follows:

- Plantation cost includes soil preparation, purchase and transportation of cladodes, and planting proper. These represent 60% of the total investment cost, including labor, which amounts to 80 man-days per hectare. These figures were established on the basis of actual development schemes (Monjauze and Le Houérou, 1965); they amounted to $104 U.S. in 1965, that is, $324 at 1980 prices.[2] Barrachette (1980) estimated them at $430/ha, while Government Services allow the figure of $265/ha as maximum investment cost for the allocation of planting loans and subsidies. The average of the two latter figures ($347/ha) is close to the experimental data found by Monjauze and Le Houérou; we finally admitted the assumption of $350/ha as representing planting cost in 1980.
- Maintenance cost for the 3 years consecutive to planting (two plowings for weed control, patrolling, and opportunity cost of the prohibited grazing) were estimated at $75 U.S./ha/yr.

---

[2] Costs are reevaluated using the UN index of unit values of manufactured goods exported by developed countries (UNCTAD, 1980). The following values are for 1960 to 1980.

1960	61	62	63	64	65	66	67	68	69	70	71	72	73	74	75	76
84	84	85	85	86	88	90	91	91	94	100	105	113	133	162	182	183

1977	78	79	80
199	225	260	300

- The cost of establishing a fence depends, as discussed earlier, on whether metallic fence or thorn hedges are considered. Cost of metallic fence (four barbed wires) is about $1 U.S. per linear meter, that is, $150/ha for plantations of about 10 ha in size. A fence made of a double row of spiny cactus would cost less than $60 per hectare, but it should be established at least 2 years before planting.

On these bases, Table II gives the cost of establishment of a cactus plantation.

In all cases operating costs include the fixed costs of guarding estimated at $12/U.S./ha/yr. Variable costs, in the cut-and-carry management scenario, include the cost of cutting and of transport estimated $6 per ton of fresh product, that is, $60 per ton of DM. Cactus are usually exploited 4 to 6 years after planting and reach maturity between 7 and 10 years; they may be kept productive for many decades when management is adequate. Yield assumptions retained are 1 to 6 tons DM/ha/yr with a feed value of 0.5 SFU/kg DM; variable operating costs are, of course, directly related to production levels. The value of production was estimated using the shadow price of barley grain in Tunisia in 1980 ($0.137 U.S./kg) as equivalent to the value of the one SFU. The value of annual production per hectare amounts to $68–411 according to the production assumption considered (500 to 3000 SFU/ha/yr). We have moreover reckoned that the herbage removed from grazing represents some 220 SFU/ha/yr, valued at $30 on the basis of the shadow price mentioned above (which is a very large overestimation as this grazing is virtually free).

In the second approach shadow prices are the regional prices of energy and DCP in concentrates as calculated above: $0.16 and 0.24 U.S. per SFU and per kilogram DCP, respectively.

In the third approach, based on the shadow price of mutton meat in Tunisia ($2.25/kg liveweight in 1980) and on a conversion rate of 10 SFU and 1 kg DCP per kilogram of liveweight gain, the value of the production comes to $112–675/ha/yr, which is an increase of 65% over the first method and 37% over the second. See Tables III, IV, and V.

It should be kept in mind, however, that given its poor protein content, cactus should not be fed alone but combined with *Acacia* or *Atriplex*

Table II. Establishment costs for a cactus plantation

Fence type	Cost per shrub (U.S. $)	Cost per hectare (U.S. $)
No fence	0.210	420.00
Thorn hedge	0.240	480.00
Barbed wire fence	0.285	570.00

Table III. Evaluation of production of fodder cactus in Tunisia

	Production assumptions			
	1	2	3	4
Fresh matter (kg/ha/yr)	10,000	20,000	40,000	60,000
Dry matter (kg/ha/yr)	1,000	2,000	4,000	6,000
Net energy (SFU/ha/yr)	500	1,000	2,000	3,000
Monetary value when in full production (U.S. $/ha/yr)				
Approach 1[a]	68[b]	137[c]	274[d]	411[e]
Approach 2[f]	82	165	330	495
Approach 3(i)[g]	112	226	452	678
Approach 3(ii)[h]	74	150	300	452
Approach 3(iii)[i]	56	112	225	325

[a] Shadow price SFU = $0.137 (average official price of barley grain in Tunisia in 1980).

[b] From year 5 to *n*.

[c] From year 6 to *n:* U.S. $68, 82, 112, 74, 56 for year 5.

[d] From year 7 to *n:* U.S. $68, 82, 112, 74, 56 for year 5; $137, 165, 226, 150, 112 for year 6.

[e] From year 8 to *n:* U.S. $68, 82, 112, 74, 56 for year 5; $137, 165, 226, 150, 112, for year 6; $274, 330, 452, 300, 225 for year 7.

[f] Shadow price SFU = $0.16 and $0.24/kg DCP (concentrate values on the international market).

[g] Shadow price SFU = $0.225 (average price of mutton on the hoof: $2.250 U.S.; conversion rate: 10 SFU or 20 kg DM per kilogram of weight gain, hence 2.25 ÷ 10 SFU = $0.225/SFU or $0.112/kg DM.
In assumption 3(i), all the production value is ascribed to cactus, the complement in the diet coming from grazing (range or stubble or fallow) which are virtually free, and urea.

[h] In assumption 3(ii), the value of the production is shared on a 66/33% basis between cactus and other browse (*Acacia, Atriplex*, tree medic, etc.) rich in protein. The 66/33% ratio represents the respective approximate proportions of cactus and other browse in a balanced diet, on a dry matter basis.

[i] In assumption 3(iii), the value of the production is shared on a 50/50% basis between cactus and other browse as cactus yields almost 80% of the energy and *Atriplex/Acacia* 80% of the protein.

browse or with straw and urea or grazing and urea. The combination with *Acacia/Atriplex* browse is a highly effective one in technical terms as shown in large-scale sheep feeding experiments done recently in Libya (Le Houérou *et al.*, 1983), where liveweight gains of 100 g/day were recorded in mature ewes on pure browse diets combining cactus and *Atriplex* or cactus and *Acacia*. On the other hand, diets combining cactus, straw, and urea (4 to 5 kg FM, 0.2 to 0.4 kg, 10 g/head/day, respectively) are able to maintain indefinitely the body weight in sheep, or even with a slight gain of 20 to 50 g/day, as shown from a 12-month experiment in Algeria (Delhaye *et al.*, 1974).

Table IV. Internal rates of return of spineless cactus plantations in Tunisia

Management system:	Direct browsing		Zero grazing		
Enclosure:	Hedge	Metal fence	No fence	Hedge	Metal fence
Assumption 1 (500 SFU/ha/yr)					
Approach 1	4.0	5.0	0.1	0.1	0.1
Approach 2	2.0	3.4	0.1	0.1	0.1
Assumption 2 (1000 SFU/ha/yr)					
Approach 1	11	12	0.1	0.1	0.1
Approach 2	10	12	0.1	0.1	0.1
Assumption 3 (2000 SFU/ha/yr)					
Approach 1	18.0	19.0	8.0	6.0	6.0
Approach 2	17.4	19.2	8.9	5.2	6.7
Assumption 4 (3000 SFU/ha/yr)					
Approach 1	22.0	23.0	12.0	10.0	10.0
Approach 2	21.5	23.4	14.1	10.2	11.6

Table V. Cost price per SFU and kilogram of DCP of spineless cactus in Tunisia (1 SFU = 2 kg DM)

Management system:	Direct grazing				Zero grazing					
Enclosure:	Hedge		Metal fence		No fence		Hedge		Metal fence	
IRR (%)	10	15	10	15	10	15	10	15	10	15
Yield assumptions										
500 SFU/ha/yr	0.42	0.99	0.31	0.53	0.87	1.76	3.09		1.04	2.16
1000 SFU/ha/yr	0.16	0.28	0.14	0.22	0.28	0.39	0.39	0.64	0.32	0.46
2000 SFU/ha/yr	0.08	0.12	0.07	0.11	0.17	0.21	0.20	0.27	0.19	0.24
3000 SFU/ha/yr	0.05	0.08	0.05	0.08	0.14	0.17	0.16	0.20	0.15	0.18

Note: Dashed line shows cost below shadow price for approaches 1 and 2.

The following are the production costs of various feeds in Tunisia (1980 prices, per SFU):

Barley grain	$0.137 U.S.	Industrial concentrate = (fattening)	$0.110 U.S.
Vetch/oats/hay	0.153	Industrial concentrate = (milk production)	0.121
Silage	0.132		
Sow pasture forage	0.147	Cactus =	0.107
Soya bean meal	0.195	*Atriplex* =	0.034
Wheat bran	0.050	*Acacia* =	0.025

As mentioned before, the computation of IRR shows clearly the overriding importance of the type of management on financial performance. Under the browsing management scenario, the threshold of 10% IRR is attained with an annual production of 2000 kg DM (1000 SFU) using the shadow price of cereals. The same threshold is reached toward a production of 1500 kg under approach 2(i) based on a shadow price of energy derived from the meat price.

Under the cut-and-carry management scenario this threshold is reached with 4000 kg DM/ha/yr when the shadow price of energy is based on meat (approach 2(i)) or toward 6000 kg DM/ha/yr when the shadow price of energy is based on cereals. A cactus plantation is always profitable whenever the yield reaches 6000 kg DM/ha/yr, a figure which is attained only in fairly well managed plantations and under adequate ecological conditions. Directly browsed plantations, however, would be profitable at only one-third of this yield, that is, in more difficult ecological conditions or under poorer management. It would therefore seem that the cut-and-carry system could be profitable under semiarid conditions, while in the arid zone the threshold of profitability could only be reached under direct browsing conditions or with high standard management.

B. Atriplex Plantations in Tunisia

Atriplex species are highly resistant to drought and can grow on heavy and salty or alkaline soils with an average rainfall of at least 150 mm per year. Like cacti, they do not adapt well in some arid tropical zones such as the West African Sahel, but on the other hand they appear to be well suited to conditions found in the dry zones of eastern Africa. They provide better quality browse than cactus joints owing to their high crude protein (CP) content (15 to 25% of DM) and, unlike cactus plantations, they can be directly grazed without incurring any specific management problems, since they are little browsed when green grass is plentiful. The grass stratum can thus be grazed at the same time as the browse as soon as the plantations reach maturity. Finally, *Atriplex* plantations can also be used for producing wood, although its quality is rather poor and producer prices are definitely low owing to transport costs.

Wood yields from *Atriplex* plantations are roughly similar in terms of dry weight to the leaf production used for browse. Browse yields are generally lower than those for cactus, however. The dual production objectives and the rich protein content of *Atriplex* leaves nevertheless mean that *Atriplex* plantations can yield financial results distinctly superior to those for cactus.

The establishment costs for a plantation of *Atriplex nummularia* were studied in Tunisia by Franclet and Le Hoúerou (1971) and in Israel by Orev (1972). Although the studies used very different experimental conditions, manual planting in Tunisia and mechanized drilling in Israel, they reach very similar results: $80 U.S./ha in Tunisia, with *A. nummularia* in 1969,[3] that is, $245 in 1980 prices, and $70 U.S./ha using *A. halimus* in Israel in 1962, that is, a 1980 cost of $220. On the other hand, Barrachette (1980a) calculates investment costs at $475 U.S./ha for plantations of 2000 stocks/ha in Tunisia in 1980, with the costs spread over a period of 2 years, counting $400 for the first year and $75 for the second. If the enclosure costs of $150 U.S./ha are also taken into account, total establishment costs for a plantation of *Atriplex* can be evaluated at over $600 U.S./ha, that is, 31.2 cents per plant, or 23.7 cents per plant without enclosures. The latter estimates were the ones used for our own profitability calculations.[4]

Because the *Atriplex* wood is marketed, the management system allows the animals to browse the leaves whenever the branches are cut. As a result, operating costs primarily consist of patrolling the plantation, estimated at $12 U.S./ha/yr, and wood cutting, estimated at $12 U.S. (4 man-days), for an output of 2.5 metric tons of wood.

Atriplex plantations established with either plants raised in the nursery or by direct drilling reach maturity in 2 or 3 years. If properly managed, leaf and wood production could reach 2.5 to 5 tons of DM each during the development phase between 4 and 7 years. Nevertheless, output was assumed to be well below this figure to take into account lower management capabilities at the small landholder level, and browse production levels between 1.25 and 5 tons of DM/ha were adopted, that is, between 500 and 2000 SFU. On this basis, wood cutting costs are estimated between $6 and $24 U.S./ha/yr, depending on the assumption with regard to production.

As in the case of cactus plantations, SFU and DCP shadow prices are derived from livestock feed costs in Tunisia in 1980, that is, $0.137 U.S./SFU and $0.24 U.S./kg of DCP. Owing to its inferior quality, the costs of *Atriplex* wood have been estimated at half those of *Acacia*

[3] Planting manually in Tunisia (nursery, soil preparation, transport, planting out, and watering) requires 40 to 50 man-days/ha with a plant density of 2000 bushes/ha, i.e., 45 bushes per man-day.

[4] In Chile, planting costs with antierosion banks and including both planting and enclosures have been estimated at $200/ha by Benjamin (1980). These plantations, established in the Norte Chico region with an average rainfall of 100 to 200 mm, involved *Atriplex repanda, A. nummularia, A. semibaccata, Galenia secunda,* and *Mairena brevefolia* (Kochia) with browse production between 1000 and 2000 kg of DM/ha/yr.

Table VI. Production of *Atriplex* plantations in Tunisia (fodder and wood)

Production assumption	1		2		3		4	
	W	F	W	F	W	F	W	F
DM kg/ha/yr	1250	1250	2500	2500	3750	3750	5000	5000
SFU/ha/yr[a]	—	500	—	1000	—	1500	—	2000
DCP kg/ha/yr	—	150	—	300	—	450	—	600
Monetary value when in full production (U.S. $/ha/yr)								
Approach 1	32[b]	70	64	140	96	210	128	280
Approach 2[c]	10	110	20	232	30	348	40	464
Approach 3[d]	32	56	64	113	96	168	128	225

[a] 0.4 SFU/kg DM.

[b] Shadow price approach 1: $0.137 U.S./SFU; wood = $0.025/kg (*Acacia* wood = $0.050 in Tunisia in 1980).

[c] Shadow price approach 2: $0.16 U.S./SFU and $0.24/kg DCP.

[d] Shadow price approach 3: Conversion rate of 600 g DCP/kg of liveweight gain, i.e., $0.225 ÷ 0.600 = $0.375/kg DCP; as DCP content in *Atriplex* DM averages 12%, the shadow price per kilogram of forage DM is thus $0.375 × 0.12 = $0.045, to which should be added $0.025 per kilogram of wood DM, i.e., an overall shadow price of $0.070 per kilogram of total aboveground biomass produced annually since the leaf/stem ratio is about 1/1.

species, amounting to $7.8 U.S./ton.[5] Overall, the value of output varies from $102 to $400 U.S./ha (Table VI). It was also assumed that the plantations were established on grazing land producing about 220 SFU/yr, that is, having a value of $42 U.S. on the basis of SFU shadow prices, and that the land cannot be grazed during the first 3 years of predevelopment, or the first 5 years when the plantation is enclosed with thorn hedges, in other words, before it reaches maturity.

The IRR is over 20% when browse and wood production reach 2.5 tons of DM/ha, and is still above 10% when output is equal to or above 1.25 tons of DM/ha (14% when no enclosure costs are included). When yields become more substantial the IRR is over 25% and even reaches 30% without enclosures. The SFU cost price at this level is only $0.3–0.5 U.S./SFU, with a 10% opportunity cost of capital, and $0.4–0.8 U.S. for an IRR of 15%, a level well below the shadow price (Tables VII and VIII). According to the results in Table VIII, the SFU and DCP cost prices are only higher than shadow prices when browse production is very low (500 SFU) and when the opportunity cost of capital reaches 15%, whether or

[5] In Senegal the cost of *Acacia* wood was around $50 U.S. per metric ton in urban areas in 1980. On the other hand, *Pterocarpus lucens* wood was priced at under $30 per ton in Niono, Mali, at the same time, after the seller had devoted between 24 to 30 hr collecting it in the bush. Taking into account the opportunity cost of his labor and other outlays (depreciation of the donkey and cart used for transport), the cost price of wood in the bush would certainly not be over $15–16 U.S. per ton. To avoid any risk of overestimation, this was the level chosen for the shadow price of wood (*Acacia*) used in the IRR calculations.

Table VII. Internal rates of return in *Atriplex* plantations in Tunisia

Production assumption	No fence		Metal fence	
	Approach 1	Approach 2	Approach 1	Approach 2
500 SFU/ha/yr	11.0	14.0	8.0	10.7
1000 SFU/ha/yr	21.0	24.5	17.0	20.3
1500 SFU/ha/yr	27.0	30.4	22.0	25.8
2000 SFU/ha/yr	39.0	33.6	30.0	28.9

Table VIII. Cost price per SFU in *Atriplex* plantations in Tunisia

Management system:	With fence		Without fence	
IRR (%):	10	15	10	15
Yield assumption				
500 SFU/ha/yr	0.18	0.28	0.14	0.21
1000 SFU/ha/yr	0.08	0.12	0.06	0.09
5000 SFU/ha/yr	0.05	0.08	0.04	0.06
2000 SFU/ha/yr	0.03	0.04	0.02	0.02

Note: Dashed line shows cost below shadow price for approaches 1 and 2.

not enclosure costs are included. Even with IRR at 10%, cost prices remain below SFU and DCP shadow prices at this low level of production only when the *Atriplex* plantations are provided with enclosures and are not used for wood at the same time as for forage.

To sum up, *Atriplex* plantations have an obvious advantage over cactus plantations, and in Tunisia at least they allow browse with a high nutritive value (good protein content) to be produced at moderate cost as soon as yields are over 1000 FU/ha.

C. Acacia saligna[6] Plantations in Tunisia

Acacia is a genus of the Leguminosae family, consisting of over 900 species that vary considerably in appearance from low bush to tree and that are distributed almost throughout the arid tropical zones of the world. Many of them adapt well to sandy soils and can be used for stabilizing sand dunes and protecting the environment, while others, such as *Acacia albida*, were grown for centuries in agropastoral systems, usually involving millet, or raised for the production of gum arabic as in the case of *Acacia senegal*. About a dozen of these species are cultivated for their leaves and pods,

[6] *A. saligna* (Labill.) Wendl. = *A. cyanophylla* Lindl.

which form an excellent-quality forage that is rich in protein and phosphorus although sometimes poor in glucides. Browse species of *Acacia* can grow in very different kinds of environments, a factor that makes their classification regarding economic performance difficult. In the following their economic and financial performance is examined in one specific case only; a number of other cases were studied in De Montgolfier-Kouevi and Le Houérou (1980, 1981).

Acacia cyanophylla, as well as, to a lesser degree, other species related to the phyllodineous Australian acacias (*A. salicina, A. ligulata, A. pycnantha, A. cyclops,* and *A. pendula*), has been used in forestry for 60 to 100 years on many thousand hectares in North Africa from the humid coastal strip to the arid zone, mostly for fixing coastal sand dunes but sometimes those of the interior also. The browse output from phyllodes, twigs, and pods usually lies between that of cacti and *Atriplex,* and may reach 6 tons of forage DM per hectare on well-managed plantations (2000 FU). On the other hand, growth of the grass stratum is low and may even approach zero when the planting density is around 800 to 1000 trees per hectare. Wood production is high, and its quality is better than that of *Atriplex.*[7] The tree can be used by cutting and carrying, by trimming followed by direct grazing, or by direct browsing with periodic pruning. The impact of the various management methods on long-term productivity is, however, little understood, and experiments to compare them have yet to be carried out.

Establishment costs for a plantation with a density of 1000 bushes per hectare are about $600 U.S./ha ($560 for the first year and $50 for the second), using 125 man-days. In addition, enclosure costs are about $150/ha in Tunisia. Operating costs are fairly low when direct grazing after trimming is the management method adopted. They are estimated at $12 U.S./ha for patrolling and $12 for cutting and transporting 2.5 tons of wood, the same figures as for *Atriplex.*

Production mainly involving browse and wood can generally begin after 3 years, building up gradually to full development toward the sixth or seventh year. Expressed in terms of DM, wood and leaf production are identical, so that 3 kg of wood are produced for each SFU. The feed value of the leaves is around 0.33 SFU/kg of DM, with 200 g of DP per SFU. A properly managed plantation above the 200-mm isohyet annually produces 3000 kg of DM in phyllodes and 3000 kg of wood per hectare. However, four different assumptions regarding production have been chosen to represent management systems of varying efficiency (Table IX). On this basis, and taking into account the shadow prices of *Acacia* browse and wood, the value of output varies between $136 and $721 U.S. per hectare,

---

[7] Energy value is 4500–5000 kcal/kg of dry wood.

Table IX. Production of wood and fodder from *Acacia saligna* in Tunisia

	Production assumption							
	1		2		3		4	
	W	F	W	F	W	F	W	F
kg DM/ha/yr	1500	1500	3000	3000	4500	4500	6000	6000
SFU/ha/yr[a]	—	500	—	1000	—	1500	—	2000
DCP kg/ha/yr	—	180	—	360	—	540	—	720
Monetary value when in full production (U.S. $/ha/yr)								
Approach 1[b]	68	68	136	136	204	204	272	272
Approach 2[c]	23	104	47	208	70	312	94	416
Approach 3[d]	68	68	136	135	204	203	272	270

[a] 0.33 SFU/kg DM.
[b] Shadow prices: 1 SFU = $0.137 U.S.; wood = $0.050/kg DM.
[c] Shadow prices: 1 SFU = $0.160 U.S.; wood = $0.050/kg DM.
[d] Shadow prices: 1 kg DCP = $0.375 U.S.; wood = $0.050/kg DM. 1 kg DM = $0.045; wood = $0.050/kg DM.

with 38 to 50% attributable to wood and 50–62% to browse. It has also been assumed that the grass stratum would be unable to grow at this tree density, so that the value of the original grazing is lost throughout the development period, amounting to $42 U.S./ha on the basis of an output of 220 SFU with a DCP content of 125 g/SFU.

At equal production levels, and despite a higher shadow price of wood, IRR levels are lower than for *Atriplex* plantations (Table VI). They are below 6 and 9%, respectively, in approaches 1 and 2, when browse production is 500 SFU/ha, and above 13 and 22%, respectively, when it reaches 1000 SFU (3 tons of DM/ha), a level roughly equivalent to that achieved on properly managed plantations. The IRR settles between 20 and 40% when production reaches about 6 tons of DM/ha (2000 SFU). The SFU and DCP cost prices at this level are fairly low for a 10% opportunity cost of capital, especially if wood is produced at the same time as browse.

When browse production is around 1000 SFU/ha, the SFU and DCP cost prices are only lower than shadow prices when certain favorable conditions are also fulfilled, namely, when IRR is 10% and no enclosures are used, or when IRR is 10% and both wood and forage are produced if the plantations are enclosed (Table X). Finally, when production is very low (500 SFU/ha), SFU and DCP cost prices are 2.5 to 6 times higher than shadow prices. Cost prices are thus highly sensitive to variations in yields, when these are low.

Other case studies were examined in De Montgolfier and Le Houérou (1980, 1981) and were concerned with *Acacia senegal* in the arid and semiarid African tropics, phyllodineous acacias in Senegal, *Faidherbia*

Table X.   Internal rates of return in *Acacia saligna*
plantations in Tunisia

Management type	With fence[a]	Without fence
Assumption 1[b]		
Approach 1[c]	5.0	7.0
Approach 2[d]	1.4	3.1
Assumption 2		
Approach 1	14.0	17.0
Approach 2	11.5	13.7
Assumption 3		
Approach 1	19.0	23.0
Approach 2	16.5	18.9
Assumption 4		
Approach 1	22.0	25.0
Approach 2	19.7	22.2

[a] Four-stranded barbed wire fence.

[b] Production assumptions as in Table IX.

[c] Shadow price = $0.137 U.S./SFU and $0.050/kg DM of wood.

[d] Shadow price = $0.160 U.S./SFU and $0.050/kg DM of
wood.

albida agroforestry systems in the Sahelian and Sudanian ecoclimatic
zones, *Prosopis juliflora* and *Parkinsonia aculeata* plantations in the Cape
Verde Islands, and *Laucaena leucocephala* plantations in Malawi. Later
studies dealt with fodder shrub plantations in Libya, mainly *Acacia saligna*
and *Atriplex* (Le Houérou and Barghati, 1982) (Table XI). The various
data collected on costs of establishment, production, and profitability
thresholds for countries within and outside Africa are shown in Table XII.

Table XI.   Cost price of SFU in *Acacia saligna* plantations in Tunisia

IRR (%)	10				15			
Fencing:	Fence		No fence		Fence		No fence	
Type of cost:	Marginal	Average	M	A	M	A	M	A
Assumption 1[a]	0.45	0.53	0.31	0.42	1.08	1.19	0.80	0.94
Assumption 2	0.05	0.12	0.01	0.09	0.17	0.22	0.10	0.17
Assumption 3	—[b]	0.06	—[b]	0.05	0.06	0.11	0.01	0.09
Assumption 4	—	0.04	—	0.03	0.01	0.08	—[b]	0.06

Notes: Duration of the project was 20 years. Dashed line shows cost below shadow price for
approaches 1 and 2.

[a] Yield assumptions alone.

[b] At this level, production for the IRR, considered wood production alone, permits one to balance
the operation so that the marginal cost of SFU becomes zero.

Table XII. Summary table: Inputs, outputs, and profitability thresholds (approximate figures; see text)

Planting	Cost of planting and 3 years' maintenance (U.S. $)		Fodder production				Cost of production (U.S. $, 1980)		Profitability threshold (ha/yr)					
			kg DM		SFU				IRR = 0		IRR = 10%		IRR = 15%	
	Hectare	Shrub	Hectare	Shrub	Hectare	Shrub	kg DM	SFU	kg DM	SFU	kg DM	SFU	kg DM	SFU
Spineless cactus Tunisia	565	0.25	1000/6000	0.5–3.0	500/3000	0.25/1.50	0.01/0.06	0.02/0.11	412	206	2000	1000	4000	2000
Atriplex Tunisia	545	0.27	1250/5000	0.6–2.5	500/2000	0.25/1.00	0.06/0.25	0.012/0.030	500	200	1250	500	2500	1000
Acacia saligna Tunisia	715	0.71	1500/6000	1.5–6.0	500/2000	0.20/0.50	0.01/0.04	0.003/0.12	800	280	3000	1000	4500	1500
Acacia senegal Senegal	300	0.48	620	1.0	200	0.32	0.02	0.08	500	160	800	260	3000	960
Sudan	248	0.40	620	1.0	200	0.32	0.02	0.06	450	140	720	230	2700	860
Phyllodineous wattles Senegal	700	0.50	1800/3600	1.2–3.6	600/1200	0.6/1.2	0.16/0.033	0.05/0.10	840	240	3000	1000	4500	1500
Atriplex Chile	200	0.20	1000/2000	0.5–1.0	200/800	0.20/0.40	0.003/0.007	0.017/0.034	125	50	—	—	—	—
Leucaena Malawi	300	0.002	2000/6000	0.013/0.024	1200/3600	0.008/0.024	0.013/0.039	0.022/0.066	200	140	—	—	—	—
Faidherbia Senegal	100	0.050	500/1000	10–20	350/700	7.0/14.0	0.0006/0.0035	0.002/0.005	36	25	108	75	180	125
Parkinsonia Cape Verde	210	0.52	400/1200	3.0–20.0	300/400	0.6/0.8	—	—	200	66	1000	350	1450	500

V. Discussion

It is rather difficult to determine the economic value of browse plantations for various reasons:

(i) There is no one overall satisfactory method to evaluate the shadow price to be ascribed to browse and the economic performance calculated depends rather strongly on the method of assessment of the shadow price that is used; we have therefore used three methods in the above described case studies. The result may vary by 50% in the case of cacti in Tunisia (Table III), by 40% in *Atriplex* (Table VI), but only by 7% in the case of *Acacia saligna* (Table IX).

(ii) The method of establishment of the plantations of fodder shrubs bears extremely significant consequences on the investment cost and hence on the economic feasibility of any operation. There are two main methods in use: the transplanting of nursery-grown seedlings, which ensures a high degree of success of establishment, but at a very high cost, of the order of magnitude of $500 U.S. per hectare in 1980, and sometimes much more; and direct sowing, which is much more risky, particularly in arid zones, but costs are also much less, by a factor of 10 to 1 compared to the transplanting method. Naturally the risk increases with aridity and so does the cost. Recently a new method has been developed that combines the advantages of the two above-mentioned methods, but it requires more skill: the direct sowing of treated and pregerminated seeds. This method may be nearly as secure as transplanting seedlings provided some precautions are taken against possible dry spells that could cause failure. One of these precautions is to wait until a certain amount of water is in the soil profile that would statistically safeguard against water stress before sowing is actually carried out. Usually 50 to 100 mm of water storage in the soil profile in the first half of the rainy season would guarantee successful establishment in 80% of the cases. But this is where the skill interferes: in the statistical evaluation of rainfall probabilities and their interpretation as a function of soil characteristics (texture, structure, depth, topographic position, etc.). This method also requires a high degree of efficiency: when the rainfall and soil conditions are adequate, action must be taken without delay. Timing seed and equipment availability are essential factors of success.

(iii) Establishment is also strongly influenced by management techniques in the first phases, that is, the avoidance of soil moisture loss through evaporation from the soil surface, which implies timely hoeing or mulching, and loss of soil water from transpiration by weeds, which implies timely weeding (one hoeing equals two irrigations, as the proverb goes).

(iv) Fencing bears very strongly on the cost and the economic efficiency of any operation as mentioned earlier. Analysis of IRR shows that this factor is perhaps the single most important factor in cost/benefit ratios.

(v) Yields and managerial skill. Yields depend on two main groups of factors: ecological conditions and adaptation of the species selected to these conditions and managerial skill of the operator. It is well known that overbrowsing may considerably reduce production, all other conditions being equal. But the method of management elected may have a strong influence as well, for instance, direct browsing versus cut-and-carry; the former may be more efficient in some socioeconomic conditions while the latter may be mandatory in different conditions. This viewpoint has been discussed regarding cacti, but may apply as well to other species.

(vi) The difficulty to assess in monetary terms the value of browse plantations (erosion control, wildlife shelter and feed, amenities, desertization control, beekeeping, maintenance and improvement of land fertility and productivity, stabilization of animal production, watershed management and water spreading, multiple use of range and agroforestry and agropastoral systems) inevitably leads to a systematic underestimation of the economic impact and validity of fodder shrub plantations. The figures found in the present study are therefore definitely biased on the low side.

VI. Summary and Conclusions

To sum up, the economic viability of browse tree and shrub plantations appears uncertain from many aspects when all the factors likely to limit profitability under current African conditions are taken into account. Given environmental constraints, intial efforts to improve this situation should probably involve lowering the investment cost of enclosures and maintaining the option to use the grass stratum, so that investment expenditure is kept at a sufficiently low level not only to enable growth of net forage output to be maximized but also to provide a high-quality supply during periods when livestock are severely underfed (Table XIII). Seen from this angle, browse tree and shrub plantations would appear to provide some solution, and probably a more efficient one than the unreliable supply of feed concentrates, to the problems of livestock feed in Africa.

Table XIII. Impact of investment costs and yields on IRR for browse tree and shrub plantations in Tunisia

	Investment		Production		
	No enclosure	Barbed wire	500 SFU	1000 SFU	2000 SFU
Cactus[a]					
Direct grazing	—	—	2.7	10.6	18.3
Cut-and-carry	5.8	4.6	0.1	0.1	7.8
Atriplex[a]	25.6	21.4	12.4	22.4	31.4
Acacia cyanophylla[a]	14.5	12.3	2.2	12.6	21.0
Total[b]	15.3	12.7	4.3	11.4	19.3
Investment/ha (U.S. $)	503	653			

[a] Project life is 20 years (for *A. albida*, 30 years); shadow prices are $0.16 U.S./SFU and $0.24 U.S./kg of DP.

[b] Average of IRRs.

Indeed, their potential contribution to the avoidance of severe herd losses during periods of drought is a major point in their favor, since the elimination of such losses would undoubtedly have positive effects on herd productivity over the medium and longer term. Again, the value of browse plantations is undeniable if their other advantages in terms of energy supplies (wood) and environmental protection are also taken into account. Efforts should therefore be made to gain a better understanding of the very real opportunities offered by various species and of the conditions under which they can grow and be used to help satisfy the vast browse and energy requirements of the arid, semiarid, and highland zones of tropical Africa.

However optimistic, such a prospect nevertheless leaves unsolved the problem of effectively implementing plantations and organizing their utilization by the pastoral population. Utilization would under any circumstances have to rely on a fair price for the services rendered.

References

Barachette, R. (1980a). "L'intérêt économique de divers types d'aménagement agricoles et anti-érosifs dans les terres privées" (mimeo), FAO, Tun. 77/007 Dir. Forêts Minist. Agric., Tunis.

Barachette, R. (1980b). "L'intérêt économique de divers types d'aménagements forestiers et pastoraux anti-érosifs" (mimeo), FAO, Tun. 77/007. Dir. Forêts, Minist. Agric., Tunis.

Beale, C. I. A. (1980). Economic aspects of developing *Leucaena* as a cash crop. A review of pre-investment studies in Malawi, 1974–79. *In* "Browse in Africa: The Current State of Knowledge" (H. N. Le Houérou, ed.), pp. 419–426. International Livestock Center for Africa, Addis Ababa, Ethiopia.

Benjamin, R. W. (1980). The use of forage shrubs in the Norte Chico region of Chile. *In*

"Browse in Africa: The Current State of Knowledge" (H. N. Le Houérou, ed.), pp. 299–302. International Livestock Center for Africa, Addis Ababa, Ethiopia.

Cordier, G. (1947). De la composition de quelques produits fourragers tunisiens et de leur valeur dans l'alimentation du mouton. *Ann. Serv. Bot. Agron. Tunis.* **20,** 25–108.

De Kock, G. C. (1980). Drought resistant fodder shrub crops in South Africa. *In* "Browse in Africa: The Current State of Knowledge" (H. N. Le Houérou, ed.), pp. 399–410. International Livestock Center for Africa, Addis Ababa, Ethiopia.

Delhaye, R., Le Houérou, H. N., and Sarson M., (1974). "Amélioration des pâturages et de l'élévage dans la région du Hodna," AGS/DD/ALG66/09. FAO, Rome.

De Montgolfier-Kouevi, C., and Le Houérou, H. N. (1980). Study on the economic viability of browse plantations in Africa. *In* "Browse in Africa: The Current State of Knowledge" (H. N. Le Houérou, ed.), pp. 449–464, International Livestock Center for Africa, Addis Ababa, Ethiopia.

De Montgolfier-Kouevi, C., and Le Houérou, H. N. (1981). Economic aspects of browse development. *ILCA Bull.* **12,** 3–19.

Dumancic, D., and Le Houérou, H. N. (1981). *Acacia cyanophylla* Lindl, as supplementary feed for small stock in Libya. *J. Arid Environ.* **4,** 161–167.

Franclet, A., and Le Houérou, H. N. (1971). "Les *Atriplex* en Tunisie et en Afrique du Nord,." FO:SF/Tun 1, Rapp. Tech. No. 7. FAO, Rome.

Hamel, O. (1980). Acclimatation et utilisation des *Acacia* à phyllodes d'origine australienne au Sénégal. *In* "Browse in Africa: The Current State of Knowledge" (H. N. Le Houérou, ed.), pp. 361–374. International Livestock Center for Africa, Addis Ababa, Ethiopia.

Jarrige, R. (1980). "Alimentation des ruminants." Inst. Natl. Rech. Agron., Paris.

Le Houérou, H. N. (1980a). Browse in northern Africa. *In* "Browse in Africa: The Current State of Knowledge" (H. N. Le Houérou, ed.), pp. 55–82. International Livestock Center for Africa, Addis Ababa, Ethiopia.

Le Houérou, H. N. (1980b). The role of browse in the Sahelian and Sudanian zones. *In* Browse in Africa: The Current State of Knowledge" (H. N. Le Houérou, ed.), pp. 83–102. International Livestock Center for Africa, Addis Ababa, Ethiopia.

Le Houérou, H. N., (1980c). Chemical composition and nutritive value of browse in West Africa. *In* "Browse in Africa: The Current State of Knowledge" (H. N. Le Houérou, ed.), pp. 261–290. International Livestock Center for Africa, Addis Ababa, Ethiopia.

Le Houérou, H. N. (1987). "Systémes agroforestiers dans le Bassin Arachidier du Sénégal." FAO Investment Center and IFAD, Rome.

Le Houérou, H. N., and Barghati, M. S. (1982) "An Evaluation of Fodder Shrubs Plantations in the Benghazi Plains" (mimeo), Tech. Pap. No. 45, Proj. Lib. 18. FAO, Tripoli.

Le Houérou, H. N., and Pontanier, R. (1987). "Evaluation des plantations sylvo-pastorales en zone aride de Tunisie," Notes Tech. du MAB. UNESCO, Paris.

Le Houérou, H. N. Dumancic, D., Schweisguth, D., and Telahique, T. (1982). "Anatomy and physiology of a Browsing Trial" (mimeo), Tech. Pap. No. 28, Proj. Lib. 18. FAO, Tripoli.

Le Houérou, H. N., Dumancic, D., and Eskileh M. (1983). "Feeding Shrubs to Sheep in Libya: Intake, Feed Value and Performance" (mimeo), Techn. Pap. No. 50, Proj. Lib. 18. FAO, Tripoli.

Leone, G. (1924). Consolidamento ed imboschimento delle zone dunose della Tripolitania. *l'Agric. Colon.* **18**(9), 299–308.

Lepape, M. C. (1980). Aperçus sur les fourrage ligneux dans les Iles du Cap Vert; étude préliminaire. *In* "Browse in Africa: The Current State of Knowledge" (H. N. Le Houérou, ed.), pp. 123–126. International Livestock Center for Africa, Addis Ababa, Ethiopia.

Monjauze, A., and Le Houérou, H. N. (1965) Le rôle des *Opuntia* dans l'économie agricole nord-africaine. *Bull. Ec. Nat. Super. Agron. Tunis.* **8–9**, 85–164.

Orev, Y. (1972) Seeding saltbush astride the margin cultivation in southern Israel. *In* "Wildland Shrubs: Their Biology and Utilization" (C. M. McKell, J. P. Blaisdell, and J. R. Goodin, eds.), USDA For. Serv. Gen. Tech. Rep. INT-1, pp. 405–406. Utah State University, Logan.

Peyre de Fabrégues, B. (1966) "Les cactées fourragères dans le Nord-Est Brésilien, Etude Ecologique," Et. Agrost. No. 12. IEMVT, Maisons-Alfort.

Wilson, R. T., De Leeuw, P. M., and De Haan, C. (1983). Recherches sur les systèmes de production animale des zones arides du Mali. Re'sultats préliminaires. Research Report No. 5, ILCA, Addis Ababa, Ethiopia.

Index

631

DATE DUE

HIGHSMITH   45230